SAVANNAH GREY

A Tale of Antebellum Georgia

Jim Jordan

Cover Illustration: *View of Savannah, 1837* by Firmin Cerveau
courtesy of the Georgia Historical Society.

This is a work of fiction. The names, characters, dialogue, organizations, and incidents included herein are either the product of the author's imagination or are used fictitiously.

This book was printed in the United States of America.

To order additional copies of this book, contact:
Xlibris Corporation
1-888-795-4274
www.Xlibris.com
Orders@Xlibris.com
38984

CONTENTS

To my lovely, patient wife

Kathleen

The computer is all yours

ACKNOWLEDGMENTS

I would like to thank the following people and institutions for their assistance in making this book possible.

I am especially grateful to the people who read the entire manuscript and provided so many valuable insights and corrected so many errors: Steve Hoffius of Charleston, my editor; Dr. John Duncan, Professor Emeritus at Armstrong Atlantic State University and proprietor of V. & J. Duncan Antique Maps, Prints & Books in Savannah; Dale Couch, Senior Archivist at the Georgia State Archives, Morrow, Georgia; Hugh Harrington, Milledgeville author and historian; Karl DeVries, Assistant Director of the Ships of Sea Museum in Savannah; and Kathleen Jordan, my understanding wife.

I would also like to thank those individuals who provided much needed expertise: for bricks and mortar, Steve Elkins of Savannah and Jimmy Price of Monroe, Virginia; for things nautical, Karl DeVries and Bill Julavits of Callawassie Island; for fire fighting, Windy Brieze of Woodbine, Georgia; for architecture, Jeff Mansell, former director of Historic Beaufort Foundation; for the Andrew Low house and family, Alice Daily; for the Governor's Mansion in Milledgeville, Matt Davis; for social customs of the "Old South," Steve Hoffius, Dale Couch, Dr. John Duncan, and Alice Daily; for Jekyll Island and the Dubignon family, John S. Hunter III of the Jekyll Island Authority; for antebellum railroads, Allen Tuten and Ed Mims; for the Georgia State Lunatic Asylum, Bud Merritt; and for the Independent Presbyterian Church in Savannah (and a vertigo-inducing climb up the steeple steps), Richard Hinely.

Historical societies and libraries were critical to performing the research on which this book is based. I am especially indebted to the Georgia Historical Society, my home away from home, and employees, past and present, notably: Susan Dick Hoffius, Jewell Anderson, Mandi Johnson, Luciana Spracher, Nora Galler, and Stephany Kretchmar.

Other institutions that provided much material are the Georgia State Archives, the National Archives in Atlanta and Washington, D.C., the New York Public Library, the Hargrett Library at the University of Georgia, the Furman University Library, the Georgia College and State University Library in Milledgeville, the Reese Library at Augusta State University, The Augusta Museum of History, the Augusta Genealogical Society, the South Carolina Historical Society, the Charleston Public Library, the Charleston Library Society, the Macon Public Library, the Ships of the

Sea Museum, Savannah, Georgia; the Clerk's Office of the City of Savannah; the Jen Library of the Savannah College of Art and Design, the Bull Street branch of the Live Oak Public Libraries, the Beaufort (S.C.) County Library, the St. Augustine Historical Society, the Historic Wilmington (N.C.) Foundation, the New Hanover (N.C.) County Public Library, the Special Collections and Archives at Emory University, the New Hampshire Historical Society, the Portsmouth Public Library, and the Armstrong Atlantic University Library.

Special thanks are due to Paul Rossmann of Charleston, who designed the book jacket. Let's hope you can tell a book by its cover.

Other individuals who deserve my deepest appreciation for their efforts are Dirk Hardison, Gordon Smith, and Adam Keuhl (for the back cover photo), all of Savannah, Dr. Larry Rowland and Ron Grindle of Beaufort, Susan Julavits of Callawassie Island, and Polly Gregg of Phoenix.

And finally, to all those people, black and white, whose labors and sacrifices have made Savannah, Georgia the most beautiful city in the world.

INTRODUCTION

Savannah Grey is told by an omniscient voice from the time of the novel, the 1830s until 1861. The narrative captures the style and norms of that time. Therefore, the word negro is used rather than African American, and it is not capitalized as it wouldn't have been at the time. Jekyll Island is spelled Jekyl, a cigar is a segar, a witness was afraid of "criminating" oneself, etc.

The story includes both fictional and non-fictional characters. An appendix listing the non-fictional characters is included at the end of the book to help the reader distinguish between them.

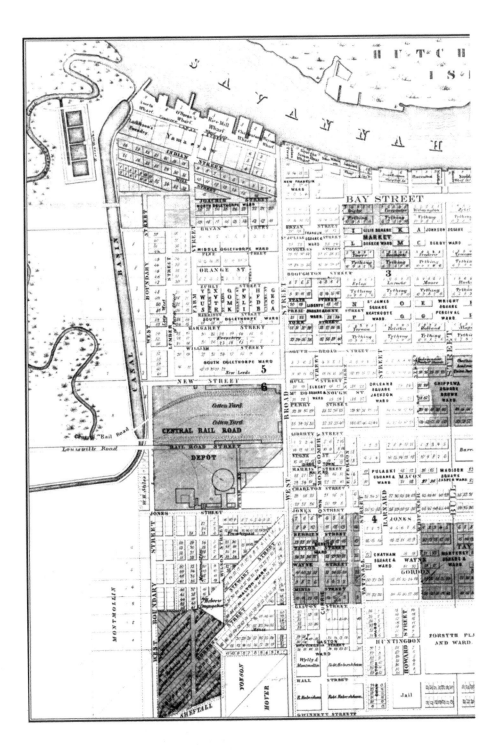

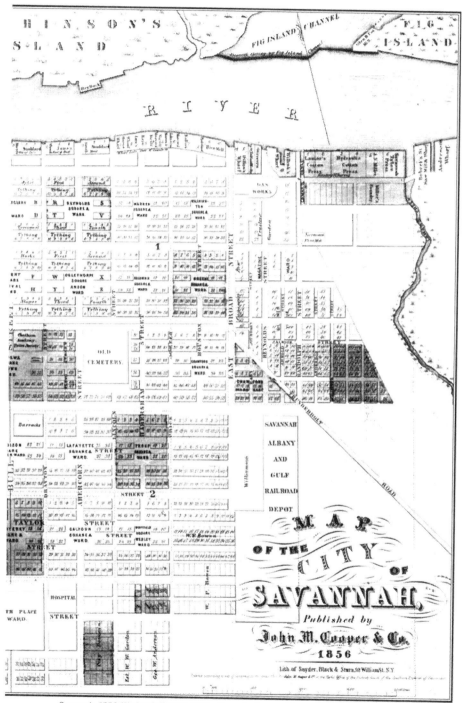

Savannah, 1856, Waring Collection 1018, volume 2, plate no. 26, courtesy of the Georgia Historical Society.

TALLULAH FALLS ◎

◎ ATHENS

◎ ATLANTA

AUGUSTA◎

Ogeechee R.

LOUISVILLE
◎

MILLEDGEVILLE
◎

Savannah R.

MACON ◎ GORDON

Georgia Central RR

Oconee R.

Ogeechee R.

◎ COLUMBUS

Ocmulgee R.

Cannouchee R.

SAVANNAH
◎
TYBEE ISL

OSSABAW ISL

ST CATHERINES ISL

Little Satilla R.

Altamaha R.

DARIEN ◎ *SAPELO ISL*

Satilla R.

ST SIMONS ISL

BRUNSWICK ◎ *JEKYL ISL*

St Andrews Sound
CUMBERLAND ISL

St. Mary's R.

◎
ST. MARYS

Map of Georgia

CHAPTER 1

A Free Man of Color

March 21, 1850

Freedom seemed far heavier than anything Andrew had carried before. His neck muscles strained like taut strands of rope as he stared down at the desk in front of him, though he held only a Bible in his hand.

Andrew had no reason to be nervous. This registration at the city clerk's office was just a formality. All the requirements with the state had been fulfilled, thanks to Amy McBain, the daughter of Andrew's former owner. Andrew had already advanced to a new status in life, the only one possible for a negro slave in Georgia. But Andrew would not relax until his name was recorded.

Joseph McBain, Amy's brother, could not have been prouder of his life-long friend. Joseph knew what this moment meant to Andrew, and thought of the many experiences they had shared. He was amazed they had even lived to see this day.

Mr. Edward Wilson, the city clerk, returned to the room and interrupted everyone's thoughts. "I can never find this register when I need it," he said to no one in particular, though Joseph, his father James, and his grandfather Daniel were seated to the side.

Wilson dropped the heavy book on the pockmarked wooden table, causing thousands of particles of dust to dance in the rays of the late morning sun filtering through the office window. The title embossed on the cover read: "Register of Free Persons of Color-Chatham County." He sat heavily in his old chair, causing air to rush noisily out of a breach in its leather covering, and opened to the page headed "1850."

Wilson thought this to be one of the more thankless tasks of his position. He had registered many a free negro in his day, and usually felt that he had given yet another black person license to be disrespectful to whites. But he knew that Andrew McBain was one of the better negroes in town and would not use his new status inappropriately.

Wilson dipped his quill into the ink well and said, "Alrighty, Andrew. Please answer my questions and you'll be on your way. What is your last name?"

Andrew clutched his Bible and stood straighter. "McBain, sir."

The thin-haired, middle-aged, portly man peered at the page through the wire-rimmed spectacles resting at the tip of his nose, and wrote cautiously, moving his lips without speaking. He then mumbled, "First name is Andrew," not bothering to take his eyes from the page, as he answered his own question.

Wilson finally looked up. "Your age?"

"Thirty years old yesterday, sir."

As Wilson recorded Andrew's age, he said, "Hmmm. Thirty, eh? It seems like yesterday I saw you and Joseph McBain running in the streets, causing all kinds of trouble." Andrew forced himself not to look at Joseph, but could imagine him grinning like a mischievous boy.

Wilson raised his eyes. "Nativity?"

Andrew pointed straight ahead, to the west wall of the office. "The Heritage Plantation, sir. Just outside of Savannah."

"Yes, a fine place. Occupation?"

Andrew finally managed a smile. "Bricklayer, sir."

Joseph called out, "And the best one in all Savannah, by God!" James and Daniel McBain laughed out loud. Andrew looked down and shook his head in embarrassment.

Even Mr. Wilson chortled. He asked, "Is that true, Andrew?"

Andrew glanced sideways at Joseph and then replied to Mr. Wilson, "There are so many good ones in town, sir. I'm just fortunate to be working here."

Wilson said, "Good answer. I saw your stucco work on Mr. Low's house. Excellent, if I must say so. Now, if Mr. Joseph McBain will permit, let's move on." Wilson peered at Joseph, who eased back in his chair.

Wilson then asked James McBain, "Sir, I assume you have been issued Letters of Guardian by the court and will serve as Andrew's guardian?"

McBain held up a document. "Of course, Mr. Wilson." Free negroes were required by law to have white male guardians, who agreed to look after their interests.

Wilson recorded James McBain's name as guardian, and the date, March 21. He placed the quill in its holder, applied a blotter to the page, and blew on it. He then picked up some papers and stood to face Andrew. "Andrew, I need to advise you of a couple of matters. As you know, you have special responsibilities as a free negro. Listen carefully, because it's up to you to know these laws."

Andrew pressed his Bible against his belly. "Yes, sir."

Wilson studied the papers as he rocked slightly on the balls of his feet. "First, you need to register here at the Office of the Clerk of Council every year as long as you reside in Chatham County. If you intend to move to another place in Georgia, you need to notify us of that, too. You cannot leave Georgia, other than to go to an adjoining state, and then only on a temporary basis." The administrator paused, waiting for a response, but Andrew remained silent.

"Second, as a free male negro over fifteen and under sixty years of age, you are required to serve as a fireman for the city at no pay, though you'll be exempt from the poll tax."

Andrew nodded. "I look forward to that opportunity, sir." Free negroes served proudly in the city fire department.

"And don't forget, as a free negro, you have the honor of paying taxes. They're due here in the City Exchange every January."

"Lucky fellow," Grandfather McBain muttered, loud enough for all to hear in the quiet room. Joseph tried to muffle a laugh in his hand.

Wilson glanced at the eccentric old man, who shrugged his shoulders. Wilson said, "Now, now, Mr. McBain. Where would we be if we didn't pay our taxes?"

Grandfather waved a finger in the air. "We'd be a dern sight better off, that's where! The founding fathers didn't give their lives so our so-called representatives could tear the hides off the bodies of its citizens!"

James McBain patted his father on the back to calm him down. He then said to Mr. Wilson, "Sir, it might be best if you don't mention the subject of taxes again."

Wilson said, "Yes, Mr. McBain." He then re-focused on Andrew. "Andrew, there are laws that apply to both free persons of color and slaves, and you should already know them. I will remind you of a few of the more important ones." He looked at Andrew as he turned to a new page. "You need a general pass from your guardian to be out on the streets between the nighttime bell and ten p.m. After ten o'clock you need a special pass, which must state the hour that pass is to expire. Past midnight, it must also state your destination. If not, you'll spend a night in jail."

Andrew stood like a statue. Wilson continued. "You know, Andrew, as long as you're a bricklayer in Savannah, you need a badge. Costs ten dollars a year."

Andrew pulled a badge from his pocket to show Mr. Wilson. "Yes, sir. I'd never forget it."

Wilson nodded. "Good. And remember, Andrew, you're not allowed to teach other negroes to read or write."

Little beads of sweat formed on Andrew's forehead, though the temperature in the room was comfortable. Andrew had never disobeyed a law in his life, save that one. He was afraid Mr. Wilson might discover it right there, revoke his new freedom, and send him out on the street a slave once again.

James McBain sensed Andrew's nervousness, leaned forward in his chair, and spoke barely louder than a whisper. "Mr. Wilson, is all this necessary?"

Wilson wagged the papers from which he had been reading to justify his actions. "Sir, I know that Andrew understands these laws, and that you've taught him well. But it's my job to inform any newly registered free negro."

Andrew broke in. "I'm well aware of the ordinance, sir." He removed a white kerchief from his rear pants pocket and wiped his face.

James sat back in his seat. Joseph and Grandfather looked at each other, remembering the day Andrew first learned of that law.

Wilson returned his attention to Andrew. "And Andrew, never hide a runaway slave, or a slave that has committed a crime. If you do, you'll have mighty hell to pay. Tell me you understand that."

Andrew stuffed his kerchief back into his pocket. "Yes, sir. I do."

"Good. As I said, there are many more ordinances governing the conduct of free persons of color, and it's your responsibility to know and abide by them."

James stood and adjusted his cravat. "Thank you for your time, Mr. Wilson."

Wilson dropped the papers on the desk. "You know I don't write these laws, Mr. McBain. I just see to it they're understood. That makes life easier for us all."

"I understand, Mr. Wilson. Thank you, again."

Mr. Wilson turned to Andrew and said, "That's it. You're now registered as a free negro in Chatham County. Allow me to say that I've never had a family attend this registration. You should feel honored."

Andrew said, "I certainly do." He then turned to James McBain, shook his hand, and said with a smile that could light up a midnight sky, "Thank you so much, sir."

Andrew then embraced Grandfather McBain, held him for a few seconds, and said, "I love you, Grampah!" The old man, with every one of ninety years written on his face, swallowed hard.

Next, Andrew hugged Joseph. "We did it, Master Joseph. We really did it!"

Joseph stepped back, put his hands on Andrew's shoulders, and said, "You did it, Andrew. Well, you and Amy." Both men laughed.

The McBains bade good day to Mr. Wilson and left the City Exchange building. They stepped onto the sidewalk of the Bay, as the locals called Bay Street, and paused to appreciate the sunny, clear day. Grandfather McBain removed a faded, blue-and-white print kerchief from his pocket and tied it over his nose and mouth.

Someone called out, "Hello, Mr. McBain." The men looked across the Bay to the building site of the new United States Custom House and saw John Norris, the New York architect who had been working in Savannah for a few years and gaining quite a reputation.

The McBains waved. Andrew called, "I'll see you in a little while, sir."

Norris replied, "Take your time."

The McBains walked the short distance to their coach, where their coachman, Hercules, was waiting. He threw his arm around Andrew's shoulders and pulled him close.

The city leaders never considered registering a free person of color as a cause for celebration, but it held great significance for Andrew. He could finally marry Patience. He could keep his promise to Grampah and write that letter to the Queen of England. And he could realize his lifelong dream to leave his mark, that of a free negro, on the most beautiful city in the world, Savannah, Georgia.

Part 1

Boat Rides

1830s

CHAPTER 2

Saving Jumbo

April 1831

Joseph McBain didn't know what a free person of color was until he was eleven years old. He had always assumed that all negroes were servants. He learned otherwise the day they almost lost Jumbo.

As a boy, Joseph spent most of his time on his family's plantation. There were few better places to be raised. The Heritage was as scenic as any place he had ever seen, bordered by the Savannah River on the north, the Augusta Road on the south, and other plantations on the east and west, with hundreds of acres of fields, woods, and streams to explore. It was also the location of the McBain family businesses—bricks, lumber, and iron castings—which Joseph knew he would one day manage with his father.

But going to Savannah was the most thrilling diversion. All the people, shops, and squares were so different compared to the country atmosphere of the Heritage. As far as Joseph was concerned, he never visited enough.

So on a weekday afternoon in April 1831, when Grandfather McBain announced that he needed to go shopping, Joseph and Andrew, who had finished his brick-making work for the day, jumped into the coach before they were invited. Grandfather entered the cab and saw the two grinning boys. Joseph was dressed handsomely in a white shirt, gray and red waistcoat, black pantaloons, and shiny black boots. Andrew wore his best shirt and pantaloons. Grandfather said, "I don't recall asking you two buzzards."

Joseph claimed, "You know it wouldn't be any fun without us." Grandfather leaned across the cab and tickled the boys on their sides. They erupted in mild hysterics.

Hercules started the horses up the avenue of oaks. Both sides of this drive were lined with great live oak trees, whose thick, gnarly branches formed a shady, sheltering canopy. In ten minutes they were on the Augusta Road, heading to Savannah. The one-hour journey provided scenic views of the countryside, with vast, cool pine forests on the south side and flat, cultivated lands that rolled to the river on the north. The road passed Vale Royal, the first plantation on the river west of Savannah, and its brown, barren rice fields, which had been converted, unsuccessfully, to a crop that did not require flooding.

The Augusta Road merged into the Louisville Road, which soon crossed Musgrove Creek. Minutes later they entered town. The coach turned north onto West Broad Street and proceeded towards the river. Before Joseph could say a word, Andrew pointed to a classical, two-story, stucco house and shouted, "Built for Master Scarbrough by Master Jay." Identifying houses and buildings was a game the two played every time they visited town. Grandfather, who invented the game and served as the judge, nodded.

Hercules turned east onto the Bay, the northernmost street on the bluff upon which Savannah sits. Grandfather put on his kerchief like an outlaw. The streets of Savannah were all sand and dirt, and while children liked playing in them, adults constantly complained about the clouds of dust that billowed whenever a horse cantered or a carriage rolled by. Walking through the sand was a task, and shoes and the lower parts of pants and dresses became filthy, even after the modern convenience of wooden and brick crosswalks. Traversing the streets after a rainstorm was a nightmare.

Grandfather groused, "If I wanted to live in a desert, I'd move to Arabia." He never failed to remind Joseph and Andrew that about one hundred years of horse dung and urine were deposited in that sand and he didn't particularly like the taste. The kerchief was his protection against inhaling evil things. Locals referred to him as "Ol' Cottonmouth." To that, Grandfather replied, "It's a dern sight better than Old Dung Mouth." Joseph thought his grandfather had a point, but he did look silly.

"Jisso hawss, jisso," Hercules called to the horses in Gullah, the language of the negroes. The coach stopped and in seconds Hercules was helping Grandfather and the boys onto the sidewalk in front of the City Hotel. Joseph and Andrew looked about at the glorious sights, the different types of carriages, the buildings, and the river. The town was struggling economically and the population wasn't much more than it had been in 1820, when Andrew and Joseph were born. But that didn't matter to two eleven-year-old boys whose senses were just beginning to develop. They could see, hear, and smell so much more of the place than in the past.

They turned their attention back to Grandfather, who was talking to a white-haired man in a Continental Army uniform, complete with a blue, three-pointed, cocked hat, blue coat, white knee breeches, white silk stockings, and shiny black shoes. The sight of Grandfather, whose handkerchief billowed in and out as he spoke to the oddly dressed man, was too much for Joseph. He started to giggle and turned away, but a hand like a vice gripped his shoulder and made him face the stranger. Even at age seventy, Grandfather had the strength of a young iron forger. "Joseph and Andrew, I want you to meet Mr. Sheftall, a friend and one of the great Americans who fought to free this country from the tyranny of the British. Mr. Sheftall, I would like you to meet my grandson, Joseph. And this is Andrew."

Mr. Sheftall eyed the boys from head to toe as if they were new recruits to his brigade. "Well, what fine looking young soldiers you have here, Daniel. Pleased to meet you, Joseph. And you too, Andrew."

Joseph's mouth hung open slightly, but replied, "It's a pleasure, sir."

Andrew said, "Pleased to meet you, Master Sheftall."

As they stood on the Bay, several people walked by. Most bade the two old men good day. However, one woman glared at Mr. Sheftall. Grandfather and Mr. Sheftall took no notice of her, though Andrew and Joseph shivered at her nasty face.

Grandfather then informed the boys, "Mr. Sheftall and I are going inside the hotel for a few minutes to discuss business. You two stay here and make some attempt at behaving. Hercules, please look after them. If they act up, take them to the city jail."

Hercules looked down his nose at the boys. "Yassuh, Gran' Massa."

The two men headed directly to the hotel barroom, the prime meeting spot for gentlemen to discuss the news of the day while satisfying their thirst. Andrew and Joseph looked at Hercules, who did not speak. He simply folded his arms across his chest and stared at them. His message was clear: "Don't cause any trouble, or I will!"

Hercules was in charge of the Heritage's horses, mules, and carriages, and had four negroes working for him. He also served as coachman. Although he was just twenty years old at the time, James McBain entrusted with him those responsibilities, and Hercules took them seriously. The stables and carriage house were immaculately clean, the horses well-groomed and exercised, and the coach, carriage, gig, and Rockaway brightly polished and well-oiled.

About five years earlier, in 1826, a Savannah River planter encountered financial difficulties and had been forced to sell all his property. The owner of a rice plantation in Darien had made an attractive offer for the negroes. McBain, who had been impressed by his neighbor's stables and the gifted, orphaned young negro who worked in them, stepped in and purchased Hercules, saving him from a lifetime of bondage in those sickly rice fields. Young Hercules understood the fate from which he had been spared and was fiercely loyal to Mr. McBain.

By the time Hercules was twenty, he was almost six feet tall and as muscular as a blacksmith. With the money he earned from side jobs, he bought clothes. He especially liked white cotton shirts and black pantaloons. He wore a silver chain, using the skull of a rattlesnake as the pendant. All of the negro girls on the plantation and in town smiled when Hercules walked by.

Hercules did not speak any more than necessary. He wasn't shy, he just let his facial expressions talk for him, and they spoke loudly. But not even Hercules could prevent Joseph from getting into unfortunate situations. Joseph's mother once said that if there were but an ounce of trouble hidden under a boulder in a forest, Joseph would find it. Hercules replied, "It fine he!"

While Hercules turned his attention to wiping the dust from the coach and brushing the horses, Andrew and Joseph focused on an area across the Bay. Andrew pointed and said, in a husky voice imitating Grandfather McBain's, "Right over yonder! That's where General Oglethorpe first climbed up the bluff from the river to found the colony of Georgia and meet Chief Tomochichi in the Year of our Lord 1733." Joseph laughed at Andrew's accurate rendition.

The boys heard the clanging of a bell from the direction of the river. Joseph, unable to control his curiosity, asked Hercules if he and Andrew could cross the street. He replied suspiciously, "Don' mek me come aftuh oonuh!"

They dashed across the Bay, having to avoid a jangling stagecoach, and stood at the fence at the edge of the bluff. They looked down the forty-foot rise, past the warehouses and River Street to the harbor, crowded with white-masted sailing ships and puffing side-wheeled steamers towing barges laden with products from inland Georgia. They spotted the schooner *Charlotte*, with her large foremast and mainmast, at a wharf, boarding passengers. The single-mast sloop *Rising Sun* floated calmly in the river, waiting for a place to dock and take on cargo. The entire riverfront was a beehive of activity, as scurrying workmen loaded and unloaded ships. Even though these were not prosperous times, the port was still a busy spot, and for Andrew and Joseph a theatre for their fantasies. They dreamed of sailing around the world to mysterious countries whose names they could not pronounce, finding sparkling treasures, and fighting villainous pirates along the way.

After what seemed to be only minutes, a loud, sharp whistle penetrated the air. Hercules was calling them back, and he didn't like to do it twice. They returned to the coach and continued their visual examination of the town.

For most of the length of the Bay, a wide grassy strip of land called the "Strand" separated the street and the edge of the bluff. It added beauty to the area, accommodated patriotic celebrations like Independence Day, and served as a welcoming ground for honored visitors who entered the city from the river.

Breaking the Strand into two sections was the City Exchange, the seat of city government, which sat commandingly at the foot of Bull Street. The Exchange had three stories capped with a cupola. The front gabled roofline formed a large triangular pediment. Within its surface was a tall, narrow, arched window, standing between two oval windows on their sides. It reminded Joseph of a cross-eyed man with a big nose.

"Let's do some shopping," Grandfather announced, tying on his kerchief as he emerged from the City Hotel alone, his business with Mr. Sheftall apparently finished. They walked east on the Bay towards Bull Street, past the Federal-style, brick row buildings with their round-top front doors, which housed so many of Savannah's commercial enterprises.

"Who was that man?" Joseph asked, looking up to his grandfather.

"Sheftall Sheftall? Just as I said, a Revolutionary War hero." Grandfather threw his shoulders back, as he always did when he talked about the war.

Joseph closed one eye. "His first and last names are the same?"

"Yes," replied Grandfather. "It's a noble name."

"Why does he dress that way?"

"Because he loves America. That's how he expresses it. I don't know of a better way." That made sense to Joseph. He loved America, too. He wondered if he could have such a uniform made in his size.

Andrew asked, "How do you know him, Grampah?"

Grandfather turned, placed a hand on Andrew's shoulder, and pointed to the west side of town, back towards the Heritage. "Over yonder, at the edge of Musgrove Creek, better than fifty years ago, running from the British, who were cutting us to pieces. My brother and I barely escaped by swimming across the creek. Sheftall was only fourteen and couldn't swim."

"What happened, Grandfather?"

"That's a long story, Joseph, for another day. But I'll tell you this, he didn't drown." Joseph looked at the ground and scratched his head. He looked at Grandfather, who was smiling.

They reached the corner of Bay and Bull Street and entered Gaudry and Legriel's Grocery. While Grandfather placed his order, the boys tip-toed up and down the squeaky plank aisles, gazing and sniffing at the goods from all over the world. There were barrels of sugar from St. Croix, hams from Virginia, tobacco leaves from Havana, wine from France and Malaga, pale and brown sherry from Madeira, coffee from Porto Rico, tea from Ceylon, sacks of salt from Liverpool, drums of fresh figs, and much more. These products from far-away lands inspired the boys' imaginations as much as the ships in the harbor. The aromas also sharpened their appetites.

They returned to the front counter, where Grandfather was settling the charges with Mr. Gaudry. Grandfather asked Hercules to load the coach with the packages and wait for them. Then he told Andrew and Joseph to follow him back towards the City Hotel to William Thorne Williams's bookstore.

Mr. Williams was one of the most learned men in Savannah. When locals wanted to discuss world affairs or new books, they went to his shop, often preceded or followed by a visit to the City Hotel bar next door.

Mr. Williams, a friend of Grandfather McBain for many years, greeted them as they entered. "Good afternoon, boys. Hello to you, Daniel."

Grandfather removed his kerchief. "Good day, William. How are you?"

"Well, we're still above ground, are we not?" replied Mr. Williams, wiping the dust from a book with a piece of cloth.

That's all Grandfather needed to get started. "We won't be for long if this dern tariff isn't done away with! There's talk Old Hickory is going to hit us again next year."

While the tariff was one of the divisive political issues of the day, it didn't mean much to Andrew and Joseph. They escaped the tedious conversation to examine the shelves of books along the walls. Joseph pulled one down and opened it, but it was in a foreign language he didn't recognize. He handed it to Andrew and said, "Read this."

Andrew tried to pronounce the words, which sounded funny and made no sense, and the boys started to laugh uncontrollably. Joseph put the book back and moved down the aisle seeking books in English.

Andrew selected one and read, "*Poor Richard's, Alman, ah, ah, ak, Almanac. Poor Richard's Almanac.* What's an almanac and why would a poor man write one?"

Joseph looked at the floor as he considered the question. Then he looked up and saw the woman who had sneered at Mr. Sheftall on the street standing next to them. She pointed the book in her hand at Andrew and chastised him. "You, boy! Just where did you learn to read? And you have no business being in this store!"

Andrew was speechless as he stepped back from the red-faced woman, whose black hair was pulled back so tightly in a bun her head looked as if it were about to explode. Finally he squeaked, "I'm sorry, missus."

"Sorry won't do! Now you get out of here!"

Though intimidated by the woman, Joseph spoke up for his companion. "Ma'am, he's with me. He's not causing any trouble."

"You shut your fresh mouth! I'm not addressing you. You should know better than to bring him in here. You're as bad as he is! Who raised you, anyway?" A small dot of saliva came out of her mouth and rested on her lower lip.

Grandfather and Mr. Williams, hearing the sharp comments, walked over to the boys. Grandfather placed his hand on Andrew's back and said, "Ma'am, please lower your voice when you speak to my . . . . "

"Let me handle this, Daniel," Mr. Williams said, stepping in front of Grandfather. He then asked, "Is there a problem, madam?"

"Yes, this negro boy. He's both reading a book and in this store, two things he is not allowed to do!"

"Well, I own this store," replied Mr. Williams, "and he or any other boy is allowed here as long as he behaves. He is behaving, and is therefore welcome."

"He is not allowed to read! That is against the law!"

Again, Mr. Williams responded calmly. "Actually, madam, he *is* allowed to read. The law states only that it is illegal for someone to teach him to read. The boy is breaking no law."

"How rude of you! Somebody please call the mayor. He'll settle this!"

"Madam, I was the mayor just last year. I know of what I speak."

The woman thrust down the book she'd been holding and stomped towards the door. She grabbed onto the handle and barked, "I don't know why we moved to this uncivilized outpost of hell!" Slam!

Andrew remained frozen, his eyes as big as silver dollars. Grandfather squeezed his shoulder and said, "Andrew, the earth belches up some strange things from time to time, and you just met one of them. She is one gruesome woman. Pay no mind."

Mr. Williams said, "I've not seen her before and she doesn't sound like she's from these parts."

Andrew still didn't move, and Grandfather realized he needed to do something special. He clapped his hands and announced, "I think it's time to visit Mrs. Mirault!"

Joseph yelled, "Yes!" and charged for the door, with a subdued Andrew close behind. The boys piled into the coach, eagerly anticipating the best ice cream ever made. Grandfather followed slowly, having failed to solve the tariff problem with Mr. Williams.

Hercules turned the coach from the Bay onto Bull, the main road that ran through the middle of town from north to south, and had to maneuver around two cows lying lazily in the street. Joseph and Andrew's attention was drawn to the old, one-story wooden cottage on the east side of Bull owned by Mr. Dure. It was one of the very first houses built in Georgia, soon after the colony's founding. General Oglethorpe had boarded there when he stayed in Savannah. The structure had miraculously survived the great fires of 1796 and 1820 and stood as Savannah's most visible link to Georgia's beginnings. As they passed this relic, Joseph imagined the great general pacing back and forth in the parlor, dressed smartly in his military uniform, his sheathed sword swaying at his hip, devising ingenious ways to defeat his dreaded enemy, the Spaniards.

The horses clopped past the old cottage and started to circle Johnson Square, the first one laid out by Oglethorpe and Colonel William Bull in 1733.

Savannah is known, more than anything, for its physical layout, which is highlighted by its evenly placed squares, fifteen of which existed in 1831. The concept was Oglethorpe's, and was based on a unit called a ward. The square sits in the center of the ward, and is surrounded by eight large lots, two on each side. Those on the north and south sides were set aside for houses, ten each, and were referred to as tything lots. Those on the east and west sides were for public buildings and churches and were called trust lots. Although the functional plan for the wards with squares ended soon after Oglethorpe left Georgia, the physical plan was continued by generations of city government.

Oglethorpe started the town with four wards. As Savannah grew, more were added. Because the wards were about the same size, and were laid out plumb to each other like tiles on a floor, a person could stand in the center of one square, look along the intersecting streets and see two, three, or four others.

The squares had many purposes. They served as parks where people could meet, stroll, and relax, and where children could play. Political rallies, public events, and celebrations were staged in them. They contained pumps for the public water supply.

They were home to fire houses, which had to be located throughout the city for quick response to dreaded conflagrations. Cisterns were sunk in most of the squares to provide a ready water source for the thirsty fire engines. To keep grazing cows, hogs, and other animals from the public wells, many of the squares were enclosed with fences. Access was gained through turnstiles.

Andrew and Joseph stuck their heads out the coach window to get a closer look at the new monument to Revolutionary War heroes Nathanael Greene and Casimir Pulaski. The fifty-foot, white pillar dominated the center of Johnson Square and towered over the nearby trees. Andrew said, "It looks like a giant sword sticking in the air."

Grandfather said, "It's called an obelisk, Andrew. Many locals think it's too plain, that Greene and Pulaski deserve something better. But it's all that the city could afford, and I think it's dern smart, all things considered. People aren't happy if they can't complain about something." It sure looked impressive to the boys, the white, New York marble gleaming in the sun.

Joseph's attention was diverted by a negro woman moving through the square. She had a basket balanced on her head. A white baby's face peered over the edge. Despite many people milling about, she never once reached up to secure the basket.

Andrew pointed to a two-story red brick building with a towering, white cupola and announced, "Christ Church! Destroyed in the Great Fire of 1796, rebuilt in 1814."

Not to be outdone, Joseph pointed across the street to a two-story, brick building with large round-top windows in the front and white blocks at the corners. "The Bank of the State of Georgia." Andrew and Joseph learned about the structures in Savannah by asking Mr. McBain and Grandfather questions each time they came to town.

As they played their game, Hercules drove the coach half way around the square and continued south, parking at the northeastern corner of Bull and Broughton. Andrew and Joseph abruptly ended their discussion and shot out of the coach to Mirault's Confectionery store. The shop was clean and bright, with a gleaming, polished, dark wood counter. They hopped on high, wooden stools, making their ravenous presence known to all. A woman appeared from the back room to greet them. Her brown skin glowed against her dark eyes, long, silky, black hair, and white, high-buttoned blouse. Mrs. Mirault owned the most popular confectionery shop in town.

"Bon jour, Monsieur McBain. I see you bring zee Chat ham Militia wis you. How may I help?" Mrs. Mirault's French accent made her even more beautiful to Joseph.

"I think three dishes of ice cream would be a popular request, Mrs. Mirault."

"And zee fla vours?"

"Peach!" Joseph shouted, almost before she finished asking.

"Me, too," Andrew added, placing full trust in Joseph's choice.

Grandfather said, "That will be three peaches, Madam." A brown-skinned man, who stood behind Mrs. Mirault, walked to a back room to fill the request.

Joseph asked, "Mrs. Mirault, how do you make ice cream?" This had been on his mind for months.

Mrs. Mirault placed her hands on her hips. "Now, Monsieur Joseph, zis is a very beeg see cret, and difficult to explain. But one day, I shall show you how to do eet."

"When?"

She looked to the ceiling in thought. "When? Hmmm. When you do somesing zat makes your grandpere and me very proud of you. N'est-ce pas?"

Joseph tensed up his face, wondering what he could possibly do. The arrival of the ice cream in ceramic bowls ended his concentration and he scooped a spoonful into his mouth. It tasted like a cold peach infused with sweet cream. The boys quickly devoured the treat.

As they waited for Grandfather to finish, they tried to see into the back room, to peek at the mysterious process that created something so delicious. They knew that ice came from up north. In the winter, big blocks of it were sawed from frozen, fresh-water lakes and put in the dark holds of ships, which sailed south, making deliveries at ports and some of the bigger plantations, including the Heritage. When the ship arrived in Savannah, the ice was loaded onto drays and carted to local icehouses. Customers then hauled it home to their iceboxes. But how it got from a chunk of ice to a creamy, sweet, fruity, frozen mass was beyond them.

Grandfather stood, patted his belly, and said, "Delicious." They bade good day to Mrs. Mirault and headed home. Hercules guided the coach southward down Bull Street, across Broughton, a residential street in those days, and around Wright Square, also known as Court House Square.

They passed the grand, stucco-over-brick house of Congressman James Moore Wayne and crossed South Broad Street, the most beautiful in all Savannah. It ran east to west for the width of the city and had a promenade of grass down the middle. Both sides of the street were lined with chinaberry trees, which bloomed in fragrant light pink flowers in the spring and provided a cover of shade in the summer.

Across South Broad, Andrew pointed to the McBain family church, with its masonry body, Greek entranceway, and white wooden steeple that soared higher than anything else in town. "Independent Presbyterian Church! President James Madison was at the dedication."

"Monroe," Grandfather corrected. "President James Monroe."

"Oh, I always get them mixed up." Andrew hung his head.

They circled around the next Bull Street square, Chippewa. It was home to the Savannah Theatre, which served as a venue for plays and lectures, and made the ward one of the more fashionable in town.

Soon they were at Liberty Street, the southern border of Savannah. Hercules turned west towards the Louisville Road and home. Joseph sat back and closed his eyes, exhausted from the excitement of the afternoon. Two minutes hadn't passed when he heard Andrew shout, "Look! It's Jumbo." Andrew pointed to Elbert Square, two short blocks to the north on Montgomery Street. Grandfather called their new destination to Hercules.

"Tu'n hawss, tu'n." Hercules steered the coach to the edge of the quiet, sparsely developed, residential square. Andrew and Joseph jumped out and ran through the turnstile to Jumbo, a scrawny black man who was manipulating something on his lap. He saw the boys, smiled, and returned to his handiwork. They plopped down on the ground at his feet.

Jumbo stood just over five feet tall and weighed about one hundred pounds, not much bigger than Andrew or Joseph. He was as black as night with flecks of gray in his hair and many lines on his face. Everyone in Savannah knew Jumbo from his two talents. He could turn a few strands of a palmetto frond into a perfect replica of a rose, which he sold to passersby. And he also performed magic tricks.

Without raising his head, Jumbo said, "Kin ah he'p oonuh tuhday?" Jumbo rarely looked at people when he spoke; he looked at his own hands, which were always occupied.

Just then, Grandfather came over. "Hello, Jumbo."

"Hello, Massa Cottonmouf." Jumbo continued working on a rose.

"How much for two roses, Jumbo? I need to make the ladies at home happy."

"Wut ebuh oonuh wan' tuh pay, massa." Jumbo always let his customers set the price. He found he almost always got more than the one shilling he would have charged.

"How about two shillings?"

"Dat good fuh me. Ah gwine mek anudduh."

"Take your time." Grandfather stepped over to Jumbo, whispered something in his ear and turned to Joseph. "You two stay right here with Jumbo. I need to ask Hercules to go back to Mrs. Mirault's. That dern ice cream was so good, I forgot all about the cakes your mother asked me to buy. Then I'm going to buy some segars. I'll be back in a few minutes."

Joseph replied, "Yes, sir," and turned back to watch Jumbo. Besides the three of them, the square was empty. At one point, a negro appeared at the public pump in the center of the square, noisily filled a bucket of water, and left.

Jumbo eventually asked Andrew, "Wut dat behine oonuh yez?"

Andrew brushed his ears with his hands. "Nothing, Jumbo."

Jumbo displayed his empty hand, reached behind Andrew's head, and pulled back. He looked questioningly at his fist, then opened it to reveal a shilling coin.

"Lawdy, lookee wut ah fine." He handed it to Andrew.

Then Jumbo squinted at the side of Joseph's head. "Ah see anudduh!" He put his hand by Joseph's ear, pulled out a shilling, and handed it to him.

Andrew and Joseph looked at each other, wondering how much money could be behind their ears. Then they heard someone from behind them say, "Now that there's a real good trick. Where'd ya learn it, boy?"

Andrew and Joseph turned around to see a tall, skinny white man with dark hair that grew straight up, wearing dirty blue overalls and a dull red shirt. Joseph felt uncomfortable in his presence and looked for Grandfather or Hercules, but saw neither. In fact, he saw no one on the streets around the desolate square. He glanced at Andrew, who was looking back at him.

"Ah jes laa'n it," Jumbo replied softly as he concentrated on his rose.

"Maybe you can teach me to make a purdy flower." The intruder grinned and leaned forward with his hand out, expecting Jumbo to give him part of a frond.

Jumbo shook his head. "Ah don' t'ink ah kin."

The stranger straightened, his smile gone. "Who owns you, boy?"

Jumbo placed the finished flower on the bench. "Ain' hab no massa."

The man's eyes darted around the square. "Well, you do now!" Instantly, two men appeared from behind nearby trees and pounced on Jumbo. They held him down as the man in the red shirt tried to tie leather strips around Jumbo's wrists and ankles.

Andrew stood up and screamed, "Hercules, help! Help!"

Joseph hollered, too. He saw a two-horse wagon at the edge of the square. He waved frantically at the driver, who yelled, "Hurry on up!" to the attackers.

The three men were having trouble binding Jumbo as he squirmed away from their grasp. The man in the red shirt said, "Hold still, boy, or I'll kill you now!" Andrew jumped on the man's back and wrapped his arms around his neck. The man straightened and grabbed at Andrew's hands, twisting to cast him off, which caused Andrew's body to swing back and forth, almost parallel to the ground. But Andrew, so strong from working with bricks, could not be pried loose.

"What's going on?" Grandfather called, running across the square, unable to see clearly, but sensing that something was wrong. The two men trying to secure Jumbo raised their heads. Unimpressed by the old man wearing a kerchief, they returned to their task, but were unable to bind the wiry negro.

Joseph ran to help Andrew and wrapped his arms around the man's legs, but a kick caught Joseph squarely on the forehead, sprawling him on the ground. His head stung and something wet ran down his face. He heard Grandfather yell, "Stay there, Joseph!"

Joseph saw Grandfather lift one of the men off Jumbo and his spirits rose, convinced they would now thrash these criminals. Then Joseph heard a sickening crack and saw Grandfather fall like a board to the ground. The wagon driver, a shovel in his hands, stood over the old man. He was fat with a full, curly brown beard. He shouted angrily, "You sorry mules can't even lick two boys and an ol' coot!" He then swung the shovel at Jumbo, hitting him on the shoulder. Jumbo continued to fight but the next swing hit him flush on the back of his head and his body relaxed.

The man pointed to Jumbo with the shovel and said to the two men holding the leather straps, "Now tie that little nigger up and lit's git outta here!" They bound Jumbo's arms and legs and carried him like a hog to slaughter.

The man in the red shirt finally pried Andrew's arms apart and threw him off. Andrew landed with a flop. As he rose on his hands and knees, the man kicked him in the stomach. Andrew expelled an "ooof" and folded up. The man kneeled, grabbed Andrew's feet and said to the driver, "Let's take this one, too. He'll bring a price, even after I whip the tar outta him."

"Just be quick about it!" the driver ordered.

The man dragged Andrew to the wagon. Joseph struggled to his feet, charged, and wrapped his arms around the man's legs again, but he was easily kicked away. As Joseph lay stunned on the ground, he felt a hand at his neck. It tore away his necklace, the possession he valued most in the whole world.

Joseph saw the man in the red shirt and the driver lift Andrew over the fence while the two others loaded Jumbo into the back of the wagon. Jumbo looked at Joseph and begged, "Please he'p me!" but Joseph was helpless, too. He closed his eyes and bowed his head.

Joseph heard the crack of a whip and expected to hear the wagon pull away, but instead he heard a scream. He looked up and saw the driver clutching at his neck, the tail of a whip wrapped around it. Hercules pulled the whip handle to him, delivering the man with it. He punched the driver in the face so hard it opened up like a smashed tomato. The man dropped the shovel and fell to his knees. Blood flowed out his nose, over his mouth, and disappeared into the top of his beard.

The man in the red shirt dove for the shovel, reaching it as Hercules stepped on the shaft. The thief looked up just in time to see a blur of a fist slam into his face. He fell backwards, his split eyebrow spurting blood.

Hercules looked in the wagon for Jumbo. One of the men who had carried Jumbo was at the driver's bench trying to release the brake. The other was in the back, aiming a shotgun at Hercules's head. "Don't you move," he yelled, as his two bleeding cohorts crawled into the wagon. Hercules stood, defenseless, looking for somewhere to jump.

"Blast his brains out!" yelled the driver, blood spraying from his mouth. The man cocked the gun. But, at that very moment, the other man released the brake and yanked the reins too hard. As the horses lurched ahead, the wagon jerked violently, causing the man with the gun to fall forward, and shoot his own foot. The blast frightened the horses even more, and they reared back. Hercules leaped onto the back end of the wagon and grabbed the sack that was Jumbo. As the horses strained forward, Hercules fell backwards and hit the ground. He was followed by Jumbo, who landed with a thud, becoming perhaps the only person thankful for those sandy Savannah streets.

The bandits raced down Montgomery Street, two holding their faces and one his foot, all hollering in agony into the wind.

Grandfather carried Joseph to the water pump in the center of the square, but became exhausted by the effort and sat on Jumbo's bench. Hercules untied Jumbo, then carried Andrew next to Joseph. Jumbo staggered to them and sat beside Grandfather.

Several men from the houses bordering the square ran up to the recovering warriors. One asked Grandfather, "Sir, we heard a gunshot. Are you all right?"

The old man said, "We can manage, thanks."

The residents took a few steps back and stared at the huffing men and boys.

Hercules got a cloth from the coach, pumped water on it, and cleaned the blood from Joseph. He asked, "Gran' Massa, oonuh wan' me tuh fetch Doctuh Minis?"

Grandfather barely shook his head. "Wait a few minutes. We'll drive over."

They sat in silence in the serene, tree-filled square, trying to regain their strength from the encounter, though it had lasted only a few minutes. Soon, Grandfather and Joseph were able to stand, but Andrew could still not get off the ground. Hercules cradled him in his arms and they hobbled to the coach.

Inside the cab, Grandfather called out, "Jumbo, come with us. Let our doctor look at you."

"No, massa. Don' bodduh fuh me."

Grandfather limped over to Jumbo, put some coins in his shirt pocket, patted him on the back, and whispered something. Jumbo lowered his face into his cupped hands, those same hands that could make living roses out of dying fronds and snare glittering coins out of thin air. They now had to heal a battered soul.

Hercules drove to Dr. Minis's office on Johnson Square, where the doctor tended to the cuts, lumps, and bruises. Minis told them the wounds would heal quickly and promised to visit the plantation in a few days to check on them.

They left the doctor's office, ointments glistening and snowy white bandages in place, a hobbled but victorious army, and headed home in silence. During the ride, Joseph eventually asked, "Who were those men, Grandfather?"

Grandfather labored to answer the question. "I guess thieves, Joseph. They wanted to steal Jumbo. Probably to sell him in another state."

Joseph asked, "Wouldn't Jumbo's owner come after him?"

"Jumbo doesn't have an owner, Joseph. He's a free person of color."

Joseph narrowed his eyes. "What's that?"

Grandfather breathed deeply as he decided how to proceed with the conversation. He replied, "Just as it sounds. A negro that's free."

Joseph tilted his head. "You mean free, like white people?"

"No. But more free than a slave. He's not owned by anyone."

Joseph looked at Andrew to see if he was listening, but his friend stared out the coach window, his arms hugging his mid-section. "How does that happen, Grandfather?"

Grandfather shifted in his seat to get a better look at Joseph's wounds. "Well, each state is different, but in Georgia, there are several ways. Before the year of our Lord 1801, owners were allowed to free their servants any time they wanted. Servants could even save money and buy their freedom if their master agreed. However, the white community became concerned that too many free negroes would be a bad influence on the slaves and a nuisance to whites, so the state legislature passed a law prohibiting voluntary freeing of slaves. After that, owners needed permission from the state. The legislature has never been too generous in that way."

Joseph pointed in the direction of town. "What about Mrs. Mirault?"

"She escaped to Savannah from the revolution in Hayti as a young girl with her family. That was before the authorities put a stop to that immigration." Joseph was relieved. He couldn't imagine her being owned by anyone.

"Is there any other way to free a negro?" Joseph asked, thinking of Andrew.

"Children of free negro women are free. I believe that's how Jumbo came to be free."

It was almost dark, and Hercules had quickened the pace of the horses, causing Grandfather and the boys to bounce inside the cab. Joseph's forehead throbbed with each bump. Their voices vibrated. It made them all the wearier. But Joseph was still curious. "Why would someone want to kidnap a free person of color who makes roses out of palmetto fronds?"

Grandfather lightly touched the lump on his head. He winced and pulled his hand away. "I guess they were going to kidnap him in any case. They didn't care if he was slave or free."

Joseph thought back to the incident. "Before they jumped on Jumbo, one of the men asked him who owned him. Jumbo said he didn't have a master."

The old man nodded. "That makes sense. I'm certain they wanted to steal a free negro."

"Why?" Joseph was not giving up.

Grandfather sighed. "Each free negro must have a white guardian, and though the relationship might be close, the guardian may not want to spend the time or money trying to find him if he's missing. However, slaves are valuable pieces of property and their owners make mighty attempts to recover them. Kidnappers are dealt with severely."

Something still didn't make sense to Joseph. "Why would a servant want to become free? They have food to eat, clothes to wear, and a place to live."

Grandfather closed his eyes for a few seconds before replying, "That's enough for today, Joseph. I'm very tired."

Joseph sat back in his seat, fascinated about what he'd just learned, and what it might mean for Andrew. He turned to his friend, who was still staring out the window. Joseph squinted into the night, but couldn't tell where they were on the Augusta Road, even with a bright, full moon. He suddenly felt sad. He touched his neck, and looked at his grandfather. The old man seemed to have aged many years in the last few hours. Clumps of his white hair stood up and the skin on his deeply lined face drooped as if no longer anchored to his bones. "Grandfather, those men stole my necklace."

Grandfather strained to see Joseph in the darkness. He got up, sat on the bench next to his grandson, and put his arm around Joseph's shoulders. "Don't be upset. We still have all the memories that my father gave us many years ago when he came to Georgia. Someone can take a necklace, but no one can ever take our memories. We must never forget them."

They rode the rest of the way in silence.

CHAPTER 3

The Necklace's Journey

April 1831

As soon as they heard the approaching horses, Joseph's parents ran up the avenue of oaks carrying lanterns. Hercules stopped to let them in the coach. Sarah McBain's mouth opened in shock as the light from her lamp exposed the bandaged and bruised faces. She hung the lantern on the lamp hook, squeezed between Grandfather and Joseph, and gave them both one-arm hugs. Mr. McBain sat on the bench seat next to Andrew and said, "My good Lord, Father! What in the world happened?"

Grandfather folded his arms across his chest. "We were in Elbert Square with Jumbo. Bandits tried to kidnap him. We stopped them."

James McBain looked at Joseph, still locked in his mother's embrace, and tried to make sense of Grandfather's words. "Some . . . someone tried to kidnap Jumbo with Hercules there?"

Grandfather said, "Hercules and I weren't there at the outset, so Joseph and Andrew had to take care of things. And they did, like real Highlanders." He punctuated that statement with an emphatic nod of his head.

James stared at Sarah, his eyes asking, "Do you believe this?" He then squinted at the purple lump on Grandfather's head.

Sarah finally released Joseph. James leaned across the cab, rested his hand on his son's knee and inspected his bandage. "How are you, Joseph?"

"I'm fine, Father," Joseph lied. "Just a little sore."

Mr. McBain put his hand near Joseph's forehead, and his son pulled back. McBain asked, "Dr. Minis?"

Grandfather said, "Yes. And the boys didn't make a peep."

McBain turned to Andrew, saw him hunched over, and put an arm around his shoulders. "And you, Andrew? Your ribs?"

Andrew tried to sit up. "No, sir. I got kicked in the stomach. But the doctor said I'm fine. Nothing broken or torn."

They reached the front gate to the house and Hercules was at the coach door. Sarah stepped out first, and Joseph followed. About one hundred negroes, eerily silent in the torch light, crowded around the coach. As Joseph stepped to the ground, his sister Amy, one year older, rushed forward and hugged him. Joseph was too tired to defend himself.

Andrew exited next. The negroes strained to see if he was hurt, knowing something bad had happened. McBain then appeared and called for Nurse Rynah to take Andrew to the plantation hospital for a bath and supper.

Grandfather emerged last. He stood on the top step of the coach and saw the throng of servants staring up at him. He raised his arms high in the air in a show of triumph. The negroes cheered. Some raised their arms as well and danced in place.

McBain held Hercules's arm and said, "Thank you for protecting my family." Hercules nodded.

After the family disappeared into the house, the negroes surged around Hercules like hounds at feeding time, hungry to hear his story. Hercules did his best as he led the horses to the stables, getting bumped and jostled the entire way. After learning of the ordeal, the servants congratulated each other on the grand victory for the plantation.

The McBains' supper went untouched as Grandfather repeated the story in greater detail. The house servants huddled beyond the doorway and listened. Joseph, tired and sad, slumped in his chair, anxious to go to bed. But a rejuvenated Grandfather kept describing Joseph's and Andrew's bravery, lifting Joseph's spirits, at least temporarily. McBain patted Joseph on the back and said, "I'm going to town tomorrow, son. We'll find those men. They'll pay for this."

Grandfather said, "Go ahead, but if those bandits were Murrellites as I suspect, you'll never see them again in these parts. Even if you pay some men, they won't know where to start." He was referring to a large gang of professional thieves who operated throughout the South.

McBain, exhausted as well, massaged his eyes. "Maybe you're right. Why don't you get some sleep and we'll talk about it tomorrow?"

As the family stood, Joseph confessed. "Father, those men stole Great-grandfather's necklace. It's been in the family for one hundred years, and I lost it." Joseph touched his bare neck.

His mother said, "Joseph, you're alive and healthy. That's what's important. Necklaces can be replaced." She gently kissed his cheek.

"Not this one." Joseph fought back tears.

Joseph dreamed of the fight. The men were pulling away with Andrew in their wagon. Joseph was on the ground, paralyzed. He tried to scream for help but couldn't make a sound. He was no Highlander.

"Joseph! Joseph! You're having bad dreams! I can hear you in my room." Joseph awoke and saw Amy looking down at him. He was covered with sweat. He blinked to make sure he was no longer dreaming. "Do you want me to sleep with you?"

Joseph considered her offer. He wanted someone to protect him, but not necessarily his sister. "No. I'll be all right, Amy."

Amy pulled her robe tightly around herself. "I'll see you in the morning then. Do you want to take your lessons?"

"Of course. I don't want to anger Miss Kelly." He was certain of that. He'd rather have angered the wild hogs that scavenged their vegetable plots.

Amy kissed Joseph on the cheek and left.

Joseph awoke the next morning looking forward to something else to occupy his thoughts, which he knew would not be easy. He couldn't move without pain. It felt like a knife had stuck in his head and Dr. Minis forgot to remove it. With some difficulty, he washed at the large metal basin in his room, dressed, and went downstairs to breakfast. Amy was finishing her meal. He slowly sat at his place at the table.

Jinny, one of the cooks, lifted his spirits as she placed in front of him a dish of his favorite breakfast—sweet potato waffles covered with bacon and a special treat, maple syrup, imported from New England. The smoky, sweet aroma made his stomach growl. As he hungrily cut into the food, Jinny stood behind him. She placed both hands on his shoulders, lightly kissed the top of his head and said, "Good morning, li'l Massa Oglet'orpe." Amy laughed out loud, and a piece of bacon flew out of her mouth. No one on Heritage Plantation escaped Grandfather's stories, certainly not the negroes. They all knew of the great Oglethorpe, and Joseph's and Andrew's fascination with him.

After allowing Joseph time to devour his food, Amy said, "Come, Joseph. Miss Kelly is waiting."

Miss Kelly, their private teacher, did not care whose children they were, lessons started at 7:30 sharp. Amy and Joseph walked to the plantation schoolhouse, a small whitewashed brick cottage about twenty-five yards to the west of their house and away from the manufacturing activity. It was spring and Miss Kelly's garden was exploding with spicy pink and red roses. On the way, Joseph looked to the clay pits by the river and saw Andrew, slightly crouched, helping the older negroes. Joseph knew he'd be there, even though he should have been recovering. Bricks were building materials, and Andrew wanted to build.

Just as Joseph sat at his desk, Miss Kelly walked into the classroom followed by Mary, Rebecca, and John Stiles of Vale Royal Plantation and Catherine and George Williamson of Brampton Plantation, neighbors who shared their teacher. They saw Joseph's bandaged head and huddled around him. Miss Kelly said, "Children, please go to your desks right now."

The children scampered to their seats, except George, who said, "Joseph, you're not wearing your necklace. Where is it?"

Joseph sighed and looked out the schoolhouse window. In the distance he saw the Savannah River flowing by. He thought about his necklace, and the journey it had made.

Andrew and Joseph both were born on the night of March 20, 1820, at the Heritage Plantation. Mr. McBain had sent for Dr. Jones when Rynah, the plantation nurse, said the missus was ready. As Grandfather told it, Joseph shot out like a cannonball. Were the doctor not there to catch him, Joseph would have flown out the window and would still be hanging off the branch of a tree, "a cryin' and a squirmin'."

While Dr. Jones, Mr. McBain, and Grandfather were sharing a congratulatory glass of port, Gully came knocking at the big house door. His pregnant wife Lucy was having pains. Rynah rose to attend to her midwife duties. Dr. Jones said, "As long as I'm here, I might as well join you."

Rynah hesitated, knowing that most of the negroes preferred her to a white doctor. But she gathered her wits and said, "Thank you, Massa Doctuh." Thirty minutes later, Andrew entered this world.

Joseph was named for his great-grandfather, the first of the McBains of Georgia. Andrew was named for Andrew Bryan, the founder of what would become known as the First African Baptist Church in Savannah.

Because of the timing of their births, Andrew was destined to be Joseph's companion, playmate, and personal servant. This was especially fortunate for Andrew, whose parents died months after he had been born.

During their early years, they played together all day under the supervision of the older, female servants, or maumas, who were addressed as "Maum." Once Joseph started school at the age of six, Andrew played with the other negro children until Joseph was done with his studies.

Joseph attended classes with Amy and several neighbors' children five days a week. They had two short breaks, and then finished around two o'clock. After the midday meal, Joseph worked on study lessons assigned by Miss Kelly. Playtime with Andrew started at five o'clock.

One day, about six months after Joseph had started school, Andrew came into Joseph's room early, ready to play. Joseph put him off, saying he had to finish his lessons first. Andrew lowered his head, so Joseph asked him to sit and wait. Andrew did, and his eyes followed Joseph's hand as he wrote. Joseph noticed Andrew's fascination, and explained what he had learned that day, and how he prepared his lessons. Andrew asked Joseph to teach him how to write something. Joseph chose the letters, "a," "b," and "c." Andrew did them correctly, the first time.

Andrew came back early the next day and just about every day thereafter for the next twelve years, even after he started working on brick production at the age of ten. As Joseph learned the alphabet, he taught it to Andrew. As Joseph learned arithmetic tables, he taught them to Andrew. The same was true for history, geography, spelling, grammar, writing, and all the other subjects. This made study time more fun for Joseph. And Andrew received what very few negroes in Georgia had, an academic education.

Every day the boys were allowed about two hours of playtime. Sometimes they played with the other negro boys on the plantation, and sometimes by themselves. In either case, they often had to escape Grandfather, who felt everyone, white and black, should be aware of the history of the McBain family, Savannah, Georgia, America, Scotland, Europe, and the rest of the world. Because of his age and poor eyesight, he spent less time working on the plantation businesses and more time trying to find audiences for his stories. After a full day of school and homework, Joseph wanted to play. So the boys snuck out of the house and ran to a field or the river.

Grandfather knew their escape routes and hiding places. If he wanted to talk, he would find them. Grandfather preferred one topic to any other, and that was his hero, General James Oglethorpe. After all, his father knew and fought alongside the man. Grandfather felt that to understand Georgia, one had to know its founder, and he made certain that Joseph and Andrew did. As frequent as the stories were, the boys never tired of hearing them, and at an early age they knew well of the general's adventurous life.

James Edward Oglethorpe was born in 1696 in London, England. His father died five years later, leaving James, his brothers, and sisters to be raised by their mother. James received a commission in the British Army when he was seventeen, and went to the best schools, including Corpus Christi College at Oxford. After a year at college, he resigned his commission, left school, and traveled to Paris to attend a military academy. After graduating, he worked as an aide-de-camp to Prince Eugene of Savoy, the commander of troops of the Holy Roman Empire, which was at war with the Ottoman Empire. After Prince Eugene defeated the Turks, Oglethorpe returned to England and school. But college no longer held excitement for him, and he moved home to the family estate, looking for something to do with his life. He decided to serve in the government and was elected to Parliament at the age of twenty-five, to a seat held previously by his father and two older brothers. James performed dutifully, if not notably, for six years, before he made a name for himself as an advocate for the rights of British sailors.

While Oglethorpe was waging this campaign, an architect friend, Robert Castell, wrote and published a book titled *Villas of the Ancients Illustrated*. In doing so, Castell had fallen into debt and was thrown in jail, where he contracted small pox and died.

Oglethorpe was angered by his friend's unnecessary death and pressed Parliament to investigate English prisons. A committee was formed, with Oglethorpe chosen to head it. A year later the committee issued reports criticizing three prisons and its wardens. Some measures were taken, but the experience left Oglethorpe feeling unfulfilled. There had to be a better alternative for the honest, hard-working poor people of England. His solution set his life on a path he could not have imagined.

When Andrew and Joseph were just nine years old, Grandfather told them about Oglethorpe's friend, Robert Castell, and his book. Grandfather had to explain many things to them, but they gained an understanding of Castell's accomplishment.

The boys were so inspired by Castell they invented a new game that day. They lay on their backs in a field near the house, closed their eyes, and tried to envision an ancient villa. Joseph told Andrew he saw a big, stone building surrounded by columns on a mountaintop. There were statues of warriors on the roof. Andrew said he saw a big white house, with an old man sitting on a rocking chair on the front porch, being served a glass of lemonade by an even older servant.

After they had exhausted their blind visions, they opened their eyes and tried to spot villas in the clouds of the late afternoon sky. They saw dozens in all shapes and sizes and would have stayed there for hours if Joseph's mother hadn't called him for supper. They agreed to play the game again the next day.

Several months later, Grandfather saw the two lying on the grass by the house, pointing to the sky, and asked what they were doing. Joseph told him. Grandfather said, "So, you little buzzards liked that story about Castell?" He motioned them to follow him inside the house and sat them at the table in the parlor. Grandfather went downstairs, and they waited.

The old man returned with a book almost as big as Joseph's desk top at school, and placed it gently on the table. He had Joseph move over one chair so he could sit between them. He opened the front cover and the title jumped out like a green tree frog: *The Villas of the Ancients Illustrated*. Andrew and Joseph gawked at each other. Grandfather actually had The Book. They felt like the most special boys in the world. It was as if Mr. Castell was in the room, a long lost friend paying them a visit.

Grandfather paged to the preface and explained that Castell wanted to translate and explain some fellow named Vitruvius, a name Andrew and Joseph had difficulty pronouncing. While Vitruvius was a great architect, he did not cover to any great extent the situating of Roman villas, which Castell was attempting to do. The boys had no idea what this meant and buried Grandfather with questions.

The next page listed the subscribers to the book and the number each had purchased. The boys knelt on the chair seats to get a closer look. There were important-sounding names, like the lord of this and the earl of that. One duke had even bought six copies. However, they did not see the name they were looking for. Then Grandfather turned the page, revealing more names. Joseph inspected each one until he came upon it. "James Oglethorpe, Esq., 2 copies." Andrew put his finger on it and smiled at Joseph.

Grandfather continued turning, and the boys saw something they could understand, a drawing. It was an engraving of a floor plan of the rooms of the master's house and its grounds. Mr. Castell had placed a letter of the alphabet on each section of the engraving, and on the side of the page, he explained it. There was a summer dining room and, on the opposite side, a winter dining room. There were summer apartments and winter apartments. Even the farmhouse had many rooms, including a winepress and cellar, an oil press and cellar, a husbandman's lodge and storeroom, a bathing room, and a sweating room. And on the grounds, there was a hen house and a dunghill. Around the borders of the engraving were strange words. Joseph asked, "Grandfather, what does *So-lan-us* mean?"

Grandfather's eyes scanned the page. "Those are the names of the winds, placed in the direction from which they blow. Vitruvius said it was important to position the house to protect against unhealthy winds."

Healthy and unhealthy winds? Joseph always thought wind was wind. *The Villas of the Ancients* was becoming more mysterious with every page.

They spent an hour going through the book, asking questions, and severely testing Grandfather's patience. But as they looked at the engravings, they could imagine the buildings not just as flat depictions on paper, but grand houses, with soaring towers and columns, with rooms so large they made voices echo, and with chandeliers that sparkled like diamonds.

At one point, Joseph saw the word "beast," and asked Grandfather if the beasts were alligators.

Grandfather lowered his head closer to the page, found the word, and silently read the sentence. "Mmmm. Before the ancients built a house or started a town, they killed a cow or a sheep that lived in the area and cut out its liver to see if the organ was healthy. If it wasn't, they wouldn't build there because the people might suffer the same fate, eating food from the same soil and drinking the same water."

Andrew's forehead creased and he said, "Poor cows." Then he asked, "What did they build the villas with, Grampah?"

Grandfather pulled his head away from the book. "Whatever they had available. Probably bricks, stone, or wood. Maybe even marble."

Andrew's eyes widened at the mention of bricks. "Bricks like we make here at the Heritage?"

"Not exactly like we make, but close. Bricks have been around for a long time."

Andrew gently ran his hand over the page with the illustration of Villa Laurentinum. "Grampah, how did they know how to build big, beautiful villas? How did they know to build a wine cellar or a dunghill?"

"Well, the owner of the property hired an architect and described what he wanted in his villa—the number of rooms—and how he wanted the villa to look. The architect then prepared drawings, and if the owner liked them, he had the villa built, usually with the help of the architect." Grandfather lightly tapped the page with the tip of his finger.

Andrew cocked his head. "Someone really gets to draw houses as work?"

Grandfather smiled. "Yes, Andrew. And it's very important. Look at these illustrations. Drawing well is a small part. You must know what to draw and where." Grandfather then swept his arm around, indicating the propriety of the house in which they were sitting.

Andrew started to say something and then stopped. He looked at Joseph and then back at Grampah. "Grampah, can a servant be a, a, you know, an *arctic*?"

Grandfather placed a hand on Andrew's head and rubbed it gently. "I don't know of one, Andrew, but that doesn't mean it can't happen. Servants do all sorts of work."

Andrew rested his chin on his hands and examined the book in silence.

A few weeks after Grandfather first showed the boys Castell's book, Joseph asked him if they could see it again. Grandfather asked, "Are you thinking of building a villa?"

Joseph said, "No. We want to draw one."

Grandfather saluted like a soldier and retrieved the book. He let them page through it, amused by their curiosity. Finally, Andrew asked, "Grampah, how did you get this book? It looks like it's hundreds of years old."

"That's a long story, Andrew." Of course, everything told by Grandfather was a long story. "But to answer your question, my father gave it to me."

"He did? How did he get it? Did he buy it?" Joseph fired questions, his curiosity building. Grandfather put up his hand to slow Joseph.

After waiting a few seconds, Grandfather said, "Oglethorpe gave it to him."

Andrew's jaw dropped. Joseph looked to the book and then back to Grandfather. Finally, Joseph uttered, "You mean the real General Oglethorpe? He actually gave it to my great-grandfather? In person?"

"Yes, he did. As a gift." Grandfather beamed at disclosing this fact that linked the McBains with the founder of Georgia.

Joseph's eyes twinkled. "A gift? How did he know him?"

"My father served him." Grandfather often made Joseph beg once the old man saw the boy was excited to learn something, feeding him just tiny bits of information.

"Grandfather, stop teasing! Tell me everything."

Grandfather laughed, realizing Joseph had figured out his game. "Remember when Castell died?" The boys nodded. "That was Oglethorpe's motivation to come to America, to help poor people like his friend. He got a group of men together, and they asked King George for permission to found a colony named Georgia, and he agreed. Those men, the trustees, raised money, chartered a ship, found people who wanted to settle here, and sent them on the voyage in the year of our Lord 1732.

"Oglethorpe led the expedition and convinced Chief Tomochichi of the Yamacraw tribe to allow them to settle here. He spent over a year getting the colony started. He laid out the town in its pattern of wards and squares. He had the colonists clear the trees and construct houses. For protection, he built a fort and a guardhouse, erected a seventeen-foot wooden wall around the town, and established several smaller communities ringing the town. At the wishes of the trustees, he laid out a ten-acre garden for experimental plantings to determine which crops would grow here. He also saw to it that mulberry trees were planted for a silk industry.

He established a system of government where tythingmen and constables kept the peace and bailiffs held court and enforced the law. He negotiated with Tomochichi and other Indians and signed a peace treaty with them. He welcomed newly arriving settlers and awarded land grants, usually fifty acres to each family. He personally attended to the people, and grieved with them as sickness took about twenty lives just months after they arrived."

Joseph interrupted, "Great-grandfather was one of those first colonists?"

"No. After the first fifteen months, Oglethorpe returned to England. He had successfully settled the northern border of Georgia with Savannah as the main town. But there was the threat of invasion from the south by the Spaniards in Florida and the French in the Mississippi River basin. Oglethorpe knew he had to settle the southern border, the Altamaha River, but getting people to go there would be difficult. They had to be good farmers who could survive in the worst conditions and also be fearless fighters. The trustees went to the Highlands of Scotland, the land of our ancestors, to find such people. My grandfather had a small cattle farm there but was killed in the Scottish Uprising of 1715, leaving my grandmother to raise her two infant sons. She died twenty years later, God rest her soul, just when the trustees sent recruiters to Inverness to find volunteers to settle the southern part of Georgia. My father was just twenty at the time, and decided to start a new life in America. He left his older brother Daniel, after whom I'm named, and sailed here as an indentured servant to the trustees."

By this time Andrew and Joseph were practically in Grandfather's lap. Joseph asked, "Was Oglethorpe on that ship?"

Grandfather had each boy stand by his side and put an arm around each. "No, but Chief Tomochichi and a few of the Yamacraws were. Oglethorpe had taken them to England with him to meet the trustees and the King, and they returned on the same ship as my father and the other Highlanders. That's when he became friends with Tomochichi's nephew, Toonahowi, who gave my father the necklace your father now wears."

Joseph voice went so high, it squeaked. "Really? He got it from one of the Indians? That's the most beautiful necklace in the world."

"Yes, it is. My father treasured it, as did I. Your father does, too." Grandfather stopped for a moment at the warm memory. "After my father and the Highlanders arrived in Georgia, they founded New Inverness, which is now called Darien. He helped build the town, and when Oglethorpe went to war with the Spaniards, my father fought alongside him. He even saved Oglethorpe's life when the general's own men of the 42nd Regiment of Foot rebelled on Cumberland Island. My father was at Fort Mose when the Spaniards slaughtered the Highlanders and South Carolinians during Oglethorpe's siege of St. Augustine. And he was at Oglethorpe's side when the general defeated the Spaniards on St. Simon's Island. Shortly after that, in the year of our Lord 1743, Oglethorpe returned to England. For the last time, as it turned out. Before he left Georgia, he personally arranged for my father a grant of good cattle-raising land on the Savannah River, about ten miles west of here. He also gave him a gift of a few books. *Villas of the Ancients* was one."

Andrew and Joseph looked at each other in disbelief. Not only did they have the book, it was one of Oglethorpe's two copies.

Andrew's inquisitiveness took hold. "Grampah, would General Oglethorpe have discovered Georgia if Master Castell hadn't died in prison?"

Grandfather laid his hand on the book and wondered how a nine-year-old would think to ask such a question. "I don't rightly know, Andrew. Georgia would have been settled eventually, but whether it would have been by Oglethorpe or some other Englishman or even a Spaniard, no one can really say."

Andrew mused, "I'm sad that Master Castell died, Grampah, but I'm happy General Oglethorpe discovered Georgia."

"So am I, Andrew. So am I," Grandfather said. He hugged both boys and left. Andrew and Joseph agreed to play the discovery of Georgia the next day. Joseph would be Oglethorpe and Andrew would be Tomochichi. The day after, they'd switch. Then they drew their first villa.

That night at dinner, Grandfather told the family about the day's lesson. Mr. McBain turned to Joseph and said, "Son, does that make you proud to be a McBain?"

Joseph sat up straight. "Yes, sir!"

James McBain unbuttoned his shirt collar, removed the leather string of teeth and colored stones from his neck, and placed it around Joseph's neck. Sarah McBain, Amy, and Grandfather clapped lightly as he did. Joseph carefully fingered his new necklace. His father had entrusted him, at the age of nine, with the honor and responsibility of carrying on the McBain heritage.

"Joseph! Joseph! Please pay attention. You're doing poorly enough in grammar as it is," Miss Kelly scolded.

Joseph looked around and saw the other children snickering at him. He sat up in his chair. "I'm sorry, Miss Kelly." Joseph forced himself to follow the lesson.

When he joined Andrew later that day, Joseph asked his companion how he was feeling. Andrew replied, "Still hurts, Master Joseph. How about you?"

Joseph stretched out his arms and grimaced. "I ache all over. Grandfather says we fought like Highlanders, but every time I think about the necklace, I feel terrible."

They worked on Joseph's study lessons. Afterwards, they drew a villa with a moat around it, to keep out the bad men of the world.

CHAPTER 4

Southern Honor

1832

James Hamilton Couper picked up the piece of paper from the table in James McBain's study. He held it in both hands, extended his arms, and studied it. "What is this, James?" he finally asked McBain, who was standing with his two other guests, William Washington Gordon and Gazaway Bugg Lamar.

McBain looked at the paper. "A drawing of a house. Pretty good, don't you think?"

"Yes," responded Couper. "May I ask who did it?" Couper resembled McBain. They were both Scotsmen, almost six feet tall with muscular builds, and had black, wavy hair. McBain had hazel eyes and longer hair, but they could be taken for brothers.

"My son and his negro companion, Andrew. They're quite taken by architecture. They left it here for me to review." McBain had seen several drawings over the past year, and this one was his favorite.

Couper raised his eyebrows. "A negro, you say? How old is this Andrew?"

"Twelve, the same as my son. They were born just minutes apart."

"Well, this is quite an effort for twelve year-olds." Couper was one of the richest planters in Georgia. He owned half of Hopeton Plantation in Glynn County, with thousands of acres and hundreds of slaves. He was also a horticulturist, geologist, archaeologist, ornithologist, herpetologist, and an amateur architect. He had even designed his own family mansion. McBain knew that Couper's compliment of the drawing was not to be taken lightly.

Gordon stepped over and said, "It looks like a house from a foreign land."

Lamar joined them and added, "I like it. It really is quite well drawn. Even the cow."

The drawing was the front elevation of a house, which had two stories over a ground floor. The portico was reached by two curved stairways. The main body had five sets of vertical openings, called bays, across the rectangular face. Circular wings, resembling castle towers, were attached to each side of the house. A dome sat in the center of the roof, flanked by statues of warriors with swords drawn. A smiling cow stood at the foot of the stairs.

"And this?" Gordon asked, pointing to another paper with columns of figures.

McBain picked it up. "Oh! When the boys finish drawing a house, Joseph calculates the cost to build it."

The stout Lamar studied the paper. "This isn't far off. He lists costs for tree clearing, excavation, bricks, mortar, nails, marble, lumber, iron, windows, furnishings, painting, and labor." Lamar then whistled lightly. "The total is two hundred thousand dollars and the architect's fee is fifty thousand! The boys appreciate a handsome profit. I like that." The men laughed.

McBain said, "Well, shall we talk?" They took seats at the table. McBain suggested, "Mr. Gordon, why don't you start things off?"

McBain had run into Gordon in town a few days before and told him of Couper's upcoming visit. Gordon requested a meeting with the two men to discuss a business proposition, and McBain arranged this day's get together.

Gordon said to McBain, "Thank you for letting me use Mr. Couper's visit to discuss this matter." Then, enthusiastically, Gordon stood and rubbed his palms together as he spoke. "Mr. Couper, I've always been intrigued by the Board of Public Works's report in 1826 about a statewide transportation system. I know you played an important role in it. It seems obvious, as you said, that laying tracks would be easier and less expensive than digging huge ditches for canals. Trains can travel at far greater speeds than barges, and linking our rail system with those of other states will be far easier than connecting rivers. There's still a place for canals in our economy, but not as the backbone. You've helped save this state an untold expense. I, for one, would like to thank you." Gordon took a deep breath and sat down.

Excitement over canals had been sweeping the country. The Erie Canal had been completed in 1825 and was hailed as one of the great engineering achievements of the time. Locally, construction on the Savannah-Ogeechee Canal began in 1826. However, Couper did not believe this mode of transportation offered Georgia the best opportunities and advised against it.

Couper remained seated and replied, "Thank you, Mr. Gordon, but it wasn't so obvious to others. Many Georgians have large investments in canals, including some of my friends and associates. They weren't too happy with our conclusion. That report was issued over five years ago, and no action on a railroad has yet been taken. Pretty slow getting off the mark, if you ask me." Couper had become involved in rowboat racing and often spoke in sporting terms.

Gordon sprung off his chair like a gymnast. "You're right, Mr. Couper, and we're the worse off for it!" Gordon was the first Georgian to graduate from West Point, the first engineering school in America. He returned to Savannah and became a lawyer. While building his practice, he had an idea, thanks in part to Couper, which had become an obsession. "But the world of commerce changes very quickly, and we must be prepared to change with it, even if some of us are involved in the canal. Look at South Carolina. They started on their railroad line from Charleston to Hamburg in 1829 when barely any track had been laid in America. With the road almost completed, and with Hamburg directly across the Savannah River from Augusta, Charleston threatens to capture a good part of the business of Georgia planters in that region. The railroad will deliver products to Charleston faster than our slow riverboats can get them to Savannah. Railroads are our future, which you so bravely pointed out to the governor. It's time for Savannah to start on a road to link it to the interior. I intend to see that we do."

Couper exclaimed, "That's excellent news, Mr. Gordon! A railroad will change the face of Savannah. Georgia, too." Couper leaned back in his chair. "Of course, railroads are susceptible to the same construction and financing problems as canals."

Gordon paced around the table. "Yes, I'm aware of that. One simply needs to organize, plan, and manage better. Whatever the potential difficulties, action must be taken. We either stand up to our challenges or play second fiddle to South Carolina, a glum prospect indeed."

McBain folded his hands on the table. He liked the idea, but was concerned about its cost, size, and complexity. He did not get excited about anything without first analyzing it thoroughly. "I agree, Mr. Gordon. How do you plan to proceed?"

Gordon stopped pacing and clutched the back of his chair. "We'll establish a corporation, and then we'll apply for a charter from the state. As soon as we receive it, we'll start selling shares, and we'll hire an engineer to plan the route. Of course, we need to get the city of Macon as enthusiastic as we are."

"It sounds like you have all your oars in the water, Mr. Gordon," Couper complimented. "How can we help?"

Gordon gulped from a glass of water. "This will be an enormous undertaking. To put it in your racing terms, Mr. Couper, we need some skilled captains. Would either of you be willing to take an active role? Your services would be most helpful, and I can assure you it will be well worth your while." Gordon smiled, trying to put the best face on his offer.

Couper responded first. "I'm interested, yes, but available, no. I'm starting a cottonseed oil company. I'm about to open plants in Alabama and Mississippi. My boat is quite full, with that and the plantation, not to mention my growing family. Little Hamilton is already three and quite a handful."

Gordon's smile faded. "Oh? I didn't know your plans. I certainly wish you well." But Gordon was not about to accept rejection. "Of course, if you're busy, we could work out something on a modified basis. You'll have plenty of time to devote to other endeavors."

Couper shook his head. "I'm awfully sorry, but I'll be traveling so much. I don't see how I could do your project justice. However, I support your mission and will gladly invest in it. I'm certain I can convince others to do the same."

"Thank you, Mr. Couper. I appreciate your trust." Gordon turned to McBain. "Sir?"

McBain drummed his fingers on the table. "I'm in a similar position. You all know the government is building a new fort on Cockspur Island at the mouth of the Savannah River. The plans call for artillery-resistant, seven-foot thick walls. They're going to need bricks, and lots of them. I'm already falling behind in my production schedule. But I'd like to help in some limited capacity, if we could work it out." McBain had no time for the project, but was intrigued enough to keep the door open on his participation.

Gordon said, "That's excellent, Mr. McBain. You can't imagine how much your presence alone would mean to the spirit of the undertaking." Of course, Gordon would have liked greater involvement from both men—they were astute and highly respected in the community. But Gordon was happy he could entice McBain in some small way and perhaps he could later expand his role.

Gordon had one last request of McBain. "Mr. McBain, could you supply any of the rail? I know you manufactured some for the railroad you built here on your plantation several years ago." In fact, it was the first railroad built in America. It was mule-drawn and moved a wooden frame-like structure between two kilns about forty yards apart to protect the green bricks from moisture during the stacking process.

McBain looked out the window towards the foundry in thought. "I'm not certain my facility is large enough to fill the requirements. How many miles will the road be?"

"About two hundred from here to Macon."

McBain picked up his quill and started writing numbers on a piece of paper. "Our facility is aimed at meeting the demands of builders. We might be able to help with some smaller orders."

Gordon said, "That could be quite helpful getting things started."

Gazaway Lamar, an observer of the discussion, marveled at Gordon's energy, passion, and perseverance. He knew Gordon would succeed even if Couper and McBain didn't join him. Lamar also had a profound interest in the South Carolina railroad. His boats carried cotton from Augusta to Savannah and stood to suffer. But he had a different solution to the problem. He was investigating the construction of an iron-hulled ship that could draft in shallower waters than a wooden one, providing quicker and more reliable river transport. However, iron-hulled ships were almost non-existent in America. Lamar had wanted to discuss sources of the metal with McBain, who invited Lamar to attend this meeting.

Lamar offered his thoughts. "What about political connections, Mr. Gordon? You'll need those as much as anything. It will help to have friendly state legislators, not to mention the governor, to obtain the charter and settle right-of-way issues. Support from the mayor of Savannah will be important. If you can't sell all the stock to the public, the city could buy it."

Gordon turned to Lamar and said, "Mmm. Yes, you're quite correct, sir."

Lamar continued. "And when you apply to the state for the charter, you might consider setting up a banking company as part of the railroad. It will help with the financing. You can't underestimate the capital requirements." Gazaway Lamar did not have the first-class education that Couper, Gordon, or McBain did, but he had a keen mind for business, perhaps the best in the room. He knew what it took to make a dollar.

Gordon was impressed with Lamar's suggestions and contemplated asking Lamar if he would be interested in participating when Couper interrupted his thoughts.

"You're on the mark with your plans, Mr. Gordon. You mustn't waste a moment. Now, get those oars moving!" Couper added with pat on the table. "Savannah needs a railroad to make it a thriving port once again."

McBain went to the cabinet, grabbed a bottle of port and four glasses, poured, and toasted, "To Savannah's railroad and the man who'll build it: William Gordon!"

The men stood and chimed, "Hear, hear!"

They lifted their glasses and sipped. There were a few moments of silence as the men looked admiringly at the purplish liquid in their glasses, and felt the sweet, burning sensation in their throats. Mr. Couper smacked his lips. Mr. Gordon nodded approvingly. McBain passed around a box of Havanas.

Joseph opened the door to his father's study, unaware that he had guests. Four sets of eyes behind a white-gray cloud of segar smoke greeted him. Though the windows were open, the fumes seemed content to float lazily in the room. He started to cough. "I'm sorry, Father. I didn't know you had company." Joseph turned to leave.

McBain called Joseph in and put his arm around his son's shoulders. "That's all right. We're just finishing. I want you to meet my guests. Gentlemen, meet my son, Joseph."

Joseph shook hands with each of the men. He had met Mr. Couper several times.

Lamar reminded Joseph that they had met years ago when Joseph was just a boy. Lamar flattened his hand and lowered it as long as his arm allowed, indicating how small Joseph was. "When Lafayette visited Savannah, in March of 1825. My son, Charlie, was baptized at Christ Church. Lafayette was there. Afterwards, I met you with your sister and parents."

Joseph thought for a moment and replied, "I remember seeing Lafayette, I think."

Couper picked up the drawing of the house and said, "I understand you're interested in architecture, Joseph?"

"Yes, sir! I am. It's fun!" Joseph beamed. "My friend Andrew and I did that." Joseph looked towards the doorway.

His father asked, "Is Andrew here?"

Joseph craned his head to spot Andrew. "I think he's in the hall."

McBain called, "Andrew, are you there?"

After a few seconds of silence, there were a few creaks from the floor, and Andrew stood at the doorway, looking in with narrow eyes. "Sir?"

Andrew and Joseph had grown quickly in the past few years, as people often observed. Joseph was taller, taking after his father and grandfather, but Andrew was more muscular. The whitest eyes and teeth dominated his round face. In fact, when first looking at Andrew, that's all anyone noticed. Andrew was shy and rarely started a conversation with white people, except Grandfather and Joseph. His eyes were windows to his mood. When they opened wide, he was happy, excited, or interested. When they narrowed, he was nervous, defensive, or sad. If there was a way to get Andrew talking, to widen those eyes, one merely had to ask him about bricks or architecture.

"Andrew, please come in," McBain said. The negro stepped slowly into the study to Joseph's side.

McBain introduced Andrew to the men. Couper held up the drawing and asked, "Tell me, boys, where did you get the ideas for this house?"

Joseph looked to Andrew to answer the question. Andrew responded slowly. "Several places, Master Couper. From Master Jay's houses in town. And from Master Castell's book, *Villas of the Ancients*. Grampah McBain has a copy of it, one of General Oglethorpe's own. It has more floor plans than elevations. My favorite is Laurentinum, built for Pliny the Younger."

The men looked at each other. White people always took note of how well Andrew spoke. His awareness of architecture doubly impressed McBain's guests.

Gordon bent slightly from the waist to address Andrew eye to eye. "Andrew, where did you learn of William Jay?"

"From Grampah McBain, sir. When we go to Savannah, he points out the buildings and tells us who designed them. Master Jay has several there."

The men looked at the drawing again. It had similarities to a Jay house, especially the front stairs and portico.

Couper asked, "What about these circular wings on each side of the house?"

Andrew hesitated. He drew them because Maum Beddy told him his ancestors in Africa had lived in round houses, and he wanted a place for them to stay, if they ever visited. But he didn't dare say that. "I just added them, sir, for variety and contrast."

Lamar pointed to the paper, "And these words along the sides?"

Andrew glanced at Joseph before answering. "Those are the names of the winds in Master Castell's book. Master Vitruvius, a great ancient architect, said the house must be situated to protect against the unhealthy winds. I don't understand them yet, but I will one day."

Lamar patted Andrew on the back. "I have no doubt you will."

Gordon asked, "Would you like to see the inside of one of those Jay houses?"

The boys looked at each other as if they had just been invited to Mrs. Mirault's for ice cream. Joseph spoke for both of them. "We'd love to, sir. But how?"

"Do you know the house on Bull and South Broad?"

Joseph said, "You mean Congressman Wayne's house?"

"Yes. I recently bought it from him. He's my wife's uncle. You're welcome to see it any time. If you're interested in architecture, you must see the interior as well as the exterior."

"Thank you, sir." Joseph remembered Grandfather saying there was some debate about how much of a role Jay had in the design of that house, but Joseph was still thrilled at the chance to see it. It certainly looked like a Jay house to him.

McBain said, "That's very kind of you, Mr. Gordon. I appreciate your generosity. We'll try to plan it." Then he addressed all the men. "Gentlemen, this has been a most interesting conversation. I'll be in town tomorrow. Maybe we can talk more."

Gordon replied, "I have an appointment with Dr. Minis in the morning. Perhaps afterwards. Have you heard about this trouble between him and James Stark?"

Philip Minis was the McBain's doctor, and had been since Dr. Jones started to devote more time to his Anti-Dueling Society responsibilities and less time on medicine. Minis was a descendant of the colony's first Hebrews, who had arrived in Georgia just five months after Oglethorpe. James Jones Stark lived in Glynn County, south of Savannah, near Couper's plantation. He was a member of the state legislature and had many ties with Savannah.

As Gordon explained, the trouble started when Stark reportedly called Dr. Minis a "damned Israelite." Minis, who was not present, heard about it and demanded an apology. He thought he received one and forgot about the matter. McBain and his guests agreed that this was an unfortunate situation, but, if the story were true, Stark was out of line.

After the guests left, Joseph asked his father when they could see Mr. Gordon's house. McBain said, "Soon, be a little patient," knowing that was impossible for Joseph. But with the business from the new fort, his father quickly forgot about the invitation. Joseph didn't, but he knew to wait a while before mentioning it again.

The spring of 1832 flew by. Joseph busied himself with schooling through June. Miss Kelly returned home to Boston for July and August and he had the summer off. Many wealthy southern families traveled to the northern states or inland to the mountains of Georgia and the Carolinas to escape the oppressive summer heat and autumnal fevers. After the deadly yellow fever epidemic of 1820, the McBains, except James, and some of their negroes went to their house in the pine forests up the Savannah River above Augusta. However, with the great demand for bricks, Grandfather decided to stay to help James. After much pleading with his mother, Joseph was allowed to stay, too.

Joseph spent most of his summer on the plantation, swimming in the river and playing games with Andrew and the other negro boys when they weren't working. One of those other boys was named Dante.

Dante was two years younger than Joseph and Andrew. Despite his age, he had already earned a reputation as the plantation thief. He learned his craft from his father, Daymon. Other than stealing and climbing trees, Dante had no discernable talents.

He was also annoying. He always complained about feeling sick, being too hot, too cold, too tired, too something, and none of the other boys liked him.

Above all, he wasn't good at games. Dante always scored the worst at quoits. The game involved trying to toss a circular metal disk with a hole in its center around a nine-inch high stake in the ground twenty feet away. Dante would grab the disk, close one eye to aim, swing his arm back and forth several times, and stick out his tongue. Then, with a mighty heave, he released the disk, throwing it straight up into the air and sending everyone scrambling.

He wasn't any better at town ball, which required using a stick to hit a rubber ball thrown by an opponent and running around a square course. The runner had to touch each corner of the course and return to the original corner without being tagged with the ball by an opponent. Dante rarely hit the ball. When he did, he ran the wrong way. His teammates yelled at him and pointed in the other direction while his opponents rolled on the field in laughter.

For a reason no one understood, Andrew protected Dante and always picked him to play on his team when no one else would.

A few others felt sorry for Dante. Jinny the cook did, because Dante's mother, Handy, was a mean old witch. Handy slapped Dante relentlessly when she wasn't in a good mood, which was always.

Amy also had compassion for Dante. The year before, Amy had been given a kitten by her neighbors. She loved that cat as much as anything. One day Feathers climbed his first pine tree, only to realize he couldn't climb down, and started to meow. Amy heard the cries and located the tree. She called to him, but the kitty was afraid to move. Frantic, Amy tried to recruit a rescuer. She begged Joseph to help, but he told his sister to let the dumb animal learn for itself. So Amy sat under the tree and sobbed. Dante wandered by and learned of Amy's distress. He placed his hands on the side of the tree, jumped up so that his feet were against it, and climbed, almost walked, up the tree. He had the kitten back in Amy's hands in minutes. That act of heroism earned Dante a defender for years.

A week after Dante rescued Feathers, Amy snitched on Joseph after he took two pomegranates from the kitchen and handed them to six negro boys, who chased Dante around the plantation, spitting seeds at him. Upon learning of this, Sarah McBain took Joseph by the ear and marched him to Dante's cabin. Joseph protested on the way, saying Dante had stolen a pair of shoes, which was true. Sarah reminded her son that it was not up to him to dole out punishment.

Mr. McBain had advised Joseph of the rules of the plantation as soon as his son was old enough to understand them, and repeated them as often as necessary. Joseph was to address the older female negroes as Miss, Missus, or Maum followed by their given name. He could never use the word "nigger," even though the negroes called each other that. He was never to give orders to a servant. If he wanted something, he was to ask politely, followed by "please," and always offer thanks. If his parents left him under the charge of one of the servants, Joseph was to do as he was told. He was never to raise his voice to any servant, and he was forbidden from striking one. If he had a problem with any of the negroes, he was to tell his father or mother, who would settle the matter.

When Dante's mother answered the door and saw Mrs. McBain holding Joseph by the ear, his face contorted in pain, she walked back inside the cabin. In seconds, the slapping began. Mrs. McBain called inside, "Please, Handy, don't hit him. He didn't do anything!"

Handy returned to the door. "'E muh chile, an' ah flam 'e ef ah wan'!"

Sarah ignored Handy's response. "I brought Joseph here to apologize to Dante!"

"Don' need no 'pology, missus," Handy replied, and retreated back to her cabin. Dante screamed again.

Fishing was very popular among the negroes. In addition to their weekly ration of food, they could eat anything they grew in their gardens, trapped in the woods, or caught in the river. Almost every evening before supper, the wharves at the Heritage were crowded with men and children sitting quietly, side by side, holding their poles. Joseph spent many summer evenings with the servants, his shoulders sloped, waiting for a bite. Usually, he gave his catch to the people sitting around him.

Hercules took Joseph horseback riding a few times a week, and Joseph improved considerably over that summer. One evening he felt confident enough to challenge Hercules to a two-mile race along the Augusta Road to the avenue of oaks if Hercules would spot him a big lead. Hercules gave him a quarter-mile. With two hundred yards to go, Joseph saw the backside of the Hercules' horse, Bonaparte, and of Hercules, who was hunched forward and moving to the horse's gait. Joseph had trouble telling where Hercules ended and Bonaparte began.

They raced several times after that. Each time Hercules extended the lead a little, each time with the same result.

That summer, Grandfather taught Joseph how to fire a rifle at a range on the western side of their land, near the border of the Brampton Plantation. Although they practiced far away from plantation housing and activities, the sight of the old man, with his thick spectacles, carrying a rifle sent a wave of fear through the negro community.

Joseph was surprised at the heaviness of the rifle, but he loved the feel of the wooden stock in his arms and the top of the butt end against his face as he aimed. The linseed oil smell of the stock was intoxicating.

Grandfather showed him how to load the muzzle with powder and ball, and how to hold and aim the weapon. After the boy knocked a block of wood off a tree stump from fifty yards, Grandfather gave Joseph a cow horn powder carrier. By the end of the summer, Joseph was accurate at one hundred yards.

One day, Grandfather had Joseph take the rifle to the range while he carried a dark, gleaming mahogany case. When Grandfather opened it, Joseph saw two dueling pistols lying on a soft cotton lining. The guns glistened from years of cleaning and care. The polished light brown wooden stocks supported ten-inch-long barrels and flint locks. Grandfather explained that handling dueling pistols was something all southern men had to master. For the next two hours, he showed Joseph how to load, aim, fire, and clean the weapons. The pistol was so heavy Joseph needed two hands to aim it. But Joseph was so excited he decided to ask his father for his own dueling pistols for Christmas.

One steamy August night when the McBain men sat for supper, James squeezed Joseph's shoulder and announced, "This has been quite a day. I saw Mr. Gordon, and we arranged for you and Andrew to see his house tomorrow."

Joseph froze. This was the best news he had received all summer. "Really? Can I tell Andrew?"

McBain spooned fish stew into his mouth and said, "After dinner." Joseph groaned his disappointment.

Grandfather looked at his son. "Is that what you call 'quite a day,' James?"

McBain replied, "Oh, yes. Dr. Arnold told me that Dr. Minis backed out of a duel he sought with James Stark."

Grandfather thrust his head forward. "What's that you say?"

McBain picked a fish bone from his stew. "I thought the matter was over last April when Stark apologized. It seems that there was confusion about the apology. A friend of Minis wrote to Stark asking him to clear the air. Stark wrote back and admitted having done Minis an unnecessary injustice, but it was not an apology. Once Minis heard about this, he wrote to Stark demanding an apology."

Grandfather's voice rose in pitch. He took affairs of honor seriously. "If Stark's willing to admit it was an unnecessary injustice, why not apologize?"

McBain shrugged. "Dr. Arnold said Stark never responded to the demand and Minis challenged him. Stark accepted and the matter was handed over to the seconds. Stark's second delivered the articles of the duel to Minis's second at noon today. Stark called for rifles as weapons and picked Screven's Ferry at five o'clock today. Philip replied that his rifle was being repaired. Anytime tomorrow would be suitable."

Grandfather practically shouted, "Five hours notice is not right! A man needs reasonable time to put his affairs in order. Stark's a horse's arse. And I mean no disrespect to the horse."

McBain said, "Stark and his second were at Screven's Ferry at five." Dueling had been illegal in Georgia since 1809, so duelers rowed in separate boats across the river to a deserted area in South Carolina named Screven's Ferry to settle the matter.

Grandfather slapped his hand on the table, causing his fork to fly off. "That's not possible! Both men have to agree to the articles."

McBain help his palms upward. "Apparently, that didn't matter to Stark. When Minis didn't show, Stark fired his gun into the air, returned to the City Hotel bar, claimed victory, and declared Minis a coward."

Grandfather shook his head, still trying to make sense of the situation. "It doesn't sound like Minis backed out."

McBain stood, ready for a cooling stroll by the river. "I agree, but the challenge wasn't met. Stark could simply refuse any further challenge on the grounds that Minis had already backed down. Minis could lose his reputation. He may even have to move from here. I need to see him tomorrow to settle for the month. I'll try to speak to him about it."

Joseph listened to the conversation as if he were watching a play. It couldn't be real. He knew men had duels, and they were serious affairs. But he never personally knew anybody involved in one. He liked Dr. Minis and was horrified that someone would call him a coward, perhaps the worst of all insults.

Joseph hardly slept that night. While talk of the duel remained in the back of his mind, the prospect of seeing Mr. Gordon's house consumed him. The boys' excitement grew the next morning when Mr. McBain told them he was so impressed with their interest in architecture, he had decided to teach them some basic concepts on the ride to town. As Hercules started the horses, McBain pulled out a book, opened it, and handed it to them. "Tell me what you see."

The boys took the book and laid it across their legs, expecting to see an illustration of an ancient temple. Instead, Joseph blushed. Andrew felt his face burning. McBain smiled. "Well?"

Finally, Joseph summoned the courage. "I see a naked man with four arms and legs and his lizard hanging out."

Father laughed at his son's analysis. "It's called a penis, son. Now, believe it or not, this might be the most important architectural drawing you'll ever see."

"A naked man?" Joseph glanced at Andrew to see if his friend had solved the riddle. Andrew just stared at the illustration.

Father said, "Yes, a naked man. Do you have any idea why the drawing is so important?" His eyes darted from Joseph to Andrew.

Joseph couldn't speak. He had no idea what his father was talking about.

McBain decided to help. "I'll give you a hint. The drawing is called 'Vitruvian Man.' It's very famous."

Andrew looked up. "Does it have to do with Vitruvius, Master McBain?"

McBain leaned forward and gave Andrew a congratulatory slap on the knee. "Exactly, Andrew. What do you know about Vitruvius?"

Joseph answered, "Castell talks about him in *Villas of the Ancients*. He said he was a great man who wrote a book on architecture. He worried about unhealthy winds."

McBain slapped his son on the knee. "Yes! He lived during the height of the Roman Empire, around the birth of Christ. Vitruvius studied the structures of the Greeks and the Romans and wrote the *Ten Books of Architecture*. It's the oldest surviving book on architecture. He said man was the perfect creation of nature, and building should be based on this perfection. That's what that picture is all about."

Joseph asked, "Father, isn't man the creation of God?"

"Remember, son, Vitruvius lived before and during the life of Christ. Christianity and its beliefs did not exist then."

Andrew and Joseph studied the picture, feeling very proud of their new knowledge. Andrew asked, "Master McBain, did Vitruvius draw this?"

"No, Andrew. An artist named Leonardo DaVinci did, not long after Vitruvius's book was first published around 1486."

Andrew scrunched up his face. "I still don't understand, Master McBain. How is a building like a naked man?"

McBain took the book, rested it on his knee, and pointed to the picture. "Vitruvius said that a well-shaped man was in perfect proportion. All his parts are of a correct size. They are neither too big nor too small, on their own or in relation to other parts of his body. He even defined the relationships. For example, the height of a man is equal to the arm span from fingertip to fingertip. The length of a man's foot is one sixth of his height. The length of the open hand from the tip of the middle finger to the wrist is the same as the face from the chin to the hairline. A temple must also be in perfect proportion, with all its parts in harmony. DaVinci illustrates Vitruvius's theory."

This was a stunning revelation to two boys just starting their education in architecture. Andrew realized he had been drawing without this information and felt dumb.

Joseph pressed his open hand to his face. Andrew spread his arms out, almost hitting Joseph in the head. Joseph tried to measure his height in foot lengths while sitting in the coach.

McBain chortled as the boys tied themselves in knots. "Columns are good examples. They're comprised of three major parts—a base, a shaft, and a capital—each of which consist of many minor parts. Their sizes must be quite precise. Just like man."

Andrew stopped measuring his body parts and stated, "But all columns aren't the same, Master McBain. I've seen different sizes in Savannah."

"Yes, Andrew. But they should be in the same proportion. A column that is one foot in diameter and six feet high is not the same size as a column that is two feet in diameter and twelve feet high. But they are in the same proportion, are they not?"

"Of course," whispered Andrew, as the great revelation took hold in his mind. He poked Joseph in the arm to let him know that he understood.

McBain gave the boys a few seconds to let that concept sink in. "That's a simple example. But all the parts of a temple have proper proportions; the length and width of the temple, the column and its parts, the beam above the columns, the spaces between the columns, the doors, the rooms, the ceiling heights, and all the other elements."

Andrew asked, "Are all ancient temples in the same proportion, Master McBain?"

McBain replaced the book on the boys' legs. "No, Andrew. Vitruvius's proportions are based on the human body. That means man and woman. So proportions of buildings are based on the bodies of men and women, plus there is a set for maidens. The three types are called orders. The Greeks and Romans called them Doric, Ionic, and Corinthian. Let's wait till we get to town, and I'll show you."

Andrew and Joseph stared at Vitruvian Man in a new light. He was no longer just a naked man. The boys had entered a new world, the mysterious world of the ancients, and they were learning its secrets.

They arrived in town twenty minutes before their appointment. McBain had Hercules drive to St. Julian and Drayton streets and led the boys to the sidewalk in front of the Bank of the United States. Andrew and Joseph had seen it before, but not with the knowledge of Vitruvius. The entranceway was reached by seven stairs and its portico was supported by six columns.

McBain said, "Whenever you see a building for the first time, look at its entirety. Not the individual parts. Try to grasp the feeling that it gives."

The boys surveyed the building. Andrew's head moved up and down, and side to side. He finally said, "Master McBain, I feel the importance of this building. I feel it commands respect from anyone who looks upon it."

McBain looked twice at Andrew. "Good, Andrew. Quite good."

Joseph couldn't wait to discuss the details. "What order is this, Father?"

McBain used his hand to direct the boys' attention. "The order is comprised of two parts, the column and the entablature. You know what a column is. The entablature is the horizontal beam that rests upon the capitals of the columns. The easiest way to identify the order is by the capital, but the difference among the orders is much more than that. This is the Doric order, named after an ancient tribe of Greeks called the Dorians. Its capital is a flat square block sitting atop a circular disk or neck. It's a masculine order, which the ancients used in temples to male gods, like Zeus." McBain examined their faces to see if he had gone too far.

Andrew asked, "So this bank is a temple to male gods?"

McBain realized it was going to take a lot more to overwhelm Andrew. "That's how the Greeks used the orders for their temples, Andrew. The Romans added a few orders, and they've pretty much been followed for two thousand years. But over time, people selected the orders based on personal preference, not just masculinity. Expense was also a factor. But the masculine order is appropriate for a bank, don't you think?"

Andrew hopped up the stairs and slapped one of the columns. "Yes, Master McBain. Strength to guard all the money inside." Joseph followed Andrew and leaned against the column, as if trying to push it over. They both returned to McBain's side.

In all the time they had spent appreciating the buildings of Savannah, the boys never really knew what they were looking at. Now they had an idea, and they studied the exterior. They walked from the front to the side in silence. They would have stayed for the rest of the day if Hercules hadn't called, "Massa, tahm tuh git."

McBain waved to Hercules. "Be right there." He turned to the boys and said, "Just two other things. The Greek Doric columns have no base, because men didn't wear shoes in the days of the Dorians. Also, since they represent man, they have a swelling in the middle. The Greeks call it an *entasis*." He patted his belly and the boys laughed. Then he pointed to the middle of the columns, and sure enough, the columns bulged slightly. "Now we need to go. We don't want to keep Mr. Gordon waiting."

They arrived to learn that Gordon had been called to an emergency business meeting and would return in an hour. McBain told the butler that they would come back at that time. McBain said to the boys, "Well, I have to see Dr. Minis and Dr. Arnold. I might as well take care of that."

They drove to Dr. Minis's office on Johnson Square only to learn the doctor had gone to the City Hotel. McBain said, "Not my lucky day. He's probably having lunch. I'll try Dr. Arnold at the Exchange. I need to place an advertisement in his newspaper." Dr. Arnold owned a half-interest in *The Georgian*, a Savannah daily.

Hercules parked at the corner of Bull and the Bay in front of Mr. Dure's house. McBain told Joseph to go to the restaurant at the City Hotel and tell Dr. Minis that he would be by in a few minutes, after he was done with Dr. Arnold. Joseph told Andrew he'd be right back and ran the short distance down the Bay.

He entered the formal dining room, but did not see Dr. Minis. He walked across the lobby to the wide entrance to the barroom and stood there, as his father had prohibited him from going into any bar. The large room was smoky, crowded, and noisy. Joseph squinted, but couldn't recognize a face. He was distracted by the bar itself, which was made of a gleaming dark wood. The wall in back of the bar was a giant mirror with shelves of dozens of variously shaped bottles containing different colored liquids, an alcoholic rainbow. The two white bartenders, handsomely dressed in blue vests, white shirts, and yellow armbands, moved effortlessly, taking orders, making and serving drinks, and chatting casually with customers. Joseph thought, "No wonder Grandfather likes it here so much."

Joseph was about to return to the coach when he heard a voice call out so loudly it scared him. "I pronounce James Stark a coward!" Joseph saw Dr. Minis standing twelve feet away at the other end of the entrance to the bar. The room fell silent. Every pair of eyes was focused on Dr. Minis. Joseph was about to give him Father's message, but something told him not to.

Dr. Minis's head jerked nervously as he scanned the barroom. Joseph heard footsteps on the stairs, which led to the entrance to the bar, near where Dr. Minis was standing. A man's body slowly came into view as it descended the stairs, first black leather boots, then legs, then body, then a head. The man in the black suit and bushy moustache reached the landing, stepped into the bar, and, seeing Dr. Minis, stopped and smiled. The two men stared at each other. Finally, the man said, "Dr. Minis. What brings you here? I didn't think you'd have the nerve to show your face in public."

Minis replied, "I'm here to see you, Stark."

The two men continued staring. Then Stark casually moved a hand towards his jacket. In a flash, Dr. Minis brandished a pistol, and there was a deafening blast, a tongue of flame, and a cloud of white smoke. Stark stepped backward while bending forward. He bounced off the banister, crashed against the end of the bar, and dropped to the floor. He didn't move, and for a time, neither did anyone else in the room. They all gawked at the body, while the gunshot rang endlessly in their ears. Joseph smelled the burnt gunpowder. He was frightened and wanted to run, but his knees were too weak. Minis also stood still, his left arm at his side, his right hand extended, limply holding the gun. A patron cautiously approached him and gently tried to take the pistol away. Minis, in shock, wouldn't give it up. Then two others tried to get hold of the weapon. Minis came to his senses, pulled another pistol from his jacket with his left hand, and pointed the gun at them. The men scattered like mice to the far end of the bar while everyone else dropped to the floor.

Joseph had to pee. He heard someone shout his name, and in a moment, his father had his arms around him. Two other men, Dr. Arnold and Dr. Waring, the mayor, rushed to Dr. Minis's side and spoke to him. Minis gave up his guns, and the men walked him out of the hotel.

The McBains did not see Mr. Gordon's house that day. Gordon understood.

Philip Minis, a good man with a proud heritage, was taken to jail to await his trial for murder. He didn't regain his honor. It turned out that Stark was not armed, and was not reaching for a pistol when he moved his hands to his jacket. Most town folks felt that Minis had murdered Stark. This was not how southern gentlemen settled a dispute.

McBain visited Dr. Minis the next day. Minis thanked him for his friendship, but said it would be best if he used Dr. Arnold. Minis explained he would likely be in jail for many years to come, and even if he were freed, he could not continue his practice in Savannah. McBain promised that when Minis was found innocent and released, he could have their business back.

That's how the McBains came to change doctors.

In the days following their trip to Savannah, Andrew and Joseph wrote down everything they had learned about Vitruvian Man and the Greek orders. Andrew sketched a temple in the Doric order, making every effort to draw it in proportion, by the few rules he knew.

Despite deciding not to ask his father for a gift of dueling pistols, Joseph still accompanied Grandfather to the range. One day, while the old man was giving him pistol instructions, Joseph asked, "Grandfather, why do men duel?"

Grandfather dropped a ball into the barrel. "To defend their honor."

Joseph handed the old man the ramrod. "Who defines honor?"

The old man used the ramrod and returned it to Joseph. He lifted the gun and aimed it at the target. "That's a good question, Joseph. If a man feels his honor has been maligned, then he does. But what is real honor? That's harder to define. Maybe it's living an honest, moral life, obeying God, taking care of your family, loving your country, keeping your word, and respecting your fellow man." Grandfather handed the pistol to Joseph.

Joseph, with one hand, aimed the pistol. Then he lowered it to his side. "Do the McBains have honor, Grandfather?"

Grandfather put his arm around Joseph's shoulders. "More than you know, Joseph. More than you know."

Joseph re-aimed and wondered if he would ever have to defend it.

CHAPTER 5

Heritage Plantation

1833

"No, Mistuh Huhclee. Uh yent t'ief it! Ah swaytuh Gawd," Dante screamed.

When Hercules couldn't find his silver neck chain, he knew where to go. He grasped Dante by the back of the collar and the seat of his pants and swung him back and forth by the brickworks' soaking pits. The negroes working nearby laughed. "Ah t'ink you do steal it," replied Hercules. Dante flailed his arms and kicked his legs. Hercules swung Dante over his head. "An' ah gwi' tell you ma!"

No threat could frighten Dante more. "Noooo! Please! Ah fine it," Dante pleaded.

Hercules stopped the swinging and held Dante like a sack of rice. "You got but one hour. The snake head, too. Hear?"

"Yassuh, Mistuh Huhclee!"

Hercules dropped Dante to the ground and walked back to the stables. Dante got up, covered with clumps of clay, and ran to the river, crying.

Andrew and Joseph, who were working at the molding tables, could hear his wails. They looked at each other and speculated on what Dante might have stolen this time. Then they got back to work. It was the spring of 1833, and the plantation was turning out as many bricks as possible. James McBain had figured right.

McBain had completed his education at Yale in 1812, at age twenty. He returned home to the cattle farm thirteen miles west of Savannah, ready to help his father, Daniel, run it. James soon realized he didn't want to raise livestock. He wanted to build. But Daniel's poor eyesight was making him more dependent on his son. James knew he had to decide about his future.

In pondering his alternatives, James traveled to Savannah and saw something promising in those sandy streets lined with sagging wooden buildings. The deep-water port on a wide river, the unique layout of the town, and the prospect of a huge cotton trade as a result of the recent invention of the cotton gin on nearby Mulberry Grove Plantation had convinced him that Savannah would boom. He wanted to be part of it.

Of course, Daniel McBain had emotional ties to his farm. It was the land Oglethorpe had awarded to his father. It was where he and his twin brother were born and raised. It was where he had lived with his wife. But he knew James would not be happy there. Daniel had been lonely since his wife and parents had died so many years before in the fire of 1796, and his son still hadn't found a wife. He sensed living close to town might be better for both of them.

With a loan from his father, James purchased acreage on the Savannah River just three miles west of the town. A year later, in 1815, his father sold the cattle farm, but kept the negroes, horses, and a few head of cattle, and they moved into an old house on the new homestead.

As it turned out, beneath the surface of the land was a huge layer of clay ideal for making bricks. The raw clay had a grey color, and the bricks it produced became known as "Savannah Greys," even though their color after firing ranged from an orange-red to a dull red. McBain set about clearing two areas for kilns and built a wharf on the river for shipping the bricks. He also bought pinelands further up the Savannah River. Felled trees were floated on rafts to the sawmill he built by the river. He constructed another wharf for lumber shipments. Next, he erected a foundry to make iron castings, and an accompanying wharf for the iron products.

Over the next few years, as the operations grew, James built a new family house, a kitchen, a milk and butter house, brick cabins for the negroes, a hospital, a guest cottage, stables, a cattle barn, a slaughterhouse, a smokehouse, and an overseer's house. He also fenced in a cattle pasture, and planted fields of corn, wheat, potatoes, and peas.

One spring evening in 1817 at a party held by neighbors, James met and fell in love with brown-haired, brown-eyed, dimple-chinned Sarah Potter. They spent almost every Sunday for the rest of the year together, attending church, horseback riding, boating, and picnicking. Early the following year, they married on the Potter plantation, Coleraine, overlooking the Savannah River, just a few miles west of McBain's plantation. In January 1819 Sarah gave birth to Amy.

By 1820, in just five years, McBain had established a thriving building-products business and owned 125 negroes. This was the world into which Joseph and Andrew had been born.

McBain was proud of what he had accomplished. He owed his success to the sacrifices his father and grandfather had made trying to make a good life in America. To honor their legacy, James named the plantation the "Heritage."

"It sounds like Dante is up to his tricks," Joseph said to Andrew as he took a handful of clay and dashed it into the mold.

"Yes, and it sounds like he's performing them for Hercules," replied Andrew, keeping an eye on Joseph's work. Andrew had started working at the age of ten, and by thirteen he had performed many of the tasks in the production of bricks and was quite skilled in them. "Make sure you spread enough sand into the mold before adding the clay. They'll pop out much easier."

Joseph had just graduated to the molding tables. For the past year, he had been working two days a week after school. His father wanted him to learn every aspect of the business. Joseph had started in the clay pits, digging up and turning over the clay in the ground. This "winning" was done throughout the late fall and winter, as exposure to the frost broke down the huge clumps of clay, making them easier to handle. In the spring, he shoveled the clay into wheelbarrows and ran them to the soaking pit, where the clay was mixed with water and trampled by foot and kneaded by hand into a smooth, moist mass. Fortunately, the soaking pit was soon replaced by a pug mill, which was worked by mules walking in circles, moving oar-like paddles within a circular wooden shell.

Once the clay reached the proper consistency, it was removed on planks to the molding tables. Joseph considered all these jobs back-breakers. Four hours at any one of them exhausted him. The only benefit, he felt, was to the development of his muscles, and the bond he formed with the servants.

The molding tables were different. Though still physically demanding, Joseph actually made bricks. Molders rolled handfuls of clay on a table spread with sand. Next, they wetted a box mold, which held individual casings for two bricks, sprinkled sand onto it, and pressed in the clay. Excess clay was removed from the molds with a water-soaked stick called a strike. The molders set the filled box mold, weighing close to twenty-five pounds, to the side, where negro boys between the ages of ten and twelve carried them to a covered, drying area. There, negro men extracted the bricks and stacked them on pallets. Six weeks later they were ready for the kiln. It wasn't easy work. Speed and proficiency were demanded. Joseph was thankful Andrew worked by his side.

"Oops," was all Joseph could say as he applied more sand to his box mold. His father told Mr. Bones, the overseer, to make sure Joseph did his work correctly and held up his part. Joseph did, according to Andrew, but he was never able to please Mr. Bones, who resented the presence of the owner's trouble-making son in the gang. Andrew once overheard the overseer complaining that Joseph caused more problems than all the darkies combined.

The molders did not talk much at the tables, as it angered Mr. Bones. However, they often sang. This made the work more pleasant and productive. Joseph never sang because he couldn't carry a tune. But that day was different. For some reason, he felt like one of the gang. He worked as hard as anyone and sweated just as much. So when the molders started to sing, Joseph hummed along. After a few minutes, he was working faster. The louder he hummed, the better he moved. He knew he was on key. He tapped his foot and swayed his body as he dashed clay into the molds. After a while, he looked up, grinning and moving to the music. The negroes were silent. Twenty sets of eyes strained at him. Apparently, he wasn't in tune. Joseph felt his face flush and stopped humming. Even Andrew, his faithful companion, had his shoulder pressed against the side of his head, as if he just had an ear removed with a rusty trowel. The negroes exhaled. One wiped his brow. They went back to work and cautiously resumed singing.

One of the molders started to laugh. One by one the others joined him. Soon, they were all laughing. Joseph looked for some support from Andrew, who couldn't meet Joseph's eyes. At first, Joseph was offended that his musical talents were causing a riot. But everyone was so amused he had to laugh as well. The moment was soon crushed by Mr. Bones, who came running over, screaming, "What's going on here? You have work to do!" Quiet returned as quickly as it had departed, and everyone returned to their molds.

Mr. Bones knew where the trouble had to have started. He stepped so close to Joseph their faces almost touched. "Is there a problem here, Mr. McBain?" Bones was five feet and a few inches tall, thin, all muscle, with closely cropped hair, and a face and neck that had veins and arteries popping out like mole tunnels. When he spoke to Joseph, they pulsated, like fat worms trying to wiggle into holes in the ground. He was a humorless man, and the negroes, who called him 'de Bone' behind his back, said only God knew if he ever smiled.

"No, sir, Mr. Bones. I told a joke. It's my fault." Joseph lowered his head, pretending to be remorseful. Joseph didn't much like de Bone. The overseer spent his days growling at something or other. Things generally ran smoothly, but this was because of Isaac, a short, full-bearded, religious negro who was the driver of the brick operation. He knew everything about bricks. Grandfather once told Joseph he overheard Isaac talking to a Savannah Grey, and the brick replied.

Bones barked, "Don't tell your jokes on my time! When you're around, there's always some kind of ruckus. Do you want me to tell your pa?"

"Yes, sir. No, sir! I'm sorry." Joseph prayed that de Bone would go away.

"One more stunt like that and I will!" De Bone turned to the negroes. "And that goes for all of you! Got it?"

As work ended for the day, the folks at the molding tables heard a loud howl. Joseph and Andrew saw Dante running away from the stables, holding his backside with both hands. Hercules walked out, fastening a silver chain around his neck.

At supper that evening, Amy told the family about Joseph's day at the molding tables, as she had heard it from Teenah, her personal servant, who had heard it from someone else. The McBains thought the incident was amusing. As Plesant served the turtle soup, Grandfather asked him if he had heard Joseph singing.

"No, gran' massa, but some ub de gals, dey done yeddy. Dey say Massa Joesup need gwi' tuh Affricky tuh laa'n tuh sing."

Amy sniped, "If he goes, maybe he could learn to dance, too." Joseph's face turned pink. Sensing her brother's unease, Amy continued, "I can teach Joseph to dance, if he'd only let me."

Once, she had been his loving, protective older sister, making sure he made it through each day unharmed. About the time she turned thirteen, the year before, when she thought she had become a full-fledged woman, that all changed. Joseph was no longer a defenseless, precious boy, but a bothersome lout. Nothing pleased her more than passing judgment on him.

Joseph snarled at Amy. "I can dance just fine!"

Amy threw her head back with a short laugh. "Hah! You can't either. You look like a pair of overalls hanging out to dry on a windy day."

"That will be enough, Amy," her mother chastened.

Amy's tone softened. "I shouldn't tell you this, Joseph, but Rebecca Stiles thinks you're cute. She'd like to dance with you." When Amy said something nice about Joseph, he knew she was laying a trap, into which he couldn't help but step.

"Rebecca?" Joseph asked, embarrassed but curious about his neighbor, just a year younger than he, from Vale Royal. He was beginning to notice girls, but was scared of them. He had no idea what to say to one, especially if he liked her. Mother had started taking him to dance and piano lessons on Saturdays in Savannah to provide him with some "social currency," as she called it. But the lessons didn't give him the currency, or the courage, to approach Rebecca.

Amy grinned. "Yes, Rebecca. But I think it was one of her moments of temporary lunacy. She has them, you know." Amy then stuck her tongue out at Joseph.

"Amy!" called Mother, shaking her head at the girl.

Joseph attributed Amy's change of character not just to her claim of womanhood, but also to her conviction that she was the most beautiful female in all of Georgia. She was pretty, even Joseph would admit that, under moderate torture. Amy was taller than her girlfriends, and her mother called her "willowy." She had her father's hazel eyes and her mother's light brown hair, which fell to her shoulders when she removed all those combs and pins. Somehow, Teenah made it shine.

Amy picked up her fan and started waving it. "Mother, I'm just concerned about baby brother. How ever are we going to marry him off? He lacks grace. I do hate to say this, but we may have to take him up north to find a wife."

"Amy, leave your brother alone!" Sarah persisted. "He doesn't have to worry about a wife for quite a while. When he does, the ladies will come flocking."

The fan quickened. "Yes, like buzzards to a dead deer. It pains me to criticize Joseph, but I don't think any of our servants would have him. A Yankee girl is our only hope. I do worry about him so."

Grandfather and James couldn't help but chortle at her performance. Joseph heard the house servants cackling from beyond the dining room door. The entire plantation would know of the conversation by morning.

Father saved Joseph's evening. "Well, I have some news. I bought a negro couple from Mr. Stiles, Rebecca's father. The husband, William, is very handy around the house. His wife Celia is an excellent seamstress." McBain was very selective in purchasing servants and was quick to claim that he had the smartest negroes in the South.

"When might we expect them?" asked Sarah, who had more than a passing interest. She was in charge of the house servants. At a plantation the size of the Heritage, this was a considerable responsibility. The McBains had three cooks, two weavers, three seamstresses, two washerwomen, and five house servants for serving, cleaning, polishing, and dusting. In addition, Plesant served as the butler and Mr. McBain's personal servant. Milsey was Mrs. McBain's personal servant. Maum Lilah and Maum Beddy, who nursed and raised Amy and Joseph, did pretty much as they pleased. Of course, there were Andrew and Teenah.

"As soon as I can build a cabin for them, dear." Father looked casually at Joseph. "Son, would you and Andrew like to help Isaac build it?"

Joseph's eyes grew as big as his dinner dish. "Really?" Making bricks was one thing, but using them was quite another. This would be the start of their building careers.

"Yes. It's an excellent opportunity to learn bricklaying." McBain leaned over and slapped his son on the back. He knew what this meant to him.

"Can I go tell Andrew?" Joseph pushed his chair away from the table in anticipation of receiving permission.

"Finish your supper first, Joseph," his mother ordered. Joseph wondered why finishing a meal was so important to parents. But he didn't argue. Three enormous gulps later, without chewing, and his dish was clean. His family winced.

Joseph bared his teeth. "That was delicious. May I be excused now?"

"Yes, you may go now," Sarah replied, shaking her head in defeat, and appreciating Amy's concern about his grace.

Powered by a foundation-shaking, window-rattling belch, Joseph was out of the house. He heard Amy screaming after him.

Joseph bounded down the front stairs, up the path, through the front gate of the fence-enclosed yard and onto the avenue of the oaks. In a few minutes he passed the overseer's house, a two-story affair, far too big for Mr. Bones, who lived by himself since his wife and son moved away the year before. Joseph noticed a low light from one of the front rooms and wondered how de Bone spent his time, as he rarely showed himself after work. Joseph guessed he was working on other requirements of his employment: calculating, ordering, and disbursing the weekly food rations for the servants, as well as keeping production records.

Someone called "Ebnin', Massa Joesup." Joseph turned and saw Nurse Rynah standing in front of the plantation hospital, directly across the avenue from the overseer's house. It was also a two-story building, the top floor for the male negroes, the bottom for the women and children. During the day, the negro women too old to work at regular plantation jobs looked after the servant children too young to work.

Joseph waved to Rynah and moved on. In a minute he entered the area where the servants lived. It was called the "Quarter." The plantation slaves, who by 1833 numbered about 175, formed a small town. Besides the house servants and the negroes who worked on the plantation businesses, there was a blacksmith, two coopers, two carpenters, two butchers, a tanner, four stablemen, three dairymen and women, five farmers, two boatmen, two mechanics, and three footmen for general work.

While servant houses in the South were usually made of wood, which was plentiful and cheap, Mr. McBain constructed his with Savannah Greys. He built one for each family. Unmarried women and men lived four to a cabin at opposite ends of the Quarter. By 1833, there were about forty cabins.

Each dwelling consisted of three rooms. One room had a fireplace and served as a kitchen, dining room, and sitting room. The other two were bedrooms. The cabins were built in a square formation, with twelve in a group. This layout formed a large, common backyard, where each family grew vegetables and raised chickens. What the negroes didn't use themselves, they sold to the missus. What she didn't buy, they sold at the City Market on Saturdays.

As far as Joseph was concerned, nighttime was the best time on the plantation. After the evening meal, the negroes sat outside their houses and tended to their lives, weaving baskets, mending clothes, grinding corn, scolding children, telling stories, and singing. Their voices filled the night air, somehow melding in harmony with the starry sky, the flowing river, and the wind-swept trees.

Many nights, Amy and Joseph visited the Quarter to listen to the singing and stories. Sometimes Maum Beddy made fried apples for them. The delicious, sweet fruit had the consistency of butter. Eating them right out of the skillet, and risking burning their mouths was part of the fun.

That night, Joseph ran to Hercules's house to tell Andrew the news. Hercules and Andrew had been living together for the past year, after Rynah told the missus it was time for Andrew to have the influence of a man. The door was slightly open. Joseph was about to knock when he heard Hercules's voice. He stood and listened.

"This dis . . . discovry was made only four years since, and J Old . . . Old." Hercules hesitated.

"Oldridge," Joseph heard Andrew say.

"Oldridge," Hercules continued, "feels much e . . . elated at the unparled"

Andrew broke in again, "un-par-a-lleled. That's a difficult one. Skip over it."

"Success dat hab, that have, attended it."

Joseph couldn't figure what was happening in the room. He knocked on the door and heard Hercules say, "Come in." Joseph entered and saw Hercules sitting at the table in the middle of the candle-lighted room with Andrew beside him. A newspaper, the *Daily Georgian,* was spread on the table. The negroes looked like they had been caught stealing.

"Hello, Hercules. Hi, Andrew." Joseph invited himself in and perused the paper. In the middle of the page was an advertisement for Oldridge's Hair Balm of Columbia. "Hercules, are you losing your hair?"

Hercules winced. "No, Massa Joseph," he replied, and looked at Andrew for help.

Andrew said, "I'm helping Hercules read, Master Joseph."

Joseph had noticed that Hercules was speaking much better, and thought it was because he spent considerable time around his father. As it turned out, Andrew had been instructing him at night for the past year.

Joseph asked Hercules to continue, which he did, reluctantly. Joseph was impressed by the coachman's effort. "Can you write, Hercules?"

"The alphabet and a few words," Hercules said, unable to look Joseph in the eye.

"Well, next time we'll have a writing lesson. It's easy." Joseph expected Hercules to be excited at the offer.

"You don' have to, Massa Joseph. Andrew's help is good." Hercules wanted to learn from a negro, and not the white boy who was so often in his care. Joseph sensed Hercules's reluctance and turned the page to read another story. An advertisement caught his eye.

"$30 Reward. Ran away from Darien Plantation on Saturday last, three negro men: Anthony, about 35 years old and intelligent. Left ear deformed. Hal, about 35 years old, his front teeth grown wide apart. Ena, about 40 years old, stout built and slow movement. Supposed they will make for South Carolina and then north. The above reward will be given for their delivery to the subscribers or lodged in any jail of the adjoining counties or districts. J. Stone & Co."

Joseph didn't want Hercules reading that, and abruptly closed the paper. Runaways were a fact of life in the South, and owners didn't want their blacks to have any encouragement. "That's enough for tonight. You read very well, Hercules."

Hercules said, "Please don' tell massa."

"He wouldn't mind, Hercules." At least Joseph didn't think he would.

"Just the same." Hercules didn't have to say more.

"I won't mention a word to him then. You can trust me on that." Joseph was confused, even hurt, by Hercules's refusal of his help.

Just then, Joseph heard Amy calling. "Joseph, are you in there? Adam is going to tell a story. Come on out."

"I'll be right there." As they left the house, Joseph said, "Andrew, I almost forgot. Father wants us to help Isaac build a new cabin and learn to lay bricks!"

Andrew stopped in his tracks. "Build? You mean walls and such? With real bricks and mortar?"

Joseph put his arm around his friend's shoulder as they walked outside. "Of course! What else?"

Andrew, Amy, and Joseph joined a circle of about thirty negroes. Adam's story about Luther was plenty creepy, especially the ending. "An' de man an' de gal dey gone tuh de cem'try, tuh de grabe. De gal step on de grabe an' say, "Thar Luthuh, ah hab proob muh lub lukkuh oonuh ast. Now kin us git marri'd?" The negroes laughed nervously at Adam's imitation of a white woman. "An' Luthuh step 'way. An' de gal say, "Luthuh, wut so funny? Ah skayd." An' Luthuh step back eben mo', an' tek off he hat. An' de gal see he face, jes' a skull. An' she scream tuh de Lawd." Adam screamed, and the frightened listeners lifted in the air from their sitting positions. He had to wait a moment for them to calm down. "An' he step back eben mo'. De gal, she cry, 'Luthuh, Luthuh,' an' she step tuh he, but uh han' come oudduh de grabe an' grab she leg an' pull she down! She holluh mo' loud, 'Luthuh! Please he'p me!' An' de han' pull she slam een de groun'. Den Luthuh, he retu'n f'um de grabeyaa'd fuh he udda gal."

Amy and Joseph walked back to the house in the darkness, their knees shaking. About half way back, in front of the hospital, a strong wind blew through the trees, making a whistling sound. Amy gasped and stopped, looking for Luther. As she turned, Joseph slowly bent down and grabbed her ankle. Amy let out a shriek that woke most of the living and a few of the dead from Savannah to Charleston. She ran to the house, crying all the way. Sarah was at the door to calm her hysterical daughter, while Joseph tried, unsuccessfully, to hide his glee.

When Amy calmed down, Mother said, "Tomorrow is Saturday. Amy, you have your finishing school. Joseph, you have your dance and piano lessons. Please be ready."

"I shall have my revenge, Joseph! You just wait and see," Amy thrust her finger at him, not giving an owl's hoot about the next day.

"Perchance we can dance together," Joseph grinned as he tried to hold his sister for a reel.

Amy hollered, "Get away from me, you barbarian!"

Joseph bent forward and puckered. "Where's my kiss goodnight?"

"Yuucch!" Amy ran upstairs.

Joseph said, "Yes, Mother. See you tomorrow morning."

CHAPTER 6

City Market

1833

At seven the next morning, the McBain men were standing on the lumber mill wharf, ready to take a boat to town. And not just any boat. Rowboat racing was becoming a popular sport for gentlemen along coastal Georgia, especially around Brunswick, Darien, and St. Marys. James Hamilton Couper had convinced James McBain to purchase a four-oared, cypress dugout, twenty-seven feet long and three and a half feet wide. McBain had it painted a dull red, the color of a Savannah Grey, and called her *Amy*.

McBain didn't do much with it. Although a few men along the river had rowboats, a boat club had not yet been formed in Savannah, as they had in other coastal towns. These clubs organized races and furnished the oarsmen, local men who rowed for sport and exercise. Without a crew, McBain was training some of his stronger negroes. Saturdays, City Market day, was an ideal time. He started taking the race boat instead of the larger, flat-bottomed, canopied boat, more suited to passenger travel.

As space was tight in the race boat, Sarah and Amy went to town in the coach with Hercules, who took Teenah to the City Market every Saturday to sell the baskets and other goods of the Heritage servants.

Joseph and Andrew sat in the bow and McBain and Grandfather in the stern. The rowers sat in the middle. They left the wharf and glided past the long dock on Marsh Island, which McBain had built so the hogs he kept there could seek safety during freshets and very high tides. This island, often referred to as Hog Island, is one of a long string that divides the Savannah River into two winding channels over thirty miles long. The southern channel provides access to Georgia, the northern channel to South Carolina.

They next passed Hutchinson Island, the longest in the river. It held the vast rice fields of the Habershams and the Marshalls. The tide was high and they could see over the tops of the rice plants for miles, a green, waving carpet. Negroes were working in the fields, and their songs filled the entire basin.

The green soon turned brown, and the voices faded away. The rice fields after the Habersham tract were dormant as a result of the city government's efforts to prevent the deadly yellow fever outbreaks that had so frequently devastated the town. Local doctors believed the standing water in the rice fields created sickly gases, called miasmas. As a result, the city council passed an ordinance prohibiting owners of land within a three-mile radius of town from planting crops that required flooded fields. The planters, though compensated for the land by the city, protested bitterly this policy of "dry culture." After a few years of reduced outbreaks, the plan seemed to have worked. Then, an epidemic hit in 1820, killing hundreds and sending thousands fleeing. Included in those deaths were Gully and Lucy, Andrew's parents, when he was just eight months old, leaving Andrew to be raised by the unmarried maumas. Still, the dry culture ordinance remained in force.

McBain observed his oarsmen carefully as they bent forward, extended their arms, and leaned back, pulling their arms to their chests. He found himself breathing to their rhythm. He called to them only when their motions were not coordinated. He was pleased at how quickly they had picked up the fundamentals.

In less than an hour, they entered the harbor and docked at the public wharf near Barnard Street. They climbed the steep stairs up the bluff and went their separate ways. Joseph walked to his dance school. James McBain attended to business affairs. Andrew walked to the City Market to meet Hercules and Teenah.

Grandfather accompanied the oarsmen to the market, giving them the opportunity to buy clothes and foods like coffee and sugar, which were not rationed on the plantation. He then escorted the men back to the boat and headed to Mr. Williams's bookstore.

Hercules drove Amy to her school and Sarah to meet her friends for morning tea. Then he parked and helped Teenah carry the goods of the Heritage negroes to the City Market.

No place in Savannah held more excitement than the City Market on Saturday. It occupied all of Ellis Square, which was better known as Market Square. The quadrangular, brick structure was a four-sided affair that formed a square around an open courtyard. The building's interior was sectioned into stalls, which were rented out by the city, and tended by negro women.

Family farmers from the country, called crackers by the town folk, loaded their wagons with produce and traveled from a few hours to a few days just to be at the market on Saturday. They drove into town from all accesses on Friday evenings and Saturday mornings, clogging Savannah's streets. They sold their goods from their wagons on the streets bordering the square. What an array of things they brought: eggs piled so high they looked like baskets of cotton balls, mounds of onions shedding their flaky skins, bright red tomatoes the size of baby pumpkins, golden peaches, melons so big two hands were necessary to carry them, dressed poultry including turkey, duck, and partridge, venison, dried meats, and sausages.

Local fishermen sold crabs, oysters, shrimps, and other fish from wooden baskets in the open-air, center of the market, which contained a pump to wash away the eye-watering smells.

Negroes like Teenah who paid six dollars and fifty cents a year for a hawker's badge sold everything they grew or made on their plantations from the sidewalk outside the market. Jumbo sold his roses. The women wore dresses and turbans of reds, yellows, oranges, and purples, and called out their goods to passersby.

The market was one of the few social and racial equalizers in Savannah. Everyone—rich and poor, merchant and laborer, black and white, Democrat and Unionist, State Righter and Nullifier—shopped side-by-side.

While Hercules helped Teenah settle on the sidewalk, Andrew decided to stroll around the market. He was intrigued by the different goods offered by the country farmers, and stopped by each wagon to inspect them. He passed an old dray with animal skins and furs. As he tried to identify them, he looked up and noticed the biggest, darkest eyes he had ever seen. "Hello," he peeped to the beautiful young girl he thought to be about his age of thirteen years. His heart started to bounce around his chest.

"Hello," she replied, with the slightest trace of a smile. Her black hair fell to her waist. She wore a wrinkled, well-worn black dress and a necklace of purple stones. "Do you want to buy something?"

"Uhhh, no, I don't think so. I mean, I like the furs." Andrew was as comfortable with girls as Joseph was, and he felt his hands sweat. The girl patted the skins and started to move away. Andrew didn't want to lose her attention. "Where are you from?"

The girl turned and appraised Andrew, noticing how well he spoke and that he was better dressed than the other negro boys in town. "Far from here. Where are you from?"

Andrew felt his skin tingle. "I live on Heritage Plantation just three miles up the river. I make bricks."

"Oh, you work on a plantation?" she replied. Her eyes wandered from Andrew.

Andrew's stomach tightened. The implication was clear. She knew he was a slave. He was inferior to the girl. He had to try to be more to her. "Yes, but I'm going to be a free person of color one day. And an architect, in the style of Vitruvius."

She blinked a few times and shrugged indifferently. "That's nice."

As Andrew searched his clouded mind for something to say, he noticed a man glaring at him from the other side of the wagon. He was tall, about the height of Master McBain, with a dark complexion and long, black hair streaked with strands of gray. His face was covered with many lines. He wore a black hat, black pants, a black shirt with a red string tie, and a black jacket. Andrew realized he was an Indian, one of the first he had ever seen. The man said, "Sally, come here," and the girl obeyed.

Andrew watched her until he felt a hand on his shoulder. "Hercules!"

"Andrew, let's walk." Hercules guided Andrew away and leaned close to him. "They Cherokees. Not many 'round yuh. They live far to the west. I hear gran' massa say the white man is tryin' to run 'em from yuh."

"Why?" Andrew was concerned he would never see the girl again.

"They livin' on Georgia land. The buckra run off the Creeks years ago. Cherokees got to go, too, is my guess. The Indians, they never goin' to have a home. Soon as they git to where the white man sends 'em, he take that land, too."

Andrew stopped and turned, but the Indian wagon was beyond his sight. He tried to think of a way he could meet Sally again when Hercules said, "You just mind one thing. President Jackson, he free the slaves 'fore that girl's daddy lets you near her."

"I don't like her like that, Hercules."

Hercules laughed and patted Andrew on the back. They walked back to Teenah.

The McBains met at City Market after their morning appointments. Teenah had sold most of the baskets and had a bag stuffed with coins to distribute at the Heritage. Hercules and Andrew were eating apples they had bought in the market. Joseph noticed that Andrew kept looking towards the farmers' carts.

Joseph's parents wanted to shop in the market before having dinner and took Amy and Hercules with them. Sarah told Joseph to meet them by Teenah in an hour.

Andrew and Joseph wandered by the crowded stalls on their own, inspecting the people as well as the merchandise. Joseph recognized a woman, but couldn't place her. She was large, though not fat. She wore a plain gray blouse and a long, black skirt. Her black hair sat in a tight bun on top of her head. "Andrew, see that woman by the hat stall? Does she look familiar?"

Andrew looked and stopped in his tracks. He grabbed Joseph's arm. "That's that gruesome woman! Don't you remember? She tried to get me kicked out of Master Williams's bookstore a few years ago. Let's get out of here!"

Joseph stared at her. "You're right. That is the old cow. Don't worry, she can't do anything to you. You're allowed in the market."

Andrew tugged Joseph away. "I was allowed in the bookstore, too, and that didn't stop her."

They darted to the open, center area of the market and a wave of noise washed over them as the negroes called out their goods. "Yeh oshta, yeh swimps, yeh crab, crab b'yuh!"

An old black man stood by several big baskets of live crabs. They frantically tried to crawl over the sides of their wooden-walled prisons, but couldn't quite make it to the top. Joseph and Andrew stopped to watch. Joseph didn't like all the messy work necessary to get the little meat a crab yielded, and rarely bothered with them. However, for a few days in spring, the crabs molted. These soft-bodied creatures required no endless shell-cracking or cheek-imploding sucking. One ate the entire critter whole. Jinny covered them in flour and fried them in butter. They were Joseph's favorite meal.

Joseph studied the crabs. He couldn't tell if they had soft or hard shells. His mouth started to water at the thought of devouring a freshly fried crab with its crunchy covering and soft center. He just had to find out. He bent down to touch the back of one of the crabs. His finger had barely entered the basket when, in a flash, three crabs clamped onto his hand with their sharp claws. Joseph yelled and jerked his hand away, sending them flying through the market air. Two landed helplessly on the brick floor and skittered away. The third was not as fortunate, and landed on the blouse of the Gruesome Woman, who had just entered the area. Like the other two, the crab tried to hide, and somehow, he crawled under her blouse.

The woman's shriek even frightened the fish. The other shoppers turned to see a large woman, mouth wide open, a clump of hair sticking up from her bun, her spectacles askew on her nose, tearing at her blouse. When she ripped it off, the cause of her alarm was revealed. The intruder was hanging onto her corset for dear life. Her howls became louder as she pulled at the garment. It came down with a giant snap and the poor crustacean shot through the market air, its claws flapping like a bird.

Very few in the crowd watched the crab take flight. Their eyes remained on the enormous breasts of the woman. When she realized her attacker had left and she was half-naked in front of a throng of strangers, she gasped, covered her chest with her arms, and fainted, falling onto the floor of Savannah Greys.

Andrew and Joseph took off. They hurried past the crowd that had circled around the woman, and Joseph took a last peek. Her eyes were closed, but the scowl was still there. The boys ran until they found Joseph's parents, who had just finished shopping. "What's that noise from the fish market, Joseph?" his mother asked.

Joseph held up his hands, wiggled his fingers, and said. "A wild crab attacked a woman." Andrew turned away, giggling.

Sarah McBain tilted her head and glared at Joseph, as Hercules would. She waited for a better explanation when James McBain said, "I think we best go to dinner."

The McBains left Andrew, Hercules, and Teenah and walked the short distance to the hotel. Grandfather was sitting at the bar, the one in which Dr. Minis had shot and killed James Stark less than a year before. Grandfather placed some coins on the counter and joined the family. They were led to a table where the manager held Mrs. McBain's chair. After she had been seated, he bowed.

By a strange reflex, Joseph followed the manager's lead and held Amy's chair. As he prepared to bow, Amy said loud enough to reach most ears in the dining room, "Why, Joseph! What a perfect little boy you're becoming. Those classes finally seem to be doing some good."

Joseph felt his face steam as he saw Amy look cross-eyed at him. He took his seat and avoided visual contact with her. He looked past the dining room, into the bar. He reflected on the day he was in there, and thought he smelled the burnt gunpowder of Dr. Minis's gun. Minis had remained in jail for six months awaiting his trial. It lasted six days. Although most Savannahians believed he was guilty of murdering Stark, the ones that mattered, the jury, returned a verdict of not guilty after only a few hours of deliberation. Minis celebrated his freedom by leaving town. Joseph missed the doctor, and wondered where he was, and if he had regained his honor.

After dinner, the McBains strolled back to the market. Sarah, Amy, and Teenah boarded the coach with Hercules and headed home. The McBain men returned to the boat. The oarsmen helped them in and pushed away from the wharf. They easily maneuvered around large ships in the harbor to the southern channel of the river.

After they passed Yamacraw, a negro section of town, a loud voice broke their concentration. "Well, good afternoon to the McBains." It was Charles Manigault, who owned Gowrie Plantation on Argyle Island, just a few miles west of the Heritage. Manigault was a Charlestonian, one of several South Carolina rice planters who were buying land on the Savannah River. He had just purchased Gowrie but had met James and Daniel McBain several times. McBain was fascinated by Manigault's use of the task system, in which the slaves were given a quota of work each day. Once they completed it, they had the rest of the day to hunt, fish, or whatever they chose. Manigault claimed the system inspired his negroes to complete their tasks more quickly.

Manigault stood in a four-oared boat about the same size as McBain's. However, it was plank style and his oarsmen were white.

McBain saluted, happy to see his neighbor. "Good afternoon, Mr. Manigault. How are you on this fine day?"

Manigault replied, "Could not be better." He then introduced a man sitting beside him, a cousin from Charleston, and his oarsmen, sporting men from a Charleston boat club. Manigault eyed McBain's boat. "I'd heard you purchased a boat. How do you like it?"

"I'm still getting used to it," McBain replied, preparing for what he knew was to come.

"I see it's one of those Indian boats," Manigault quipped. He was referring to the dugout style, often called a pirogue, which was used almost exclusively in the South.

McBain replied, "And yours is a Yankee boat. I've not seen many in these waters. I find it odd you'd have one." The northern boats were made of planks. There was a heated debate between northern and southern boatmen about which style was the faster.

Manigault bent at the knees and slapped the side of the boat. "I just had it shipped from Philadelphia. I've studied the two types quite closely. I'm certain the plank is faster, but I haven't yet had the chance to prove it." Manigault raised an eyebrow. "Might you give me that opportunity, my good sir?"

McBain said, "I fear not. I'm carrying two more riders than you." He then looked at his negroes and added, "Besides, my oarsmen have never raced before."

Manigault put his hands on his hips and grinned. "Mr. McBain, did you call those negroes 'oarsmen?' They look like sunburned, northern college boys." His men laughed.

Grandfather stood and jabbed his finger in the direction of the South Carolinian. "These negroes can swallow you up in their wake, Manigault!" Joseph elbowed Andrew lightly in the side, appreciating Grandfather's spirit. The boys wanted to race.

The rice planter held his belly and bellowed. "That sounds like a challenge, sir! And one that should be accompanied by a respectable wager between gentlemen."

McBain put his hand on Grandfather's back and asked him to sit. His heart wasn't in the competition, but he couldn't back out now. "Is twenty dollars to the Heritage lumber mill wharf respectable enough for you, Mr. Manigault?" Joseph was surprised that his father would make such a large wager. McBain was not a gambler, and always warned Joseph against it.

"Twenty dollars? Why, that's hardly a pallet of bricks. Fifty dollars would be even more respectable, what with the price of fine Scotch whiskey these days." Manigault's cousin and rowers smirked at each other. Joseph heard his father gasp at the counter offer.

McBain shook his head. He wasn't sure his men were ready, and he would never race for that amount of money. He was about to refuse the challenge when Manigault said, "I understand your reluctance. Losing is no fun, especially when you've lost before the race even begins. I'll tell you what. Two of my men against the four of yours."

Grandfather stood again, shook his fist, and shouted, "I'll buy you a drink out of my winnings, Manigault, you cocky little fart. Two hundred dollars for a drink won't break a man of your means." McBain turned so quickly to face Grandfather he nearly fell over.

Manigault laughed and hollered, "You have a substantial set of balls, Grandfather McBain. You also have a wager."

McBain whispered to Grandfather, "Are you insane?"

The old man shouted, "I'll not have that arrogant gamecock insult our negroes!"

McBain groaned and accepted the inevitable. He yelled, "We'll await your arrival at the wharf, Mr. Manigault!"

Manigault cupped his hands around his mouth and called, "To the Heritage, men!" and his team started to row. McBain's negroes needed no order, but before they knew it, they were behind by a boat length. The blacks rowed hard, but their oars were not slicing into the water in unison and they couldn't keep a straight line.

Joseph stood to cheer the negroes on, and rocked the boat. McBain scolded him to sit and be still. Joseph sat and he and Andrew clasped their hands together, bouncing their knees up and down. McBain called to his men, "Smoothly, smoothly. We have two miles. Find your stroke." While McBain tried to gain control, he kept glancing at Manigault. Grandfather repeatedly slapped his right hand into his left palm.

After a half-mile, the plank boat was ahead by almost three lengths. Manigault looked back at the McBains, laughed, and thrust his fist into the air. His cousin sat and called a cadence to his men.

"Calmly, men. Find your stroke. Forward, pull, forward, pull!" McBain urged, trying to build a rhythm. His men were doing better. They were not falling any further behind, but they were not gaining either. With a mile left to go, it looked like a lost cause.

Joshua, McBain's strongest oarsman, started to sing. His strong voice pierced the still river air. The other rowers joined in the chorus.

> Lawd tek muh han' an' ease muh burden
> Oh ay mah ay mah ay
> Tek muh han' an' show me heben
> Oh ay mah ay mah ay
> Mah ay mah ay oh ay mah ay
> Mah ay mah ay oh ay mah ay

Their oars started slicing into the water like knives and their bodies pulled back and bent forward as one. Their skin glistened with sweat.

> Life so hard ah cyan' keep tryin'
> Oh ay mah ay mah ay
> Lawd stay near and ease muh burden
> Oh ay mah ay mah ay
> Mah ay mah ay oh ay mah ay
> Mah ay mah ay oh ay mah ay

Joseph could see shoulder and back muscles straining with each pull. They were beginning to gain on the other boat. Manigault kept punching the air with one hand while holding his top hat with the other. Joseph and Andrew moved forward and back in time with the oarsmen.

As they passed Hutchinson Island, the negroes working in the rice fields heard the oarsmen and sang with them. Soon the whole river basin was engulfed in song:

> The Lawd hear muh prayer but he won' tek me
> Oh ay mah ay mah ay
> Say muh burden can nebuh break me
> Oh ay mah ay mah ay
> Mah ay mah ay oh ay mah ay
> Mah ay mah ay oh ay mah ay

McBain's men heard the Lord answer them. They rowed harder and gained on their opponent. Sweat poured off their bodies as they grunted with each pull. Joseph thought their muscles would burst out of their skin. Grandfather started slapping his thigh and screamed "Row, Row, Row!" With less than a half-mile left, only a boat length separated the two. Joseph saw a crowd of Heritage servants jammed on the steam mill wharf, jumping up and down and waving their arms.

Mah ay mah ay oh ay mah ay
Mah ay mah ay oh ay mah ay

They continued to gain. With fifty yards to go only a few feet separated them. Manigault turned and recoiled at the closeness of the dugout. Both sets of oarsmen kept pulling with all they had, their teeth bared and faces grimacing, summoning every bit of strength in their bodies. Joseph could hear the cheers of the Heritage negroes. He and Andrew yelled along with Grandfather, "Row! Row! Row!" They were about to pull even. "Row! Row! Row!"

As they neared the wharf, Joseph noticed a thick tree branch about ten feet long floating in the middle of the river. McBain saw it, too, and called to his men to stroke harder on the right. Joseph glanced at the wharf and thought he saw something move beneath it. Then he heard Manigault scream to his men, "Look out!" It was too late. They hit the branch flush. The boat swerved violently. Manigault took off in flight, like a great, pregnant blue heron in a top hat. He plunged into the river with an enormous splash as the *Amy* passed the wharf.

Amidst the joy of victory, McBain ordered his men to turn the boat around to fish the struggling loser from the river. McBain was out of his shoes and jacket and in the water in seconds, supporting his flailing opponent. With all their energy, the drained oarsmen heaved the vanquished man into the boat, almost capsizing it in the process. Then they pulled in McBain.

The negro oarsmen congratulated each other with slaps on the back. Joseph and Andrew clapped their hands and whistled. Grandfather attempted a victory jig, to the delight of the servants on the wharf, almost capsizing the boat again. McBain called for everyone to calm down as he stood over Manigault, who lay motionless on the bottom of the boat. Then, as if somebody had dropped a hot coal down his drawers, he jumped to his feet, almost knocking McBain back into the river.

"Well, Mr. Manigault! You're standing in the winning boat, as you predicted. Sadly, you lost!" McBain tried to be a good winner and conceal his jubilation. It was difficult.

Manigault protested, spraying water in all directions. "What in damnation? That was no race. We hit a felled oak. That cancels the outcome!"

McBain brushed his dripping hair from his forehead. "Sorry, old man, but we were ahead of you at the finish line. We were able to avoid the branch. You could have, too, with proper captaining."

Manigault held his arms out like a scarecrow, as if to dry his soaking clothes. "I want to know how that branch just happened to come floating out on the river at the finish line as I was thrashing you."

"Father." Joseph wanted to say he saw the branch float from under the wharf.

"Not now, son," McBain replied, enjoying the debate. He returned to Manigault. "Branches float in rivers. We passed several during the race. The river is wide enough to row around them. And, yes, we do accept wet currency." Andrew and Joseph laughed at McBain's gloating. Joseph had never seen him so happy.

Manigault shook his head like a wet dog. "That was a damned good race, even if I must say so myself. I will pay Grandfather McBain the two hundred dollars you won under highly questionable circumstances, but only if you consent to a rematch."

McBain slapped Manigault's shoulder. "I agree, within the month. Now, let's get into dry clothes and have that drink!"

The three Darien runaways waited in the cool water under the wharf, and watched as the men climbed up the ladder. They prayed that they would soon be able to cross the river and continue on their journey. One week earlier they decided that freedom was worth any cost, including their lives. Each had been born on a rice plantation near Darien, and started work in the fields at nine years. They worked from sun up to sun down, six days a week, and lived in a drafty, one-room log cabin with seven other unmarried men. There were only four beds, so the men took turns sleeping on the earthen floor, except in the winter, when the need for warmth forced them to sleep together. An old, female slave cooked their meals at the servants' mess house. Not one of them had ever eaten at a table. One of the men, Anthony, had seen his father and mother get whipped for stealing one of massa's chickens.

Anthony, Hal, and Ena left the plantation at night. They stole a small rowboat and moved north by the coastline, hoping to get as far away from the bonds of servitude as possible. They abandoned the boat at daybreak and proceeded by land. In four days they reached the Yamacraw section of Savannah where they met a negro who knew of a free man in Beaufort who hid runaways and sent them to the next safe house.

They left Savannah at night and headed west a mile to cross the Savannah River away from the activity of the city. They cut through the barren rice fields of the Vale Royal Plantation and were at the river just before sunrise. Hal found a big live oak branch. The men clung to it and paddled towards an island, but the strong tide carried them up-river. The sun was peeking over the horizon, so they decided to go back to the Georgia shore and hide under a nearby wharf.

As they planned their next move, people gathered on the deck above them. A boat came by, boarded people, and left. By that time, it was daylight and the runaways heard the activity of the plantation near them. It was too risky to enter the river without being seen. They also realized they would need a boat in the strong currents. Anthony suggested they wait until the boat came back. They would steal it or take it by force if necessary and row to South Carolina at night. Hal and Ena agreed. Ena, heavy and a weak swimmer, held onto the branch, just in case.

They waited in the water, held onto a piling, and tried to determine the plantation work being performed from the sounds. The screeching of the steam-powered saw confused them, but they knew it wasn't a rice field. When the tide went out, they huddled on the bank under the wharf and dozed on a bed of mud. The hours passed, and the tide returned. The hungry runaways were up to their necks in water again and concluded the boat may not be coming back. They couldn't wait another day. They had to use the branch to cross the river and risk being seen. They planned to go to the island in the river, catch one of the hogs they'd heard, cook it, eat their fill, and take what they could.

They moved to the front pilings and readied themselves. As they were about to push off, they saw two narrow boats racing side by side in their direction. Then they heard singing. Soon, people were cheering and trampling on the wharf above them. They thought the dock was about to collapse and retreated back under it. As they did, Ena lost his grip on the branch and it floated into the river.

"I had you beat when that tree floated by," Manigault announced again in the parlor of the McBain house. James feigned a yawn. He had beaten Manigault at his own game and was enjoying every moment, especially when the loser had to peel apart seventy dollars in wet bills to partially pay the wager.

McBain said, "I think you need that drink now."

Manigault replied, "I have to decline, sir. There's no house on Gowrie. We were just going to have a look around. We need to row there and return to Savannah before nightfall. Do you have the time?"

McBain reached for his watch and realized he was not wearing his jacket. In all the excitement, he forgot he had taken it off in the boat before he jumped in the water. "It seems I left my jacket on my boat. Joseph, would you fetch it?"

"Yes, Father." Joseph frowned. He enjoyed watching his father toy with Mr. Manigault and didn't want to miss a minute. He ran to the river as fast as he could.

"Pa?" Dante whispered as he sat outside his cabin with his father, as massa and the buckra disappeared into the big house.

"Wut?" his father, Daymon, replied, not wanting to be bothered.

"Ah gwine tuh de whaa'f." Though only eleven, and not considered smart, Dante was observant. Few things happened around him that escaped his notice. This was invaluable in his development as a thief.

"Wuffuh?" Daymon readied his hand to slap his son on the head.

Dante jumped up. "Massa leabe he jacket een de boat. Ah gwi' fetch it fuh 'um."

Daymon spat on the ground. "Lit massa git it hese'f."

"Ah t'ink he leabe he watch een it."

Daymon stood and headed for the wharf, with Dante scurrying behind. They heard Handy, yell, "Wuh oonuh gwine?"

"Nebuh oonuh mine!" Daymon replied, without turning to look at her, as he cursed his double dose of slavery. When they reached the end of the wharf, Daymon turned around and descended the ladder to McBain's boat. As he stepped onto it, a hand was around his mouth and a knife was at his throat. He felt himself being pulled to the middle of the boat, which started to rock. He saw Dante back down the ladder and receive the same welcome from another man.

The two had arrived just as the runaways were about to push off. Anthony whispered in Daymon's ear that if he or the boy made a sound, they would both die.

Daymon nodded. He knew the men had to be runaways, and desperate. His heart slammed so loud in his chest, he could hardly hear his captor.

Anthony couldn't leave the man and boy behind to tell their massa. Yet Anthony couldn't kill them. He had no choice. He told Daymon that he and his friends would take him and the boy across the river and would release them on the other side. Anthony pressed the knife against Daymon's neck.

Daymon nodded. He had to think fast as well. He hated his bondage. He couldn't stand his wife or his son. When Anthony removed his hand from Daymon's mouth, Daymon whispered, "Tek me wid oonuh! Ah know de way."

Anthony froze, not expecting that. Knowledge of the route would be helpful. But taking the man would increase the chances that his massa would come after them. Still, Anthony was certain massa would search for them anyway. "Wut 'bout de boy chile?"

Daymon, who hadn't the slightest idea of the roads but hoped it would convince his captors to take him, couldn't leave his son at the wharf. "Leabe he on de udda side. Massa fine he lookin' fuh me."

Anthony liked the solution. "Tell de chile tuh hush. Now us gitway."

They settled in the boat and were about to leave. Then they heard more footsteps.

As Joseph approached the wharf, he heard voices nearby and assumed they were servants fishing. He backed down the ladder, hopped into the boat, turned, and saw Dante, Daymon, and three strange negroes looking at him. The biggest one jumped on him. All Joseph noticed about the man was his ear, which looked like a small, dried fig. Joseph screamed for help before the man covered his mouth with his hand. Joseph struggled but the negro was too powerful. He felt the boat push away from the dock. He heard Dante cry and saw Daymon clasp a hand over his son's mouth.

Joseph's heart raced like a frightened rabbit. After a minute he heard someone shout from a distance, "Stop, or I'll shoot!" He saw Mr. Bones standing at the edge of the wharf with a musket pointed at them.

Joseph heard the negro holding him shout, "Keep rowin'!"

Mr. Bones fired the gun and a musket ball hit the boat. Thwack! It startled everyone. Joseph's captor flinched and loosened his grip. Joseph bolted free and jumped overboard. As soon as he felt the cool river water embrace him, he wanted to scream for joy. He floated to the surface, shook his head and waved to the people gathered on the wharf, about one hundred yards away. It took but a few seconds for him to realize that his wet clothing and boots were like anchors on his body. The currents pulled him down, but he managed to struggle to the surface. He screamed for help, and took a mouthful of water. Joseph tried to swim but could barely move his arms. He tried to rip off his shirt, but went under and swallowed more water. He tried to take in air so he could hold his breath and remove his boots, but he couldn't manage it. As he tried to float, ripples washed over his face. He swallowed more water than air, and knew he couldn't stay above the surface much longer. He looked to the wharf. People were getting into a boat, but they were too far away to reach him in time. He glanced at the boat from which he had escaped, just twenty yards away. His black captors stared at him. Joseph knew he was going to die.

Using his last bit of energy, he wiggled his arms and legs to raise his head just two inches higher to keep his nose and mouth above water. He couldn't do it. He gulped more water. There was no air to breathe. As Joseph sank below the surface, he said goodbye to his parents, Amy, and Andrew.

Joseph saw a bright light and tried to reach it, but he couldn't move. The light came closer. He felt God lifting him to heaven. He felt air. He gulped for it, but couldn't get any down. He coughed and water came out. He gulped again, as if trying to bite an apple. He took in some air in but coughed up more water. His chest burned and felt like it was going to explode and he started to retch. He tried to move his hands to wipe the water away from his mouth, but couldn't raise them. He twisted his body in an attempt to quicken his assent. He was surprised going to heaven was so painful. Then he heard God say, "Whoa, lil' buckra. Us gwi' ride de tide. Us gwi' ride de tide." He was even more surprised God was a negro.

Joseph continued fighting to get air into his lungs, but it seemed he only vomited water out. In the distance he heard an angel shout, "Grab this rope." Then someone pulled him up, and he was lying face down on a hard surface. It wasn't what Joseph had imagined heaven to be. Someone started pushing on his back. Someone else shouted, "Tie up that negro!" Then Joseph blacked out.

*　　*　　*

Isaac pointed to the items on the ground. "Oonuh hab de brick, de mawtuh, an' de traw'l. All oonuh wan' fuh build dis wall." It was five days after the river incident. As McBain had promised, Joseph and Andrew were starting their bricklaying careers.

Isaac dropped to one knee to show them how to lay bricks using the American bond style. Five rows exposing the long side of the brick, called the stretcher, are laid, alternated with one row exposing the head of the brick, called the header. The stretcher is eight inches long and the header four. The middle of a brick in one row must align over the meeting joint of two bricks on the row below. The thickness of the wall plays a big part in laying the bricks. The slave cabins had eight-inch thick walls, so when laying a stretcher row, two bricks had to be placed side by side, inside and out. The header row required one.

Isaac scooped some mortar with the trowel, slapped it on top of the lower row of bricks, and spread it evenly with the trowel. Then he picked up a brick and spread some mortar on one of the header ends, as if he were buttering a piece of bread. He laid the brick, pressing the header end with the pre-applied mortar against the previously laid brick. He tapped the top of the brick, scraped off the excess that oozed out, and flicked it back in the mortar pan. He then handed the trowel to Andrew.

Andrew smiled at Joseph, knelt, and laid his first brick. Andrew worked slowly, but it was clear that he grasped the concept. Isaac stopped him once to explain the application of the mortar, but Isaac was clearly impressed.

Joseph's turn came. He squatted and spread mortar on the lower row. Andrew handed him a brick. Though it weighed five pounds, to Joseph it felt like a ton. He was still sore from his struggle in the water. He scooped some mortar from the tray and applied it to the header.

Isaac said, "'Nuf!"

Joseph dropped the brick. Isaac groaned. Joseph picked up the brick, scraped off the old mortar, applied some new, and pressed the brick down gently. He scraped off the excess mortar.

"Mmmm," Isaac offered, charitably, as he adjusted the crooked brick by hand.

After Joseph laid a few more, Isaac said, "Ah hab udduh wu'k, an' ah cyan' watch obuh oonuh fuhebbuh. Wu'k dis wall cause he don' hab no window. An' do it right. Ah yent hab no tahm tuh fix a mess." With that, Isaac left.

Andrew went first. After cautiously handling the first few, he picked up speed and laid the bricks perfectly. Then Joseph tried. He was not as fast as Andrew, but he made an admirable effort. Isaac came by every thirty minutes to inspect. He made a few adjustments and didn't criticize them, which was a good sign. The boys weren't ready for villas in Savannah, but they were finally building.

As Andrew worked, he looked up and asked, "How are you feeling, Master Joseph?"

Joseph hadn't discussed his ordeal with anyone except his father, and that was a cold recounting from the time he left the house to fetch the jacket. "I'm still sore."

"I didn't think your father and Mr. Bones would reach you in time. When I saw you go under, I closed my eyes and prayed to God. When I opened my eyes, I saw one of the runaways holding you."

Joseph said, "You know, when I thought all was lost, I said goodbye to you and my family. And I prayed for Amy to take care of you. I think that was my last thought."

Andrew nodded, laid two more bricks, and stood. Joseph threw his arm around Andrew's shoulders and said, "Friends forever."

Andrew handed the trowel to Joseph and smiled. "Friends forever."

CHAPTER 7

Quiet Goose

1834

In the nine months since he met Sally, Andrew looked forward to Saturdays at the City Market more than laying bricks. She and her father, Quiet Goose, appeared sporadically, about once a month. When they did show, Quiet Goose expected her to sell hides, not socialize. Still, when business slowed in the afternoon, he allowed Sally to chat for a few minutes with Andrew, who paced on the sidewalk by the Heritage servants as they hawked their goods. Sally's smile was the signal that he could come over. When Quiet Goose placed his top hat on the wagon, it was time for Andrew to leave.

Their limited conversations were friendly. Sally asked him about his duties at the plantation, the family who owned it, and his interest in building. She avoided questions about herself. One day in March 1834 that changed.

Sally ran her hands through her long hair and said, "It's time to go, Andrew."

Andrew saw the hat on the wagon. He asked, "Will you be back next month?"

Sally looked down. "I don't know. We never know if we're coming back."

Andrew glanced at Quiet Goose, who was talking to a customer. "Why not?"

"Because the government is trying to take our land and make us leave Georgia."

Andrew remembered Hercules telling him that, but it didn't make sense. "How can they do that if you own it?"

Sally's eyes flared. "The white man doesn't care. They take it anyway. They found gold on some of our lands. Others are good for growing cotton. Georgia passed an act to move us out west and then sold our land by lottery. Even their Supreme Court said the state couldn't do it, but that didn't stop them. But my father says he'll never leave. They'll have to kill him first." Sally's voice wavered. "He means it." She rearranged the hides, although they didn't need it.

Andrew heard Quiet Goose tapping his hat on the wagon. "I hope that doesn't happen, Sally. I hope I see you again."

Sally patted Andrew's hand. "I hope to see you, too, Andrew." Then she walked to the other side of the wagon. Andrew, with a lump in his throat, went to find Joseph to ask about the Cherokees.

"There's Andrew," Joseph said as he got up from his seat on the sidewalk next to Teenah.

Andrew approached Joseph and said, "I need to speak to you, Master Joseph." Just then, Amy ran up to tell Joseph their parents were waiting at Mrs. Platt's Boarding House for dinner. Joseph told Andrew he would see him later and left with Amy.

As they entered the dining room, Mr. McBain stood to greet them. "Joseph, you remember Mr. Lamar?" Gazaway and two other men stood.

"I certainly do. It's a pleasure to meet you again, sir." Joseph reached across the table to shake hands.

Gazaway said, "Good to see you, Joseph. I think it's been two years." Then Gazaway introduced Joseph to his cousins, Mirabeau Bonaparte Lamar and Judge Lucius Quintas Cincinatus Lamar.

As Joseph shook each man's hand, he thought about the distinctive Lamar names. Gazaway Bugg? Mirabeau Bonaparte? Lucius Quintas Cincinnatus? They took personal identification to new heights. They were more than just names. They were gilt-edged human picture frames.

Gazaway told his cousins about Joseph's interest in architecture. Mirabeau and Judge Lamar were impressed and asked Joseph questions about the source of his inspiration. When the food was served, the three Lamar men spoke mainly to James, Sarah, and Amy. Amy's beauty and wit overshadowed Joseph's career in building. At fifteen years, she talked easily and confidently with men.

As an observer, Joseph learned many things. Gazaway Lamar had recently moved to Savannah from Augusta with his wife and four children. His shipping business thrived and he had become a commission merchant in town. He was also a director of the Planter's Bank of the State of Georgia. And he talked about running for city alderman on the State Rights ticket.

Judge Lucius Quintas Cincinnatus Lamar lived in Milledgeville, the state capitol. Joseph's father showed him great respect. Joseph noticed the judge hardly smiled.

Mirabeau Lamar talked about losing a bid for a congressional seat in 1832 and was preparing for another run. He spoke mostly about his interest in the Texas territory.

As they finished eating, two boys, about ten years old, ran to the table. Both were covered in sand, telltale signs of a frolic in the streets of Savannah. One of the boys, panting hard, asked Judge Lamar, "Father, may I stay in Savannah with Cousin Charlie this summer?"

Before Judge Lamar could respond, the other boy asked Gazaway, "Yes, Father. Can Lushe stay with us?"

Gazaway said to the boy, "Catch your breath, Charlie. I'd like you to meet some friends of mine." Gazaway looked at the McBains. "James and Sarah, Amy and Joseph, please meet my son, Charles Augustus Lafayette Lamar. We call him Charlie. Charlie, meet Mr. and Mrs. McBain and Amy and Joseph."

Charlie bent a little from the shoulders, breathed heavily with his tongue hanging out, like a retriever, then stood up straight. He flashed a toothy, freckled smile and chirped, "Hello, everybody."

"What an adorable boy," chimed Amy.

Judge Lamar then introduced his son, Lushe, to the McBains and explained, "He's really Lucius Quintas Cincinnatus, Junior."

Lushe tugged at his father's sleeve, "Can I, Father? Can I spend the summer here?"

Judge Lamar brightened when he spoke to his son. "We'll have to ask your mother. It's up to her."

Gazaway clapped his hands together. "In any case, you must come down for the launching of the ship. It will be around the fourth of July. We can all celebrate Independence Day together. We'll have a grand time."

"I don't know, Gaz. I'll be riding the circuit then. It would be difficult for me," replied Judge Lamar, sounding tired. Everything on his face pointed down—the corners of his eyes, his mouth, and the lines on his forehead.

Charlie asked, "Uncle Lucius, what's 'riding the circuit' mean?"

Lucius placed a hand on Charlie's shoulder. "Well, judges have to hold court in many different places. We call traveling to each of the counties 'riding the circuit'."

"Who do you ride with?" Charlie asked what Joseph was thinking.

"There's the solicitor general for the circuit, and the lawyers who plead the cases. We travel together in a big group. You could think of it as a parade of lawyers."

Charlie's eyebrows bunched together as he thought that over. "I think I like the circus parade better, Uncle Lucius." The adults laughed.

Judge Lamar mussed Charlie's hair. "Sometimes there's not much of a difference." The judge managed a smile. "We'll do our best to be here in July."

Lushe and Charlie cheered.

James McBain accepted Gazaway's invitation to the family to attend the launching and the parties bid good day.

*　　*　　*

The McBains struggled to get through the crowd gathered around Mr. Cant's shipyard near the foot of West Broad Street. The Strand was packed as tight as it had been in years. Grandfather McBain said it was a fine turnout, considering the people had gathered to honor a ship and not a war hero. Gazaway Lamar's idea of an iron-hulled, steam-powered boat that could navigate the shallows of the Savannah River had become a reality. When he couldn't find a builder in America, he located one in England. Lamar hired William Scarbrough to go to London to supervise the construction. Scarbrough had been a partner in the *S. S. Savannah*, the first steamship to cross the Atlantic, in 1819. He had since fallen on hard times and was working for the new shipping entrepreneur in town.

To eliminate any potential damage from an oceanic voyage, the builder constructed the ship in pieces and sent them to Savannah as cargo. The parts arrived in Savannah in March 1834 and were assembled at John Cant's shipyard according to written instructions. The anticipation of the launch had been building for weeks. It was yet another first for Savannah. Lamar called the ship the *John Randolph*, for the fiery state-rights senator from Virginia.

The McBains finally squeezed onto the ship. Gazaway had to raise his voice above the din of the crowd, the engine, and the band to introduce them to his family and other guests. Mr. and Mrs. McBain and Amy spent time talking with Mr. Lamar's wife, Jane Meek Cresswell Lamar. Joseph stood next to Charlie Lamar and asked him if his cousin Lushe had come for the occasion. Charlie lowered his head and put his hands in his pockets. He said Lushe was supposed to but never arrived.

The band stopped abruptly. All Joseph could hear was the hum of the ship's engine. A man in a black robe stood on the wharf and blessed the vessel. All the people on the *John Randolph* and those on the wharf, mostly workers from Cant's and the band, removed their hats and bowed their heads. When the pastor finished, the band struck up, "The Star Spangled Banner." The workers huzzahed and waved their hats in the air as the captain blew the whistle. Sailors untied the lines and threw them on the ship, which slowly churned up thousands of bubbles as it pulled away from the wharf. Joseph looked to the bluff and saw people applauding. He proudly stood erect and waved back.

The boat made it to mid-stream and glided up and down the harbor a few times. It floated like a piece of cork. Other ships blew their horns as the *John Randolph* passed by. Charlie was so excited he banged both his hands against the railing of the boat like a drum. Some of the passengers commented that it felt like they were on a cloud. Joseph couldn't wait to tell Andrew about the miracle ride.

After docking, Gazaway invited his guests to his house on Broughton Street for a celebration. McBain accepted. Grandfather said he would be along after he first visited the open field on West Broad Street, as he did around every Independence Day. The last few years he had taken Joseph with him.

Charlie, standing next to Joseph, was interested to know why anyone would want to walk around that field. He asked Gazaway, "Father, may I go with Grandfather McBain and Joseph?"

Gazaway replied, "I don't know, Charlie. They might want to be by themselves."

Grandfather said, "Charlie's welcome to join us." It was a private matter, but he always enjoyed having children around. Charlie pulled his cap on tight, ready to go.

Hercules drove Joseph, Charlie, and Grandfather to West Broad and the southern edge of town before taking Amy and her parents to the Lamar house. Grandfather donned his kerchief and walked onto the open field overrun with weeds. Joseph and Charlie followed close behind. The old man walked to the center of the field and stopped. He closed his eyes and prayed silently. Joseph did the same. Charlie didn't understand the moment, but copied Joseph while keeping an eye on Grandfather McBain.

When Grandfather finished he ambled to another spot, knelt, pulled up a clump of grass, and rolled the soil in his fingertips. He reached into his jacket pocket, pulled out a crumpled red rose, and dropped it to the ground.

After a minute of silence, Charlie asked, "Sir, why do you always wear that kerchief outdoors?"

Grandfather stood and rested a hand on Charlie's shoulder. He explained how he and his twin brother, James Edward, grew up on their father's cattle farm and how they joined the Continental Army at seventeen years of age to fight for American independence. He told Charlie how he and his brother and thousands of Americans and Frenchmen fought on the very ground on which they were standing to retake Savannah from the British, and how his brother and hundreds of others were killed during the battle, their blood still deep in the earth. He recounted how he was wounded during that same disastrous siege and how, during the American Army's retreat to Charleston, a young nurse dressed his wound, and how that nurse gave him her handkerchief to wear so he didn't have to breathe the dust kicked up by the hundreds of other wagons ahead of him. He recalled how he and his parents rebuilt their ravaged farm after the war in the free air and soil of Georgia. And how, on the Savannah bluff on a warm day in May of the year of our Lord 1791, waiting for the greatest American of them all, President George Washington, and wearing his kerchief, he met the nurse who gave it to him twelve years earlier. And how they married and had a son before she and his parents died in the great fire of 1796.

"That's why I wear it, Charlie. To remember those I love. Especially those no longer with me. Life's precious. Don't forget that."

Charlie, trying to comprehend what he had just heard, simply said, "Yes, sir." The old man and the two boys trudged back to West Broad Street.

Hercules was waiting. As they drove to the Lamar house, Joseph promised Charlie that one day he and Hercules would teach him how to ride a horse. Charlie was so excited he said he would ask his father for permission as soon as they reached the house. When they arrived, Hercules opened the coach door and Charlie got out first. Joseph was about to exit when Hercules held up his hand, commanding him to stay put. Joseph saw his father on the sidewalk talking to Gazaway, who kept rubbing his eyes with unsteady hands. Then, James, Sarah, and Amy climbed into the coach. Joseph saw Mr. Lamar hug Charlie.

Joseph asked, "What's wrong, Father? What about the celebration?"

"Mr. Lamar just learned Judge Lamar committed suicide a few days ago. Shot himself in the head. They need to be alone."

Charlie never did get to ride horses at the Heritage.

∗　　∗　　∗

Andrew didn't see Sally at the City Market for many months. As each Saturday passed without a sign of her, Andrew became sadder and quieter. His heart almost danced out of his chest when he saw the Indian wagon at the market one afternoon in the fall of 1834, just months after Judge Lamar had killed himself. Quiet Goose hadn't changed. Andrew had to sit on the sidewalk and wait for a lull in business. With the McBains meeting the Lamars for dinner for the first time since the launch of the *John Randolph*, Andrew had plenty of time.

Sally finally smiled and Andrew darted over. He asked her where she had been for so many months, but she ignored the question and asked Andrew about bricks. Andrew got the hint. He didn't care, as long as he was with her.

Andrew became so engrossed in his conversation he didn't notice that Master McBain had returned and was talking with Master Lamar and a boy a few yards away.

McBain said, "That was a most enjoyable meal, Gaz. I'm glad to hear Judge Lamar's family is recovering. I hope Mississippi serves them well."

Gazaway squeezed Charlie's shoulder. "Charlie is sad Lushe's moved so far away." The boy's face was expressionless. He missed his cousin.

A passerby interrupted the two men. "Hello, Mr. McBain. Hello, Mr. Lamar," said William Washington Gordon.

"Hello, Mr. Gordon!" replied McBain, happy to see his friend. He noticed that Gordon was with his wife and another couple. The other man was unmistakable.

Gazaway tipped his hat. "Yes. Good to see you, Mr. Gordon."

Gordon shook both men's hands. "Mr. Lamar, congratulations on the *John Randolph*."

"Thank you, Mr. Gordon. And congratulations to you. You've made considerable progress, indeed." Since they had met at the Heritage two years before, Gordon had been elected alderman for the City of Savannah in September 1833. In December of that year, the legislature had granted a charter to Gordon's company, the Central of Georgia Railroad and Canal Company. Gordon was elected alderman again in 1834, and his fellow aldermen in turn elected him mayor. In fact, Lamar had run for alderman on the State Rights ticket, the one opposing Gordon's victorious Union and State Rights ticket. A month later Gordon was elected to the Georgia House of Representatives. He had heeded Lamar's advice of making political connections.

Gordon said to the men, "I'd like you to meet my wife, and Congressman Wayne and his wife." As the folks exchanged greetings, passersby stared at James Moore Wayne. He was the most recognizable and controversial politician in Savannah. A lawyer, he had served in the Georgia legislature and as the mayor of Savannah. He had been a judge for the city and the state. In 1828 he was elected to the United States House of Representatives. When Andrew Jackson needed a few southern votes to pass his hotly debated tariffs, Wayne supported him, incurring the anger of many Georgians, including Grandfather McBain, while gaining the respect of President Jackson. Still, Wayne remained a popular figure, and had been re-elected three times to the Congress.

As the adults conversed, Charlie turned away and noticed a negro boy talking with a pretty Indian girl by a wagon. An older Indian man was standing nearby, staring at the people with his father. Charlie edged a little closer to hear what the negro was saying.

"The bricks, about fifty thousand of them, are stacked high with tunnels, or fire eyes, in the base. That's where the wood is placed for the fire. The cover, which keeps the bricks dry during loading, is moved and fire is lighted. The covering, a big wooden structure like the frame of a house with a roof, actually rests on a big wagon with grooved wheels that sit on rails. The wagon is rolled to another firing area about forty yards away, and another kiln is built with green bricks while the first kiln is fired."

What a strange conversation, Charlie thought. The girl looked directly at the negro and nodded as he talked. The negro spoke like a white and with authority. Charlie didn't know how to make bricks, but he believed every word the boy said.

The Indian girl asked, "What happens if it rains after the roof is wheeled away?"

The negro replied, "The fire has been lighted and is so hot, any rain evaporates before it falls on the bricks. We start the fire slowly to get rid of any moisture still in the clay, otherwise the bricks explode. After a day, we increase the temperature with hotter-burning Georgia pine. The entire burn lasts about seven days and must be tended to twenty-four hours a day."

Charlie heard the adults bidding goodbye to each other and stepped to his father's side. As the Gordons and Waynes turned to leave, a loud voice pierced the air.

"Excuse me, your Excellency!" called Quiet Goose. "Excuse me, sir!" The voice was as loud and deep as a ship's horn and caught the attention of everyone in the area. Joseph, who was standing with Hercules, heard it and hurried to his father's side.

Quiet Goose marched past Andrew and Sally to meet the congressman. Sally grabbed Andrew's arm. He could feel her tremble.

Congressman Wayne turned and saw the Indian approaching him. Wayne asked, "Are you talking to me, sir?"

The Indian stopped a few feet from the congressman. "I am, your Excellency. You must do something to help my people." The McBains, Lamars, Gordons, and Mary Wayne froze, as if they were about to witness an accident they couldn't prevent.

Wayne appraised the man from hat to boot. Strangers didn't call out to him on the street. This was a brazen, insolent move. "And what is it that I should be doing, sir?"

Quiet Goose knew he was being rude. But he saw a representative of the government that was trying to displace his people from their ancestral lands. He wasn't going to waste the opportunity. "I think you know, Excellency. The white man is forcing us from our lands. We have lived in what you call Georgia and Alabama for hundreds of years. The Cherokees have copied your ways, just as the white man wanted. We are what you call civilized. We have a constitution and a court system. We have schools and are educated. We have our own newspaper. We are farmers. We dress like you. We don't make war. Many of our people worship your God. Yet your government, especially your president, wants us off the few acres we have left. I beg you, sir, please help my people. We won't give up what little you have not already taken."

Wayne looked around and saw the huge crowd of on-lookers gathered on the sidewalk and street. He hooked his fingers in his vest. "We're not taking anything, sir."

Quiet Goose adjusted his hat. "I am aware of your address to Congress, Excellency. Yes, I am." In that address made a few years earlier, Wayne had made the case that the Indians did not own all the land they claimed because they did not use it all to feed their people. They only had the right to land necessary to meet their basic needs.

Wayne considered the situation. He could have walked away and no one would have blamed him. But he did not. The Indian had to be answered and put in his place. "We will soon have a treaty, our nation and yours. You will be treated fairly by its terms."

"It will not be fair, and you know that, Excellency Wayne! The white man will find a few of us who will sign that lie you call a treaty, and all Cherokees will be forced to live by it, as you did to the Creeks."

This was just as Andrew had learned from Sally. He respected Quiet Goose's courage to confront Master Wayne with this information.

Wayne, deciding to end the conversation, replied, "As I said, I will see to it that the treaty is fair. That's the best I can offer you. I have no other power."

The Indian responded quickly, before Wayne could walk away. "We took our case to your Supreme Court, and they said you had illegally seized our land. Yet your president refused to enforce the decision. I ask you, Excellency, if President Jackson doesn't follow your laws, how fair will the treaty be? We are tired of running to suit people who want our territory. I will stay on my homestead, sir. Your soldiers won't move me, as they have done to so many of my ancestors." There was total silence in the normally noisy area. Quiet Goose called, "Sally!"

The Indian's daughter replied from behind him, "Yes, Father."

"Come here."

Sally left Andrew and pushed through the thick crowd to her father's side. Andrew wondered why Quiet Goose would want his daughter at a time like this. He worked his way next to Joseph and Mr. McBain to watch the confrontation.

"Excellency Wayne, this is my daughter, my only child. Her mother is too sick to leave our village. Friends must watch over her when we come to market to sell our goods. Your 'fair' treaty will kill my wife. My daughter and I will stay by her side, even if it kills us. I want you to see one person you will be destroying. A face of life, of hope. Not my old, beaten face."

Wayne looked at the shivering girl. "We are not destroying anything, sir."

Quiet Goose took out a hunting knife, still in its sheath, and handed it, handle first, to James Wayne, who stepped back and looked at it as if it were a live rattlesnake. He would not take it. "Kill her now! Kill me now! You need to see what your deeds do. You pass acts that kill my people, but you do not see the dead. We die far from where you make your laws, in infertile fields, on barren trails. If you are a man, thrust that knife into my daughter, just so you can see what you do to my people." The air was stuffy and still. Andrew could hear only the stomping hooves of horses trotting by on the street. Joseph, with memories of Dr. Minis fresh in his mind, looked to his father, whose swarthy face had turned pale.

Wayne said, "Sir, please put that knife away. You must trust that we will provide for your well being and safety. We have no reason to do otherwise."

Quiet Goose unsheathed the knife, and James Moore Wayne flinched. People in the crowd gasped. Mrs. Wayne took hold of her husband's arm to lead him away. Wayne yanked it back.

Quiet Goose, with his eyes on Wayne, pulled his daughter in front of him and held her close from behind. He then put the tip of the blade six inches from her chest. Someone in the crowd screamed. Sally closed her eyes. Tears ran down her cheeks. Andrew's gut turned to ice.

"If I kill my own daughter, and you see it, you will have me arrested and executed. If you murder my daughter, you go home to your family and have supper with the best wines from France. And you call that justice." Quiet Goose released the frightened girl, put the knife back in its case, and tucked it under his belt.

Wayne shouted as if he were debating a bitter foe in the House. "We do not murder, sir! The Cherokee are treated well. You will be compensated generously for your land."

Quiet Goose ignored the response. He cupped his hands around his mouth, raised his head to the sky and cried, "I declare Excellency Wayne a coward!" He turned around to face the huge throng behind him, most of whom were standing on tiptoes to see the goings on, and repeated the insult. People looked at each other in disbelief at the unbelievable affront. Quiet Goose once again faced Wayne. "Your Excellency, I challenge you to a duel. That is how you defend your white honor, is it not? I have just insulted you in front of hundreds of your supporters. And I do not apologize. Let us go to South Carolina and duel, sir. If you kill me, a jury of whites will acquit you. And you will see and remember always how your treaties work."

James Wayne looked at the man's daughter. He wanted to hug her and tell her everything would be all right. Instead, he offered, "Good day, sir." Wayne took his wife by the arm and walked away, with the Gordon's in tow.

Quiet Goose called after him. "This is not an empty threat, Excellency! I will die on Cherokee land! By your hand! By your treaty!" When Wayne disappeared from view, Quiet Goose put his arm around his daughter and walked back to their wagon.

Andrew did not have the chance to say goodbye to Sally. He wasn't sure he would ever see her again. Joseph was relieved no one was hurt. But he couldn't forget the Indian, and his willingness to die for what he believed.

If James Moore Wayne had any intention of using his influence to see that Congress produced a fair treaty with the Cherokees, he never got the opportunity. In January 1835, a few months after his confrontation with Quiet Goose, President Andrew Jackson named Wayne to fill an opening on the Supreme Court of the United States.

Quiet Goose's prediction came true. The United States government negotiated a treaty with a minority of Cherokees, giving the entire tribe two years to move themselves west of the Mississippi. Although a majority of the Cherokees signed a protest against the treaty, the United States Senate still ratified it by a one-vote margin in May of 1836.

Quiet Goose had until May of 1838 to relocate his family to the new Indian lands. But he already knew what he had to do.

CHAPTER 8

A View of Savannah

1836-1837

"Fetch de wood," Anthony said to no one in particular. "An' staa't de fiah." Joseph and two friends walked to the woods lining the beach as the bright Georgia sun made its first appearance of the day. Anthony readied the boat to go fishing. It was late October 1836. They were on a maroon.

A few times a year, Joseph and some friends, in the care of servants, took a boat to a secluded spot on Tybee Island beach, where they camped. The negroes fished, wrapped the catch in wet cornhusks, and roasted them in the fire. The boys sat around the fire, ate, and drank sweet coffee. They told stories, joked, sang songs deep into the night, and slept under the stars. The next morning, they went swimming in the ocean while the negroes caught more fish and made more coffee. After breakfast, they played games on the beach until they were exhausted. Then they went home.

That particular morning, Anthony was organizing Joseph and his friends. Joseph was glad Anthony was there.

After Joseph had been pulled from the river that nightmarish evening three years before, he found himself on the wharf, dizzy, nauseous, and lying face down. Someone was pushing on his back, making him cough up water. He heard his mother cry, "I think he's safe! Oh, thank God!" He tried to move but didn't have the strength.

He heard his father say, "You're going to be all right, son. Stay still. We want to get the water out of you." Joseph tried to say that he understood, but coughed until his chest hurt. Then he heard his father shout, "Untie that man!"

Mr. Bones said, "But sir, he must be a runaway!"

McBain stood and glared at his overseer. "He likely is! And he saved my son's life. Now untie him." Mr. Bones removed the leather straps.

Anthony never said why he abandoned his flight to freedom to save the life of a white boy he didn't know. Whatever the reason, Anthony, standing in the rowboat and watching Joseph drown, told Hal and Ena he would meet them in Beaufort.

Then he jumped into the river. But standing in front of Mr. Bones, the consequences of his decision were beginning to dawn on him.

With the situation seemingly under control, Mr. Manigault asked, "Mr. McBain, is there anything we can do before we leave?"

McBain glanced around the area. "No, thank you. We'll be fine."

Manigault and his men started to leave when a loud wail that sounded like a distant, braying animal filled the air. McBain said, "What could that be?"

Joseph croaked, "Maybe Dante."

McBain kneeled next to Joseph. "What did you say, son?"

Joseph coughed out, "Dante. He and Daymon were on the boat."

"Well, law me," McBain whispered, looking to the river. There was more to this saga than he knew. "Do you know what they were doing on the boat, Joseph?"

Talking hurt his chest and throat so much, Joseph squeezed his eyes shut as he spoke. "No. They were there when I arrived." With everyone concentrating on saving Joseph, no one had noticed Dante being thrown overboard near the shore of Hog Island.

McBain asked Hercules to carry Joseph to the house. Then he asked, "Mr. Manigault, would you mind helping me locate that crying and retrieve my boat?"

Manigault replied, "Not at all." They rowed in the dusk towards the screams. Sitting on the end of the pier on Hog Island, being observed by several hogs, was Dante, sobbing, drenched, and fatherless.

Handy had just learned that her husband and son had gone off with runaways when a rescued Dante ran to her. He was greeted with a full-force slap in the face and dropped to the ground like a brick. Handy screamed, "Wut oonuh done tuh dribe he 'way?" She stormed into her cabin.

The servants who witnessed the scene mumbled to each other. None of them blamed Daymon for leaving. Hercules said he'd rather crawl headfirst up a sick alligator's arse than spend a night with Handy.

Two days later, while Joseph was still in bed recuperating, his father told him that he was purchasing Anthony and would have him help take care of the Heritage boats. Though happy at the news, Joseph asked, "Won't he try to run away from here?"

McBain sat on the edge of the bed. "I hope not, Joseph. We'll treat him much better than he was used to. He saved your life when he didn't have to. I can't send him back to his owner."

If Anthony had any thoughts of escaping from the Heritage, they were cooled by the news of Hal, Ena, and Daymon. Days after the three had escaped they were caught stealing vegetables and chickens from a plantation near Beaufort, South Carolina. Daymon was shot dead. Hal and Ena were captured and returned to their owner. Anthony had trouble eating the night he learned of it. He knew the price Hal and Ena would pay.

Three years after he saved Joseph's life, Anthony was on Tybee beach, watching the sunrise and preparing to catch breakfast. Bondage at the Heritage was a vast improvement over his previous plantation. He dutifully kept care of massa's boats and was never scolded or threatened with the whip. Massa even complimented him on his work. McBain gave him the opportunity to make extra money by helping neighbors repair their boats. Andrew had even taught him to read. Anthony still had plans for freedom, but they weren't as urgent as before.

One of Joseph's friends broke the early morning quiet by pointing out to sea and shouting, "Now what in Lawdy's name is that?"

A small sailing ship that should have been tacking towards the mouth of the Savannah River was heading towards the beach. They watched as the boat, packed with passengers, drifted with the tide, rose onto the bar, spun around, and tilted on her keel.

One of the passengers seemed to fall out—or was thrown. He stood in the water up to his knees and waded towards the beach as the others in the boat yelled at him and shook their fists. When he was about halfway to the shore, the shallow shelf dropped off and the man disappeared to the cheers of the passengers. In five seconds his head reappeared, to jeers. He forged ahead.

The man struggled onto the beach and the marooners gathered around him. He was balding, short, had a flushed red face, and was stark naked. He bent at the waist with his hands on his knees, trying to catch his breath. He straightened, with his privates fully displayed. He looked at the boys and said, "Well, lads, can ya' give us a hand, then?"

Joseph stepped forward, "Where do you want to go?"

The naked man said, "On shore right 'ere would be a dandy start."

Anthony looked at the tilting boat and the passengers struggling to remain upright. He asked, "Tell dem pussons tuh leabe de boat. Us hab tuh pull she obuh de bah."

The man turned to Anthony. "Now, I appreciate the way you think, my good man. To whom might you belong?"

Anthony nodded at Joseph. "Massa Joseph McBain."

"A Scotsman?" The stranger opened his arms, as if to greet a long lost friend.

"Yes . . . sir," Joseph hesitated. He didn't want to embrace a naked man.

The man dropped his arms. "We Irish and the Scots are like brothers!"

Joseph said, "I guess," and asked the man, "Who are the folks in the boat?"

"Some Irish lads just come from the 'oold country, to find work. They 'ear there's jobs to be 'ad in Georgia, on the railrood."

The boys, Anthony, Andrew, and Dante stripped to their underdrawers and waded to the craft. There were about twenty-five men. They looked somewhere between weak and sick, with ribbed, pale white bodies and unshaven faces. Joseph guessed they were in their twenties and thirties, though a few looked to be about his age of seventeen.

At Anthony's request, the men removed their clothes, left them in the boat, jumped into the shallow water, and pulled the boat over the bar. The captain anchored the boat fifteen yards from shore as the refugees crawled onto the beach and collapsed.

Anthony, Andrew, and Dante jumped in the McBain boat and returned in an hour with a large catch of trout, whiting, and mullet. Joseph and his friends had the fire roaring. The starving Irishmen enjoyed their first maroon. Not one of them could remember a better meal. They had to share what little coffee was left, taking sips from the cups and passing them around. No one complained.

Joseph sat next to the man he took to be the leader. He called himself Shamus Riley. He was Andrew's height, but thinner, with straight, dark red hair, old scars over each eye, and a protruding chin, which gave his face the profile of a quarter moon. Joseph asked him how they came to Savannah.

Shamus said they had left their families in Ireland to find work in America. They sailed to New York but jobs were scarce, so they made their way south to Charleston, South Carolina. They met Captain Gleeson in a rundown tavern. The captain told them the railroad in Georgia was looking for men, and there were more Irishmen in Savannah than in all of Dublin. The captain offered to take the men on his luxury ship at just fifty pence per head, half payable on the spot. The men, down to their last shillings, agreed.

Before continuing with the story, Shamus picked up an oyster shell and threw it at the captain, who let the object bounce off his shoulder without comment. Shamus then related how the Irishmen arrived at the wharf the next morning and saw the "luxury" ship. The thirty-foot tub was a single-mast sloop with a patched, dirty, drooping sail. The rigging was rusty. Barnacles and seaweed flourished on the hull just below the waterline. Gleeson stood on the bow, tipping a sweat-stained sailor's hat. The men debated whether to risk their lives in it. But they were desperate to get to Savannah and they packed in, sitting on the smelly, slimy deck. Within an hour they hit moderately choppy seas which, in Gleeson's ship, felt like a gale, and all but a few bent over the side, giving up what little they had in their stomachs to the fishes. After recovering, they threatened to throw the captain overboard. When cornered, Gleeson miraculously produced four bottles of something vile he called whiskey. It saved his life, for the time being.

Fortunately, the nighttime sky was clear, which allowed the captain to maintain his course. In the morning, they spotted the mouth of the Savannah River and, in celebration, finished off the last of the whiskey. Captain Gleeson felt a strong wind come up, moving his ship briskly through the water, and cried out triumphantly, "See, me lads, I tell ya she's a 'ell of a luxury ship!"

Just then, another strong gust came up and cracked one of the yardarms. The ship started to drift with the tide and settled on a sandbar near shore. That's when they spotted the boys and, exhausted, weak, and hungry, threw the captain over the side to find help.

Anthony and Dante went to the woods with their machetes. Shamus said, "Well, cappy, 'ave you figured out 'ow to complete our journey, then?"

The captain, relaxed after his meal, patted his belly and belched. Then, one man yelled, "Where's me fookin' money, you son of a 'airless, toothless whore!"

The captain started to say something when Joseph interrupted, "I think Anthony is fixing your spreader." All the heads turned to the woods and heard the sound of wood being hacked.

Shamus said, "You ain't getting the other 'alf for the passage, cappy. It's all we got left. An' you sure didn't 'airn it." The others shouted their agreement.

Captain Gleeson protested, claiming that the men would be getting to Savannah nearly on time, with the bonus of a tasty meal under their belts. Some of the men moved towards the captain. He quickly said, "I guess I can accept the second class fare."

Soon, Anthony and Dante had a makeshift four-foot spreader ready. They waded to the ship and replaced the broken one. The tide was up. The men thanked Joseph and the others. As they were about to leave, Joseph pulled out his pouch. He said to Shamus, "Here, this isn't much, but you'll need something to live on while you find work." Joseph's friends did the same. The foreigners protested but Joseph wouldn't relent. The Irish told the boys they would never forget their generosity. They waded back to Captain Gleeson's tub, put on their clothes, and sailed towards the mouth of the Savannah River.

Joseph stood next to Andrew, watching them sail away. He said, "They're sailing to new lives, just as Oglethorpe had planned it."

Andrew laughed. "I don't think Oglethorpe ever imagined a boat like that."

*　　*　　*

Joseph spent the next year concentrating on his studies and selecting a college. His father wanted him to get the best education possible. His mother wanted him as close to home as possible. In the fall of 1837 he prepared a letter requesting admission to the College of New Jersey in Princeton. He and Andrew joined Mr. McBain one day on a trip to Savannah to post it. During the ride, McBain asked, "What are your plans in town today?"

Joseph said, "We're going to see the new squares." The city had just completed surveying three new wards—Pulaski, Jasper, and Lafayette—bringing the total to eighteen. Despite the financial panic of 1837, the city needed room to accommodate its growth.

Hercules parked in front of the City Hotel on the Bay. McBain told the boys he'd meet them in front of the Exchange in an hour and hurried to his meeting. Hercules began his errands.

After Joseph posted the letter in the Exchange, he and Andrew ran down the front steps and brushed by four boys about their age walking on the Bay. The tallest member of the group was a little shorter than Joseph, had a scab under one eye, and wore tattered shirt and pants. He said to Joseph, "Why don't you watch where you're going!"

Joseph recognized them as members of a gang from the Old Fort section on the east side of town. For many of the youth in Savannah, there were no schools to attend, or jobs to be had. So the boys joined gangs and looked for fights to pass the time.

Joseph was unafraid. At the age of seventeen, he had sprouted up like a mushroom, according to Grandfather, or a weed, according to Amy. He was two inches less than his father's six feet, and lean. Andrew was about five and a half feet tall, but stockier and more muscular than Joseph. Working with bricks for so long had given them considerable strength.

"I am watching where I'm going," Joseph replied, standing straight, trying to accentuate his height advantage.

The biggest one stepped towards Joseph. "You charged right into us!"

"We did not. We walked by you. We have no problem with you," Joseph barked. Two men in suits strolled by and paid no attention to the quarreling boys.

The leader snarled, "Is that so? Well, maybe we have a problem with you." He moved his shoulders back and forth, limbering up for battle. Then he called, "Okay, boys. Donnie, you and me take pretty boy. Johnny and Billy, take the darkie."

Andrew raised his fists in front of his chest. The two boys took a step back and considered renegotiating their assignment.

Joseph said to the leader, "Why not you and me? Can't you handle a fair fight?"

The tough stepped back and rolled up his sleeves, a sure sign of impending fisticuffs. "I want to share you with my friends. Ready, boys? When I count to three."

Joseph tensed up. He didn't think the gang would start a fight in front of the Exchange. But the leader crouched into a warrior stance and said, "One. Two." Then something dropped from the sky and smacked the leader on the head. He screamed, "Ooouch!" His face was multi-colored. Joseph stood open-mouthed.

A voice called from above. They all looked up and saw two men peering down at them from the top of the Exchange. One was wearing the hat of a watchman. Donnie screamed, "It's the Watch! Let's get out of here!" and the gang ran towards Old Fort.

Joseph bent down and picked up a piece of wood smeared with paint. A short man, about thirty years old, with bushy black hair and a thin black moustache, ran out of the Exchange. He said with an accent, pointing upwards, "I am so sorry! I am painting! I put my palette on the ledge and I knock her off by mistake! Do I hurt someone?"

Joseph uttered, "Uh, no. We're fine." Joseph handed the palette to the man. "You say you were painting the Exchange?"

The man fluttered his free hand as he spoke. "No! I am not painting the Exchange! I am painting a painting in the Exchange." The boys squinted at the top of the building. The man said, "Come, I show you." They followed him into the building, walked up three flights of stairs, and through a door to a narrower stairwell. They ascended it through a trap door. To their amazement, they were standing in the bell tower. The view was breathtaking. They could see all of the city and the forest beyond to the south. Joseph saw smoke billowing from the iron foundry furnace at the Heritage to the west. They turned and saw the endless green rice fields of South Carolina to the north, and the river all the way to Tybee Island to the east.

Another man in the tower said, "Afternoon, boys." He gave a quick salute and returned to surveying the city, moving his head back and forth. He was a watchman, employed to spot fires as soon as they started and alert the fire companies below.

The boys froze when they saw the painting on a wooden stand. They looked at each other, wide-eyed. They tiptoed over and stooped to inspect it. It captured the entire city from the perspective of the tower, from north to south, and in such detail that it seemed to include every structure and tree in the town. Joseph focused on the Nathanael Greene monument in Johnson Square. Then he recognized Christ Church, the Independent Presbyterian Church, the City Market, Mr. Dure's house, and on and on. He identified a locomotive and two cars moving down the new railroad tracks of the Central of Georgia Railroad. Joseph turned to the painter, who was cleaning his palette, and said, "Sir, this view of Savannah is amazing."

"Cerveau, Monsieur. Joseph Louis Firmin Cerveau."

"My name is Joseph McBain." He reached out his hand. "And this is Andrew. Mr. Cerveau, for whom are you painting this?"

"For nobody, Joseph. I sell her when she is finished." Cerveau explained that he had come to America from Izmir, Turkey on the Aegean Coast and settled in Savannah in 1830 when he was eighteen. He was a commercial artist, painted china, and gave drawing lessons.

Joseph asked, "Do you come here every day to paint?"

Cerveau inspected his brush of squirrel hair and said, "No. I make a sketch from here and do most painting in my studio. It is too difficult to bring here all my paints." Cerveau pointed to a bunch of brown, bulbous-looking pouches on a small table. They were pig bladders, which he used to store individual paints. "I bring the painting today to check my colors."

Joseph eyed the pouches. Then he and Andrew returned their attention to the painting. Joseph said, "Look! That's Sheftall Sheftall. And there's the City Hotel!"

Andrew pointed at the area of Reynolds Square. "There's the Planters Bank. And the Bank of the United States. He then pointed to the middle of the canvas. That must be the military barracks with the flag!"

They inspected the painting in silence. After a few minutes, they heard Mr. Cerveau tapping his palette with the wood end of his brush. They thanked him for showing them the painting and bid goodbye.

They left the Exchange and saw Mr. McBain chatting with James Hamilton Couper and another man. Mr. Couper greeted Andrew and Joseph warmly. Joseph wanted to ask his father to buy Mr. Cerveau's painting, but decided to approach him later.

"How are your architecture careers progressing?" Mr. Couper asked.

Joseph put his hand on Andrew's shoulder. "Very well, sir. Andrew is an excellent bricklayer. He's ready for Savannah."

Andrew swiped the ground with the toe of his shoe, and said, "I still have lots to learn, but Isaac at the Heritage is a good teacher."

Couper then introduced the boys to the other man, Amos Scudder. "Mr. Scudder is the top mason here in Savannah. Maybe when he sees your work, Andrew, he'll put you on one of his projects. That is, if Mr. McBain approves."

McBain said, "That's a fine idea, James. When Joseph begins college next year, it might be wise to let Andrew get some experience under the eye of the best man in town."

As McBain knew, Amos Scudder was more than just a mason. He had worked on many of Savannah's most distinctive buildings, including the Savannah Theatre, the Green-Pulaski monument, the City Hotel, the First Baptist Church and the Independent Presbyterian Church, most of which had been built with Savannah Greys. He had also been a city alderman for six straight terms.

Scudder said, "We can always use good bricklayers," not sounding as enthusiastic as Joseph would have liked.

After some light banter, Couper and Scudder bade good day and left. McBain said to the boys, "Anthony is at the wharf. I'm going back to the plantation by boat. Wait for Hercules. Help him with the shopping and come home. And Joseph, please stay out of trouble." This was more of a plea than an order.

Joseph said, "You don't have to worry, Father. Those days are over." Andrew rolled his eyes, though neither Joseph nor Mr. McBain could see.

"Let's hope so," McBain said before heading down the steps to River Street.

As Andrew and Joseph waited for Hercules, a man ran by them into the Exchange. A few minutes later the same man charged out of the building. Joseph called after him, "Is there a problem?"

Without stopping, the man yelled, "The railroad workers, the Irish! They're marching on Savannah! The mayor is calling up the militia."

Joseph said to Andrew, "Calling up the militia? Do you think there's going to be fighting?" Andrew shrugged, not wanting to pursue this adventure.

Just then, Hercules pulled up. Joseph announced, "Hercules, the railroad workers are marching on Savannah and the mayor is calling up the militia. Let's go see!"

Hercules shook his head. "Sounds like trouble, Massa Joseph. An' we got work to do."

Joseph ignored Hercules's use of 'we.' "Then Andrew and I will go. We'll meet you here in an hour."

Hercules sighed. "You best be back. Don't make me come huntin' after you. I'm not gettin' in trouble with massa for this."

Joseph said, "You won't, Hercules. Those days are over. I promise." Then he turned and ran, with Andrew following, and shaking his head.

A few minutes later they were on the west side of town and made their way to a group of people congregating by the Louisville Road. About fifty local militiamen stood in formation on the city side of the bridge that crossed the Savannah-Ogeechee Canal. Several more stood on the bridge, aside two cannons. About a mile away, a large group of men, who Joseph concluded were the Irish workers, marched towards them.

Joseph and Andrew squeezed to the front of the crowd until they were twenty yards behind the militia. An officer stomped over and ordered the onlookers to disperse. No one moved. The officer's face turned as red as his military jacket. Before he could holler again, a soldier called him back. The workers were within two hundred yards of the bridge.

The marchers were white, dressed in dirty workmen's coveralls and caps, and carried clubs and sticks. An officer walked to the front of the bridge. When the Irish were within twenty-five yards, he raised his arms in the air and screamed, "Halt as you are!"

The leader of the marchers held up an arm and the others stopped. He stepped forward. Joseph saw it was Shamus, the man he met on Tybee beach. He was heavier than the previous year, but the chin that stuck out like the bottom half of a banana was the same. He shouted, "Move out of our way, you and your boys with guns. We want to see the railroad folks. They owe us our bloody wages."

A man in a suit stepped from the line of militiamen and stood next to the militia officer. Joseph recognized him as the mayor of Savannah, John C. Nicoll. He called to Shamus, "I'm certain they're aware of that. I'll pass on your message anyway. You don't need one hundred men with clubs to deliver it. Now turn around and go back to work."

Shamus said, "We're bein' robbed, sir. The deal is, we work, and then we get paid. Well, we done the work. We done our part. The company don't do theirs. We're not goin' anywhere 'til we get our wages." The men waved their clubs in the air.

Nicoll held up a palm to quiet them. "If you lay down those weapons and act peacefully, I can't prevent you from coming into town."

Shamus said, "We come this far, we're completin' the job, sir. We want to speak to the company. If those soldier boys want to fire on innocent men, tell 'em to get ready." Shamus faced his men. "We're marchin' into toon!" The men cheered.

Mayor Nicoll said to the officer, "Don't allow them any further, Captain."

The officer faced his soldiers and shouted, "Ready, men!" He raised his right arm into the air, and walked to the side of the road with the mayor. The militiamen raised their muskets. The crowd hushed. They had come to see a fight, not an execution.

Shamus Riley called out, "Get ready, men!"

Joseph's knees felt weak. The Irish lads were about to be slaughtered. Andrew wanted to leave, but there was no way to fight through the huge crowd.

"Prepare to fire!"

"Hold it!" someone cried. All heads turned to the voice. A white-haired man dressed in a black suit and white collar emerged from the crowd, not far from Joseph and Andrew. He approached the mayor and whispered. Nicoll signaled to the officer, who ordered his men to lower their guns. The white-haired man walked to Shamus.

Shamus listened patiently. He stared at the ground and nodded his head, like a boy being reprimanded by his father. The two shook hands. Shamus looked back at his men and told them their protest was over and that food would be served at the Catholic Church of St. Johns on Liberty Street. The marchers dropped their weapons, which hit the ground in a collective thump. A man standing in back of Joseph said, "Father O'Neill's the only man in Savannah who could have averted that blood bath."

Just like that, the confrontation ended. The spectators dispersed, grumbling that the mob had marched all this way for a fight only to be talked out of their rage by a Catholic priest. The railroad workers milled about, murmuring to each other.

Joseph decided it was not a good time to greet Shamus. He said to Andrew, "Let's go back before Hercules comes looking for us," satisfied that he had been able to stay out of trouble.

Andrew said, "That's two fights we've avoided today."

They walked through Oglethorpe Ward, the poorest section of town. The houses, which accommodated large numbers of people, were gray, wooden, one-story affairs with side gable roofs that sagged. Rarely did a window frame hold a window. They looked as if they had been built long ago, with thrift in mind. Negro men of all ages sat on the porches and stairs, watching the activity on the streets. Dogs barked in every lane. Swarms of flies hovered over strewn pieces of garbage.

The boys were surprised to hear someone call, "Massa! Andrew!" They saw Jumbo jumping up and down from the other side of West Boundary Street. He then ran to them. "Massa! Dem buckra, dey yuh een Sabannuh!"

Joseph said, "Hello, Jumbo. What men?"

"De buckra, massa! Us fight 'um!"

Joseph grabbed Jumbo's arm. "You mean from Elbert Square? That was five or six years ago. Are you sure?"

"Yassuh, fuh sutt'n! Two men, dey een uh saloon on Fahm Street." Jumbo's body seemed to vibrate as he spoke. The old wounds still festered. He had seen the men earlier and ran all over town looking for someone to tell, though it was unclear what anyone could do. With a stroke of luck, he saw Joseph and Andrew.

Joseph looked at Andrew. If the men were in Savannah, he couldn't let them get away. "Andrew, we have to make certain these are the men before we do anything." Joseph turned to Jumbo. "Take us to them."

Within minutes they were standing in front of a run-down saloon patronized by the poor whites of Oglethorpe Ward. Joseph knew he would have to go in by himself, as it was illegal to sell liquor to negroes. He also knew he would be out of place with his young face and nice clothes. "Andrew, let's walk around the back. We need to change clothes. Jumbo, you stay here and keep watch."

They walked to the yard in back of the saloon and changed quickly. Andrew could barely button Joseph's trousers or shirt, and the shirtsleeves extended to his fingertips. Andrew's trousers hardly reached to Joseph's ankles, and Joseph could barely keep them up. Andrew's shirtsleeves ended a few inches above Joseph's wrists. Still, Joseph looked a little bit less like the son of a rich planter than before.

They returned to the front of the saloon. When Jumbo saw them, he burst out laughing, but stopped instantly.

Joseph said, "Wait here. I'll be right out." He pulled up his trousers and hopped up the three creaky wooden stairs, and strode through the single, swinging door like a soldier marching in a parade. It was dark inside, even in the middle of the afternoon, and he had trouble focusing his eyes. He wrinkled his nose at the odor of the ghosts of so many cigarettes and segars. When he reached the bar, he glanced around. Men sat quietly at tables, drinks and cigarettes in hand. Two men stood at the other end of the bar, but Joseph couldn't make out their faces. There was no confusing this place with the City Hotel. There were no discussions of the year's crops, cotton prices, or the upcoming boat races. The men were there to drink. They had no place else to go.

The bartender slapped the counter to get Joseph's attention. "What can I get you, son?"

Joseph turned sideways and rested one arm on the bar. "A glass of port, please,"

The bartender and the men at the nearby tables laughed. "Sorry, sonny. You're in the wrong place for a glass of port."

Joseph felt himself flush and attempted a recovery. "Yeah, I was just in the mood for port. I don't know why. Can't stand the stuff, actually. Give me a glass of whiskey."

"One whiskey coming up." The bartender shook his head as he filled the order.

Joseph's eyes finally adjusted to the darkness. He looked around the room for the men. He didn't recognize anyone at the tables. The two men at the far end of the bar were in deep conversation. One lifted his head and looked towards Joseph. It was him! It was the man who had worn the red shirt. Joseph turned away, even though the man would never recognize him now.

The bartender placed the glass on the bar and said, "That'll be six pence."

Joseph reached inside his trouser pockets and realized his money was in his pants on Andrew. "I'll be back in a few seconds." Joseph heard laughter as he left.

Andrew and Jumbo were standing on the other side of Fahm Street. Joseph charged over. "Andrew, give me the money in my pants."

"What's going on, Master Joseph?" Andrew asked as he dug into his pockets.

"That's them, all right. Be ready!" Joseph had no time to explain, and, in any case, he didn't know what they should be ready for.

Joseph returned to the bar and dropped two six-pence coins on the counter. "Keep the change."

"Thanks, sonny," the bartender said.

Joseph took a sip, banged the glass on the bar and gagged at the searing heat in his throat. He heard even more laughter. He had become a source of entertainment for the aimless folks in the saloon. He dried his tears on his sleeve and summoned the courage to approach the two men. He clutched the front of his pants and walked down the room on shaky legs. He recognized the second bearded man. The men looked at Joseph, who drew his lips back, producing the smile of an inbred imbecile. The men looked at each other and turned back to the bar.

Joseph heard the first man say to the bearded man, "Let's get outta here, Lem."

Lem replied, "Damnation, Zach. Let me finish." Lem drained his drink.

Joseph couldn't let them leave. He shouted, "Barkeep, give these two gentlemen a drink. On me."

Lem and Zach looked at Joseph as if he were a clown from the circus who forgot to take off his costume. Joseph terminated his smile. He felt his insides rumble, but he was determined to make these men pay for their actions.

Zach said, "Thanks, kid. What's on yer mind?"

"Nothing's on my mind, I just want to buy some neighbors a drink," Joseph quipped, hoping to relax them.

"We ain't yer neighbors, kid," replied Lem, who scratched his beard as if he was trying to catch something in it. They did not want to have anything to do with him, other than a free drink.

The bartender served two whiskeys. Zach reached over for his. As he did, the top of his shirt parted, revealing a necklace of animal teeth and colored stones. Joseph's heart started to pound against his chest. He had come after these men to avenge his, Andrew's, and Jumbo's honor. Now he was also getting the chance to regain the McBain family history. His nervousness disappeared. He suddenly felt angry. "Nice necklace. Where'd you buy it?"

Zach looked down at his chest and then at Joseph. "You got a nose for stuff that don't concern you, kid. It can get you in trouble." He sucked air through his teeth and returned to his drink.

Joseph wanted to punch the man on the spot, but that wouldn't do any good. It could also get him killed. He had to get them outside with Andrew and Jumbo.

"I was just asking. You don't see a necklace like that every day. I'll buy you a drink for it."

The men downed their drinks. Zach spat out, "Get lost!" and the two headed for the door.

Joseph walked after them, preparing to jump on one when they reached the street. He heard himself call out, "Don't you remember me?"

The men stepped one by one through the swinging door, first Lem and then Zach. As soon as Zach had cleared the door, he heard Andrew say loudly, "Don't you remember me?"

Joseph heard a cracking sound, and Zach flew backwards through the door, landing on the floor in a heap, his nose busted open. Joseph jumped on him and punched him in the face. He felt a pain in his knuckle and decided he had avenged his honor enough. He ripped the necklace from Zach's neck and put it in his pocket. He had it! Joseph got to his feet and started to run but Zach grabbed his leg and pulled him down. As Joseph fell, he grabbed hold of a bottle on a table. He hit the floor. Zach moved to get on top of him, and Joseph swung the bottle, hitting Zach on the side of the head. He cried out, put his hands on his face, and rolled onto his side. Joseph got up, ready to hit Zach with the bottle again, but the bartender and several customers took hold of him and threw him out of the saloon. He landed on the dirt of Fahm Street. Seconds later, Zach landed next to him, flat on his back, and soaked in blood. Zach made no effort to get up, though he blinked his eyes skyward several times. Joseph saw Andrew on the other side of the street, trying to pull Jumbo off Lem. Jumbo punched him repeatedly in his face, five years of rage behind each blow. Several negroes stood by casually, as if they were watching a turtle cross the road. Fights were not unusual in Oglethorpe Ward, though this one featured a black man beating a white.

Joseph saw some white men at the far end of Fahm Street running towards them. One was wearing a floppy-brimmed, straw hat. He screamed, "Lemuel! Zachariah!"

Joseph called out, "Andrew, let's get out of here! Their friends are coming!" Andrew pulled Jumbo off Lem and they ran to Hercules.

They reached the Bay and realized they weren't being followed. They stopped to catch their breath. Joseph said, "We did it, Andrew! Look what I got!" Joseph pulled the necklace out and showed it to Andrew. Andrew smiled as he rubbed the knuckles on his right hand. Jumbo paced back and forth. He still had some fight left in him.

They continued up the Bay to the coach. Hercules saw them approaching, with Andrew and Joseph wearing each other's clothes, and had to look twice. He buried his face in his hands, afraid of what he was about to hear. He looked at Joseph and said, "You gonna tell me about it, 'fore I face massa?"

Joseph explained what had happened. Hercules groaned and pointed to the cab door. As Joseph and Andrew entered the coach, Hercules asked, "Jumbo, need a ride?"

Jumbo grabbed the door handle and said, "Wes' Boundary an' Willyum Street."

They started home and the boys bragged about their victory. In five minutes, as they crossed Fahm Street, Joseph saw Mr. Cerveau walking around like a lost child. Joseph called for Hercules to stop, and he and Andrew ran to the painter. "Mr. Cerveau, what's wrong?"

"Joseph! Andrew! Thanks God! Some men, they steal my painting of Savannah! Please help me to find them. I give reward." Cerveau was near tears.

Joseph's face burned with fury. "When did this happen? Who were they? What did they look like?"

Cerveau took out a kerchief and wiped is brow. "Maybe thirty minutes ago, as I am walking to my shop on Congress Street. They were white, four of them, looking like farmers in a covered wagon. One has a knife in his hand and threatens me. I have to give her up, just like that. He is wearing a beeg straw hat."

"Oh no," Joseph uttered, the memory of the fight fresh in my mind. "What about the watchman in the bell tower? Did you tell him?"

"Yes! He say the other watchmen do not start street duty until the night, and he cannot leave the tower! He must look for fires!" This was true. During the day Savannah was policed by just the city marshal and five constables.

Joseph asked, "What about the marshal?"

"I cannot find! Joseph, I have no time. I see the wagon drive to this direction. I must have my painting! I work on her for months. She is my child!" Cerveau buried his face in his handkerchief.

Joseph started for the coach. "Come with us, Mr. Cerveau. We'll find the marshal or a constable."

Cerveau took one last look around the street and his eyes popped open. He slapped Joseph on the arm. "Joseph! Look! That wagon. That's them!"

Joseph saw a covered wagon on Fahm Street heading towards them. Three men sat on the driver's bench. Lem, the bearded one, was driving, his eyes bruised and puffy. The man next to him wore an old straw hat. Joseph didn't recognize the third man.

Joseph ran to the middle of the street in front of the thieves' wagon. Andrew, Cerveau, and Jumbo were right behind him. Lem stopped the horses two feet in front of them. Joseph heard Hercules call out, "Massa Joseph!" but he paid no mind to the coachman.

Lem squinted at the two whites and two blacks in front of him. His mouth opened. Only an intrusive bug got him to close it. He spat and said, "You!"

"That's heem. He's the one to take my painting!" cried Cerveau, pointing to the man with the straw hat.

Three heads poked out from the wagon cover in back of the driver's bench. One was wrapped in rags that served as bandages. It was Zach. Lem said through clenched teeth to Joseph, "Kid, why don't you and your friends go away before someone gets hurt real bad? If you do, I might not come back and kill you and those two niggers."

Joseph answered, "Give us the painting you just stole and we'll let you go."

Lem spat again, hitting the rump of one of the horses. "I mean it. Move away. I'm in no mood to fuss with you."

Just then, Hercules appeared next to Joseph. "I'm sorry, sir. You ain't touchin' no one here." Hercules recognized the fat, bearded Lem. "Good to see you again. Looks like you come on more hard times."

Lem stared at the negro. Though he had committed many robberies in the last five years, he remembered well the face of the black man who had beaten him so soundly. Lem asked the man in the straw hat, "You ready, Pooler? You too, Zach?"

Zach and the two others disappeared into the wagon. Joseph heard shuffling sounds, and saw five men come out from the back. The three men on the front bench got down. Joseph, Andrew, Jumbo, and Cerveau took a few steps back, but Hercules stood his ground against the eight men.

The third man from the driver's bench said, "Step back, men, and let me have a word with our colored friend." The man, the tallest of all, thin, and with a dark red blotch occupying one side of his face, had kept his right arm close by his side. He moved it to reveal a large machete. "Now, all of you just walk away and we'll get back in our wagon and nobody gets hurt. We're in a hurry."

Hercules looked around and noticed the large crowd of onlookers which had gathered on the side of the street. He couldn't believe the situation in which he found himself. One second he's driving home, the next he's facing eight thieves, one with a machete. Joseph drew trouble like manure drew flies. Hercules had to get to the Heritage with Joseph unharmed or massa would have his hide. Without taking his eyes off the men, he said, "Joseph, Andrew, Jumbo, do as the man say. Go to the coach. Do it now!"

They started to retreat, but Cerveau screamed, "No, my painting! Please don't take my painting!" and ran to the back of the wagon. Two of the men grabbed him, picked him up, and threw him at Hercules's feet.

Hercules said, "Sir, get back there. I mean it!" Cerveau got up and joined the others at the coach.

Hercules started to retreat. Lem shouted, "Stay right there, boy! We have some unfinished business." Hercules stopped.

The other thieves quickly surrounded Hercules. Lem pulled a knife. "Now let's see how strong you are."

Joseph ran to Hercules's side and yelled, "Get away from him! Take your damned wagon and leave us alone."

Lem said, "Zachariah, take care of this pest once and for all."

Zach pulled a knife and started towards Joseph, who retreated about ten steps before tripping and falling on his back. Zach stepped on Joseph's chest pinning him down. Zach bent down, moving his knife back and forth inches in front of

Joseph's face. Joseph rolled his head from side to side to avoid the tip of the blade. Zach laughed.

"Joseph, Andrew, me lads. Is that you?"

Joseph turned his head and saw about twenty-five white men walking towards them. "Shamus!" Zach straightened to see what was going on.

"I thought you looked familiar," Shamus replied as his friends encircled the thieves and quickly disarmed Lem, Zach, and the man with the machete. "We were just leaving town and noticed this little gathering. Are these fellows causing you a problem?"

Joseph leapt to his feet and appraised his antagonists. Their menacing looks had vanished. "As a matter of fact, Shamus, they were trying to kill us."

Shamus sneered at Zach. "Is that the bloody truth? We've 'ad a miserable day ourselves. We don't appreciate big men pickin' on smaller ones." Shamus turned to Lem. "You worthless pigs know you were fookin' with me friends?" The thieves were speechless. "The lads an' me aren't very 'appy. We walked turtee miles to get 'ere, and we 'ave to walk turtee more to get back, and for noothin'." Shamus's men moved closer around the outlaws.

Hercules spoke up. "You don't have to walk back, sir. There's a wagon with two fine horses. After we take a painting from the back, they're yours."

"Hey, that's . . ." Pooler never finished his sentence. His straw hat flew off his head and he was sprawled on the ground a second after an oak club cracked against the back of his skull.

Shamus asked Joseph, "Is this Anthony?"

Joseph replied, "No, this is Hercules."

"Well named. That's very kind of you, 'aircules."

"Give me a minute." Hercules drove the McBain coach next to the covered wagon and disappeared into it. As he did, Joseph told the Irishmen about their original meeting with Lem and Zach five years before, and how they met them that day.

Hercules reappeared from the back of the wagon with Cerveau's painting, holding it up for the large crowd to see. Someone said, "My good Lawdy."

Shamus and his men walked towards the wagon, prodding their prisoners along. The crowd on the sidewalk converged to see the beautiful painting of Savannah. Shamus gasped, "Mother of Jesus. That's bloody beautiful! What's it called?"

Cerveau stepped onto the wagon. "I think I call her 'A View of Savannah.'" Hercules and Cerveau then carried the painting to the coach.

Joseph took a deep breath. "Thank God! Now we better be getting home."

Hercules called, "Not so fast, Master Joseph. There's more." He waved Joseph over and re-entered the back of the covered wagon.

"Holy!" gasped Joseph as he peered into the back. The wagon was full of the thieves' haul: rugs, jewelry boxes, paintings, rifles, vases, and other valuables. It had been a big few days for the gang. No wonder they wanted to get out of town so fast.

Joseph said, "Shamus, we're in a hurry. Do you mind taking these gentlemen and their bounty to the city jail. I'm sure the marshal and the mayor will be appreciative. And I'm certain no one will say a word when you drive off in their wagon."

Shamus said they'd be happy to help. After the friends said goodbye, the Irishmen marched their prisoners away.

Jumbo also said goodbye. He was as happy as Cerveau. He reached behind Joseph's ear and pulled his hand back, opening it and revealing a six-pence piece. Joseph grabbed behind his ear, trying to find the place where so many secret coins were stored.

Then Joseph, Andrew, and Cerveau hopped in the coach with the "View of Savannah." Hercules drove to Cerveau's china store on Congress Street and they helped him carry the painting into his shop. The painter hugged and kissed each new friend on the cheeks.

Finally, they headed home. On the way back, Andrew said, "We did it, Master Joseph!" Joseph put his hands up and started to punch the air in front of him. Andrew laughed and did the same. Joseph moved from his bench and sat next to Andrew. He put his arm around his companion. It was a great ride home.

Joseph's family was waiting in front of the house. Father was about to scold him when he was rendered speechless by seeing Joseph and Andrew in each other's clothing. When he stammered, "Wh . . . what in the world?" Joseph spread the top of his shirt and revealed the McBain family necklace.

Joseph recounted the events of the day over a supper of pork chops and sweet pepper rice. Mr. McBain stopped eating to rub his temples. Mrs. McBain never touched her food. Amy reminded Joseph how childish he was and that she would never introduce him to any of her girlfriends. Ever! And Grandfather slapped Joseph on the back, again and again, grinning in delight.

After supper, the men sat on the piazza. McBain said to Joseph, "Son, you'll be going to college soon. I think it will help you grow into a man. And I pray it will keep you out of trouble. Your mother and I need to sleep soundly once again."

"I won't cause you or Mother any worry ever again, Father." Joseph sat back in his chair for a moment, enjoying the silence of the Heritage night. He leaned forward and patted his father's knee. "But we did give those thieves an awfully good thrashing." Joseph leaned back with a smile on his face. He felt ready for college.

CHAPTER 9

Only One Night at Sea

June 1838

Joseph climbed the gangway on his journey to manhood. It was June 1838. He was booked on Gazaway Lamar's luxury ship, the *SS Pulaski*, bound for Baltimore, and advertised as "Only one night at sea." From Baltimore, Joseph would take a train to Philadelphia and then a coach to Princeton. He had plenty of time to see some of the North before school started in the fall.

Grandfather was escorting Joseph. Andrew and Anthony went along to carry baggage. James, of course, was too busy to go, but he promised to visit his son in a few months.

Joseph was going to miss home. The night before his departure, the negroes held a party for him in the Quarter. They fried chicken, sang, and danced. But Joseph was going to miss Andrew more than anyone.

The *Pulaski* was over two hundred feet long and twenty-five feet wide, with side paddle wheels, two copper, low-pressure boilers, and a 225-horsepower engine. She also had two large sailing masts, one fore and one aft. The promenade deck had plenty of room for passengers to stroll or relax on settees. Two companionways aft and one fore led to the first deck, where two private staterooms and the women's sleeping quarters were located. A companionway aft led to the second deck and the men's sleeping quarters.

Captain Dubois and the sailing master, Captain Pearson, in their crisp, white uniforms and hats, welcomed the McBains at the top the gangway. Anthony, Hercules, and Mr. McBain helped Grandfather and Joseph settle in the men's quarters, with its bunk-style berths. Then Anthony and Andrew claimed their bunks in the men's servants' quarters, also on the second deck. Afterwards, they all met on the promenade deck to watch the other passengers board.

One family that garnered much attention from the ship's crew was Gazaway Lamar, his wife, three young daughters, three young sons, sister, and niece. Charlie Lamar, fourteen years old, wavy reddish-brown hair sticking out from under his cap, brought up the rear. In front of him were his two younger brothers, William and

Thomas, both with straighter, blonder hair than Charlie, handsomely dressed in blue shorts, white shirts and blue caps. The two captains bowed slightly at the waist and tipped their caps as the Lamars gained the deck. Captain Pearson saluted Charlie, William, and Thomas. The boys came to attention and saluted back.

The McBains also saw James Hamilton Couper board with several women and children whom he was escorting to the North.

At the first blast of the ship's whistle, James, Sarah, and Amy kissed Joseph goodbye and left the ship. Joseph stood with Grandfather and waved to his family on the wharf. The whistle blew again, and soon the ship chugged away. Savannah slowly shrank from sight. Joseph felt a lump in his throat at leaving those he loved.

The churning paddle wheels propelled the ship by the islands that bisect the river from Savannah to the Atlantic—Hutchinson, Fig, Marsh, Elba, Long, and Cockspur. The captain blew the whistle as they passed the immense fort under construction on Cockspur Island. The workers stopped and waved.

The ship cleared the river and headed north on its day-long trip to Charleston, where it would dock for the night. Anthony, Andrew, and Joseph stood by the railing on the promenade deck with other passengers, watching the coast of South Carolina and its lush green sea-islands pass by. Grandfather rested on a settee.

Someone on the ocean side of the deck shouted, "Sea monsters!" Everyone dashed over and saw giant fishes gliding in and out of the water. The sea seemed to be full of them. Joseph put his hand on Andrew's shoulder and pointed to a big fish. "That's a porpoise." Then he pointed further out and said, "I believe that's a grampus." Andrew nodded. Then Joseph screamed, "My Lord! A whale!" Sure enough, what looked like the inverted hull of a ship broke the ocean surface, spraying water into the air. The sea monsters swam next to the boat for a spell, shooting out of the water, their larger-than-human, glistening, gray bodies serving as personal escorts.

As the ocean entertained the passengers, James Hamilton Couper appeared on deck. Joseph and Andrew greeted him. Couper told Andrew he had spoken to Mr. Scudder about him working on the new Christ Church. Couper asked Andrew if he were familiar with the newest architectural style so popular in the South, the Greek Revival. Andrew's eyes opened wide and said he had seen some examples in Savannah—the Second Bank of the United States on Drayton Street and the Chatham County Courthouse by Wright Square. Andrew admitted he was disappointed that the courthouse had been built flat on the ground and was not elevated, detracting from its monumentality. Couper agreed.

Couper also asked Andrew if he knew of the Ionic order, the one to be used in Christ Church. Andrew said he learned from Master McBain that it had evolved from the Ionian tribe in ancient Greece and was a feminine order, used by the Greeks when building temples to woman Gods. He understood the rounded volutes in the capitals represented the ringlets of a woman's hair, and the proportions were more slender than the masculine Doric order.

Couper raised his eyebrows and said, "Very good, Andrew. Your architectural education seems to be progressing well."

A sea monster could have shot out of the water, danced on its tail, and played the fiddle, and Andrew would not have noticed, nor cared.

As they chatted, Charlie Lamar, his two brothers, three young sisters, and niece climbed up the aft stairs and marched across the deck to the railing, in single file. They looked like a family of ducks crossing a lane.

After Mr. Couper excused himself, Joseph and Andrew walked over to Charlie. Charlie introduced Joseph to his brothers and sisters and his niece. The two boys stayed close by Charlie's side, while the little girls wandered off to play with other girls. Charlie explained that his family was going north for the summer, but he hoped to return to Savannah soon to work in his father's business. Charlie kept a watchful eye on his brothers, though they just stood at the railing watching the sea monsters. At one point Thomas's collar stood straight up in the sea breeze, and Charlie quickly patted it down.

Joseph introduced Andrew, and Charlie recalled him from the day in City Market as the brick expert speaking to the pretty Indian girl. They chatted until Gazaway Lamar came on deck to gather the children for dinner. Gazaway greeted Joseph and Andrew and said he hoped they all would have a chance to talk later. Joseph congratulated Lamar on his spectacular ship.

Joseph, Andrew, and Anthony remained on deck and watched the ocean. Before they knew it, the whistle blew. It was late afternoon. They were arriving in Charleston.

After taking supper on the ship, Grandfather and Joseph strolled into town. Though Joseph had never traveled outside of Georgia, he'd always assumed Savannah to be the most beautiful city on earth. But Charleston was its equal. It wasn't laid out in wards, but had its own distinct charm, with its narrow streets, gaslight street lamps, and elegant houses. Joseph asked why the short side of many of the houses faced the street, while the front, with double-tiered piazzas, faced a garden. Grandfather said that it was to shield the house from excessive sunlight. Joseph thought that maybe houses should be built that way in Savannah, though he also thought the style made many of the houses look the same.

Joseph slept soundly on the docked ship and awoke at six in the morning to the ship's movement. The *Pulaski* was leaving Charleston. Soon, they were thirty miles out to sea. They would arrive in Baltimore the following afternoon.

That evening after supper, Joseph and Grandfather sat with Gazaway, his wife Jane, his sister Rebecca, and Charlie on the promenade deck. Grandfather congratulated Lamar on the success of his cousin, Mirabeau Bonaparte Lamar, who had recently become the second President of the Republic of Texas. Gazaway confided that he had tried to sell the *Pulaski* to the new republic but it didn't have the money, so he put the ship into the Atlantic Coast service.

They also talked about Gazaway's recent proposal to the city council. When the Central of Georgia Railroad announced plans to build its terminus on West Broad Street and the Louisville Road, it meant the cargo, mostly five hundred pound bales of cotton, would have to be taken off the railroad cars, loaded onto wagons, and driven to River Street. Gazaway proposed, for a small fee per bale, to lay tracks across town, with connector tracks to River Street, avoiding the time-consuming and costly task of the unloading, carting, and reloading process. The city council rejected it.

Gazaway then recollected the first time he'd met Joseph on the day Lafayette laid the cornerstones to the monuments for Nathanael Greene and Casimir Pulaski. Charlie had just been baptized at Christ Church and the marquis was in attendance. From that day on, Charlie became Charles Augustus Lafayette Lamar.

Gazaway told a story that James McBain had told him. It happened on the first day of Lafayette's visit, as everyone waited on the Strand for the hero's arrival. Joseph was sitting on his father's shoulders when someone fired a cannon. The loud blast scared everyone half to death, and shattered Mr. Ryerson's drug store window on the Bay. Ryerson came running out of his store. He jumped up and down and waved his arms in anger, causing great hilarity among the large crowd. Mr. McBain joined in the merriment until he felt something warm running down his back. Joseph had been so frightened by the blast that he peed in his pants and so, all over his father.

As the Lamars and Grandfather laughed loudly at the story, Joseph hid his red face in his hands. Gazaway also told Joseph that his father had bought him a little Georgia flag that day, and Joseph waved it for hours without stopping. Mr. McBain said that was the day Joseph became a true Georgian.

Grandfather slapped Joseph's leg and said, "He still is, and always will be." Joseph made a mental note to ask his father about those stories.

The folks soon retired for the night. Joseph lay in his bed and dreamed about Lafayette's visit, the people, the river, the bunting, and the cannon.

The blast seemed so real it woke Joseph. It took him a moment to realize he was not on his father's shoulders. There were no roaring crowds, just darkness and silence. He couldn't hear the hum of the ship's engines that had lulled him to sleep. He felt his bed tilting to starboard. Someone grabbed his shoulder. He heard Grandfather say, "Joseph, something's happened. Get your clothes on while I investigate."

As Joseph dressed, he heard the other men in the bunks start to grumble. A few minutes later, Grandfather stuck his head in the door and shouted, "Joseph, come with me! Now!" Joseph ran into the passageway. A passing crewman accidentally knocked him into the wall and didn't bother to apologize. Grandfather looked Joseph in the eye. "A boiler's exploded. It's ripped a hole in the ship. Get Andrew and Anthony and meet me on the promenade. Be quick, Joseph! We must help the women and children into lifeboats. Then we need to save ourselves."

Joseph recoiled, but did as he was told. As he ran to the servants' room, he could feel the ship listing. He tried to open the door but it was jammed. He heard shouts from the room, and lunged against the door. Pain shot from his shoulder through his arm, but the door still wouldn't open. He grabbed a small red hatchet hanging on the wall nearby and yelled, "Stand back!" He hacked a hole through the top half of the door. Once the opening was big enough, ten black hands from inside grabbed onto the wood and ripped it away. Joseph helped the negroes climb out.

Andrew and Anthony emerged and they hurried to the aft companionway. When they reached the first deck, Joseph looked down the passageway and saw Gazaway's sister, Rebecca, and her niece, Eliza. He told Anthony and Andrew to go upstairs, and he'd follow shortly.

Joseph ran to Rebecca. She was bending, talking to a negro man on his hands and knees. His eyes were squeezed shut and his lips pulled back, revealing clamped white teeth. Little Eliza looked on, her trembling hands covering her mouth. Joseph heard the man say, "Oh missus, muh feet done burnt off!" Joseph looked to where the negro's feet should have been. Two bloody stumps, still smoldering, protruded from his trousers. Joseph fought the urge to vomit.

Joseph told Miss Lamar to take Eliza upstairs where the lifeboats were being readied. Joseph knelt by the husky negro, too heavy for Joseph to carry, and told him to crawl on his hands and knees and Joseph would help him up the stairs. The man shook his head. "It muh tahm, massa. It muh tahm."

Joseph told him, "No! We'll get you out of here. Crawl this way."

The man squeezed his eyes tight, fighting the unbearable pain. "No, massa. Sabe oonuh se'f. But ah need uh fabuh. Ah Noah. Ah wid Massa Parkman ub Sabannuh. Tell muh wife Daisy ah bin t'inking ub she tuh de end. Do me dat kindness, massa!"

"Come with me, Noah. We'll get out of here." Joseph grabbed Noah's arm.

Noah pulled away. "Massa, oonuh haffuh beliebe me. Gawd bless oonuh."

"God bless you, Noah." Joseph stood, looked at the doomed man, and left.

Joseph reached the promenade and froze. The moon and stars shone so bright he could see the entire deck. It was packed with people moving slowly, trying to maintain their balance on the tilting ship, while trying to find a way to safety. He heard a few shouts and babies crying, but there was no mass panic. He stood next to an old negro man who was lashing two settees together. The man saw Joseph looking at him. "Gwine tuh sabe muh massa!" he explained.

There were no lifeboats on the deck and the starboard side was only ten feet above water. Joseph removed his shoes and trousers, remembering his day in the Savannah River. He tried to spot Grandfather, Andrew, and Anthony. He called out their names, but no one responded. He made out a lifeboat in the water next to the ship with the Lamars and another family. He called to Gazaway, who waved him over.

Joseph took half steps to the side of the boat when another explosion propelled him through the air. He landed in the ocean, the cool water stinging his nostrils. He floated quickly to the surface and was surprised at his buoyancy. He blew through his nose, shook the water from his eyes and saw the most horrible sight. The *Pulaski* had broken in two. The stern and the bow were sticking vertically into the air, both on fire, further illuminating the night. He heard screaming and crying all around him. People were thrashing about wildly, trying to stay afloat. A little girl near him cried for her mother. He swam to her and held her. She wrapped her arms around his neck so tight he had trouble breathing. It was one of the little girls who had played with the Lamar children earlier in the evening.

She beat her little arms and cried, "Mummy, mummy, where are you mummy?"

Joseph looked around and saw people standing on a piece of wreckage twenty yards away. "You're all right! I'm taking you to mommy now. Please be still."

He paddled with one arm to the wreckage while cradling the whimpering child in the other. He reached the side and a man took her from Joseph. The man said, "Good work, son!"

Joseph pushed away to search for more survivors. There were fewer cries for help than just minutes before. He saw a body in a white nightgown floating face down just a few yards away. He swam to it, turned the body over, and lifted the head out of the water. The hair hung down like strands of a wet mop. The head rolled lifelessly in his hand, the eyes and mouth wide open. Mrs. Gazaway Lamar was dead.

A loud, gurgling noise like a thunderstorm dominated the night air. Joseph saw the bow and stern slowly sink together in a macabre ballet. There were a few screams from within, and then the *Pulaski* was gone.

Joseph heard a few distant sobs and prayers, but he was too exhausted to search them out. He had no idea how long he'd been in the water. He located the wreckage where he had left the little girl and swam towards it. Two men pulled him on.

From his knees, Joseph examined the "craft" in the moonlight. It was approximately twenty feet square, and probably was once part of the promenade deck. It floated a few inches under water. A cable box about four feet high, four feet long, and three feet wide stood in the middle. It was the only dry place on the wreck. All the people were soaked, with their clothes clinging to their bodies.

A man held the little girl Joseph had rescued. He turned out to be Mr. Hutchinson from Savannah and the little girl was his daughter, Connie. The man to whom Joseph had given Connie stood at the edge of the wreck, looking for other survivors. There were other people on the floating piece of debris: Mrs. Smith, who lost her husband, Dr. Ash, Dr. Stewart and his servant, Caroline, Mr. McRae, Mr. Brown, and an old negro mauma.

Joseph was elated to see Gazaway, his sister Rebecca, and young Thomas Lamar. He stood and sloshed over to them. Gazaway embraced him. "Thank God you're alive, Joseph." He then asked, "We were in the lifeboat when the ship split in two. It capsized us. Rebecca, Thomas, and I were able to swim here. Have you seen any of my family?"

"No sir," Joseph lied. Gazaway closed his eyes, and his shoulders slumped. Abruptly, he stood upright, pushed the sorrow out of his mind, and replaced it with the challenge at hand.

He called out, "Please, Mrs. Smith, sit on the cable box. All women and children please sit on the cable box, out of the water!"

Over the next few hours, the men stood at the perimeter of the vessel and called into the darkness for survivors. Captain Hubbard and two shipmates found them, but that was it. No one else responded. Deflated, the men sat in the carpet of water.

The survivors had time to think about their losses. Joseph's pain was unbearable. Grandfather, Andrew, and Anthony were likely dead, all because Joseph was going to college in New Jersey. He would never hear Grandfather's stories again, or build villas with Andrew. He would never be able to reward Anthony for saving his life.

Joseph was fighting back tears when a cry for help grabbed everyone's attention. Gazaway shouted, "Please speak again! Who are you?"

A male voice gurgled, "I am Colonel Ball. I'm with my wife and daughter. Help us! We're drowning."

Joseph shouted, "Keep talking, Colonel Ball. I will find you!" He jumped in the water and swam towards the voice. He called, "Please talk, sir. Where are you?" Mr. Lamar and the other men yelled as well. But they heard no reply. Joseph swam back to the wreck. Three more good people, he was certain, were dead.

The survivors sat quietly through the night, unable to sleep or speak of the horrible tragedy. Daylight didn't help. It unveiled a scene of complete destruction. The surface of the sea was littered with pieces of wood, big and small, clothing, papers, boxes, valises, and other rubbish from the ship. The people looked for life and any debris that might be useful. Their search was interrupted when Rebecca Lamar cried, "Oh my God!" A body had floated upon their craft during the night. Mr. Hutchinson turned the corpse over. It was Mr. Parkman of Savannah, an associate of Gazaway.

Mr. Hutchinson was about to push the dead man back to sea when Gazaway said, "Don't!" Hutchinson did not question the order. The body remained with them, a grim reminder of their looming fate.

The folks sat quietly until Mrs. Smith started to bawl. Gazaway sat next to her and said, "Our losses are devastating, ma'am. We need to find salvation in the Lord."

Mrs. Smith looked up at Lamar with tears pouring from her eyes and whispered, "I have to go." She dropped her head in embarrassment.

Lamar patted her back. As if the living nightmare these people had just experienced wasn't bad enough, they now had to relieve themselves in the open, in front of total strangers. Lamar announced as he pointed out to sea, "Could everybody sit facing the east to allow some privacy for those who need it."

The survivors quietly shifted. Mrs. Smith crept to the edge of the wreck, squatted, and, while facing the backs of the others, sobbed as she heeded nature's call.

An empty lifeboat half-filled with water floated by. Dr. Ash secured it to the wreck. He and Hutchinson tipped the boat over to dump out the water and then plugged the holes with rags. Someone spotted a wicker basket with two bottles of wine bobbing in the water. Joseph retrieved it. The men agreed that the wine would be rationed to the women and children.

At midday, the spirits of the survivors were lifted when another lifeboat with two men found them. One was Mr. Smith, the husband of the woman on their wreck. They had a tearful reunion. No one knew the other man. He sat on the cable box, his head hanging down and his hands on his knees.

Rebecca informed the man that the cable box was for women and children. He moved onto the deck without comment. As Joseph secured the boat to the wreck and plugged the holes, the man screamed, "Four stinking lifeboats for two hundred people! Mother of God!" That was the only time Joseph heard him speak.

Gazaway, an owner of the *Pulaski,* turned away and looked out to sea. The two lifeboats attached to their wreck were of the four that the ship provided, and they both leaked like old rusty cans. Joseph wondered what happened to the other two.

At that point, nineteen people and one corpse claimed the wreckage as home.

Then Gazaway yelled, "Look yonder!" Two people on settees tied together drifted to them. An older man and a younger woman, about Joseph's age, were barely conscious. It gave the survivors hope that their loved ones might be out there as well. However, the man died within an hour and despondency returned. His body was placed alongside Mr. Parkman's.

It was still Friday, about twelve hours after the sinking of the *Pulaski*, when Joseph realized he was wearing only mid-calf drawers. Modesty was not an issue, but Joseph felt the sun beating on his neck, back, and lower legs. He looked for something to wrap around him. The only available fabrics were the clothes on the two dead men. Joseph wondered if anyone would be angry if he took a shirt off one of them.

Someone shouted, "What's that?" interrupting Joseph's dilemma. In the distance, he saw debris that looked like it could be part of the wheelhouse. As it floated closer, Mr. Hutchinson said he saw something moving on it. Rebecca held Joseph's arm in anticipation. At about one hundred yards, Joseph saw arms working in a rowing motion.

As the object came closer, Dr. Stewart called out, "Do you see us?" One of those arms waved. It was black! Joseph couldn't make out the face, and he couldn't wait. He jumped into the water and swam.

Joseph saw a white set of eyes and teeth. "Andrew!" The rower waved both hands. Joseph swam to him and grabbed his wrist. "You're alive! I can't believe it! Tell me I'm not dreaming!"

Andrew smiled weakly. "You're not dreaming, Master Joseph."

Joseph glanced on the hunk of debris and saw Charlie Lamar and an older man and woman. Charlie's face had a green pallor. "Charlie, you're alive too! Your father's on our raft. So are Tommy and your Aunt Rebecca!" Charlie barely nodded. Joseph got behind them and pushed them to the wreck, which must have seemed like a grand ship compared to their tiny vessel.

While Joseph embraced Andrew, and Gazaway and Rebecca Lamar smothered Charlie, the others aided the older couple.

Joseph helped Andrew sit on the watery craft, still not believing his companion had survived. "Andrew, what happened to you?"

Andrew leaned against the cable box, his arms lying limply on the watery deck. He spoke haltingly. "I was on the promenade deck with Anthony and Grampah, waiting for you. The ship was about to go under. Anthony told us to jump in the water and swim away from the ship to avoid getting sucked down with it. Then the ship split in two and we were thrown into the water. It was horrible, Joseph. I tried to find Anthony and Grampah, but I couldn't. I heard screaming all around me." Andrew took a deep breath. Joseph noticed everyone was listening to his story. "I swam around until I saw this torn-up section of the ship." Andrew pointed at the hunk of debris. "I climbed on it and started to paddle, looking for people. I saw someone struggling in the water. It was Master Charles. I was able to pull him up. We just drifted. At daybreak, we spotted Reverend and Mrs. Woart holding onto a plank. We pulled them on. The Reverend led us in prayer. God was there, Master Joseph. I felt him!" Andrew clutched Joseph's arm.

Gazaway patted Andrew on the shoulder; "You're a fine lad, Andrew. You saved my boy. I'll never forget it."

"God saved him, Master Lamar."

There were twenty-four people on the wreck. While each new survivor lifted their spirits, the raft became more crowded and there was no food or drink, save two bottles of wine.

Joseph thought about God and what Andrew had said. He regretted not being more religious and envied Andrew's faith. He hoped God would forgive him because he was so young, and would give him the courage to survive.

The elation from finding Andrew and the others soon faded. The pretty woman who had floated on the settee just hours before lost consciousness. She never regained it, and soon died. Then, the top of the cable box broke under the weight of those resting on it. Everyone had to sit in water through a long and uncomfortable night. Andrew and Joseph, both practically naked, huddled together for warmth.

Early Saturday morning they saw ships on the horizon. Andrew and Joseph stood, yelled and waved their arms, to no avail. Captain Hubbard said they were too far from the shipping lanes to be spotted. Dr. Stewart wondered out loud what they should do if no one could see them.

Hubbard recommended that six men who could swim should take one of the lifeboats and head to land. If the boat capsized in the breakers, at least one of them would be able to make it to shore for help. The other men agreed. Joseph volunteered Andrew and himself but Mr. Lamar wanted them to take care of the women and children. Lamar and Hubbard selected themselves, the two shipmates, Dr. Stewart, and the man to whom Joseph gave Connie Hutchinson.

Lamar took Joseph by the arm and whispered in his ear, "Joseph, please look after my family. I beg of you." Lamar then kissed Thomas, Charlie, and Rebecca, and told them he would be back shortly. They pushed off, with the two shipmates rowing. Gazaway turned around and waved. Seventeen survivors remained on the wreck.

As soon as the six men left, Joseph removed Mr. Parkman's shirt and put it on. Andrew and Mr. Hutchinson moved the three corpses to the edge of the raft. Reverend Woart led them in prayer. Then Joseph pushed the bodies into the sea.

Everyone sat, left with their thoughts. Joseph tried to calculate when they could expect Gazaway to return. But he didn't know how far they were from land or how fast the men could row. The hours passed with a growing sense of gloom. The survivors hadn't had anything to eat or drink for almost two days, other than the few drops of wine for the women and children. The sun beat down on them, feeling like thousands of tiny needles piercing their salt-caked skin. Their mouths felt like dry, sour rags.

Mr. Brown broke the silence by screaming, "I can't take it anymore!" He walked over to the side of the wreck, cupped his hands, and started to drink seawater.

Andrew rushed over and grabbed hold of him. "Don't do that, sir. You'll only make things worse." The man struggled unsuccessfully to release himself from Andrew's grasp. His body went limp, and he started to quake. Then he started to retch. He went to the edge of the wreck, got on his knees and vomited for what seemed to be hours. The others looked out to sea, shielding their eyes and covering their burning bodies, trying to ignore Mr. Brown.

Late that afternoon, Reverend Woart approached Rebecca Lamar as she doled out the wine. His hands were clasped in front of his waist. "Excuse me, madam, but may I please have a drop of the wine? Just to place on my tongue?"

Rebecca cradled the bottle in her arms. "Reverend, you know it's just for the women and children."

"I know, and I feel ashamed for having to ask, but, you see, I don't think I'm going to make it." He stuck his tongue out. It looked like an unfired Savannah Grey. Joseph turned away.

Rebecca fought back the urge to cry. "Reverend, I would love to give everyone some, but I simply cannot. You are putting me in a most difficult situation."

"Aunt Rebecca, you can give him my share," Charlie said. "I'll be all right." Charlie then huddled close to Tommy.

The others stared at Charlie. He did not look well, and had hardly spoken since he boarded the wreck. But he was giving up his share of wine for this pitiful man.

"You are a noble boy," said the Reverend, placing his hand on Charlie's head.

Rebecca carefully placed two drops on Woart's tongue. The Reverend thanked Rebecca and Charlie again and returned to his semi-conscious wife. He never asked for another drop, and led the people in prayer every few hours.

Saturday night brought a thunderstorm. The sea started to buck gently, as small caps broke over the side of the wreck. The survivors sat with their heads back and mouths open, trying to catch as many drops as possible. Joseph thought of a painting he had seen of baby birds being fed by their mother. He looked around for vessels to collect the rainwater, but didn't see any.

The storm soon brought rougher seas, and larger waves started to rock the wreck and wash over it. Suddenly, they were lifted into the air and dropped roughly by a large wave. Joseph heard their vessel creak and felt it bend beneath him. He told everyone to sit in a circle in the middle of the wreck and lock arms to prevent any one person from being washed overboard. There the seventeen sat, adrift on the ocean, in the middle of a gale, in total darkness, praying for their lives.

The storm raged most of the night. The wreckage rode up and down the huge swells. Joseph thought he must be in hell and this was how he would spend eternity, scared out of his mind. Andrew made promises to God in exchange for everyone's survival. But besides the howling of the wind and the creaking of the wreck, the only noise was the black mauma chanting a prayer. No one else, not even little Connie Hutchinson or Tommy Lamar, cried or spoke.

The first words came from the Reverend Woart, who said, "My poor, dear wife." Joseph looked up and in the darkness barely made out Mrs. Woart, her head rolling around lifelessly on her shoulders. The Reverend unlocked his arm from his other partner, Charlie Lamar, and tried to move his wife out of the chain. Just then, a large wave lifted the wreck and both Reverend Woart and his wife flew off. Fifteen remained.

Charlie Lamar swiveled over and locked arms with Mr. Hutchinson.

The storm died down just before daybreak. The seas calmed and the stars came out. No one had the energy to move or talk, and they stayed in a circle in the middle of the wreck. Joseph noticed the other lifeboat was gone.

Connie Hutchinson, who was lying on her father's lap and looking up to him, spoke in a weak voice. But in the still night, everyone heard it. "Daddy?"

"Yes, sweetheart?" Hutchinson gently moved the girl's wet hair from her face.

"I see angels, daddy." Her eyelids fluttered. Her soaked, ripped dress clung to her tiny body, making her look like a discarded doll.

"Are they nice angels, sweetheart?"

"Yes, daddy. They want me to go with them. Can I go, daddy?"

Hutchinson paused. His voice cracked. "Not now, sweetheart. You're safe here with me. You're my little angel, and I need you here." He continued to stroke her hair.

"They're such nice angels. I'll only go for a little while. I'll come back, daddy." She slowly raised her tiny arm and touched her father's cheek.

"Please stay here, sweetheart. We'll be having tea soon with mother."

"Oh daddy, I want so much to have tea with mummy. Mmmmm. Can I have two lumps of sugar in my tea, daddy?"

"Of course you can, dear."

"I'm going to invite the angels, daddy. Caroline and Eliza. And Martha."

Charlie and Rebecca, who had shut their eyes during the conversation, raised their heads, hearing the names of Charlie's sisters, and looked at the dying girl.

"Yes, invite the angels, Connie. Have them come here."

"I want to visit them, daddy."

Hutchinson could barely speak. "Please, darling. Stay with me. Please." Connie didn't respond. Her hand dropped from her father's cheek and relaxed at her side. He said, "I love you, my dear little sweetheart."

Connie whispered, "I love you, daddy." Those were her last words. Connie left to play with the angels.

Mr. Hutchinson, who had lost his wife and two children, held his daughter close until sunrise. Without asking anyone to join him in prayer, he walked to the edge of the wreck, squatted, bowed his head, and gently laid his little daughter on the surface of the heartless ocean. He stood and watched her disappear into the deep.

Andrew and Joseph watched Hutchinson closely. They needed him alive. Neither was sure he would return from this cruelest of burials. Eventually, he did. Just fourteen remained.

After several hours, in the early morning light, Mr. McRae shouted, "Look, there's a ship!" The others looked, hopefully, but saw nothing. Joseph stood to get a better view, and simply shook his head.

Dr. Ash said, "I don't see a ship, sir. Where are you pointing?"

Mr. Brown said, "Yes, I see it, too!"

The man who arrived with Mr. Smith stood, grinned, and waved at the horizon.

Dr. Ash said, "Men, there is no ship out there." The doctor looked to the other people to make sure he wasn't the crazy one.

McRae paid no attention. "I'm not waiting here any longer. I'm going to the ship." He got up, straightened out his damp shirt, strode to the edge of the wreck, and fell over the side. Charlie grabbed his leg. Andrew and Joseph splashed over and pulled him back in. They held him down as he tried to wiggle away.

Dr. Ash announced his diagnosis. "This man is delirious!"

After a while, McRae relaxed and Andrew and Joseph released him. He sat silently. But an hour later, he called, "There she is again, boys," and darted off the wreck, followed instantly by Brown and the nameless man. No one was quick enough to stop them. McRae flailed his arms and shouted, "Wait for us!" Joseph and Andrew could see six arms beating the water. Then they saw none. Eleven remained.

The rest of Sunday moved slowly. The survivors had hoped Gazaway would have returned by then. But without any sign of help, their depression grew.

Sunday night marked the fourth on the wreck. Joseph sat next to Andrew. He wanted to thank him for his friendship. His mouth and throat were so dry he could only croak a sound. Andrew whispered in a raspy voice, "Don't give up, Master Joseph! Never give up!" Joseph hugged his knees and shivered in the nighttime air.

It had been virtually impossible to sleep on the partially submerged craft. Andrew suggested that the people sit back to back. The others followed Joseph's and

Andrew's lead. Tommy and Charlie Lamar leaned against Rebecca Lamar. Dr. Ash leaned against Mr. Hutchinson. Mr. and Mrs. Smith had each other. Dr. Stewart's servant and the black mauma paired up.

The Monday morning light woke them. The sun seemed to pierce Joseph's skin. In minutes he thought he was in a frying pan. Mr. Smith drew their attention to something on the horizon. Joseph thought, "Not again," but there was an indeed an object. It wasn't moving. They debated whether it was a ship or not. Mr. Smith said that he would have a look.

Andrew said, "Sir, that object is miles from here. You can't just go have a look. You'll drown for sure."

Smith assured Andrew that he had swum and rowed all his life. He proceeded to pick through the pile of debris on the deck, took some planks, tied them together to form a cross, and stood by the edge of the wreck.

Rebecca begged Mrs. Smith to speak to her husband. Mrs. Smith shrugged and said, "It's no use even trying when he sets his mind to something."

Smith tossed his vessel in the water, shouted, "I'm on my way!" and jumped on it. He had trouble balancing himself at first, but once he did, he started to paddle with his hands. Within minutes, he disappeared. Mrs. Smith fiddled with the ring on her finger.

The ten survivors, so used to death, soon forgot about Smith and fixed their attention on the object on the horizon. Dr. Stewart's servant, Caroline, speechless for four days, started to sob, "Ah gwine tuh die! Ah gwine tuh die! Tek me now, Lawd." She cried for a few minutes and lay down on the watery floor. Andrew sat by her and placed her head on his lap.

Charlie Lamar went mad on Monday night. He cried for his dog, and then thought he saw him drowning in the water. Charlie wanted to save him, but Aunt Rebecca calmed the boy. Joseph sat next to Charlie to make sure he didn't try to save his dog again.

Joseph couldn't sleep. He noticed that Rebecca looked uneasy and was going to ask her if she wanted Charlie or Tommy to sleep leaning against him. Joseph saw little Tommy squirming on her lap. At first, Joseph thought he was just uncomfortable. Rebecca, half asleep, tried to shift him around, but no matter what she did, Tommy continued to wriggle. Tommy opened his eyes and looked straight up to the sky. He moaned softly, and his body went limp. Rebecca tried to shift him again, thinking he had fallen asleep. She soon realized the truth. She bent forward and kissed his forehead. Her pained face, with her mouth wide open and her eyes just slits, showed that she was crying, but no sound came from her.

Joseph spent the rest of the night wondering if Tommy Lamar and Connie Hutchinson would meet in heaven, get married, have a family, and never suffer any pain like they did on earth. Maybe they would have a big wedding, and invite all those who perished on the Pulaski. Soft, gay music would be provided from violins played by little angels. They would have all the tea and cakes they wanted. Women would be dressed in frilly, yellow skirts, holding parasols to shade them from the afternoon sunshine.

Joseph jerked awake. He checked to see if he had been dreaming, but Tommy's lifeless body still lay on Rebecca's lap. Joseph counted survivors. Dr. Stewart's servant and the mauma were gone. So was Dr. Ash. Joseph closed his eyes. Six remained.

Rebecca woke Joseph. She claimed she needed to go to Savannah to catch a ship, but she wasn't dressed for the occasion. She rambled for a few minutes and stopped. Then she started up again, ignoring Tommy's body floating at her feet.

Joseph leaned over and placed his hand on hers. He strained to speak. "Miss Lamar, Mr. Lamar is getting help. He'll be back soon. It's all right."

Rebecca looked to the sky and answered, "Gazaway, my dear brother. Why, he's in Savannah waiting for me. He'll be angry if I don't get there in time!" Her blistered, sunburned face had white residue caked at the sides of her eyes and mouth.

"He won't be angry, Miss Lamar," Joseph assured her, patting her arm. She stopped her ranting. They all tried to sleep, the only escape from the hell around them. They knew they were going to die very soon.

The Tuesday morning sunrise brought Joseph out of his doze. He looked around to see if they had lost anybody. Rebecca and Charlie Lamar, Mrs. Smith, Mr. Hutchinson and Andrew were sleeping, so Joseph closed his eyes. He was awakened by a scream.

"Look! Look!" Mrs. Smith cried.

Joseph opened his eyes with a lack of enthusiasm. He had started off the last two mornings the same way. But there it was. A ship headed towards them, with sails so white, the brightness hurt his eyes. Andrew and Joseph staggered to their feet and leaned on each other for support. It was real! Andrew hugged his master. "Never give up, Master Joseph! Never give up!" They weakly waved their arms, though the ship had obviously sighted them.

A lifeboat was lowered. Rebecca sat still, oblivious to her rescue. Charlie lay motionless against his aunt, his head dangling. Joseph knew he was dead. Tommy still floated at her feet. If the boat could have only come a few hours earlier, the Lamar boys might have lived.

Joseph vaguely remembered being brought onto the good ship *Henry Camerdon* and sipping a sweet liquid. The next thing he knew, he was in a bed in a small but comfortable room. A woman was staring at him. Joseph took in his strange surroundings. He was confused. "Where am I, ma'am?"

"You're safe in my house in Wilmington, North Carolina. Rest while I fetch the doctor."

Joseph felt better. He laid back and slept until someone gently shook his shoulder. A silver-haired man looked down at him. "How are you feeling, young man?"

"Tired, sir. My skin is on fire."

"I'm not surprised." He touched Joseph's scalp and temples and various parts of his body. He lifted his eyelids and peered into the boy's eyes. "What's your name, son?"

"Joseph McBain, sir. Of Savannah, Georgia," he was happy to add.

The doctor packed his medical bag. "Joseph, you've survived a horrible disaster. You need to rest and eat, and get your strength back. Your face, neck, and legs are burnt and covered with blisters from exposure to the sun, but you'll heal. We've applied a lotion. Our hospital is full. You were brought here yesterday after the ship arrived, once we were certain you were out of danger. I'll check back every day. You eat and drink everything Mrs. Carruthers serves you. Your courage has made us all proud."

"Thank you, sir. And, ah, sir, I need to know one other thing. I was on the raft with a negro. He's my companion, my servant. Have you seen him?"

"Andrew? Yes, he's in the next room. He's under the same care as you and is doing well. He awoke several hours ago. You can see him after you have some food."

Joseph closed his eyes, thanked God, and held the doctor's hand in gratitude. "Thank you again, sir."

Mrs. Carruthers brought up a platter of eggs, grits, cornbread and butter, and a glass of milk. No meal, not Jinny's soft-shell crabs or the roasted fish on a maroon, tasted better. Mrs. Carruthers told Joseph that once he was able to digest the eggs, he could have some ham and bacon. Joseph thought the eggs and grits were just fine.

After his meal, Joseph sat on the edge of the bed. He looked at his legs, which were a deep red, puffy and covered in blisters. He tried to get up but felt dizzy and sat back down. Finally, he was able to stand and noticed he was wearing someone else's nightshirt. He walked out of the room. His neck and legs stung. He heard voices from downstairs, and went to find them. As he got closer, he recognized Andrew's voice.

"After the fire is out and the bricks have cooled, we sort them by type. Not all bricks get the same heat during the burn, and have different strength and color."

Joseph stood in the doorway. Andrew was sitting at the table with his back to him talking to Mr. and Mrs. Carruthers. Mrs. Carruthers looked at Joseph. Andrew turned around, jumped up, and embraced Joseph. It hurt, but Joseph didn't care.

Mrs. Carruthers said, "Now don't get too excited, you two. You heard the doctor. Plenty of rest and food. Joseph, meet my husband, Mr. Carruthers."

"Yes ma'am. It's a pleasure, sir." The man stood and the two shook hands.

Mrs. Carruthers continued. "Horace will get some clothes for you. I'm sure you don't want to walk around in nightclothes all the time. I also suspect you'll want to go to church as soon as you can."

"Yes ma'am." She was so nice Joseph couldn't refuse her. But with his skin as it was, he decided to stay in a loose fitting nightshirt a while longer.

They all sat on the front porch. Strangers passed by and called out greetings: "Welcome!" and "God bless you!"

Mrs. Carruthers said, "Joseph, until your parents arrive, you and Andrew treat this home as your own. You're both so brave."

Joseph said, "Thank you, ma'am. My father will compensate you for your costs."

Mrs. Carruthers wagged a finger at Joseph. "You hush, young man. Being a Christian does not call for compensation." She winked at Horace.

They sat quietly in the evening dusk, sipping lemonade. Joseph had so much to say, but he didn't know where to begin. All of the horror of the *Pulaski* had caught up to him. He hung his head, fighting back tears. He felt a hand on his shoulder but he didn't respond. Joseph didn't want any sympathy. He just wanted to purge the last five days.

"Tell me when you come up for air, Joseph, so I can say hello to my grandson."

"Grandfather?" Joseph turned and saw his grandfather, grinning like a raccoon. He jumped up and hugged the old man.

As he held his grandson, Daniel McBain said, "Dear Joseph, I thought I had lost you. I didn't think there was any chance I would see either of you again. Then I heard more survivors had been found. I tracked you here. Andrew was awake but you weren't. I stood at the foot of your bed. I was so happy I couldn't resist calling your name. When I did, you released a mighty blast of wind. Dern near blew the covers off the bed. I knew you'd be all right."

Joseph stepped back and laughed out loud. Andrew coughed to hide his embarrassment. The Carruthers looked at the ceiling, pretending not to have heard the remark.

"But Grandfather, how on earth did you survive?"

"Have a seat," the old man said. He told them of his experience.

Grandfather was thrown into the ocean when the ship broke in two. He lost his spectacles and could hardly see. He floated on his back and called for help. After a time he felt something poking him. He screamed, thinking it was a sea monster, the kind that ate humans. It turned out to be an oar. Several men had been able to release the two other lifeboats just before the *Pulaski* exploded. Fortunately, those boats had been stored under tarpaulin and had no leaks. The men rowed around, searching for life. Grandfather was the last person they could fit.

Grandfather called for Joseph to see if he was on his boat, but no one answered. He and the others sat in the boats, listening to the screams and pleas for help around them. But there was nothing they could do. Finally, a man in Grandfather's boat called to a Mr. Couper in the other boat, saying it was senseless to remain. It was time to head to land. The other man agreed.

Grandfather called out, "James Hamilton Couper of Glynn County. Is that you?"

"Yes, who is that calling?" Couper responded.

"Daniel McBain of Heritage Plantation."

"Mr. McBain. You're alive! Thank God!" Couper shouted.

"Tell me, Mr. Couper, is Joseph or Andrew, his negro, in your boat?"

"No. I'm sorry to say they aren't, sir."

Grandfather's heart sunk in his chest. "Can we take some time and look for them?"

"We're in two rowboats, Mr. McBain, and both are over full. We can't take on another person without sinking."

"If you find Joseph, I'll jump out so that he can come on. He has a whole life ahead of him. I'm an old man ready to die!"

A voice from Grandfather's boat interrupted. "I'm afraid that's impossible, sir. We can't row around asking drowning people if they're your grandson, and if they are not, leave them to die. We can't in good conscience do that. The Lord has placed us in these boats. We must accept that and seek safety."

"Captain Hibbert is right, Mr. McBain," Couper called. "We have no choice. We must go on. I'm sorry for Joseph and Andrew. I know how much you love them. May God rest their souls. Many families are facing the same tragedy tonight."

Grandfather hung his head.

Eleven people were in Grandfather's boat and twelve in Couper's. They left the area of the *Pulaski* in the middle of night and headed west, towards land. They arrived off the coast at about 4 p.m. on Friday, after thirteen hours of rowing. There was no easy access to the turbulent North Carolina shore. They would have to go over violent breakers to make it to the beach, which the boats could not do without capsizing. Couper suggested they continue along the coast until they found a calm inlet. Mr. Hibbert agreed but the two oarsmen in each boat, deck hands from the *Pulaski*, were too tired and refused. They would take their chances in the crashing waves ahead of them.

Couper and Hibbert had to agree. There weren't four strong men to replace the rowers. They did convince the oarsmen to go in one boat at a time to allow the men from the first boat to help the people in the second boat after it broke up. Grandfather's boat went first. To no one's surprise, it flipped over. Grandfather tried to swim but he couldn't see the waves, and kept getting smashed into the surf. Finally, he felt the ocean floor. He tried to walk towards the shore, but oncoming waves kept knocking him down hard. Then, the powerful tow sucked him back. When he realized he didn't have the strength to make it in, someone, Grandfather never found out who, pulled him onto the beach. However, five people from his boat drowned in the surf just yards from shore.

Couper's boat also overturned. But with the aid of the men on the first boat, and through Couper's own efforts, all twelve made it safely to shore.

They found help and were put up by residents of a nearby town. This was Friday night. On Sunday they were moved to Wilmington. On Monday, Grandfather wrote to James to come to Wilmington immediately.

Grandfather said, "Andrew was able to fill me in on some of your ordeal. We all need to rest. Today is Wednesday. Your father should receive my letter today and will be here by the weekend, depending on the ship schedule. We have time to catch up."

Joseph leaned forward in his chair. "Grandfather, what about Anthony?"

Grandfather shook his head. "I haven't heard a thing."

Joseph looked to the street, sad once again. Grandfather did tell them that twenty-six people had been found on a piece of wreckage and were brought in with them on the *Henry Camerdon*. In fact, those people had been rescued first and told the captain they thought they'd seen other survivors in the water, thus saving Joseph and the others.

Andrew and Joseph felt a tide of exhaustion and retired to their bedrooms for the evening. Grandfather returned to his hotel.

Joseph slept for fifteen more hours and awoke on Thursday. He was still sore and couldn't wear more than a loose nightshirt over his sunburn. He went downstairs and joined Andrew, Grandfather, and the Carruthers. At the advice of the doctor, they spent the day chatting.

On Friday, they ventured outside. The boys dressed in loose fitting clothes that Grandfather had bought at a local store. Everyone in Wilmington seemed to know who they were and greeted them with kind words.

As they walked on Market Street towards the riverfront, Joseph spotted Gazaway Lamar and ran to him. "Sir, you made it! I thought, well . . . we didn't hear from . . ." Joseph didn't know how to ask him questions without saying the wrong thing.

Lamar forced a smile through bloodshot, baggy eyes. "It's good to see you made it, Joseph." As Andrew and Grandfather approached, Gazaway said, "Oh, thank God you're all alive." He shook Grandfather's and Andrew's hand. "Andrew, thank you again for saving my boy's life."

Joseph thought it odd Lamar said that, since Charlie had died. Then Joseph noticed a boy walking slowly and unsteadily towards them. "Charlie, you made it!" Charlie looked so frail Joseph wondered why he was even on the street.

Charlie leaned against his father and said hello to the McBains. He asked Joseph if he had heard of any more survivors. Joseph shook his head. Charlie looked away.

Joseph finally found the words to ask Mr. Lamar what was on his mind. "Sir, what happened after you left us?" In an unsteady voice, Gazaway told them.

After departing the wreck on Saturday morning, he and the five others made it to the coast off the New River Inlet in North Carolina late Saturday afternoon, at the start of the storm. Their boat crashed on the breakers but all six made it to shore. Lamar went to the local fishermen and told them what had happened. He offered them money to send a ship. The fishermen declined. They said few ships and certainly no piece of debris could survive the brewing gale. Lamar offered to pay a local man to go to Wilmington, fifty miles south, and inform the people of the disaster and to send out rescue ships. The man also refused, claiming it was a hopeless mission. With all his money, Lamar could not find anyone to save the remnants of his family.

On Wednesday morning, word came from Wilmington. Survivors had been recovered and taken there. Lamar hired a carriage and arrived in Wilmington on Thursday to find Rebecca and Charlie barely alive, but learned little Thomas had died. Gazaway Lamar had lost his wife, three daughters, two sons, and a niece. No family suffered more in the disaster.

They strolled together silently on Market Street for a few minutes. Lamar told the McBains he was going back to the hospital to check on Rebecca. They bade goodbye. Joseph watched father and son walk away, their feet scraping the ground, hunched over with their hands in their pockets.

There were six survivors from Joseph's and Andrew's wreckage, seventeen from the two lifeboats which saved Grandfather, six men in Gazaway Lamar's lifeboat, twenty-six from the other piece of wreckage, and eight others who survived by clinging onto debris and floating to shore.

Of the approximately 193 passengers and crew, 130 perished and sixty-three survived. Savannah, and America, wept.

CHAPTER 10

Moving On

1838-1839

The coach turned onto the avenue of oaks from the Augusta Road. Andrew rode on the driver's bench with Hercules. Joseph sat inside with his family. Eight days had passed since the *Henry Camerdon* plucked the two from the ocean.

The female servants working in the vegetable fields at the top of the avenue, having seen Andrew, ran alongside the coach, waving with one hand, and holding their dresses in the other.

Before Joseph's parents and Amy had left for Wilmington, McBain addressed the plantation with news of the disaster. He told them Grandfather McBain was alive, but he had no news of Joseph, Andrew, or Anthony. As soon as he learned more, he would send word to them. Until then, he asked that they all pray for the missing. Their return was the first the negroes had learned of Joseph's and Andrew's fate.

The servants mobbed Grandfather, Joseph, and Andrew with pats on the back and embraces. Father had a hog roasted for the plantation. There was great merriment throughout the supper.

At the end of the evening, Joseph stood on an old chair in the Quarter and called the two hundred negroes and his family together. He asked for silence as he eulogized Anthony, and then led them in a prayer. The McBains were both surprised and impressed by Joseph's action.

Joseph spent the following day reading and fishing by himself. His family respected his introspection. The day after, his father joined him on the wharf. After an hour of watching their lines lay unmolested in the water, James asked Joseph if he were ready to consider returning to college. Joseph said he was but wanted to be closer to home. McBain suggested Franklin College in Athens, Georgia. Dr. Arnold had been a trustee at the school and could help get Joseph admitted for the fall. Joseph agreed. A great weight was lifted from his mind.

All of Savannah mourned the loss of the *Pulaski*. Almost every resident knew someone who had died. The tragedy was all anyone spoke of. Residents wore black crepe armbands for a month. The Independence Day celebration, usually such a joyous event in Savannah, was canceled for the first time in memory.

Added to the sadness were scattered voices of anger. Gazaway Lamar complained that the men on the ship could have saved more women and children if they hadn't been so concerned about themselves. Lamar came in for criticism himself, as survivors complained about the number and condition of the lifeboats. All Savannahians were incensed to learn that several captains of passing ships, upon reaching Charleston, had reported spotting debris in the water the day after the accident. Yet not one of them, until Captain Davis of the *Henry Camerdon*, made an attempt to investigate.

A week after Joseph had returned, he summoned the courage to keep his word to Noah. He had Hercules take him to the Parkman home in town.

A negro woman who Joseph guessed to be about twenty-five years of age answered the door. She was wearing a house servant's outfit, black with a white collar. Her hair was cut in a perfect semi-circle ending at her ears. Joseph removed his hat. "Good morning. Are you Daisy?"

"Yes, sir, I am." Daisy took a step back and stared at Joseph, not knowing what this white man intended.

"My name is Joseph McBain. I'm from the Heritage Plantation."

Daisy nodded slowly. "Yes, sir. Were you one of the McBains on the *Pulaski*?" Even the negroes in town knew the names of the survivors.

"Yes, ma'am. I was on my way to college. God chose a few of us to survive, and I was one." Though Joseph was unclear about his relationship with God, he always invoked Him to explain the unexplainable.

"He has his reasons, Master McBain. I have to accept them, even if I don't understand them." The woman seemed to be bearing up better than Joseph.

Joseph looked past Daisy. "I wonder if I could talk with you. Inside?"

"Yes, of course, sir. I'm so sorry. Please come in." She took Joseph's hat and led him into the parlor, where much of the furniture was covered with sheets.

Joseph sat on a couch while Daisy remained standing. He said, "Please. Sit down." Daisy sat on the other end of the couch. A lone tear ran down her right cheek, leaving a glistening track. She pulled a white kerchief from her sleeve. Joseph looked around the room, trying to give her some privacy to weep. The house was quiet, apparently empty of people, except the two of them. It seemed as if the building itself were grieving. Daisy saw Joseph inspecting the room. "The family is selling everything, the house, the furniture, the horse and buggy. Me."

Joseph didn't know how to respond. He had planned to converse with Daisy for a while to put her at ease. But he felt a sudden urge to keep his promise, as if Noah's spirit was poking him from behind with a stick. "Daisy, I saw your husband, Noah, that night." Her eyes opened wide, as if she wanted to say something, but Joseph knew that if he paused he might never finish. "The boiler exploded. People were running everywhere. Noah was on the first deck trying to calm the women and children and direct them to the lifeboats on the top deck. I told him to go to the promenade deck. He said he had to make sure Mr. Parkman and his three girls were safe. He told me to save myself. I tried to convince him to come with me, but he wouldn't. He asked me to tell you that he was thinking of you then. And that he loved you always, and always would."

Daisy stared at her lap. Tears ran down her face. A few drops fell on her dress before she used her kerchief. She swallowed several times. Then she faced Joseph. "I thank you, Master McBain, for telling me that. You don't know how much it means to hear Noah's words from someone who was with him. It gives me peace to know that he was thinking of me. But I must confess, this is so difficult." She closed her eyes tightly, but they couldn't hold in the sorrow.

Joseph thought he might break down, too, but he gathered his strength. When she composed herself, he asked, "Daisy, is there anything I can do for you?"

She looked towards the parlor window. "Master McBain, I had one dream in life, to have Noah's children. That's no longer possible." She paused. Joseph kept quiet. This conversation required a verbal delicacy he did not possess. Daisy asked, "Do you want to have a family, Master McBain?"

Joseph scratched his head as he thought of an answer. "I guess so. But I'll have to get married first. And if you must know, Daisy, I'm scared to death of women."

Daisy interrupted her grief with a short burst of laughter. "Well, you be fighting them off soon, I can assure you." She pulled at the lace edges of her kerchief and shook her head. "No, sir, there's nothing you can do for me."

They sat quietly for a minute. Joseph had done his job, but he couldn't leave. "What's going to happen to you, Daisy?"

She patted her nose. "I don't know, sir. It's not up to me."

Joseph knew it was time to leave. "God bless you, Daisy." He left her on the couch and escorted himself out of the house.

For days afterwards, Joseph couldn't get Noah's physical suffering and dignity in the face of death or Daisy's mental anguish and dignity in the face of an uncertain future out of his mind. He wondered if white people would have acted any differently, or better.

At some point the survivors of the *Pulaski,* relatives and friends of those who died, and Savannah had to put the disaster behind them.

Andrew had suffered every bit as much as Joseph. Fortunately, he had something to occupy his mind. The morning after they arrived from Wilmington, Andrew was stacking bricks on the kiln.

A few weeks later, Joseph and Andrew were sitting outside Andrew's cabin. Andrew confessed that he had made three promises to himself if he survived. He would get closer to God. He would become Savannah's first negro architect. And he would ask Quiet Goose for Sally's hand in marriage, if Mr. McBain approved.

The third promise grabbed Joseph's attention. Andrew liked Sally. That was no secret. But he'd rarely seen her in the five years since they met, and they were not adults during that time. In fact, for the two years following Quiet Goose's confrontation with James Moore Wayne in 1834, Sally and her father hadn't appeared once at the market. When Grampah told Andrew that the United States Senate had ratified a treaty with the Cherokees in May 1836 giving the Indians two years to move out of Georgia, Andrew assumed he would never see Sally again.

However, one Saturday in late 1836, Sally and Quiet Goose appeared at the City Market. Andrew's heart beat like a woodpecker's head at feeding time. Sally had grown and become even more beautiful in his eyes. After that day, the Indians came to the market once a month. Quiet Goose's rules allowing Sally to talk to Andrew did not soften with time. For a year and a half they spoke once a month for fifteen minutes.

When in May 1838 Andrew told Sally he was accompanying Joseph on a trip to New Jersey and might not see her the next month, Sally said she looked forward to his return. Andrew asked her about the treaty that would force the Cherokees to move. Sally told Andrew that her father would never leave his land. Andrew had no reason to doubt her. Now he was preparing to propose marriage.

Joseph thought that jumping to marriage from those once-a-month chats was a giant leap. "Andrew, we're only eighteen. I know people marry at that age, even younger. But we don't have much experience with women."

Andrew said, "The government is trying to run the Cherokees from the state. This might be my last chance. I made the promise out at sea, Master Joseph. I'm going to keep it. I can't lose her."

Joseph knew reasoning with Andrew would not be easy. Joseph sat closer to his friend and spoke in a whisper. "Andrew, do you really think Quiet Goose will let you marry her? Do you think she even wants to get married? What will my father say? Where would you live?"

Andrew hesitated, confused by Joseph's questions. "I don't have all those answers, Master Joseph. I just know I have to try."

"Listen. We're going to town on Saturday. If they're at the market, I guess the first step is to ask Quiet Goose if he'll let Sally marry you."

"I'd feel more comfortable asking Sally first, knowing if she'd even marry me, before I go to her father. I've never really spoken to him."

Feathers, Amy's cat, appeared and rubbed against Joseph's leg. He idly petted the animal and asked, "How would you address him? Call him Master Goose?"

Andrew chuckled. "I don't have to worry about that until Sally accepts."

That next Saturday they traveled by rowboat into Savannah. Andrew was unusually quiet. Mr. McBain asked him if he were feeling well. Joseph had considered telling his father about Andrew's plan, but decided not to. If Sally rejected Andrew, no mention need be made.

Joseph and Andrew waited all morning. Andrew had walked around the market at least ten times, looking for the wagon. The Indians never appeared that day. Nor did they for the next eight Saturdays.

Joseph finally told Grandfather of Andrew's plans and asked if he knew anything of the Cherokees. Grandfather shook his head sadly and explained that when the deadline came for the Cherokees to relocate, only two of eighteen thousand had 'volunteered' to leave. In late May, General Winfield Scott was ordered to lead federal and state troops to the area to assist the reluctant Indians. Grandfather assumed that the tribe had been force-marched to their new home. Joseph didn't have the heart to tell Andrew of this.

What Grandfather did not know, nor would ever learn, was that Sally's sickly mother had died in May, just days after Sally and Quiet Goose had returned from their last trip to Savannah, and they had the solemn task of burying her. Quiet Goose refused to leave his log cabin when the troops came. He had made a promise to his wife on her deathbed that he would not leave their land, and he would never leave her. Their spirits would be united forever. When he heard that the federal troops were a day away from his village, Quiet Goose, confident that his nineteen-year-old daughter could survive without him, dug a grave next to his wife's, put in a simple casket, lay down in it, and shot himself in the head. He left Sally a note, explaining his actions, and asking her to put the top on the casket and shovel the dirt on top of it. He told her he loved her, and where she could find his money. By late June, about the time when Andrew was waiting in City Market to propose, Sally was marching with sixteen thousand other Cherokees to holding stockades in Tennessee, where they would be penned up like cattle for the summer, awaiting another march to their new home in Oklahoma.

As the summer wore on with no sign of Sally, Andrew grew more morose. Joseph still could not bring himself to say anything to his heartbroken friend.

As Sally languished in the sickly stockades, Joseph made plans to attend Franklin College. This time there were no inspirational talks from his parents about studying hard, acting like an adult, and avoiding trouble. His father told him to do his best and his mother made him promise to write every day so she'd know he was all right. Nor was there singing or dancing in the Quarter the night before he left; just some farewells from the servants.

Joseph's parents, Hercules, and Andrew accompanied Joseph to Athens in September of 1838. Although he was attending college in Georgia, the riverboat from Savannah to Augusta and the stagecoaches from Augusta to Athens took almost as long as the trip to New Jersey would have. There were no accidents. It was a dull journey.

His parents stayed for a few days, saw the college, and met the faculty and administrators. They felt confident Joseph would be safe there.

The night before his parents were to return to Savannah, Joseph and Andrew had a private moment to talk in Joseph's room. "You know, Andrew, you could have stayed here with me in Athens. I asked Father about it. He said it was up to me, but that you might get a chance to work in Savannah. He thought it would be best for you to stay at the Heritage. I agreed. Now that you're about to leave, I'm not so sure."

Andrew sat on the edge of Joseph's bed. "It's going to be different without you, Master Joseph. I wasn't looking forward to saying goodbye to you in New Jersey. I'm not looking forward to tomorrow. But I appreciate what Master McBain is trying to do for me. I want to be an architect. That's one of my promises, and I've already failed at another. I have to succeed."

Joseph sat next to Andrew. "You will for certain, Andrew. I know it. When college is over, we'll be partners."

"I can't wait for that day, Master Joseph."

Joseph threw his arm around Andrew. "Friends forever."

When Andrew returned to the Heritage, he made bricks and built cabins. He also continued to sketch. By the end of the year, he had designed a house, a church, and a memorial to Anthony, all in the Greek Revival style. But Andrew soon became captivated by the Corinthian order, with its sleekness and the intricate capitals of acanthus leaves, upon studying William Jay's semi-circular portico on Archibald Bulloch's House on Barnard Street. Andrew used the order in most of his designs.

Yet Andrew rarely smiled or joked. The experience of the *Pulaski*, the loss of Sally, and the departure of Joseph within a few months were too much to cast aside. His melancholy did not escape Mr. McBain. He felt badly for Andrew for all he had gone through.

One December day, McBain called Andrew to the study. "Andrew, please have a seat. I've been so busy I haven't had much time to talk. I have some news for you. Reconstruction on Christ Church is about to begin. You'll be working as a bricklayer for Mr. Scudder."

Andrew held onto the arms of his chair as if to keep from floating off. In his sadness, Andrew didn't believe this would really happen. "Thank you, sir! I'll do a good job, I promise."

"I have no doubt you will, Andrew. This is just a first step in a very successful building career." McBain paused for a moment. "Also, I've rented a house in Savannah, on Orleans Square. I'm spending more time in town for business and need a place to stay. Grandfather McBain will live there, as well. In Savannah he can be near his friends. Lilly the cook, Molly, Chloe, William, and Celia will move, too. You'll live there while working on the church."

Andrew was speechless. He had always dreamed he might one day live in the town that Oglethorpe designed.

"And while you're here, Andrew." McBain opened his desk drawer, removed a package, placed it on the desk, and pushed it towards Andrew. "Here, we McBains have a small present for you, for all you did on the *Pulaski*. And for being such a good friend to Joseph."

The flat package was wrapped in dark blue paper with a beige ribbon. Andrew stared at it. Someone had prepared it with great care. Mr. McBain nodded. Andrew carefully untied the ribbon and placed it aside. Then he slowly unfolded the paper, sealed at strategic points with drops of wax. McBain thought Andrew could have built a house in the time it took him to unwrap the gift. Finally, the contents were revealed. It was a book, the size of *Villas of the Ancients*. Andrew lifted the cover to the first page. It read:

Andrea Palladio
The Four Books of Architecture

"Master McBain!" Andrew's eyes opened wider than a bullfrog laying eggs. "I've read about this but I never thought I'd see a copy."

"Go ahead, take a look." McBain watched Andrew inspect the precious tome, placing his fingers on the edge of the pages to turn them. "I suggest you keep the book in our safe and read it here when you have the time. Just let Grandfather McBain or me know."

"Yes, sir. I agree. It needs to be preserved." Andrew could not even begin to comprehend how much the book cost or how much effort Master McBain had gone through to obtain it. "Sir, I don't know how to thank you. This is the greatest gift ever. I'll never forget it."

McBain leaned across the desk and patted Andrew's arm. "Thanks aren't necessary. You must know about Palladio if you're interested in classicism. He was responsible more than anyone for reviving the ideals of Vitruvius in the late fifteenth century. Of course, he added his own ideas. His buildings were based on a central pedimented unit often flanked by symmetrical dependencies. They are referred to as the three-part and five-part plans. You read that book and we'll discuss it another day. Take a few minutes now and page through it." McBain and Andrew stood and shook hands. "I can't tell you how proud we are of all you've done."

Andrew ducked his head and said, "Sir." He then sat in a corner chair and read for an hour, until Plesant told him that Isaac was looking for him to get back to the kilns.

Andrew lay in his bed that night, unable to sleep. For the first time in many years, he played his and Joseph's childhood game, Villas of the Ancients, in his mind's eye. He saw a square in Savannah. Occupying the two east side trust lots was a church in the style of an ancient Greek temple. Nineteen steps led to the front landing. Columns of the Corinthian order bordered the entire structure, eight in the front and back, fifteen on the sides.

Standing on the two trust lots on the west side of the square was a Palladio-inspired house in the three-part style. The two-story central unit had a two-tiered portico. The bottom tier had six Doric columns; the top, six Corinthian columns. Loggias extended from the sides, connecting to two circular units for his ancestors.

Bordering the rest of the square were classical houses, Georgian, Federal, Adam, and Greek Revival, representing all the orders, in perfect symmetry and proportion. Hundreds of people walked around the square, marveling at the structures, and wondered who had designed them. Andrew fell asleep happy for the first time in months.

McBain had also noticed Amy moping around. She was an excellent student, read her Bible regularly, sang in the church choir, and had always been able to avoid the trouble Joseph found so easily. Her parents were eternally grateful for this. At nineteen years, she was expected by her family and friends to either marry or help her mother with her plantation duties until she did. Then she would have children and servants of her own.

Amy followed the plan and supervised the seamstresses, weavers, washerwomen, house servants, and cooks. But it bored her. So did the men she met at the balls and parties she attended.

One day McBain asked his daughter why she seemed so glum. She told him she wanted to advance her education, learn new things, and see the world beyond the Heritage, just as Joseph was doing. Her father hugged her and asked for some time to work things out. James spoke to Sarah about Amy's future. Sarah couldn't bear to have both her children away from home, but agreed that Amy should have the same opportunities as Joseph.

It only took McBain a few days to find a solution. A new college, the Georgia Female College, had just opened in Macon. It was the first college for women in America and they were eager for applicants. Classes were being offered in European languages, English letters and science, music, drawing, painting, and domestic economy. Amy had never been more excited in her life. She was sad to be leaving the plantation and Feathers, but she knew one day she would be back. In early January 1839 James and Sarah took Amy to Macon, where she boarded at the school facilities.

Grandfather McBain, almost eighty years old, was as hopeful about the future as any other McBain. He would be living in Savannah and seeing his friends at the local taverns and bookstores anytime he wished.

Most of all, he would have a chance to play a part in the recording of Georgia history. A Savannah bank employee and an autograph collector had the idea of forming a society to store documents relating to Georgia's history. In late spring of 1839, the Georgia Historical Society was organized. Its officers included some of the most prominent citizens of Savannah. A former United States senator and attorney general was elected president. James Moore Wayne, associate Supreme Court justice, became one of the vice presidents. Grandfather McBain was asked by the family doctor, Richard Arnold, another founder, to be a curator, along with Grandfather's friends William Thorne Williams and John

C. Nicoll. Grandfather could finally talk about history to people who wouldn't try to escape.

While the McBains got on with their lives after the *Pulaski*, others did not fare as well. Gazaway Lamar tried his best to recover from his staggering loss. At Rebecca's suggestion, Charlie moved to Augusta to live with her until Gazaway could put his life in order. Lamar reluctantly parted from the only remaining member of his immediate family. But he had to dispose of his family's personal belongings and settle all the other legal matters. It was best that Charlie not witness that painful process.

Lamar methodically took care of closing his family's affairs and managing his business interests. But he was crushed by the loneliness of waking up in the morning and returning in the evening to a silent house, empty except for the servants. Prior to the *Pulaski*, he had been greeted from work by a pack of laughing children. Charlie had to peel his brothers and sisters off his father so he could enter the house. Now, Gazaway returned to solitude. In attempting to maintain his sanity, he buried himself even deeper into his business affairs.

Charlie was better off living with his aunt and being close to his cousins in Augusta. Rebecca placed Charlie in a private school and he made an attempt to keep up with his studies.

But Charlie missed his father. He wanted to talk to him about his lost family, and what they were doing in heaven. Even though Gazaway visited Charlie frequently in Augusta while attending to business interests, he was always too busy to discuss these matters with his son.

In a year's time, Gazaway wrote to Rebecca that he was planning to remarry and take Charlie home. Rebecca understood that her brother could not live long without a woman. Gazaway said he was confident Charlie would accept his wife-to-be. Rebecca, who knew Charlie better than anybody, had her doubts.

In June 1839 Gazaway journeyed to Augusta. As soon as he entered her house, Charlie was there to greet him. "Are we really going home, Father?"

Gazaway stepped back and looked at his fifteen-year-old son. He was growing into a young man. "Yes, Charlie. You're looking handsomer and healthier than ever."

"Aunt Rebecca has taken proper care of me." Charlie stepped to his aunt's side and kissed her cheek. He saw she had a handkerchief in her hand. Charlie was leaving the woman he loved most in the world. He had thought this over and devised a solution. He'd ask his father to invite her to live with them in Savannah. His father needed a woman around the house, and he loved his sister.

Rebecca said, "You've been a joy, Charlie. Now, I need to go out for a while. You can spend some time with your father. I'll be back soon."

"Yes, Aunt Rebecca." Charlie would use her absence to present his plan to his father. He watched his aunt place a shawl around her shoulders and walk out the door.

"Charlie, let's sit inside." Gazaway swept his arm towards the parlor door.

"Yes, Father." Charlie hurried into the room.

They sat on chairs facing each other. They talked awhile about school, relatives, and Charlie's passion, horseback riding. When those topics were exhausted, Gazaway stared at his boy for a few moments. The silence became uncomfortable for Charlie and he squirmed in his chair. Finally, Gazaway spoke. "Son, I have some very exciting news to tell you. I've met a wonderful woman. You'll like her very much. We're getting married. We'll be a family once again." Gazaway clasped his hands together and smiled.

Charlie felt as if he had just been slammed in the chest with a hammer. He never even thought about his father remarrying. His lower lip started to tremble. "Father, I still miss Mother and my brothers and sisters. I can't leave them now."

"Son, we're not leaving them. They're safe in heaven. They'll always be in our hearts. But we must go forward here on earth. Mother would want us to move on with our lives. She wouldn't want us to mourn forever."

Tears formed in Charlie's eyes. "Father, it's only been a year. It feels like yesterday. I can't live with a stranger now. I want to stay with Aunt Rebecca."

Gazaway pressed his palms together. "Charlie, you'll love Miss Casenove. I wouldn't think of marrying a woman you wouldn't like. You must trust me, son."

"How did you meet her?" Charlie's sadness turned to anger. The tears disappeared.

"She's related to the people who took care of me at New River Inlet."

Charlie's voice rose as he challenged his father for the first time in his life. "You mean our family had just drowned and you met this woman?"

Gazaway tried to keep calm. "Charlie, I must ask you to change your tone. I am your father. Remember that. You mustn't speak to me in that manner. For your information, I met Miss Casenove there. I didn't see her again until just a few months ago, while I was in Virginia on business."

Charlie put his throbbing head in his hands. He thought he was going to be sick.

Gazaway Lamar leaned forward in his chair. "We'll return to Savannah. Then we'll move to Alexandria, Virginia. I have business interests there. Miss Casenove and I will get married and we'll all be together. A family, Charlie. That's what we need. We won't be alone any longer. There are excellent schools in Alexandria and many boys to make friends with. They have many riding academies."

Charlie kept his head in his hands. His breathing became louder. He looked up at his father, screamed "Nooooo!" and leapt off his chair. He plowed into his father as he was trying to stand. Charlie knocked him back into the chair and they tumbled over in a mass of twisting arms and legs onto the floor. Gazaway quickly rolled on top of his son, who was flailing away with his fists, and grabbed his son's wrists. Charlie's body went limp. He sobbed, "No, no, no! I won't go! I won't!"

Neither heard Rebecca Lamar open the front door. "Oh, my God!" she cried when she saw her brother sitting on the floor, straddling Charlie.

Gazaway sprang to his feet, and pulled his son up. Charlie ran to his room without looking at his aunt. Gazaway couldn't face his sister. He picked up the chair and inspected it to see if there was any damage. He then straightened the rug. Rebecca started to weep. "I'll take care of it, Gaz."

Gazaway hugged her. "Things will work out, Rebecca. Charlie will be all right. He's been through a lot."

Lamar married Harriett Casenove in the summer of 1839 in Alexandria, Virginia. Charlie behaved like a young gentleman at the service and reception. Gazaway rented a house in Alexandria. Charlie attended yet another school and adjusted to his new family and home. He obeyed his father and stepmother, and showed genuine happiness at the birth of a sister. He and his father had a family again.

William Washington Gordon continued to devote his life to the future of Savannah, the Central of Georgia Railroad. A year after the Financial Panic of 1837 and the Irish workers' march on Savannah, trains were running regularly over forty-six miles of track. And though money problems continued to plague the operation, by late 1839 eighty miles of the projected 190 had been laid. Most of the laborers by then were slaves. Shamus Riley and his friends had moved back to Savannah to find work.

Despite all the problems, it seemed certain that Savannah, in a few years, would have its road to Macon. The 1840s were certain to be exciting and prosperous times. The McBains eagerly anticipated them.

Part 2

Train Rides

1840s

CHAPTER 11

Christ Church

1840

"You sold your racing boat?" James Hamilton Couper asked as he stood by the fireplace in the drawing room of his Hopeton Plantation mansion.

James McBain, his hand resting against the dark green marble mantel, responded, "I'm afraid so. I just don't have the time for it."

It was the autumn of 1840. The McBains were guests of James Hamilton and Carolyn Wylly Couper at their plantation near Darien for the local regatta. They were enjoying pre-supper conversation with the Coupers and their other guests, Pierce Butler, a local plantation owner, and his wife, Fanny Kemble Butler.

Carolyn Couper, sitting on one of two matching settees with the other women, wasn't interested in discussing the races. "How are the children, Sarah?"

"Very well. Joseph is at Franklin College in Athens and Amy's attending the Georgia Female College in Macon. She's enjoying meeting other young ladies from all over the South. She has informed us that she wants to travel to Europe when she graduates. She says Georgia is so provincial and she needs to experience other cultures to broaden her understanding of life."

Mrs. Couper said, "Well, good for her. I think it's wonderful that intelligent young women have the opportunity of an advanced education in the South and the chance to see other parts of the world. It will make her more intriguing to wealthy suitors."

Sarah shook her head. "Amy complains that the young men she meets are still boys, just in bigger bodies." Sarah paused to taste her wine. "She's not an easy one to understand." Sarah's main goal in life was seeing that her children married as soon as possible and started families. Recently, she had become concerned about Amy.

"She sounds ever so interesting. I should enjoy meeting her one day," Fanny Kemble Butler said in her proper British accent. Fanny was a Shakespearean actress, one of England's most renowned, and had been one of the most sought-after personalities in London society. However, in the summer of 1832 at the age of twenty-nine, to help her father pay his mounting debts, she agreed to a two-year tour of the American stage. The Americans adored her. She met United States presidents and played to filled theatres in all the prominent northeastern venues.

Sarah smiled at the praise from such a famous person. "I'm certain she would enjoy meeting you, Mrs. Butler."

"That would ruin Miss McBain for certain," Mr. Butler added. During her tour, Fanny had attracted many dashing bachelors. For richer or poorer, she chose Pierce Butler of Philadelphia to be her Romeo for life. They married in June of 1834, shortly before her tour ended. She gave up her acting career for her husband.

"Mr. Butler!" Fanny responded, covering her mouth with a hand in mock indignation.

Couper, uncertain if Pierce and Fanny were about to have one of their famous spats, broke in and said, "You'd also like meeting one of Mr. McBain's negroes, Mrs. Butler." Couper knew well of Fanny's anti-slavery sentiments—she didn't keep them hidden, much to her husband's regret—and thought Andrew's story might soften her attitude on the peculiar institution.

Just then, Mr. Couper's butler, Willie, stepped into the parlor and said, "Excuse me, Master Couper. The first course is served."

The three couples walked across the center hall into the dining room. A dark mahogany dining table, covered with a green, felt-like baize cloth under a light yellow linen damask cloth, was situated in the middle of the rectangular room. A glittering chandelier hung over the table. The men seated their wives in scroll-back, cushioned fancy chairs, and then seated themselves.

Sarah McBain took in her surroundings. A large fireplace with a black Italian marble mantel sat beneath a painting of an English fox-hunting scene. The far wall had a full-length curtained window overlooking a canal which fed into the Altamaha River. Against another wall sat a mahogany sideboard with four sets of wine glasses, each forming a crescent, at the corners. In the center were stacks of plates for additional courses, more silverware, and several cruet stands, all arranged in perfect symmetry. On either side of the sideboard were side tables, also piled with plates and bowls.

Covered platters of food were waiting on the dining table. As Willie poured the wine, two female servants wearing black dresses and white blouses removed the covers. The first course consisted of a tureen of turtle soup, a leg of boiled mutton, a boiled ham, macaroni pie with parmesan cheese, crispy bacon, and a platter of dumb fish.

Willie said, "Master Couper, the oysters will be out shortly."

Couper thanked him, then raised his flower-etched wine glass to his guests and toasted their good health and prosperity. The diners echoed the toast.

From a seated position, Mr. Couper carved the ham while Mrs. Couper carved the mutton. The women servants helped serve the food to the guests.

After sampling the mutton, Fanny asked, "Mr. Couper, you were saying about one of Mr. McBain's negroes?" Pierce winced upon hearing his wife's question, but continued eating.

The Butlers had lived in Philadelphia for two years after their marriage. In 1836 they were elated to learn that Pierce had inherited two prosperous plantations in Darien, Georgia. For Fanny, that joy was short-lived when she realized they had also become among the largest slaveholders in the state. Pierce, acutely sensitive to his wife's abolitionist views and her loose lips, refused to allow her to travel to Darien with him on business trips. But in 1838 the longtime overseer of the plantations retired and Pierce had no choice but to move with Fanny and their two young daughters to manage things until he could hire a replacement. Pierce went first. Fanny and the girls arrived in late December 1838 after a ten-day trip, during which Fanny complained about anything and everything: the trains, the ships, the food, the inns, the whites, the blacks, and on and on. After four months of living on her husband's plantations, Butler Island and Hampton Point, Fanny was more repelled than ever by human bondage and continued to harangue her husband about it. The Butlers moved back to Philadelphia in April of 1839. Pierce had to return to Georgia the following year for business and reluctantly brought Fanny with him. Her potential to express her feelings in public or private kept him constantly on edge. On top of that, it especially irked Pierce that his deeply principled wife had no trouble spending the wealth the plantations produced.

As Couper carved, he explained, "He's a bricklayer with an interest in classical architecture. He knows more about it than most white builders." The McBains nodded in agreement.

"Classical architecture?" Fanny cocked her head as if she hadn't heard Couper correctly. "How did that happen down here?"

Sarah McBain explained the story to Fanny, whose eyes moved from Sarah to Mr. Couper to see if they were teasing her.

When Sarah finished, Couper said to McBain, "Andrew certainly impressed Amos Scudder with his work at Christ Church. Scudder didn't want to take on a negro. Said it might cause dissension with the other workers, who were all white. But he did a favor for me. Now he can't stop singing his praises."

McBain said, "Andrew values the experience, James, I can tell you that. I can't thank you enough for your help."

"Yes," replied Sarah McBain. "His going to jail was so unfortunate."

"Jail?" the Coupers and Butlers replied in chorus.

"Sadly, yes. I get angry just thinking about it," McBain said.

*   *   *

The plans for Christ Church had been ambitious. The rectangular building would occupy the southeast trust lot on Johnson Square, as did its predecessor. Its Greek entranceway with six colossal columns in the Ionic order would be reached by climbing fifteen steps.

On Andrew's first day, Amos Scudder explained to the bricklayers that the wall was to be three feet thick and laid in the modified American bonding pattern of five rows of stretchers alternated with one row of headers. From the start, Andrew's talent and willingness to work hard caught the eye of Scudder.

One morning, a few weeks after the project had begun, Andrew took note of the brick some of the men were using and said, "Excuse me, you shouldn't use that brick."

One of the men, who had ignored Andrew from the start, said, "Who asked you? You too lazy to work?" and returned to laying bricks.

Andrew spoke at the man's back. "I'm not lazy, sir. But this is not the right brick for an exterior wall." The other men stopped working and stood, holding their bricks and trowels, to witness the confrontation.

The white man continued working and said, "Is that so? How would you know?"

Scudder spotted the men standing around and approached them. "What's all the talk about? Get to work! We're already behind schedule."

The white bricklayer replied, "We're trying to, Mr. Scudder, but this darkie here is telling us not to."

Scudder glared at Andrew. While he liked the young negro's work, he wouldn't tolerate any friction his presence might cause. "Is that true, Andrew?"

Andrew picked up a brick from the pallet and held it out. "Sir, this is salmon brick. It shouldn't be used on the exterior wall."

Scudder looked at the brick. Andrew was correct. The strongest bricks from a burn were those stacked nearest the center of the kiln, closest to the fire. A darker color, they are laid on the exterior side of the wall, which needs the greatest strength. The bricks on the perimeter of the kiln do not get as much heat and are not quite as strong. Because of their lighter color, they are called "salmon" or "back-up" brick, and are used for the interior side of the wall, which does not require the same strength.

"Andrew's right. Get the right brick over here. Tear out the salmon brick, and hurry! Time's a-wasting." Scudder walked away without acknowledging Andrew, but was grateful that he had caught the problem in time. The previous church had been torn down because of structural problems, possibly by using the wrong brick. The men returned to work realizing Andrew knew what he was talking about.

For the better part of 1839 and early 1840, Andrew worked on the church, and he made the most of the opportunity. He not only gained experience as a bricklayer, he learned about other construction techniques. Scudder personally showed Andrew how to erect the scaffolding on which the men stood to lay bricks at higher levels. Eventually, Scudder put Andrew in charge of the plumb rule and the level, making certain the bricks were laid level and square. In time, some of the white workers went to Andrew when they had a problem, and sometimes included him when they had jokes to tell.

Andrew even tried to teach a few of the whites the negro habit of balancing a wooden hod piled with bricks on their heads as they moved along the scaffolding so their hands would be free. For safety reasons, Andrew had to stop the lessons. The whites continued to carry the hod by hand.

Walking to the site one day, Andrew saw Shamus Riley and Ryan Daly on the street. They were looking for employment. Andrew, knowing that Scudder needed workers, asked them if they could lay bricks. Shamus said, "A wee bit." Andrew told Scudder he had some men for the job. The next day the Irishmen were working on the church.

Andrew lived in McBain's rented house on West Hull Street. He arrived at work at seven a.m. each day and departed at six p.m. It was a long routine but one he enjoyed. He was helping to build one of the most important structures in Savannah, and he got to traverse Oglethorpe's landscape regularly.

One evening in early 1840, as Andrew passed through Wright Square on his way home, he heard someone call, "Hello, Brother Andrew." A neatly dressed black man with white curly hair smiled down at him from a gig.

"Reverend Marshall. Good evening!" Marshall was the minister at the First African Baptist Church and the most influential negro in Savannah. He was a free man and owned a profitable dray business. His booming sermons, which promised freedom in heaven for the enslaved on earth, filled the old wooden church on Franklin Square every Sunday. Andrew had met him several years before when he accompanied Isaac to the church on a few Sundays. Andrew was surprised that the man remembered him.

"Andrew, I understand the Lord has been looking over you. Even out at sea."

"He surely has, sir." Though Andrew was unaware of it, many blacks in town had heard of the negro boy who was a hero on the *Pulaski*, and remembered him more than a year later.

Marshall leaned towards Andrew and said in a low, strong voice, "Andrew, don't you think it would be a good idea to show Him your appreciation by visiting His house?"

Andrew looked at the ground as if he had been caught fibbing. "Yes, sir. I've been meaning to. Now that I'm living at Master McBain's house in Savannah, I'll be able to go. I had been attending Isaac's sermons at the Heritage on Sundays."

"That's good, Brother Andrew. Tell me, what work . . . ."

They were distracted by an unmistakable scream, one known throughout town. In the center of Wright Square stood Moko, thin, tall, and black, wearing a red print dress, an orange-patterned headdress, and large, gold-colored hoop earrings. She was arguing with imaginary acquaintances. She picked up her stringy carpetbag and walked through the square towards the Bay. A group of six white boys appeared and taunted her from behind, trying to tug on the back of her dress. Moko turned and chased after them. The boys squealed with laughter as they escaped. Moko stopped at the fence and cursed at them. Then she started laughing and continued on her way. The boys regrouped, reentered the square, and marched in step behind her.

Moko took after them again. As she did, she ran into the corner of the water cistern cover and fell to the ground. She let out a wail.

Marshall and Andrew dashed to her. As they helped her sit up, she screamed. Marshall asked, "Sister Moko, are you all right?"

"Dey cyan' fool ol' Moko," mumbled the delirious woman.

Andrew noticed a lump on Moko's forehead and a cut on her ankle. Reverend Marshall took a kerchief from his pocket, tied it around the wound, and said to Andrew, "She must have hit her head when she fell. And that cut's pretty bad. Stay with her while I pull my gig to the square. We'll take her to the infirmary."

Andrew knelt next to Moko and tried to calm her. She seemed dazed, but hollered, "Don' wan' dem man-chillun ketch de higguhri-hee!"

"Moko, there's no horned owl here," Andrew offered, trying to make sense to her.

Reverend Marshall returned. "We best carry her!"

The men picked up Moko by her underarms and legs, which she didn't appreciate. Despite her yelling, they lifted her over the fence and onto the gig. "I know this isn't pleasant, Brother Andrew, but we have to help our sister."

They seated Moko between them and Reverend Marshall started driving south on Bull. She seemed to relax and started singing in a pitch higher than a bobwhite. "Ah need uh man tuh gib me dymins, real dymins f'um muh lub."

When Andrew was certain she wasn't going to escape, he asked, "Reverend Marshall, where is the infirmary?"

"About a mile and a half south of town." The reverend held the reins loosely and concentrated on the street ahead.

"I've never heard of it. Do they accept negroes?"

Marshall nodded. "It's just for negroes. It's been open for eight years. Built with money provided in the will of a white man. God bless him. May he rest in peace."

Moko continued to sing. Andrew leaned back, closed his eyes, and put his hands in his pockets. Just then, Moko shrieked, jumped over him, off the gig onto Jones Street, and ran towards the dense wooded area to the south. Andrew leapt to give chase but stumbled as he exited the moving gig and fell flat on his face. Marshall pulled to the side of the street and ran to Andrew, who was able to dust off the sand, but not his embarrassment.

Marshall grabbed Andrew by the arm and said, "Hurry! We need to find her."

The men searched the woods for half an hour, but Moko knew every tree and gully in the area and evaded her rescuers. With nighttime upon them, Marshall said, "We'll never find her in the dark. Let's go. I've tried to get her to the infirmary before and have never yet succeeded."

As they rode back to the center of town, Marshall asked, "Will we see you at church on Sunday, Brother Andrew?"

"I'll be there soon, sir. You have my word."

As they drove around Chippewa Square and onto Hull Street, a white man in a uniform stepped in front of the gig and called, "Hold it right there." It was the

Watch. He approached the reverend's side. "May I see your passes?" Marshall reached into his pocket and pulled out a piece of paper. He unfolded it and handed it to the man. "Pull your gig over to the post so I can read this." The city was illuminated by oil-fueled lampposts, which were located at public water pumps, the wharves, the Exchange, and the guardhouse. The light provided a dull, eerie beauty to Savannah, as it made the trees and their shaggy clumps of hanging moss glow. But the lamps barely provided enough light to see the streets, no less to read.

The watchman squinted at the pass. He handed it back without saying a word. The watchman said to Andrew. "You, too."

Andrew felt his insides freeze. He didn't have a pass. He looked at the reverend. The elder negro turned to the watchman. "Sir, we were on our way home when we saw Moko hurt herself. We tried to take her to the infirmary, but she escaped into the woods south of Jones Street. We searched for her but stopped when it turned dark. We were just on our way home. We had no intention of being out past the bell."

The watchman asked, "Did you hear the bell?"

Marshall replied, "No, sir. We must have been in the woods."

The watchman looked at Andrew. "Do you have a pass?"

Andrew's voice wavered. "No, sir."

"Who is your master and what is your name?"

"Master James McBain of Heritage Plantation, sir. My name is Andrew."

The watchman's eyebrows rose. "McBain? What are you doing in Savannah?"

Andrew realized his hands were moist. "I'm a bricklayer at Christ Church. Master McBain rents a house here on Hull Street by Orleans Square. I live there."

The watchman rested a foot on the gig. "Is Mr. McBain or any other white person at the house now?"

"No, sir, I don't believe so. Master McBain and Grandfather McBain are at the Heritage tonight. They're due in town tomorrow morning." Andrew knew his answers were not satisfying the watchman.

The man studied Andrew. The negro spoke well and was owned by a respected family. And he was with Reverend Marshall. But with no white person at the McBain house, it was too much of a risk to let him go. The boy could get into negro trouble, like stealing, fighting, or drinking. "Andrew, step down and come with me."

Marshall pleaded, "Officer, please leave him in my care until tomorrow. Andrew's no problem to anyone."

The watchman's expression did not change. "You know the law as well as I do, Reverend. Let's go, Andrew."

Andrew stepped down from the wagon, landed on shaky legs, and followed the man. Marshall watched them walk across Chippewa Square, in the glow of the Savannah night. He bowed his head. He hadn't felt so sad in a long time. But there was nothing he could do. And it was too late to travel to the Heritage. He would have to wait till morning.

A guard opened the heavy gate in the fifteen-foot high brick wall that surrounded the grounds of the city jail on a trust lot by Lafayette Square. The jail itself was four stories, and even in darkness one could taste the soot and dirt. The watchman and Andrew climbed the stairs and walked through the front door into a smoke-filled room. They approached a man in a baggy gray uniform sitting behind a desk, a freshly rolled cigarette dangling from his lips.

The watchman asked, "Can I leave this boy here? The guardhouse is full."

"Yes," the guard replied. He asked the watchman about Andrew's arrest, recorded the answers in a log, and then called, "Bart!" Another guard came through a thick iron door that led to the rest of the floor. "Take this boy to central cell."

"Yes, sir," Bart replied. He mockingly saluted Andrew. "Follow me."

Andrew walked through the doorway and stumbled over his own fear. He was a criminal, thrown in jail for helping a demented woman. He had brought shame on himself and the entire plantation. He was even going to jail before Dante.

"In here." Bart opened an iron-rod cell door to a large room with eight men sitting on the floor and using the grimy walls as back rests. Six were white and two were black. In the city jail, the races were equal. "Enjoy your stay." Bart locked the door with a key as big as a hammer and left.

Andrew avoided looking at the other men. He sat on the floor a few feet away from them and leaned against the wall. He folded his arms and closed his eyes.

"Oonuh! Wuffuh oonuh yuh?"

Andrew opened one eye. One of the negro prisoners was pointing at him. The other men stared, awaiting an explanation. Andrew wiped his face with his hand. "I was on the street past the bell without a ticket."

A white man dressed in a business suit, sitting near Andrew, slurred, "You'd shink zey'd have more important shings to do zan arresht negrosh wishout pashes." The smell of alcohol made Andrew nauseous.

"Excuse me, young man. To whom do you belong?" asked another man, dressed like a circus barker in a black and white checked jacket, white shirt and red cravat.

Andrew rested his arms on his bent knees. "My name is Andrew, sir. I belong to the McBains of the Heritage Plantation."

The barker said, "Now, that's what I admire. A respectful negro who knows to call a white stranger 'Sir.' You've been raised with manners, I see." He glared at the negro who first spoke to Andrew. The negro snorted at the white man.

"Don't worry. Your master will be here tomorrow to get you out. You'll be all right," said another white man. He was middle-aged, properly dressed in a business suit, though it was crumpled. His hands were dirty and his face unshaven for days.

The barker explained to Andrew, "Jed is a debtor and will be here a lot longer than a day unless a miracle happens." Jed looked at the floor.

"A debtor? Master Jed, you're in jail because you're in debt?" Andrew asked, his rising voice laced with disbelief.

Jed raised his head and considered Andrew. "Yes. You sound surprised."

"Sir, I am. General Oglethorpe founded Georgia to protect the poor people in England from debtors' prisons," Andrew stated, as if that would free Jed.

The other prisoners stared at Andrew for a moment. First, the barker started to laugh, slapping his leg as he did. Then the others, including the negroes, started to laugh. Loudly. Even Jed smiled. Someone from down the hall yelled, "Quiet!" Andrew's body tensed. How could anyone laugh at the great Oglethorpe?

The drunk slurred, "We've come a long way . . . *burp* . . . haven't we?" and the men started laughing again.

Andrew, looking like he had been stung by a bee, turned to the others for some sympathy. He got none.

The other negro in the cell, an older man named Gus, whose master lodged him in jail while he went out of town, said, "Now oonuh gwine say Uggatop din' 'low slabery."

Andrew sat straight up. "He didn't! He had the trustees ban slavery in Georgia! It was illegal for fifteen years!"

The first negro, mimicking the drunk, said, "Us come uh long way, habunt us?"

The men laughed raucously again. Prisoners down the hall banged on their cell bars. Jed recognized Andrew's discomfort. "Andrew, please excuse us. We're all down on our luck for one reason or another, and some of us are debtors. I admire your knowledge of our history and your admiration for our state's founder. But when you're in jail, the lofty goals of our forefathers don't mean very much. I have a family and I don't know when I'll see them again. I don't know who'll provide for them. I'm powerless to do anything about it." Jed's voice started to break.

"I'm sorry, Master Jed," replied Andrew, feeling worse than before.

There was silence in the room. As if they had just acted out a scene in a play, the men returned to the positions they'd been in when Andrew had entered the cell. No one spoke for the rest of the night. They eventually lay down on their straw mats and slept.

Loud cries woke Andrew early the next morning. He saw Jed and Gus lying on their mats with their eyes open. Then he recognized the crack of the whip before each scream. Andrew whispered, "What is it, Master Jed?"

Jed whispered back, "Most likely a negro getting whipped."

After hearing more cries, Andrew asked, "What could he have done?"

"I don't know. It could be for a crime. Or maybe his owner brought him here to be whipped. For a small fee, of course. Don't worry. He can't get more than thirty-nine lashes in a day. It's the law."

Andrew wrapped his arms around his body, frightened and repulsed. Finally, the whipping stopped. He looked at the other men. Only Jed and Gus had their eyes open, as best as Andrew could see. He wondered how anyone could sleep through that.

Andrew heard the opening of the main door to the cell area. Two jailers walked by his cell, supporting a moaning negro whose feet dragged along the hallway floor.

He heard a cell door open at the other end of the hall and then he heard it lock. Andrew looked at Gus, who was staring back at him.

Gus said softly, "Us come uh long way, habunt us?"

"Andrew McBain," the guard called as he opened the door. "Follow me."

Andrew nodded to his mates and left the cell without saying goodbye, thinking he'd be returning. He was led to the entry room and saw Mr. McBain talking to a gentleman and banging his fist on the desk. McBain saw Andrew and hurried to him. "Good Lord! Are you all right?"

"Yes, sir." Andrew rasped, too embarrassed to look Mr. McBain in the eye.

McBain said, "Good. Let's get out of here." He turned to the man and said, "Good day, Marshal."

The morning sunlight momentarily blinded Andrew and he raised a hand to shield his eyes. He made his way to the carriage and saw Hercules on the driver's bench. Andrew gave a single wave. Hercules shook his head and waved back.

After Andrew settled in the cab, McBain said, "Reverend Marshall was waiting at the house this morning when I arrived. He told me all about your evening. Do you want to go home?"

"No, sir. I want to go to work. The walls are almost done. I want to be there through the entire job. Please don't tell Master Scudder about this."

McBain called to Hercules to drive to Christ Church. On the way over, McBain stared out the window and breathed like a tormented bull. As the carriage pulled up to the church, Andrew spotted Moko sitting on a bench in Johnson Square with a kerchief wrapped around her lower leg, and talking to people only she could see.

*   *   *

"How could the watchman do that?" Mrs. Couper asked loudly. "Just after the bell, heading home? With Reverend Marshall, no less? Just for his share of the fine?"

"It's very sad," said Fanny. "Hopefully this will not discourage your Andrew from his architectural career." Butler again stiffened in his seat at his wife's comment.

McBain answered, "I'm certain it won't."

A servant announced, "Fresh oshtuhs, plum' and joocey, see boo play!"

Sarah McBain looked up and smiled. "Why, thank you, Dante. You speak French so well!"

Dante beamed as he placed the platter of oysters on the table.

Dante's life had taken a curious turn. After Daymon's death, Dante's mother, Handy, became even meaner, probably because she had only one male, Dante, left to torment. Her beatings of her son increased, which angered many of the other Heritage servants.

Like most of the blacks, Handy believed in spirits, root doctors, fixers, and conjures. About a year after Daymon had been killed, Handy started accusing another servant, Betsy, of putting a spell on her husband, causing him to run away and get shot.

Betsy told Handy she was crazy, that a fixer had got hold of her mind. Over time, the animosity between the two festered. One night, sitting around the communal fire, Handy started mumbling to herself. She started to slap Dante on the head. A few servants, including Betsy, told her to stop. Handy leaped across the fire at Betsy. They fought like mad hogs until there was a scream. Handy fell into the fire with a knife sticking in her chest.

Master McBain reported the death to the marshal and investigated it himself. No one saw anyone stick a knife in Handy. And no one admitted to it.

Dante, parentless at fifteen, moved in with Andrew and Hercules. Neither were able to cure his laziness or thievery, but Dante didn't dare steal from his two roommates.

A few years later, Jinny, who had always felt sorry for Dante, asked Mrs. McBain to allow the boy, then seventeen, to assist her, Ruby, and Lilly in the kitchen with menial jobs. Dante couldn't do anything well, and he annoyed the other workers at the clay pits. Sarah agreed.

One day, Dante was helping Jinny in the kitchen when she had to go to the dairy house. She asked Dante to stir the pot of stew and not take anything. While she was gone, Dante looked about for something to steal. He first decided to taste the stew. It was good, he thought, but it needed something to enhance the flavor. He looked around the kitchen, saw some rosemary and red peppers, chopped them up, and added them to the pot. After ten minutes he tasted the food again. "Dat mo' bedduh," he thought.

Jinny returned and sampled the stew. It was tastier. She saw the remains of the pepper on the chopping block and looked at Dante.

"Ah add 'mary an' peppuhs, fuh tas'e." Jinny was speechless. Dante explained, "Ah alltime cook fuh ma."

The McBains told Jinny the supper was delicious. She explained to the missus what had happened. The McBains thought she was joking.

Dante had found something he enjoyed, could do well, and that was a benefit to the McBains. With Lilly moving to the house in Savannah, Dante was assigned to work for Jinny. Of course, details had to be resolved. Initially, he could not be left alone in the kitchen, and he was subject to regular body searches by Jinny, Ruby, and Plesant.

A year later, Dante and Jinny accompanied Mr. and Mrs. McBain to Hopeton Plantation to work for François, the Coupers' chef, reputably the best in all Georgia. It was common to bring servants on trips in the South, but not one's own cook. With François's reputation, McBain thought it might be beneficial for Jinny and Dante to work in his kitchen and wrote to Couper. Couper agreed only after François grudgingly consented. McBain warned Dante to be on his best behavior and told Jinny and Plesant, who also made the trip, not to let Dante out of their sight.

"Mussy boocoo, Muhdam McBain," Dante said, trying to sound like the French-speaking mulatto chef. The diners roared at Dante's affectations.

As the people sampled the oysters, Mr. Couper explained the problems he had in the cottonseed-oil business, and why he finally had to sell it at a loss, in 1836. The McBains listened intently, surprised Couper had actually failed at a project.

After the diners finished the first course, Mr. Couper nodded to Willie. The servants cleared the table and retrieved more dishes and silverware from the sideboard. Everyone was distracted when they heard Françoise shouting, "Out, out!" all the way from the kitchen, an outbuilding near the big house. McBain stood, thinking he needed to save Dante from François.

The Coupers laughed. Mr. Couper tried to calm McBain. "Please relax, James. It's just François clearing the kitchen. No one is allowed to watch while he readies the turkey, not even Mrs. Couper. It's a secret he learned from his father, Sans Foix, who was my father's chef."

Mrs. Couper added, "You'll see in just a little while." Fowl was normally served as part of the first course. But not when François prepared turkey. It was its own course, and the feature of the evening.

Fanny Butler said, "I can't begin to imagine. Can you, Pierce darling?"

Pierce Butler shrugged and wondered why he had brought his wife on this trip.

Eleven-year-old Hamilton Couper entered the dining room to say goodnight to his parents and guests. The boy told everyone he wanted to race rowboats when he grew up. At his father's instigation, Hamilton performed his best hog calls, and went to bed.

As soon as young Hamilton left, the people heard loud voices and a door slamming. They looked to the dining room entrance. François walked in first, dressed in a white shirt, white trousers, and a white chef's hat. One of Mr. Couper's butlers followed, holding a large silver tray with a silver dome. François's assistant cook came next, carrying another covered silver platter. Then, in single file, marched two of Mr. Couper's house servants, Jinny, and Dante. They stood in a line and turned as one to face the dinner guests, just as François had instructed them. The chef stepped forward and bowed slightly from the waist. In his French accent, he spoke to each person, "Madam et Monsieur But lair, Madam et Monsieur McBain, Madam et Monsieur Coo pair, it is an hon air to serve you." He bowed again, straightened, and waved a hand in the air.

Impala, the butler, stepped to the dining table, holding the domed platter waist high. François lifted the cover. A large plume of steam billowed, momentarily engulfing Impala. The steam cleared, revealing a large, plump, golden turkey. François stepped towards each guest with Impala following. They viewed the bird and smelled the gamey aroma. Pierce Butler's stomach growled like an angry dog. He put a hand on his belly and hoped no one heard it.

Impala then placed the tray on a small serving table. François stepped to the table and, with a flourish, produced a large carving knife and fork. He stood over the turkey and gently stuck the fork in it. Clear juices flowed out. François sliced through the entire bird in one smooth stroke, the meat floating to the plate. The guests stared at the platter. McBain said, "A boneless turkey?"

Mrs. Couper announced, "That's François's great secret. He can de-bone the entire turkey and put it back together in its original state. One merely has to slice without a care about the bones. You could pick it up in your hands and eat it whole, with the proper appetite. And a lack of manners."

"How in the world does he do it?" replied Mrs. McBain. François put down the knife and placed his right index finger to his lips.

François then served white and dark meat on each plate, while two of Mr. Couper's house servants followed with potatoes, onions, and peas. James Hamilton Couper raised his wine glass and toasted to a good weekend of racing. Then the diners tasted the turkey. The meat was moist, flavorful, and so delicate it practically dissolved in one's mouth without chewing. McBain and Butler groaned in appreciation. Sarah McBain said, "This is so delicious. I've never tasted turkey like it." Mrs. Couper put her knife and fork down, and applauded politely. The others joined her. François bowed. The other servants followed his lead, including Jinny and Dante.

François said, "Merci," turned on a penny, and walked out. The kitchen staff followed, in single file, an epicurean parade, while the servers went to their positions in the dining room.

François had one job—to make supper at the Coupers' house the most sought-after invitation in coastal Georgia. He succeeded, and was rewarded with whatever he requested in the kitchen. He had total control over his domain.

Cooks were among the most valued servants. Big planters had two or three. But cooks' lives were far from easy. Their work included gathering wood for the fire, grinding corn for the cornbread and hominy, going to the hen house for eggs, the smokehouse for meats, the dairy house for milk and butter, the ice house, the garden for fresh vegetables, to other servants for chickens or freshly caught fish, and then preparing a multi-course meal. Afterwards, the cook had to clean dishes, pots, and pans, and prepare for the next meal. There was rarely a break, unless the cook was François.

Jinny was an excellent cook, but she had no desire to be like François. Dante did. He was in awe of the mulatto. That entire weekend, he observed his cooking style, mannerisms, and speech. Several times François had to tell Dante to "Stand away!" which Dante did, only to return. If the McBains had stayed one more day, François might have de-boned Dante.

The three couples ate hungrily and conversation was temporarily suspended. After they had finished, they all sat back, exhausted. As the dishes were cleared, a servant placed champagne glasses in front of each guest and Willie poured. Mr. Couper talked about the races scheduled for the weekend. He said the Dubignons of Jekyl Island had a strong boat, but he and Mr. Spaulding were the men to beat.

Before they knew it, the servants had brought the next course, which consisted of bread pudding, cherry pies, and six tall glasses of syllabub. At first, the women demurred. But the men made such a fuss over the thick, creamy syllabub which evaporated in their mouths, leaving the smooth taste of the sweet sherry with which it had been flavored, that the women ate theirs too.

The servants quietly cleared the table for the dessert course. Fanny Butler spoke. "Mr. McBain, please forgive me asking, but your negro who is so interested in architecture. What are your plans for him?" Pierce Butler's jaw muscles bunched up.

McBain sat back and patted his mouth with his napkin. "Let him work in Savannah for builders like Mr. Scudder and develop his talents."

Fanny Butler looked at the table in thought, carefully choosing her words. "But even so, he could never advance beyond the status of a common workman, could he?"

Pierce interrupted, "Frances, Andrew is Mr. McBain's to deal with. Please let him be."

During the evening McBain had sensed Mr. Butler's tension each time Mrs. Butler spoke. Couper had told McBain of Fanny's feelings on slavery and the problems it had caused in the Butlers' marriage, but McBain thought Fanny was merely being inquisitive. McBain had no problem explaining his handling of Andrew, or his views on slavery. "That's all right, Mr. Butler. I don't mind discussing this if it's on Mrs. Butler's mind."

Fanny said to Pierce, "Darling, I'm simply interested in the possibilities for a talented negro in this . . . this unfortunate society." Fanny tried, but had difficulty refraining from voicing her opinion.

Carolyn Couper took a deep breath and glanced at Sarah.

Pierce stood and said to his wife, "Would you please keep those comments to yourself!" He threw his napkin on the table and marched from the room. Mr. Couper, of whom Fanny was very fond, gave a hand signal to Willie for the servants to leave the room. Willie closed the pocket doors behind him.

Fanny had watched her husband leave. She appeared as if she would follow after him, but settled back into her chair instead and said, "I apologize, Mr. McBain, for that choice of words. I am not trying to bait you. I'm just trying to understand. You were saying?"

McBain pondered how to proceed with the conversation. He certainly did not want to start a confrontation between the Butlers. He looked at Mr. Couper, who gave him a slight nod. "I will do everything in my power to help Andrew. It may not be easy, but I have some influence."

"But Mr. McBain, you must see the problems with the institution of slavery if men like Andrew cannot be free to develop under it."

McBain arched his eyebrows. "Mrs. Butler, you are aware how the institution came to the colonies, I trust?"

Fanny nodded, "I am, sir. But the English recognized their mistake and corrected it."

McBain sipped his wine. "They took their time in doing so. If memory serves me, while slavery was banned in England in the 1770s, the slave trade was allowed until 1807, just about the time America outlawed it. And England didn't ban slavery in its colonies in the West Indies until 1833. Even then, the English had to resort to the guise of African apprenticeship to circumvent the ban. That's just a few years ago. You see, the English founded the American colonies, introduced slavery here, and made a fortune trading the Africans. The English are the major purchasers of the products grown by slave labor, and now, a few years after they end it, they condemn us for maintaining the institution. It may take us some time, but we will resolve it as well."

"I hope so, Mr. McBain." Fanny decided it was best to drop the subject. "And I appreciate your willingness to discuss this. Not everyone is so considerate."

They were interrupted by the loud opening of the pocket doors. Pierce strode into the room with a platter of fruit and cheese. He placed it on the table, turned to his wife, folded his arms, glared, and said through clenched teeth, "Darling, the dessert course is served. This conversation is over. Is it not?"

Fanny Butler looked at the McBains and Coupers and said, "Of course, Darling. I'm sorry." She smiled at Mr. Couper. "This is a wonderful dinner, sir. I'm so grateful you included us."

Pierce took his seat, forced a smile, and consumed his glass of wine. Mr. Couper called the servants back into the room.

The conversation returned to the rowboat races and the amount of money rumored to be wagered on the competition. After the dessert course, servants set down finger glasses. When everyone had cleansed, the Coupers led their guests, Madeira in hand, to the gallery at the back of the house overlooking the expansive garden, lawn, and some of the plantation outbuildings. The men leaned against a white fluted Corinthian column, while the women sat in large green plank-bottomed chairs.

Three negro men walked onto the torch-lit lawn, one holding a fiddle, one a clarinet, and the other bagpipes, and started to play.

*   *   *

Not long after the McBains' visit to Hopeton, Dante, Hercules, and Andrew walked across Franklin Square on a Sunday morning. Andrew had finally arranged to go to church and had invited Dante and Hercules to join him. They hopped up the three steps to the front door of the creaky structure and walked in. They were submerged in a wave of song.

The entire congregation was on its feet, swaying from side to side, clapping their hands, and singing from their souls. The building vibrated and seemed as if it would explode if the doors and windows were not opened to release the energy. A man standing at the front, on a raised platform, sang a line, and the audience repeated it. On the right side of the stage, a choir of about twenty-five black men and women sang and led the worshippers. And to the left Reverend Marshall looked approvingly at his flock.

Hercules led them to a bench in the last row. The three men immediately joined in, swaying, stomping their feet, and clapping their hands. Andrew felt something good wash over him.

CHAPTER 12

The Tour Guide

1841

"Yes, sir?" Andrew asked as he stepped into Mr. McBain's study in town. Andrew had finished his work on Christ Church and was working on another job for Mr. Scudder.

McBain sat back in his chair. "Andrew. Please come in. I need to ask a favor of you. Some customers are arriving from New York by ship this evening. I'm scheduled to meet with them tomorrow morning, but I won't be able to see them until the afternoon. Would you mind showing them Savannah until I'm free? Grandfather McBain usually does that, but he's not feeling up to it."

Andrew turned an ear towards his owner. "Show . . . show people Savannah, sir?"

McBain clasped his hands behind his head. "Yes. Show them the sights, tell them stories of the town. They're in the building business. They'll be interested in our architecture."

"But Master McBain, I've never given a tour."

"Andrew, you know as much about Savannah history and architecture as anybody. Take the carriage with Hercules and pick up the men at the Pulaski Hotel. I'll give you a letter of introduction to hand to them."

The next morning, Andrew and Hercules were standing on the sidewalk on Bryan Street in front of the hotel, both dressed smartly in black pants and white shirts, waiting for the doorman to fetch Messrs. Gilles and Patterson. Two men emerged, with the negro doorman behind them. Hercules and Andrew approached the men and Andrew said, "Good morning, gentlemen."

The New Yorkers, startled by the two black strangers, hurried back into the hotel. The doorman followed them and explained. The visitors re-emerged and Andrew handed McBain's letter of introduction to Mr. Gilles, the taller of the two. After reading the letter, Gilles said to Patterson, "Let's see Savannah." Andrew and Hercules introduced themselves and ushered the guests into the open-top carriage.

Hercules drove to the Bay and Andrew escorted the men across the Strand to the edge of the bluff. As soon as Andrew explained Oglethorpe's vision for Georgia and his initial voyage to America, the men began to relax. By the time Andrew showed them Johnson Square and explained Oglethorpe's ward plan, and how Nathanael Greene saved the South during the Revolutionary War the men started to enjoy themselves.

Hercules proceeded to Oglethorpe Square in front of George Welshman Owens's residence. Andrew gave the men a minute to study the five-bay, two-story-over-a-ground-floor, stucco house. Gilles murmured, "Beautiful."

Andrew stepped from the carriage onto the square and the visitors followed. "I think this is the most innovative design in Savannah. It was William Jay's first house here. Have you heard of him?"

Patterson replied apologetically, "No, I'm sorry we haven't."

Andrew pointed at the structure. "Master Jay designed this house while in England when he was only twenty-four years old for Master Richard Richardson, who knew Jay through family connections. Jay sent the plans here and building began. He came to Savannah the next year to supervise the remainder of the construction. When the house was completed in 1819, it stood amongst predominately wooden Colonial, Georgian, and Federal houses."

The men continued their examination. Gilles asked, "What style would you call it?"

"Master McBain refers to it as the Adam style, named after architect Robert Adam. The Federal style in America evolved from it."

Mr. Gilles took a few steps to view the south side of the house and returned to Andrew. "I've heard of Adam. A Scotsman, I believe. Supposed to be a genius."

Andrew explained, "He certainly was. Master McBain said Adam was influenced by his research at Diocletian's Palace in Split, a visit to Rome, and the discovery of the lost cities of Pompeii and Heraculaneum. This encouraged him to break away from the strict rules of eighteenth-century English Palladianism, the source of the Georgian style of architecture in America. He did this by introducing movement to his designs using new forms and contrasts. His ideas came to America in pattern books, and through the interpretations of American builders became the Federal style. Exteriors have elliptical or semi-circular windows over the front doors. But the main difference between Federal and Georgian is in the interiors. The ornamentation, such as ceiling medallions, is more intricate. Mantel designs are more elaborate. Stairways are curved and spiraled, and balusters are thinner. Walls of rooms are rounded."

Patterson asked, "Did Mr. Jay work for Robert Adam?"

"No, sir. He was a few years before Master Jay's time. Jay learned from Adam's disciples in England, and brought the pure form of the Adam style directly here. Master McBain says we're fortunate to have had him. He doesn't know of any other city in America that has such fine examples of Adam architecture." Andrew pointed as he spoke. "Look at Master Owens's house. Here he especially uses the curve; in the elliptical, dual front stairways, in the curved alcove housing the front door, in the curved fascia of the portico, in the round-top window over the portico, and in the recessed arches over the windows. The front elevation is still symmetrical and proportional, as a classical style must be, but it has a novel expression."

Patterson squinted, "Now that you say that, it's apparent."

Andrew added, "I once saw the inside of this house with Master McBain. Master Jay used decorative forms in plaster, bright colors, and varying room shapes. He was especially ingenious in the staircase design and bringing light into the house. He even put a cistern on the roof to catch rainwater to provide an internal water source."

Andrew turned to the Northerners, who were no longer looking at the house but at him. Andrew felt uneasy and rubbed the back of his neck. "Would you like to see a few other Jay houses? The Telfair and Scarbrough houses are more classical than this. The Bulloch and Habersham houses are also masterpieces. At least I think so."

The guests climbed into the carriage. Patterson said, "Whatever you say, Andrew."

Andrew knocked on the open door of McBain's study. It had been two days since Andrew conducted his tour. "Sir, you called for me?"

McBain closed his ledger. "Yes, Andrew. My meetings with Gilles and Patterson went very well. We may be doing business together. They were quite impressed with you. I wanted to thank you for a job well done. You put them in a positive frame of mind." Of course, McBain purposely chose Andrew to show the New Yorkers another side of the negro in the South. He knew Andrew would leave them speechless.

Andrew's chest swelled. "Thank you, sir. I enjoyed doing it."

"You did so well, I want you to do me another favor. The men are leaving for Augusta tomorrow. Why don't you and Hercules pick them up at the hotel before work and drive them to the ship? I think they'd enjoy seeing you again."

The next morning, after Andrew and Hercules had carried the guests' baggage to the ship and started back to the carriage on River Street, Gilles asked Andrew to stay behind for a minute. "Andrew, I have a question to ask you. I'd like you to keep this between just you, Mr. Patterson, and me."

Andrew hesitated. He had no idea why Gilles would be asking him a confidential question. But he couldn't refuse a request from a guest of Master McBain. "Yes, sir?"

Gilles stepped closer. "Andrew, we don't have much time, so I'll get to the point. Mr. Patterson and I have a thriving company in New York. We sell building materials and are in construction. We always have a need for good workers. Would you be interested in coming north and working for us?"

Andrew was so startled by the proposition that he flinched. "I apologize, sir, but I don't understand. What do you mean?"

Gilles anticipated Andrew's confusion. "I'm offering that we buy you from Mr. McBain and take you to New York. We'd arrange a convenient way for you to repay us. You'd work in our company, use your skills, and make a good wage. And you'd be a free man." Gilles tapped his walking stick on the ground, hammering in the last point.

Andrew nervously looked for Hercules, but he was on the coach talking to another driver. "Sir, I'm part of Master McBain's family. He'd never sell me."

Gilles grunted a short laugh. The contempt was not lost on Andrew. "We know he's fond of you, Andrew, but you're a slave, a piece of property. Surely you know that. And all property has its price. Slaves are bought and sold everyday in the South. We may have to pay a premium, but believe me, we'd be able to acquire you. It will all be handled very properly, with Mr. McBain's consent. You'll come to New York and be free to work, marry, raise a family, educate your children, save money, repay us, and build your own house one day."

Andrew was angry that Gilles would comment on his relationship with Master McBain when he knew nothing about it. But in truth he knew he was a piece of property. Could Gilles be right? "I . . . I don't know what to say, sir. I've never thought about leaving here. The McBains have been so good to me."

Patterson asked, "How old are you, Andrew?"

"Twenty-one, sir."

Gilles said, "You're a young man, Andrew. You have so much to live for in freedom. We wish we had more time to become acquainted, but we don't. So we have to be blunt. You have no rights here. You can't vote or do anything on your own without the permission of your owner. If Mr. McBain wants the best for you, he'll let you go."

Andrew slid his hands into his rear trouser pockets and looked at the ship on which the men were traveling. All he could think to ask was, "Can I vote in New York?"

Gilles leaned even closer, till their arms were touching. "Well, if you own enough property. But one day you will be able to, freely. Much sooner than here. Andrew, in New York your dreams can come true. They never will in Georgia."

"Master Gilles, I . . ."

"Please, Andrew, call me Mr. Gilles. I'm not your master."

"Yes, sir, Mr. Gilles. I'm told that the negro is treated much better in the South. In the North the black man is still denied most rights, opportunities, and education."

"That's what Southerners claim, Andrew. No disrespect to Mr. McBain. It's true that the negro does not have all the freedom that a white man does in the North, but the negroes are free. Those rights will come. Runaway slaves arrive in New York every day. They don't have a penny to their name, and most haven't eaten for days. Yet they risk everything to escape bondage. Mr. Patterson and I try to help them."

Andrew's mouth felt as dry as hot sand. Gilles pressed ahead. "Andrew, I've never met a finer gentleman than Mr. McBain. I assume he treats you as well as you say. But what would happen if he sells you, for whatever reason? He sells the plantation.

He goes bankrupt. He retires. Heaven forbid, he dies. Your next owner may not be like Mr. McBain. You'd have no say in the matter."

"One day, Master Joseph will own me. He's my closest friend."

Gilles held Andrew's shoulder and shook it gently. "Andrew, can you hear yourself? 'One day, Master Joseph will *own* me!' Does that sound right?"

The ship's whistle blew. Patterson said, "Andrew, you think about it and we'll talk again when we return from Augusta. Please don't mention this to anybody." They shook hands and the men walked to the ship.

Andrew returned to the carriage and climbed onto the bench next to Hercules, who asked, "You done?"

Andrew nodded without meeting Hercules's eye. Hercules started the horses. For the next ten minutes, Andrew dusted his boots, hitched up his pants, studied the stitching on his shirt, and cleaned his fingernails. Hercules finally broke the silence when they reached the Augusta road. "You talked to those men a long time."

"I did?" Andrew removed his hat and examined it. A few minutes later, he said, "They offered to purchase me from Master McBain and take me to New York to work in their company."

Hercules stopped the horses in the middle of the road. "They what?"

Andrew finally faced Hercules. "Just what I said."

"Can they do that?"

"They seem to think so." Another coach pulled up behind them. Hercules pulled to the side of the road and let it pass. Andrew watched the negro driver wave without turning around. Then Andrew related the conversation with the New Yorkers to Hercules. "I didn't know what to say. They're certain Master McBain would sell me for the right price. Do you believe that, Hercules? Would he?"

"Whew!" Hercules exhaled and started the horses again. He didn't think so, but he had to be honest. "The McBains are the finest white people I know. You like a son to them. But if a buckra gives massa a thousand dollars more than you worth, I don't know."

Andrew shivered, though he wasn't cold. "What should I do?"

Hercules cracked the whip and the horses picked up the pace. "I don't know. But if a nigguh has the chance to be free, without getting killed, I think he's got to take it."

Andrew hunched over. "Joseph's my best friend. You're my brother. The McBains and the Heritage negroes are my family. How do I just leave? What would I do when I get to New York? Where would I live? By myself?"

Hercules pulled hard on the reins and the horses stopped. He swiveled in his seat to face Andrew. "You afraid?"

Andrew shook his head. "I don't know."

Hercules reasoned for Andrew. "I think most slaves run away 'cause they tired of getting whipped, not 'cause they so hungry to be free. Look at Anthony and his friends. And you ain't never been whipped."

"Do you think we'd be treated better in the North?"

Hercules shrugged. "Maybe. Don't plan on it. But you be free."

Hercules was about to crack the whip, but Andrew reached out and grabbed his wrist. "Hercules, you could come with me! I could ask the men from New York. We'd go together. We could live together. You're the best horse trainer around. You could get work easily."

Hercules twisted his hand free. "I got the same questions you do, Andrew. Besides, they asked you, not me. Don't ruin it for yourself. You got big dreams. You can become a great builder one day. Maybe these men can really help."

Hercules started the horses. They did not speak the rest of the way to the Heritage. Andrew spent the next days working at the kilns and the nights thinking of his choices. He didn't want to leave the McBains, whom he loved. But he was being offered a unique chance and never wanted to regret having passed it up. He decided to ask Master McBain to sell him.

"Master McBain?" The Scotsman looked up from his desk in the Heritage study. "Sir, may I have a word with you?"

"Certainly, Andrew. Have a seat." McBain pointed to a chair with his pen. Andrew eased his body down. He felt a bead of sweat running down his back.

Mr. McBain went back to writing numbers in a book. "Yes, Andrew?"

Andrew crossed one leg over the other. "Sir, I need to talk to you."

McBain sensed Andrew's seriousness and put his pen down. "Sorry, Andrew. I was just catching up on some record keeping. What is it?"

The big moment had arrived. But Andrew couldn't find the courage. He stared blankly at McBain's ledger.

McBain leaned forward in his chair. "Andrew, what did you want to discuss?"

Andrew shifted in the chair and switched legs. Before he had entered the study, he was confident he would be able to make his request.

McBain drummed his fingers on the desk, but Andrew remained speechless. Just as Andrew was about to speak, McBain said, "Well, while you think about it, I have something to tell you. I was going to wait until next week, but now that you're here. I've purchased a trust lot on Pulaski Square. I'm going to build a house in Savannah. I'm spending more time there, as will Joseph when he returns from college. Grandfather McBain prefers being there. It doesn't make sense to rent. The timing depends on the availability of the architect. I plan on using Mr. Charles Cluskey. He's designed Greek Revival buildings in Augusta and Milledgeville. He just built Mr. Sorrell's house on Madison Square." McBain sat back and let Andrew ponder that.

Andrew mumbled, "Is that the new, pumpkin-colored house?"

"Yes, Andrew, and I want you to work with Cluskey through every step of the process, from the design to the construction. Of course, your involvement will be to listen and learn. But few men your age have the opportunity to work on a project with such a fine architect. I must warn you, though, he may not appreciate your presence at first. Architects can be very protective of their work. Still, this will be an enormous educational experience for you."

Andrew moved his lips, but words did not come out. Finally, he managed, "Sir, this is more than I ever imagined."

McBain stood and sat on the edge of the desk next to Andrew. "Andrew, I told you I'll do what I can to help you develop your talent for architecture. This is a significant step." McBain leaned forward and patted Andrew on the shoulder. "Now, what did you want to ask me?"

Andrew cleared his throat. "Uh . . . sir, do you think I could ever become an architect? Here, in Georgia?"

McBain returned to his seat, picked up a piece of quartz he used as a paperweight, and started to turn it over in his hand. "I won't mislead you, Andrew. It won't be easy. But there are possibilities. For now, you need to learn as much as you can. I know what it means to you, and I'll do everything to assist you." McBain paused, but Andrew didn't speak. "Is there anything else?"

Andrew wanted to ask Mr. McBain if he considered him more than a piece of property and if he would ever sell him. Instead, he shook his head. "No, sir."

McBain replaced the paperweight. "Good. It might be a while before Cluskey is available, so be patient. I'll let you know when we begin. In the meantime, Mr. Scudder has plenty of work for you."

Andrew left the office more confused than before he had entered it.

"You going to New York?" Hercules asked Andrew that night as they sat in front of their cabin.

Andrew picked up a pine cone and tossed it across the avenue of oaks. "No. I'm staying."

Hercules bent forward so he could look into Andrew's eyes. "Did you ask massa to sell you?"

Andrew tossed another cone. "No. I went to him, but I didn't have the courage. I prayed for strength but before I could ask, he told me he's going to build a house in Savannah. He wants me to work with the architect. I couldn't ask him after that. I don't know what it is, Hercules. Whether I'm afraid to be on my own, or I just can't bear to leave the McBains, or I just don't believe the North will be any better than the South. I kept thinking about Master Gilles's and Patterson's reaction when they first saw us at the hotel, until they knew we were sent by Master McBain. They ran like we were ghosts."

Hercules nodded at the memory.

"Hercules, I want to be an architect, to design buildings that will make people stop and look. Buildings that will make Savannah proud, that will make black folk proud. I can do it, I know I can!"

Hercules considered asking Andrew if he wanted that more than freedom. But he knew that if there were any black man who could prove the negro was the white man's equal, it was Andrew. Maybe it was God's plan to have Andrew stay in the South. "When do the buckra return from Augusta?"

"Today. We have to go to Savannah tomorrow to take them to their ship. I'll tell them of my decision then. Please, Hercules. Don't mention this to a soul."

Hercules said, "You know you don't have to worry about that."

They sat quietly, watching the other negroes. Standing by the side of their cabin, invisible in the darkness, was Dante.

Mr. Gilles kept shaking his head upon learning of Andrew's decision. "Andrew, let's say that you attend all these meetings, help build the house, and become the best architect in the entire South. What can you do with it? Will anybody engage you?"

Andrew, unable to look Gilles in the eye, looked towards the harbor. "Master McBain said he would help me."

Gilles waited for some passengers to walk by. "Andrew, Mr. McBain is very reputable, but what can he do? There are no negro architects in the South."

"Sir, are there any in the North?"

Gilles voice rose in frustration. "I don't know of any, Andrew, but at least you'll have a chance in the North, especially with your skills. And you would be working for me. I have plenty of contacts. If architectural work came up, I would involve you."

"I appreciate that, Mr. Gilles, but I just couldn't ask Master McBain. It was too difficult for me. I guess I'll have to chase my dream in Savannah."

Gilles dug into his pocket and handed Andrew a piece of paper. "Andrew, I realize we're asking you to make a big decision. If you change your mind, write to me. Here's my address in New York. Good luck to you." They shook hands and the New Yorker headed to the ship.

Andrew left the wharf and made his way to Bull Street on his way to work by Chippewa Square. He was relieved. He had made his choice and felt it was the right one. Somehow, he would become Georgia's first black architect.

As he passed through Wright Square, he saw a large crowd by the courthouse steps on the east side of Bull Street. A white man stood at the entranceway with a group of negroes off to the side. It was the first Tuesday of the month, the day of the sheriff's sale to liquidate the property of debtors.

Andrew stopped in the square and watched. The sheriff called a black man and woman to his side. A little black girl about four years of age held the woman's hand. Some white men moved closer to get a better look at the negroes. The white men asked the sheriff questions, which Andrew could not hear. The sheriff responded and at one point turned to the negro man, who nodded his head. He pulled his shirt over his head and stood there, bare-chested. One of the men in the crowd walked up to the negro man and spoke to him. The slave opened his mouth and stuck out his tongue. The white man then pulled the man's lips up and down and walked back to the crowd. The bidding lasted about three minutes. When it ended, the black woman covered her face with her hand. The little girl wrapped her arms around the woman's leg.

Andrew left with an empty feeling in his stomach. As he walked, he fingered the business card in his pocket.

CHAPTER 13

The Professor of Mesmerization

1842-1843

The McBains were catching up with Joseph in the parlor of the Orleans Square house when Amy, who was standing by the floor-to-ceiling, red-curtained window, spotted Andrew on the street. "He's here!"

Joseph sprung from his chair and said to his father, "Let's call him up now."

Amy said, "Give him a chance to relax. He just got home from work. You can see him after supper. I told the servants not to tell him you're home."

Joseph had arrived from college earlier that day in November 1842. It had taken him a little extra time to graduate, but that was behind him now. He was ready to work for his father, selling Heritage products and taking care of administration from their new Savannah office on the corner of the Bay and Abercorn. He was happy to be back with his family and excited about seeing Andrew again. He had never forgotten about their dream of building villas together.

While Joseph was still in Athens, Amy had graduated from the Macon Female College in May of 1842. She returned to the Heritage and asked her parents for permission to go to Europe with two friends from school. The parents of one of the girls, Elizabeth Harden of Augusta, were making the tour and invited their daughter and a few friends. The McBains agreed.

The girls spent the next four months traveling in foreign countries, mostly England, France, and Italy, experiencing ancient cities, strange cultures, new foods, and fascinating people, all under the watchful eyes of Mr. and Mrs. Harden. They returned in October, and Amy's friends spent a week at the Heritage. Elizabeth talked about all the beautiful churches, buildings, and gardens they toured. Charlene, from Milledgeville, talked about all the handsome men they met. Amy talked about all the poverty and needy people she saw.

After her friends left, Amy helped her mother manage the house servants. In two weeks she pronounced it boring and informed her parents she was going to visit Charlene in Milledgeville.

James and Sarah had hoped Amy's independent behavior would have quelled after attending college and touring Europe. But, apparently, it hadn't. She had grown into a beautiful woman. She was more willowy than ever at five feet three inches. Instead of a dimple on her chin, as her mother had, she had them on her cheeks, and they grew to quarter-moons when she smiled. Her parents thought she could pick any bachelor she wanted. They were still hopeful she would soon want to settle down, and they let her go to Milledgeville.

Amy returned just a few days before Joseph had arrived from Athens. James, Sarah, and Grandfather couldn't have been happier that the two were home again.

After the McBains finished supper, Chloe knocked on Andrew's door and told him that Mrs. McBain wanted to see him in the family parlor. Andrew closed the *Four Books of Architecture*, placed it under his bed, washed his face, hands, and armpits in the bowl of water in his room, put on a clean shirt and pants, and went upstairs.

Andrew froze when he saw Joseph. The two embraced. Joseph stepped back, and said, "So this is what the best mason in all of Georgia looks like!"

They talked for hours. Andrew told of his building experiences. Then Amy talked about her trip to Europe and all the poor people in the world. When Amy paused, Andrew said, "It's been so long, Master Joseph. Tell me about your last year at college."

Amy interrupted, with a smirk on her face. "Yes, Joseph. Please tell us all about it. I heard you were involved in a medical experiment."

"Amy!" Sarah said abruptly, as her daughter had broken a solemn promise never to mention her knowledge of it.

Joseph glared at his mother. "How did she hear about that, Mother?

Before Sarah could respond, Amy said, "I haven't seen my dear brother in a year. I need to catch up, especially now that he's famous."

James McBain leaned back in his chair, ready for the assault. He knew Joseph couldn't escape. His survival depended on Amy's sense of mercy. "If you must know, Amy," Joseph replied, "I did take part in a medical experiment."

Amy scanned the people in the room before shouting, "Hah! Some experiment! Walking through the streets of Athens in your underdrawers with two other boys at night! Singing *Hark the Herald Angels Sing* with a snowman ornament tied to the front of your garment!"

"That's a dern lie!" Joseph cried, feeling his face on fire. "It was a reindeer!"

Amy wiped away imaginary tears. Andrew buried his face in his hands to hide his laughter. Joseph heard the giggles of the house servants from a nearby room.

Amy said, "Please continue. Don't leave Andrew in suspense."

Joseph turned to Andrew. "I've wanted to tell you, Andrew, but it's not something one can describe in a letter. Last year I had made the acquaintance of a very fine doctor who had a practice not far from the college. One night last January, we were having a party when Dr. Long appeared. It just so happened he was experimenting with gasses he thought might negate pain during an operation. As fate would have it, he had some ingredients with him. In the name of research, he asked for volunteers to inhale the gas."

Amy interrupted, "That's a big fib. You were having an ether party!"

"I'll ignore that, Amy." Joseph continued, sticking to the lie he had already sworn to his parents. "I wanted to do my part for the medical advancement of the community, so I volunteered, not knowing all the risks."

Amy added, "Yes, but knowing a local girl was kissing your ear!"

"Amy!" Sarah McBain shrieked, putting her hands over her face.

Joseph adjusted his cravat. "Thank you, Mother. Sister must have left her senses in a ghetto in Europe. Anyway, Andrew, the gas had a most amazing effect. I started finding humor in anything and everything. All who had sampled the gas did. One lad was so consumed with joy he toppled over a table and sprained his ankle. Though he had trouble standing, he felt no pain. The experiment worked!" Joseph noticed Andrew looking at him suspiciously.

In fact, at that moment, Andrew was recalling that Mrs. McBain had to make an emergency trip to Athens the previous January, taking only her personal servant Milsey. Now he knew why.

Joseph continued before Andrew could start asking questions. "Someone said we should try to prove the theory further, but without subjecting ourselves to bodily injury. Since it was January, one fellow wondered how long we could be exposed to the elements. Andrew, I don't remember ever taking my clothes off, or walking the streets, or tying anything to the front of my underdrawers, but apparently I was able to go outside half naked without feeling the effects of the frigid winter night."

Grandfather laughed and said, "It happens to me all the time."

Joseph concluded his side of the story. "You should know, Andrew, that a few months after I participated in that experiment, Dr. Long applied the ether treatment during an operation without the patient feeling any pain. Surgery can now be painless. Do you realize what that means to the advancement of society? In no small way, I contributed. And I'm not asking for thanks."

"Oh, good Lord," Amy gasped, holding her stomach.

As it turned out, Mrs. McBain had to make a case to the college president why Joseph should not be expelled. She succeeded, with Joseph having to take extra classes.

Joseph began working for his father the next day. Savannah had recovered from the financial crisis of 1837. Mr. Gordon's railroad was operating over 80 percent of the line and the building business was strong. Joseph settled into a comfortable weekday routine—work during the day, a drink afterwards at a tavern with friends and business associates, and then home for supper prepared by Dante. Mr. McBain had moved Dante from the Heritage to Savannah to work with Lilly in anticipation of Joseph's and Amy's return. While much had changed during his absence, nothing surprised Joseph more than how well Dante cooked. Though no one trusted Dante alone in a room, they all thought his meals were superb.

After supper, Andrew and Joseph often strolled around town, where they evaluated designs of houses and planned their first project. One evening they walked on Congress Street and passed D. H. Stewart's Ten Pin Alley. Joseph had bowled at college and offered to teach Andrew. They walked in and Joseph obtained a lane from the clerk. A minute later a man stockier and a few years older than Joseph approached them. "Excuse me. My name is Daniel Stewart. I own this place. What do you think you're doing?"

Joseph replied, "Good evening, Mr. Stewart. I'm Joseph McBain. We'd like to bowl."

The man pointed to Andrew. "Not with him you're not."

Despite the fact that Savannah was a slave society, there was a fair amount of social and commercial mixing of the races. Its extent was defined by custom, not law. Whites and blacks shopped side by side in the City Market. Coloreds lived in every ward of the city. Servants, of course, often lived with their masters, but free persons of color owned or rented dwellings, even in the predominately white wards. Blacks and whites interacted daily at work. Negroes were often allowed to attend amusements such as minstrel, magician, and acrobat shows in the various halls in the city, usually at half price, and sat in negro galleries. For the circus, they were often permitted to sit alongside whites. White children of slave-owning families were likely raised in part by a servant and grew up with black playmates. Some white churches allowed bi-racial services, though most had negro entrances and galleries. Whites, should they attend a black church, sat with the negroes.

Of course, a black would not enter a white establishment as a patron in the white wards, alone or with other negroes.

However, there were gray areas, especially when a servant was in the company of his or her owner. In such instances, it was understood that the black was in the care of the white person and would behave appropriately. There were times when the owner or manager of the business might have to exercise discretion in deciding whether to allow admittance to the negro.

If a white woman entered a shop with her children in the care of a servant, a common occurrence, the negro would not be denied entry. After all, she was performing her job. Of course, she would have to behave and show deference to the whites, but her presence would be accepted.

Less commonly, if a white man and his negro servant frequented a white establishment for amusement, as when Joseph and Andrew went to the bowling alley, the owner could decide if the negro was welcome. The owner might not object because he would trust the white to exercise proper control. Also, he might not want to turn away business. However, if another white customer objected, the owner had to decide whether to ask the negro to leave. Mr. Stewart chose to have a clear policy—no black patrons.

Joseph replied, "Mr. Stewart, he's under my care. He will not misbehave."

Stewart said, "That may be, but his presence makes my other customers uncomfortable. I don't want that, nor do I want it known that I welcome negroes."

Joseph looked at the other bowlers, who were involved in their fun and not paying any attention to Andrew. "I'm sorry to have caused you any inconvenience, sir. We'll leave now."

Joseph and Andrew headed for the exit. Though Joseph was angry, he knew it was Stewart's decision to make. Stewart called out, "Thank you for understanding, Mr. McBain."

Andrew was also angry. He was a grown man, skilled in the building trade, and earning a living. He was properly dressed and respectful. And he was with a member of one of the most respected families in town. But Andrew knew his place.

These were the obstacles that Andrew and Joseph, as friends, had to negotiate living in Savannah. After they left Stewart's Ten Pin, they walked to a run-down, dimly lighted billiards parlor in Oglethorpe Ward, where Andrew won fifty cents from his master.

Sometimes, Grandfather joined Joseph and Andrew on their evening strolls. He had plenty of energy at eighty-four years and especially enjoyed going to the amusements. He still loved the circus. He had always taken Amy and Joseph when they were younger. When they lost interest, he brought the female Heritage servants and their children. The negroes shrieked and hollered at the animals, magicians, and acrobats. But no one made more noise than Grandfather.

Grandfather rarely missed a minstrel show or an equestrian troupe. But there was one entertainment he liked more than any other. "Joseph, guess who's at Armory Hall?" the old man asked the moment Joseph walked into the house from work one spring evening in 1843.

"Who?" Joseph replied, as he plopped into a chair in the family parlor.

Grandfather stood over Joseph, waving the newspaper with the advertisement. "The Professor of Mesmerization, Doctor Swift! Do you want to go?"

Joseph laughed at his grandfather's enthusiasm. "Sure. What about Andrew?"

"Of course. Ask Hercules and Dante. They'll love the professor."

The professor invited people in the audience to the stage to face their past lives. He put his subjects in a trance and they said the most amazing things. Patrons argued endlessly whether the professor and his volunteers were legitimate. Joseph and Andrew were skeptical. Grandfather was a firm believer in Dr. Swift.

After supper, Grandfather, Joseph, Andrew, Dante, and Hercules walked along deserted, dimly lit Barnard Street to Armory Hall. Once they turned onto Broughton, they saw a huge crowd blocking the sidewalk in front of the theatre. Whites and blacks talked animatedly, reliving past performances by the professor.

Grandfather, surprisingly mobile, pushed through the crowd, purchased the tickets, and moved directly into the hall to get seats close to the stage so he could see better. The first tier, usually the negro gallery, was closed, so coloreds had to sit in a side section in the orchestra. Grandfather settled with Joseph in the first row by the aisle next to the negro section. Andrew, Dante, and Hercules sat in the same row across the aisle. Grandfather winked at Joseph. "This is going to be a good night. I can feel it."

Joseph scanned the interior, which held well over a thousand people when full. A floor-to-ceiling, deep-red curtain shielded the stage. About thirty lamps lined the side and back walls. A giant rosette decorated the ceiling.

A drum roll sent everyone scurrying to their seats. The patrons chatted with their neighbors, speculating what the professor had in store for them. Ushers in white shirts and red vests ran down the side aisles and dimmed the wall lamps. The drum roll stopped and the people hushed. The curtain opened from the center, revealing a barren stage save one wooden chair, which faced the audience. A slim, tall man in a white suit and black shirt, with straight, silver hair to his shoulders, and a tanned face strode onto stage and the crowd applauded. He stopped at the center of the stage and faced the audience. He held out his arms at his waist and slowly raised them, the crowd's cheers intensifying with their ascent. Once his arms were straight over his head, the professor smiled and yelled, "Hey-lowwwww Savannahhhhhhhh!"

The crowd jumped to their feet and roared. Dr. Swift kept his arms stretched over his head, draining every drop of adulation from the people. He lowered his arms and the cheers gradually subsided, until there was silence again and everyone sat. These folks were believers.

Swift put his hands on his hips. "We think we know ourselves! We think we're our own masters. But oh, no, no, no, no! We know so very little. Why, you wonder? Because we have all lived before. Many, many, many lives. Good lives, adventurous lives, dangerous lives, mysterious lives, even naughty lives. Yes, you and you and you!" He jabbed the air with his finger, targeting everyone in the theatre. "Who of you knows anything of your prior lives, I ask? Who of you even has the courage to face them?"

The professor bent slightly forward and narrowed his eyes, peering at the audience. "I need a person of courage. I need someone unafraid to face the past."

A buzz of whispers like a swarm of bees covered the theatre, but there were no volunteers. Joseph looked across the aisle and saw Dante, Andrew, and Hercules sink into their seats, trying to hide from the professor's sight. Then, a male voice from the back of the auditorium yelled, "Here, professor!"

The people turned to locate the man. He was standing, pulling on the arm of a seated woman, trying to coax her up. Dr. Swift said loudly, "Don't be shy, madam. This will be the single most important moment of your current life!"

The man called out to the professor, "Excuse me, Doctor. My wife is shy. She claims she's had a life before this one. She wants to know more about it."

Finally, the woman stood, lifted her chin, throwing her curly blond ringlets back, and walked proudly to the stage. The audience applauded politely, hopefully. She was pretty and Joseph guessed her to be not much older than himself. She wore a simple green print day dress. As she walked by, Grandfather started to chuckle. Joseph, Andrew, and Hercules squirmed in their chairs, while Dante clapped with the crowd.

The cheers grew louder as she mounted the stage. "Please sit here, madam." Dr. Swift pointed to the chair in the middle of the stage.

She sat stiffly, her back as flat as a board, and fidgeted with the sleeves of her dress. She looked up at the professor. "Madam, you say you're aware of a prior life?"

"It's the strangest feeling, doctor." The professor interrupted and asked her to speak louder. She obeyed. "I sometimes do or say something, and it seems I've lived that moment before. My husband makes fun of me when I tell him about it."

Dr. Swift scowled at the grinning husband, who was standing at the foot of the steps to the stage, between the McBains and their servants. The doctor reprimanded, "This is not funny!" The husband shrugged. He thought it was. Swift returned to his work. "You're a brave woman."

"Thank you, Doctor."

"Now, I want you to relax your body and your mind." Joseph saw her close her eyes. Her chest rose as she took a deep breath.

She asked, "This won't hurt, will it?"

"No, no," the professor replied. She eased into the chair and extended her legs. "Now, please take three deep breaths. I want you to count to yourself, very slowly, and just look at the emerald stone on the chain around my neck. Onnnnne, twooooo, threeeeee." As the professor counted, he moved his palm up and down just inches in front of her delicate nose.

Her head and shoulders slumped. Her eyes became slits. She was mesmerized! The crowd started to buzz again. Dr. Swift raised his hand and quiet returned. Joseph looked across the aisle at Andrew, who made wide-eyes in disbelief.

"Are you comfortable, madam?"

"Yes," she replied very softly. People from the back of the theatre moved forward, packing the aisles, to hear the woman. Ushers forced the patrons to return to their seats.

Dr. Swift knelt by her side, facing the audience as well. He spoke loudly, so everyone could hear him. "I want you to travel back, way back, as far back as you can."

"Back, back," she whispered. The professor repeated her answers for the crowd to hear.

He waited a moment for the woman to complete her journey. "Are you there, madam?"

Her eyelids fluttered like butterflies. She answered in a language no one understood.

"Madam, I know you're in a land far away, but can you speak in English?"

She moved her mouth, but no sounds came out. She finally managed to say, "Yes."

"Where are you, madam?"

"In Egypt. In Cairo."

The husband's mocking smile grew wider. He faced the audience and pointed a finger at his head. Someone was crazy.

"What are you doing in Cairo, madam?"

The eyelids fluttered. "I'm in a room. There's a chair and a mattress."

"Are you alone?"

"There's someone else. A man."

The professor stood and repeated her answer with an emphasis on 'A man.' The audience went, "Oooouuuuuu."

The doctor squatted again. "Who is the man? Do you know him?"

"No. He's a stranger. He's very big. He's bald. I'm afraid of him." The woman's husband flexed his muscles to mock his wife. Someone hissed at him.

"A very big stranger? Is anybody else in the room, madam?"

"No. Just us."

"Just you two? What is the man doing?"

"He's giving me money." The husband turned and looked at his wife.

"Why is he giving you money, madam?" She tried to speak but could not. She seemed to be choking. "Please, take your time. You're safe. No one can hurt you."

"I'm naked. He's about to come into my bed."

When the professor repeated the woman's answer, a gasp erupted from the crowd. Joseph heard a woman shriek in the back of the theatre. Hercules and Andrew sat straight up. Dante leaned forward, his chin almost resting on the stage. The husband stuck his head toward the stage, as if he hadn't heard that response correctly.

Dr. Swift, who knew he had a performance brewing that would draw in crowds for months, helped the husband. "Repeat that, madam. Why is he giving you money?"

"I give men pleasure for money. I'm very poor. It is the only way I can feed my family." Dr. Swift repeated the answer to the stunned audience.

The people talked loudly, their voices collectively sounding like a waterfall. The professor stood and held up his hands for silence. The husband looked around the hall and saw people laughing at him. He called out to the professor, "Stop right now!" and climbed the stairs to the stage. The audience whistled and jeered at the humiliated man, his grin long gone.

The professor moved towards the husband to keep him off the stage. "I'm sorry, sir, but . . ." Then the crowd exploded. The doctor turned and saw the mesmerized woman had stepped out of her dress and was undoing her corset. It was off in a blink.

She stood only in her underdrawers, exposing a chest that mesmerized every man in the theatre, including the professor. She sat on her chair, raised her arms over her head, and leaned back, ready to receive her customer. Dr. Swift's jaw dropped.

The husband charged his wife and wrapped his jacket around her. The woman started screaming and banging her fists on her husband's chest. Joseph wondered if she thought she was being attacked by her customer. The husband tried to pull his hysterical spouse from the stage. Dr. Swift tried to pull the man away. The husband took a swing at the doctor and missed, and the two men toppled to the floor in a heap. As they wrestled, the woman started to remove her underdrawers. The theatre was in an uproar. The professor screamed at the husband, "I must remove her from her trance! She thinks she's in Egypt! Let me bring her back!"

The husband sat in shock on the stage as the professor got the half-naked woman back on her chair. But she wrapped her arms around his neck and legs around his waist and kissed his face. The professor staggered back as he lost his balance, but the woman stayed attached like an appendage. Many in the audience rushed the stage, knocking away the ushers like bowling pins. Joseph, Andrew, Hercules, Dante, and Grandfather found themselves on their feet, hollering with the crowd. Dr. Swift finally pried the woman from his body and got her on the chair. He yelled to her over the din of the crowd and waved his hand in front of her face. She stared straight ahead for a moment. Her cheeks twitched and her eyes opened wide. She looked at her exposed body and started to shake. Her mouth formed the words, "What's happening?" Her husband jumped up and helped her pull on her dress. He picked up the other articles of clothing and they ran off the stage, down the aisle, and from the theatre.

The audience was on its feet, and made so much noise Dante covered his ears with his hands. Dr. Swift stood at the edge of the stage and screamed, "Ladies and gentlemen, please return to your seats and remain calm!" to no avail. He thought he saw plaster falling from the ceiling and began to worry. He then felt someone pulling on the leg of his trousers. He looked down and saw an old, white-haired man wearing thick spectacles with some bills in his hand. The professor kneeled and listened. He looked around, nodded his head, and took the money.

"Ladies and gentlemen! We need order! Please return to your seats!" It took ten minutes for the crowd to settle down.

"Thank you, kind people. That was a very, very, very brave woman indeed! She confronted her past, and will be better off for it. I think she deserves some applause."

The crowd cheered wildly. Gentlemen's hats flew through the air. The professor slowly raised his arms upward and the applause intensified. The theatre began to vibrate. He dropped them back to his sides, and the noise stopped. He was back in control.

"Now, we need another person with bravery and courage. Someone who is not afraid to look deeply within, and learn secrets that will improve the self." He leveled his right arm and moved it back and forth, pointing to the audience. All the patrons, except Grandfather, were terrified the finger might select them, and curled into their seats. The finger traveled over the theatre two more times. Then it stopped. The professor yelled, "You! Yes, you. The handsome negro in the first row!"

Dante looked like he had seen the Holy Ghost. The audience stood, trying to catch a glimpse of the next victim. Dante shook his head violently, as if to ward away an invading wasp. "No, suh! Ain' gwine tuh mus muh eyes! No, suh!"

Doctor Swift started to raise his arms slowly and the crowd began to stomp their feet. Grandfather stepped across the aisle and nudged Dante on his shoulder. Amidst the cheers, Dante said to Grandfather, "No suh, Massa Grumpuh, uh yent gwine dey!"

Grandfather shouted in Dante's ear, "I'll give you five dollars."

"Fibe dolluh?" Dante scratched his chin. This was an amount that had to be considered. He stood, hitched up his pants, and asked, "Wuffuh he wan' me?"

Grandfather shrugged, "Luck, I guess."

Dante mounted the stairs to the applause of the crowd. The negroes in the audience stood and waved. Dante, realizing he was the center of attention, turned to the crowd and waved back.

The professor knew the first act would be hard to beat. He was already planning on spreading the word to other towns about the Egyptian prostitute. Nothing but packed houses loomed. Still, he needed to complete the show.

"Please sit here, young man. And what is your name?"

Dante grinned at the crowd. "Dante, massa."

"This is very brave of you, Dante."

"Brabe yent mattuh. Massa Grumpuh gib me fibe dolluh fuh dis." The crowd roared.

"Now Dante, sit back on this chair and relax." Dante paid no mind to him, fully enjoying the attention he was receiving.

"Dante!" Dr. Swift said sharply. "Sit back and relax!"

Dante did as he was told. The professor looked into his eyes and said, "Dante, pretend you're trying to sleep. I want you to count, one, two, three, and look at the stone in my necklace as you do. Onnnnne, twoooooo, threeeee." The professor moved his right hand slowly in front of Dante's eyes. Dante easily fell under his spell.

The professor knelt next to Dante, facing the crowd. "Dante, I see you like being on stage. Do you like to sing?"

Dante nodded. "Yassuh. Ah sing alltime."

"You do? What's your favorite song?"

Dante didn't hesitate. "Yankee Doodle Dandy."

Andrew looked at Hercules and mouthed, "Yankee Doodle Dandy?" Hercules turned his palms upward. He was as confounded as Andrew.

Dr. Swift stood and stepped aside. "Please stand and sing it for us, Dante."

Dante rose, faced the audience, and started to sing the song in perfect English. As he sang, he marched in place swinging his arms to and fro. Soon, the audience sang along. When he finished, the crowd stood and cheered. Dante bowed repeatedly until the professor forcefully guided him back to the chair. The professor was pleased. The negro was an entertainer.

The professor kneeled. "Dante, do you take things that don't belong to you?" Joseph, Andrew, and Hercules stared at Grandfather. He didn't notice. He was fixed on the stage.

Dante's smile dissolved. "Yassuh."

The patrons emitted a low, "Oooouuuu."

The professor eyed the crowd as he asked, "Why do you do that, Dante?"

"Us fambly. Dey t'ings belong tuh all ub us." The whites in the crowd laughed.

Grandfather winked at Joseph. Joseph thought, this is one wily old man.

Swift wagged his finger. "Things in your house belong to you. Things in other peoples' houses belong to them. Do you understand, Dante?"

"Yassuh."

"Do you like dogs, Dante?"

"No suh! Uh yent luk no dawg!"

"If you ever take anything again that doesn't belong to you, you'll turn into a dog and bark the rest of your life. Now, I need to be certain you understand, Dante. Get on your hands and knees and bark like a dog." Dante kneeled slowly and started barking, his lips pulled back, and his teeth bared. Many in the crowd started barking and howling, too. The professor finally ordered, "Stop!" Dante crawled on his hands and knees to the chair. "Dante, did you like that?"

Dante shook his head. "No suh. Ah yent tek nuttin' ebuh agin."

The whites in the audience stood and cheered. The professor held his arms open wide, proud that he was able to please the folks with the negro.

Dante soon distracted him. "Massa Mus muh eyesuh, kin ah t'ief secrits?"

Swift looked at Dante. "What? Steal secrets? No, Dante. You can't steal anything. If you do, you'll bark like a dog forever."

Dante lowered his head. "Yassuh."

But Dr. Swift was a showman, not a moralist. His curiosity was aroused. This could be a rich moment. "Do you know any secrets, Dante?"

"One, massa."

Swift put his hands on his hips. "All right, Dante. I'll let you tell one secret, and that's all. Then you can't steal anything, or you bark like a dog the rest of your life. Now, what is the one secret, Dante?"

"Andrew gwine run'way nord wid two buckra."

The professor repeated, "Andrew's going to run away with two white men?" The remark, which no one understood, save Andrew and Hercules, sucked the life out of the crowd. Joseph and Grandfather looked at Andrew, who sank into his seat.

A disappointed professor brought Dante out of his trance. It was time to get the negro off the stage. He put an arm around Dante and raised his other, calling for the audience to show its appreciation for the negro. The crowd barked and howled.

It wasn't until Swift was in his dressing room that he realized his necklace was missing.

"I was never going to leave. Some men asked me if I wanted to go. I told them no," Andrew explained to Grandfather and Joseph as he paced back and forth in the study after the professor's performance. "I'm still here, Grampah."

It was a long, silent walk back to the house. Joseph was so upset that he had temporarily forgotten about the Egyptian prostitute's chest. Dante was oblivious to what he had done, but sensed something was amiss. Even hypnotized, he was trouble. But he had five dollars and a necklace for his efforts.

"Do you want to reveal who these gentlemen are, Andrew?" Grandfather asked, sitting in a chair.

Andrew stopped pacing. "No, Grampah. They asked me in confidence, and I refused them in confidence. I'd like to let it pass."

Of course, Grandfather knew who it must have been. "It's been a long evening. Let's get some sleep. You both have work tomorrow."

Andrew stepped to Grandfather, bent over, and kissed the old man on the top of his head. "I love you, Grampah. I wouldn't leave you." He then left the room.

As he reached the door, Grandfather called out, "Andrew?" Andrew stopped in the doorway. "I'm glad you stayed."

Andrew looked at Grandfather and Joseph and left.

After Joseph was certain they were alone, he whispered, "I can't believe that Andrew actually thought about leaving us."

Grandfather removed his spectacles and rubbed his eyes. "Don't be surprised, Joseph. Not for a second."

"Why? It's like a family member leaving. Like if Amy left."

"But he's not, Joseph. He's a slave. One we love and we think we treat like family, but he's still a slave. He's far too intelligent not to realize it. The chance to be free must have seemed mighty appealing. If you must know, I'm a little surprised he didn't take it."

The truth finally hit Joseph. One day Andrew would leave. He couldn't imagine life without his friend. "What can we do to make him want to stay? Can we give him his freedom?"

"I don't know, Joseph. Let me think about it. But let's keep tonight just between us. I'll speak to Hercules and Dante. There's no reason for your father to learn of this."

It was just a few days after the evening with the professor that the family was in Savannah together having supper. Grandfather retold some of the events of that evening, which kept Mr. and Mrs. McBain laughing throughout the meal. McBain had already heard about the mystery woman. It had been the talk of the town. In fact, the city marshal was rumored to be trying to arrest her for indecent exposure. Grandfather learned this from Dr. Swift, who had tracked him down the next day, looking for his necklace. But no one in town knew who the couple was, and no one had seen them after they ran from the theatre. Of course, this rekindled the speculation that the incident was planned. Grandfather wouldn't hear of it.

James, Sarah, and Amy could hardly believe the story about Dante being mesmerized, but they thought it was a great idea. Time would tell if he would stop stealing, though Sarah said it didn't seem to stop Dante from taking the professor's necklace, which Grandfather had found during a search of Dante's room.

Amy managed a smile or two during the conversation, but mostly toyed with her food. Over cranberry pie, her mother asked, "Dear, are you feeling all right?"

Amy folded her napkin neatly and placed it on the table. "I'm fine, Mother. I have an announcement to make. I might as well do it now."

Joseph groaned at Amy's sense of drama.

Amy kept her eyes fixed on her plate. "I have decided to do something useful with my life." Sarah slowly moved a hand to her glass of wine. "I'm moving to Milledgeville. I'm going to work at the new lunatic asylum."

All movement halted. James McBain's mouth remained half open, revealing a freshly bitten piece of pie. Sarah lifted her glass of wine and gulped. She said, calmly, "I'm sorry, dear. Where did you say you were working?"

Amy raised her voice. "I said I'm going to work as an attendant at the new state lunatic asylum in Milledgeville."

Sarah looked to William to refill her glass, and then asked, "Amy, is that what you want to do with your fine college education?"

Amy fiddled with a strand of her hair. "Yes, Mother. I want to help people."

James said, "There are plenty of people right here to help, dear. Even ones who will know you're helping them without trying to kill you for it."

"Father, you don't understand. These people have deep problems and no one to care. It's a big issue, otherwise the state wouldn't have put up so much money to build an asylum."

Amy was correct. There had never been a facility in Georgia for handling the mentally ill. Local officials had had to deal with the problem. The insane deemed to be harmless and who were not cared for by relatives were allowed to roam, and settle where they may. When their presence became objectionable, they were usually confined to poorhouses, workhouses, or jails. The violently insane were sent to jails where they were subject to the same treatment as other inmates. Finally, in the 1830s, the state legislature recognized it had to do something for the idiots, lunatics, and insane of Georgia. Grandfather claimed that covered 90 percent of the population. A facility was built, and the first patients were admitted in 1842.

Milledgeville, on the banks of the Oconee, was the state capitol. It had grown rapidly with the burgeoning cotton economy, but was primarily a government town. When the legislature was in session, from November to February, its population swelled. Being the seat of government, the town was the first choice for government-sponsored institutions. It was already home to the state penitentiary.

Sarah asked, "How did you hear about this, this opportunity, Amy?"

Amy sipped her water, knowing her mother would not like her answer. "From Charlene, when I visited her last month."

Sarah took a deep breath, recalling the fuss Charlene had made over European men. "Oh, yes, Charlene."

McBain asked, "Do you already have this so-called employment?"

"Yes. I was interviewed by Dr. Tomlinson Fort, one of the trustees of the asylum, and by Dr. David Cooper, the superintendent. I just received the offer in the mail. I start next month."

"And where do you intend to live?" asked Sarah.

Amy glanced at Joseph, seeking support from the interrogation by her parents. Joseph just stared, and Amy looked at her mother. "Dr. Cooper has a guest cottage on his grounds, which he'll rent to me. He'll also make his coachman available."

Sarah wasn't giving up. "Dear, you can get a good job here. Even one helping people, if that's so important to you. And there are so many more eligible young men in Savannah."

Amy's voice rose along with her frustration. "Mother, I'm not interested in finding eligible young men anywhere. I don't want to spend the rest of my life raising children and looking after a house and servants."

Her mother picked up her fan. "Dear, there's nothing wrong with running a plantation home. It's necessary, challenging, and rewarding."

Amy, realizing she had insulted her mother, walked around the table and hugged her from behind. "I'm sorry, Mother. I didn't mean to offend you. You raised us well and the Heritage is the best plantation in all of Georgia. But I want to do something different. I want to see the world beyond Savannah."

Her father tapped the table with his finger. "Ah, Amy, do I need to remind you that you were just in Europe? You've seen the world. And don't you think this is something you should have discussed with us first?"

Amy kept her hands on her mother's shoulders. "Father, I'm almost twenty-four years old. I'm a woman. I can make my own decisions. I'm going to work at the asylum."

McBain slapped the table. "No! I'm sorry Amy, but I absolutely will not allow it."

CHAPTER 14

Amy and the Lunatics

November 1843

"Train to Macon, Jawwwjuh! All aboarrrd!" the conductor shouted over the din of the locomotive. James, Sarah, Joseph, and Andrew were on their way to Milledgeville to visit Amy.

They had arrived at the depot on the west side of Savannah at 5:45 one morning in November 1843, just weeks after the line from Savannah to Macon had been completed, making the 191-mile railroad the longest in the world. The accomplishment had been greeted with celebrations in both towns. William Washington Gordon's dream had come true. Unfortunately, he didn't live to see it. The fevers that had killed so many of his workers took him as well in 1842. But he had left a legacy which would change the face of Savannah forever.

As Hercules tended to the luggage and Joseph's parents picked up the tickets, Joseph and Andrew inspected the train. The locomotive, inscribed "W. W. Gordon," was only about twelve feet long. The mass of iron and steel shivered as dark smoke, with the smell of burning wood on a crisp winter day, funneled up from the smokestack. The vibrating locomotive reminded Joseph of a snorting, black bull penned-up in its stall, ready to charge at the opening of the gate. A cowcatcher that looked like a shiny piece of fence was attached to the front. The engine sat upon two sets of wheels, a smaller set in the front and a larger set at the back. A small platform for the engineer to stand and control the levers was located on the end of the engine casing.

The tender car, a dull-yellow, roofless box that stored the wood fuel, was attached to the locomotive. The baggage car followed. It was a larger, enclosed wooden box with one door on each side. A workman on the ground handed luggage to another man inside the car.

As Joseph and Andrew walked by, they noticed people squished together on two benches in the back of the car. Baggage car class cost four dollars and fifty cents to Macon, while passenger car class was seven dollars. The savings were significant if one could stand the darkness and discomfort. Slaves usually had no choice.

Two apple-red passenger cars were next. Five flat, wooden-railed, empty freight cars brought up the rear. They had carried bales of cotton to Savannah and were returning to the interior for more of the precious cargo.

The whistle blew and Joseph saw his parents boarding the train. He and Andrew hurried to join them. Double-hung sash windows lined the long walls of the passenger cars. Twelve rows of unpadded bench seats with backrests occupied each side of the car, creating a center aisle. Mr. and Mrs. McBain sat on one side of the aisle, and Andrew and Joseph sat opposite them. A coal-burning stove sat in the center of the car. Fortunately, for those who valued their lungs, it was not fired-up that day. There was not a feature in the car built for comfort, but no one seemed to care.

The cars were full with mostly adult male passengers dressed in suits. The state legislature opened its annual session on the first Monday in November, and legislators, lobbyists, lawyers, and other interested persons were flocking to the capitol.

Just as the McBains settled in, the whistle blew again. It was precisely six a.m., departure time. Since there were no external lights on the engines, travel was scheduled in daylight as much as possible.

The locomotive did not charge out like an angry bull. Instead, it strained to get started, like a tired, old mule, and did so with a jerk, causing the McBains to bounce in their seats. The train inched ahead as the engineer generously blew the whistle, waking everyone on the west side of town. Joseph wondered if walking might be quicker. But after a few minutes, the train gained speed and soon roared along at twenty miles per hour, so much faster than any steamship or stagecoach. The McBains grabbed onto their seats, both exhilarated and nervous at the sensation of sliding over the ground so rapidly.

They passed through a stagnant, watery basin clogged with cypress trees, whose roots popped in and out of the water, looking like giant gray snakes. The train then entered a pine forest, the trees so tall Joseph had to press his face against the window to see their tops. Soon, the train chugged through vast brown fields of corn, whose plants had recently been harvested. The passengers chatted excitedly, pointing out sights to each other, even though everyone could plainly see them. Before they had a chance to settle down, the whistle blew and the passengers flew out of their seats. They were approaching Station Number 1.

Stations were located every ten miles and were identified by number. Driving into one of them required great skill, for all that connected the cars was a strong chain. If the engineer braked too quickly, all the cars bumped into each other one by one, from front to back, throwing passengers forward when they hit the car in front, then jerked backwards when hit by the car behind. The McBains yelped at their first railroad jostle. They sensed it would not be their last.

While the train took on fuel, the passengers got off to exercise their legs and look around, though there was not much to see. The stations were located in desolate, open areas, with a water pump, wood pile, and wooden platforms to load and unload freight.

As the McBains chatted by the train, a thin, bespectacled man in a suit approached Andrew. "Excuse me," he said in a northern accent, "But are you allowed in this car?"

Andrew looked at the car. Before he could respond, Mr. McBain stepped forward and said, "Yes, he is. Why do you ask?"

The man walked away. Joseph said, using the pejorative term southern whites used for northern whites, "I guess wooly-heads don't care to travel with negroes." Andrew thought of Messrs. Gilles and Patterson from New York, and how they retreated into the hotel upon first seeing Hercules and him.

The railroad did not specify where negroes had to sit. Custom prevailed. A master transporting his slaves would normally put them in the baggage car, and not just because it was cheaper. It was the proper thing to do. However, if a white family traveled with a servant who was tending to the children, the negro would ride with the family in the passenger car. This was also true in stagecoaches.

Andrew was properly dressed and behaved, and in the care of the McBains. The other passengers saw this and accepted him. If a passenger had complained to a railroad employee about his presence, the employee would have to settle the matter.

That day, a Northerner objected, and only to Mr. McBain. It would be a cold day in hell before James would yield to a wooly-head complaining about Andrew. Of course, the stranger confirmed to the McBains what Southerners already knew: that they treated and tolerated negroes much better than did Northerners.

Soon they were back on the train, continuing their journey. Station Number 3 had an inn within a few minutes walk and the McBains dined on a breakfast of eggs, bacon, and hoe cakes. Joseph brought a plate of food to Andrew, who ate outside the inn sitting on the ground beneath a tree. Traveling together and dining together were two different matters.

The folks heard the whistle and hurried back to the train. By eleven o'clock, the Georgia sun started to unleash its power. The passengers opened the windows to let in fresh air. Along with the air came the smoke from the smokestack. It had lost its intoxicating odor and had become obnoxious. Passengers fanned their faces with their hands, hats, or newspapers and coughed loudly. Joseph felt little stings like insect bites on his scalp and scratched his head. After a few minutes, the passengers agreed that being too warm was better than choking on the fumes and closed the windows.

As Joseph gazed at the sights, he noticed something shoot past his shoulder, followed by a noise of something hitting metal. He turned and saw the man behind him wiping his mouth with the back of his hand. He was chewing tobacco and using the stove as a target. While Joseph watched, the chewer let fly a long stream of brown liquid, propelled by a spurting noise. It flew like a small bird. It splattered against the non-functioning stove. Many men chewed tobacco, and the results had to go somewhere. The designers of the railroad cars hadn't thought of everything.

Sarah McBain said to the man, neatly dressed in a suit, "Sir, do you mind?"

"Pardon me, madam," he replied politely. He leaned across his bench mate, opened the lower sash of the window, and spat out the wad of tobacco, spraying the people on the seat in back of his. He then lighted a segar, the smoke from which, in a confined space, created a thick, permeating odor. Realizing that she could not win, Sarah worked her fan.

The McBains heard the whistle and clutched their seats. They were arriving at the next station. When Joseph got off the train, he noticed small black dots on his white shirt. He tried to swipe them away but they wouldn't move. When he picked at the material, he found they were little holes. The engine smoke that blew into the windows contained small burning embers. Joseph looked up and saw other passengers swatting futilely at their ruined garb.

And so the trip went. They rarely saw houses or towns from the train. Despite the noise, heat, tobacco juice, engine smoke, segar smoke, bumps, jostles, and ruined clothing, the passengers seemed thrilled by the experience. The 170-mile journey to Gordon took eleven hours. The train made fifteen stops before arriving at five in the afternoon. The McBains hired a coach to take them to a small inn a few miles outside of town.

As the inn had no rooms for negroes, Andrew was given a blanket and slept on a pile of hay in the coach house while father and son shared a bed with a lumpy mattress in an unheated room with two other men. Sarah shared a room with two women and a baby.

Early the next morning, they took the stagecoach to Milledgeville. The ride reminded the people of the improvement of train travel. The morning air was freezing, both outside and inside the coach. The lung-clogging stove on the train would have been welcomed.

The riders bounced in their seats like nervous frogs. There were three benches. The ones at each end of the cab had backrests. The bench in the middle, where Joseph and Andrew sat, did not. Three people fit comfortably on each bench, for a total of nine passengers. Some lines allowed a passenger to sit outside on the driver's bench, but that was not the case on the Hawkinsville stage. Anyone other than an experienced driver could easily fly off the coach from the slightest bump.

Fortunately, the day warmed and the ride became more pleasant. Andrew noticed a farm house of a style he had not seen before. Two small cabins were built next to each other, with a passageway in between, and were covered with one large, gabled roof. He pointed out the window, "Master McBain, which style is that house?"

McBain lowered his newspaper. "A 'dog-trot.' It's a common style of architecture in the South. It suits the needs of the area. There's no architect involved. When poor farmers settled in the South, they built simple log cabins. If they needed more room, they built another cabin to the side, leaving space in between for the dogs.

They eventually put one roof over the two cabins, turning the open space into a breezeway. It became, along with a dog run, a place for the family to sit and enjoy the breezes. Because of the original purpose, they're called dog-trots. Soon, the farmers built the houses in that design from the start. Many high-style houses are designed with a center-hall plan based on a central breezeway."

"The farmers were concerned about the winds, just like Vitruvius," Andrew replied. McBain laughed. The other men in the coach stared at the negro.

They arrived in Milledgeville in the afternoon. Amy was waiting for them. It was a joyous reunion. Joseph even hugged his sister. She accompanied them to their hotel, the Lafayette, where Joseph had his own room. The basement in the hotel had two servants' rooms, one for male and one for female, with bunk beds.

The family had supper in the hotel dining room while Andrew ate in a small servant's mess in the basement. Afterwards, they all went for a walk and chatted for hours. Amy, who lived near the asylum two miles away, stayed in the hotel for the night.

The next day, Sunday, was Amy's day off. The family attended the Presbyterian Church, while Andrew went to the Baptist Church service, which was inter-racial. They all met afterwards and strolled around town. They passed the "Anti Van Buren State Rights Hotel." Milledgeville was a political town, and its citizens wore their opinions on their sleeves.

They also saw the flat-roofed Gothic Revival state capitol building with its Gothic arches and crenellated parapet, and the Federal houses which dominated Milledgeville. At Joseph's prodding Andrew described the elements of each one. Amy and Sarah were especially impressed with Andrew's knowledge.

Later in the afternoon, the women returned to the hotel to rest while the men visited the new governor's mansion. Mr. McBain had arranged a tour through the Chatham County representative to the legislature. The building had been designed by Charles Cluskey, the architect McBain wanted for his new house in Savannah.

They stood on the sidewalk and admired the front elevation. The most prominent feature of the coral-colored, stucco-over-brick, two-story classical Greek design was the pediment, which covered the middle three bays of the seven-bay building, and the four colossal Ionic columns which supported it. Doric pilasters adorned the front corners of the house. Pedimented granite hood molds sat over the windows. A granite stairway led to the landing and the front door, which was bordered by a granite door surround.

Andrew gawked. "Master McBain, this is an impressive building."

"It certainly is." McBain was convinced that Cluskey was the architect for his house. "Follow me."

They strode to the front door. Before Mr. McBain knocked, it opened. A tall, thin, gray-haired negro dressed in a butler's suit bowed slightly and said, "Good afternoon, gentlemen."

The guests removed their hats. "Good afternoon. I'm Mr. McBain, from Savannah. Representative Flournoy arranged an appointment for us to see the mansion."

"Yes, sir. The governor is expecting you. Please come inside." The McBains stepped into a large entry hall and examined its high ceiling and walls, each of which had a door. The butler said, "Please wait here," and exited through the door on the right.

In moments, a stout, gray-haired man about Andrew's height walked into the entry hall. "Mr. McBain. It's a pleasure to meet you. I'm Governor McDonald. I've heard so much about you and your plantation from Mr. Flournoy."

As the butler gathered the McBains' hats, James said, "Governor, it's an honor to meet you. I hope we're not imposing."

"Nonsense, sir. I love showing the house. It's one of the few pleasant responsibilities of my employment."

McBain introduced Joseph and Andrew. The governor shook Joseph's hand. McDonald had been briefed by Flournoy about McBain and his gifted negro. "Andrew, I understand you're interested in architecture. What do you think so far?"

Andrew looked around the entry hall as he contemplated his reply. "Sir, from the outside, it's a beautiful Greek Revival structure, with classic Greek details. I've never noticed a building that had columns and pilasters with different capitals on the same level." McDonald rubbed his chin and wondered what Andrew was talking about.

McBain came to McDonald's aid. "Yes, Andrew. It's possible to place different capitals on the same building. However, if they are present on different stories, there is a required sequence. Doric always supports Ionic. Ionic always supports Corinthian. It cannot be violated, or Vitruvius will step out of his grave and give you a swat on the seat of your pants."

The others laughed. Andrew responded, "Yes sir, I believe Palladio wrote of that."

Governor McDonald clasped his hands together and said, "Well, you learn something new every day. Now let me show you the inside." He walked through the door opposite the front door. The McBains followed.

They entered an immense circular hall. Their eyes were drawn upwards to the most incredible architectural sight Joseph or Andrew had ever seen—a huge dome decorated with three rows of giant trapezoids, which diminished in size from bottom to top. The borders of the trapezoids were gold-gilded egg-and-dart design. At the very top of the dome was a glass window, which allowed light to flood into the hall. To Andrew it seemed like an eye, a living part of the mansion, to watch over everyone.

After giving the visitors a few moments to absorb the sight, the governor asked, "Well, what do you think?"

Andrew responded, "It's magnificent, sir. What is it called?"

The governor replied, "A rotunda."

Mr. McBain, his eyes fixed above, added, "A circular hall capped with a dome."

Andrew said, "Of course. Palladio has illustrations of rotundas, but I never imagined they'd look like this in real life. I didn't even notice the dome from the street, which makes it even more amazing to come upon inside."

McDonald smiled at the appreciation the McBains showed. He held his arm out, pointing to the next room on the tour, and the McBains marched towards it.

The excursion lasted an hour, with Andrew asking many questions. Afterwards, they thanked the governor for his time and left, in awe of the mansion and its rotunda. Andrew could not wait to meet Charles Cluskey.

The family dined at the hotel. Joseph thought Amy looked tired, a slight darkness under her eyes. She had said she wanted to help people, and she was getting the opportunity, twelve hours a day, six days a week. She helped feed, clothe, bathe, medicate, subdue, and counsel about one hundred patients. Though she rented a cottage on the grounds of Dr. Cooper's home, the asylum's supervisor, Amy often slept in one of the attendant's rooms at the asylum. Work was her life, but it seemed to be wearing her down.

Over supper she described three new patients. One was a widow who had just lost eight thousand dollars in a business venture and had lost touch with reality. Another was a young man who had gone insane by taking too many steam baths to cure congestive fever. The last was a male patient who thought he was God, but had made remarkable progress, and had plans after he recovered to stay at the asylum to help other patients.

Joseph noticed his mother chewing her food much slower than normal, and had to gulp to get it down. It was apparent she was worried for her daughter.

But Joseph's curiosity had piqued. "Amy, your work sounds fascinating. May we visit you at the asylum?"

Amy shook her head. "That's not possible, Joseph. People other than relatives, workers, and officials are not allowed in the building or near the patients. I can show you the building from the outside, but I can't take you onto the grounds."

As Joseph thought of a ploy to see the asylum, a voice interrupted them. "Mr. McBain, what are you doing in town?" a rotund, well-dressed man asked.

James McBain stood to greet his acquaintance. "Representative Cobb! I could say the same of you. Shouldn't you be in Washington?"

As the men shook hands, Cobb explained, "I'm in town for a few days to look after our plantation and to take care of some other business." Howell Cobb was only five years older than Joseph. He had also attended Franklin College and had become a lawyer. At just twenty-two years of age, Cobb became the state solicitor of the Western Circuit of Georgia and by 1843 he was serving in the House of Representatives as a moderate, Southern Democrat. James McBain was not deeply involved in politics, but he was a Democrat and a Unionist. He had met the young Cobb several times in Savannah and liked him. He knew Cobb's star was rising. McBain introduced his family to him.

Cobb then excused himself and returned with an attractive woman about Joseph's age. Eight years earlier, Cobb had married Mary Ann Lamar, daughter of Zachariah Lamar, a very wealthy Milledgeville planter who had died shortly before their wedding. Mary had inherited a fortune, including a sizable plantation, though it had been diminished by the Panic of 1837.

Cobb introduced his wife. James said, "Mrs. Cobb, I understand you're related to Gazaway Lamar. He's a friend and business acquaintance of mine."

She exclaimed, "You know cousin Gaz? How is he? I haven't written him in months."

"He's doing fine, as should be expected. Local businessmen are pleased he moved back to Savannah. We need men with his ingenuity and enterprise."

Mary Lamar Cobb stared at her husband, and mouthed, "McBain? McBain?" She looked back at Mr. McBain. "Were you the McBain on the *Pulaski*?"

"No ma'am. My son and his companion. And my father." McBain nodded at Joseph.

Mary Lamar Cobb stepped around the table and took Joseph's hand. "You're the fellow who saved dear Charlie's life! Oh, thank you! Charlie always speaks so fondly of you and a negro who pulled him from the sea."

"Andrew, my servant, really saved him. He's here with us. Tell me, how is Charlie? I haven't seen him since then."

Mary answered as she sat in a chair offered by Mr. McBain. "He's doing well. He started his own concern with his friend, William Sims. Do you know him?" Joseph shook his head. "Well, he's a darling. They're grocery and commission merchants. Charlie has a keen sense for business, just like his father."

Howell Cobb said, "Miss McBain, I hear you're doing admirable work at the asylum. I also hear every eligible bachelor in Baldwin County sends you flowers."

Joseph quickly interjected, "And she won't make it easy for a one of them." Amy's parents laughed loudest at the joke.

Amy sneered as if to say, "That wasn't funny, Joseph."

Cobb said, "Miss McBain, it just so happens that I've been invited to see the asylum facility tomorrow with some legislators. I might see you there."

"I heard we're having important guests. I look forward to seeing you."

Joseph jumped at his chance. "Mr. Cobb, would you be able to bring another visitor?" Joseph's parents and Amy glared at Joseph.

"Who would like to go? You, Joseph?" asked Mr. Cobb.

Joseph avoided his family's stares and said he would. McBain apologized. "Please excuse my son, Mr. Cobb. He's twenty-three, but he sometimes displays the manners of a boy."

Cobb waved a hand in the air. "Don't be foolish. Of course he can come. He should be able to see where his sister is working. Why don't you all come?"

Sarah said she did not care to see the place. Nor did Mary Cobb. It was finally settled. James and Joseph would join Representative Cobb, while Sarah and Mrs. Cobb would have tea. Andrew could explore the town on his own.

The next morning, McBain and Joseph joined the legislators, John Brown of Baldwin County, Charles Dubignon of Glynn County, Robert Flournoy of Chatham County, and Congressman Cobb. It took thirty minutes to traverse the two miles to Midway. As the carriage ascended a hill, Joseph saw two identical buildings perched at the top. The structures were rectangular, made of brick, with the long sides facing each other, about sixty feet apart, creating a common yard. They each had three stories atop a ground floor. The gabled roofs of wood shingles were slightly pitched and had three chimneys, each spewing a light gray, dreary smoke which seemed to coat the sky. A wooden fence surrounded the two buildings. Goose bumps popped up on Joseph's arms.

Dr. David Cooper greeted the guests at the gate. He wore a thin cotton cloak over a suit jacket. "Gentlemen, welcome to the Georgia State Lunatic Asylum. Thanks to your generosity and support we've been able to build the first lunatic asylum in Georgia, and the fifth in the entire South. Instead of lunatics, idiots, and epileptics living in the streets or causing harm and winding up in jails, we now have a facility where they can be treated for their problems and become productive citizens again. If they cannot be rehabilitated, they at least have a place where they can receive proper care. I will now show you the facility. All violent and dangerous patients are properly restrained, so you are not to fear anyone you see walking freely in the area. The more we treat them as normal people, they faster they'll recover."

Dr. Cooper walked to the East Building. The visitors followed. The stairwell was a covered wooden attachment to the side of the building and provided access to each floor. Dr. Cooper led them through the ground floor door. He said, "This is the basement floor, for male patients. The kitchen is located here and meals are distributed to the other floors using a dumbwaiter. At the far end of the floor is a stove, which heats the building with pipes. These first two rooms on the left and right are for the male staff. Because we have so few workers, we need to have them here from six o'clock in the morning until nighttime, and we provide sleeping quarters. We have two male servants in one room and a watchman and a male attendant in another room. The steward and I live nearby.

"Since we are a young facility and have more rooms than patients, we place one person per room. However, we are prepared to have several non-violent patients together. Of course, the violent ones are confined to their own quarters."

Cooper walked slowly down the aisle, holding a small notebook, looking into the windows of iron bars in the solid oak doors of each room, and saying good morning to the men inside. The visitors followed the doctor, almost on tip toes, as if one misstep would unleash an outbreak of unrestrained lunacy. At the far end of the floor, outside the kitchen, Dr. Cooper spoke in a low voice. The six men huddled around him. "As you may know, only the courts can commit lunatics, idiots, and epileptics to our facility. Normally, a relative applies to the court to commit an individual. A trial is held and one of the seven jurors must be a doctor. If the person is considered so deranged as to be a threat to the community, he is sent here, and is treated at the expense of the state. The man in that middle cell on the right was a farmer, committed by his family. The court agreed. There was no question he was a lunatic. He was violent, had hallucinations, and screamed and cursed all day and night. When he first arrived, we had to chain him to the floor of his room and put him in a straight jacket. We puked him several times a day, which weakened him and allowed us to perform further treatments. We gave him nauseants for more puking, cathartics for his bowels, digitalis to stimulate his heart, and anodyne to relieve pain. In addition, we gave him cold baths twice a day. This treatment had a positive effect. He soon stopped his ranting, swearing, and violent nature. He reads the Bible regularly, and is no longer confined to his room."

Joseph's sphincter curled up like a frightened spider. He made a mental note not to be committed to the lunatic asylum.

The doctor led them back down the aisle to the stairs, and to the second floor. "On this floor are twenty-three more rooms for male patients, and several rooms for attendants. We also give treatments here."

The doctor walked down the aisle. A negro appeared from one of the rooms and said, "Mawnin', massas."

Dr. Cooper responded, "Good morning, Sheets." Then he turned to the visitors. "Our servants help our attendants. The attendants assist the patients for all non-medical needs. They help bathe and feed those who cannot do for themselves. They make certain that the patients are using their time productively, either by reading, cleaning the building, working in the yard, or performing other chores. We depend on them to be pleasant to the patients and put them in a cheerful state of mind. Of course, they may be called upon to assist the steward or me with the difficult patients."

As the doctor explained this, Joseph developed a new respect for his sister. She actually performed these menial, often disgusting tasks. A man walked out of the room from which the negro had just exited and said, "Good morning, Dr. Cooper."

"Good morning, Evan. How are you feeling today?"

"I feel the Lord right beside me, sir, and that's a fine feeling." The man was about thirty-five years old and five inches shorter than Joseph's six feet. He had straight black hair that reached his shoulders. His neatly cropped beard revealed considerably more gray than the hair on his head. His swarthy complexion highlighted his smile of white teeth. Crow's feet radiated from the sides of his gray eyes, his most prominent feature.

"Right you are. Evan, I want you to meet some gentlemen." The doctor introduced him to the men. Evan looked at Joseph for an extra second. Joseph felt his skin crawl. The doctor explained, "Evan is one of our real successes since he came here three months ago. His father had been a lunatic and committed suicide trying to fly off a cliff to prove he had special powers. Sadly, Evan witnessed this when he was only nine years old. Evan grew up thinking he had special powers, too. Because of his persuasiveness, he convinced others he was God, and they followed him. Evan became violent, especially to those who tried to leave his so-called church. But since he's been here, he's lost all aggressive tendencies, believes in the one real God, and spends his time helping others. He'll be here for a while yet, but he's on his way to recovery."

Evan flashed a smile that Joseph guessed the inmate could produce as easily as breathing. "I'm happiest when I can help people, sir. It's what the Lord wants me to do."

The guests said goodbye to Evan and continued their tour. On the third floor the doctor said, "This and the fourth floor are the women's wards. Like the second floor, there are a few rooms for attendants and for treatments, and twenty-three rooms for patients."

A heavy white woman in a cotton cloak similar to the doctor's appeared from a room and approached them. She nodded at the visitors. Dr. Cooper introduced her as the matron. Dr. Cooper asked her how the morning was going. She replied, "Fine, except for Valerie. But I think we finally have her under control."

Dr. Cooper studied a page in his notebook and then said to her, "That's good. I'm going to show these men the floor, so please make sure the ladies are decent."

Dr. Cooper turned to the guests and lowered his voice. "Before, I told you that a patient had to be sent here by a jury of the inferior court. That's only the case for Georgians who are committed by their families and can't afford their own care. Applicants from Georgia and other states who pay one hundred dollars in advance for a year's stay are also admitted. That fee covers food, a room, clothing, and care. The woman in the corner cell is from Beaufort, South Carolina, and her family can well afford the money.

Joseph asked the first question of the day. "Excuse me, Dr. Cooper, but who would want to come here if they didn't have to?"

Dr. Cooper took a step closer to the men. "Good question, Mr. McBain. Believe it or not, some people feel they need a change from their normal lives. We now have a female patient, married no less, who wanted time away from her friends and relatives. She paid her money and is here today. However, she is very stubborn. When she caught a fever and we tried to treat her, she refused. We forced down a cathartic to purge her bowels, administered cold water douches, and changed her diet. She responded quite favorably and has even expressed a desire to leave us before her year is up."

Mr. Brown asked, "Is it always obvious to relatives when a family member needs help?"

Doctor Cooper pulled a pipe from his jacket pocket and held it as he spoke. "Sometimes the mental problems start very innocently. Most people are not trained to notice gradual changes in personality. We have one female patient who first started showing signs of mental sickness by refusing to do her housework. When forced by her husband, she became violent and started to hallucinate. When she arrived here, we had to put her in a straight jacket. We treated her with cold douches, cold baths, and nauseants. This did little good, and we were going to bleed her, but a large dosage of laudanum, an opiate, calmed her considerably. After several weeks, she's made remarkable progress. She now makes her own bed without being asked!"

Joseph wondered if the ether he had tried at college would be useful on these patients.

"Kiss my stinking arse, you dirty whore!" a voice bellowed from one of the rooms. The matron ran into it. More screams came from the room, which set off a reaction of shouting from the other patients on the floor. A negro woman in a black dress ran into the room.

Dr. Cooper said, "Please excuse me," and followed the negress. The cries from the room escalated, and then stopped. Soon, the other screaming ceased. It became uncomfortably quiet. Dr. Cooper emerged from the room, running his hand through his hair and smoothing his cloak. He said to no one, "That's better."

He gathered the men around him and whispered, "Valerie is a single woman and a lunatic. Whenever a man left her, which was all too often, she had epileptic seizures. She turned violent and suffered hallucinations. Soon, she no longer had to lose a man to have these reactions. She just had to think of it. We treat her with calomel as a purgative, and her convulsions have decreased, but she is still very ill."

Amy then walked out of Valerie's room. She blew away the loose hair hanging over her face and approached the visitors, smiling wearily at her father and brother. Dr. Cooper said, "It's workers like this that make our asylum a success. Yes, we use medical treatments, but the care and attention given to the patients by Miss McBain and the others does more than all the drug therapy in the world. Mr. McBain, you should be very proud of the courageous young woman you've raised."

McBain, aghast at seeing the wretched souls with whom his daughter worked all day, hadn't said a word during the tour. He had been thinking how to convince Amy to leave the asylum. "Yes, I'm very proud of her."

Amy squeezed next to her father and held his hand. "My father had doubts about me coming here at first, but now I think he realizes how important this work is. We're helping people rejected by everyone else. If not for the asylum, these poor folks would be on the streets, a danger to themselves and society. I want to thank everyone who's made this possible."

Mr. Dubignon said, "You can count on us to do everything in our power to support this worthy institution." Flournoy and Cobb voiced their assent. Amy could have had these legislators emptying their pockets if she wished.

McBain kissed Amy on the forehead. He asked Dr. Cooper, "May I request an early release for my daughter tonight so she may have supper with her family?"

Dr. Cooper winked at Amy and said to McBain, "I think that can be arranged."

Amy said she would meet them at the Lafayette at 7:30 and went back to Valerie's room. The men moved to the top floor. A bell rang. Dr. Cooper explained it was the signal for the patients to go to the yard.

The fourth floor was also for women and had the same arrangement of rooms as the second and third floors. Dr. Cooper explained some other cases, and the visitors asked questions. Howell Cobb asked if they accepted negroes as patients. Dr. Cooper said they did not, but such a facility was much in need. Joseph thought of Moko.

Dr. Cooper thanked the men for their support and led them outside. As they waited for the coach to come around, Cobb asked, "Mr. McBain, why don't you and your family join Mrs. Cobb and me for supper?"

McBain said, "That's a splendid idea."

Cobb said, "How about Huson's Hotel at 7:30? They have an excellent kitchen." Cobb's physique indicated the congressman knew about good kitchens.

Joseph interrupted. "Father, Amy's coming to our hotel then."

McBain snapped his fingers. "That's right, Joseph. Would you go inside and tell her to meet us at Huson's at 7:30."

Dr. Cooper said, "Wait, Joseph. You can't go in there alone. One of our staff will escort you." Cooper then called Sheets, who was in the yard watching the patients, to take Joseph into the building to find Amy.

Joseph followed the negro up the stairs. Sheets peeked into the door to the second floor, saw nothing, and was about to close it when he thought he heard voices from one of the unoccupied attendants' rooms. He and Joseph entered the floor and stood by the door. They heard a panting male voice say, "Oh, I want to share your soul. I can't live without you. I promise to come back for you."

A female voice gasped, "I need you so. I'll be waiting for you."

Sheets closed one eye, scratched his head, and glanced at Joseph as he deliberated what to do. He finally peeked through the barred window and his jaw dropped. Joseph looked in as well. Evan was running his hands over Amy's body while kissing her on her open mouth. Sheets said, "Oh, Lawdy!" and ran away.

A pain shot through Joseph's chest as he charged into the room. Evan saw Joseph and pulled away from Amy, who blushed as she tried to smooth her dress. She pleaded, "Joseph, wait. It's not what you think. We love each other."

Joseph said, "No! Not with this pig. He's evil, Amy! I can see it in his eyes."

Amy patted down her mussed hair. "Joseph, he's so kind. He wants to help."

Joseph stopped a few feet from her. "Amy, what crap you're saying. He's a hustling pig."

Evan held his arms out in a gesture of conciliation. "Joseph, let us help you understand. Why don't you join us? There's so much we can do. We can . . ."

"Shut your rotten mouth, devil eyes!" Joseph stepped towards Evan, who pulled out a small, makeshift knife.

Joseph stopped in his tracks. "Put that thing away before I stick it up your arse!"

Amy grabbed her brother's arm and begged, "Joseph, please don't fight him. He's not violent. And please don't tell Father."

Joseph glared at Evan, who eased his knife-wielding hand to his side. "You mean, don't tell Father you were kissing an inmate at the lunatic asylum?"

Amy pleaded as tears welled up in her eyes. "Joseph, I'm a woman. I can do as I please. It will do no good to tell him."

Joseph had had enough. He said, "There's been a change in plans, Amy. We're meeting the Cobbs at 7:30 at Huson's Hotel. I'll see you then." Joseph then pointed at Evan. "If I ever catch you with my sister again, I'll kill you." Joseph returned to the coach, his head throbbing.

The McBains and the Cobbs stood in front of the hotel waiting for Amy. It was almost eight o'clock. Joseph wasn't hungry. He couldn't erase the incident from his mind. Amy was an adult, free to make her own decisions. But that didn't mean she always made the right decisions. Now, she was acting downright blind, stupid even. Joseph thought he was the only one who could save her from Evan's deception. He decided not to tell his father. Maybe she'd come to her senses on her own after the surprise encounter.

Joseph's parents were chatting with Mary Lamar Cobb. Andrew was engrossed in conversation with Howell Cobb. Joseph stepped over, hoping to join their discussion. He heard Andrew say, "Greek Revival is considered to be the first style of architecture in America that did not come from England. The feeling of independence after the War of 1812 inspired American architects to find new sources for their cultural ideals. They supposedly found inspiration in the Greeks, who were fighting for their freedom from the Turks. But there was a Greek Revival movement in England just before the War of 1812. How anyone knows the style came directly from Greece and not England, I can't say. But that's not important. America was ready for a change from the delicateness of the Federal. A new style, one of strength and monumentality, has captured the soul of the South. It's well reflected in the Governor's Mansion."

Cobb said, "Fascinating, Andrew. I've never heard anyone talk so passionately about architecture."

As it was past eight o'clock, McBain suggested they go to the dining room. The Cobbs thanked Andrew for saving Charlie, and they went inside. Andrew returned to his room.

They sat at the table and discussed the day at the asylum. Mr. Cobb talked about the need for a negro facility. Just then, a breathless Dr. Cooper interrupted them. "Mr. McBain, may I have a word with you? It's urgent." McBain followed him to the lobby.

In a minute, McBain returned. His voice trembled. "A patient has escaped from the asylum. He's kidnapped Amy."

Sarah placed her hands on her chest and gasped out loud, attracting stares from other tables. Joseph's heart sank to his bowels. "Wh, wh, which patient, Father?"

"That fellow we saw today. Evan. He's escaped before. They thought he had been cured. Joseph, come with Dr. Cooper and me. He couldn't have gotten very far."

Joseph stood and said, "I'm getting Andrew. I'll see you outside."

Howell Cobb also stood. "Mr. McBain, I'm coming, too."

"If you wish, Mr. Cobb. I'd appreciate all the help I can get. Sarah, you stay here. If Amy escapes from this fiend, she'll probably return here."

In a flash they were all out of the hotel and on Cooper's two-horse wagon. Cooper said, "Evan is from the Augusta area. He'll likely head there. I've left a message for the marshal. When he hears, he'll get some men and join us."

They were off into the darkness to find Amy. No one said a word until they were well on the road to Augusta. But Joseph's mind was racing. He had to have some answers. "Dr. Cooper, how was Evan able to kidnap her?"

Keeping his eyes focused on the barely visible road ahead, Cooper replied, "I'm not certain. We found a key made from a spoon in Amy's room at the asylum. But no one heard any noise or saw them leave. He must have overpowered her and carried her off. One of our horses is missing."

Joseph wondered how Evan could have taken her by force with no one noticing. Could she have gone willingly? Did Joseph prompt this by his intrusion? He didn't dare say anything to his father. They had to catch them and find Amy safe.

Driving was difficult. The moon was bright, but the thick line of trees bordering the road muted it, and the horses would barely trot. After an hour in the chilly night, they saw a campfire in the woods to the side of the road. Cooper parked the wagon and they trekked single-file on a narrow trail towards the flames. Couper called out, "It's Dr. Cooper of Milledgeville," to avoid surprising any nervous man with a gun.

They came upon three men sitting around a fire and drinking from tin cups. The campers looked up with smiles, though one had a shotgun across his lap, a hand gripping the stock firmly.

"Good evening," Dr. Cooper said calmly, an unlighted pipe in his mouth.

"How do," the man with the shotgun replied, as he eyed the five visitors. He looked twice at Howell Cobb.

Cooper removed the pipe. "My name is Dr. Cooper, from Milledgeville. We're looking for an escapee from the lunatic asylum, a male about forty with long black hair and a black and gray beard. About my height. He's traveling with a woman. Have you seen anyone like that?"

"No, sir, we surely haven't," replied the man with the gun, easing his grip. "How long ago did they escape?"

Cooper replied, "About two hours ago. We believe on horseback. We're not sure they came this way, but it's our best guess."

The armed camper said, "If they're on this road, some teamster will see them." These men were wagon drivers, also called wagoners or teamsters, for the cotton planters. It was harvest time and the teamsters were bringing the five hundred-pound bales to a railroad station or a river, where they would be transported to a port with ocean access. During the season the country roads were full of these wagons. As the trip usually took several days, the teamsters made camps at night by fresh water creeks near the roadside.

Cooper said, "We'll keep moving, then. If you should see a man fitting that description, and he answers to the name of Evan, take custody and return him to the lunatic asylum in Milledgeville. The one hundred dollar reward will make it worth your time."

"A hunnerd dollars?" replied one of the men.

McBain added, "If you bring back the girl, who goes by the name of Amy McBain, it will be another three hundred." If the eyebrows of the wagoners had not been attached to their foreheads, they would have flown off their faces like frightened starlings. Four hundred dollars was better than a year's wages.

The man with the gun stood and said, "Sir, we might just take a little ride around the area tonight. That girl must be very important to you."

McBain said, "Yes, she is." He and the others hurried back to Cooper's wagon.

They journeyed into the night, hunched over, their breath now visible white clouds. Joseph and Andrew scanned the darkness, looking and sniffing for any sign of a fire. McBain stood, facing backwards, silently praying for the safe return of Amy. Cobb dozed in his seat.

They met three more groups of wagoners within four hours and offered the same reward. As they rode on, Joseph sank deeper into his guilt. He concluded he had to tell his father, but he did not want to do it in front of the other men. He would wait until they stopped again, and would pull him aside.

They continued in silence, their senses tuned. The first dim glow of sunrise depressed Joseph even further. The men were exhausted, as were the horses. It was clear they were not going to find Amy or Evan. Joseph closed his eyes and regretted finding the two together.

The gun blast split the early morning stillness. Cobb almost fell off his seat as Cooper jerked the wagon around in the direction of the sound. After a quarter-mile, they heard shouts from the woods. Cooper parked the wagon and the men ran through the brush towards the voices. Cooper called out repeatedly, "It's Dr. Cooper, don't shoot!" They reached a clearing and stopped cold. Joseph saw a teamster with a shotgun in the crook of his arm, looking to the ground. Amy and Evan were lying flat on their backs fifteen feet apart. Evan's shirt had a dark red hole in the center.

McBain rushed to Amy's side, knelt, and placed his hand on her heart. "Amy, my little girl." Joseph moved to his father's side.

Just then Amy opened her eyes, scaring the hoe cake out of both of them. She was alive! She looked up at her father, then rolled her head to the side, and saw the lifeless body of Evan. She put her hands to her face and bawled.

McBain took her in his arms and tried to console her. "You're all right, sweetheart. He can't hurt you now."

Joseph stared at Evan, half expecting him to get up. He kept his fists clenched. Cooper asked the teamster, "What happened?"

"After you tell us of the missing girl, me and Josiah decide to take some hosses and have a little look-see. I seen this heeyah fiyah on this side of the road, away from the stream, which I think's a might odd. I come upon this little camp and see this heeyah man looking back at me with a pistol in his hand. That lady theyah was sitting by the fiyah with two otha ladies and a young man. The man theya says to me, 'You safe heeyah, we you friends,' or some such. I says, 'I'm lookin' for a man looks jest like you, and a young lady name of Amy Mc something.' So he looks at the lady strange like, and says to me, 'I give you twenny dollahs if you turn around and leave.' I tellum, 'Nope, he's worth a lot more'n that to me.' And he says, 'How much?' And I say, 'The fun's ovuh, drop the gun and come with me, you and the girl called Amy.' So he says, 'You cain't hurt me, I'm God,' and starts to lift his gun. I don't need to heeyah no more. I blows that theyah hole in his chest. Really nuthin' to it at this range. This heeyah lady looks at the dead fella, screams, and blacks out. The other folks ran away on theyah hosses. Josiah took after um. I been callin' out to him to git back heeyah. They wasn't worth no money. My gut tells me this nice lady heeyah is Amy. I could sure use them four hunnerd dollahs."

They carried Evan to the wagon and drove home with just the sound of the horse hooves and wagon wheels against the hard road, and Amy's muffled sobs against her father's chest. McBain patted her shoulder. Joseph and Andrew sat in the back, as Amy's cries cut into them. They passed many teamsters in the early morning, driving their loaded wagons toward Augusta, helping to build the prosperity of Georgia.

The McBains extended their stay for a few days until Amy recovered from her trauma. Sarah rarely left her daughter's side. Sarah and James tried to convince her to return to the Heritage. Amy wouldn't hear of it. She was staying until she could no longer help others.

The night before the McBains departed, they had supper with the Cobbs and the Coopers. Everyone seemed happy, but Amy, who mostly stared at her plate. After the meal, Joseph said he needed fresh air and asked Amy to join him. As they strolled, Joseph said, "I haven't said a word to Mother or Father. Don't worry." She thanked him.

Joseph turned up his jacket collar and shoved his hands in his pockets. "Amy, what happened?"

Amy wrapped her arms around herself and shivered. "Forget about it, Joseph. It's over. I wish to forget. Please let me."

Joseph stopped and turned to his sister. "I will if you just answer a few questions. Then I'll never mention it again."

Amy stopped, too, but didn't face her brother. "All right, Joseph. I shall answer them if I'm able."

"This is tough to ask, Amy, but I will anyway. Did he take you or did you go with him?"

Amy started walking. Joseph followed. Eventually, she stopped and said, "Do you think I'd run away with him with all of you here?"

"You didn't answer the question."

Amy started walking again. "Next question."

Joseph, still a half-step behind Amy, asked, "Who were the people at the camp with you and Evan, the ones that got away?"

Amy used a pinkie to wipe away a tear from the corner of her eye. "The man and one of the women were followers of Evan."

"What were they doing there?"

"They met Evan about a mile from the asylum, to help him escape."

Joseph laid a hand on Amy's shoulder. "Who was the other woman?"

Amy stopped and turned to Joseph. "Evan's wife!" She then started back to the hotel.

Joseph followed her. He asked no more questions, though he wanted to. He was mostly sad that his own sister could have fallen for a fraud like Evan. He prayed she would return to Savannah, where he could protect her.

They walked the rest of the way in silence, broken only by Amy's sniffling. Her pain was deeper than he had imagined. He put his arm around her shoulders and held her close. When they reached the hotel, Joseph promised Amy he wouldn't tell a soul. He offered to give her twenty dollars to keep Sheets quiet. She refused, saying she could handle the negro.

Amy hugged Joseph. "You're a wonderful brother. Have I ever told you that?"

Joseph kissed her cheek. "Not in those words."

CHAPTER 15

A Trip to Mexico

1845-1847

"Here's to Joseph McBain and the spirit of his great grandfather and namesake," James McBain announced, standing at the head of the dining table. Grandfather and Sarah raised their glasses. Joseph patted his necklace of animal teeth and stones.

It was May 1845. Joseph had just announced that he had become an Irish Jasper Green. Every able-bodied man in Savannah was expected to join one of the several volunteer militia groups and be prepared to defend his country. These units also served as the main social clubs in town and made the selection all the more important. Despite being a Scotsman, Joseph opted for the Greens because his father said he should serve under the best possible leader. There was none better than Henry Rootes Jackson. The Yale graduate was considered one of Savannah's most brilliant lawyers and military officers.

"We're dern proud of you, young man," Grandfather said, as he donned his raggedy, seventy year-old, three-pointed continental army hat for the occasion.

"Have you written your sister?" his mother asked. "She'll be so proud of you."

"Yes, but I haven't mentioned the Greens." In the aftermath of the incident at the asylum, Amy and Joseph had become closer and corresponded regularly. Amy had recovered from her ordeal and continued devoting her life to those who needed assistance. She had recently written Joseph that she was spending her Sunday afternoons with a lawyer from Milledgeville. Joseph thought that only a marginal improvement over Evan, but didn't tell her so.

Once they had finished toasting, McBain delivered more good news. "I'm finally going to see Charles Cluskey about our new house."

Joseph, who was trying on Grandfather's hat, asked, "Does Andrew know?"

McBain had to stifle a laugh at the sight of his son, whose eyes were barely visible under the hat. "I'll tell him when I see him. He's going to attend our meetings."

Joseph said, "Cluskey's a Jasper Green, you know."

Before McBain could respond, Grandfather snatched his hat from Joseph's head. He said, "How do you think Mr. Cluskey is going to react to Andrew?"

McBain sipped his wine. "I'll tell him. Andrew will stay out of his way. Cluskey won't be happy, but he'll accept it."

Grandfather pulled the hat onto his head. "How can you be so sure? The best architect in Georgia being told a negro will attend his design meetings? The man who helped organize that gathering of Savannah mechanics a few years back to protest the use of negro contractors by local businessmen? It doesn't sound likely to me, James."

James nodded but didn't respond. The night's celebration was for Joseph, and he didn't want to draw attention elsewhere. But Cluskey was still on McBain's mind.

Charles Cluskey had immigrated to New York from Ireland in 1827, when he was twenty years old, and moved to Savannah two years later. He traveled to the interior of Georgia to find architectural work. In 1834 he was jointly awarded the commission for the Medical College in Augusta. The classic Greek Revival design was Cluskey's first significant success. Other projects soon followed, including the main building of Oglethorpe College at Midway and the Governor's Mansion in Milledgeville. By 1839, Cluskey had established himself as a premier architect.

With his reputation bolstered, Cluskey returned to Savannah and was soon building the town's finest houses since William Jay. However, Cluskey could never manage his finances and accepted work that was less befitting a great architect. He won contracts to build five brick storehouses in the side of the bluff east of the Exchange, to lay a sidewalk on Whitaker Street, to dig a ditch across Forsyth Park, and to build a cistern in Warren Square. The work wasn't classical, but it paid expenses.

Still, Cluskey fell deeper in debt. His wife died in 1842, leaving him to raise their daughters alone, and within a year he filed for bankruptcy. McBain knew the Irishman would accept anyone's presence at the meeting, as long as he got paid.

*   *   *

"Welcome, Mr. Cluskey," McBain said as he invited the architect into the rented house on Orleans Square. "We're finally getting started. Follow me." Cluskey trailed behind his host, inspecting the crown moldings on the way.

They entered the study. McBain said, "Mr. Cluskey, please meet Andrew. He's the lad I mentioned would be observing our meetings. He's quite keen on architecture."

Andrew stood at the side of the room and said, "It's an honor to meet you, sir." Cluskey gave an imperceptible nod and turned back to his host.

McBain offered a chair for the Irishman and asked, "How is business, Mr. Cluskey?"

Cluskey laid down his papers and writing tools and wiped his hands on his jacket. "Better, sir. I'm finishing the convent for the Sisters of Mercy on Liberty Street. And the government has appropriated thirty thousand dollars for the new

Custom House. I'm optimistic I'll get that. I need a public building in Savannah to my credit."

"I'm sure you'll get it, Mr. Cluskey." The men sat at the desk while Andrew took a seat at the side of the room. McBain told Cluskey he wanted a two-story, center-hall-entry, Greek Revival house with a Corinthian portico. He specified the rooms on each floor. Cluskey asked him questions, elevation by elevation, room by room, and took thorough notes. Occasionally, Cluskey sketched to clarify a point. The meeting lasted most of the afternoon. At its conclusion Cluskey told McBain he would have some drawings in a month. The architect left without acknowledging Andrew.

When McBain returned from escorting Cluskey from the house, he sat on the corner of the desk and asked Andrew, "Well, what do you think?"

Andrew hadn't moved from his spot at the corner of the room. "I would never have thought to ask the questions he did, sir, like the patterns of movement between rooms. It makes me realize how little I know."

McBain waved Andrew over to the desk. "Don't be impatient with yourself, Andrew. You're learning how to design a house. That doesn't come easily. I know you're busy working for Isaac and Mr. Scudder, but I'd like you to prepare a set of drawings based on what Mr. Cluskey and I talked about today."

Andrew slowly made a motion in the air with a finger. "You mean actual drawings, sir?"

McBain prodded Andrew. "Yes, that's exactly what I mean. You've been drawing houses on your own since you were nine years old. That's sixteen years. This should be no problem."

"I can never do what Master Cluskey can."

McBain slapped Andrew on the shoulder. "I'm not expecting you to. But I want you to go through the process. You want to become an architect. Well, you're on your way. Don't fight it."

As Andrew left the room, McBain made a mental note to speak to Isaac about Andrew's schedule. While the McBains had been visiting Amy in Milledgeville, Mr. Bones quit, claiming he needed to return to his sickly wife in Columbus. Mr. McBain needed a replacement. At Grandfather's suggestion, he gave that position to Isaac. The other negroes responded positively, and production immediately increased. But within a few weeks, some of them complained to McBain that Isaac was as bad as de Bone. McBain told Isaac to go easy and promised to take some responsibilities off his shoulders. Andrew became the driver of the brick operation and succeeded at calming things down. McBain felt comfortable letting him spend more time on his design work.

Two months after their first meeting, Cluskey informed McBain that the preliminary drawings were ready. McBain first wanted to review Andrew's plans, and asked him to present them. Andrew had designed a two-story building, with a classical

Greek entryway with four colossal columns in the Corinthian order, supporting a pediment that covered three of the five bays. The tympanum, the interior face of the pediment, contained a sculpture in relief of a man in full Highlander habit. Two curved stairs led to the front landing. The rear elevation presented a sunroom on each side, projecting past the rear entry steps, and creating a U shape. The floor plans were a standard center-hall-entry design, with a formal parlor and a family parlor on one side of the first floor, and a study and dining room on the other side. The second floor had four bedrooms. Andrew had omitted the servants' stairs, but McBain made no mention of it.

McBain was impressed by the professionalism of Andrew's work. He asked Andrew several questions about his design. He tapped the drawings and said, "Excellent, Andrew. I'm proud of you. Wasn't this worth the effort? If Mr. Cluskey had given me these, I'd have been very pleased. Now, let's see what he has to offer."

Andrew peeped, "Thank you, sir." He stood up and hardly felt the floor under his feet.

In early August the architect entered the study with several rolls of paper in his arms. He ignored Andrew, and offered his hand to McBain. "I apologize for the delay, sir, but the convent took more time than I had thought. I've also been involved in the Custom House discussions."

McBain said, "Oh? What's the latest?" The project was a hot topic in town.

Cluskey started to unroll his drawings on the desk. "Some locals, including the collector of customs, have written to the secretary of the treasury recommending me. I'm certain to get it. I've been asked to submit plans."

McBain helped place paper weights on the corners of the drawings. "When do you think construction will start?"

Cluskey blew some dust off the front elevation. "They still need to select the location. Since Mr. Dure's house was destroyed, the corner of Bull and Bay is the preferred spot. If all goes well, we should start by the end of the year." Mr. Dure's house, the city's oldest landmark, had burned in February 1845, after having survived the two great fires and several hurricanes.

"I certainly wish you luck, sir. My house should fit nicely within your schedule. Now, let's have a look at your plans." McBain waved Andrew over from the other side of the room. He sat as far from the men as possible while still able to see the papers.

McBain studied the plans, asking Cluskey many questions about materials and the design. When he finished, he said, "Mr. Cluskey, this is fine work. Please leave the drawings and allow me a few days to organize my thoughts. Then we'll finalize this."

Cluskey nodded his assent, bade good day to McBain, and left.

McBain asked, "Your thoughts, Andrew?"

Andrew looked at the desk. "The plans are remarkable, sir. It will be the grandest house in Savannah."

McBain pulled the front elevation from the pile and placed it on top. "Do you have any comments about the design?"

Andrew thought for a moment, started to point to the sketch, but withdrew his hand as if he'd touched a hot skillet. "Sir, who am I to criticize Master Cluskey?"

"Andrew, I'd like your opinion. This is between you and me."

Andrew answered, "In one respect it's similar to Master Eastman's on Chippewa Square. The front of that house faces McDonough Street and has no distinguishing elements except the small Doric portico and the curved stairs, and is overlooked. The side gallery faces the square and is more impressive in design and size than the front portico. I think the front should be the most significant elevation. Passersby see the side gallery. Guests and residents walk through the portico. The Eastman house is still beautiful. As brilliant as Master Cluskey is, perhaps Master Eastman insisted on the design and Cluskey agreed, but I would not recommend that for you, sir."

McBain smiled at Andrew. That was his own major objection to Cluskey's design. "What would you propose, Andrew?"

"I believe the front of your house should face Pulaski Square, and that the portico be two stories instead of just one, with colossal columns. That would make it more monumental, sir. There's room for a tiered piazza on the Macon Street side of the house. It will provide a handsome view of the square. Of course, the house will be longer than it is wide. That will change Master Cluskey's floor plans."

McBain met with Cluskey a few days later and asked him to alter the plans. Cluskey grumbled, but made the adjustments. McBain approved the final drafts and the cost estimate by the end of October. He even paid Cluskey fifty dollars over his requested fee, which the Irishman happily accepted. Cluskey started organizing workers and ordering materials. McBain's only request was that Andrew and his crew serve as the bricklayers. Cluskey didn't argue. He knew McBain was committed to his negro. Cluskey would complain at the right time—when he caught Andrew doing shoddy work.

Cluskey's rudeness towards Andrew began to change when Andrew introduced his crew of Shamus Riley, Ryan Daly, Billy McNeely, and a negro named Shadrack. The three Irish bricklayers talked with Cluskey about Ireland for half an hour while Andrew and Shadrack stood by like lamp posts.

Andrew had met Shadrack at church. Shadrack had recently been auctioned at a sheriff's sale for eight hundred dollars. His new owner, Mr. Jones, a commission merchant, had no need for a bricklayer, but he did want a good investment. He told Shadrack to find work and a place to live. All Mr. Jones requested from Shadrack was eight dollars per month. Anything Shadrack made above that was his. Shadrack, having a skill, earned one dollar and twenty-five cents a day and worked an average of twenty-six days a month. After paying his master, Shadrack had an ample twenty-two dollars and fifty cents on which to rent rooms in Oglethorpe Ward, and feed and clothe his wife and child. Shadrack's owner received ninety-six dollars a year for a handsome annual return of 12 percent, and Shadrack got to live almost like a free man. As long as Shadrack kept working, he and Mr. Jones were happy.

When construction started, Cluskey kept a close watch on Andrew's brickwork, waiting for an opportunity to criticize him. He never got it. He soon recognized that Andrew was a first-class bricklayer, one of the best with whom he'd worked. However, one day he saw Andrew's crew cleaning up around the site, and not laying bricks. He confronted Andrew for an explanation. Andrew told him the men had already laid seven rows of bricks that day, and anymore would put too much weight on the wet mortar on the bottom row. Cluskey responded, "Oh, yes," and walked away.

Andrew studied everything Cluskey did. Despite being ignored by the architect, Andrew thought the man was a genius and wanted to learn all he could from him. He even hoped Cluskey might use him on the Custom House.

One day Andrew approached the architect, who'd been absent from the site for a week and asked if he could order more bricks. "I don't care what you do," Cluskey snarled, and walked away, leaving Andrew holding his trowel at his side.

That evening, Andrew joined Mr. McBain, Grandfather, and Joseph on the piazza after supper. Andrew recounted the incident with Cluskey. McBain slapped his forehead. "Oh! I should have warned you. Cluskey just learned the government selected someone else for the Custom House. Everyone in Savannah is outraged that an outsider got it." The Irishman was highly regarded in town. Not only was he a prominent architect adding to the beauty of Savannah, but he was the city surveyor, a member of the Hibernian Society, and a member of one of the white fire companies.

Andrew asked, "Who did get the commission, sir?"

"A New Yorker named John Norris. He just completed the Custom House in Wilmington, North Carolina. Cluskey's likely to be in a foul mood for a while. Just do your job and stay out of his way. If he becomes too difficult, let me know. I do feel badly for him. He was counting on that project."

Construction on the house progressed, and with it the excitement in the McBain family also grew. Joseph couldn't wait for it to be completed and told his mother so at dinner one March evening. Sarah didn't respond. She had other things on her mind.

"Stop worrying, Mother. I'm not going anywhere," Joseph said, reaching across the table to hold her hand. "Men are volunteering in huge numbers all over the country. It's more likely the man in the moon will be sent to Mexico than the Jasper Greens."

Mexico had been a problem to America since a group of settlers, mostly Americans, had fought for and won independence for Texas from their mother country in 1836. As soon as it became the Republic of Texas, many in America and Texas pushed for annexation. Through political chicanery on pro-annexation politicians' part, and a Constitutional Convention and popular vote on Texas's part, Texas became the twenty-eighth state on December 29, 1845. Mexico wasn't happy. Not only was the annexation a diplomatic insult, but the boundaries of the new state were in dispute. War seemed inevitable.

Sarah pushed her dinner plate aside and stared at the table. "You can't just tell a mother to stop worrying and have her stop worrying."

James tried to calm her. "Dear, it's what every young man does to serve his country. That's what makes America so strong. It's highly unlikely Joseph will go to Mexico, but if he does, it will be with Henry Jackson."

"Isn't that wonderful?" Sarah said sarcastically, folding her arms. "At his age, Joseph should be here, finding a wife and raising a family."

"I won't be going anywhere!" Joseph's voice rose in frustration. He got up, walked around the table, and kissed his mother's cheek.

A few months later, in early June 1846, Joseph was waiting to board a train at six a.m. at the Central of Georgia depot to the music of a military band. He was bound for Columbus, Georgia, and then Mexico with the Irish Jasper Greens.

The United States and Mexico had been unable to avoid hostilities. After American troops had ventured into the disputed territory, they were attacked and almost wiped out by the Mexican army. President James K. Polk called for war. Congress granted him permission to deploy the American military and call up fifty thousand volunteers. Ten Georgia units with 910 men were called, including the Jasper Greens.

Joseph stood silently with his family. Sarah, kerchief in hand, sniffled. When Henry Jackson called for the Greens to board, Joseph embraced everyone, including Andrew and Hercules. Then he walked down the boarding path. Jackson greeted him and directed him into a car. Soon, the whistle blew, and the McBains watched the train roll away.

By mid-June all the Georgia units, called the First Regiment of Georgia Volunteers, had reached Columbus, and Henry Jackson was elected colonel. The conditions in camp were unbelievably poor. Joseph thought he was a prisoner, not a soldier. The men lived in crowded, dirty tents, drank rancid water, and ate putrid food. Some became so sick and weak that they puked and crapped where they lay. Joseph slept outside, often in the rain, to avoid the odors and moans. There were few doctors and no medicine. And they hadn't left Georgia yet. Joseph missed home more than he thought possible. He'd lay awake at night, thinking of his family, Andrew, and the new house.

The construction moved ahead smoothly. By late July, most of the brickwork had been completed. Cluskey had so much confidence in Andrew that he spent more time trying to fight the selection of John Norris for the Custom House commission.

Norris had created a firestorm by hiring a few non-local mechanics and workmen for the project, and Cluskey tried to exploit that anger. Also, there was talk of enlarging the project to include a post office and federal court house. New plans might have to be submitted, possibly necessitating a request for new bids.

Andrew concentrated on the house. One day, he was making mortar on the lot when a man in a suit walked by, watched Andrew for a few minutes, and asked him how he made it.

Andrew was only too happy to explain. He leaned on his mortar hoe. "For lime we cook oyster shells in a pit, what we call a lime rick, at our plantation and send them here in barrels. There's an endless supply of shells. Indians lived in the area for hundreds of years and ate a lot of oysters. They threw the shells in piles, called middens, which, over the years grew to be enormous mounds. We sure need them. A house requires a huge amount of mortar to lay the bricks and coat the inside and outside of the house. I put a batch of cooked shells in this pan and add water. The mixture boils. I stir it with this mortar hoe and add sand until it reaches a smooth consistency. I put it in a pit for a few days, and then I pound more sand into it. For laying bricks or the first coat on the exterior, I'll use mortar that's set for just a few days. For the exterior finish coat, I use a finer, aged mortar. For the interior finish coat, I use mortar that's aged even longer and has been pressed through a sieve to remove any lumps or unburned shells."

The man pointed to the ground near Andrew's feet. "Why did you run the sand on that white sheet?"

"Excuse me!" Cluskey shouted as he ran across the lot to Andrew and the stranger. Red-faced, Cluskey demanded, "What business do you have here?"

Andrew looked at the man and back to Cluskey, shocked by the Irishman's behavior. "Master Cluskey, he was just asking about . . ."

"Shut up, Andrew!" Cluskey yelled. His eyes stayed fixed on the man and did not see Andrew recoil. "Now, if you haven't business here, Mr. Norris, be on your way."

Andrew stiffened. Norris was the man who had been making Cluskey's life so miserable. But Norris didn't move. Cluskey pulled the mortar hoe from Andrew's hands. Andrew said, "Master Cluskey, I don't think . . ."

Cluskey sneered at Andrew. "I told you to shut up or start looking for other work!"

The two white men glared at each other. Cluskey raised the hoe to his chest, but Norris didn't move. Finally, Norris said to Andrew, "I like your work, Andrew. I'm sorry if I caused you a problem." Norris tipped his hat and walked away.

When Norris had disappeared from view, Andrew said, "Master Cluskey, he just asked me about making mortar."

Cluskey's face was still red. "Do you know who that was?"

"You called him Mr. Norris. I assume he's the architect for the Custom House."

"Not yet, Andrew. Not yet! And don't ever disobey my orders again!" Cluskey threw down the hoe, kicking up dirt into Andrew's new batch of mortar, and walked away.

Andrew didn't tell Mr. McBain about the incident. But Cluskey did several weeks later, out of embarrassment for his behavior. McBain told Grandfather about it one night on the piazza. "Cluskey said Andrew stayed away from him for days. However, Andrew finished the chimney and had to show Cluskey. Cluskey asked Andrew if he planned to put a brick arch over the top as a cap. Andrew looked up at the chimney and asked why that was important. Just then a big turkey buzzard perches on the chimney, lets out a shriek, rolls its head around, and pukes right into it."

Grandfather howled with laughter at the story. "What did Andrew do?"

McBain puffed on his segar. "What could he do? Everyone at the site was laughing so hard. He had to get a chimney sweep to clean up the mess. Then he built a cap. The incident relieved the strained feelings between them."

Grandfather sat back in his chair in the warm September night while McBain read his newspaper. They were both lonely without Joseph and Amy at home. And Sarah was in the mountains for the summer and wouldn't be back until late October. The old man dozed until he heard, "Oh, my good Lord!"

Grandfather bolted up. "What is it James?"

McBain squinted at the paper in the weak gaslight. "It says here the Jasper Greens were involved in a fight. There was a loss of life."

"They fought the Mexicans?" Grandfather tried to grab the newspaper.

McBain pulled the paper to his chest. "No! Not the Mexicans. It was a brawl with the Kennesaw Rangers. Another Georgia militia unit."

"Well, law me! What does it say?" Grandfather demanded. McBain studied the paper, reading the article for a second time. Grandfather got impatient. "James, read the dern report!"

James held the paper closer to his face. "It says the Georgia regiment was camped at the mouth of the Rio Grande when they and some other companies were shipped upriver to another camp. During the trip, some Rangers bullied two brothers from the Greens. A Ranger struck one of them. They were about to attack the other one when a Green came to his aid. A Scotsman."

Grandfather took a deep breath and exhaled noisily. "Please, James. Continue."

"One of the Rangers hit the Scotsman in the head with a claret bottle. A fight ensued but the captains quickly broke it up. Both companies were given strict orders to stop any offensive conduct. Things quieted down until the next day. As they were docked along the river to transfer to another boat, the Rangers started to harass the Scotsman again. They insulted his forebears!"

"That's us!" Grandfather snapped forward, ready to fight the Rangers himself.

McBain waited for his father to settle back in his seat. "The Scotsman offered to fight any Ranger who thought he was man enough. No one accepted." McBain peeked over the paper. Grandfather was smiling. "An officer intervened and prevented a disturbance. Then most of the men from the two companies boarded the other boat, but some camped on shore, as the ship was not to leave until the next day. Apparently they had no further trouble. Until later that night. Both companies were sleeping on the ship when they heard a loud cry for help from the riverbank. The men on the ship ran to help their companions on shore. The two companies reached the top of the gangway at the same time, but were repelled by the sentries. They started fighting on the boat. Just at that moment, a militia unit from Illinois marched by. They heard the noise and for some reason charged up the stairs to the trouble. Swords were drawn, and shots were fired. Men are reported dead and wounded."

Grandfather closed his eyes. "Any names?"

McBain dropped the paper on the floor. "No. I guess we're just going to have to wait."

While they waited, Cluskey finished the house, as fine a structure as any in Savannah. In early December, in Cluskey's honor, James McBain held a party. He wanted to keep it small since neither Amy nor Joseph could attend, and invited only 150 guests. Twelve servants from the Heritage had to be transported to Savannah to assist with the preparations, which took several days. While Jinny, Lilly, and Dante cooked some of the food, McBain had the Pulaski Hotel provide the bulk of the evening's repast, dishes, glasses, silverware, and servers. Aspasia Mirault provided the cakes and pies.

McBain had Andrew work as one of the butlers helping Plesant and William answer the door, take coats, and ensure the guests had everything they needed. Several of the guests knew Andrew, and he spent as much time talking as he did working. This, of course, was McBain's plan. He told his guests of Andrew's role and asked that they compliment the negro.

Andrew greeted Dr. Minis, who had returned to Savannah from his self-imposed exile and opened a drug store. He talked about architecture with James Hamilton Couper. Couper even went to the kitchen to compliment Dante on the delicious food and commented that the weekend with François seemed to have served him well.

Later, while Andrew was cleaning up some spilled wine, McBain summoned him. "Andrew, some old friends would like to say hello."

Andrew followed McBain into the study and recognized the older man. "Master Lamar!" He was not sure of the younger man. "Master Charles?"

Charlie shook hands vigorously with Andrew. "Yes, it's me Andrew. Good to see you again." Charlie had not seen Andrew in eight years, since the *Pulaski* disaster.

The Lamars had moved back to Savannah in 1840 after a brief stay in Virginia. Gazaway sold his shipping company, though he maintained ownership of a few ships, and expanded his commission merchant business. He owned the Eastern Wharves, the largest cotton-warehousing facility in Savannah. He had also dabbled in politics again. He was elected a commissioner of pilotage in 1841 and an alderman for the city for the 1845 term. But his second wife's health was poor and he had no choice but to relocate to the north. Lamar was a businessman, and there was no better place to practice that craft than New York City. He moved there in late 1845, leaving his Augusta interests in the care of his brother, George Washington Lamar, and his Savannah operations in the hands of his son. Gazaway happened to be visiting Charlie at the time of McBain's party.

When Charlie moved to Savannah from Virginia with his new family, he had no intention of attending college. He wanted to be rich, just like his father, but without his father's help. He started a grocery-commission company with his friend, William Sims. They soon opened a grocery store, but the young men couldn't run either business successfully and had to close them. Charlie then went to work for his father.

McBain said to the twenty-two year-old, "Congratulations, Charlie, on your marriage to Miss Nicoll." The previous February, Charlie had married the daughter of Judge John C. Nicoll. Nicoll was one of the most influential men in Savannah. He had been the captain of the Republican Blues, the mayor of Savannah, a founding member of the Georgia Historical Society, a judge of the Court of Common Pleas and Oyer and Terminer for the city of Savannah, and was currently a judge for the Superior Court of Georgia. McBain pondered the power behind the marriage of a Lamar and a Nicoll.

Charlie bowed slightly from the waist. "Thank you, sir. Marrying Caro was the best thing that ever happened to me."

McBain said, "I wish you a lifetime of happiness and many children."

Andrew added, "I do too, Master Charles."

Charlie said, "Andrew, if it weren't for you, I wouldn't even be here."

Sarah approached the men. "James, it's time to toast Mr. Cluskey." McBain and Andrew said goodbye to the Lamars.

Guests continued to congratulate Andrew on his work on the house. It was one of the happiest nights of his life. He wished Joseph were there to share it with him. He wondered how Joseph was faring.

*   *   *

"I understand Massa Joseph was cleared of that trouble in Mexico," Hercules said to Andrew as they stood with Dante in the back of the First African Baptist Church one Sunday in January 1847.

Andrew palmed his Bible. "Thank God. Everyone was so worried."

Hercules sighed. "Massa Joseph sure keeps the Lord busy."

Just then, a pretty girl in a white dress and white ribbons in her hair approached the three. Hercules bowed to her. She said, "It's such a beautiful day, we're having lemonade and cakes in Franklin Square. Please join us." She fixed her eyes on Andrew, smiled, and left.

Dante and Hercules looked at Andrew, who was as stiff as a Georgia pine. Hercules said, "Andrew, you look like you need a glass of lemonade." Hercules and Dante guided him from the church to the square and left him alone.

Patience Low was the pretty sixteen year-old daughter of Deacon James Low, the coachman for Andrew Low, one of the wealthiest commission merchants in town. Her skin was coal-black, and she always wore a white dress with a white flower or ribbon in her hair to church. Since she was five years of age, she never missed Sunday school, the only form of education available to negroes. And her parents read the Bible to her every night before bed. She spoke as well as most whites.

In the past year she had developed from a girl into a young lady and drew the attention of every unmarried man at the church. Her father was never far away.

Andrew stood near Patience in the square, but she was so busy serving the other members of the congregation, he didn't get a chance to talk to her. Yet, every time he emptied his glass, she rushed over with a smile and refilled it from a sweating, metal pitcher. Finally, Andrew rejoined Hercules and Dante.

Dante punched Andrew playfully on the arm. "She hab de eye fuh oonuh."

Andrew avoided looking at his friends. "I don't know. She's nice to everyone. It's her nature to smile."

Hercules placed a hand on Andrew's back. "Andrew, you can see one of those Greek orders you always talking about from ten miles in the dark, but you can't spot a woman's interest in you when it's right in you face. She's sixteen. At that age, girls have something on their minds when they smile sweetly at a man. You best present youself. You can't wait forever."

Andrew looked at Hercules like the coachman just asked him to leap over the Savannah River. "How do I do that?"

Hercules rolled his eyes. "Next Sunday, after services, you ask Miss Patience if she want to take a stroll. You got to ask her daddy for permission first. Ask him to join you. Try to put him at ease, though that's impossible."

Andrew finally blinked. He realized he was embarking on the biggest project of his life. The brickwork at the McBain house was minor in comparison.

A few days later Hercules asked Andrew to join him for a haircut by Ulysses, the best negro barber in town. Other Heritage servants had always cut Andrew's hair and he was looking forward to having it done professionally. Maybe Patience would notice. Ulysses had a tiny shop in Oglethorpe Ward, not more than ten feet wide and ten feet deep. Four old chairs that he had bought from Peter, a slave of the city scavenger, lined one wall. In the middle of the shop was a sturdier wooden chair.

Hercules and Andrew waited as Ulysses attended to a customer. The barber was short and wore a white shirt that hung neatly outside of his brown trousers. He had a thin moustache that looked like a black line drawn with a quill.

When their turn came, Hercules stood and said, "Ulysses, meet my friend, Andrew. Please take care of him."

Ulysses smiled and pointed to the chair. Andrew sat and Ulysses draped a towel around his shoulders. He faced Andrew and studied his head, as a doctor would inspect a wound. He placed a thumb under Andrew's chin and lifted it gently. He placed his fingers on the side of Andrew's head and coaxed it to a level position. Ulysses murmured "Uh huh," and began to cut.

Andrew didn't dare move his head. His eyes darted around, taking in the shop. His gaze froze on shelves on the wall. They were lined with carvings of people's faces. He recognized the one with the sharp prominent nose and the curls of the periwig tumbling down. It was Oglethorpe, just as Andrew had seen in Joseph's books!

He felt Ulysses's fingers on his head. "Please keep still, Andrew."

"I'm sorry. But those carvings. One is General Oglethorpe."

The barber kept cutting. Eventually, he said, "Very good, Andrew."

Andrew examined the other faces. He recognized George Washington. "Who are the men next to George Washington?"

While concentrating on Andrew's hair, Ulysses named every president from John Adams to James Polk.

Andrew's eyes bounced from figure to figure as Ulysses announced each name. "You carved all those after cutting hair all day?"

"Uh huh. There you go." Ulysses whipped the towel away from Andrew's shoulders with one hand and held a small, round, rusty-handled mirror about two feet away from Andrew's face with the other.

Andrew moved his head from side to side and smiled, happy with the results. He thought he looked more prosperous. He thanked Ulysses and paid his ten cents. While Andrew waited for Hercules, he inspected the carvings up close. After that, he had his hair cut by Ulysses every other Saturday.

It took Andrew a few weeks, but he finally approached Patience one Sunday as she was cleaning up after services and said what he had been practicing for days. "HelloPatience.ThatsurewasaninspiringsermonbyReverendMarshalldon'tyouthink?" Andrew wished his heart would slow down.

Patience turned to him and beamed. Her teeth were like pearls. "Why, Andrew! You scared me half to death. Yes, that was a beautiful service. I'm so happy you came over to talk to me. Let me finish here and I can spend more time with you."

Andrew barely maintained consciousness. "Yes, I'll just wait over there. Take your time." Andrew stepped to the side of the church and wondered why Patience, ten years younger than he, was so much more composed. He pretended to inspect the church interior and noticed Hercules looking at him, nodding positively. Dante stood next to Hercules, with fingers in the corners of his mouth, pulling his lips apart, and sticking out his tongue. Andrew grimaced at Dante's antics. Hercules noticed and slapped Dante on the back of his head, almost causing Dante to bite off his tongue.

"I'm ready, Andrew. Would you like some cake?"

Andrew snapped to attention. "Er, well, actually, I'd like to get some fresh air. It's a little hot in here. Would you like to take a walk? I could show you the house I helped build for Master McBain. Of course, if your father approves."

Patience clasped her hands in front of her chest and said, "Why, Andrew! How sweet of you! Yes, please ask Father. He'd want that."

"I'll go ask him now," he replied, hoping something would save him from having to do so. Since Quiet Goose, fathers of girls intimidated him.

Patience giggled, "Good. I'll wait right here."

Fighting rumbling bowels, Andrew found Deacon Low. "Excuse me, sir. How are you today?"

The deacon appraised Andrew from head to toe. "Fine, Brother Andrew. And you?"

Andrew took out his kerchief and dabbed his forehead. "Real fine, sir. I have so much hope after Reverend Marshall's sermons. Sir, it's mighty warm in here. Would you permit me to take Miss Patience for a walk? I'd like to show her the house I helped build for Master McBain. It's on Pulaski Square. We'll be back in no time."

The deacon looked around the church for his daughter. He caught her eye and she waved. Deacon Low returned his attention to Andrew, who wanted to apologize for taking the deacon's time and run from the church. "Yes, Andrew. You may walk with Patience. But I'd like her back here in an hour." The deacon pulled out his time piece and studied it a little longer than necessary.

Andrew took out his watch and glanced at it. "Yes, sir. You can depend on that."

The deacon moved closer to Andrew and held his gaze. Then he said in a low voice, "Andrew, that girl is the most important thing in my life. Do you understand?"

Andrew thought he could feel his eyeballs shaking. "Yes, sir. I certainly do."

"Enjoy your walk."

"Andrew, it's a beautiful house. And you built it. I'm so proud of you!" Patience said as she took in the house from Pulaski Square.

Andrew gazed at the house as well, with his chest puffed up, not only because of his part in creating it, but because Patience was by his side. "Master Cluskey really built it. But I did the brickwork and the stucco. I oversaw that part."

Patience took hold of Andrew's arm. "That's the best part of the whole house. Was Master Cluskey nice to work for?"

Andrew's heart began to race, feeling Patience touching him. "I guess. He sure has a temper. But I learned so much. I'd like to work for him again. Master McBain told me he has a petition signed by two hundred local men demanding that he be named the architect for the Custom House. He's going to Washington soon to deliver it personally to President Polk. If he succeeds, he might ask me to work on it."

Though Patience didn't understand everything Andrew said about building, she nodded her head as if she did. "That would be so exciting, Andrew."

They walked around the house and Andrew explained the design. Neither saw the McBain servants peeking out the window at them. They sat on a bench in the square for a few minutes before returning to the church. They were gone fifty-eight minutes. Patience told Andrew how much she enjoyed their stroll. Andrew said he'd like to do it again. She squeezed his arm and went to find her father, who was ten feet away, holding his watch.

*   *   *

On a June evening in 1847, one year after they had departed, the Irish Jasper Greens disembarked from the train at the Savannah depot. There were no bands or flag waving. Joseph's family greeted him. His mother gasped when she saw how much weight he had lost. She hugged him for a full minute. Then she touched his cheeks and sighed, "Oh, Joseph."

They drove the short distance to Pulaski Square, and Joseph saw the completed house for the first time. He asked to be let out so he could take it in. He stood in front, his hands on his hips, flanked by his father and Andrew. After surveying the structure, he put an arm around both of them, and they walked to the house.

Joseph was overwhelmed by the beauty of the interior, the high ceilings, the columns separating the rooms, the crown moldings in the Greek key, the chandeliers, the paintings, the pocket doors, and the rugs. He wanted to ask Andrew all about it, but didn't have the strength. As they entered the parlor, the house servants greeted Joseph. His father called out, "Speech!"

Joseph took a drink of water before he started. He looked at the glass. "What I would have paid for this a few months ago." He then faced the folks. "I wish I could tell you all that I fought like a Highlander and did the McBain name proud. But I can't. I hardly saw a Mexican. I only fought other Georgians. I marched from one post to another for the entire year. I was told on the train ride home that of the 910 men of the First Georgia Regiment, only 450 were mustered out. One hundred forty-five men died and 315 were discharged, mostly due to sickness. I can't tell you that I did a thing to defend our country. But I can tell you how happy I am to be back home with the people I love."

Everyone applauded. Sarah said, "Joseph, what is the first thing you want to do in your new home?"

He didn't hesitate. "Take a bath."

His mother had anticipated Joseph's request and had the bath ready. Joseph lowered himself into the tub and groaned with pleasure. He submerged his head and slowly re-emerged. He closed his eyes and started to doze. He didn't want to fall asleep in the water. He sat up, scrubbed himself, trying to wash away a year of grime. He had to force himself to get out and dress. His old clothes hung loosely on him.

He made it through the mock turtle soup before he slumped over, asleep, in his chair. McBain and Hercules helped him upstairs to his bed.

CHAPTER 16

A Free Man of Color

1849-1850

One Sunday in the spring of 1849 Andrew entered the church but Patience wasn't there to greet him, as she had most Sundays for the past two years. After the service, Andrew searched for her. Deacon Low approached him. "Andrew, I want to speak to you. Outside, please." The deacon turned and headed for the door. Andrew's heart began to race.

When they reached Franklin Square, the deacon faced Andrew. "I'm sorry, Andrew. Your Sunday walks with Patience must end."

Andrew thought he had been punched in the stomach. He rubbed his gut, the pain was so real. He had been planning to ask the deacon for permission to marry Patience. "Why, sir? I love and respect Patience. We have such a fine time together."

Deacon Low clasped his hands behind his back like a military officer and looked into Andrew's eyes. "Andrew, you're a good, decent man. That's why I allowed you to see my daughter in the first place. I saw no harm in it. But Patience is now eighteen. She's a young woman and I need to make decisions for her own good. I only want one thing for her, and that's her freedom." He coughed into his fist and looked about the square. He saw no one near them. Through clenched teeth, he spewed his fury. "Of course, as a nigger, I'm powerless to do that!" The deacon closed his eyes for a moment. Then the controlled voice returned. "Please, forgive me for that, Andrew."

Andrew observed the anguished man. He'd never seen him lose his temper. But he couldn't think of anything to say. His mind was full of dark clouds.

The deacon continued. "I once asked Master Low if he would free Patience if I paid him. He said that wasn't possible. So the best I can do to give the gift of freedom to my little girl without running away is to have her marry a free man of color. When she does, Master Low says he'll sell Patience to him. She'll still be a slave, but she'll be owned by the man she chooses to love and protect her for life. I shouldn't have allowed you and Patience to spend so much time together in the first place. Now she's so fond of you, I have to end it."

Andrew felt dizzy. He started to sweat and wiped his face with a kerchief. "Deacon Low, I make a good living. I have more work than I can handle. I have money saved. Master McBain wouldn't interfere with my marriage. Patience and I could live in Savannah on our own just like free people. Thousands of slaves do it now."

The deacon maintained his military bearing. "I'm sorry, Andrew. You're still a slave. If something should happen to Mr. McBain, you and Patience could be sold anywhere. Or sold apart. That's not what I want for my daughter. I know you'd take care of her, but there's too much beyond your control."

Andrew pressed his palms together. "Sir, I love Patience. I want to spend my life with her and raise a family."

"Andrew, I don't want to discuss this any further. I'm relying on you to be a man and honor my request. Patience is too hurt right now. Pay no attention to her at church. I'm sorry it's turned out this way. May God bless you." The deacon headed back to the church. His head ached. Informing Andrew had been even harder than he had expected.

"Sir?" Andrew called. Deacon Low stopped. "What if I were a free man?"

The deacon turned around. "It's not possible, Andrew. Mind what I say. Hear?"

Andrew stared at the church long after the deacon had entered it. He didn't have the strength to return. He had already lost one woman he wanted to marry. Now he was losing another. He sat on a bench and waited for Hercules and Dante to come looking for him. When they did, Andrew didn't say a word until they returned to Pulaski Square and he could speak privately to Hercules.

"I love her, Hercules. I don't want to lose her," Andrew said as he leaned against the coach in the carriage house.

Hercules was brushing one of the horses. "You still have some hope."

Andrew looked up. "What hope do I have?"

Hercules continued brushing. "You can ask massa to free you. I don't know why he wouldn't. Master Joseph told you many times he wanted to."

"Master Low told Deacon Low it's not possible."

Hercules put the brush down and leaned against the coach next to Andrew. "It can't hurt to ask. Maybe massa has more friends in Milledgeville than Master Low. Maybe he has more money. You know how these things work."

Andrew didn't answer. He pushed himself off the carriage and paced the floor. He stopped to pat one of the horses on the rump. The horse neighed. Hercules said, "Do you still have the address of that buckra from New York?"

Andrew rubbed his forehead and mumbled, "Yes. I have it somewhere." He turned to Hercules and thrust his fist into his palm. "You're right! He could purchase both of us and take us to New York and I can pay him back. That man Gilles said he could do it."

Hercules picked up the brush and returned to the horse. "It's a chance, Andrew. I don't know how the deacon will feel about you taking Patience away from him. Master McBain and Master Low got to approve. But you got choices most niggers don't."

After a few stomach-tightening Sundays of watching Patience but unable to talk to her, followed by sweaty, restless nights, Andrew decided to discuss the situation with Joseph. With his consent, Andrew would ask Master McBain to manumit him. If he refused, Andrew would write to Mr. Gilles. Andrew felt he had to move fast. He didn't know how long Patience would wait for him.

A few mornings later, in early May, Andrew and Joseph were walking to work along Whitaker Street. As Andrew was about to raise the subject, he was distracted by a group of twenty negroes running past them towards the Bay. Joseph said, "What in the world?" Soon another group of ten charged past them.

Joseph turned and saw at least fifty more blacks running in their direction. He said to Andrew, "Something's going on. Let's see." They quickened their pace. When they reached the Bay, they were swept up in a flood tide of hundreds of giddy negroes. They were carried past the Exchange, where hundreds more blacks crammed the Strand. Joseph and Andrew pushed their way to the edge of the bluff.

Joseph looked to the harbor and blinked several times in disbelief. Thousands more negroes were packed along River Street and the wharves. It seemed as if every one of Savannah's six thousand blacks had overrun the town. Joseph wasn't scared, but he was far from comfortable. He surveyed the area and saw a few white faces in the second- and third-floor windows of the office buildings on the Bay, staring at the proceedings like schoolmasters watching a yard full of misbehaving boys.

The negroes were waving and shouting at black passengers on a docked ship. The crewmen, Joseph saw, were white. Then he saw the ship's name. "Of course," he thought. He had completely forgotten about it, as it was several weeks late.

"What is it, Master Joseph?" Andrew had to yell above the din, though he was standing directly in back of Joseph.

Joseph wedged aside to make room for Andrew. "It's the *Huma!*"

Andrew looked at the ship and thought, "My God, it's finally here."

In 1816, several prominent white men gathered in Washington City to form the American Colonization Society. They believed free negroes would never be accepted into white society in America and wanted to offer them the chance of settling in Africa. The society raised money from philanthropists and by selling memberships in the organization. In 1820, the society sent three white agents and eighty-eight blacks across the Atlantic to found an African colony. Soon after settling an area on the Upper Guinea coast, the three whites and twenty-four of the blacks died of fever. The survivors evacuated to nearby Sierra Leone, which the British had established in 1787 to settle slaves who had escaped America during the Revolutionary War. A few years later, despite a shortage of funds, threat of sickness, and hostility from local tribes, the society successfully settled another area. Over the ensuing years, several thousand free negroes in America had seized the opportunity to remove to Africa, and by 1847, the colony, Liberia, had become an independent nation, governed by negroes.

A few auxiliaries of the society formed in Georgia, but they didn't generate much local support or funding. Still, the society pressed ahead with its mission. In 1849 it chartered the *Huma* to relocate free negroes from Charleston, Augusta, and Savannah. The response was overwhelming. Free negroes flowed into Savannah. The local slave population turned out in thousands to send off 184 of their brothers and sisters.

After a few minutes of watching the unbelievable assemblage, Andrew shook Joseph's shoulder and hollered in his ear, "Look! Isn't that Jumbo on the ship?"

It took Joseph a while to scan the deck, but he finally spotted Jumbo, the friendly rose-maker and magician, acknowledging the boisterous crowd with his hands clasped over his head like a triumphant prizefighter. Joseph called out to him, but his shouts didn't carry two feet past his mouth. Joseph and Andrew waved as wildly as the others in the crowd, but Jumbo was as unlikely to see as hear them.

One black and three white pastors stood at the foot of the wharf and read from Bibles. After they blessed the ship and prayed for the passengers, a tug towed the *Huma* away from the dock and towards Tybee Island. The crowd cheered even louder. Jumbo and the other emigrants were on their way to Liberia. Joseph wondered what the local reaction to this spectacle would be. Andrew wondered what Africa was like.

Part of the crowd on the bluff ran up the Bay, keeping pace with the *Huma*, while the rest lingered. The celebration over, Joseph and Andrew left for work. When they reached the Bay, they heard someone call, "Good morning, Brother Andrew. Good morning, Mr. McBain."

"Reverend Marshall!" Andrew hadn't spoken to him in two months, as he had been leaving the church right after services, since he was unable to speak to Patience. He was embarrassed facing Marshall and hoped Deacon Low had explained the situation to him.

The ninety-four year old reverend leaned on his cane and said, "This is a great day. So many of us are going home." Marshall pointed in the direction of the ocean and said, "That home." He then pointed skyward. "Not that home."

Joseph and Andrew laughed. Andrew then asked, "Reverend, I thought I saw Brother Titus, his wife, and children on the ship. Aren't they slaves?"

The reverend shifted his cane to his other hand. "They are, or were. Why?"

Andrew stammered, "I, I thought the American Colonization Society only took free persons to Africa."

Marshall nodded. "That's true. Titus and his family were manumitted."

Andrew glanced at Joseph, and then faced the minister. "I didn't think that was possible."

"His owner died. The will provided for Titus's return to Liberia. Left him a nice amount of money, too. The courts have ruled that foreign manumission is legal. Any master, living or dead, can free his slaves as long as he sends them to Africa."

Andrew looked to the river and the fading *Huma*. He had another option. Going to Africa wouldn't be ideal, but at least he would be with Patience.

Joseph and Andrew bade good day to Marshall and went their separate ways. Andrew only had to walk across the Bay to the Custom House site. "Sorry I'm late, Mr. Norris. I got caught up in the crowd."

Norris replied, "So did a lot of people, Andrew. The whole town is standing still."

Despite the constant petitioning by Charles Cluskey, local mechanics, and artisans against John Norris, the New Yorker remained the architect of the Custom House. The start-up had been a slow process as the scope of the project grew to include a post office and courtroom and the increased appropriation had to be approved by Congress. Also, an adjoining lot had to be purchased to accommodate the larger building.

While this was transpiring, Norris opened an office in Savannah and offered his services to the general public. And he used local workers. Soon, he won bids for the Georgia Historical Society building on Bryan Street, the Chatham Artillery Armory on Wright Square, and two lighthouses in the Savannah River.

Norris had employed local builder Matthew Luftburrow for the Custom House. While the Greek Revival building was to be constructed of imported granite and marble, the foundation and floor supports would be brick. Norris asked Luftburrow if he knew of a negro bricklayer named Andrew who worked for Charles Cluskey. The builder said there was one who belonged to the largest brick maker in Savannah and was supposed to be the equal of any white. Norris asked him if he would hire the negro if he were available. Luftburrow said he wouldn't mind. Norris went to McBain's house and asked him if he could hire Andrew. Andrew had been working on the project for the past year and impressed Norris with his skill and commitment.

"It's an amazing sight, sir," Andrew replied, observing the scene on Bay Street.

"It certainly is." Norris didn't think it was possible in the South. He also never thought he would see so many negroes working in so many jobs in Savannah. The whites and blacks did not interact socially, but they lived and worked together with no apparent problems. Of course, something was brewing beneath the surface, as the turnout for the *Huma* showed.

Norris found nothing more surprising than Andrew McBain, a first-rate black bricklayer interested in classical architecture and conversant in Vitruvius and Palladio. "Andrew, you'll soon be finished with your duties here. I'm working on a house and could use your help finishing it up. Will you have time?"

Andrew folded his arms in thought, trying to conceal his excitement. Norris was as great an architect as Cluskey, and nicer to work for. Andrew thought it an honor that Norris requested him for another job. "I believe so, sir. I need to ask Master McBain if he has anything planned for me. Where is the house?"

"On Lafayette Square. Where the city jail used to be."

Andrew stepped back. "Master Low's new house?"

"Yes. You know of it?"

"Yes, sir, I do." The discussion had brought back to mind his predicament with Patience. He had missed his opportunity to talk to Joseph that morning. He had to try again that evening. "I'll ask Master McBain about working on Master Low's house when I see him. I'm certain he'll approve."

"Master Joseph, do you have time to talk?" Andrew asked after the McBains had finished supper.

Joseph made a motion like he was aiming a pool cue. "Sure. How about the billiards parlor? I owe you two dollars from the last time. I need to win my money back."

"I'd like to talk here, alone, if that's all right."

Joseph said, "Of course. Let's go on the piazza. It's a beautiful night."

They sat and Joseph lighted a Havana. He blew a long trail of smoke that floated towards the square. They watched it make its journey until it disappeared into the night.

Andrew spoke in a hushed voice, "Joseph, I need to ask you a big favor."

Joseph sat up. "You sound serious."

Andrew explained the situation with Patience and her father. Joseph drew heavily on his segar, his eyes almost crossing as he focused on the glowing red tip. He had met Patience many times during her Sunday strolls with Andrew. Joseph thought she was beautiful and was elated for his friend, who had told Joseph of his plans to propose. "He won't let you see her? Ever?"

"Good evening, gents. Mind if I join you?" Grandfather said as he settled in a chair. "Is that a Havana I smell?" Joseph fetched a segar, clipped it, and handed it to the old man, who asked, "Did you hear about the commotion in town today?"

Joseph eased back into his seat. "You mean the *Huma*? We saw the whole thing."

Grandfather waved his unlit segar as he spoke. "Some people are mighty upset. I was at the Pulaski House this afternoon. They're already talking about banning American Colonization Society ships from here. One alderman is recommending a two hundred dollar tax on all free negroes who come to Savannah."

Joseph said, "This isn't what Sir James Oglethorpe planned when he founded Georgia."

Grandfather rested his feet on the front part of Joseph's chair. "No, I'm afraid it's not. And for your information, he isn't *Sir* James. He was never knighted."

Joseph coughed on his segar smoke. He cleared his throat and said, "He wasn't? I always assumed he was. Didn't you tell us he was?"

"No. It's the one thing about him I never told you. One of the great shames of history. It still rattles my arse." Grandfather leaned on his side and slapped his buttock. "That's why I never mention it."

Andrew stiffened. "After founding Savannah from a pine forest? After all he sacrificed, including his own fortune, to save Georgia? After banning slavery? After defeating the Spanish in America? Why not?"

"I don't rightly know, Andrew. As I told you, he came from a family of Jacobites, something the ruling Hanovers never took kindly to. The Duke of Cumberland, who led the English forces, blamed Oglethorpe when Bonnie Prince Charlie escaped a battle during the Uprising of '45. Had him court-martialed. Thankfully, he was cleared."

Andrew asked, "If he was cleared, why would he be denied knighthood?"

Grandfather saw that Andrew was upset about this news of his hero. "I guess his Jacobite past and the fact that he even had charges brought against him were too much to overcome. He had a strong personality, Andrew. Made some enemies along the way. Folks in South Carolina wouldn't have wanted him knighted after the slaughter of their soldiers at Fort Mose during the siege of St. Augustine. But life is full of injustices. You try to change them. If you can't, you just have to live with them."

Andrew stared into the night and thought about injustices. He heard himself say, "Someone should write a letter to the Queen. Let her hear a Georgian's opinion of Oglethorpe."

Joseph and Grandfather both looked at Andrew, inadvertently blowing streams of smoke at him. He fanned the fumes away with his hand. Grandfather said, "Why don't you do it, Andrew? Make your case and ask her to knight Oglethorpe posthumously. You just might convince her."

Andrew looked at the floor. "I don't think that would work, Grampah. Why would she listen to me? I'm just a . . ." Andrew caught himself. It was an unfortunate slip of the tongue, but it was all that he had been thinking about recently.

Grandfather read his mind. "Precisely because you are."

Andrew thought about what he had said. Would the Queen of England, if she even cared to listen, be sympathetic to an American slave? "I don't know. I wouldn't feel comfortable writing to her." Andrew took a deep breath and said, "Grampah, when you walked in tonight I was just about to discuss something with Master Joseph. I want you to hear what I have to say."

Grandfather said, "If you wish."

After Andrew finished explaining his troubles, Grandfather said, "Andrew, Mr. McBain and I have often talked about freeing you. I guess it never became a pressing issue. That's just changed. I'll speak to him when he comes to town tomorrow. You do realize one of our representatives to the legislature must submit a bill to manumit you and it has to pass both houses. We won't know who our representatives will be until the October elections. As soon as we know, James will have a word with him."

Andrew said, "Thank you, Grampah. I'll speak to Deacon Low. Maybe he'll reconsider letting me see Patience."

The men stood. Grandfather grabbed Andrew's hand to shake it. He asked, "Andrew, if you're manumitted, would you feel more comfortable writing to the Queen?"

Andrew smiled. "If I'm ever listed on the free persons register, I'll proudly write to Queen Victoria."

Grandfather squeezed Andrew's hand. "I'll hold you to that. The more I think of it, the better it sounds: a negro in Georgia asking the Queen of England to knight the great Oglethorpe. If she has any heart at all, she can't refuse."

"Would you mind repeating that, James," John W. Anderson, asked. "I didn't quite hear you." It was October 1849. Anderson had just been elected to the house of the state legislature from Chatham County and was preparing to leave for Milledgeville.

"I said, I'd like you to introduce a bill to manumit one of my negroes." McBain had stopped by Anderson's office to congratulate him on his election.

Anderson removed his spectacles, blew hot air on them, wiped them against his shirt, and put them back on. "I did hear you correctly. James, I think it's been a while since a negro was manumitted by the legislature."

McBain pulled up a chair and sat. "We have to try. Andrew is like a son to Sarah and me. He's as hardworking, honest, and faithful as any man I know, black or white."

Anderson countered, "He could be the Lord's first born! If he's a slave, the legislature isn't likely to free him. Free negroes are considered to be lazy troublemakers."

McBain banged the desk with his fist. "Andrew is no lazy troublemaker, believe me. And I'm certain if we use our collective influence, we can accomplish it."

Anderson was indeed an influential fellow. He had been an alderman, a congressman, and a state legislator. He was a director of the Central of Georgia Railroad and Banking Company. He had also been a captain of the Republican Blues militia unit. If he couldn't help Andrew, few could. "Thank you for your confidence, James. It'll be like spitting into the wind, but I'll try. There are hundreds of men in Georgia who feel their servants are special. Make your request to me in writing. Make a case for the boy. You're one of the most respected businessmen in the state. The legislature will listen, at least. But don't get your hopes up. Word is there's going to be a very heavy docket."

McBain told Anderson he would have the letter to him the next day. He then paid a visit to Thomas Purse, one of the biggest booksellers in town, and the new state senator from Chatham County. McBain received no better encouragement from him.

The rest of the year passed with high expectations. Andrew had a talk with Deacon Low at church informing him that Master McBain was seeking his manumission. Deacon Low said he was happy to hear it, but still didn't allow him to see Patience. Andrew was not aware that Patience had told her father she would never again look at another man, slave or free. But the deacon maintained he knew what was best for her.

Joseph enjoyed the life of a bachelor. At twenty-nine years, he was one of the most eligible in Savannah. At six feet he was slightly taller than his father, more muscular, and wore his light brown hair to his shoulders. And he was rich. He met ladies as most single men did: at soirees, dinner parties, and at church. He displayed a greater interest in a few and met their parents. He attended the annual Jasper Greens ball, a precursor to an engagement, with Kathleen Habersham. But, to his mother's dismay, Joseph never got engaged. He was having fun. But he did miss his sister.

Amy had written to her parents that she wouldn't be home for Christmas, but she did announce that she was leaving her position in February and would be returning to Savannah for good. She was tired. The McBains were thrilled. Sarah couldn't wait to bring her daughter home. She was certain that now, at last, Amy was ready to find a husband and start a family.

Sarah left for Milledgeville in early February 1850 to bring Amy, and all her belongings, back to Savannah. She was accompanied by Teenah and her husband, Jefferson, who worked for Hercules in the stables and also served as a coachman.

Before Sarah departed, James told her he had not heard from Anderson about the status of Andrew's bill. He said he had written to Anderson informing him to expect a visit from her, and to show Mrs. McBain every courtesy, as it wasn't customary for a woman to approach a legislator about legislation.

The morning after she had arrived, Sarah visited the capitol building, but Anderson was in session all day and she did not see him. She tried again the next day and caught him during a break as he hurried from the building to another meeting. When she called his name, he said that he didn't have time. Then he realized it was Sarah and stopped. He explained that he'd been so busy he hadn't had time to introduce the bill and didn't think he would before the end of the session.

That evening, Amy's last day at the asylum, Sarah sat and cried as she recounted the conversation with the legislator to her daughter. "With only two weeks left, he doesn't think he'll be able to introduce it. And we're leaving in two days."

Amy massaged the back of her sobbing mother. "That's wrong, Mother. He's had plenty of time. I can't understand it. Mr. Anderson is such an honorable man."

Sarah sniffled, "Andrew will be crushed. He's so in love with that girl."

Amy paced around the room looking at the floor, her arms folded. She stopped and turned to her mother. "Unpack those bags! We're not leaving."

Sarah lifted her head. "What are you talking about, Amy?"

Amy kneeled next to her mother's chair. "I've lived here for six years, Mother. I know a lot of people in this town. We're not leaving until Andrew is free, or at least gets a hearing. Now, we need to get organized. Tomorrow, we'll telegraph Father and tell him we'll be a few weeks late. I'll talk to Dr. Cooper about staying on at the cottage. Then we need to speak to every legislator. We don't have much time, and they're in session all day. We'll have to divide up the list. Is Mary Lamar Cobb in town?"

Sarah said, "Yes. We've written to each other. We were going to arrange a visit but she hasn't been feeling well."

Amy stood and started pacing again. "I hope she's well enough to help us. I'll send her a message to meet us tomorrow. And I need to pay a visit to Mr. Anderson."

"When?"

Amy stepped to the coat tree. "Right now. I know where he's living. The bill must be introduced immediately or all is lost."

As Amy tied her bonnet and put on her shawl, Sarah said, "Amy, he told me just today he doesn't have the time."

Amy wrapped a shawl around her mother's shoulders. "We'll see. I'll have Jefferson get the carriage."

Anderson was surprised to see the women at his front door. He thought he had fully informed Mrs. McBain of his schedule. He had a pile of bills to read for the next day's business. Being speaker of the house didn't allow him a second of free time. As it was, he didn't think he'd be going to bed before two o'clock. Still, a gentleman, he invited them in. They sat in chairs in front of a crackling fireplace.

Anderson puffed on his pipe. "How may I help, Mrs. and Miss McBain?"

Amy relaxed in her chair as if she were about to catch up with an old friend. "I would like to know about the bill to manumit one of our servants."

Anderson picked up some papers from a side table and put them on his lap. Then he presented the status to Amy just as he had done to her mother; slowly, explaining the legislative procedure, as if addressing a young child. As he spoke, he occasionally glanced at the papers.

Amy stood and pushed her chair two feet from Anderson's. She took the papers from his lap and placed them back on the table. She sat on the front edge of her chair and glared at the man. "Sir, you told my father that you would introduce that bill during this legislative session. He felt comfortable with your promise because of your reputation and friendship. Speaking for my father, I expect you to keep your word."

Anderson put his pipe down. "Miss McBain, you must understand I serve many people and businesses. They all have requests. I do my best to meet them. Some are easier than others. The legislative session is limited and I can only do so much. I had informed your father of the heavy schedule and warned him not to get his hopes up."

Amy calmly asked, "Did you give your personal word to each one of your constituents, sir? Your solemn promise?"

"Miss McBain, if every one of my constituents required action on their special interests, I'd get nothing done." Anderson was flustered by Amy's direct approach. He reached for his pipe. Just as he was about to stick it in his mouth, Amy stood, pulled it from his hand, and tapped its smoldering contents into the fireplace. She stood over him. The representative looked as if he were about to have a tooth pulled.

She pointed the pipe at him. "No excuses, sir! You gave your word."

Amy's rising voice caused Anderson to press back in the chair. "Yes, Miss McBain."

"Good." Amy sat again. She noticed her mother, who didn't have her fan, rapidly tapping her chest, her face as white as a ball of cotton. "Let's move ahead. I want to know where each representative resides in Milledgeville, so I can contact them."

"Miss McBain, you won't have time to contact them all. There are one hundred of us."

Amy slapped the bowl of Anderson's pipe in her palm. "Sir, please don't tell me what's not possible. Tell me what *is* possible."

"Miss McBain, I'll appoint a committee to discuss the bill tomorrow. That's the procedure. I'll make sure the committee recommends its introduction. After it's read the first time, I'll have a good idea of who is in favor and who isn't. You can concentrate your efforts on those who are uncertain or against it."

Amy handed the pipe to Anderson. "That's an excellent suggestion, sir. That's what you're known for. But remember you have only two weeks to the end of the session. The bill must be read and passed in the house and the senate."

Anderson stuck the pipe in his mouth. "I'm well aware of that, Miss McBain. I'll do what I can. I'm seeing Senator Purse and the president of the senate, Mr. Wofford, tomorrow. I'll mention the issue to them as well. But I must warn you, I have no power in the senate. And the senators are not enthusiastic about manumission."

Amy said, "I'll deal with the gentlemen there when the time comes. Thank you for your time." Amy stood and her mother and Mr. Anderson followed. When they reached the front door, Amy said, "Sir, you can't imagine how important the passage of this bill is to us. Good evening." After the women left, Anderson paid a visit to the liquor cabinet.

Sarah and Amy met Mary Lamar Cobb the next day. She seemed distracted, unable to concentrate on any topic for long. Two of her sons had died the year before in Washington, where her husband was serving as a congressman and speaker of the house. Her fortune was dwindling fast, thanks to Howell's lavish spending. Mr. Cobb hardly wrote to her as he was involved in some compromise to preserve the union. She told Sarah and Amy she hated politics and wished her husband had been a country lawyer. Mary did say she remembered the negro who had saved Charlie and would speak to anyone, if she had the energy.

True to his word, Mr. Anderson appointed a committee of six representatives to prepare and report a bill to emancipate a negro man named Andrew, currently the property of James McBain of Savannah. The committee recommended the reading of the bill. After its first reading, John Anderson gave Amy the names of the men he thought were undecided. That list included about half of the legislators. Sarah, Amy, and Mary Lamar Cobb spent the next four days lobbying those representatives. The mood of the representatives was surprisingly favorable. Several agreed with Amy that one more free negro couldn't hurt. Others, after almost four grueling months in Milledgeville, would do anything to wrap up matters and go home. The bill was read two more times on consecutive days and passed by a vote of fifty-five to forty-five. The bill was sent to the Senate with just six days remaining in the session.

That evening, Sarah and Amy went to Thomas Purse's house. He was cordial but not optimistic about the bill's chances in the Senate. The mood there was different, he explained. Senators considered themselves a more deliberative lot. Mr. Purse also made it known he had no power to push it through.

The women then went to the residence of the president of the Senate, William B. Wofford. He was from another district and owed nothing to the McBains. But he was impressed by the commitment of the two women. Amy, properly perfumed with her hair flowing loosely to her shoulders, made her presentation, standing closer to the politician than her mother thought necessary. As they left, Wofford said he would make sure the bill was read the next day, but claimed its passage would be a tough hill to climb.

Back at the cottage, Sarah said, "Amy, could you have been any more seductive to Mr. Wofford?"

"He said he's going to have the bill read tomorrow, didn't he?" Amy sat next to her mother on the couch. "I can handle him, Mother. Please leave that to me. Tomorrow night we'll visit him and see where we stand." Sarah took a deep breath. The frightened girl after the incident with Evan had become a hardened young woman.

The bill was read for the first time the next day and the McBains saw Wofford that night. Based on his conversations with his colleagues, he said it seemed they were about ten votes short, an insurmountable deficit.

Over the next three days, the women visited every man Wofford named as uncertain or moderately opposed. Amy spent extra time making herself up, under the narrowed-eyed glares of her mother. They pleaded, cajoled, and hinted at support from the influential McBain family.

The bill was read a second time on the next to last day of the session. Wofford told Amy that they had made great headway, but he figured they were still down by three, with the bill being read the third time and voted on the next and final day.

Amy dropped Jefferson off at the cottage and drove her mother and herself to the residences of the senators and a few of the better known restaurants to find the men and again plead their case. Two senators succumbed and promised to vote for manumission.

The McBains visited Wofford's house at eleven p.m. They sat around a table in the study and reviewed the list of senators. Wofford said, "It looks like you're a vote short. If you can just turn one man, you'll have it. But I know these men, Miss McBain. They are dead set against freeing negroes in principle. You won't change any more minds."

Amy buried her head in her hands and rubbed her temples. Wofford felt sorry for the women. He had seen few lobby as hard. Amy abruptly raised her head, picked up the list of names and said, "We need to leave now, sir. Thank you for your help. If you can think of a way to change a vote, I'll be eternally grateful."

As soon as the women boarded the carriage, Amy said, "Mother, I need to visit someone. I'm taking you to the cottage. You shouldn't see where I'm going. You'll be uncomfortable."

Sarah's mouth turned down. "Amy, I'm as deeply involved in this as you. We succeed together or fail together."

Amy snapped the reins. "I have no time to argue, Mother. If you insist, I'll bring you. Just never question me about where we're going."

"Of course I won't, dear. I would never do that."

Amy did not speak as she drove to the outskirts of Milledgeville. Sarah could make out the outlines of poorly constructed houses. She heard dogs barking and babies crying and smelled burning wood. Amy pulled the carriage to a house and tied the horse to a post. Lighted lamps glowed behind blinds in every window in the house. Sarah heard muted laughter from within.

Amy climbed down and said, "Follow me, Mother. We're going inside. I need to speak to someone and then we'll leave. Remember, you wanted to come." Sarah moved slowly, wondering if she had done the right thing.

Amy walked along a dirt path and up uneven steps to the front porch. She opened the door and entered a large room full of negroes, some men and mostly women, sitting on three well-worn couches, threads and tears everywhere. Two of the women were sitting on men's laps. All the women wore dresses with low-cut necklines revealing pushed-up mounds of breasts that looked like shiny black melons. The negroes fell silent as the two white women entered the room. The stares of strange black faces, the heavy smell of cheap perfume and tobacco smoke, and the laughter from nearby rooms weakened Sarah's knees. She saw thousands of specks of white lights flashing before her. Her own daughter had brought her to a negro house of ill fame.

She heard Amy somewhere in the distance say, "Sit here, Mother." Sarah felt someone guide her to a chair and she plopped down. She felt herself being fanned. Her dizziness slowly cleared and she saw Amy sitting on the arm of her chair. "Mother, are you all right?"

"I'm fine, Amy, why do you ask?" Amy handed the fan to her mother and was about to say something when they heard stomping of heavy feet on the stairs. A large black woman adorned in a blonde wig and bright red dress with fluffy black trim entered the room.

"How may . . . Why Mistus Amy! Wut a suhprise, chile! Sheets tole me you leabin' town!" The negress hugged Amy. Sarah felt faint again. The madam personally knew her daughter.

"I'm fine, Dolly. Dolly, please meet my mother, Mrs. McBain." Sarah gaped at the woman, unable to speak.

"Hello, missus. Look at you, chile! Now ah know wuffuh Mistus Amy so beautiful."

The negroes in the room erupted in laughter. Sarah worked her fan. "Thank you, Dolly. You're very kind."

Dolly bent and rested her hands on her knees to speak face-to-face with Sarah. "May ah git you some tea, missus? Uh drink uh some kine?"

Sarah nodded. "Yes, please. Tea would be fine."

Amy said, "Dolly, may I speak to you for a minute?"

"Sholy can, mistus. C'mon inside."

Amy said to Sarah, "I'll be right back, Mother. Relax and have your tea."

Dolly led Amy through a beaded curtain and into another room. Sarah smiled uncomfortably at her neighbors and elevated the pace of her fan. The negroes smiled back. Then one of the men resumed telling a joke to the others.

Twenty minutes later Amy reappeared to find her mother listening intently to one of the negroes, who was saying, "An' he say tuh de gent'men, 'Ah know you jes' lef' dere cause you wearin' muh shirt.'" The negroes screamed in laughter. Sarah smiled.

Amy broke up the party. "Ready, Mother?"

"Oh, yes, dear." Sarah stood. "Good night, Flower and Angel, Cyrus and John."

The negroes stood. One said, "Ebnin', missus. C'mon back wen you kin."

A recovered Sarah followed Amy out. "Where are we going now?"

"Not we. This time I'm taking you home first. There's no place for you to sit or wait where I'm going." Amy had made up her mind.

"No, Amy!" Sarah was beginning to enjoy her adventure.

"Yes, Mother. Yes! You can't be a part of this. That's final."

Sarah accepted her daughter's decision. Amy took her to the cottage and drove off. Sarah realized her relationship with her daughter had changed forever.

Amy drove for ten minutes, parked the carriage in front of the house, walked to the front door, and knocked. A servant answered the door. "Yes, Missus?"

"Is Senator Flint in?"

"Yes'm. Who is calling?"

"Miss Amy McBain."

Amy and Sarah woke up late Saturday and spent the day packing. Sarah wanted to go to the state house and wait for the outcome of the vote, but Amy refused. She claimed she didn't want to do anything to embarrass the family. They didn't say much to each other. Amy handed clothes to Teenah, who folded them and handed them to Mrs. McBain, who packed them. Occasionally, Sarah asked Amy where she had bought an article of clothing, but otherwise they were silent. They had done all they could for Andrew, and were planning to visit Mr. Purse that evening to get the news before leaving for Savannah the next morning.

Late in the afternoon, they heard a knock at the door and froze. Teenah went downstairs to answer it. Amy and Sarah stared at each other, hardly breathing. They heard voices, then Teenah climbing the stairs. "Master Wuffud fuh oonuh, Miss Amy."

Amy patted her hair and straightened out her dress, and she noticed her hand was shaking. She descended the stairs and walked to the door. "Mr. Wofford, please come in."

Wofford stepped into the house, removed his hat, greeted Amy, and saw Mrs. McBain standing on the middle of the stairway. His face was expressionless. He said to Amy, "I don't know how you did it, Miss McBain. I didn't think there was a chance. But the bill passed by one vote. Your negro has been manumitted. Congratulations. I wish you'd come work for me."

Amy raised her hands to her face and said, "Thank you so much, sir!"

Sarah ran downstairs and wrapped her arms around Amy. Teenah followed Sarah, hugging Amy from behind, creating a bundle of humans. Teenah started to bounce up and down on the balls of her feet. Amy felt her movement and followed along. So did Sarah. They bounced together, laughing, crying, and moving to freedom's beat.

Wofford looked on, and couldn't help but smile.

Part 3

Freedom Rides

1850-1861

CHAPTER 17

The Wedding

1850-1852

Amy stood beside Andrew as the McBains waited for Hercules to bring the coach to the front of the house on Pulaski Square and whispered, "Are you excited?"

Andrew was dressed in a black suit, white shirt, and necktie. Though he was only three inches taller than Amy, his top hat made him look a foot bigger. He smiled at Amy. "I certainly am, thanks to you." It was several weeks after Andrew first registered as a free person of color. The family was going to Mr. Low's house to meet Patience and for Mr. Low to meet Andrew.

Amy held Andrew's arm and said, "Patience is a lucky woman, Andrew."

Andrew blushed and said, "I'm the lucky one, Miss Amy."

Amy looked to the square and thought about the events that made this night possible. Over the years at the asylum, Amy had met several members of Sheets's family, including his aunt Dolly, the proprietor of a popular, local house of ill fame. Dolly had asked Amy several times if she could buy her things like soaps and perfumes that could only be purchased at white stores. Amy always obliged. Dolly was eternally grateful and told Amy she'd like to return the kindness. Amy told her it wasn't necessary. Then Amy needed one vote to free Andrew. She frantically searched her mind for any idea that might produce it. She thought of Dolly and the dirty little secrets she might have about the legislators who were her customers.

Amy also had a surprise for Andrew, but wanted to keep it secret until after meeting with the Lows. Joseph, her partner in it, agreed. She looked around to make sure her parents could not hear her. They would be surprised, too. "Andrew, with your experience, do you think you could build a house? You know, design and construct it?"

Andrew pursed his lips in thought. "I think I could, but I've never done it before. I'd need help. I'd have trouble getting all the workers to take orders from me."

Amy tugged gently on his sleeve. "Don't be bashful, Andrew. If you had help, you could do it? There's a first time for everyone."

Hercules pulled the coach to the front of the house and the family climbed in.

The McBains stepped from the coach and stood at the gate of Mr. Low's new house to admire the landscaping. The path to the front stairs divided the garden into two parts, both in perfect symmetry. The beds on either side were the same size and shape, and the flowers they held—spicy pink, fair white, and red roses, geraniums, and syringa—were the same. Mr. McBain opened the gate and said, "Andrew, don't you think landscape design can add as much beauty to a house as the architecture?"

Andrew said, "I had finished my work before the garden was laid out. Seeing it now, I wish I'd been here. Look at all the swirls of colors. It's like Master Cerveau painted it. You know when it comes to flowers, all colors blend. They never contrast."

The family walked up the path. They all stared at the house, a classic Greek Revival, two-story-over a-basement-floor, five-bay, center-hall design in coral-colored stucco. The front door surround had Tower-of-the-Winds columns with one row of acanthus leaves in the capital, and was capped with a pediment.

The family climbed up the stairs and Low's butler, Tom Milledge, dressed in a suit, welcomed them at the door with a slow bow at the waist. He then escorted them into the hall. Andrew Low, several inches shorter than the McBain men and grayer in hair, appeared from one of the rooms. He held out his arms and announced, "Welcome to the McBain family. Good to see you, James." Low acknowledged Sarah and Amy with a smile and a bow, and shook hands with James, Joseph, and Grandfather.

McBain then introduced Andrew. Low said, "Yes, Andrew, I saw you often working on the house."

Andrew bowed and said, "It's a pleasure to meet you, sir."

Low led the folks into the study. Had Low received the McBains without the presence of negroes, he would have entertained them in the guest parlor. However, for this occasion, with a mixing of races, the less formal study was more appropriate, as would have been the piazza.

Low's two daughters, Hattie and Amy, two and three years old, his sister-in-law, Elizabeth Hunter, Deacon and Mrs. Low, and Patience were waiting. Andrew Low took the little girls from Elizabeth's arms and introduced them to his guests. The girls buried their heads in their father's shoulders. Low handed his little treasures back to Aunt Elizabeth. Andrew Low's wife, Sarah Hunter Low, had died during childbirth in May of the previous year and his four year-old son, Andrew, Jr., the year before that. Low, an Englishman and one of the wealthiest commission merchants in town, asked his wife's sister, Elizabeth Hunter, to move in and help raise the girls.

Low introduced the McBains to the others. The deacon bowed and Polly and Patience Low curtsied, all with smiles, Patience's being the most sincere. Patience then stepped over to Andrew and held his arm. She was wearing a high-waisted, white and pink print full gown with dropped shoulders and leg-of-mutton sleeves.

The hem reached her instep. She wore a white flower in her hair. Andrew thought she was even more beautiful and graceful than usual.

Mr. Low looked around the room, beaming, and said, "What a fine moment this is. I can't believe our little Patience is a woman and ready to marry."

Marriages involving negroes were not legal in the state of Georgia. Slaves were property and could not make contracts, and free negroes were not citizens. But most whites recognized negro unions. Slave owners considered these "marriages" important events for the stability and additional slaves they produced.

Of course, owners set the rules for slave marriages. A harsh master might pair his servants up, not allowing them to select their own mates. But most owners let their slaves make their own choices.

The master also decided whether to allow a wedding ceremony, and many performed the service themselves. A common ritual, with roots to African traditions, involved laying a broom stick on the floor. The couple, holding hands, would step backwards over it.

If a church was nearby, or there was a plantation chapel, the master might even have a white minister administer the vows. Most masters allowed a simple celebration afterwards. If they didn't, the servants would have one anyway, away from the eye of the master.

Matters became more complicated when slaves of different owners wanted to marry, since the two masters had to agree. Once they did, they also had to resolve the living arrangements. Often, the husband and wife stayed with their respective owners and were allowed to visit each another once or twice a week. However, one master might purchase the other slave so the couple could live together.

When two Heritage servants wanted to marry, the man approached Mr. McBain for permission. Mrs. McBain had a seamstress make a simple dress for the bride, though on several occasions, for favored servants, Amy had lent clothes and jewelry to the bride for the ceremony. Mr. McBain performed the service in the big house. This was followed by a modest celebration in the yard of the house or in the Quarter, with cakes served. Sarah McBain often attended the festivities, as did Amy and Joseph when they lived at the Heritage.

That James McBain and Andrew Low would want to meet the prospective spouses of their charges, and allow the parents of the bride-to-be to attend the meeting, wasn't a common occurrence. But it was reflective of the paternalistic feelings some owners had for their servants.

Andrew, being a free man, did not need Mr. McBain's permission, but the McBains were his family, and he coveted their approval.

Andrew Low continued, "Deacon, why don't you say some words?"

"Yes, sir, Master Low." Deacon Low's jaw muscles clenched as he deferred to another man who had the ultimate approval of his own daughter's marriage, and would receive hundreds of dollars for selling her. But he held his hands behind his back and spoke. "There is no event so happy and so sad at the same time as the day a father gives away his daughter in marriage. Happy for the lifetime she will share with her new husband, sad because she is leaving our home. She's not going far, praise the Lord, but she's still leaving. I will no longer be greeted each morning and evening by that smile. I will no longer read the Bible to my baby each night, or tell her stories at bedtime. Not that I have done that recently." The folks laughed. "If my wife and I had to find the best man for her, an honest, hard-working, God-fearing man, we could not have found one better than Andrew McBain. May the Lord bless this couple and their marriage."

"Hear, hear," McBain called.

Patience hugged her father and mother.

Mr. Low said, "Please sit," and pointed to the two leather-covered settees and some chairs. The McBains, Elizabeth Hunter, and little Hattie and Amy sat while the negroes remained standing. Patience handed Amy and Joseph each a tube of paper tied with blue ribbons. Joseph turned it around in his hand, unsure of its purpose.

Patience said, "Master Joseph, please open it."

Joseph untied the ribbon and unrolled the paper. He read to himself and smiled.

"Well, don't keep us in suspense, Joseph," Sarah said.

Joseph blushed faintly. "I can't. You read it, Mother." He handed her the paper.

Sarah silently perused it and smiled at Patience. She then read,

> "Master Joseph, so successful, tall, and handsome
> Has the ladies of Savannah offering a ransom
> When will Master Joseph heed the call
> And stop their guessing, one and all"

Everyone applauded. Joseph said, "That was very thoughtful of you, Patience." Amy, less bashful than Joseph, unrolled her poem and read aloud.

> "Miss Amy left Savannah in a flourish
> A life of helping others she hoped to nourish
> Now she's back the bachelors take heed
> Of a woman so beautiful and strong they're all afraid"

More applause. "Thank you, Patience. I enjoyed that." Amy smiled. "And they should be afraid."

In the chatting that followed, Patience asked Mrs. McBain to tell stories of Andrew as a child. She did, and so did Grandfather, to the delight of everyone, except Andrew.

Tom Milledge brought in a tray of small cakes and offered it to the McBains, then set it on the table. The little girls knelt on the floor and started to sample each piece before their auntie motioned them away. The negroes made no move towards the cakes.

McBain asked about a wedding date. Deacon Low said a year was proper, if that met with Mr. Low's approval. The deacon wasn't letting go too quickly. Mr. Low nodded. One year was fine with him. Andrew sighed. He had hoped they could have married at once.

Polly Low then proclaimed they'd be married by the Reverend Marshall at the First African Baptist. She was worried Patience and Andrew would leave that church for the Second African Baptist on Greene Square, where most free Baptists of color in Savannah worshipped. Patience had assured her they would never leave the reverend. Andrew said little. He would marry Patience on Hog Island if he had to.

After about an hour, Mr. Low said, "James, I agree with the deacon. Patience could not have found a better man." Low turned to the happy couple. "May you two share a lifetime of happiness with my blessings." Andrew and Patience thanked him.

When the McBains returned to their house, Amy said, "I have an announcement to make. I'd like everyone including Andrew to gather in the family parlor."

Amy stood in front of the fireplace while everyone else sat. "I've been thinking about what I'm going to do here in Savannah. This town is growing so fast and there's limited space for people to live. With my savings, and a small loan from Grandfather, I've decided to build a paired townhouse, two houses in one building, as an investment. I'll rent both of them." Amy held a hand out. "Please meet my architects and builders, Joseph and Andrew McBain."

Andrew turned to Joseph, who was sitting next to him on the couch. Joseph slapped Andrew's back. "Congratulations, partner."

Andrew stood and held Amy's hand in both of his. "Thank you, Miss Amy. I can't tell you what this means."

McBain stared at his daughter, who winked at him. He realized her plan. She was giving Andrew the chance to be an architect, with Joseph acting as a front to the white community. Sarah beamed, realizing how much Amy was like her father. Grandfather hugged her.

A month later, Amy purchased a lot on Harris Street by Madison Square. The ward had been laid out in 1837 but was largely undeveloped in 1850. Charles Cluskey had built a beautiful Greek Revival house on the northwest corner of Bull and Harris in the early 1840s, setting the tone for a fashionable area.

Amy met with Andrew a few weeks later to discuss the design, which she wanted to be Greek Revival, constructed of exposed brick—Savannah Greys, of course. She told Andrew not to mention to anyone other than Patience that he was the architect and builder. Andrew knew that, but asked for and received permission to tell John Norris.

Norris congratulated Andrew and lent him his copy of *The Modern Builder's Guide* by Minard Lafever, one of the great American Greek Revival architects.

It took more than a month for Andrew to complete the first set of drawings. He asked Norris to review them. Norris, duly impressed, gave Andrew some suggestions, including recessing the front doors, adding iron balconies to the first floor windows, and adding two-story galleries on the back, all of which Andrew incorporated into his design.

At the end of June, he reviewed the plans with Amy. The entranceways were at either end of the building and reached by a single stairway. The doors were fronted with a portico of Ionic columns, and capped with a pediment. The front doors were six paneled, with rectangular over-lights and sidelights. Each unit consisted of two bays, with the windows in a three-part pattern—a different size window on each floor, from largest up to smallest, as Charles Cluskey had shown Andrew. A simple dentil pattern lined the cornice. The brickwork was in the Flemish bond pattern, with each row alternating a header with a stretcher.

Amy was especially interested in the lighting scheme. A gas works had just been completed, built on the location of the Old Fort on the east side of town. As the works were constructed, the city had pipes laid under the streets. Amy's house would be one of the first in Savannah to have gas piped in.

Amy was also surprised to see the designs in relief in the tympanums in the portico pediments. Andrew explained that Ulysses the barber would sculpt them.

Andrew spent a week updating the drawings for Amy's comments. The next time they met, Joseph attended. Andrew gave Amy the cost estimates and a construction schedule. In addition to his responsibilities for the family businesses, Joseph would hire and pay the workers, order the materials, and visit the site daily to provide management, all based on Andrew's advice. Amy ended the meeting by telling Andrew and Joseph the project was in their hands. She and Sarah were leaving the hellhole of Savannah in summer for a new retreat, Tallulah Falls, in western Georgia.

Andrew and Joseph started immediately and by November, when Amy returned, she saw the shell of a house. That very evening, Dante asked Andrew to help him in the kitchen. Despite a tiring day at the site, Andrew obliged.

Dante's cooking continued to delight everyone. And ever since his session with the professor of mesmerization, he seemed to have stopped stealing. He was a few inches taller than Andrew, but slimmer. His hair grew in every direction, and sat atop a slightly lopsided face dominated by eyes that were so close together they almost touched at the bridge of his nose.

Dante stood at the chopping block, sizing up a freshly plucked chicken, and said casually, "Ah gladdee oonuh free."

Andrew concentrated on peeling a potato. "It wasn't easy, Dante. Thank God Miss Amy was in Milledgeville to help me."

Dante hacked the bird. "Leas' massa he'p oonuh. He yent mannimit no udda slabe."

Andrew put down the knife and dried his hands on a towel. Dante was making more than passing conversation. "What are you meaning to say, Dante?"

Dante tossed some chicken parts in a bucket. "Oonuh spend mos' de tahm wen uh chile in de big house playin' wid Massa Joesup. An oonuh laa'n tuh read an' write. Oonuh nebuh lib lukkuh slabe."

Andrew stood and wrung the towel in his hands. "I worked at the Heritage just as hard as anyone, in the pits, at the tables, at the kilns, at the wharf. Just remember that. It's true my friendship with Master Joseph gave me an advantage. I got an education. The McBains became my family. When I needed to be freed, they helped me. I'm not sorry for anything."

"Dat berry good fuh oonuh." Chop, chop.

Andrew took a deep breath. He had always befriended Dante when others wouldn't. Now Dante was hostile because of Andrew's success. "I can't change slavery, Dante. I do what I can to make things a little better. When we're finally free, we'll have to be educated to survive, or nothing will change. I tried to help you, but you never had the time."

"Mussy boocoo. Us yent nebuh gwine fuh free. Wuffuh wait fuh it?"

"You have to have faith, Dante. Reverend Marshall knows the day will come."

Dante held up a chicken leg and pointed it at Andrew. "He uh hunnud yeah ole. He stillyet waitin'. He waitin' een heben soon."

Andrew threw the towel on a chair, shocked at Dante's comment. "Dante, if you don't have faith in God, what have you got?"

"Ain' hab nuttin', Andrew, jes' lukkuh all de udda nigguhs. If dey bin uh God, wuffuh dey slabery?" Dante dropped the chicken leg on the block. Whack!

"Dante, we're just slaves on earth. We'll be free in heaven."

"Andrew, fuh summun so smaa't, oonuh sho uh dum nigguh." Andrew took a step towards Dante, who quickly decided to take a different line. "Oonuh t'ink massa mannimit me an' he'p me buy uh restran'?"

"What?!!" Andrew leaned forward and placed his hands on the table, as if to prevent himself from falling over. "You want to buy a restaurant? There aren't any negro restaurant owners in Savannah."

Dante crumbled some sweet basil into the pot. "Dey ent no nigguh builduh in Sabannah, an' oonuh buildin' uh house fuh Miss Amy, ness pah?"

Andrew collapsed in a chair. "Dante, I'm free to do my work. You still have to cook for the McBains. When would you have the time to cook for a restaurant?"

Dante put down the knife and sat in a chair across from Andrew. "If massa mannimit me, lukkuh he done fuh oonuh, ah hab de tahm, see boo play."

Andrew pointed up at the ceiling. "What's wrong with cooking for the McBains? I thought you liked it."

"Mos' de tahm, ah jes' cookin' fuh Massa Joesep, Miss Amy, an' gran massa."

"But that's what you're expected to do. And they appreciate your cooking."

Dante tossed a potato in the air. "Ah talk tuh Brutus. He cookin' fuh Ow House Restran'. He say white folk wan' tuh meet he ebry night."

Andrew finally realized what Dante was getting at. Being a family cook for the McBains was no longer good enough. He wanted wider recognition for his talents, like Brutus got. Andrew did not want to tell Dante that he did not inspire confidence in others. Yet he was an excellent cook, according to Mr. McBain. And he was finally showing some ambition. That Dante would even think in such terms intrigued Andrew. "Dante, let me think about this. You won't be manumitted, or be allowed to own a restaurant. That's just the way it is. The only way this could happen would be to get Master McBain to change your schedule to free up your evenings. Then maybe you could get a job as a chef in a restaurant."

Dante went back to the chopping block. "No buckra gwine tek uh nigguh wid no 'sperience. Ah hab tuh buy de restran'."

"I told you that's not possible. Besides, many of Master McBain's friends know you're a good cook."

Dante ignored Andrew's point. "De Miraults, dey hab uh restran'."

Andrew considered that. The Miraults were confectioners. And they were mulattoes, slightly more acceptable to whites than blacks. But Andrew was interested by Dante's request. He thought out loud, "Maybe if we had the money, Master Joseph could buy a restaurant and you could be the cook. He could hire people to do the other work." He then said to Dante, "But you must ask yourself why Master Joseph would go through all the trouble just so you can be a cook in a restaurant?"

Dante looked at the floor. He had no answer.

"How much money do you have, Dante?"

Dante answered softly, "Fibe dolluh."

"What do you do with the money you make when Master McBain lets you cook at parties for other people? Or with the money Grampah gives you?"

"Spen' it."

Andrew folded his hands on the table and chose his words carefully. "Dante, you always ask others for help but do nothing to help yourself. You have to save the money. I wouldn't think of going to Master Joseph unless you have the money."

"Hummuch?"

Andrew shook his head. "I don't know. I've never owned a restaurant. At least two hundred dollars. Think about it, Dante. You can't just say you want a restaurant. You have to plan it, assuming Master Joseph would even help. Would he need a license? Where would the restaurant be located? How much would the rent be? Would you have to make renovations? Buy tables and chairs, plates, pots, skillets, and things for the kitchen? Who would do the serving and cleaning up, and how much would you have to pay them? How much would you charge for each dish? Who would do the shopping? There are so many things you have to know."

Dante threw the potatoes into the pot and grumbled, "All de folks luk muh gumbo."

Andrew stood next to Dante. "Dante, you're a great cook. But you have to go about this properly or you'll fail. No one's going to do it for you. You take some time and come up with answers, and I'll write them down. You also come up with the money, and I'll go to Master Joseph. The chances are very slim. But if you're willing to make an effort, I'll help you."

Andrew gave Dante an inspirational pat on the back and left the kitchen. Andrew was heartened by Dante's spirit but knew, with all the work and money needed, he would never hear about it again.

Dante watched his friend leave and thought, "Cyan' eben aks uh fabuh. Andrew ain' no diffren' den de buckra."

Despite a festive and exhausting evening helping to welcome home Mrs. McBain and Miss Amy from their summer retreat, Andrew hardly slept. Dante's comments stuck in his mind. He anxiously awaited Hercules's arrival the next day.

"What?" Hercules asked as he prepared to feed the horses in the carriage house.

Andrew followed Hercules. "I said, do the Heritage slaves think I betrayed them by my relationship with the McBains?"

Hercules snorted a laugh, sounding like a horse.

"I'm serious."

Hercules put the feed bucket down and faced Andrew. "I know you are. I laughed because you waited so long to ask. I think most slaves are glad for you. They proud you doin' good. It reflects on them. They also know you a black man, and that you never be accepted by white folks, no matter what you do. But there are two hundred of us at the Heritage, and some must think you get special treatment. Some think that of me. The house servants, too."

Andrew picked up the bucket and carried it to the horses. "Mrs. McBain wants to have a party at the Heritage after Patience and I get married in Savannah at the church. I don't want that if the others don't."

"That's dumb, Andrew. The folks want to celebrate the wedding with you. You their hope. They say Andrew is doin' what the white man does, even better. And you started by workin' right beside them."

Andrew handed the bucket to Hercules and said, "Dante wants to open a restaurant. He wants me to help him."

Hercules dropped the bucket, spilling feed on the floor. "He what?!"

Andrew recounted his conversation with Dante.

"So he's jealous of you being free. And he wants people to praise him. That started when he came back from Master Couper's years ago talkin' French. Now Brutus. I hope you gave him a hard kick in the arse."

Andrew knelt and swept the feed back into the bucket with his hand. "I said I'd help him if he saved the money and found out what it would take."

Hercules pulled Andrew up by the arm. "Andrew, has the fever caught hold of you? You want to help that worthless pile of manure?"

"He's not worthless, Hercules! He's a good cook. And he's twenty-eight years old. Look how far he's come. Now he's showing some ambition. I couldn't just turn him away. But we both know he'll never do what I asked of him."

Hercules released Andrew's arm. "True, but we also know he's not done askin' for favors. Let Dante learn to take care of himself. Helping him will only get you in trouble."

Andrew picked up the water bucket and headed for the backyard pump. "Deep down, he's a good man and a good friend, Hercules. I really believe that."

Hercules shook his head.

*   *   *

"Yuh hay f'um he comb, Launzy. Oonuh sendum uh conjuh," Dante said in a hushed voice to one of the old maumas, who was also the Heritage's conjure doctor. They were standing by the side of the plantation hospital. Dante was angry with Andrew. He went to his friend for a simple favor, and all he got was a bunch of conditions. It would take years to save two hundred dollars. And what was this about a plan? The slaves would be free before he could do all that. Even then, Andrew said he doubted Joseph would help him. Andrew had changed once he became a free man. He forgot about his friends.

"Wuffuh kine ub conjuh, Donnie?" The short, round-shouldered woman asked as she pulled the black curly hairs from the comb.

"Hmmm. Mebe sumptin' spile de house he buildin' fuh Miss Amy."

"Oonuh hab two dolluh?" Launzy asked as she fiddled with a plant root.

"Two dolluh?" Dante dug deep into his pocket, and took his time about it, waiting for the old witch to lower the price. He finally gave her the money. "Oonuh don' mine takin' money f'um uh slabe."

"Muh powuhs ain' free." Launzy never liked Dante and didn't want to hear his whining. "An' hush 'fo ah call oonuh ma obuh yuh."

"Wuh?"

"Oonuh ma. Ah see huh ghos'. Ah see huh all de tahm. Now, gi 'way f'um yuh!"

"Don' beliebe een no ghoses."

"Ah kin sees 'um." Launzy nodded and chewed on the root for a moment. "Ah bawn wid de caul, uh membrin, obuh muh face. Ah see de ghoses. Oonuh ma dey dey." Launzy pointed to one of the live oaks by the avenue.

Dante squinted at the tree, moving his head from side to side to see it from all angles. He turned back to Launzy. "Pit de conjuh on Andrew, dat's all."

"Ah callin' oonuh ma."

"Nooo!" Dante ran to find Hercules to go back to Savannah.

Launzy watched the pest run away. She didn't want to put a conjure on Andrew, but business was business.

On a Sunday in March 1851, Reverend Marshall performed a ceremony for Andrew and Patience McBain at the First African Baptist Church in front of the congregation, the McBains, and the Lows. Patience wore the white dress her mother had made for her. Andrew wore a new, gray suit and top hat Grandfather had bought him as a wedding gift. The chorus sang and the negroes prayed for the couple. Then they had lemonade and cakes in Franklin Square.

After, the McBains went to Mr. Low's house where they held a small party in the backyard with Mr. Low's servants.

In the late afternoon Patience and Andrew boarded the Rockaway. Hercules closed the door after them, stepped up to the driver's bench and started the horses to the Heritage. The McBains followed in the coach, driven by Jefferson.

Andrew sat close to his bride, held her hand and explained the sights. She squeezed Andrew's hand as he recounted how Grandfather and his twin brother swam across Musgrove Creek to escape the British in 1778. It was the same creek in which Patience and Andrew had been baptized.

It was just nightfall as they reached the top of the avenue of oaks. Hercules drove the Rockaway past the Quarter, which was deserted, and stopped. He opened the door on Patience's side, and signaled for her and Andrew to step out. Standing on the road and seeing the lights of the big house in the distance confused Patience. Andrew stared blankly at her. She turned around and saw the McBains standing in the road as well. She looked back at Andrew and saw several people lighting pine-pitch torches lining either side of the road all the way to the house. Soon, there was a lighted pathway with the underside of the branches of the huge oak trees illuminated. When Patience's eyes adjusted, she recognized servants dressed in their best clothes standing alongside the road between the poles. They started singing and clapping their hands. Patience looked at Andrew, who, beaming, offered his arm. She took it and they walked down the avenue. The McBains followed.

When they reached the house, Patience hugged her husband once again. In the yard beside the house someone started to light more torches, and Patience saw several long tables. Two negroes, one with a banjo and the other with a fiddle, began to play. Andrew escorted her to the music, took her in his arms and started to dance, just as Joseph had shown him that afternoon. When they finished the other servants joined in the merriment, singing and dancing.

The McBains sat at a separate table and enjoyed themselves as much as the negroes. Joseph and Amy danced together for the first time in years. Grandfather did a jig, to the cheers of the negroes, and only fell over once, to the cheers of the negroes. Andrew and Patience danced for hours. It was a night Patience would never forget.

The next day the McBains, with Andrew and Patience, returned to the house in Savannah. Patience moved into Andrew's room on the ground floor.

In the afternoon, Mr. McBain, Joseph, and Andrew went to the Planters Bank by Reynolds Square. McBain gave Andrew the money he had earned on outside jobs over the past ten years, better than fifteen hundred dollars, a small fortune for most whites, let alone negroes. Then Joseph opened an account for Andrew, held in trust by Joseph McBain.

Later that day, in Mr. Low's study, Andrew paid seven hundred dollars to Mr. Low, and received a bill of sale, witnessed by James McBain. Patience was Andrew's, body and soul. Every January thereafter, Andrew would have to pay a property tax of three dollars on his slave wife.

A few days later, using part of Andrew's savings, Joseph purchased a lot on Greene Square for his friend, the deed held in trust by Joseph McBain. This evaded the city law prohibiting free negroes from owning real property in Savannah.

As they walked home after completing the transaction, Andrew said, "Thank you for all your help, Master Joseph."

Joseph replied, "You're a free man, Andrew. I think you can call me Joseph now."

Patience continued to cook for Mr. Low for one dollar a day. The walk from Pulaski to Lafayette Square took ten minutes. She saw her parents almost everyday, and did what she liked best, cooking and playing with little Amy and Hattie.

Two months later, Andrew and Patience rented a house on Washington Square from Aspasia Mirault until Andrew could build a house of their own. Things could not be working out better for two negroes in Savannah, Georgia, in 1851.

*   *   *

To Andrew's frustration, the construction of Amy's house encountered the same obstacles as the construction of any house, and took longer than he had planned. Materials were not delivered on time. The wrong materials were delivered. Workers did not always show up on schedule. Workers who did show up got into fights. There were too many rainy days. Materials were stolen. The city issued fines for petty violations.

Joseph was on site early in the morning and at the end of the day, and whenever a new crew first showed. The negro workers and the white bricklayers took direction from Andrew, and even though everyone was civil to each other, Joseph had to deal with the other white workers.

One afternoon, Andrew asked one of the carpenters to replace a floor joist. The man told Andrew to go back to Africa. Andrew told him that talk wasn't necessary. The white man said it was and shoved Andrew, but the negro didn't budge. Joseph walked in during the stand-off and asked the carpenter for an explanation. The man told Joseph, who told the worker he was off the job. The other workers looked on. They grumbled amongst themselves but said nothing to Joseph.

Eventually, Andrew and Joseph overcame the problems. By the end of June 1851, the only major job remaining was installing the blinds and sashes, though a long list of small tasks had to be finished.

Twenty-four years after they had first played Villas of the Ancients, they stood together on Harris Street and looked upon their first house. Joseph put his arm around his friend. "We did it, Andrew! We really did it!" Andrew wiped away a tear. Indeed they did.

The next day, the blinds and sashes were installed. "Thank you, Master Van Horn. Miss McBain will be very pleased with your work," Andrew said.

Charles Van Horn, whom Andrew had met through John Norris, put his tools in a box and headed for the door. Without looking at Andrew, he said, "If I can be of service, have Joseph or Miss McBain contact me."

Andrew, trying to compliment Van Horn, said, "I'll surely do that, sir. You've put very fine touches on Miss Amy's house. They fit in perfectly with Joseph's overall design."

Van Horn turned to Andrew. "Mr. McBain is very capable, but he didn't design this house." Besides owning the window-sash and blind company, Van Horn was also a builder, and had built the Chatham Artillery for John Norris.

Andrew followed Van Horn to the door. "Don't underestimate him, sir. He followed Master Lafever's book."

Van Horn stopped and pointed a finger at Andrew, "Listen to me. There are a lot of hard-working white men in town who don't fancy losing their livelihood to darkies. They don't like it at all! Just watch yourself!" Van Horn walked out the door.

Andrew felt numb. He didn't know how to respond. He followed Van Horn down the steps to the street, and watched him climb into his dray and drive away.

Andrew turned back to the sidewalk, where a group of people had gathered. They were looking up at the tympanums in the porticoes, which bore portraits in relief of James Oglethorpe and George Washington, as sculpted by Ulysses. He forgot about Van Horn.

The paired houses also drew many curious negroes. Word had spread in the colored community that the house was designed by a black man and was as fine as any in Savannah. It also became well known at the Heritage that Andrew had built Miss Amy's house. Isaac told Mr. McBain that the servants wanted to see it. Father agreed to let Jefferson take a few of them into Savannah each Saturday afternoon. McBain would have allowed more, but a city ordinance, passed shortly after the *Huma* incident, prohibited more than two slaves from any one plantation from coming into town at the same time. Whether they saw it or not, the Heritage servants were proud of Andrew.

Amy first saw the house in early November, the day after she returned from Tallulah Falls, and was so excited she hugged Joseph and Andrew. A week later, the three watched from the first floor parlor as negroes carried the tenant's furniture up the stairs to the second floor.

As Amy explained to Joseph and Andrew that she had decided to open a millinery and woman's clothing shop with her friend, Marilyn Gardner, they heard creaking from the floor above. They looked to the ceiling and saw cracks began to spread in the surface. Then a piece of mortar dropped from it. Without saying a word, Andrew bounded up the stairs and ordered the movers to leave the house. Amy and Joseph stared at each other while they heard Andrew walk on the floor above.

Andrew returned looking as if he had just been handed a death sentence. He told Amy and Joseph he would be right back, and not to let anyone upstairs.

Ten minutes later he returned with John Norris. Norris said hello to Amy and Joseph and hurried upstairs with Andrew. When they returned to the parlor, Norris stared at the ceiling while Andrew fetched a ladder, hammer, and crowbar.

Norris laid down a large sheet in the center of the room, placed the ladder on it and climbed up. Using the hammer, Norris lightly tapped the ceiling, listening for a solid sound. Then, with the hammer and crowbar, he ripped away at the smooth stucco and ceiling laths. Amy gasped loudly at the destruction of the new ceiling. Norris heard her and called out, "Sorry, Miss McBain. But this is necessary. We can fix it."

Norris poked around, shook his head, and descended the ladder. He faced Andrew. "What size beam did you request?"

"Six by fourteen."

"Who was your carpenter?"

Andrew, who was already having trouble breathing, forced out, "Mr. Johnson."

Norris looked back at the ceiling and scratched his ear. "That's odd. My experience with him is quite good."

Amy asked, "Mr. Norris, what's wrong?"

Norris shook his head. "The beam is too small to carry the weight of the floor above and all the furniture sitting on it. It's causing the ceiling to sag."

Amy groaned and leaned against the wall. "Can it be fixed?"

Norris looked to Andrew and then at Amy. "Yes. We could put a supporting wall underneath it. But I think the best way is to tear out this ceiling, and replace the beam with the proper size. Then repair the ceiling."

Andrew's mouth was so dry he sounded as if he had a sore throat. "I'm sorry, Miss Amy. I don't know how this happened. I'll repair it at my expense."

Norris heard Andrew's wavering voice and jumped to his aid. "It's not as bad as it sounds, Miss McBain. Thankfully, Andrew noticed it right away. It could have been much worse. I'm going to check the rest of the framing. I'll lend some of my men to help Andrew. It shouldn't take more than a week or two."

Amy was weak-kneed at the defiling of her house and the thought of telling her tenants they couldn't move in as promised. "Thank . . . thank you so much for your help, Mr. Norris. I guess it's not that bad if it will only take a few weeks to fix."

Norris said, "I'm happy to help. Is there any furniture in the other house?" Amy shook her head. "Then I'm going to look at it with Andrew." Norris turned to Joseph. "Mr. McBain, could you arrange to have the furniture moved downstairs while we do?"

"Yes, Mr. Norris. I'll have it done right away." Joseph hurried out the front door.

Andrew pulled a handkerchief from his pocket and wiped his face. "Miss Amy. I don't know what to say. I let you down."

Amy saw Andrew sweating. She stepped over to him and patted his arm. "Don't worry about this, Andrew. Problems come with building a house. We haven't had any major ones until this. We'll fix it and move on."

Andrew thought out loud. "I saw the beams as they were delivered. I'd swear they were the right size. But I should have checked the installation. That's my job."

Norris jumped in. "Don't be too quick to judge yourself, Andrew. This sounds very strange. Any good carpenter should have known the right size beam. We can investigate this later. Now, let's take a look at the rest of the framing."

Norris and Andrew examined both houses by tapping on the ceiling and walls. As far as they could tell, only the one beam was undersized. Norris went to see Mr. Johnson and explained the problem. Johnson swore he delivered the proper materials to the site.

With Norris's help, Andrew corrected the problem. Two weeks later, Amy's tenants moved in. During that time, Andrew repeatedly thought of the events that might have caused the problem. He remembered the worker that Joseph had removed, and of Van Horn's comment, but he never mentioned anything to Joseph.

One evening shortly after Amy's house problem, Andrew was at the McBains' house. He told Dante what happened with Amy's house. Dante said, "Oh? Ah got tuh git tuh de kitchen," and left without saying another word.

After he completed Amy's house, and with a loan from Mr. McBain, Andrew started a house for Patience and himself. As before, he used Joseph to order materials, and hire and supervise white workers when necessary. Andrew and Patience decided on a one-story over a ground floor brick house on Greene Square with a portico of four Doric columns. Patience spent considerable time with Andrew reviewing the plans and even helped design the kitchen.

One evening in February 1852, Joseph saddled his mount to visit Andrew. Savannah Grey had been a gift from his father on Joseph's thirtieth birthday. She was a speedy filly. Joseph kept her in the city and loved taking her for runs on country roads on Sunday afternoons. As he rode along South Broad Street, he heard someone call, "Not a bad looking hossy, thar!"

"Charlie Lamar! How are you?" While Joseph and Charlie did not mix socially, Savannah was small enough that they ran into each other frequently. It was hard for anyone in town to ignore Charlie.

It had been six years since Gazaway Lamar moved to New York and left his Savannah business interests in the hands of his son. In 1850 Charlie had built the largest cotton press and warehouse in Savannah. The next year, at the age of twenty-seven, Charlie had become the captain of the Georgia Hussars, one of Savannah's most prominent militia units, a testament to Charlie's horsemanship, prowess with firearms, fighting spirit, patriotism, and leadership skills. He was also a member of the Chatham Democratic Party. But horses were Charlie's real passion, and riding Black Cloud at dangerous speeds through the streets of Savannah was his way to relax.

Charlie fell in with Joseph heading east on South Broad. "Could not be better, Joseph. Business is good and my horses are fast. And you?"

Joseph leaned forward and stroked Savannah Grey's neck. "Very well. Everybody's building something made of brick, lumber, or iron. How's your father?"

Charlie eyed Joseph's horse as he answered. "He's still living in Brooklyn. It's a healthier situation for his wife. He factors the cotton I send to England. He and some associates are about to open a new bank. He sees profits in it."

Joseph said, "Gazaway sees profits on the moon."

Charlie laughed loudly. "And beyond! How's your family?"

"Everyone's fine. Amy lives at the house on Pulaski Square. She just opened a millinery shop with a friend on Congress Street."

Charlie waved to two men who had called his name. He then said to Joseph, "So I've heard. She's caught the notice of every bachelor in town. But no one understands her. She's beautiful, unmarried, owns a shop, and turns down every proposal for marriage." Charlie then asked, "Tell me, how is your negro, Andrew?"

"Andrew isn't my negro anymore. We freed him two years ago. He's married to one of Mr. Low's servants. He helped me build a house for Amy and now we're building one for him on Greene Square. I'm going there now."

"I'm glad to hear that." Charlie gently patted Black Cloud. "If I ever need to build something, I'll ask Andrew. Let him know that!" As they crossed Whitaker, Charlie asked, "Can that filly of yours do more than trot?"

"A bit. But we can't run any faster than a trot, Charlie. It's the law."

"Oh, really?" Charlie stood in his stirrups, looked around, and eased back into the saddle. "That law doesn't apply to Charlie Lamar. Race you to Habersham!"

Charlie smacked Black Cloud's flanks and took off. Joseph followed in hot pursuit, the horses kicking up the sand of South Broad. As they charged across town, Joseph heard people yelling at them to slow down. He pulled back on the reins, but Charlie leaned further forward. As they crossed Drayton, a woman in the middle of the street screamed, threw her packages in the air and ran back to the sidewalk. Joseph crossed Habersham several lengths behind. Even if he hadn't slowed down, he wouldn't have caught Charlie. Black Cloud was too much horse.

The two sat together on their horses and had a hearty laugh. Joseph was peeved that he had been drawn into breaking the law, but enjoyed the race.

"Good mule, Joseph. Not too many horses can keep up with Black Cloud. Why don't you come to the racetrack and meet some of the fellows?"

"Halt, halt I say," called a fat constable as he waddled down the street towards Joseph and Charlie. When the constable finally reached them, he was so winded he could hardly talk. He handed up his musket to Charlie and said, "Here, hold this!" He tucked his shirt back into his trousers and took his musket back. "Charlie, you know you can't ride your horse through the city streets like that."

"Bob, that was nothing more than a canter. I violated no law. You're turning this city into a prison for honest, hard-working citizens," Charlie reasoned.

"A canter?" The constable paused to catch his breath. "You almost killed Mrs. Battersby on Drayton Street."

Charlie leaned forward and spoke in a low tone, as if he didn't want Mrs. Battersby to hear. "That old sow has to watch where she's going. She causes a clutter in Savannah every time she sets foot outside her house."

Bob turned to see if Mrs. Battersby was near. She was still picking up her packages in the street. Bob said, "Charlie, that might be true . . ."

Charlie cut him off. "Bob, how're your lovely wife and children?"

"Oh, they're getting by, Charlie. Things are tough on a constable's wages."

Charlie reached into his pocket and removed some coins. "I know, Bob. Now here, you take this and you buy those boys some toys. And you tell them that when they're big enough, Charlie Lamar is going to show them how to ride a horse like a man. You hear me now? With all the service you constables give to this community, you should never want at all."

Bob dropped the coins in his pockets. "Thanks, Charlie. But please don't race in the streets. Take them to the track."

"You have my word, Bob." Charlie winked at Joseph.

"And good day to you, Mr. McBain. Sorry we didn't have a chance to talk."

They watched the constable walk away.

Charlie turned to Joseph. "You think about joining us at the race track, Joseph. Meet some of the boys and you just might win a few dollars from them. Not from me, but maybe from the others."

Joseph thought racing his horses would be fun. "Thanks for the invitation. I'll let you know when I can make it."

"Give your family my regards." Charlie called out "Heyahhhhh!" and charged his horse in the direction from which they came. Poor Mrs. Battersby, once again trying to cross South Broad, was sent screaming back to the sidewalk, tossing her packages all over the street.

Joseph heard Charlie holler above the old lady's howls and Black Cloud's stampeding hooves.

CHAPTER 18

Charlie Lamar

1852-1853

Andrew stiffened like a pole when he heard the clanging of the bell. His head jerked side to side, like a squirrel sensing a lurking hawk. At the boom of a musket, he dropped his trowel and called out, "Got to go, Mr. Norris, got to go!"

John Norris emerged from the shell of the unfinished house by Madison Square and saw Andrew run towards Wright Square. Norris understood. This was the price local businessmen paid for employing free negroes.

The bell that Andrew heard on that April afternoon in 1852 was coming from the cupola in the Exchange. The watchman was pulling the bell rope for dear life. Men at the guardhouse on Whitaker and President streets and at the Independent Presbyterian Church on Bull Street started ringing their bells, too. The watchmen on the streets fired their muskets in the air, shook rattles, and screamed "Fire!" In less than a minute, every soul in Savannah knew there was a conflagration. The memories of the great fires of 1796 and 1820 hung in the air as heavily as black smoke.

As Andrew ran along Bull Street, people on the sidewalk stepped aside, knowing their lives and property were in the hands of negroes. After the 1820 fire, the City Council acted to do more to protect its residents. In 1825 the Savannah Fire Department was formed, headed by three white men, and comprised of several individual fire-fighting companies located in the squares. Each company, or "Engine," as they were often called, had two white managers and were manned with free men of color between the ages of fifteen and sixty. It soon became clear there weren't enough free negroes to staff all the companies, and the department received permission from the City Council to hire slaves as firemen at twelve and one-half cents an hour. Even when private white companies started forming in the 1840s, blacks made up the vast majority of Savannah's firemen.

When Andrew reached the intersection of Bull and South Broad, the ringing of the Exchange bell stopped. Then one ring was followed by momentary silence, then another solitary clang. The fire was in district one, whose boundaries ran from the river, south to South Broad Street, west to Bull Street and east to East Broad

Street. While this was still a large area to pinpoint a fire, it was an improvement over the days before 1846, when the watchman in the Exchange cupola indicated the direction of the fire to the men below by pointing a pole.

Andrew was the first man to arrive at the Engine House Number 4 in Wright Square. Within minutes, more than half of the company's sixty free negro members had appeared. Under the command of Solomon Ziegler, the white manager, the company swung into action. The men grabbed the two drag ropes affixed to the front of the heavy, suction-and-discharge, Hunneman engine, and pulled it onto Bull Street.

Henry Linville, the other white officer, charged up to them. "A cotton warehouse at the east end of River Street!" Ten men, including Andrew, grabbed onto each of the two front drag ropes, and four men ran to the back of the machine and placed their hands flat against it. The remaining men lined up in single file on either side of the engine.

Andrew's entire body tensed up as he awaited the orders. Abel, the head negro fireman, called out, "Ready, my brothers!" All the men started running in place, with short, choppy steps, kicking up sand around them. Then Abel shouted, "Step to, my brothers, step to!" The men grunted forward and, like a giant palmetto bug, the red, black, and yellow engine started moving slowly around the square, twenty men pulling, four men pushing, and thirty-six men running alongside.

They gained speed as they headed north on Bull, slowed down to circle half way around Johnson Square, and then sped up to the Bay. All other wagons moved to the sides of the street. Andrew heard the huffing of the other firemen and felt his own sweat running down his face as he focused on the rump of the man ahead of him.

Abel cried, "Right onto the Bay, my brothers, right onto the Bay!"

The engine swung onto the Bay, barely slowing. As the team straightened, Abel yelled, "Change right, my brothers, change right!" Ten men running alongside the right side of the engine replaced the men on the right drag rope, so quickly and coordinated that the engine hardly slowed. There was also a change of the men pushing from behind. Then Abel called, "Change left, my brothers, change left!" and the maneuver was repeated with precision. People on the sidewalk applauded the efforts of the negroes, as smooth as any acrobats they had ever seen.

Andrew, now running alongside the engine, saw huge funnels of black smoke rising over the river at the foot of East Broad Street and invoked the Lord under his breath. As they neared the East Broad ramp, the teams of men switched once more, with Andrew back on the drag rope.

The city was still awash in the clanging of bells, musket fire, rattles, and screaming. "Left down East Broad ramp, my brothers, left down East Broad ramp!" The four men pushing from behind backed away and ten men grabbed the two tail ropes attached to the back of the engine to slow its descent down the ramp.

"Right onto River Street, my brothers, right onto River!" Thomas Baty, ahead of Andrew on the left drag rope, stumbled and fell. Andrew tripped over him but maintained his footing. Then, Andrew heard a scream. He knew the wheel of the engine must have run over Baty. Stopping was out of the question, and another fireman jumped in to take Baty's place. Andrew prayed Thomas was not hurt too badly and that bystanders would take care of him.

Andrew's nostrils filled with smoke as the team moved down River Street. They passed the new gas works on the right and Willink's Wharf on the left. A ladder company had just arrived at the scene. The men of Engine Number 4 pulled the Hunneman to the river and dropped the suction hose into it. Solomon Ziegler ran to the chief of the Savannah Fire Company, A. N. Miller, who was trotting back and forth in front of the burning warehouse, trying to determine if anyone was still in it.

Chief Miller yelled, "Laddermen, axmen, ventilate the building!" Teams of men with ladders held high over their heads ran to the building as far from the hungry flames as possible and dropped them against the side of the warehouse. Axmen scampered up the ladders to the roof and started hacking holes in it. Smoke billowed out from the building's interior, allowing firemen, should they go inside, to see and breathe better.

Andrew heard the neighing of horses in a stall under the warehouse, which was on piers. They were trapped and would surely perish. He ran to the gate, opened it, and screamed at the animals. While they were escaping, the floor of the structure collapsed in a smoldering, spark-filled explosion.

Andrew returned to his company and saw the axmen descend the ladders like spiders dropping down their webs. Abel yelled, "Pump, my brothers, pump!" Andrew and twenty-three other men, twelve on each side, grabbed hold of the large wooden bars, called brakes, and started pumping. In seconds a stream of water gushed through the hose, held by two men, blasted out of the play pipe, and disappeared into the bursting flames. The water came out with such force that the hose holders crouched to brace their legs to control the stream, which soared through the air a distance of fifty feet.

Eight other negro companies and three white companies had arrived at the scene, all under the command of Chief Miller, all working to extinguish the conflagration. Hundreds of men, black and white, pumped fiercely, alternating frequently on the brakes to obtain maximum effort. Chief Miller looked on, praying that the thousands of gallons of water would do their job.

Someone screamed that two ships docked near the warehouse had caught fire. Chief Miller yelled, "Oglethorpe Company! Save those ships!" The all-white company swung into action. They dragged their engine to a flat boat next to the *Isabella* and *Jane Hammond*, boarded it, and fought the fire from the river.

Chief Miller returned his attention to the warehouse. He could hear the firemen crying out with each pump, pushing themselves to keep the geysers of water strong and high. But the fire was spreading, its crackling sound echoed like laughter at the fire fighters' efforts. After a muscle-straining hour, the skeletal building started to collapse. Miller knew the battle was lost. Still, he had the men pump water for another two hours on the smoldering ruins to ensure the fire wouldn't spread. Then he called, "Halt! Stop pumping!"

The managers of each company repeated the order. The streams of water sputtered and trickled. The cadence of the men and the shouts of encouragement ceased. Firefighters panted like spent hunting dogs as they watched the axmen approach the building and hack down any standing boards.

Exhausted and dispirited, the firemen sought areas to rest. The men of Engine Number 4 trudged to the safety of Willink's Wharf and collapsed. Tears covered their faces and saliva dripped from their mouths. The stench of the fire would fill their nostrils and lungs for days. A few sat on a large log that served as a railing, but most lay on their backs, like fallen soldiers, gasping and coughing.

After several minutes, a shaken but firm voice cut through the noise and spoke to them. "Solomon, men, I want to thank you. You were the first to arrive here even though I know you came from Wright Square. You did your best to put this fire out. It spread so quickly, God couldn't have saved those sheds."

The men barely had the strength to lift their heads to see the stocky, reddish-brown haired man with a closely cropped beard. "I also want to thank the man who freed my horses."

Solomon Ziegler surveyed his men, and pointed to Andrew. "There, Charlie."

Andrew sat up, wiped the tears from his eyes and focused on the speaker. The man looked at Andrew. "Andrew McBain, is that you?"

The other firemen looked at Andrew. Andrew said, "Master Charles?"

"Good heavens, Andrew, are you alright? Jesus!" Charlie Lamar stepped over a few bodies, and kneeled next to the negro.

"I'm all right, Master Charles. Just need to catch my breath."

Charlie called to one of his assistants, who was still transfixed at the steaming pile that used to be Lamar's Cotton Press. "Mr. Woolhopter, get some fresh water out here immediately! These men just offered their lives to save my business."

"Where should I fetch it, sir?" the assistant replied, as he eyed the negroes.

Charlie barked, "Fetch it out your arse if you need to, just get it here! And get enough for all the other companies. Commandeer some onlookers if you must. Go to Claghorns and put the buckets on my account!"

"Right away, Mr. Lamar." Woolhopter ran down River Street to the store.

Charlie turned back to Andrew. "I can't thank you enough. You saved Black Cloud and five other horses. Only one perished. I have to get back to my business, or what's left of it. If you ever need anything, Andrew, you let me know. I mean it!" Lamar patted Andrew on the shoulder, stood, and left.

Andrew watched him thank the men of the Oglethorpe Fire Company, who did not want anything to do with the negro companies. They were sitting by a warehouse on River Street, every bit as exhausted as the other firefighters. They were able to save the *Jane Hammond* and the *Isabella*, ships that had just been loaded with cotton from Lamar's warehouse.

The men of Engine Number 4 recovered, rolled up their hoses, gathered their equipment, and pulled their engine back to Wright Square, singing as they went. Mr. Zeigler told them that Thomas Baty had a broken leg. He would not be able to work for months. The members of the Second African Baptist Church would have to take up a collection to pay his rent and feed his family until he healed.

As they trudged back, Andrew saw Charlie Lamar walking along the Bay, his head down and his hands in his pockets. Charlie was on his way to the telegraph office, composing in his head a communication to his father.

The elder Lamar had quickly made his mark in New York. His cotton commission business was thriving, and he had become the first president of the Bank of the Republic. He was also planning to establish a fire-insurance company. He had felt comfortable leaving the Savannah operations in his son's hands, and by all outward appearances, Charlie seemed to be performing admirably. However, the destruction of the foundation of the Lamar empire in Savannah, the cotton press and warehouse, was a considerable blow to Charlie's confidence.

Gazaway left New York for Savannah immediately upon hearing of the fire and went directly from the ship to the Lamar office to give support and counsel to his son. Charlie eagerly awaited his father, who always had wise advice and comforting words.

"You what?" Gazaway shouted, as he stood over the seated Charlie.

"I cancelled the insurance." Charlie's normally strong voice weakened in the face of his father's anger. He seemed to be shrinking as he looked up at Gazaway.

"Charlie, tell me you're joking. Please tell me that," Gazaway pleaded.

"The premiums were too high. They were sucking everything from the business."

"Too high, Charlie? We own wooden sheds filled with cotton, one of the most flammable combinations known to man. Of course they're high. Insurance is a cost of doing business, just like payroll and shipping and all others. You pay it because without it you could lose everything, and you never put yourself in that position. Never!"

Using his feet, Charlie pushed his chair backwards a few inches, but there was no escape. "Father, think of the money we saved not paying those premiums for two years."

Gazaway looked at the ceiling. "I can't believe my own son is saying this. How much more than those premiums did we just lose?"

"I'm convinced someone started the fire, Father. I've put up a reward of one thousand dollars. Once I get my hands on him, I'll take the losses out of his hide."

Gazaway shook his head. "The reward doesn't seem to be exposing anyone. If someone did set it, it's emboldening him. Didn't you tell me the cotton saved from the *Jane Hammond* was destroyed by fire while drying out in a field?"

"That just shows you what I'm up against. But they won't outsmart me, Father."

Gazaway sunk back into his chair as if his legs had given way. "What's next, Charlie, besides finding the person responsible?"

Charlie sat straight in his chair again. "I've already spoken to the loan officer at the bank. We'll have a new building before you know it. We'll make our losses back in no time. Besides, cotton is too risky. It takes nothing to send it into flames, and the prices are too uncertain. You can go broke in cotton."

Gazaway groaned. "Charlie, people make fortunes in cotton. The whole world buys it. We can't grow it fast enough. Yes, there are times when demand gets soft. You plan things so when prices go down, you have reserves to wait it out. The demand will eventually return. It always does. That's business, Charlie. I thought you'd learned that."

"Don't worry, Father. New business opportunities appear all the time that will replace the cotton profits. I'm already involved in one."

"How can you be thinking about other business opportunities when the heart of our operations has been destroyed?" Charlie did not respond. Though hesitant to ask, Gazaway summoned the courage, knowing it would cost him one way or another. "What business is that?"

"Plank roads!" Charlie had recently helped form the Ogeechee Plank Road Company and had become a director. Overland travel to areas not serviced by railroads or rivers was essential, yet the uneven surfaces of the dirt roads made for slow speeds and were unusable in rainy weather. To remedy this situation, companies laid wooden planks on the roads, allowing vehicles to move more quickly, smoothly, and reliably. The companies charged tolls for use of the roads.

Gazaway ran his hands through his hair. "I believe you've mentioned this before. It doesn't sound like a good idea, son."

Charlie pointed to a ledger book on the desk. "I keep the subscription books. We just put the road under contract. We're not fully subscribed, but will be soon. When the road is finished, the revenue from the tolls will pour in. People will beg for shares."

Gazaway glanced at the book. "Plank roads require a large capital investment, need constant maintenance, and are in danger of being replaced by railroads. There's no future in them. And you know nothing about them. Besides, you have a business to rebuild."

Charlie folded his arms. "Father, you second-guess everything I do."

Gazaway ignored his son's attitude. "Charlie, I'll lend you the money to rebuild the cotton sheds and buy new presses. In the meantime, we need to rent some space to keep the warehousing business going. I'll help you out while I'm here. You need to get it taken care of before you come to New York next month. And Charlie, running our operations here is a full-time proposition. You don't have time for plank roads. You're trying to do too much."

"I can manage it. I'm even considering another challenge, one that will help all our operations." Gazaway took a deep breath. He wanted to cover his ears with his hands. Charlie continued, "I'm going to run for city alderman. Just like you did."

Gazaway pursed his lips. His son had surprised him. "That's not a bad idea, but only if you have time for it."

Charlie slapped the desk. "I'll make time. This city is run by a bunch of jack asses. We need someone who will fight for the business community."

"You'd be a good representative, son. Just don't do it at the expense of our other interests. Now, I must be going to another meeting. We have to rebuild the press and the warehouse immediately. And please buy that insurance."

Gazaway left Charlie and walked on the Bay to his next meeting, his head throbbing from learning of the fire loss. He had to cross to the other side of the street to avoid the construction area in front of Savannah's newest architectural wonder, the United States Custom House.

A month later, the building that had caused so much controversy had finally been completed. It was worth the wait. The Greek Revival structure of granite and marble, and its six Tower-of-the-Winds columns without bases stood commandingly on the Bay. It gave magnificence to the city's landscape. In the minds of many, John Norris was the top architect in Savannah and perhaps the entire South.

In October, a few months after the dedication, Joseph passed the building, which he considered to be the symbol of Savannah's growth. He didn't even think to admire it as he hurried to his office after an extended business luncheon. As he cleared the row of buildings by the intersection of Bay and Abercorn, he slammed into someone who was moving rapidly on Abercorn towards the river. He heard a shriek. He stumbled and regained his footing to see a pair of boots sticking up into the air. They belonged to a lady in a light green, floral print day dress, who was sprawled on the sidewalk, her straw bonnet askew on the side of her head. One of her two valises lay in the street, partially open. An approaching carriage couldn't avoid rolling over it. The lady looked in horror as her clothing and papers blew down the Bay.

Joseph attempted to help her up. "I'm terribly sorry. I didn't see you coming around the corner. Are you all right?"

She looked past Joseph to the street. "My things! My God, they're all over the street! I'll miss my ship!"

Joseph scampered to recover her belongings. In a few minutes he returned with his hands full. She ripped the garments from his hand. Tears rolled down her cheeks. She dragged the crushed valise from the street to the sidewalk.

Joseph felt his face on fire. "I'm sorry. I'm trying to help. Honest."

The lady struggled to close her grip. "Then gather my letters. They're all over the street. I'll take care of the clothing, thank you."

It took Joseph ten minutes to collect them all, and he almost got run over by a stagecoach in the process. When he approached her, she was shaking the sand out of her clothes, tears still flowing. Joseph felt sick to his stomach. She tried to close the damaged suitcase, but it was ruined. She knelt, wrapped her arms around it, stood, and turned around to see Joseph holding her papers. She gasped, placed the case back on the sidewalk, and opened it. A hostile gust of wind grabbed a pair of her underdrawers and blew them down the street. Joseph ran to retrieve them, and returned to find her sitting on her opened luggage, her head buried in a nightshirt. She looked up at Joseph. He held out the garment, now decorated with bits of fresh horse dung, compliments of the streets of Savannah. Her chin dropped to her chest.

Joseph decided to take command. "Are you catching a ship? The river's right here. We can make it. I'll carry your luggage. You run ahead."

As soon as he said that, he heard a ship's whistle. Joseph squinted towards the river and saw a ship leaving a wharf. "Were you by any chance booked on the *Texas*?" Without lifting her head, she nodded.

Joseph groaned and sat next to her on the sidewalk. He ignored the passersby staring at them. "There are other ships. This isn't the last one. Where are you going?"

She didn't answer. Joseph looked at his boots and wondered what to do next. He heard her say, "New York." He looked at her as she raised her head. For the first time he realized she was beautiful, even through the tears, mussed hair, and crooked bonnet. They held each other's gaze. Then she adjusted her bonnet, packed the letters, and stood. "I need to book passage on the next ship to New York. Then I must send a telegram. I guess I'll need to buy a new suitcase and find a place to stay." She looked to the left and right, uncertain of how to proceed.

He took her damaged bag. "My name is Joseph. Joseph McBain. I can't tell you how sorry I am. I'm very clumsy. Always have been. That's what happens when I dance. I wind up sprawled on the floor. But I'll make it up to you."

The lady lifted the undamaged valise. "It's really my fault for being so late. My name is Emily Hulett. I appreciate your help, Mr. McBain."

Joseph hugged the grip tightly and said, "I have a friend who's a shipping agent, Miss Hulett. He'll book you on the next ship to New York. His office is just a block away on Drayton." Joseph started to walk and she followed in silence. Joseph felt relieved that he was allowed to help. When they got to the corner of the Bay and Drayton, Joseph saw Charlie Lamar leaving his office and called to him.

Lamar came over, looked at Emily's unkempt state and Joseph clutching a smashed suitcase. "Hello, Joseph. Is there a problem?"

Joseph wanted to shake Charlie's hand but couldn't loosen his hold on the suitcase. "Hello, Charlie. Miss Hulett here just missed her ship to New York due to my clumsiness. I'd like to book her on the next ship. Miss Hulett, please meet my friend, Mr. Charlie Lamar."

Emily smiled. "Pleased to meet you, Mr. Lamar."

Charlie tipped his top hat and bowed. "It's my pleasure, Miss Hulett. Yes, I can book your passage. There's another ship to New York in two days. Let me have your old ticket and I'll see what I can do. Where do you want the ticket delivered?"

Joseph said, "We still have to find a room for Miss Hulett. Just drop it off at my office. If there are extra charges, put them on my account."

Charlie replied, "I'll have it there in a few hours. And Joseph, don't forget about the aquatic club. I'm counting on you to join us." Joseph nodded.

Emily smiled and said, "Thank you so much, Mr. Lamar."

Charlie tipped his hat again and walked towards the river.

Emily and Joseph watched Charlie leave. Emily said, "What a charming gentleman. Isn't he the one who rides that black stallion so recklessly around town?"

"That's Charlie. He just got back from New York himself."

"Oh. Did he enjoy it?"

Joseph adjusted his hold on the suitcase. "No, unfortunately. His year-old son took sick and died. They returned and had funeral services. It was quite sad. He acts the part of the warrior, but he can't escape the sorrows of life."

"I'm so sorry. There must be nothing sadder for a parent than losing a child."

They headed to the telegraph office. Joseph stayed to the side as Emily wrote the message for the telegraph operator. Joseph, still hugging the ruined valise, inched over to see if she was notifying a beau. She looked at him and he shuffled back to the wall.

After Emily paid for the telegram, she picked up her suitcase and said, "Now, I need a place to stay for two nights. I can't go back to Mrs. Church's house. My replacement arrived there today. I don't have much money with me and may have to borrow some. I promise to repay you as soon as I arrive in New York."

Joseph followed Emily out of the office. "I'm the reason you missed the boat," he said. "You must allow me to pay for your room. I'm taking you to the Pulaski Hotel."

Emily answered over her shoulder, "No, that's too expensive, Mr. McBain. I simply can't allow it."

Joseph finally reached her side. "Then I'm taking you to the Marshall House. It's new and also first class."

She started to protest, but Joseph said, "First, I'm buying you a new bag." He gained a step in front of Emily and led her to a nearby shop. She selected a new suitcase and went to a back room to transfer her belongings.

With Joseph carrying both grips, they walked the few blocks to the hotel on Broughton Street. The manager greeted Joseph, who placed the luggage on the tiled floor. "Mr. McBain, how may I help you today?"

Joseph acted in control, though he feared making a fool of himself. It was in crucial situations when he was at his worst. "Please put Miss Hulett into a room for two nights and charge my account. And make sure she enjoys every convenience."

The manager bowed at Emily. "Yes, Mr. McBain. Is there anything else?"

Joseph looked at Emily, who smiled at him. Her beauty emboldened him. He said to the manager, "Yes. Would you make a reservation in the dining room for two this evening? Say, eight o'clock." Joseph looked again at Emily. "I can't allow a lady to dine alone."

She said, "That's so thoughtful of you, Mr. McBain. Eight is fine."

Joseph felt weak. "See you tonight, then." He did it! He was able to handle the situation with some finesse. He had to leave before he did something stupid. He tipped his hat and turned towards the door, tripping over her suitcases, and sprawling on the floor in the middle of the Marshall House lobby.

Joseph's announcement that he was having dinner with a young woman caused an endless stream of questions from Amy and Grandfather. As soon as Dante heard about it, he was unhappy that Joseph wasn't bringing her home. "She tas'e muh cookin' she ent gwi' on no boat." Joseph told him maybe the next night, when his parents were in town.

For the first time in years, it took Joseph several attempts to select the proper shirt, cravat, and jacket. Even then, he wasn't certain he looked right. He met Emily in the lobby promptly at eight o'clock. Without the bonnet she was more beautiful than in the afternoon. She wore her strawberry blond hair piled on top of her head. Her fair, freckled skin framed light brown eyes. Joseph marched into the dining room, though he concentrated on the floor, and the many hazards it held for clumsy people like him. Emily noticed and started to giggle. She couldn't stop, not as they were seated nor as they ordered supper. Finally, she passed her hand over her face, just as the professor of mesmerization would do, and stopped.

They talked. Over the first course of crab bisque, Joseph learned she had attended Oberlin College in Ohio. After graduation she wanted to travel, so she came to Savannah to teach at Mrs. Church's private school. She lived upstairs at Mrs. Church's house on the northwest corner of Broughton and Abercorn with two other teachers from the North. She spent her free time at the Lutheran Church and volunteering at the Savannah Female Asylum, a home for orphaned and wayward girls. She returned to New York for three weeks in the summer and at Christmas. After two years, she was lonely and wanted to be near her family.

Over the steamed oysters she talked about her family and New York City. Her father was a teacher at a private school and her mother was a nurse. Her brother worked on a ship as a policeman. She missed them all. Over the venison steaks Joseph talked about his family. Emily was particularly intrigued with Amy.

Over bread pudding Joseph told her about Andrew, bricklayer, architect, free negro, and Joseph's friend for life. At first, Emily was skeptical that a white man would be so friendly with a black. But she sensed Joseph's affection as he smiled and animatedly used his hands to describe their lives together.

Over Joseph's port, they talked about Savannah. She confessed that she liked Georgia, except for one thing. "Do you own any slaves, Mr. McBain?"

Joseph leaned forward and said in a low voice, "We don't call them slaves, Miss Hulett, unless we are referring to them in terms of law. We call them servants or negroes. I personally don't own any, but my father does. About two hundred."

Emily grabbed hold of the arms of her chair. "He owns two hundred living humans?"

Joseph nodded and said softly, "It's a big plantation."

Emily followed Joseph's tone of voice and whispered, "But how can you own people, force them to work, and control their lives?"

Joseph surveyed the nearby tables before replying. "We treat our servants very well. They live in brick cabins. We provide food and clothes and take care of their medical needs. We do this whether they work or not, whether they're too young, or too old, or too sick. They grow vegetables and raise chickens and hunt and fish to supplement their food rations. They make baskets, which they sell to us or at the city market and keep the money. When things are slow on our plantation, we hire them out as bricklayers or day laborers. They keep eighty per cent of their wages. They can buy food or clothes or anything else with the money. We employ the task system. The servants have a defined workload. When they finish, they have the rest of the day to themselves. Most are done by four. They don't work on the Sabbath and get days off at Christmas."

Emily chewed on her lip as she pondered that information. Though she had lived in Savannah for two years, she didn't know much about the institution. "You make it seem like heaven on earth, like being a slave, excuse me, a servant, is such a wonderful thing. But slavery is so very wrong. It's against God's will."

Joseph, who had given the subject much thought recently, answered honestly, "Yes, in a sense, it is wrong. The truth is, under the present circumstances, negroes are better off being cared for. What would happen if they were freed? What would they do? There's no alternative. Most can't read or write because the legislature made it illegal to educate them. That's the real problem. They'd be useless in society, other than for what they're doing now. They couldn't survive on their own, being free, at least not in any human way. Yes, we created that situation and we're tethered to it. You might think that's an easy excuse. But I think many slaveholders like my father know slavery is wrong, they just don't know what to do about it. And they don't want hundreds of thousands of freed negroes living by their sides."

Emily frowned, and for the first time that evening she looked sad. She said, "At least you have the courage to admit it."

Anxious to change the subject, Joseph said, "Miss Hulett, I've had a great evening. I have a busy day tomorrow, but I'd like to invite you to supper at my house, and meet my family."

Emily pouted. "Mr. McBain, I'm leaving for New York in two days. For good."

"I know, but I enjoy your company. I'd like to share it one last day."

Emily twirled her spoon and said, "All right. But only if you call me Emily."

Joseph resumed breathing. "Emily it is! And I have two small requests." She nodded. "Please call me Joseph. And please don't discuss slavery with my parents."

Joseph picked up Emily at the hotel the next evening. She wore a simple calico dress and a white cotton bonnet. He felt light-headed as he caught the scent of her honeysuckle perfume. After helping her into the Rockaway, he said, "You look lovely."

Emily blushed and said, "Thank you. I really didn't have much time to get ready." Only four hours, she thought. "I hope I look presentable for your family."

Joseph said, "You certainly do," and drove away.

Hercules was waiting, opened Emily's door, and helped her down. She smiled and thanked him. Joseph walked around the carriage and introduced Emily to Hercules, who bowed.

As Joseph walked Emily to the front door, he turned his head back to Hercules, who nodded approvingly. Chloe opened the door as they reached the landing, and Joseph ushered Emily into the entry hall. He began to feel steamy under his shirt collar.

Joseph escorted Emily into the family parlor, where the rest of the McBains, Patience, and Andrew were waiting, and introduced her. They exchanged pleasantries. Emily was stunned that the two negroes were joining them.

Much to Joseph's dismay, Amy asked Emily how she and Joseph had met. Emily answered in enough detail to amuse everyone. Grandfather asked Emily if she knew about the great Revolutionary war battles in New York. Before she could respond, he described the Battle of Brooklyn Heights and Washington's great escape to Manhattan Island.

Andrew asked Emily about her school experiences in Savannah. The question relaxed Emily as she explained her passion for teaching. As she spoke, she saw Andrew and Joseph smile at each other. The bond between them was undeniable.

When they were called to supper, Patience and Andrew bade goodbye and left.

Dante took it upon himself to impress Emily and prepared Country Captain, a well-known dish brought to Savannah from the east by a ship captain. He sautéed chunks of chicken breast in a pan with butter. In another pan he fried a diced onion. He added curry powder, some chicken broth and a small amount of cream. He combined the contents of the two pans into one, let it simmer and served it over rice. He topped the whole dish with raisins and nuts. Dante served it with his best François imitation. He had Lilly carry the platter to the dining room and stand next to Emily. Dante, wearing white trousers, shirt, and chef's cap followed. He removed the tray lid, let the steam billow out, and said, "Country Cap'in, see boo play!"

Emily was impressed by Dante and the smell of the delicious food. She said, "Merci, my talented chef."

Dante bowed, folding his right arm underneath him, until his head almost hit the table. He then said "Mussy boocoo," and marched out of the room.

The food was so good and Dante so amusing that Joseph stopped being nervous. He, Grandfather, Emily, and Amy carried most of the conversation. Emily had never met a woman as independent as Amy and who had done so many interesting things. She was fascinated by Amy's stories of the lunatic asylum. On top of that, she was beautiful and unmarried at thirty-three years of age. Emily regretted she didn't get a chance to talk more to her.

Sarah and James McBain were subdued, content to listen to the conversations. Their eyes darted from Emily to Joseph, looking for tell-tale signs of infatuation.

The evening flew by, and Joseph had to remind Emily she had a ship to catch in the morning. She said goodnight to everyone and thanked Mr. and Mrs. McBain for the wonderful evening. As she and Joseph walked down the steps to the waiting Rockaway, the McBains peered through the front door sidelights. Amy said, "I think Joseph just found his future."

Grandfather said, "That's a fact."

Sarah McBain said, "She's quite a lovely lady, isn't she?"

James McBain was silent.

Joseph picked up Emily the next morning and took her to the ship. This time they were early. After she settled in her berth, they took a walk along River Street. Mountains of cotton bales lined the road. One could not see along the riverfront because of them. All the commerce was making many people rich.

Joseph surveyed the area. "Isn't this beautiful, Emily?"

Emily gawked at the piles of cotton bales. "I must admit, I feel the excitement. When I first arrived in Savannah, Mrs. Church told me never to come here, and I never did, except to catch a ship. Now that I'm with you, I feel safe, and find this hustle and bustle so interesting. But I don't really understand it."

"It's not difficult. See that steamer." Joseph pointed to a steamship with side paddle wheels coming into the harbor. It was towing five barges piled high with bags and bales of cotton. "It's bringing cotton from the interior, from plantations close to the river. And see those large drays?" Joseph turned to River Street. "They're bringing cotton from the depot, from planters who can get their crops more easily to the railroad. One way or the other, starting in early autumn, as the cotton is harvested, the planters get their crop here as quickly as possible."

Emily's eyes followed a procession of wagons carrying the white gold. "Who are they sending it to?"

"The commission merchants, the factors here in Savannah. They do everything for the planters. They receive the cotton, have it graded, baled, weighed, counted, tagged, and warehoused. The factors sell the cotton to buyers here in Savannah. The factor takes a commission plus a charge for insurance, drayage, warehousing, and shipping. The factors do the bookkeeping, too, and keep an account for each planter. They send money to the planters when requested, and they order supplies and equipment for the planters. For a fee, of course. As you can see, they rely heavily on each other."

"I was here for two years and never saw this side of Savannah." Suddenly, Emily's attention was distracted. She looked at a nearby wharf. "Joseph, what are those negroes doing?"

Joseph turned and saw a black man run head-first into a large bale of cotton, then fall back on the seat of his pants, with six colored men standing to the side, laughing. "They're butting. They pool some money and take turns to see who can knock over the bale."

Emily's face strained. She said, "I can't believe that," as the next negro took a fifteen-foot running charge, and wound up on the deck of the wharf. "Isn't it dangerous?"

Joseph winced as another black bounced off a cotton bale. "Sure is. A few months ago a negro broke his neck and died. But they still do it. Some of the Irish lads say it's because the negroes like to gamble. But Grandfather says it's from the desperation of nothing to lose."

"Your grandfather is very wise. If he understands that, why does he own them?"

Joseph stared at the blacks on the wharf. "He loves our negroes. Some whites just say that to lessen their guilt. Grandfather means it. His parents and his wife died in the fire of 1796. All he had, besides his son—that's my father—were the servants on his cattle farm. They got him through it. They cared for him as a family would."

Emily moved on, though Joseph didn't answer her question. "I never met anyone from Savannah society before. I wish I'd met you on my first day here, not my last."

Joseph turned to Emily and put his hands on her shoulders. He knew he had to do something special to show Emily he wanted to see her again. He leaned forward and kissed her lightly on the cheek, a remarkably bold move, in public, no less. It could have earned him a slap in the face. Instead, she accepted his kiss. The ship's whistle blew. Emily took Joseph's arm and they walked back to *The Union* in silence.

At the gangway, Joseph asked, "If I write, will you write back?"

"Of course I will."

"If I write every day will you write back every day?"

She put her hands on Joseph's shoulders, rose up on her toes and kissed him on the cheek. "There had better be a letter waiting for me when I get home." She turned and walked up the gangway.

That evening, James McBain called Joseph into the study and asked him to sit. McBain remained standing, and leaned against his desk. "Son, you're thirty-two years old. Your mother and I had hoped you and Amy would have been married by now, giving us lots of grandchildren. We know it's important to find the right person to share life with and we've never interfered. But I need to say something about Miss Hulett, if you don't mind." McBain did not pause to see if Joseph minded. "She's beautiful and intelligent. But she's a Northerner, son. They're different from us. She'll never accept the way we are. You may be fond of her, but you'll only wind up miserable if you pursue this. You're a Georgian, with Georgia clay in your bones and Georgia water in your veins. There. I've said my piece. What you do is up to you."

Joseph thought of the kisses that afternoon. "I wouldn't pursue her if I didn't think she'd accept me, or us, Father."

"I pray you're correct, son."

Andrew was glad Joseph had finally met a woman who stole his heart, and told Patience so as they returned home after meeting Emily. Andrew was happily married, and knew the importance of having someone to love.

Patience was also doing well. She occasionally cooked for Mr. Low and was gaining a reputation, along with Dante, amongst the dinner party circle as one of the better private cooks in Savannah. And she enjoyed helping Andrew fix up their new house, especially the kitchen. But the one thing she was looking forward to, her real goal in life, was starting a family.

Andrew continued to work for John Norris on the Gothic Revival house for Charles Green, an English cotton merchant who was spending the unheard-of-amount of ninety-five thousand dollars for his residence on Madison Square. The Green mansion was so demanding that Norris had little time to devote to other clients. Yet he was designing the Unitarian Meeting House and another private house. Recently, he received another request. He didn't have the time for it, but he didn't want to turn down the business. He needed a good assistant to help him out.

"Andrew, please come in," Norris said as he sat in his office on the Bay. It was November 1852. "Are you working on anything besides the Green house?"

"I'm still tinkering with my house. I should be done soon."

"I was hoping you might help me with a design for a couple from New Jersey. They've lived here for about twenty years. It would be a good experience for you, and I'll pay you as the assistant architect."

Andrew felt like shouting. He had wondered whether Norris held him in lower regard since the problem with Miss Amy's house. Now, Norris was actually asking for his help to design a house. "When do we start?"

"In a week. Here, I want you to read something in the meantime." Norris handed Andrew a book, *The Architecture of Country Houses*, by Andrew Jackson Downing. "This is the best one around. Downing has excellent examples of Gothic and Italian villas. It just came out a few years ago, and every builder and architect of any repute has a copy. My clients saw villas on a recent trip to Italy and want to build one here."

Andrew's heart sank. "Italian villas are new to me, sir."

Norris pointed to the book. "No matter. You understand construction and architecture and you're creative. You read that book and you'll have plenty of ideas. I'll be here to help."

Andrew read the book in three nights. Then he sat with Norris to discuss the client's requirements, and started working on the plans immediately.

A month later, in mid December, Norris asked Andrew to meet him at his office at six that evening to review the drawings before Norris showed them to the client. Andrew came by, but Norris wasn't there, so he placed the drawings on the drafting table and started touching them up. He stopped only to answer a knock at the door.

"Is Mr. Norris in?" a man inquired. A dour woman stood next to him.

"No, sir. He's not here yet. I expect him any minute. Please come in and have a seat."

As the couple sat, Andrew overheard the woman say to her husband, "The nerve of making us wait."

The husband whispered, "Well, we are an hour early."

Andrew returned to the drafting table. After a few minutes the woman stood, stepped behind Andrew, looked over his shoulder, and said, "Just what do you think you're doing?"

Andrew looked up. "Excuse me, Missus?"

She stared at the drafting table. "Those drawings? What are you doing with those drawings? Those are our drawings! Our name is on them! Herbert! Why is a negro touching our drawings? I won't have a negro working on our house plans!"

"Ma'am, I . . ."

"You, shut up!" she screamed at Andrew.

It hit Andrew like a hammer. It was Gruesome Woman from the bookstore so many years before. She was older, heavier and gray-haired, but the scowling face and arrogance were the same. And she had caught him in the act. Andrew's heart sank to his stomach. "Missus, I . . ."

"Is there a problem?" asked a breathless John Norris as he entered the office.

The woman marched up to Norris. "Mr. Norris, I saw this negro working on our house plans. I will not tolerate such a thing! I will not suffer the humiliation."

Andrew stood. "Sir, the drawings were out and . . ."

Norris held up his hand and said, "I'll handle this, Andrew." Norris said to his clients, "Mr. and Mrs. Young, every sketch, every drawing that I present to you represents my design based on your specifications. You can be assured of that. If you see anything that doesn't suit you, please tell me and I will change it. We won't begin construction until you are satisfied and approve the plans. That is our agreement, is it not?"

Gruesome woman eyed Andrew then turned to Norris. "I should hope so! We came by early for our appointment, if you don't mind. Can you see us now?"

"Certainly." Norris said to Andrew, "That will be all for today. I'll see you tomorrow."

Andrew already had his hat in his hand. "Yes sir, Mr. Norris. Good evening, mister, missus," a fuming Andrew said as he fled from the office.

John Norris reviewed the plans with his clients without having first reviewed the latest changes with Andrew. After ten minutes, Mrs. Young had forgotten about the incident with the impudent negro. She praised John Norris for his excellent work.

After Andrew left Norris's office, he ran to Ulysses's shop. The idea had struck Andrew from out of the blue as Mrs. Young berated him. It could jeopardize his relationship with Mr. Norris, but at that moment, Andrew didn't care. He had to know if Ulysses would help him.

He got to the shop just as the barber was leaving. "Good evening, Ulysses."

Ulysses jerked around as he was locking the door. "Andrew! You frightened me. I'm closing for the day. You'll have to come by tomorrow."

Andrew panted to catch his breath. "I don't need a haircut. I have more work. Would you be available? It will be in a few months."

Ulysses dropped his key into his pocket. "Of course, Andrew. What is it? Stucco sculptures again?"

The two walked along the street together. "No. Wood carvings of people. We'll need to locate drawings of some men."

Ulysses smiled. "It sounds interesting. Just tell me when."

"I will." Andrew felt much better. He went home to Patience.

CHAPTER 19

New York

1853-1854

Joseph lay sideways on the couch laughing when Andrew told him he was designing a house for Gruesome Woman. Joseph sat up and dried his eyes. "From New Jersey, no less? Did she recognize you at all?"

"I hardly recognized her, it's been so long. Besides, I have the feeling we all look alike to her."

Joseph laughed again. "I guess she hasn't mellowed with age. You'd better keep away from her. Lord knows what she's capable of."

Andrew examined the palms of his hands. "I have a little surprise for her."

"Oh, really? What?"

"Just a little present. It's my secret. I'll tell you at the right time."

Joseph stood in front of Andrew. "You're just like Grandfather, leaving me guessing. You must tell me!"

Andrew didn't want anyone to know and regretted mentioning it to Joseph. He wanted to change subjects. With Joseph, that would be easy. "I can't now. Tell me, have you heard from Miss Emily?"

By any measure, Joseph was in love. He had a new daily routine. He kept regular office hours, but they were interrupted as soon as he heard the mail ship whistle. Thirty minutes later he hurried to the post office and paced the lobby while the mail was sorted. The workers knew him well by February 1853, four months since Emily had left, and brought his mail to him the moment it was ready.

Joseph read the letter as he returned to his office. Once he closed the door behind him, he held the letter to his nose and inhaled its honeysuckle scent. He then read the letter a second time before answering it. He got back to work, breaking every hour to reread her letter. On the way home after work, he posted his reply.

Joseph needed something else to occupy his mind and jumped at the chance to meet with Charlie Lamar one February evening to start a rowboat racing club in Savannah. Charlie said he was tired of those blowhards from Brunswick, Darien, and St. Marys talking about their boats.

Joseph arrived at the City Hotel barroom at six p.m. and was greeted by Charlie. "Joseph! Come here and meet some friends."

Before Charlie could introduce him, an older man stepped up and said, "Hello, Joseph."

"Mr. Couper!" Joseph was surprised to see the old family friend.

Charlie wondered how the two knew each other, and then realized they were all on the *Pulaski* together.

Couper said to Joseph, "You're looking fit enough to man a four-oar by yourself." While Joseph feigned embarrassment, Couper continued, "Joseph, meet my son, Hamilton. He's changed a bit since you last saw him." A handsome fellow, in his early twenties, who looked just like his father—tall, lean, fair, wavy black hair—approached and shook Joseph's hand.

After the two exchanged greetings, James Couper said, "I'm glad there are a few men in Savannah interested in boating. Charlie Lamar is a true outdoorsman."

One of the other men said, "Yes. He'd rather gamble outdoors than in!" This drew a thunderous laugh from the other men.

Charlie laughed at his own expense, threw his arm around the man, and said, "Joseph, let me introduce you to the rest of the fellows. This is my good friend, Henry Dubignon. His family owns Jekyl Island. Henry keeps a house in Savannah and is a member of the Chatham Artillery. As long as his brother John keeps growing sea-island cotton and sends Henry his share of the profits, I'll always be a successful gambler." Everyone laughed but Henry.

Charlie withdrew his arm from Dubignon and pointed to another gent. "This is Richard Akin. We made him city sheriff this year. Savannah will never be the same."

Joseph recognized Akin, who also had been the clerk of the City Council, but had never made his acquaintance before. "My pleasure, Sheriff Akin."

"And meet Randolph Spaulding, William Brailsford, and Thomas Bourke from Glynn County. We need to teach these gentlemen who the real sportsmen are."

After Charlie introduced the other men, the first meeting of the Aquatic Club of Georgia was called to order. Mr. Couper was elected president, Charlie Lamar second vice president, and Joseph third vice president. They adopted rules and regulations and agreed to stage the first regatta the following December.

Joseph worked an evening a week with the club officers over the next few months. Still, Emily was always in Joseph's thoughts. He wrote to her suggesting he visit her during the summer, the slow season for his business. She accepted and suggested July, when she had a few weeks off from teaching.

Joseph told his family at supper the day he received her reply. Sarah said, "That's very nice Joseph. We're very happy for you. She's a lovely young lady."

James simply nodded. Grandfather slapped Joseph on the back and told him to make sure he got a return ticket. Amy got up and hugged her brother.

Joseph left Savannah by ship in late June. The ride was smooth and comfortable. He caught up on his reading and thought of Emily, and what might happen at the end of his trip. He wasn't able to sleep soundly until the last night. In fact, he didn't sleep at all on the second night as they sailed past the area where the *Pulaski* had sunk.

Four days after his departure, he was looking at lower Manhattan Island, a forest of buildings, from the harbor. In contrast, he realized, Savannah was just a little country town. He stepped off the ship and found Emily and the hack driver waiting at the end of the pier. She walked up to him, hugged him, and kissed him on the cheek. She pulled back. Her smile convinced Joseph he was doing the right thing.

Joseph had tried to reserve a room at one of the famous New York hotels, the Astor, the Irving, or the Howard, but they were all booked. He happened to be in town when a new building called the Crystal Palace, modeled on a similarly named structure in London, and constructed of iron and glass, was opening. It was the venue for an international trade fair celebrating the industry of all nations, and was drawing thousands of tourists and businessmen. Emily finally found a boarding house for him at Irving Place, near 14 Street on the east side of the island.

After loading Joseph's luggage, they drove to the hotel. Joseph and Emily sat close and talked of how happy they were to be together, but Joseph was distracted by the enormity of New York. They drove up Broadway, both sides of which were lined with multi-story buildings, seemingly for miles. The streets were packed with activity, and there was a stew of sounds—people shouting, vendors bargaining, horses clopping and snorting, carriages creaking—all around them. The hack driver had to stop constantly to avoid hitting people crossing the street. Joseph thought of New York as one big City Market. He felt like a grain of sand on a beach.

The driver helped Joseph carry his bags to his room, and waited while Joseph and Emily took a stroll around the neighborhood. The boarding house was a short distance from Gramercy Park, nicely flowered, enclosed by an iron fence, and surrounded by beautiful houses, much like a Savannah square. Joseph wanted to stroll through it, but Emily explained it was restricted to the people living in the nearby houses, who paid ten dollars a year for its upkeep. Joseph didn't think excluding people was proper. Still, it reminded him of home each time he passed by.

After their walk, the hack drove them to Emily's house on West 16 Street, a six-story building in which her family occupied the ground floor. The driver helped Joseph carry a large, flat package he had brought with him from Savannah into the residence.

Emily's parents greeted Joseph with lips forced back. Unbeknownst to Joseph, when Emily had told her parents about him upon her return from Georgia, they were upset. Her father lamented, over and over, "We haven't raised our daughter to be a slave owner!" But Emily convinced them she would not consider a serious courtship with Joseph unless he swore never to own slaves. Her parents relented, for the time being.

Mr. Hulett escorted them into a sitting room. They sat on couches and chatted about his trip, the weather in Savannah, and his first impressions of New York. Then Joseph said, "I've brought a gift for you," and pointed to the package leaning against a table. "Please, open it."

Mr. Hulett stood and removed the paper wrapping, exposing a wooden casing. He fetched a hammer and removed the nails on the top. He carefully lifted the contents, a painting about four feet by three feet. Joseph and Mr. Hulett held it up. Mrs. Hulett said, "My Lord! It's beautiful, Mr. McBain. What is it?"

Joseph beamed. "It's the most beautiful city in the world. Savannah, Georgia."

Emily clutched Joseph's arm. "Joseph! How in the world?"

Joseph asked, "Do you have time for a story?" The Huletts nodded. They sat and stared at the painting as Joseph told them about the day sixteen years earlier, in 1837, when he and Andrew helped Firmin Cerveau recover his masterpiece.

Emily asked, "This is the painting?"

"No. I wanted to buy it, but never did. I always regretted it. He sold it to a man in New York. I often run into Mr. Cerveau on the street and always stop to chat. I saw him shortly after Emily had left Savannah. I don't know why, but I asked him if he could paint another view of Savannah, from the same place, the bell tower of the Exchange, with the current landscape. He accepted. After a few months, he asked me if he could have it lithographed. I agreed, and he gave me one along with the original. I thought you might enjoy it."

The Huletts again approached the print. Joseph explained the scenes, and how they differed from the original. Of course, the Custom House had replaced Mr. Dure's house, and the new Christ Church sat where the old one had been.

After a while, Mrs. Hulett gushed, "This is a most wonderful gift, Mr. McBain. The colors, the detail. I feel as if I'm standing in Savannah."

It was a good start to Joseph's visit. He couldn't wait to tell Mr. Cerveau how well the artwork had been received.

For the better part of three weeks, Joseph and Emily walked all over the city and took a hack only when they tired. One day they hiked to 42 Street and Fifth Avenue to see the Crystal Palace. It was enormous. Joseph guessed it occupied as much space as three Savannah squares put together. They arrived on the opening day and couldn't get very close. As they gawked at the swarms of people milling about, Joseph saw Howell Cobb walk by with several other men.

Joseph said to Emily, "That's the governor of Georgia. He was the speaker of the house a few years back. I guess he's here for the grand opening. I met him once. He helped us save Amy from a lunatic."

Emily said, "What?" Joseph assured her he would tell her about it sometime.

They took a hack to 59 Street and Fifth Avenue and came upon a huge expanse of woods. Emily said, "I wanted to show you this. The city is trying to make all this land, from here to Eighth Avenue to the west and from here to 106 Street to the

North, into a big park." Based on Joseph's understanding of New York City blocks, the park was going to be bigger than Savannah.

"Why do you need a park as big as Georgia?" Joseph exaggerated.

Emily playfully slapped Joseph on the arm. "There are a lot of people here. We need a place to relax with our families, to take strolls and carriage rides."

Joseph pointed to a cluster of shacks. "It looks like people live on the land now."

"Oh, just some Irish. They're all over the place. I guess the city will have to move them if they get permission from the state to claim the land to build the park."

They went on several excursions with Emily's parents. On the Fourth of July they took a boat around Staten Island and to a crowded area called the Jersey Shore. They returned in the evening to see a fireworks show by the Hudson River.

They took the Long Island Railroad, fast and clean, to Greenport, a town on the eastern part of Long Island. They stayed two days at an inn and spent their time bathing and sailing in the clear waters of the Long Island Sound.

There were so many amusements in New York Joseph had trouble deciding which ones to see. His favorite was Barnum's American Museum on the southern part of Manhattan Island. It presented every show imaginable. Joseph particularly enjoyed the bearded Swiss Lady and the human whirling phenomenon, Herr Von Spingalen.

It was during the visit to Barnum's that Emily and Joseph had their first argument. Joseph mentioned that he didn't see any negroes. Emily answered casually, "I don't think they're allowed in. The museum sets aside a few hours one day a week for them."

Joseph stopped in his tracks. "Are you serious?"

Emily replied, "Yes. Why?"

"With all the harassment we get from Northerners about our treatment of negroes, they're not allowed in here with whites? Isn't that a little hypocritical?"

"No. They're free people here."

Joseph looked about the room before replying. "Free to be excluded by whites?"

Emily raised her nose in the air. "Are they allowed in Savannah?"

Joseph nodded. "For most amusements, they are. Theatres set aside galleries for negroes. Often, owners and their families sit with their servants at the circus. I don't know of a theatre where specific hours are set aside for negroes." Joseph paused for a moment. "Now that we talk about it, I remember hearing Barnum is opening a museum in Savannah. Being good Yankees, they'll probably have separate times for negroes."

"Here we go again. You're going to tell me how wonderful Southerners treat their slaves. Oh, excuse me. I mean servants." Emily started to walk away.

Joseph followed her. "No. I told you I think slavery is wrong. But to see that the North doesn't treat its negroes as well as we do is quite surprising."

Emily stopped and turned to face Joseph. "You talk about treatment? May I remind you we don't whip negroes here."

Joseph winced. Though he had never known his father to whip or allow a whipping, some slave holders did. He, like most Southerners, was very sensitive to that accusation. He tried a different argument. "New York didn't completely abolish slavery till 1827. That's just twenty-five years ago. And it was gradual. New Yorkers had almost thirty years to sell their slaves in the South. You people weren't such angels."

An older man and woman walked by the arguing lovers and stared at them. Emily stared back. After they passed, she turned to Joseph. "At least our negroes are free, Mr. Know-it-all!"

Joseph watched the couple walk away. "Emily, I've only been here a few weeks, but I see a distinct difference between the attitude towards negroes in the North and South. It's true most Southerners believe blacks are inferior. But we live with them and grow quite fond of them individually. I grew up with them. They were a part of every day of my life. My best friend is a negro. On the other hand, Northerners think the black race should be free, but have no desire to live with or get close to them as individuals."

An edge of anger lurked in Emily's tone. "I don't know how you got that idea. We think of negroes as humans, not pieces of property that can be discarded as trash."

Joseph knew this conversation was becoming destructive. He wondered if they could ever live together. "I have a story I want you to hear, Emily. I think it may change your mind about us a little." Emily shrugged her shoulders. She didn't think it would change her opinion at all. He told it anyway. "About fifteen years ago I was on a ship that exploded at sea and sank."

Emily suddenly became concerned and took Joseph's hand. "You were? Which one?"

"The *Pulaski*."

Emily grimaced as she thought of the agony Joseph must have suffered. "I remember that. I was only twelve at the time. It was big news. Everybody talked about it. It was supposed to be horrible. You were really on it?"

"Yes. There were several groups of survivors. Andrew and I were on a piece of wreckage. Some others made it into the only two lifeboats that would float. The folks in one of those boats fished my grandfather out of the ocean. He was the last one they saved. They couldn't take on any additional people without sinking. They just sat there, unable to leave the scene, though incapable of helping anymore. Two black maumas were in the boat that saved Grandfather. Some of the most prominent people in Savannah and their children were drowning, screaming for their lives as the lifeboats floated around. There probably wasn't a white person on either boat who thought blacks were equal to whites, or were even true humans. Yet, there they were. No one suggested throwing the maumas over so they could save whites. It would have been easy to do, out in the ocean. And as it turned out, they both died in the surf trying to come ashore. Whatever you may think of us, Emily, we don't consider our negroes as trash."

Emily held Joseph's arm. "I'm sorry you went through that. Let's not discuss this anymore." She bowed her head and they exited Barnum's. Joseph wasn't certain if he had convinced Emily of anything, but he agreed that it was time to drop the issue.

Other than that argument, they behaved as young people in love, walking arm-in-arm, laughing, interested in what each other had to say, and hating to leave each other at the end of the day. Time flew too quickly, and the trip seemed to end right after it had begun. Joseph didn't need any more time to decide. He loved Emily and wanted to marry her. With just three days of the trip left, Joseph went to a jewelry store and bought a simple diamond ring. He made dinner reservations at the Irving Hotel. He planned to ask her over dessert.

To be sure, there were issues to be worked out, assuming she accepted and her parents approved. Where and when would they get married? Would she live in Savannah? Would she accept the southern way of life? But the most important thing, the one thing he had to know was, would she say yes? Everything else could be worked out, he was certain.

When they were seated, Joseph was so nervous, he couldn't think of anything to talk about. Fortunately, when the waiter brought a tray of oysters, Emily asked, "What a strange necklace. I noticed it before but I've never asked. Where did you get it?" Joseph told her about the necklace, and the saga of the McBains. It took most of the supper.

At the serving of the trifle, Emily, who had been so engrossed in the story she hardly touched her food, said, "I guess I understand your love for Georgia a little better."

This was it. He reached in his jacket pocket and felt the ring. His fingers tingled touching it. "Emily, these have been the best weeks of my life."

Emily moved her chair closer to the table. "Mine, too. I don't want you to leave."

"It's amazing you lived in Savannah for two years and we never met. I feel like I wasted two years. I don't want to waste any more, Emily."

Emily's eyes twinkled as she smiled.

Joseph was about to continue when he was interrupted, "Excuse me, sir. Is there anything else we can get you?" While Joseph enjoyed the fancy restaurants of New York, the waiters constantly hovered over the table. He couldn't raise a piece of bread near his mouth without someone asking him if he needed more butter.

Perturbed at the interruption, Joseph turned to address the negro waiter, but found himself tongue-tied. Joseph stared, trying to make certain. It couldn't possibly be. He was dead. Gray hair had replaced most of the black, and weight had been added, but the man's face and the ear were unmistakable. "Anthony?"

The waiter looked at Joseph. "My name is Anthony, sir."

Joseph rose on unsteady legs. "Anthony! It's me, Joseph. Joseph McBain!"

Anthony squinted at Joseph. It had been fifteen years. He searched his memory for something he never wanted to think about again. The eighteen-year-old boy he once knew bore but a small resemblance to the man facing him. "Master Joseph?"

"Yes!" Joseph held his arms to embrace the man who had saved his life. "My good God! You're alive! You made it!" The diners at the nearby tables stared at Joseph and whispered amongst themselves. Emily gawked.

Anthony looked around to see if he was needed elsewhere before responding. "Yes, I made it. I see you did, too."

Joseph relaxed his arms to his side, confused by Anthony's reaction. "Why didn't you contact us? We waited months for news. Father put an advertisement in the South and North Carolina papers, but we heard nothing. We prayed for you every night. The whole plantation!"

Anthony answered, "That was a long time ago. Things are different."

"What happened? How did you survive?"

"It's a long story, Master Joseph. I don't really want to talk about it. You see? I'm still calling you Master."

"Everyone will want to know. I want to know! We all thought you had perished. Then I see you in New York fifteen years later. I have to know!"

The other diners had lost interest in Joseph and Anthony and returned to their meals. Other black waiters in white shirts, black ties, and green aprons rushed around, carrying huge trays with dishes. Everything around them was in motion. Anthony spoke without emotion. "I grabbed onto a deck chair. In a day I floated to shore in North Carolina. I went north, running at night and hiding by day. I was arrested in Virginia two weeks later. I told the sheriff I had survived the *Pulaski* and I belonged to Master McBain of the Heritage Plantation in Savannah. He put me in jail for a few months, told me he put a notice in the paper but got no response, and then sold me at an auction. I worked on a tobacco plantation for ten years. Massa died and I was sold again. My new owner and his missus decided to move from Virginia to Texas. They took me and their eight other slaves. The ship first stopped in New York. Some people here heard about us, slaves on a ship in the harbor, and brought a lawsuit in court claiming we were in a free state and we could no longer be held as slaves. There was a big trial. The judge ruled in our favor. When I least expected it, I got my freedom. I don't like to look at my life before that. I became a waiter and I get along. I have a wife and a little girl."

Joseph stammered, "Do, do you want me to say anything to anyone?"

"Thank Andrew for teaching me to read and write. And tell Massa McBain that the papers he gave me were ruined in the sea, but the gold helped."

"Wh . . . what papers, what gold?"

"Excuse me, Mr. McBain. Is there a problem?" the restaurant manager said to Joseph. "We need Anthony to attend to his duties."

Joseph faced the man. "No, sir. I knew Anthony. We're just catching up on old times."

Anthony picked up a few dishes from Joseph's table and said to the manager, "I think we're caught up, sir." Then he said to Joseph, "Tell everyone I'm well, that I'm a free man." With that, Anthony walked towards the kitchen.

Joseph slumped into his chair, his legs extended on the floor. He glanced at Emily but he couldn't talk. Anthony was alive but he didn't want anything to do with him.

"Joseph? What's wrong? Who was that negro?" Emily reached across the table and opened her hand, hoping to receive Joseph's.

Joseph sighed. "Let's walk. I'll explain it to you."

An hour later, as they passed Union Square, Joseph finished his story. "We assumed he was dead. Fifteen years later, I run into him in New York City. He wasn't happy to see me."

Emily hooked her arm in his. "He said he was trying to forget his past, Joseph. Can't you see that? No person wants to be enslaved. It's against human nature, regardless of how well you think you treat them."

Joseph said nothing. He had always assumed the Heritage negroes loved his family and would stand by them through anything.

When they arrived at Emily's house, Joseph said, "We only have two days left. I'm visiting Gazaway Lamar tomorrow morning at his office. I'll pick you up after, about midday."

Emily stepped closer to Joseph and put her hands on his shoulders. "Joseph, I hate to see you so shaken. Get a good night's sleep. I love you."

Joseph kissed Emily on the forehead. "I love you, too." He walked to the hotel, his head spinning from the night's events. It wasn't until he undressed and found the ring that he realized he had forgotten to propose.

He remembered the next night at the New York Hotel. He told Emily he'd like to ask her father for permission to marry her, if she agreed. He placed the ring on her finger. Emily stood, coaxed Joseph out of his chair, and wrapped her arms around him. She heard a few gasps from nearby diners. She turned to them and held up the ring. They stood and toasted the couple.

They went to her house so Joseph could ask Emily's father for his blessing. Emily's parents had originally prayed that Joseph's visit would be an unhappy one. But during his stay, they grew fond of him. He was handsome and charming, and never talked about negroes, except for his friend, Andrew. They understood their daughter's attraction. And they loved their painting. Maybe Emily could change him.

Emily's father consented and prepared a toast of champagne. Joseph thought Mr. Hulett's approval came easier than he had imagined. Negotiations became tougher when they talked about where they'd get married. Emily's parents insisted on New York, saying it was tradition to hold the wedding at the bride's home. They didn't reveal their revulsion at the thought of traveling to a slave state. Emily claimed she wanted her friends to attend, and they wouldn't be able to travel to Savannah.

Joseph acquiesced, even though he knew his parents would be disappointed. However, Joseph didn't think he could get a proper amount of time off from work to return to New York until the following summer. He couldn't wait another year. He had to have Emily sooner. He had a private talk with Emily. Though her brother was out at sea and would miss the wedding, they agreed that Joseph would delay his return home by a week so they could marry right away. Joseph would then return to Savannah and Emily could stay behind for a few months to finish her employment and wait for the steamy Georgia summer to pass.

Over the week Emily contacted as many friends and relatives as possible and had a simple wedding dress made. Joseph sent a messenger to Gazaway Lamar's office, asking if he were free to attend his wedding. Lamar replied that he would be honored.

The day before Joseph returned to Savannah, Emily and Joseph took their vows at an English-speaking Lutheran church. Afterwards, they had a celebratory dinner with their guests at the Astor Hotel, for which Gazaway Lamar paid. The folks toasted the newlyweds repeatedly, but as far as wedding celebrations went, it was a mild affair. Despite Joseph's charm, it was clear Emily's friends did not approve of her marriage to a Southerner. Nor did they appreciate sharing a table with a southern businessman whom they surmised owned slaves.

Emily spent the night with Joseph at the hotel. He returned home the next day.

Joseph gathered his father and grandfather into the study as soon as he arrived and announced his marriage and the circumstances around it. His father embraced him, but Joseph didn't feel the strength of sincerity. Grandfather's hug was strong. Joseph promised they would have another ceremony once Emily arrived in Savannah. He said he had written to his mother and Amy, who were still in Tallulah Falls.

Joseph then called in the servants and informed them. Dante boasted it was his Country Captain that did it, and he would cook it upon Emily's return.

When everyone left the study, Joseph asked his father, "How's business?"

McBain sat at his desk. "Busy, considering the time of year. I'm glad you're back. I didn't realize how much I depended on you until you left. I'll go over the details with you tomorrow. Tell me about your trip. It apparently worked out to your liking."

Joseph sat and updated his father. He finished by stating, "And I saw Anthony."

McBain leaned back and clasped his hands behind his head. "It is a fascinating city. I always enjoy visiting . . . you saw who?"

"Anthony."

McBain looked at the desk and whispered to himself, "Anthony? Anthony?" He faced his son. "Anthony, who we lost on the *Pulaski*?"

Joseph nodded. "That Anthony. He's a waiter in a hotel in New York where Emily and I had supper. He didn't recognize me. When I introduced myself, he seemed distant, embarrassed even. He didn't want to talk. I finally convinced him to explain what had happened. It's an amazing story, really." Joseph retold it.

McBain stood and went to the window overlooking Pulaski Square. "I read about the Jonathan Lemmon case. It had Southerners up in arms as a direct attack on property rights and an assault on the Compromise of 1850. But he's alive! I just can't believe it."

Joseph shifted in his seat. "He said the papers you gave him were ruined in the sea, but the gold helped."

McBain gazed out the window as he remembered his secret deal with Anthony. "After Anthony had saved you, I wanted to reward him. I gave him a choice. I would manumit him or sneak him to the North. He chose the latter. I didn't want our other negroes to know I was doing it. I bought him from his owner in Glynn County and put him to work at the Heritage, with the understanding that at a convenient time, I would send him north. That opportunity came when you were accepted at college. He was going to escape when you arrived there. I gave him papers saying he belonged to me in case he got caught in the South, and I gave him some gold to help get settled in the North. Are you surprised?"

Joseph stood and patted his father on the arm. "Now that I understand, I'm glad you did it. But I am disappointed that he wasn't happy to see me. Does Grandfather know of your deal?"

"Yes. I told him before the trip. He'll be happy to learn Anthony's alive. But it's best you don't mention it to Andrew or Hercules."

That night Joseph visited Andrew and Patience and told them about his marriage. Andrew embraced his friend. Patience brought out a cake she had baked that day. They sat in Andrew's parlor and Joseph told them about the trip, except his and Emily's lone argument, and Anthony.

Andrew was consumed by work. In November 1853, the Youngs' beautiful Italianate house on Perry and Whitaker streets was completed. Mrs. Young rarely came to the site, and when she did, she never paid any mind to the workers. Andrew was the lead bricklayer and in charge of the stucco work. He had asked Mr. Norris if Ulysses could carve the wooden brackets that supported the eaves of the roof. Andrew said the carvings of the faces of Gods would make a fine, classical touch. Norris approved.

Much to the puzzlement of Mrs. Young, many negroes came by to admire the house. Several times she had to shoo the darkies away. She wondered what they cared about high-style architecture. As it turned out, the negroes were viewing the dark mahogany brackets carved by Ulysses. The outlines were hardly visible from the street. But by looking closely, one could see the image of Andrew Bryan, the founder of the Savannah African Baptist Church; George Liele, a black Baptist minister who had started religious services for slaves on the Brampton Plantation, and had baptized and inspired Andrew Bryan; Jesse Peter, a black Baptist minister partly responsible for ordaining Andrew Bryan; Henry Cunningham, one of the founders of the Second African Baptist Church; Reverend Andrew Marshall; and even Oglethorpe. Andrew had made Mrs. Young's house into the first outdoor tribute to the great negroes of Georgia.

While Joseph waited for Emily to move to Savannah, he busied himself with the Aquatic Club of Georgia's first regatta, scheduled for early December.

The night before the races, the club officers and members met at the City Hotel and appointed the judges for the next day's events. Joseph, Henry Dubignon, and Richard Akin were named starting judges, and Charlie a termination judge.

Before the first race, Dubignon asked Joseph if he wanted to place a wager on it. Joseph asked if it were proper for judges to gamble on the races. Dubignon responded, "Why not?" Joseph declined, but Akin was nearby, and he and Dubignon quickly negotiated a bet.

The races turned out to be a smashing success. Thousands of people lined River Street and the bluff on the Strand above to cheer the competitions. Tens of thousands of dollars reportedly changed hands. James Hamilton Couper was the big winner on the first day, as the eight-oared *Sunny South* took the four hundred dollar purse. The next day, Randolph Spaulding got even in the six-oared boats, captaining the *Kate Kenan* to victory. After each race, the negro oarsmen, in their brightly colored outfits, were loudly applauded.

After the conclusion of the regatta, the members of the club celebrated with a supper at Oglethorpe Hall. Joseph noticed a frowning Henry Dubignon pass a wad of bills to Charlie Lamar and Richard Akin. During the evening, folks approached Joseph and congratulated him on his efforts. Charlie slapped Joseph's shoulder and said, "Great job, Joseph. Savannah is mad about racing now, thanks to us. Next year will be even bigger, and we'll teach those men from Glynn County a lesson or two. Say, when is your wife coming to join you?"

"In two days, Charlie. I'm counting the minutes."

"You're a lucky man, Joseph. She's a beautiful woman."

Joseph met Emily as she walked off the ship. They hugged for minutes, partially blocking the pier, and oblivious to the grumbling passengers trying to get around them. Hercules took her luggage and escorted them to the coach. They drove to Pulaski Square where they would live until they built their own house. Despite her anxiousness to leave the city the year before, Emily was delighted to be back.

Joseph's parents treated Emily as a daughter and Amy and Emily became friends. Emily spent her first week with Sarah shopping for the two hundred servants' Christmas presents, which included their winter clothing allotment. Men received a pair of negro brogans, one hickory and one red flannel shirt, two pair of overalls, one pair of pants, undershirts and underdrawers, a blanket, and a wool hat. Women received a pair of shoes, two dresses, two headdresses, underclothing, a shawl, and a blanket.

On Christmas Day the family gathered at the Heritage, though Andrew and Patience visited with her parents. It was the first time Emily had seen the plantation. She was astounded at its size.

After Emily toured the house and was introduced to the house servants, Hercules saddled the horses and he, Joseph, and Emily toured the grounds. As they rode through the Quarter, about one hundred negroes surged alongside Emily's horse, waving, smiling, and tugging on her dress. Emily, never having been near so many blacks at one time, became frightened, and looked back at Joseph for assistance. Joseph smiled. She turned back and waved weakly at the servants.

After the ride, the family sat in Mr. McBain's study by the fireplace. The house servants filed in and Mrs. McBain handed them their gifts. They walked to Grandfather, who gave each adult two dollars and each child a bag of candy. After, Hercules stepped outside, whistled, and the rest of the negroes marched in procession from the Quarter to the big house to receive their gifts at the door. Each servant smiled and thanked the massa, missus, and gran massa. Emily was amazed at how orderly the process was, but wondered how sincere the thanks were.

After the New Year, Joseph purchased a lot on Monterey Square, which had been laid out in 1847 and was the last of the Bull Street squares. He informed Emily that Andrew would serve as their architect and builder. Emily said she eagerly anticipated working with Andrew, but secretly wondered if it were wise to let a negro design their house. She wanted it to be special.

As soon as Emily started working with Andrew, her opinion changed. Andrew recommended a two-story over a ground floor Italianate villa with a double-level side gallery. He showed her some examples from Andrew Jackson Downing's book and prepared some sketches. He answered every question she asked. In weeks, Joseph and Emily had agreed on the design and the floor plans. With Joseph again acting as the builder, construction began in February.

Included in Andrew's plans was a plumbing system. The Savannah Water Works was scheduled to begin operations in June of 1854. The pumping station was located near the river on the west side. It would draw water from the Savannah River, filter it, and pump it to a water tower in Franklin Square. From there the water would be sent through pipes to buildings throughout the city.

Less thought was given by the city on how to dispose of the water. Human waste was piped to dry wells in back yards. Other waste water was delivered to a spot in the backyard of the owner's choosing.

While Emily detested slavery, she adjusted well to having Dante and Lilly cook, Chloe clean, Celia sew and wash clothes, William greet her, and Jefferson drive her around town. But as a newlywed, she yearned to do the things she'd always dreamed of for her husband. After a month, she decided to cook supper for the McBains and marched into the kitchen to tell Dante.

Dante said, "Sorry, Missus Joesup, but oonuh got nigguhs fuh dis. Oonuh got no need fuh cookin', see boo play." Dante went back to shelling shrimp.

Emily went to Joseph, who was reading the newspaper in the study. "Joseph, I wanted to cook tonight. But Dante told me in so many words to leave the kitchen. In your own house! Are you going to allow that?"

Joseph lowered the paper and laughed. "Yes, of course."

Emily narrowed her eyes. "What? You're siding with a servant against your own wife?"

Joseph pointed to the chair next to his. "Please, Emily. Sit for a moment. You of all people should understand. They're servants, but they have their pride. Dante's an excellent cook. Guests talk about the food they eat here, and Dante knows it. That kitchen is his little kingdom. Your trying to do what he does so well is sort of an insult to him. He thinks you're unhappy with his cooking and could do better."

Emily covered her mouth with her hand. "I'm sorry. I didn't mean to insult him. I just want to cook for my husband."

"Emily, I can walk into the kitchen right now and tell him you're cooking tonight and he'll obey me. Dante won't be happy, but he'll get over it. However, in due time, I'm certain he'll let you assist him."

Emily sighed. "I guess I'll cook another day. I'm a wife, Joseph. I didn't mean to hurt anyone's feelings."

Joseph leaned over and kissed his wife. "I know that, and so do they. Just be happy you didn't try to hook the buggy to one of the horses with Hercules around."

Emily's stay in Savannah was relatively short-lived. When summer came, Joseph, fearful of the dreaded summer fevers, asked Emily to return to New York or go to Tallulah Falls with Mother and Amy. Emily claimed she lived through part of two Savannah summers, and she could tolerate another. But Joseph prevailed, and she decided to return to New York.

With building experience under his belt, Andrew was able to accomplish tasks at a faster pace. He told Joseph the house would be ready by November. As it turned out, it wouldn't.

One early August evening, Mr. McBain, Grandfather, and Joseph were interrupted by a knock at the front door. William escorted Dr. Arnold into the study. He had been the McBains' doctor and friend since Dr. Minis shot James Stark twenty years earlier. In that time, he had become one of Savannah's leading doctors, an alderman, the mayor, a co-founder of the Georgia Historical Society, a founder of the Savannah Medical College, and a founder and secretary of the American Medical Association.

He told the McBains he had just come from the east side of town and saw several cases of yellow fever. He said black vomit doesn't lie. He suggested they make plans to leave town as soon as possible.

Joseph asked if he should write his wife not to return to Savannah until things cleared up. Dr. Arnold said that would be a good idea.

Four days later James, Joseph, and Daniel McBain, Andrew and Patience, and most of the Heritage slaves moved up the Savannah River to McBain's pine forests, and all Heritage operations ceased. Mr. McBain hired two white men he knew from town to guard the plantation.

By mid-August, a full-blown yellow fever epidemic that had started in the northeast part of town had spread slowly to the southwest, reinforcing the notion that it was contagious. By late August one hundred people were dying every week. By early September one-half to two-thirds of the inhabitants had left. Savannah was practically deserted. Most business activity stopped. Dr. Arnold and several other doctors worked day and night trying to bring some comfort to the sick and dying, knowing there was no cure.

In early September, when it looked like things couldn't get worse, a gale hit Savannah, demolishing buildings, flooding outlying areas, and killing even more people.

By the end of September, the number of fever deaths started to diminish. By mid-October, residents began returning to their homes, or what was left of them. By November, the town was close to normal, and the losses could be tabulated. One thousand forty people had died, 936 of whom were white. Savannahians once more had to pick themselves up and rebuild.

While at the house in the pine forest, Grandfather took Joseph and Andrew by boat to see nearby Augusta, a city on the Savannah River that Oglethorpe had founded two years after Savannah. As they walked along the river, Grandfather described how the great Oglethorpe traveled through Augusta after he convinced most of the Indian tribes in the area to join him against the Spaniards. When he finished, the old man turned to Andrew and asked, "Speaking of Oglethorpe, did you ever write that letter to the Queen?" Andrew said he hadn't. Grandfather merely shrugged.

Full of guilt, Andrew started that evening. He couldn't find the words. He wrote and rewrote. He had asked Grampah for assistance, but the old man said, "Just write what's in your heart. That's the only way. The Queen has to feel the letter. I can't do that for you. That can only come from here." He tapped his chest.

One November evening, after they had moved back to Savannah, Andrew sat at his desk. He vowed he would not go to bed until he finished the letter. He held the pen tighter than normal. He at least wanted his writing to be clear and the grammar correct. Sometime around midnight, he heard, "Pumpkin, are you coming to bed?"

"Yes, Patience. I'm just finishing a letter."

Patience walked into the room, picked up the letter, rested her backside against the desk, and read. After completing each page, she delicately placed it on the desk. When she finished, she wrapped her arms around Andrew. "I love you, Andrew McBain. This letter is why I do."

Andrew frowned. "I don't think it will convince the Queen, if she ever gets to see it."

Patience squeezed him tighter. "It doesn't matter, Andrew. What matters is you wrote it. I know you wrote it, your Grampah knows, and I'm certain General Oglethorpe does, too."

Andrew picked up the pages. "I'm going to show it to Grampah tomorrow morning and then I'll mail it. I know he'll be excited about it."

Patience kissed the back of her husband's neck. They went to bed and tried again to conceive a child.

The next morning, Andrew and Patience were up early, hustling about to start their busy days. Andrew went to the McBains. He couldn't wait to read the letter to Grampah and see his reaction. William answered the door. "Hello, Andrew."

"Good morning, William. Is anyone home?"

He waved Andrew in. "Ebryone gone but gran' massa. He still een bed. He sleepin' laytuh an' laytuh."

"Can I wake him? I've got a surprise for him."

"Yes. An' git he down yuh fuh brekfus'."

Andrew bounded up the servants' stairs and wondered how the old man made the climb each night. He knocked on the bedroom door but didn't hear anything. He knocked again. Still no answer. He slowly opened the door, stuck his head in and called, "Grampah? It's Andrew. I have the letter!" There was no reply.

He called again, still without a response. He opened the door wider. The room was dimly lit by the sun squeezing in from the sides of the curtains. He could make out the old man lying in the bed, so very still. "Grampah? Are you awake? Grampah?"

CHAPTER 20

The Trade

1855-1856

The funeral service was held at the house on Pulaski Square. Hundreds of people came by to pay their respects. Both Sarah and Amy, dressed in black with veils, dabbed at the corners of their eyes with handkerchiefs while receiving mourners in the parlor. James and Joseph stood erect, trying to appear strong while feeling empty, as they accepted condolences. Joseph could not look at the closed, pine casket on the stand or the painting, draped in black, of Grandfather hanging on the wall.

At two o'clock the pall bearers carried Grandfather's coffin to the city-owned, two-horse, open hearse in front of the house. Amy had bought a large swath of fabric in the City Market in almost the same blue and white print as the kerchief Grandfather always wore, and placed it over the front of the coffin, folding just as the old man did.

The procession formed in the proper order, with everyone dressed in black and on foot. The sexton led, carrying his staff of office, a piece of black crepe tied to the top end. The hearse followed with the McBains walking behind. Then came friends of the family, and, lastly, McBain's Savannah servants, including Andrew and Patience.

They plodded east on Macon Street to Bull, circled around Madison Square, continued on Bull to Chippewa Square, and stopped in front of the Independent Presbyterian Church for a silent prayer. They resumed on Bull, turned west on South Broad Street to West Broad, and proceeded south to the Louisville Road. At the city line, the coffin was transferred to a McBain wagon, driven by Hercules. The McBains, Andrew, and Patience climbed into the coach driven by Jefferson, and started the journey home. About a half mile from the plantation, the two hundred Heritage servants met and fell in behind the coach, and wailed all the way back.

As James, Joseph, Andrew, Hercules, Jefferson, and Isaac removed the coffin from the wagon, servants surged forward and placed their hands on the wooden box. The six men carried the casket to the family cemetery and set it down. The McBains stood around the coffin and the blacks stood several feet in back of them.

James read a prayer to a background of muffled sobs and whippoorwill songs. Then they lowered old gran' massa into the earth. James and Joseph took off their jackets, rolled up their sleeves, grabbed shovels, and together, filled the grave.

The McBains' grief did not pass quickly. They especially felt it upon entering the house on Pulaski Square, expecting to see Grandfather appear, drink in one hand, and segar in the other, ready for a discussion or lecture of some kind. But the house was silent. James suffered the most. He and Grandfather were father and son, closest friends, and business partners.

One night in February 1855, four months after Grandfather had passed, James and Sarah were in town, reading in the family parlor. Sarah told James that she worried about his loss of weight. He assured her he would be all right. Sarah put down her book and sat next to her husband. She held him for several minutes until she heard the front door open. She darted back to her chair as Emily and Joseph entered the room.

McBain looked up and saw his son and daughter-in-law grinning. He asked, "What in the devil are you two so happy about?"

Emily took Joseph's hand and announced, "We just saw Dr. Arnold. He thinks we're having a baby!"

James and Sarah jumped up and embraced them. McBain said, "What wonderful news! This calls for a celebration! Someone call Amy! She's upstairs."

Joseph said, "I will. Then I'll have Hercules get Andrew and Patience."

McBain said, "I'll be right back!" Like a young man, he bounded down the stairs and moments later, bounced back up. He stood in the parlor doorway holding up two bottles of French champagne for all to see. To the family's applause, he wrapped a small towel around the top of one bottle, turned it, and slowly pushed the cork out. After it popped into the towel, McBain held the bottle up, a small white cloud of effervescence rising from it. He poured and made several toasts. In his excitement, he clinked Joseph's glass so hard he almost broke it. Sarah, Emily, and Amy made so much noise that James and Joseph decided to have a segar on the piazza. After a while, Andrew appeared and squeezed the breath out of his friend. Then Hercules, Dante, and William came out to offer their congratulations. The gloom around the family had lifted. The McBains would finally have an heir.

Two weeks later, Patience and Andrew visited Emily and Joseph to announce that they, too, were having a baby. Spring of 1855 was truly a new beginning.

Life improved for everyone. Andrew finally finished Joseph's house in April. There was no repeat of the problem with Amy's house. Andrew, secretly, and Joseph, openly, had checked all the work as it was performed. Andrew felt vindicated. He was leaving his mark on Savannah's architectural landscape, though few people knew it.

The house overlooked Monterey Square and the new monument to Polish Count Casimir Pulaski, the Revolutionary War hero who had died in the bloody Siege of Savannah in 1779. Lotteries had finally raised enough money to honor Pulaski separately from Nathanael Greene. The square-shaped column, topped with a figure of Lady Liberty and surrounded by an iron fence, afforded a grand view from Joseph's parlor. Joseph and Andrew agreed: Grandfather would have loved it.

A month before Emily and Joseph were to move in, McBain called Joseph into his study and asked him which servants he wanted for his new home. Joseph explained that Emily refused to have any, claiming millions of people were able to live without them, and they could, too. McBain asked Joseph who was going to do the shopping, cooking, cleaning, dusting, polishing, washing, sewing, and driving, especially after Emily had the baby. Joseph said if they needed cooks, cleaning women, or coachmen, they'd have to hire them.

McBain, whose graying hair and lined forehead bespoke his sixty-two years, asked Joseph if Emily would tolerate servants once he took over operations at the Heritage. Joseph said she would never interfere with the business. His father said nothing. He wasn't so sure.

A month after they'd moved in, Emily invited her in-laws to a supper of bean soup, chicken stew, and peach pie. Emily cooked and Joseph deftly set the table, breaking only one dish. McBain had trouble cutting his chicken with his knife, and had to chew extra before he could comfortably swallow. Even then, it felt like half the meat was wedged between his teeth. He told Emily the food was delicious.

Everyone had a grand evening. Amy seemed to be enjoying life. She said she still received compliments on her paired houses on Harris Street. She talked about the success of her millinery and women's clothing shop. Much to her mother's delight, she mentioned a certain bachelor she had met at a party.

She had even volunteered to help Emily prepare the evening's supper. But Emily wanted to try it by herself. So she helped Emily clear the dishes. As they did, Joseph told everyone about Andrew's latest project.

John Norris had asked Andrew to work on the new public school on Calhoun Square. Andrew was proud to have a part in it. The city had never had a public school, other than one for poor children started in 1817 by a group of local women and funded by private contributions. In 1841, a planter from Glynn County, Peter Massie, left five thousand dollars in his will for the education of the poor children of Savannah. The city invested the funds and by the early 1850s they had appreciated enough to finance two schools, one on the east side and one on the west.

The city selected Norris as the builder. He completed the west side school in early 1855 and started the east side school in the spring of that year, just as Andrew was finishing Joseph's house. Andrew immediately began helping Mr. Norris.

Andrew and Patience continued to attend the First African Baptist, where Reverend Marshall, one hundred years old, still preached. One Sunday after services, the reverend told Andrew that the elders desired a new church, and they wanted Andrew to be the architect and builder. Marshall said only blacks would work on it, and Andrew would not have to hide his name. Marshall explained he was traveling north over the summer to raise money for the construction, and they would discuss it further when he returned. Andrew could think of no greater honor.

Joseph kept busy as well, working with Charlie Lamar and Richard Akin on the next regatta. Charlie also convinced Joseph to help him and some other men organize an annual agricultural fair for Chatham and Effingham counties to help build the industry of the area. Having seen the turnout for the international trade fair in New York, Joseph was excited by doing something similar, though on a much smaller scale, for Savannah.

Between the regatta and the fair, Joseph saw Charlie once a week. That ended abruptly in early May, when Charlie's infant daughter died. Charlie and his wife Caro had lost two young children in three years. Joseph worried for his friend, but knew an upcoming visit by Gazaway would lift Charlie's spirits.

Gazaway went directly to the Lamar office from the ship, as was his habit. He spent an hour trying to comfort Charlie over his loss. Eventually, Gazaway asked, "How's business?"

Charlie shrugged. "Dull. So dull that I've decided to run for the state house."

Gazaway, disturbed to hear this on the first day of his three-week visit, forced a smile. "You were an excellent alderman and you'll be a better representative, son. But are you going to have time to run our operations? The legislature is in session when we're quite busy."

"I'll make the time, Father. This state needs to hear from the voice of commerce, and from someone who understands the danger from all these Catholic immigrants."

The elder Lamar sensed the first throbs of a headache. "How's the flour mill?"

"I'm about to get started. I'll be the builder. That way it will get done right."

Gazaway wanted to ask Charlie what he knew about building, but decided against it. "The sooner it gets built, the better, son. It'll be the biggest mill in town."

Charlie rested his elbows on the arms of his chair and pressed his fingertips together. "Oh, yes. And I'm investing in a new business." He left that hanging in the air, like a fat goose, until Gazaway's eyes begged him to continue. He said, "Gold mines," and sat back, waiting for praise from his father. Everyone clamored for gold.

Gazaway swallowed as if he had a peach pit caught in his throat. "What happened to plank roads?"

Charlie examined his fingernails. "They're a little slow getting started. And they can't produce profits as large or as quickly as gold mines."

Gazaway had pledged not to argue with Charlie on this trip, but he had to ask some questions, knowing he would eventually pay for his son's endeavors. "Who else is in on this?"

"Several Augusta men. You know them all, including Nelson Trowbridge. And James Gardner." Charlie gave the last name its own sentence for emphasis.

Gazaway poked his head forward. "James Gardner? Has he taken leave of his senses? He owns the *Constitutionalist* newspaper, plantations, and has a bright future in state politics. Why is he getting involved in gold mines with a slave dealer like Nelson Trowbridge?"

Charlie stood and stuck a thumb to his chest. "And me? Go ahead, say it, Father. You always do. It just so happens, Gardner sees the potential, too. If you must know, he, Trow, and I are partners in another deal. Trow's about to buy a lot of negroes from an estate in Beaufort and sell them to a customer in New Orleans at double our cost."

The joy of seeing his son for the first time in six months had evaporated in an hour. Gazaway had pledged to himself to try to make Charlie a more responsible businessman on this trip. He didn't want to attempt it on his first day, but it had become unavoidable. "Tell me, Charlie, have you lent any money to Trowbridge?"

Charlie nodded. "A little, to get into the gold mine and negro ventures. He's good for it. He finds many opportunities, Father. He has a nose for making money."

Gazaway folded his hands on the desk. "Charlie, did you ever ask yourself, if he has such a good nose, why does he have to borrow from you?" As Charlie stumbled over his words, Gazaway asked, "How much are you into the gold mines for?"

Charlie returned to his chair. "The same as the others. Fifteen thousand dollars."

Gazaway shot up. "Fifteen thousand! Charlie, you're making me nostalgic for plank roads. Gold mining takes a huge amount of capital. You need to buy the land, digging equipment, hauling equipment, mules, a stamp mill, and negroes for the labor. And then you have to clothe, feed, and shelter them."

"Father, please sit down. This is just to get the operation started. Once we do, we'll put the mines in a stock company and sell the shares on the New York Stock Exchange. That's how to make a fortune in this. Trow's going to New York to set it up."

Gazaway eased back into his seat. "You'll still need to show some results! Since the gold rush, everyone connected with the industry has moved to California. It'll be difficult finding qualified workers."

Charlie's voice rose like a ship's whistle. "Father, I'm sick and tired of you second guessing everything I do!"

Gazaway's voice elevated, too. "Charlie, you're gambling on these ventures with my money. Have you thought of that? Since I moved to New York, I've loaned you over fifty-seven thousand dollars."

Charlie blinked at the mention of the amount. "How do you figure?"

Gazaway, never one to toss out figures casually, took a sheet of paper from inside his jacket and read. "When I left for New York, I gave you the Eastern Wharves and the land they're on, nineteen negroes, cash, a cotton inventory, your house, two lots, cows, and the church pew."

"You record everything we give each other, father to son, son to father?" Charlie exclaimed, trying to peek at the paper.

"Father to son, Charlie. Only father to son. Fifty-seven thousand dollars worth. And you're going to pay me back. Because of your misfortune with the fire, I'm not going to charge interest. And I won't charge you for the wharves and land. That brings the debt to thirty-one thousand. If you don't repay me, it will be taken from your share of my estate, when my time comes."

Charlie stammered, "You're . . . you're serious? I owe you for all that?"

Gazaway folded the paper and put it back in his jacket. "Yes! They were never gifts. I told you that at the time. Charlie, you're thirty-one. You have to take responsibility for yourself. You'll never do that if you keep using my money without consequence. I failed to teach you that when you were younger. After the *Pulaski*, I could never say no to you."

Charlie's face turned plum red. He stood and said, "Father, I'm tired of your constant criticism of me. I've got news for you. I'm going to pay you every darned penny. Then you won't have to second guess me anymore."

"As long as it's my money, Charlie, I will second guess you. If you don't want my opinion, use your own resources."

Charlie walked to the office door and clutched the handle. "You heard me, Father. You'll get every one of your sacred dollars!" Charlie slammed the door as he left.

Gazaway hung his head.

Charlie went home and did not speak at supper. He kissed his wife and his little daughters good night and went to bed. After Caro tucked in the girls, she joined her husband, who said to the darkness, "No matter what I do or how hard I try, I can't please him or make him proud of me. Nothing." Charlie fought back tears.

There had been open crying in Savannah that day, not far from Charlie's bedroom. Patience had awakened in the morning with pains. Andrew ran for her mother, Polly, also a midwife. Then he went to Pulaski Square, where Emily and Joseph had been staying while awaiting the birth of their child, and brought Joseph back to his house.

Just as they arrived, Polly Low was delivering a baby boy. Tears ran down Andrew's face as he saw what he and Patience had created. The two men fetched water and towels for Polly. Then they stood in the room and gawked at the crying child.

Eventually, Andrew and Joseph sat in the parlor and talked about babies—how to hold them, how to feed them, how to bathe them. They wondered when children might start to talk and walk on their own when they heard knocking on the front door. It opened before Andrew reached it. "Dante!"

Dante stepped past Andrew and into the parlor. "Massa Joesup, Missus Emily hab she chile. Ah jes' tell Doctuh Arnie. He wid she now."

Joseph ran out the door.

"Joseph?" Andrew whispered as he walked into the McBain study the next morning.

Joseph, who had been sleeping on a chair, opened an eye. "Andrew!" He stood to greet his friend. "Isn't this incredible? Our sons born on the same day, just like us. It's a sign of something. I don't know what, but it must be."

Andrew inquired, "How are Miss Emily and the baby?"

"Both healthy! My parents came in last evening. Mother and Chloe are up there now. They let me hold him. Andrew, have you ever felt anything as wonderful as holding your own child for the first time? We're the luckiest men on earth."

Andrew nodded, "Maybe, maybe. Joseph, I was just thinking about naming my boy. But I didn't want to do anything without speaking to you first."

Joseph thought Andrew was following the custom of servants asking their masters to name their children, or at least approve of the names they chose. "You can name your son anything you'd like, Andrew."

But Andrew had another worry. "I just don't want to use the same name as you."

Joseph realized the potential for a conflict. "Emily and I had agreed upon Daniel, after Grandfather, if we had a boy. Joseph for his middle name."

Andrew said, "I thought of Daniel, too. You know how much I loved Grampah, but if I name my boy James, that honors Patience's father, your father, and Oglethorpe."

Joseph smiled. "Father will be honored. Oglethorpe, too! Have you chosen a middle name?"

"Yes. Vitruvius. James Vitruvius McBain."

Joseph laughed and threw an arm across Andrew's shoulder. "Think he might be an architect one day?"

Andrew beamed, "He just might be."

Lilly moved in with Joseph and Emily and helped cook, clean, and take care of the baby. Her presence made Joseph realize how much he missed having servants.

After four months, Emily announced she was ready to take care of Daniel by herself and Lilly could return to Pulaski Square. Joseph asked her to reconsider. Lilly made their lives so much easier. But Emily insisted they didn't need servants. She could handle it all, but she wanted Joseph home after work to help out.

Before they married, in the steamy grip of love, Joseph had promised Emily they wouldn't have servants in the house. After they married, they got along fine, especially since Emily did all the housework and Joseph used his parent's servants for sewing and transportation when he needed them. But a child changed everything. The work around the house seemed to double. And Joseph always had these tasks done for him.

Still, Joseph felt compelled to try to honor his promise to Emily. He had to cancel all other commitments, including work on the fair and the regatta. He visited Charlie one evening at his office to inform him. Charlie had another visitor. "Joseph, I'd like you to meet my friend and business partner from Augusta, Nelson

Trowbridge. We call him Trow. Trow, this is my good friend Joseph McBain." They shook hands. Trowbridge was Joseph's height, but as skinny as a reed. He had black, slicked-down hair parted in the middle, and a black moustache.

Joseph explained his situation to Charlie, who laughed to himself, knowing that's what happened when a southern boy married a Yankee girl. He said he hoped Joseph would have more time next year. Joseph told him he hoped he would.

Joseph also said he was sorry to hear about the election results, though he really wasn't. Charlie had run for a seat in the Georgia House of Representatives after leaving the Democrats to join the American Party, also known as the "Know-Nothings." Their main platform was to keep immigrants, especially Catholics from Germany and Ireland, out of America. The party had been gaining strength throughout the country, but the ticket was defeated in the Georgia elections.

"We only lost by a few votes. We'll win next time," Charlie predicted.

After exchanging a few more pleasantries, Joseph bade good day. As he put on his hat, Lamar said, "Joseph, are you interested in a good investment? It will make you a rich man, or should I say, an even richer man."

Joseph laughed. "Like what, Charlie?"

Charlie nodded towards his partner. "Tell him, Trow."

"Glad to, Chollie." Trow sat back, put his feet up on Charlie's desk, and told Joseph about the Park and Columbia gold mines near Augusta and the Beaufort negroes. Trow ended by saying they were offering this opportunity only to a few select people.

Joseph didn't have to think long. He thanked Trow but said he didn't know anything about those businesses. Joseph promised Charlie he would be in touch and left.

Joseph's attempt at being a devoted husband and father without servants lasted four months. It exhausted him. He decided he wasn't going to spend his life waking up, helping with the baby, working all day, and rushing home to help with the baby, supper, and the house, especially if he didn't have to. He wanted to be able to have a drink with friends after work. He wanted to go to the quoits club, and work on the regatta and agricultural fair. Besides, he didn't feel comfortable doing servant's work. He told Emily he was bringing in two or three servants. Emily refused. Joseph's face turned red and his voice rose. He said he was seeing his father the next day to request the servants, and for her to be prepared, whether she liked it or not. Emily, who had never seen Joseph that angry before, asked if they could hire someone; an Irish woman maybe, like her family did in New York. Joseph explained that that would be an insult to the Heritage servants, who expected to take care of him and his family. Emily, concerned about annoying Joseph more, relented, but said she's accept no more than two servants. A week later, Chloe and Jinny moved in and Jefferson, living at Pulaski Square, came by twice a day to care for the horses and Rockaway. Joseph was calm again.

Over those months caring for their child without help, Joseph did little socializing. He hardly saw Andrew, who had the same family responsibilities as he. Nor did Joseph see Charlie again until March 1856, when Charlie visited him at his office looking for Andrew. Joseph told Charlie where he could find him.

"Master Charles!" Andrew stood to greet Charlie on the site of the Massie School. Andrew was applying the exterior finishing coat of stucco.

"Hello, Andrew. Joseph said I could find you here." Charlie surveyed the two story, stucco-over-brick, Greek Revival structure. "The school certainly is handsome."

Andrew wiped his hands on a rag. "I agree, Master Charles. The Greek Revival provides the perfect setting for teaching and learning."

Charlie nodded slowly, and said, "Andrew, I need to ask you a favor. I just started building a flour mill on Randolph Street, near the river. It'll be six stories. I hired a useless drunk as a bricklayer, and I'm already behind schedule. I need to get rid of him. Can you help me out? I'll keep you busy for at least a year."

"I have a few other jobs going, Master Charles. I could start a few hours a day, maybe get some men in. I'll personally have more time in a few months."

Charlie patted Andrew on the back. "That suits me, as long as you supervise them. Can you start next Monday?"

"Not Monday, sir. I have duty at the engine house. We're practicing for the parade."

"All right. Tuesday. You'll be getting me out of a fix, Andrew. Again."

"Pump harder, my brothers, pump harder!" Abel shouted as the men of Engine 4 grunted every ounce of strength into their task. He screamed, "Got it! You got it, my brothers!" and the negroes brought their pumping to a halt. They shook hands and waved to the white and negro spectators applauding them from the edge of Wright Square. It was late March, but they already felt prepared for the water throwing competition in May.

Savannahians loved parades. They turned out in large numbers to see all the militia groups march in full colors in the four annual military parades, which celebrated the Battle of New Orleans, Washington's Birthday, May Day, and Independence Day.

The largest non-military parade was the annual colored fireman's parade held in May. All the negro companies, whose numbers totaled 650 men in 1856, marched in their uniforms through the streets of Savannah. Whites and blacks alike crammed the parade route to cheer their companies. Negroes especially enjoyed the parade since it was the only one in which they were allowed to participate, except as musicians.

After the parade, the companies gathered in a square for the water throwing competition. The winning team brought great honor to their ward. One of the contests, the one for which Engine 4 was practicing, involved shooting a stream of water at a pot held by a man standing on the top of a nearby roof. That evening, one of the negro firemen stood atop the two-story station house in Wright Square, holding a bucket.

Abel called to the men, "Master Ziegler will be pleased." The white manager of Engine 4 had left minutes earlier and asked Abel to finish the session.

A voice interrupted them. "Hey! You boys! You soaked us!" The fifty negroes watched seven white men approach them. Andrew knew these men were looking for trouble. He looked around for a policeman. Two years before, in 1854, a police department had been established to patrol the city during the day. Andrew didn't see an officer. He braced himself for the confrontation.

The biggest white man marched up to Abel, and, looking down at the black, said, "You think that's funny?"

Abel started to respond, "We didn't soak you, sir, and I don't think . . ."

Before he could finish, the man punched Abel on the chin, knocking him to the ground. Three other whites circled the negro and started kicking him. Despite the disparity in numbers, a negro did not strike back against a white outside of Oglethorpe Ward or Currytown, the negro neighborhoods, and Abel's fellow firefighters looked on helplessly.

Andrew watched in anger and felt his hands curl tightly into fists. His eyes darted around to see if any of his friends were about to rush to Abel's aid. They wanted to help but knew they would get beaten if they did. When Andrew saw that Abel could no longer hold his hands around his head to defend himself, he jumped into the circle, caught one of the white's legs, and flipped him in the air. The white landed flat on his face.

Three other whites jumped on Andrew and held his arms while the man who Andrew had flipped tried to punch him in the face. Andrew turned his head and got hit in the neck. He threw one man off him but the next punch caught him below the eye.

"Hold it! Stop or I'll break in two the next man who raises a fist!" a large, stocky white man in a brown suit and top hat hollered as he stepped between Andrew and the white man. The men holding Andrew threw him to the ground. He jumped up and helped Abel to his feet. The stranger looked around and asked, "What in damnation is going on?"

One of the white attackers by the name of Galloway said, "Marshal Stewart, we were on our way to the Kansas Meeting when these darkies soaked us."

Andrew said to the marshal, "That's not true, sir!" He then looked at Galloway. "You weren't near us or the firehouse. None of you got wet!"

Galloway moved towards Andrew but Marshal Stewart stepped in front of him, and Galloway backed off.

United States Marshal Daniel H. Stewart had no official authority to halt the confrontation, but everyone thought he had. He was physically imposing, not muscular like Hercules, but thick. Every part of his body, his arms, legs, shoulders, and neck, even the bulge around his waist looked hard. Stewart was raised poor and was driven to climb his way out of poverty. He worked at any job to make a living and had done relatively well. At the time of the confrontation, he was a bricklayer, owned a wood business, served as a director of the Republican Blues Building and Loan Association, and was the United States Marshal for the district of Georgia. He had learned early in life that serving the public provided invaluable contacts. He'd once been the city supervisor of streets and lanes, the city marshal, and the chief of the Savannah Fire Company. He knew well the white attackers, members of the Young America Engine Company.

Galloway yelled, "You niggers couldn't smell a fire, no less fight one!"

"Shut up, Galloway," Stewart barked. "I'm not going to tell you again!"

Several white men who had been watching from the side of the square hurried over. One pointed to the attackers and said, "Marshal Stewart, don't you be believin' these bad boys for a moment. They're as guilty as the devil hisself! The darkies was just doin' their jobs." If the whites of Savannah appreciated its negroes for anything, it was their service as firemen, and most didn't hesitate to support them, even against these known trouble-makers.

Stewart glared at the attackers. "Haven't you caused enough problems? You're already in danger of losing your engine."

White men wanted to be firemen, but not as part of an organization that included blacks. So in 1846, a group of whites petitioned the City Council for permission to form their own private company. The City Council consented, granting a charter to the Oglethorpe Fire Company, and stipulating that the company was responsible for purchasing its own equipment. However, it had to serve under the command of the chief of the Savannah Fire Company at fires. In the following years, three more white companies, including the Young America, were granted charters.

With separate negro and white companies, problems were bound to arise. In May 1850, just when Andrew had become a fireman, the Savannah Fire Company allowed its negroes to wear uniforms. The white companies, who already had uniforms, thought it was an insult to put the negroes on an equal footing and protested to the City Council. The council ordered the Savannah Fire Company to revoke the negroes' uniform privilege, but the company's managers objected, and the council rescinded its order.

In 1853, the City Council, sympathetic to the white companies, made decisions that further weakened the power of the Savannah Fire Company, whose white managers resigned in protest. The council accepted the resignations and appointed replacements, but that didn't end the trouble. The white companies continued to harass the black firemen. The worst offenders were the members of the Young America Company.

Stewart wanted to side with the whites. His friend Philip Russell was the second manager of the Young America Company. But they were obviously guilty and he wanted to appear to be fair in the eyes of the witnesses. He scolded the white attackers. "Mr. Russell will hear about this. He'll decide your punishment. Now get back to your business."

Nobody moved. The white man whom Andrew had flipped wobbled towards Andrew, "You better watch yourself, boy."

Stewart said, "I thought I told you to go about your business, Timmons. I mean it!" Stewart then squinted at Andrew. "You look familiar. Who's your master?"

Andrew, with a lump growing under his eye, stood tall and said, "I'm a free man, sir, and I'm a McBain."

A man who had been with Stewart, John Tucker, stepped to Stewart's side, and said, "That's Joseph McBain's negro."

Stewart searched his memory. "Mmmm. Oh, yes, a long time ago at the bowling alley. And Van Horn told me about you. You're the one taking brick work from us."

Andrew touched his bruised eye but said nothing. Tucker added, "Charlie told me he's using him on his flour mill."

Stewart was surprised Lamar would hire Andrew. He would have to leave the negro alone. "I better not catch you causing any more trouble, McBain, or I'll cause trouble you won't ever forget. Now clean up and get out of here."

The negroes moved their equipment back to the engine house.

Stewart and Tucker headed to St. Andrew's Hall. They had something more important on their minds than breaking up fights caused by the Young Americans. It was the news from Kansas. No issue had captivated the country more.

In 1820, in order to keep a balance, Congress had reached a compromise allowing Missouri to enter the union as a slave state and Maine a free state. After that, no territory north of the 36° 30' line could enter the union as a slave state. The compromise lasted over thirty years. But with the vast land gains of the Mexican-American War, Southerners demanded the right to settle in the new territories with *all* their property, and the issue of the expansion of slavery had to be revisited. One of the territories in question was Nebraska, which, according to the 1820 Compromise, would have to enter the union as a free state. To avoid a confrontation, in 1854 a senator crafted a bill dividing this territory in two, Kansas and Nebraska, and allowing their residents to decide their status by popular sovereignty. The North was outraged by the breaking of the 1820 Compromise, as it was believed Kansans would choose to be a slave state. Thousands of Southerners and Northerners began moving to Kansas to establish residence for the vote. Not surprisingly, violence erupted.

The slave states could not allow Kansas to be free. Meetings were held all over the South, including Savannah, to furnish support for the pro-slavery settlers.

Stewart and Tucker were greeted in front of St. Andrews Hall by three men, Charlie Lamar, John Montmollin, and George Wylly. Lamar and Montmollin were two of the organizers of the event.

Tucker, Montmollin, and Wylly were long-time Savannah residents and inseparable acquaintances. In 1847 they had served together in the city government, with Montmollin the marshal, Wylly the clerk of the market, and Tucker the superintendent of the city watch. They had all since prospered along with Savannah.

Montmollin asked Tucker, "Where have you been?"

"The marshal here had to break up a fight between the Young Americans and a negro engine company." John Tucker owned a plantation ten miles south of Savannah, but lived in town where he also worked as a general commission merchant. When he became a director of the Republican Blues Building and Loan Association, he brought his friend Daniel Stewart with him.

"Can't anything be done about those jackasses?" Montmollin said. He was a morose man and many people wondered why joking, party-loving men like Charlie Lamar and John Tucker kept his company. But Montmollin was wealthy and influential. He was the largest auctioneer in town, along with his partner George Wylly, he was president and a director of the Mechanics Savings Bank, and owned a plantation on the Carolina side of the Savannah River.

Marshal Stewart said, "Charlie, I hear one of those negro firemen, Andrew McBain, is an acquaintance of yours."

Charlie perked up. "Andrew? He's the finest negro in town, by God. Is he all right?"

Stewart explained. Charlie howled when he heard Andrew flipped that loud-mouth Timmons on his arse. Charlie said, "Unless you catch him committing a crime, Daniel, you leave him alone. He saved my life. And he's working on my mill."

Tucker said to the marshal, "Yes, Daniel, don't dare disturb Charlie's negro friends." Stewart, Wylly, Charlie, and even Montmollin had a good laugh. Then, they joined hundreds of others in the hall to pledge support for Kansas.

Despite the troubles in Kansas, Savannah was prospering. Cotton was being shipped in record quantities. All the commerce lent great promise to the second Chatham and Effingham Counties Agricultural Fair. The first one drew respectable crowds, but it was held twelve miles outside of town. The organizers needed a more convenient location to attract larger participation. They secured the Ten Broeck race course just three miles west of town, near the Heritage.

Joseph was invited to attend an executive committee meeting for the fair at Lamar's office in early September. Joseph was happy for the diversion. Emily and Danny were in New York with Emily's parents for the summer, and he longed for their return. Joseph missed coming home, picking up his smiling, gurgling son, swinging him around in circles, then laying him on his back and tickling his stomach. Though Emily wouldn't admit it, the servants enabled them to devote more time to Danny. But Emily was never really comfortable with the idea of being served by slaves, and wouldn't dare tell her parents or friends she had them.

Charlie greeted Joseph as he took his seat. Just then, Marshal Daniel Stewart took the chair next to Joseph. Charlie asked Stewart, "Daniel, do you know Joseph McBain?"

Stewart shook Joseph's hand and said, "We've met once, several years ago. Nice to see you again, Mr. McBain."

General George Harrison, the president of the fair committee, called the meeting to order and Charlie sat by his side. During the proceedings Joseph was named to head the building products committee and to help Charlie arrange transportation for exhibitors. Daniel Stewart was appointed to head the poultry committee.

Over the next two months, Joseph and Charlie worked on the fair together one evening a week. They wrote to farmers, planters, manufacturers, and horticulturers from around the state and advertised in local newspapers. They encouraged Savannah residents to participate in the many different livestock, poultry, vegetable, fruit, embroidery, and cooking competitions.

Joseph met Stewart several times at Charlie's office. Joseph found Stewart a difficult man with whom to talk. Yet, Stewart did everything Charlie asked. Charlie, so well connected in Savannah circles, had always introduced Stewart to his friends, and included him in events such as the fair, contacts that the socially-conscious Stewart coveted.

Two weeks before the fair, Emily and Danny returned home. Emily couldn't stop talking about New York City, and how exciting and modern it was. She reported that her parents marveled over Danny's eyes, exactly like Joseph's. Joseph had to agree. The first night, he lay on the floor with Danny on his chest, and tickled him for hours.

The fair, held in mid-November, attracted several thousand patrons and exhibitors. Large animals such as cows, bulls, horses, sheep, and pigs were penned in the infield. Smaller animals like chickens and turkeys, and fruits, vegetables, and other farm crops were shown on the open deck, along with the building products exhibitions. Cooked goods like breads and pies, household items, knitted clothes, and embroideries were exhibited under the covered deck. By mid-day, so many people were in attendance, they had trouble moving around without bumping into one another. Late in the afternoon, the awards were presented in the enclosed long room.

Afterwards, Charlie held a party at the Our House bar. Joseph saw Henry Dubignon hand Charlie some money. Joseph wondered what in the world the two could have wagered on at an agricultural fair, but he wasn't surprised.

Nelson Trowbridge approached Joseph and asked him if he had changed his mind about investing in the gold mines or negro ventures. Joseph said he had not.

Richard Akin asked Joseph if he wanted to help form a jockey club, now that his fair responsibilities were over. Joseph said he would like to, if he had the time.

Then, Charlie called for a toast for all those who contributed to the success of the fair, ending a great day for Savannah.

As soon as the party concluded, so did the euphoria over the fair. A larger, more important event was being hosted by the city in a few weeks and locals were in a frenzy preparing for it. The hotels, restaurants, and bars would be filled as never before.

For years the southern states held an annual convention to discuss the economic policies of the region. The overriding concern was ending the agricultural South's reliance on the North for manufactures, shipping, and capital. The conventions were not meant to be political. But in the atmosphere of 1856, with the Kansas conflict, the recent presidential election sending Democrat James Buchanan to the White House, and the emergence of the Republican Party, politics would be difficult to avoid.

Joseph wasn't involved in the organizing committee for the convention, but he was as interested as any other Southerner in its proceedings, and he ran across Chippewa Square to the Atheneum Theatre early one Monday morning in December 1856 to make sure he didn't miss a minute. He made his way to the men's visitors section on the first tier, took a seat, and looked upon the orchestra and one thousand of the most successful and influential men in the South. He spotted the Georgia delegation and the Savannah representatives sitting in the middle section near the stage. They included his father, Andrew Low, Dr. Richard Arnold, John Owens, a defense lawyer, John Boston, the port collector, Charles Green, and William Hodgson, the oriental scholar, diplomat, and curator of the Georgia Historical Society.

The mayor brought the meeting to order, and Mr. James Lyons of Virginia, the president of the convention, addressed the crowd. He said they were gathered to restore the commercial independence of the South, but the day might come when the South would have to exert all her powers to preserve her rights. The attendees cheered.

Mr. Lyons read the names of the members of the Committee of Business who would consider all proposed resolutions, and the discussions started. One gentleman said the South needed to start newspapers in the North to give exposure to southern views. Another man spoke of the need for the South to have a line of ocean steamers to sail directly to Europe without having to go through northern ports, even though this had been tried recently and failed. Another delegate called for the repeal of the tariff and the start of direct taxation.

That's how the morning went, much like previous years' meetings, with issues hotly debated, and little resolved. Just before one o'clock the crowd started to talk amongst themselves, ready to head to the restaurants and taverns. Many delegates stood and stretched when Mr. Lyons said, "One last speaker, please, before we adjourn." The crowd groaned. "I would like to recognize the gentleman from Georgia, Mr. William Gaulden."

People remained standing, some giving good-natured jeers, as Gaulden, a lawyer from Liberty County, took the stage. He smiled and held up his hands, as if he were acknowledging cheers. Then he stuck his fingers in his vest pockets. "Gentlemen,

I have just a few resolutions for your consideration, if you please. Then we can partake in the fine hospitality and repast of Savannah." Applause exploded from all corners of the theatre.

Gaulden waved to the crowd. "First, I would like to thank our gracious Savannah hosts for putting on such a fine convention." Huzzahs. Gaulden pointed to the second tier. "Now I ask, have you ever seen so many beautiful ladies in your whole, ever loving lives?" Cheers, hoots, and whistles.

He waited for the folks to calm down. "Getting down to business, I would sincerely hope our astute representatives in Congress will try their best to shoot down that blasted Yankee tariff." Gaulden held up his arms as if he were firing a rifle in the air, and feigned a recoil. The attendees howled. The lawyer knew how to move a crowd.

Gaulden held up his hands to quiet the folks. "I would also request our congressmen, while they're at it, to use their best efforts to repeal all laws interdicting the African slave trade." The audience froze, as if the next ice age had suddenly blown into the theatre. Joseph looked at the man next to him to make sure he heard the speaker properly. Gaulden continued, leaving no room for doubt. "The South, in support of its great institutions, needs the trade reopened if it is to remain great."

Joseph heard a few gasps around him. The audience participation spread, with everyone either applauding or jeering. Joseph found himself on his feet, booing the speaker. There was total bedlam in the theatre. The slave-trade cat was out of the bag.

After the War of Independence, a ravaged America had to rebuild. Georgia and South Carolina, whose rice economies depended on slave labor, had not been able to import Africans for almost ten years. They had lost thousands of slaves during the war to runaways, deaths, and British promises of freedom. They needed to replace that manpower, and soon after the Treaty of Paris in 1783, African slave importations reached pre-war volumes. But there was a growing discontent against the inhumanity of the trade and the issue had to be resolved before a union could be accomplished.

During the Constitutional Convention, the Georgia and South Carolina delegates would not accept a ban of the trade. Eventually, a compromise was reached, and a clause was added, stating that, "The Congress could not prohibit the importation of such persons as any of the states shall think proper to admit until the year 1808." In addition, it stated that, "If a person held to service or labor in one state escaped to another, that person had to be returned, upon a claim, to the [owner]." It was clear, even though the words "slave" or "slavery" were not used, domestic slavery and the importation of slaves from outside of America were legal.

However, the revulsion to the trade did not go away, and by 1798 every state had passed laws banning the importation of slaves from foreign places. South Carolina and Georgia had more than just humanity in mind. The bloody slave revolt in San Domingue in 1791 had made them reconsider living with dominating numbers of negroes by their side. Whatever the motivation, after the actions by the states, the trade to the United States was dead, and many believed that the institution of slavery would die of its own inertia.

But in 1803 South Carolina repealed its law banning slave importations. Ten years earlier, on a Savannah River plantation, a young man had invented an engine that could remove seeds from short-staple cotton, drastically reducing the manpower requirements for deseeding. Cotton then became a very profitable crop. Slaves, and lots of them, would be needed for the other harvesting tasks. Also, the Louisiana Purchase opened a vast new territory which would support crops using slave labor. South Carolina wanted to import as many Africans as possible before the pending federal ban. Though no other state joined South Carolina, it was clear there would be no natural death to slavery.

In March 1807, Congress passed, and President Thomas Jefferson signed, federal legislation ending the legal importation of slaves into the United States from any foreign place, effective on the earliest possible date, January 1, 1808. The act said nothing of the institution of slavery itself. Individual states continued to determine its legality, as well as the right to import slaves from other states.

Of course, the new law gave rise to an illegal trade, forcing the government to create more legislation. In 1819 and 1820, it passed laws making the importation of slaves an act of piracy. Conviction was punishable by death.

In 1842, America and Great Britain signed the Webster-Ashburton Treaty, which, among other things, established a joint patrol of warships along the West African coast to seize ships involved in the slave trade. America joined other nations including France, Spain, and Portugal, which also had squadrons on the coast. However, because the boarding of one country's ship by another could cause an international incident, the squadrons' effectiveness was reduced. Also, the coast of Africa was a long span to patrol with a limited number of ships. Men were willing to take the risk for "wool" or "ivory," as Africans were called.

So the illegal trade continued, and the cost of slaves rose, even though the price of cotton had barely moved in years. With a prime negro field hand fetching over one thousand dollars in 1856, better than half of planters' capital was tied up in slaves.

It was in this atmosphere of world condemnation of slavery, endless legislation to prevent the illegal importation of Africans, and a booming demand in cotton that William Gaulden called for re-opening the trade.

"Order, gentlemen! Order!" Mr. Lyons shouted. Several other members of the committee took the stage and held up their hands to quiet the crowd. After calm had returned, the committee agreed to lay the resolutions on the table for a later time. The delegates charged out of the Atheneum and onto the streets in a buzz.

Joseph waited outside the theatre for his father. "Can you believe that? The convention was generating such promise for the South. Then he opens his mouth and I was embarrassed to be in the theatre. Is Gaulden out of his mind?"

McBain answered, "Apparently, though I wouldn't worry about it. The trade will never be re-opened. But this is an enormous distraction to our purpose. We're here to move forwards, not backwards. Thankfully, Mr. Lyons buried the debate. Gaulden and his proposal will be forgotten as soon as the delegates get some food and drink in them."

Joseph said, "I hope so." He returned to his office, and, after work, visited the packed Pulaski Hotel barroom. The tobacco smoke was as thick as any morning mist he had ever seen. The noise of so many men talking gave him a headache. There was only one topic of conversation. Gaulden's proposition wasn't forgotten. Joseph decided to leave, troubled that anyone could be in favor of importing Africans. As he walked home, he envisioned the headlines of the Northern newspapers, accusing the entire South of wanting to re-open the slave trade.

Joseph decided not to mention the day's events to Emily, who would lecture him that if people didn't have slaves, there wouldn't be a slave trade. Over dinner, of course, she asked about the convention. Joseph was about to tell her when Andrew and Patience appeared at the door. They were both very distraught, with Patience in tears. They had just received word that Reverend Marshall, at one hundred one years of age, had died in Virginia, en route to Georgia, and they wanted Joseph to sign a pass so they could visit Patience's parents to pray. Joseph and Emily spent half an hour consoling them. Emily forgot about the meeting, at least temporarily.

The delegates flooded into Atheneum Hall the next morning, ready to discuss the economic independence of the South. Mr. Lyons called the convention to order and recognized a man, who called out from his place in the orchestra, "Mr. President, I move that we continue the debate of the honorable Mr. Gaulden's resolution!" Some stood and stomped their feet. Mr. Lyons looked around the stage, as if trying to find a higher authority. The delegate continued. "I move we hear from the honorable Leonidas Spratt of South Carolina."

Spratt, a Charleston lawyer who didn't own any slaves, was perhaps the loudest voice for re-opening the trade. As owner and editor of the *Charleston Standard*, he had started his crusade as early as 1852, but hardly made a ripple outside of South Carolina. However, earlier in 1856 Governor James Adams announced to the South Carolina Legislature that it was time to consider legalizing the trade. Though America took notice, there was still no wide support in the South. But now Spratt had a captive, influential audience before him.

Spratt spoke passionately, his fist pumping with each word. He said there was no more important issue for the convention to consider than re-opening the trade. The United States Congress had exercised power it did not have, and it was time for the South to do something about it. He wanted to hear the objections of those who disagreed.

Several delegates accepted Spratt's challenge. One man said the convention was not competent to consider the issue, and the South should think long and hard before it defied the feelings of the entire Christian world. Another said he would not endorse commerce in Africans and that the Convention should not consider it. Still another said the subject was an attack upon the Union. These men drew long applause from a majority of the assemblage.

Gaulden again defiantly strode onto the stage. "Gentlemen! Have you forgotten how your bread is buttered, your families fed? We have a labor system based on slavery. We have had it since our ancestors came here almost two hundred years ago. When we broke away from the British, our founders said slavery was just fine, and so was bringing in slaves from Africa. Then, in 1808, Congress told us slavery was still fine, we just couldn't bring in any more Africans. Now, I ask, does that make a dang wit of sense? I want some gentlemen at this august gathering to tell me, why is it right to import a negro from Virginia to a cotton field in Georgia, but not from some uncivilized jungle in Africa?" Gaulden had to let the noise die down before he could continue. "No man can explain the difference logically. So I say this now, to each and every person here. You can try to ignore this issue as if it doesn't exist. But it does. It's a part of every other issue you discuss this week. Our steamship lines, our railroads, our education, our manufactures, all depend on our peculiar institution. It's high time, gentlemen, to reclaim our true rights before the world!" He walked off the stage, which shook from the audience's cheers and cat-calls.

Mr. Lyons had no choice but to put the resolution to re-open the slave trade up for a vote by the Committee on Business. It was defeated soundly, sixty-eight nays to sixteen yeas, but wasn't forgotten. Through the rest of the convention, the issue hung in the air like the odor of a ripe skunk.

On Thursday night, the last day of the convention, Charles Green hosted a party for the delegates and other friends at his Gothic Revival mansion which Andrew had helped build. It was so crowded many folks drank and socialized outside in the chilly air on Macon Street and in Madison Square. The gathering was alive with great hope for the South. Joseph heard no talk of disunion or re-opening the trade, only of the South casting off its dependence on the North. He felt better. It had been an exhausting week, and he was ready for a good night sleep.

As Joseph left for home, he saw Leonidas Spratt and William Gaulden talking intently with Charlie Lamar.

CHAPTER 21

An Expedition to the Moon

1857-1858

Patience and Andrew sat on the parlor floor, quietly playing with Truvy, as they had taken to calling James Vitruvius. They had overcome the pain of losing Reverend Marshall as Andrew had dealt with the death of Grampah, through prayer and time. William J. Campbell, a man of compassion, had become the new reverend of the First African Baptist, and had made the transition easier for the congregation.

Andrew asked, "Is Truvy doubling in size each day, or is it my imagination?"

Patience laughed. "No. Your eyes are good." She patted her son's belly.

Andrew lay on his side and rubbed his wife's back, a signal his wife was familiar with. She caught Andrew's eye and said, "Maybe we should lie down in the bedroom."

As they stood, they heard a knock at the door. Andrew looked at Patience and left to answer it. Patience heard, "Ebnin', Andrew."

She groaned when Andrew said, "Dante! Come in."

Dante followed Andrew into the parlor. "Ebnin', Pay'shun."

"Hello, Dante," Patience said as she sat back down. She was not an admirer of Dante. She thought he was lazy, befriended questionable characters, was insincere in his faith, and only visited Andrew when he needed something.

Dante picked up eighteen-month-old Truvy and lifted the child over his head. Truvy giggled and drooled on Dante's face. Patience and Andrew laughed as Dante wrinkled his nose and gently placed Truvy on the floor.

Dante dried his nose on his shirt sleeve. Then he reached into his pocket and pulled out a wooden toy and waved it in front of Truvy, who stared at it in open-eyed wonder. It was a white boy, wearing black shorts, a shirt, and a hat. Dante pulled a string in the back and the boy's arms and legs folded up. When Dante released the string, they straightened out again. Truvy stuck his arm out. Dante handed the toy to him, and the child started to bang it on the floor.

Patience took the toy from Truvy and said, "Thank Mr. Dante for the toy, Truvy."

Truvy belched. Patience said, "Thank you, Dante. That was thoughtful of you."

Dante nodded and then turned to Andrew. "Kin ah tahk wid oonuh?"

Andrew glanced at Patience, who was dangling the toy in front of her son, and said, "Sure. Let's go into the study."

Dante followed Andrew, looking at the large rooms and paintings on the walls and thinking how lucky Andrew was to have his own house with a study. Andrew sat at his desk, but Dante stood, dug into his pocket, pulled out a roll of bills, and dropped it on the desk. Andrew eyed it and looked up at Dante. "What's this?"

"Ah ready tuh buy uh restran'."

Andrew picked up the wad and turned it around in his hand, impressed with its size. He hadn't thought about the restaurant discussion with Dante in years. "The restaurant you talked about, what, five or six years ago? I thought you'd given up on it."

Dante finally sat. "Tek tahm tuh sabe.

Andrew patted the cash. "How much is here?"

"Two hunnud an' fawdy dolluh."

Andrew went, "Mmmm." He couldn't believe Dante had the discipline to save. "That's very good. Do you mind telling me where you got it?"

"Udda wu'k fuh massa, an' he'pin Miss Amy at she shop."

Andrew pushed the roll towards Dante. "I'm impressed you were able to do this. But have you thought about the things we discussed so long ago? About a plan?"

Dante nodded emphatically. "Sho' hab."

"You remember I said it was unlikely Master Joseph would go along with this?"

Dante shoved the money into his pocket. "Ah hab tuh try."

Andrew took a deep breath and wondered if he should pursue this. He had a queasy feeling in his gut. But Dante had indeed come up with the money. Andrew opened a drawer, and grabbed a pen, ink, and paper. "All right, let's get started."

They hunched over the desk and discussed the running of a restaurant, about which they knew little. Neither had ever eaten in a proper one, but they tried to imagine what it would be like. Halfway through their exercise, Patience opened the door to say good night. She closed it before Andrew could say good night in return.

The men finished two hours later. Andrew told Dante he would discuss it with Joseph at an appropriate time, but it might take a while, perhaps a month. He urged Dante not to get his hopes up. After Dante left, Andrew tiptoed into the bedroom, undressed, and eased into bed. He faced away from Patience, hoping she was asleep.

"Andrew?"

He knew she wouldn't be. "Yes, angel?"

"What did that troublemaker want?"

Andrew told her the story, including meeting François at Master Couper's house and Brutus, the cook at Our House Restaurant. "Dante wants that, too, to be recognized."

"A negro can't own a restaurant here in white Savannah."

Andrew still faced away from Patience. "I told him that. But he was finally showing some ambition and I didn't want to destroy it. I told him maybe Joseph would buy a restaurant and let him be the cook."

Andrew felt Patience sit up in the bed. "Andrew McBain, are you in your right mind? Why should Master Joseph even consider that? He'll throw you out of his house, and rightly so. Besides, Master McBain owns Dante. It's his decision to let Dante do something like that."

Andrew turned on his other side to face his wife. "I know. But I never in a million years thought he'd come up with the money, or a plan. Now that he has, I don't know what to do. I don't want to go back on my word."

"Andrew, the last thing whites want us to have is ambition. You were fortunate with the McBains. Don't go thinking others can be as lucky. Besides, you believe Dante came upon that money honestly?"

"I don't know he didn't." Andrew yawned loudly.

Patience ignored the hint. She pulled the covers up to her neck. "What about the niggers he roams with? Andrew, listen to me. Just tell him to forget it. He's trouble. All he does is ask favors. He's never done anything for you."

Andrew thought about rubbing Patience's back, but it was inaccessible. "I know it's difficult for you to understand my feelings for Dante. It's hard even for me. When I was a child, as good as the McBains were to me, I envied everyone who had parents. Except Dante. His mother beat him all the time. And he had no friends. I tried to be an older brother to him. I wanted him to have just one person who cared about him a little. That was me, though I'm certain he was never aware of it. He went on stealing and bothering people. Then he saw his mother get killed. I wondered how much worse things could get for him. A few years later he discovers he likes cooking, and he becomes a cook, a good one. He had something important in his life. He stopped stealing and was fun to be with. Now he wants a restaurant. He deserves to have something he cares about."

Patience laid her hand on her husband's head. "Andrew, you're a saint. But don't fool yourself, Dante only thinks about himself. Not you, not anyone."

Andrew said, "Tonight, he thought to buy a toy for Truvy. That's a good sign."

Patience sighed. She knew she wasn't going to change Andrew's mind. "When are you going to ask Joseph?"

"Not for a while. He's busy working on the next fair. He's taking it on like a crusade. And I'm too busy working for Master Charles. I told Dante to be patient."

Patience slid down into the bed. "Andrew, I love you. You know that. You're the smartest man I know. But this is the dumbest thing I've ever heard."

Andrew rolled over, facing away from his wife. He had trouble falling asleep.

*   *   *

Joseph certainly was busy. Business was booming. The wealth created by the thriving cotton trade resulted in a surge of construction. The Central of Georgia Railroad was completing a large passenger, cargo, and maintenance facility on the west side of town, one of the most modern in the country. Its construction required thousands of Savannah Greys. And the Savannah, Albany & Gulf Railroad, whose depot was on the east side of town, just east of Troup Square, had just connected Savannah to the south near the Great Ogeechee River, and was about to extend further south to the Altamaha River, bringing in even more commerce to the city.

Joseph was committed to seeing Savannah become a larger trading center, and one way to do it was through the agricultural fair. He thought it his civic duty, he enjoyed the work, and he developed many valuable contacts.

One evening in April 1857 he attended a planning meeting at Charlie's office. He sat next to Daniel Stewart, and congratulated him on being appointed the city marshal. Stewart, who was still the federal marshal, had become a powerful and influential man.

General George Harrison handed out assignments for the upcoming fair to be held at the Ten Broeck race track in November. He again asked Joseph to head the transportation arrangements for exhibitors as well as the building products exhibition.

After the meeting the men went for drinks at the Screven House. As they filed out of Lamar's office, Charlie tapped Joseph on the shoulder. "Joseph, do you mind staying behind for a minute? I need to speak with you. We'll catch up with the others."

"Sure, Charlie."

Charlie closed the door as Joseph took a seat. "Joseph, may I be candid with you? I feel comfortable talking to you."

Joseph didn't like the sound of that. "Of course."

Charlie started to pace the office. "I'll get right to it, then. I've had a run of bad luck recently. Those gold mines I told you about? The yields are low and expenses are out of control. Trow's in New York trying to place the mines into a stock company so we can sell shares to the public. He's had no success yet. And the purchaser of the Beaufort negroes, a planter in New Orleans named Johnston, can't honor his notes. Not yet, anyway. On top of that, I've been taken for forty-five thousand dollars in a business deal with a thieving New Yorker. I'm strapped."

Joseph felt his body tense up. Charlie had lost a fortune. And he knew what Charlie was leading up to. "Charlie, what about all your other operations—the wharves, the cotton press, the warehouse, the commission business, the shipping agency, the insurance agency, the plank roads? You're a director at the Bank of Commerce and the Central of Georgia Railroad. I assumed you were one of the richest men in town."

Charlie continued to pace, head down. "I've had some real bad luck, Joseph. It happens to all businessmen."

Joseph thought, well, it hadn't happened to him, or anyone else he knew. The 1850s had been incredibly prosperous. It seemed everyone was doing well. Everyone, apparently, except Charlie. Joseph thought there must be others Charlie could turn to. "Can Trow help?"

Charlie laughed without mirth. "Hah! He's one of the reasons why I'm in trouble. He owes me thousands. The holders of his notes are offering them at half price."

Joseph scratched his head as he frantically searched his mind for Charlie's other friends. "What about Akin, Tucker, Montmollin, or Wylly?"

Charlie said, "They're all short on cash. Tucker is purchasing Drakies Plantation on the Savannah River. Akin has no assets."

Joseph guessed Charlie had already borrowed from everyone else he knew. Still, he wasn't giving up. "Your father?"

Charlie stopped in his tracks and looked at Joseph. "I can't ask him for any more help. Besides, all he does is criticize me."

Joseph had run out of suggestions. He sat like a can on a fence at the rifle range and waited. Charlie fired. "Can you help me out, Joseph? I'll give you a personal note. I'll be able to repay you in full by the end of the year. You have my word."

Joseph wondered what his father would do in this situation and concluded James would always help a friend. "If you're really broke, Charlie, I'll make a loan for your personal note. I can't let a friend struggle. How much do you need?"

"One hundred thousand would help me get through this."

Joseph almost lifted off his chair. "One hundred thousand dollars! Charlie, I can't lend you that much! That's a fortune!" He thought Charlie might ask for a few thousand at most. Unprepared for the request, Joseph heard himself say, "Five thousand is the best I can do."

Charlie didn't hesitate. He shook Joseph's hand and said, "Thanks, Joseph. That'll sure help. Could I get it tomorrow? You'll get it back plus interest, you have my word. Now let's get that drink. On me!"

Joseph felt numb. He told Charlie it was late and he had to get home. Charlie thanked him again and they parted. Joseph had difficulty walking in a straight line. The confident, back-slapping, boasting, drink-buying, socially prominent Charlie Lamar was broke. Yet he had managed to get Joseph to lend him five thousand dollars.

Joseph didn't dare tell his father or Emily that he had loaned Charlie money. He was so angry with himself he hardly ate for days. Joseph could afford it, though five thousand was a large sum of money. It was still on his mind in June when Andrew dropped by his office.

After asking about families, Joseph said, "Tell me, with Reverend Marshall's passing, is there still talk of building a new church?"

"Yes, but I haven't heard from Reverend Campbell. He has a lot on his mind." Andrew paused. "Actually, I have something on my mind, too, Joseph. You're not going to believe this. I told Dante I'd help him with something. I know it was wrong to do." Andrew told Joseph about Dante's idea.

Joseph tugged at his ear as if his hearing was defective. "You're serious?" Andrew nodded. "Andrew, that's impossible. I have no inclination or time to get involved in a restaurant, especially for Dante's sake. And Father would never allow it."

Andrew looked at his lap. "I know, Joseph. I'm embarrassed to even be here. I just felt I had to keep my word, even though I should never have given it."

"Andrew, you're a great friend. That's why you did it. And I'd do anything for you. But this, I can't. It's just too insane."

The two men chatted for a few more minutes and Andrew left. Joseph thought buying a restaurant was far less risky than lending money to Charlie. Still, Joseph had made one huge mistake. He wasn't about to make another.

*   *   *

Shortly after Joseph gave his decision to Andrew, Charlie was in his office telling his partner, "I'm broke, Trow. If I don't make some money soon, I'm bankrupt."

Trowbridge watched Charlie sit at his desk and nervously flip a coin in the air. Trow had been holding onto a money-making idea for weeks but had been reluctant to offer it. Now with Charlie in deep trouble, Trow figured this was the time. "There's a way to make money, Chollie. Big money. And quickly. It would solve all our problems."

Charlie continued flipping. He was afraid to tap Trow's advice, which he felt had gotten him into this mess in the first place. But Charlie could never refuse the bait of large, quick profits. Like a hungry trout, he bit. "All right, what is it, Trow?"

"Africans."

Charlie snatched the coin in mid-air. He wondered who was crazier, Trow or him. "Trow, your negro business is one of the reasons why we're in so much trouble."

Trow picked up a pen and piece of paper from the desk. "No. We're in trouble because of a bad customer. I should have known better about Johnston. Besides, those negroes were too expensive. There's a cheaper place to buy them." Trow paused. Charlie stared at him, his dark eyes demanding Trow to continue. "In Africa." Trow wrote as he spoke. "Look, I hear they cost fifty dollars each. Add in the expense of transporting them, they're still cheap. We'd have to sell them below market since they're illegal, say seven hundred dollars average. But even if we buy 450 and only 400 survive, it still puts two hundred thousand dollars in our pockets, after our costs. That's big money, Chollie."

Lamar peered at Trow's calculations. "That would bail me out. But the trade is illegal. Being broke is better than being broke and in jail or hanging in a noose."

"Chollie, people not nearly as smart as us are getting rich in the trade. We don't even have to bring them back to America. We can sell them in Cuba. Slavery is still legal there."

Charlie closed his eyes and thought. Two hundred thousand would put him right, even split with a partner. Of course, there were risks, but they were heaped on him by Northerners and spineless Southerners. Why shouldn't the South have slaves?

Charlie bolted forward and pounded the desk. "Spratt and Gaulden are correct. It's our right to have negroes. The trade should never have been prohibited in the first place. How I'd love to be the person to reopen it."

Trow pounced on Charlie's interest. "All we have to do is get a ship, hire an experienced captain, and give him some money. The captain hires a crew, buys the supplies, sails to Africa, purchases the negroes, and returns. When the ship lands, we deliver the negroes to our customers and collect the money."

Trow, as always, made it sound so easy. Charlie said, "There are plenty of ships available. Where do we find a good captain, one we can trust?"

"New York or New Orleans. That's where most of the crews are as well. I'm going to New York for the gold mines. I can find a captain."

"How much cash do we need?"

Trow continued writing, excited that Charlie liked the idea. "It depends, Chollie. A ship will cost about fifteen thousand dollars, but maybe you can buy it with paper and cash. Supplies and provisions might run ten thousand. A captain and a crew of fifteen will cost about fifteen thousand. Four hundred fifty negroes would cost twenty-five thousand. You'll need cash for bribes, say five thousand. The total will be about fifty-five thousand dollars, excluding the ship."

Charlie rubbed his temples. He didn't have any personal cash except five thousand dollars from Joseph's loan. However, if he sold some property, took cash from the business, and used cash set aside to retire some past-due notes, he could raise half the funds and his problems would be over in less than six months. "You have thirty thousand dollars, Trow?"

"I can get my hands on it, Chollie."

Charlie thought about that. If Trow could get his hands on thirty thou, why couldn't Trow pay him back? Charlie decided not to press it and risk killing the African deal. "Make sure you have your end. I have an ace in the hole, a relative who is influential in the government." Trow smiled. He knew that after James Buchanan was inaugurated President in March 1857, he had appointed Howell Cobb the Secretary of the Treasury, which included customs.

Charlie and Trow shook hands on their new partnership. Charlie said, "Now get your arse up to New York and start things rolling."

Trow couldn't convince any New York banker to underwrite shares in the gold-mining company. But he did find a captain for a slave voyage, and with the help of the captain found a ship in New York, the *E. A. Rawlins*. Trow negotiated a price, and telegraphed Charlie, who purchased the ship, half with cash and half with notes. Captain Alex Grant, Jr., told Trow he would sail the *Rawlins* to Mobile, have it outfitted on Lamar's account, and he and a crew would be in Savannah in a month. Charlie could hardly wait.

In early July, Charlie and Trow stood at the wharf and welcomed the *Rawlins*, a three-mast bark, 115 feet long, twenty-five feet wide, ten feet deep, with a burden of 273 tons. Charlie thought it looked like so many commercial ships, clean but slow, a mule on water.

After the gangway was put in place, a man with a limp hobbled down, walked up to Trow, and shook hands. Trow introduced Grant to Charlie. Charlie was ecstatic. To him, the injured leg indicated an experienced, hardened captain, afraid of nothing. He knew this was the right man for the job. After exchanging pleasantries, Charlie pointed to the ship and whispered to Grant, "You can fit 450 Africans in that?"

Grant nodded. "No problem. Probably more."

Charlie was amazed that it was possible. He couldn't imagine that many crammed in. The men retired to Charlie's office, where they planned the mission. Over the next few days, Grant and Trow bought supplies while Charlie secured twenty thousand dollars in gold and applied to customs for clearance to Funchal, Madeira, near the coast of Africa.

When the ship was finally loaded and ready to leave, Charlie sat in his office and poured a whiskey. For the first time in a long while, he truly relaxed. In a few months, everything would be right again.

*　　*　　*

Joseph arrived home from the office and heard Danny's voice in the family parlor. He entered the room, kissed Emily on the cheek, picked up his son from the settee, and swung him in the air, loving the sound of the boy's giggles. Joseph had been annoyed with Emily for refusing to go to Tallulah Falls for the summer with his mother and Amy. But seeing two-year-old Danny safe and healthy, waving his arms and laughing on the floor, Joseph was happy they had stayed.

As Joseph got on his knees and watched Danny stomp around, Emily asked, "Dear, did you see today's paper?"

Danny plopped backwards on his rump. "No. I'll read it before supper. Why?"

Emily handed Joseph the paper and pointed to an article. "That's why."

Joseph read on his knees, and said, "Whew." The article reported that Lamar's new bark, the *E. A. Rawlins*, had been ordered seized by the United States Customs in Savannah on suspicion of being a slaver, and was to be searched.

Two things about the *Rawlins* concerned the port collector, John Boston. First, it was headed for Africa. Second, its cargo could be used for transporting hundreds of people across the Atlantic; items such as thirteen thousand feet of lumber, which could make slave decks, two hundred bricks for a large, deck side oven, medicines, forty tierces of rice, 102 sacks of cowpeas, 115 barrels of pilot bread, and 283 shooks. These items did not prove the ship was a slaver, since many of them could be sold on a legitimate trading voyage, but their presence raised questions.

John Boston had been the port collector of Savannah since 1853. He had lived most of his adult life there and like so many other Savannahians, experienced a wide array of professions. Boston knew Charlie well. They had both served on the organizing committee of Savannah's first agricultural fair and the Kansas meeting. They were fellow members of the Democrat party, when Charlie wasn't flirting with the Know-Nothings. And Boston often dealt with Charlie's shipping business. But Boston was a serious public servant, and no personal relationship was going to interfere with his job. Boston had the United States marshal seize the ship.

Emily said, "Joseph, I'd prefer if you have nothing to do with Charlie anymore."

Joseph glanced at the article again. "We don't know if he's guilty, Emily. He deserves to be heard. Wait until the ship's inspected. But, beyond the agricultural fair and the jockey club, I have little reason to see him."

Emily pleaded, "Joseph, you spend so many hours on those activities. I know they're important, but you see him all the time."

Joseph handed the paper back to Emily and put Danny back on his feet. The boy took a step before falling into his father's hands. "I'll extricate myself from Charlie. It may take a while, but I will."

Emily tossed the paper aside. "I've heard from some friends at the female asylum that he's broke. If the government takes his ship, he'll be bankrupt. Then he'll probably look anywhere he can for help. Whatever you do, Joseph, don't lend him any money."

Joseph ate sparingly that night.

The next day Marshal Daniel Stewart searched the *Rawlins* and found nothing suspicious. The ship was cleared to commence its voyage. Charlie wrote Howell Cobb complaining about Boston's actions, calling the port collector a natural-born "Know Nothing," and submitted a bill for thirteen hundred dollars for the expense of having his ship laid up a week for the seizure and search. He never collected. Although annoyed with his cousin for not helping, Charlie didn't lose sleep. His knew his problems were almost over.

*   *   *

Emily was not the only woman demanding that her husband have nothing to do with Charlie Lamar.

"You never told me that!" Patience said to Andrew. They had been sitting in their parlor after returning from the funeral of Aspasia Mirault, for whom Patience had been baking. They were discussing where Patience might work next when Andrew mentioned that he was anxious to leave the employ of Charlie Lamar because Andrew had heard Lamar was rumored to be involved in the slave trade.

Andrew responded, "I just learned of it myself. It's strange how it all turned out. He's changed so much. Master Charles was such a fine young man, and so strong on the *Pulaski*."

Patience demanded, "I don't care if he walked on water. If he's a slave trader, you can't have anything to do with him. Finish that job and be done with him."

Andrew put his hands in his suit jacket and leaned back. "Thankfully, the job is almost finished, and Mr. Norris needs me on a project." Andrew's hand fiddled in his pocket, and he pulled out an envelope. He held it up and stared at it.

Patience looked at the envelope and said, "What's that?"

"The letter I wrote to the Queen of England. I guess I haven't worn this suit in a while."

Patience moved closer to Andrew on the couch, took the envelope, and inspected it. "You never sent it?"

"No. It didn't seem the same without Grampah. I was going to put it in his grave when he was buried to take with him to heaven; to remember me forever. I brought it to the funeral, but I was so sad I forgot. I guess it's been in this pocket for three years."

Patience stood and handed Andrew the envelope. "Andrew, you must send it! For your Grampah's memory, and Oglethorpe's. Please. Promise me you will."

Andrew took it. "I promise. I'll do it tomorrow."

Patience bent forward and kissed her husband on the forehead.

*   *   *

Charlie's first experience in the slave trade was no more successful than any of his other business ventures. A few months after leaving Savannah for Africa, Captain Grant saw a few British cruisers near Madeira, got cold feet, sailed into Funchal harbor, sold a portion of the supplies, and sailed back to New Orleans. He found Trowbridge, who was in town trying to collect from Johnston for the Beaufort negroes. The captain handed Trow sixteen thousand dollars of the remaining gold and disappeared.

Charlie had lost five thousand dollars on the expedition and was in deeper trouble than ever. Tens of thousands of dollars of his notes were falling due. To make matters worse, a financial panic had gripped the country. Cotton prices fell, banks failed, and economic activity shrank. Taking more cash out of the family business was impossible. Charlie's time was running out. But he wasn't giving up. He still owned the *Rawlins* and Grant did return most of the gold, which Charlie could use on another expedition. First, he had to contend with his father.

Gazaway had not planned to be in Savannah in the late autumn of 1857, but as soon as he had heard about the *Rawlins* debacle, he booked passage.

The two Lamars' relationship had improved since their falling out over Charlie's mismanagement of the business two years before. Charlie had apologized to Gazaway and they had remained in close contact. Gazaway, for his part, refrained from criticizing his son's handling of business operations, as much as it pained him. He did not want Charlie's incompetence to come between them any more than it had. Still, the news of Charlie's African venture tested the limits of his patience.

Gazaway entered the office, embraced his son, sat, and got down to business. "Charlie, the Lamars are not slave traders. An expedition to the moon would have been equally sensible!"

Charlie remained standing. He was not about to back down on an issue about which he knew he was right, though he vowed to remain calm. "Father, I'm tired of Southerners who have such a holy attitude against importing Africans, yet don't condemn slavery. What's the difference between buying negroes in Virginia and Africa?"

Gazaway's voice started to rise first. "I'll tell you the difference. A shipload of slaves from Virginia to Savannah will be treated somewhat humanely. Slaves shipped from Africa are treated no better than rats. Traders expect 10 to 20 percent to die."

Charlie threw his hands in the air. "Oh, spare me, Father. My entire life I've heard that slavery is good. Good for the planters because it supplies the only inexpensive labor source that can raise the crops of the South. Good for the Africans because it takes them out of the jungle where they live like savages and provides them productive work, food, clothing, and shelter. Good for God because the Africans are Christianized. If it's so blessed good, why can't I import all the Africans I can fit on my ships?"

Gazaway stood to face his son eye-to-eye. "Charlie, every state in the Union has banned the importation of slaves, as has the federal government, as have all countries around the world. Doesn't that tell you anything?"

Charlie sprayed spittle as he shouted, "Yes! It tells me I'm being deprived of my rights. Not one saphead who passed any of those laws knows a thing about commerce."

Gazaway dropped back into his seat and gasped, "May God forgive you for all your attempts to violate his will."

Charlie bent from his waist and placed his hands on the desk. "Let all the sin be on me, Father. I am willing to assume it all."

Gazaway shook his head as he appraised his son. "Charlie, your heroic assumption of risk has left you broke."

Charlie's face flushed. "I'm not broke, Father, I'm simply pressed for cash. And not because of my decisions. It's because of my reliance on others. I've also been hurt by this financial panic, as has everyone. I'll be all right in time, you wait and see."

Gazaway ran his fingers through his hair in frustration. He saw no alternative. "Charlie, if I advance you the money to relieve your debts, will you forget about this African business?"

Charlie pushed away from the desk. "My own father is trying to buy me? No, Father. I will not. My honor is worth more than money."

Gazaway snorted cynically. "What about your family's honor? Your conduct is embarrassing me, our cousin, Secretary Cobb, and your father-in-law, Judge Nicoll."

"If southern principles are making life difficult for the cowardly, so be it. Besides, Howell Cobb is a joke. His career as a politician in the South is finished."

"Charlie, what are you going to do to get out of your financial embarrassment? Is your self-righteousness going to pay your debts? Or will you look to me, as usual?"

Charlie turned his back on his father and looked out the window. "I'll make do. Businesses will revive. And I won't ask you again for money. You can be sure of that."

"Charlie, your paper is floating all over town and no one will touch it. Do you think I don't know that? It's hurting our business. No one wants to deal with a debtor." Gazaway arose from his seat and stood next to his son. "I have a proposition for you. I'll buy back the Eastern Wharves, the land, and the flour mill. George Wylly appraised them for me. They're worth one hundred four thousand dollars. I'm deducting the thirty thousand you owe me. That leaves seventy-four thousand dollars, which I pray will get you out of your other debt. But I'm going to limit your participation in the business. I'm going to have your cousin, Gazaway, Jr. move here from Augusta to work with you."

Charlie weakly argued his case. "Every business has a bad spell. You know that. My decisions will allow us to make more money than ever once the economy improves."

Gazaway picked up his hat and walked to the door. "I'll have a deed and bargain of sale prepared. This is the last time, Charlie. I'll bail you out no longer."

Both father and son knew that was not true. Charlie's windfall would not satisfy all his debts, but it would buy him some time. He'd have to plan another African venture. He would show his father.

*   *   *

The recession clouded the Christmas season for many Savannahians. Even slaves suffered, as their owners cut back on their presents. The McBains were better off than most and weathered the financial panic fairly well. They continued their gift giving as in years past. Still, one night at supper shortly before Christmas, Amy couldn't help but notice Dante walking slope-shouldered out of the dining room. "Does anyone know what's wrong with Dante? He's been looking miserable for a while."

Joseph said, "I think I might know. It's an unbelievable story, really." Joseph told his family about Dante's desire to own and cook in a restaurant. Silence occupied the table.

McBain said. "What a curious idea for Dante to have."

Joseph shrugged, "I agree. I was surprised Andrew approached me with it. That was months ago."

The family ate quietly for a few minutes, the only sound the clinking of silverware against plates.

"I'd like to run a restaurant." The clinking stopped. Everyone looked at Amy. "Actually, I think I'd enjoy it. I'm bored with the shop. Why is everyone staring at me?"

McBain popped a piece of cornbread into his mouth. "Amy, what do you know about running a restaurant? It's much more than cooking tasty food."

Amy laid down her fork and folded her hands on the table. "I know that, Father. I know how to run a business. I own a profitable rental property and a successful clothing shop, and I never had experience with either."

McBain responded, "You do realize that Dante is my servant? Do you think I should give him up so he can be a chef? Amy, I'm not in business to advance the careers of my negroes."

Amy countered, "If I open a restaurant, Dante would pay you interest from what he earns. It will provide a good return. He cooks mostly just for me now, anyway. You're in town only a few nights a week. He should have a chance to display his talents. Lilly is a good cook. She can handle the kitchen here on her own."

Joseph interrupted, "Amy, do you have any idea what you'd be getting yourself into? Restaurants are risky under the best of circumstances."

Sarah tapped the table with the handle of her knife and said, "Amy can accomplish anything she sets her mind to, I'll guarantee that."

Emily put her hand on Amy's. "I agree. I'd wager on Amy any day."

Amy replied, "Thank you, Mother, Emily. I see the women here have some faith in me." She then faced her father. "I'll have a word with Dante and I'll let you know my intentions."

McBain chewed his food without comment. Amy had out-maneuvered him again.

Amy spoke to Dante a few days later. She told him that she was looking for something else to do and the restaurant idea interested her. But she didn't want to spend half her life chasing around Savannah looking for him. She demanded full-time involvement, where Dante would shop, cook, and clean. And he had to invest most of his savings in the business to ensure his commitment. Dante promised to God he would do anything she asked. Amy said that if he broke his word, she'd sell him to a rice plantation. But if he did his work, she'd pay him forty dollars a month, though he would have to give ten of it to Mr. McBain. Dante wanted to start that day. Amy told him she first needed to arrange for someone to assume her tasks at the millinery shop. She also had to find space for the restaurant. It would take a while, maybe a few months.

It was the best Christmas Dante ever had. After his talk with Amy, he ran to Andrew's house to thank him.

Business life in town usually came to a halt during the Christmas season, but not for Joseph. He had traded his regatta responsibilities to become a member of the Savannah Jockey Club and helped organize the annual race week, which began right after the New Year, on January 5, 1858. This involved working closely with Richard Akin and, to a lesser extent, Charlie Lamar.

During this time, Joseph never mentioned to Charlie the note, which came due on December 31, even though Joseph knew that Charlie had sold property in the business to his father, for it was a matter of public record. Joseph planned to approach Lamar about the debt immediately after the races concluded.

Despite rainy weather and the poor economy, large crowds attended the races. Once again, Joseph proved his organizing and promotional skills. At the conclusion of the event the members of the jockey club retired to the dining area in the ladies' stand to celebrate the success. However, Danny had a fever and Joseph needed to get home, and missed the festivities.

After a restless night, Joseph set out on foot the next morning for Charlie's office. As Joseph reached Bull Street, he saw Richard Akin driving his gig in the opposite direction. Akin stopped and called, "Joseph, have you heard the news? After you left yesterday, Henry Dubignon had too much to drink, not that that's news. But he got into an argument with Charlie, and went at him with a knife. Some fellows disarmed Henry and threw him off the premises, but he came back and threatened Charlie's uncle. Charlie pulled out a pistol and shot Henry in the eye."

Joseph ran to the gig. "Good Lord! Is Dubignon alive?"

"Yes, thankfully. He'll lose the eye. The doctors probed but couldn't find the ball. I'm going to the hospital now. Charlie and Henry are going to apologize to each other. If you have a few minutes, why don't you come along? You'll have a positive influence on the meeting."

Joseph and Akin arrived at the hospital by Forsyth Park, south of Monterey Square, just as Charlie, standing at the bedside, and Henry, flat on his back with a small mountain of white bandages over his left eye, started conversing. Charlie was hunched over, and looking truly contrite. Marshal Stewart, John Tucker, John Montmollin, and George Wylly stood quietly in the corner, adding an official tone to the proceedings. Joseph and Akin joined them. Henry admitted he pressed Charlie too hard, but said Charlie was wrong to shoot him. For his part, Charlie apologized for shooting Henry. The men shook hands, and were congratulated by their friends for resolving the dispute. Joseph thought that Charlie was becoming more dangerous every day.

Afterwards, Charlie gave Joseph a ride to his office. Charlie recounted the incident and asked Joseph if he had acted wrongly. Joseph chose not to get engaged in the issue. Instead, he replied, "Charlie, your note's past due. I intend to present it at the bank today. I assume it will be honored. I know you sold the Eastern Wharves back to your father. You must have the cash."

Charlie looked at Joseph. "Joseph, I pay my debts. You know that. I have some of the money now. I just wanted to discuss something with you first." Of the seventy-five thousand dollars in cash that Charlie received from his father from the sale of the Eastern Wharves, he paid off fifty thousand of his debts, keeping his creditors temporarily at bay, and allocated twenty-five thousand dollars for another slaving venture. He had set aside twenty-five hundred for Joseph, but wanted to use it to entice him into a business deal. "I have a proposition, Joseph. I'll give you half now, and you put the balance in a partnership with me. There's no risk."

Joseph closed his eyes and murmured, "Not again. What is it this time?"

"Camels! It's a contract with the government. And there are no lawmakers telling me I can't do it."

Joseph gasped. "Camels? Who needs camels in America?"

"Texas! Henry Wayne, Justice Wayne's son, has spent time there and thinks camels are a natural for transportation in that terrain. He made a proposal to Congress to bring them in, and they're putting thirty thousand dollars into it. I have a ship and a crew ready to sail to Africa. This will be easy money."

Joseph shook his head in pity. "Forget it, Charlie. I know nothing about camels, and neither do you. Why do you consider such things?"

Charlie pulled the gig to the side of Abercorn. "Money, Joseph. If everyone that owed me paid me, I'd be as easy as an old shoe." Charlie noticed Joseph staring blankly at him. "I have to go to New Orleans next month to collect from the man who bought the Beaufort negroes. Trow is there, supposedly doing that, but he owes me so much money he doesn't answer my letters. If you don't want in on the camels, I'll give you half of what I owe you now. When I get back from Louisiana, I'll have the rest. I appreciate your patience. I'll be by in an hour with the cash and a note for the balance."

Joseph hopped down and watched Charlie turn onto the Bay. He was thrilled to be getting back twenty-five hundred dollars. But he knew he had to avoid Charlie in the future.

Two weeks later, Charlie was in the lobby of a New Orleans hotel, where he finally cornered Trow. Trow explained that Johnston had no money and couldn't pay anything. Charlie found a chair in the lobby and collapsed into it. His time was running out. Not even a successful importation of camels would get him out of the hole. He closed his eyes and let his head hang back. In the blackness, he saw floating images of the lobby plants he had just been staring at.

"Chollie? Chollie?" Trow pulled him out of his trance. "Something's come up. It's real and it's legal. I swear on the lives of my children."

Charlie looked at Trow with a glare that would have burned a hole through a Savannah Grey. "Don't tell me. Camels?"

Trow looked at Charlie as if he had grown another head. "Camels? Are you crazy? Don't joke around, Chollie. I'm serious. A state legislator here is going to present a bill to legalize the importation of African apprentices."

Charlie, exhausted from his string of bad luck, wondered what his life would be like if he had never met Trow. "All right, I'll bite. What's an African apprentice?"

"It's like a slave, but not for life. This bill sets their servitude at fifteen years. They come into the country as free negroes."

Charlie scratched his head. "What happens after fifteen years?"

Trow looked around and whispered, "Who knows? Maybe the owners will sell them in Cuba after fourteen years. Who cares? The important thing is bringing them here. I know the people involved, Chollie. The first act will provide for importing twenty-five hundred apprentices into Louisiana. We'll get the contract to do it! We'll make at least two hundred dollars per African after our costs. That's five hundred thousand dollars, even if it takes three shipments. And it'll be legal. Our problems are over!"

Charlie thought it sounded too easy. "When will this vote take place?"

"In a few days in the House. A few days after that in the Senate. It's guaranteed to pass! And what can the federal government do? They're not slaves. More like indentured servants. My contact says it's what the French are doing to supply their plantations in the West Indies."

Charlie snapped his fingers. "Just like that, Trow?"

Trow snapped his fingers in response. "Yes, Chollie. Just like that. Even if the federal government objects, it will take years to go through the courts. We'll have our money and be out of it. Have a ship and a crew ready as soon as possible. Once the bill passes, my friend will have the contract and we'll be ready to go. This is real, Chollie."

Charlie said, "The *Rawlins* is set to go on another expedition. I don't want to hold her up for this. When I reach Savannah, I'll get my other ship, the *Richard Cobden*, ready. With a contract from the state of Louisiana, we should be able to convince some people to take a piece. Trow, if this doesn't turn out, I'll have your balls."

Charlie decided to wait in New Orleans until the bill was introduced in the House of Representatives in Baton Rouge. He had been burned by Trow too often to go running back to Savannah and incur costs getting a ship ready. So Charlie strolled around town and took in the sights. He even located Mr. Johnston and had a talk with him, but it did no good. Charlie still needed a miracle.

On March 2, 1858, one day before the African Apprentice Bill was scheduled for a vote in the Louisiana House, Charlie and Trow had a drink on the hotel veranda, and gazed at the ships in the harbor. Trow tried to talk to Charlie but realized he was not listening. Charlie was staring at a beautiful, sleek schooner, sails unfurled, gliding easily past the other ships. She had long topmasts and large gaff topsails. She also had a long flying jib boom. Her bow was concave and her thin-planked decks as white as a cotton field in October. Everyone on the veranda was looking at her.

Charlie asked, "Trow, can you make out the name of that ship?"

Trow squinted. "The *Wanderer*. Out of Port Jefferson, New York."

"Oh, yes. I read about her. She was in Brunswick not long ago. Won the regatta. No one could touch her. Supposed to be the fastest thing on water. What a beauty."

The next day, the Louisiana House passed a bill authorizing the importation of twenty-five hundred free negroes from Africa, to be indentured for not less than fifteen years. Charlie Lamar was on a ship for Savannah that afternoon.

He arrived to a desk full of letters from creditors, but not a penny from debtors. He had but one hope left, to bring back a shipload of Africans for the State of Louisiana. That would put him right. He immediately started getting the *Richard Cobden* ready.

CHAPTER 22

The Favor

March-July 1858

"I'm ruined, Chollie," Trow moaned as he sat in Charlie's office, resting his sweaty forehead on the heels of his palms. The African Apprentice Bill had failed in the Louisiana Senate by just two votes, with the sponsoring senator voting against it. Trow had gone directly to Lamar upon returning from New Orleans to deliver the news.

Charlie rocked on his office chair. "Stop whining, Trow. I'm going to turn this seed into a tree. The bill may have failed, but it gave me an idea. The vote was close. It had a twenty-five-vote majority in the House, and barely failed in the Senate. I would say it was more popular than not."

Trow performed the calculation in his head. "By twenty-three votes?"

Charlie nudged his chair closer to the desk. "In a sense. Now, do you know any law which prohibits importing free immigrants into this country?"

"No, Chollie. But to be honest, I don't know much about the law."

"I do, Trow, and I don't know of one. Shiploads of Europeans arrive in America every day, and they're allowed to stay. Well, there's a state where importing African immigrants is acceptable to most of its legislators. I'll bring Africans into Louisiana, even if that bill failed. If the government contests, I'll win in the courts."

Trow turned an ear to Lamar. "Charlie, did I just hear you say you'd bring a shipload of Africans into Louisiana, in the open?"

Charlie leaned back. "Yes, and I intend to get government approval."

Trow perused Charlie's face. "Are you feeling all right, Chollie? That food in New Orleans is awfully rich. I've had gas for weeks."

Charlie stuck his tongue out as if being examined by a doctor. "Never felt better, Trow. The *Richard Cobden* is sitting at a wharf in Charleston, ready to go."

"Chollie, I hate to disagree with you, but I'll be the Pope before the government gives you permission to bring Africans here, no matter what you call them."

Charlie groaned. "Trow, that's the kind of attitude that spells failure. I've got old Howell Cobb on my side. I'll send a request for clearance to the port collector in Charleston, who'll be too scared to make a decision, and he'll pass it on to Cobb. He'll know it's my ship, even though the request must be sent under the name of my agent in Charleston. I'm confident he'll grant clearance. His future in politics depends on his handling of this."

"Chollie, you keep telling me Cobb's a joke and a failure. You must know there's a good chance he'll turn you down."

Charlie made a fist and shook it. "Just let him try. But one must be prepared for all eventualities. That leads me to my second idea. I have two ships, the *Rawlins*, which is hopefully on its way to Cuba with a load of Africans, and the *Richard Cobden*. But if I must sneak Africans into America, these ships are too risky. They're not fast and would be sitting ducks for the African squadron or revenue cutters along this coast. I need a ship no one thinks could be a slaver, and could out-run any government vessel"

Trow stammered, "Wha . . . ?"

"Do I have to spell everything out to you, Trow? The *Wanderer*!"

Trow blinked several times. "The ship we saw in New Orleans? That's a luxury schooner. You couldn't fit fifty Africans in it. It wouldn't be worth the cost. Chollie, I think you need to lie down and rest. You had a rough trip."

"Trow, please start thinking with your head and not your arse. Grant told us he could easily get 450 into the *Rawlins*. The *Wanderer* isn't much smaller. Of course, I'll need a unique captain, a sportsman, a man of distinction with balls the size of melons. I'll ask Lafitte if he knows a man of such stamp. I'll also write to Spratt."

"Chollie, how do you plan to finance it? You said you were using your last dollars on the *Cobden* and *Rawlins*."

Charlie winked. "I still have some funds from the sale of the wharves to my father. I'll also use the *Cobden* money if it isn't cleared. But I can't do it myself. I'll need partners. Now, I've got to get to work. I'll see you tomorrow. And Trow, start thinking positively."

After Trow left the office, Charlie, invigorated by the brilliance of his plan, wrote a letter under the name of his agents to the port collector in Charleston. He realized no sane man could argue with his logic. Even that idiot Cobb would see it.

*　　*　　*

In April, Amy found a ground floor-room with a kitchen for rent on Congress Street and Whitaker, by the City Market. It was a good location, though it needed renovating, cleaning, and painting. Amy hired a few Irish workers and they, she, and Dante worked on the restaurant almost every day for three months. Joseph, Andrew, Emily, and Patience even pitched in on an occasional Saturday afternoon, as three-year-olds Truvy and Danny crashed around.

By mid-June, the place had been scoured and painted, and the chairs, tables, kitchen equipment, and other supplies delivered. Amy had mirrors put on one of the walls to make the room seem bigger. She hung some paintings and Cerveau's lithograph of 1853 Savannah on another wall. At Andrew's suggestion, they exposed the ceiling beams and hung gas lamps of light blue glass from them, giving the room a soft glow.

Amy was pleased by Dante's effort. He showed up on time and did anything she asked. However, she didn't approve of Dante's friends visiting him at the restaurant as he worked, and told him so. Dante promised he would have no more visitors.

They were on schedule to open in mid-July. Of course, summer was not the best time to open a restaurant, but Amy knew a slow start would allow her and the employees to work out the problems they were bound to face.

One day in late June, Amy led Dante to the sidewalk in front of the eatery. "We need to have a sign prepared. What should we call this eatery?"

Dante looked up and down Congress Street as if searching for a name. "Dunno, Miss Amy. Ah yent t'ink uh dat."

Amy glanced at Dante and, suppressing a smile, said, "How about 'Dante's Place?'"

Dante's eyes widened. "Miss Amy!"

Amy patted Dante's back and said, "Dante's Place it is!" realizing that few people in Savannah would know the 'Dante' in the name was a negro.

The next day, one of Dante's friends, Hank, Mr. Down's coachman, walked into the restaurant, past Amy and into the kitchen. Amy fumed while they joked. When Hank left fifteen minutes later, he brushed against a broom leaning against the wall, knocking it over. It hit the tile floor with a loud crack, but Hank kept on walking.

Amy yelled after him, "You! Pick up that broom!" Hank didn't stop. As he reached the doorway, Amy yelled again, "I said pick up that broom!"

Hank turned and stared at her. "Oonuh not muh missus."

"No. I'm trying to teach you manners, so you won't be such a miserable rat!"

Dante watched the confrontation from the kitchen and feared for Miss Amy. He called, "Hank, git de brum."

Hank walked into the restaurant and lifted the broom. Amy stepped over and clutched the shaft, but Hank wouldn't release it. They scowled at each other, their faces only a foot apart. She ripped the broom from his hands and almost fell over backwards. When she regained her balance, she sneered, "Until you can act like a man, don't come near this place. Now get out!"

*   *   *

About the time Amy had found the space for the restaurant, Charlie Lamar also started on his new venture. "Please come in, sir." Charlie led William Corrie into his office. "Mr. Corrie, please meet my associate, Mr. Trowbridge."

The men exchanged pleasantries and sat around the desk. Charlie was impressed with the appearance of the potential captain of the *Wanderer*. Corrie was handsome, with straight black hair which reached his neck, and a neatly trimmed beard and mustache. He was dressed in a dark blue jacket, gray trousers, a white shirt, and a blue and white necktie.

Charlie waited for his bookkeeper, Mr. Woolhopter, to serve drinks before talking. "Mr. Lafitte speaks highly of you. He told me about your career as a lobbyist in Washington. How does one manage to survive in that place?"

Corrie picked up his glass. "Oh, quite easily, if you know the price of each politician."

Charlie laughed. "Yes, I imagine that helps." Charlie paused for a moment before asking, "Do you have a price, Mr. Corrie?"

Corrie twisted the diamond ring on his finger. "I do enjoy the finer things in life." The forty-year-old William C. Corrie was born and raised in the Charleston, South Carolina area. After attending school, he went to work in his uncle's dry goods store on King Street, where he proved to be an excellent salesman. With his charm and handsome looks, he made his way to Washington City, where he quickly established himself as one of the most effective lobbyists in town. Whether hosting elegant dinner parties, serving as a judge at yachting competitions, holding forth at the barroom at Brown's Hotel, or serving as a second in a duel between naval officers, Corrie was a visible presence in Washington. Corrie was driven by his fondness for wealth and his zeal for adventure.

Charlie asked, "Do you mind taking a risk or two?"

Corrie blew on his ring and polished it on his jacket. "Not at all, Mr. Lamar. I rather enjoy it. It makes the pay-off that much sweeter."

"Mr. Corrie, I think we may be able to do business together. Here's the proposition." Charlie explained.

Corrie mused, "I just settled a claim with the government. It would be fitting to invest their money in this venture."

Charlie grinned at Trow, appreciating the irony. Charlie said, "Of course, you must hire a discreet crew."

Corrie replied, "Certainly. The harbors of the North are full of such men. If one ever talked, he would no longer make a living in the business. There's no other way he can earn eight hundred dollars for five or six month's work. Of course, these men depend on the owners to defend them to the heavens in court, should the need arise." Charlie nodded. Corrie then pointed at the map on the desk. "The landing must be in total seclusion."

Charlie put his finger on Jekyl Island. "It's all taken care of. I have the perfect location, owned by friends. And I already have the customers. You get the Africans and land them. Trow and I will take care of the rest." The men stood and shook hands. Charlie said, "Now, Mr. Corrie, you'll need to pay Colonel Johnson a visit. I'm certain he'll be open to our offer for the *Wanderer*. Because of my undeserved reputation, the ship will need to be in your name. And I'll let you know as soon as I hear from Cobb. I never received an answer to the letter I sent to the port collector in Charleston, so I wrote to Cobb directly, explaining matters further. He probably hasn't recovered from reading it." Charlie, Trow, and Corrie had a hearty laugh over that.

Charlie's good mood ended a few days later when he read Howell Cobb's response to the application by Lafitte & Co., which asked for clearance of a ship to embark for Africa to pick up African immigrants and return to the United States, though no port was specified. Lafitte had forwarded it to Charlie. Charlie was so angry, he couldn't read it all at once. Every few paragraphs he stood and paced around his office before sitting down again. Cobb, who had suspected that Lamar was behind the application, had also released his response to the papers, and it would soon become public. Cobb made no reference to the subsequent letter sent to him directly by Charlie.

Cobb cited many points of law restricting and abolishing the slave trade. But Cobb did not limit himself to the interpretation of the law. He guessed at the motives of the applicant. He said the Africans could only be brought into the country for one of two reasons: bonded to labor, which was unquestionably against the law, or as free immigrants, which was absurd. Cobb said there was no state, free or slave, which would allow or want such immigration. States were trying to reduce their free negro populations, not increase them. Cobb added that anyone who thought that African immigrants would enjoy the rights and privileges of free men in America could be charged with mental imbecility. The real purpose had to be to import them as slaves, and the port collector must refuse clearance of the *Richard Cobden*.

Charlie was furious and, though Lafitte sent the company's official reply, he could not let it pass without a response. He wrote yet another request to Cobb for clearance to Africa and pick up African emigrants, without stating the country to which he would bring them. Cobb refused again. Charlie would seek his revenge, and would not be satisfied until he ruined his relative.

William Corrie moved ahead on the *Wanderer*. He went to New York in April and convinced Colonel Johnson to sell the ship for twenty-two thousand dollars, three thousand less than Johnson's cost to build it just a year before. Then Corrie announced that he was going on an around-the-world hunting trip and had the ship delivered to Port Jefferson, Long Island, for outfitting. He then returned to South Carolina.

Soon after the *Wanderer* arrived in Port Jefferson in early June, tanks capable of holding fifteen thousand gallons of water were installed in the bilge. This was far more water than would be necessary for a year-long trip for several gentlemen and a crew, and the port collector at Port Jefferson took notice. Soon the *Wanderer* and its men were under observation by a U. S. deputy marshal, who witnessed the delivery of a considerable amount of supplies, and the arrival of William Corrie, several foreign-looking crewmen, and two gentlemen. One of them was John Egbert

Farnum, Mexican War hero and famous filibusterer who served under Narcisco Lopez in Cuba and, more recently, William Walker in Nicaragua. The other man was Nelson Trowbridge.

The deputy notified the district attorney in New York City, who dispatched the revenue cutter *Harriet Lane*, which took possession of the *Wanderer* and a supply ship, and towed them to New York harbor.

The arrival of the seized yacht generated much local interest. Journalists speculated that, with Farnum and eight foreign-speaking crewmen, the ship might be going on a filibuster mission or serving as a privateer in the Gulf of Mexico. One suggested it could be a slaver, but the others agreed it was much too small.

The next day, U. S. Marshall Isaiah Rynders, the man several newspapermen thought was the prime reason why so many ships received clearance so easily from the port of New York to Africa, and the district attorney searched the *Wanderer* and the supply ship. Members of the press were not permitted to attend. Nothing untoward was found, just a large amount of luxury provisions appropriate for a gentleman. Also, Corrie was a member of the prestigious New York Yacht Club. Rynders released the ship and let her load the rest of the provisions. Rynders apologized to Corrie for the inconvenience.

Feeling no animus, Corrie invited several officials to lunch on the ship. When the wine was served, Corrie raised his glass and toasted; "If thine enemy hunger, feed him, and if he thirst, give him drink." The men roared and drained their glasses.

The *Wanderer* remained in New York harbor for a week before sailing to Charleston, and arrived seven days later, at the end of June.

*   *   *

It was like old times, with James McBain, Joseph, and Andrew sitting on the piazza, discussing business and architecture. McBain and Joseph smoked segars and drank port. As the men talked, they could hear Sarah, Amy, Emily, and Patience in the family parlor, playing with Danny and Truvy.

McBain caught up with Andrew, who had been working for John Norris on the Abraham Home for Indigent Females on Broughton Street at East Broad. Andrew said Norris wanted his help to add a wing onto the Screven House Hotel on Bryan Street and to build warehouses and offices for Mr. Stoddard along the Bay.

McBain commented on Norris's ability to design in so many styles. He had built memorable Greek Revival, Gothic Revival, and Italianate structures in Savannah. Even the talented Charles Cluskey didn't stray from the Greek Revival. Andrew said he felt blessed to be able to work for Norris.

McBain asked Andrew if Charlie Lamar had paid him for the work on the flour mill. Andrew said Charlie had been slow but had recently paid him the balance.

McBain mentioned that Charlie still owed him five hundred dollars for the purchase of bricks, and that his notes were floating all over town. McBain added,

"There are rumors that Charlie purchased a luxury yacht and is planning an around-the-world hunting trip, including Africa and the East Indies. Word is Captain Farnum, the Mexican War hero, is going to lead the expedition. He's in town now buying supplies."

Joseph thought that Charlie had nerve living so lavishly while still owing him money. He said, "Charlie's been having a nasty squabble with Mr. Cobb over his right to import Africans."

Andrew asked, "Why would he argue with Secretary Cobb? They're related. I remember Master Cobb speaking so well of Master Charles."

McBain said, "That all changed, Andrew. Charlie thought Cobb should allow him to bring in Africans. Cobb refused and insulted Charlie publicly. Charlie detests him for it."

Before Andrew could ask any questions about Charlie, the women appeared on the piazza. It was time to go home.

*   *   *

During the nights following the arrival of the *Wanderer* in Charleston, Captain Corrie entertained captains, port collectors, and other officials at the finest restaurants. As he did, his crew cat-footed to the *Jehossee*, just a few berths away, removed the slaver equipment Trowbridge had ordered from a local supplier, and secreted it to the *Wanderer*. The leg chains, cuffs, sacks of rice and beans, cooking pots, bricks, lumber, and hardware for the slave decks were stored under the hold deck and behind the bulkheads. The ship would be ready to begin its voyage as soon as Charlie sent additional provisions with Farnum from Savannah.

While Corrie was showing off the ship to his Charleston guests on a warm, early-July evening, Andrew was startled by a furious knocking at his back door. He opened it and was almost knocked off his feet by Dante, who charged into the house. "Dante!"

Dante was shaking. He held Andrew's arm. "Oonuh haffuh he'p me. Please he'p me!"

"What's wrong? What trouble are you in?" Dante started to sob. Andrew grabbed Dante by the arm and shook him. "Dante, speak to me."

Through tears, Dante replied, "Hank an' me gone tuh he massa's house aftuh wu'k. Massa Down drunk lukkuh sayluh. He holluh tuh Hank fuh dis an' dat. Hank, he gwi' tuh leabe, but massa grab Hank an' dey wrassle tuh de flo'. Ah try tuh pull Hank 'way! Ah swaytuh Gawd it true. Hank git up an' dey uh knife stickin' in massa. Ah yeddy uh scream, an' ah see uh gal at de do'. Den Missus Down run een an' see me an' Hank standin' obuh massa. He guhglin' an' tryin' tuh moob. Missus scream, an' ah run tuh yuh. Andrew, ah skayd tuh de't."

Andrew led Dante into the family parlor. He felt dizzy. This was a nightmare. They both flinched when they heard the front door open, and stood stiff as boards at the sound of footsteps. Patience walked into the room, but Dante didn't budge, his shoulders almost touching his ears. Patience put Truvy down and stared at her husband. "What's wrong, Andrew?"

Dante blurted, "Ah nebuh kill 'um!"

Patience shouted, "I'm not talking to you, Dante!" She turned back to her husband and asked, "Andrew, what in the Lord's name going on? What is he talking about?"

Andrew smacked his dry lips before speaking. "Dante's in trouble, Patience."

"Really? And he comes to you for help?" Patience, trying to stay calm, said to Dante, "Please go outside for a minute. I want to have a word with my husband."

Dante stood close to Andrew. "Ah cyan' go owside."

"Right now!" Patience screamed. Dante dashed out the back door.

Patience folded her arms. "Andrew, what's going on?"

Andrew told the story just as he had heard it from Dante. "He needs help."

Patience's eyes narrowed to glowing slits. "He murders a white man and you're thinking of helping him? Get him out of our house!"

"Dante could never kill anyone. You know that. I have to try to help him."

Patience stepped closer to her husband. "Just what do you propose? Do I need to remind you that you're a black man? You can't do a thing. And if you're caught helping or hiding a runaway, you'll go to jail as if you committed the crime yourself! Andrew, we've worked very hard to make something of ourselves in this society. You earned what little freedom you have. You're a builder. We have a beautiful child, and we're going to have more. We own a house and have money saved. You've always lived by the rules, and you're respected by blacks and most whites. You're not going to risk all we have for that worthless nigger!"

Andrew put his hands on Patience's shoulders. "Patience, they'll hang him. If I thought he was guilty, I wouldn't think of helping him. But I believe him. I can't let him die."

Patience pushed Andrew away and yelled at him, startling Truvy. "I said, you will not risk all we have for Dante!"

Andrew looked at the woman he loved with all his being. He saw Truvy frowning at him. He retrieved Dante. In front of Patience he said, "Dante, there's no place for you to hide. If I could help you, I would. But I can't. Let's go to Master McBain and explain what happened. He's the only person who can help."

Dante gasped, "Andrew, no buckra gwi' beliebe me."

Patience took a step towards Dante. "You have no choice!" she shouted.

Andrew stood between Patience and Dante. "Dante, we either go to Master McBain, or you go out that back door and escape. I can't do any more than that."

The loud rapping on the front door pierced their guts. Andrew motioned to Dante to go out the back door. Andrew then slowly walked to the front door. As he grabbed the handle, the knocking was repeated, harder and faster. He opened the door and faced Mr. McBain, Marshal Stewart, and Deputy Marshal Stone. He saw Hercules sitting on the Rockaway in the street.

"Master McBain, sirs, please come in." Andrew stepped aside and the men entered. Andrew led them into the parlor. Marshal Stewart looked around the room, impressed by its size and decoration.

Andrew stood next to Patience, who was holding Truvy. She strained a smile. "Master McBain, how good to see you."

McBain rubbed the top of Truvy's head. "Hello, Patience. This is Marshal Stewart and Deputy Stone."

Stewart squinted at Andrew and said, "I believe we've met. Twice."

Without waiting for Andrew's acknowledgement, McBain said, "Andrew, there's been a killing. Mr. Down was murdered in his house by two black men. His wife said one was Hank, their coachman. The other was Dante. Have you seen him this evening?"

"Yes, sir. He was here ten minutes ago. He said he was in trouble, but swore he was innocent. He didn't tell me what the problem was. He was very frightened. I told him to go to you and he would be treated fairly. He was too scared and ran away. I was just going to Pulaski Square to tell you."

Stewart stepped closer to Andrew. "So he was on his way to Mr. McBain's?"

"I don't know, sir. He just ran."

The marshal jabbed his finger at Andrew's chest. "You know the penalty for aiding or hiding a runaway wanted for a crime?"

McBain held Andrew's arm. "Marshal, Andrew is as honest as the day is long."

Stewart ignored McBain and said to his deputy, "Let's look around."

Patience's heart beat so hard in her chest she thought it would knock her over. She considered telling the marshal that Dante was outside. In a shaky voice, she offered, "Let me show you around, Marshal."

Stewart commanded, "You stay right here." He and his deputy then inspected every room in the house, searched every closet, and under and behind every piece of furniture, while McBain, Andrew, and Patience stood, looking at each other in the parlor. When the lawmen finished, they walked out the back door and slammed it shut. Andrew and Patience flinched.

Just then, Hercules came charging through the front door and hollered, "I think I just saw Dante running down Houston Street!"

McBain jumped to the back door and called to the marshals, "My coachman thinks he saw Dante on Houston Street!"

Stewart and Stone barged back into the house. Stewart asked Hercules, "Which way?"

"North, towards the river."

Stewart said, "Let's go!" He and his deputy bolted out the front door.

McBain said to Andrew, "Come to the office first thing tomorrow morning," and left. Patience collapsed on the couch and wept. Truvy crawled next to her.

Andrew waited a minute before going out back. He looked around but didn't see Dante. Andrew closed his eyes and prayed for his friend. As he turned to go back into the house, a clump of Spanish moss fell on his head and over his face. It felt like a thousand spider webs. He yelped and swiped at his face. When he realized it was moss, he looked up at the tree in the dusk.

Someone in it whispered, "Andrew!"

Andrew whispered back, "Dante? Get down here!" When Dante reached ground, Andrew said, "They're gone."

"Hank done 'um, Andrew. Ah sway!" Dante's breath was rancid with fear.

Andrew sighed. "Dante, if you're innocent, you've got to go to Master McBain. There's no choice, other than to run away."

Dante embraced Andrew. He pulled away, turned, and ran from the yard to York Street.

Andrew returned to the house. Patience was still lying on the couch. Tear tracks lined her face. "Andrew, I'm frightened. That marshal man is coming back."

Andrew sat next to her. "I agree, but Dante's gone. He just ran away."

Patience sat up. "I thought Hercules saw him escaping."

"Hercules must have been mistaken. Dante was hiding in the tree in the back. I told him to turn himself in to Master McBain. He ran off."

Neither Andrew nor Patience was able to eat or sleep. Andrew spent the night thinking of Dante, and how he would fare on the run. He knew his friend was doomed.

Andrew was up early the next morning, preparing to see Master McBain. He said goodbye to Patience, who was walking out the back door with Truvy to the privy. Seconds later he heard a scream from the backyard. He ran outside, certain that a moccasin had taken refuge in the privy. He saw Patience standing at the door, her hands over her mouth. Truvy was sitting on the ground behind her. Andrew grabbed a shovel, ready to behead the reptile. "Patience, move away so I can get at it!"

Patience stepped aside. Andrew tiptoed to the door, shovel raised, and saw Dante shivering uncontrollably on the floor. "Dante!"

In a barely audible voice, Dante said, "Ah hab no place fuh gone. Ah gwine tuh die."

Andrew said, "You stay here until I come to get you. It may be a while." Then he picked up Truvy and said to Patience, "Come inside."

In the house, Patience leaned heavily against Andrew. He said, "Go out with Truvy for the morning. I have to see Master McBain. I'll tell him Dante's here. He'll come for him. I don't want you here when he does. This will be over soon." She nodded.

When Andrew arrived outside McBain's office, he saw Hercules standing by the Rockaway. "Morning, Hercules. Is there anything I should know before I go inside?"

Hercules huddled close to Andrew. "No. We searched all over town last night, especially Oglethorpe Ward and Currytown."

Andrew, not willing to reveal even to Hercules that he was hiding Dante, asked, "In what direction did you see him run?"

Hercules looked up and down the street, and said, "I didn't see him run nowhere. When the marshal and massa went into the house, I thought I saw Dante climb a tree in the yard. When I hear the back door close, I made that up about Dante running down the street. That got them away from the house."

Andrew whispered in astonishment, "You were helping Dante, too?"

Hercules slapped Andrew's arm, hard. "I was helping you, Andrew. If you caught hiding that nigger, you going to jail for a long time. He's not worth it!"

Andrew explained to Hercules what had happened since. Hercules shook his head. "If he don't leave, you got to turn him in."

"That's what I'm going to do right now." Andrew's voice started to crack. He bowed his head then raised it again. "They're going to hang him, Hercules."

Hercules grabbed Andrew by the shirt. "Don't blame youself. He got himself into this. You go in and get this over with before the marshal finds Dante at you house."

Andrew breathed deeply. He stared at the ships in the river. He thought how nice it would be to board one with Patience and Truvy, and sail to some exotic place, away from all this trouble. Then his one boat trip, the *Pulaski,* flashed in his mind. "Hercules, I just got an idea. It's a long shot, but it may be Dante's only chance. I'm going to see Master McBain, then I've got work to do. I'll speak to you later."

As Andrew hurried into the building, Hercules called, "Don't do nothin' dumb!"

"Good morning." James, Joseph, and Amy stood to welcome Andrew. Joseph shook Andrew's hand. Joseph had thought of visiting Andrew the night before, but his father advised against it, as he sensed tension between Andrew and Patience.

McBain said, "Andrew, please sit. I explained to Marshal Stewart that Dante is not a violent person, but he said he's heard it all before. I'll do everything I can for him, but I can't change the evidence. Mrs. Down swears she saw Dante and Hank standing over her husband's body. Her niece was also there, but she's too hysterical to talk. Dante looks up to you, and he'll likely seek you out. If he does, convince him to give up. Don't help him in any way. I don't want to see you get in any trouble over this."

Amy, whose eyes were bloodshot, asked, "Andrew, did he give any indication where he might be going?"

"Miss Amy, he was so scared, I don't think he knew what to do. He just ran. But he swore he had nothing to do with it."

They discussed where Dante might hide. McBain said he would send Hercules to the Heritage to tell Isaac to be on the alert for Dante. Finally, McBain said, "That's all, Andrew. Please mind what I say. If you see him, come get me immediately. Don't do anything else for him." Andrew nodded and bade goodbye.

Andrew emerged from the building, waved to Hercules, and walked quickly along the Bay to Drayton Street.

"Andrew, this is a surprise. Please, have a seat. What can I do for you?"

Andrew eased into the chair. "Good morning, Master Charles. It's good to see you again. I hope your family is happy and healthy." Andrew paused. Charlie nodded and stared, indicating that Andrew should get on with his business. "Sir, you told me if I ever needed a favor to see you. Well, I need one. A very big one."

Charlie put his pen down. "That's true. I've said it several times, and I meant it each time. What's on your mind?"

Andrew turned in his seat and looked at the open door. He then whispered to Lamar, "First, I have a request. I must beg that you never mention to anyone what I'm about to ask, not even to the McBains. If that's not possible, I can't ask the favor."

Charlie's smile left his face. This was quite a demand by a negro of a white man. "This sounds serious, Andrew. You have my word."

Andrew rubbed his clammy hands together. "Master Charles, I have a friend in big trouble. He swears he did nothing wrong, and I believe him. But he was present when someone was killed."

Lamar's dark eyes bore into Andrew's soul. Charlie stood, walked around the desk, closed the office door, and returned to his chair. "Thaddeus Down, eh? So it was your friend who killed that no good rascal who doesn't pay his gambling debts?"

Andrew clutched the edge of the desk. "He didn't kill him, sir. He was there, but had nothing to do with it. I've known Dante all my life. He could never kill anyone."

Charlie stroked his beard. "How may I help you, Andrew?"

Andrew rubbed his face with shaky hands. "I've heard that you're taking a cruise and will be stopping in Africa. Can you take my friend with you and leave him there? That's his only chance. I'll pay for his passage."

Charlie blew air through his lips. "Andrew, are you asking me to sneak an accused murderer, a negro no less, out of the country, and risk going to jail for a very long time?"

"No, that's not . . ." Andrew lowered his head. "I guess that is what I'm asking."

Lamar examined his hands as he thought about Andrew's proposal. Andrew had saved his life, and he had never forgotten that. He also saved four of his horses. And Andrew was the reason the flour mill was completed on time. But the *Wanderer* was critical to his survival. It had to succeed or he would go under, become a debtor, possibly go to jail, and shame his family. This was too important a mission to place in jeopardy. Besides, he would have to convince Corrie to go along with it. "Andrew, I always meant what I said about that favor. I never suspected it would involve committing a crime. I'm sorry. When you have another request, one not so dangerous, come back and see me." Charlie rose from his chair.

Andrew felt a wave of depression run through his body at the rejection. He had one last shot. "I understand, sir. After all, this would certainly embarrass your cousin, Master Cobb."

Charlie dropped back in his seat. "Embarrass Cobb? How?"

"If he ever found out you were taking negroes back to Africa."

Charlie howled with laughter. "That would anger that fat cracker, wouldn't it?" The thought of sneaking a negro out of the country and bringing a shipload of Africans back in, after all Cobb had put him through, tickled Charlie. Of course, he couldn't tell Andrew the *Wanderer* was a slaver. When his mirth passed, he asked Andrew, "But how could I tell Cobb and not get in trouble? After all, your friend is wanted for murder."

"You wouldn't have to tell Master Cobb. After you return from your trip, announce you found a group of runaways hiding at the racetrack who wanted to go back to Africa, and you decided to help them, trying to please Master Cobb. You even hoped some were his slaves. You could publish the letter in all the papers in the South."

Charlie let out another hoot. The thought of humiliating Cobb excited him. "Andrew, if I decided to help your friend, how would I get him on to the ship?"

Andrew, knowing he had captured Lamar's interest, thought there was a simple solution. "Easy, sir. He could sneak on with you at night."

Charlie drummed the desk with his fingers. "Not so easy, Andrew. I'm not making the trip. Some associates are. And the ship is leaving from Charleston."

Andrew slumped in his chair. This killed his plan. "Charleston?"

"Yes. How would we get him to Charleston? I have a steam tug going there in two hours, at ten o'clock. He'd have to elude the customs inspector and the health officer."

Andrew concentrated. He had to solve this problem. Suddenly, Andrew stood up, energized by an idea. "We could do what 'Box' Brown did!" Henry Brown was a slave in Richmond, Virginia. Just two years before, in 1856, Brown's friend had packed him in a human-sized box with some water and biscuits, drilled some air holes in it, addressed it to an abolitionist in Philadelphia, and sent it by the United States mail. He arrived a few days later in good health. "That will get him by customs here and Charleston."

Lamar was impressed with Andrew's quick thinking. "Yes, that's a possibility. But once the ship leaves, what does he do for the six-week voyage?"

"Dante's an excellent cook. He'll keep the crew happy with the food, I can assure you."

Charlie thought more seriously. Corrie had hired a cook, but he could always use another. "The yacht will land somewhere along the mouth of the Congo River, depending on the whim of the captain. I guess he could leave him there."

Andrew sat back down. Lamar had made a good point. Where in Africa would Dante go? He could go to Liberia and find Jumbo, who had emigrated there nine years before on the *Huma*. But wherever he landed, it had to be better than the gallows in Savannah. "The captain can drop him off wherever he docks. I'll give my friend money to pay his way to Liberia once he's on shore."

The image of Howell Cobb cursing and stomping around his office once he learned that he had been outsmarted flashed through Charlie's mind. Lamar stood and said, "All right, Andrew. Get two boxes. Fill one with building tools, hammers, lumber, and stuff. Put your friend in the other. You have two hours. And as you leave, would you go to my wharf and ask a Captain Farnum to see me?"

Andrew smiled and said, "Yes, Master Charles. Anything you say."

Andrew turned to leave when he head Lamar say, "One last thing." Andrew stopped and faced Charlie. "You do realize the chance I'm taking here? You also know if our little deal should become known by the wrong people, at any time, I have no choice but to hold you responsible, as much as I like you? It won't be pleasant."

Andrew held Charlie's stare. "Yes, sir."

Lamar slapped the desk. "Good. Let's get going." Andrew was out the door.

Charlie sat, closed his eyes and imagined the expression on Cobb's face when he learned Charlie brought negroes back to Africa, and laughed loudly. His daydream was interrupted by a voice. "Charlie, a negro told me you wanted to see me?"

Charlie looked up. "Farnum! Come in! I found a good cook for your voyage."

Farnum was a barrel-chested man, Charlie's height, with a neatly trimmed beard and eyes in a permanent squint. He still wore his military shirt from the Mexican War. Charlie was glad that such a man was part of the expedition. Farnum said, "I thought Captain Corrie had one."

"Well, he has another one, just for the trip over." Charlie explained the situation.

Farnum held the back of the chair. "Charlie, that's ridiculous. It's too risky."

"Don't worry. We're about to smuggle five hundred negroes into this country. Surely we can smuggle one out."

Farnum sighed. "I don't like it, Charlie, not one bit. But if you insist."

"Two boxes will be here in two hours. Leave for Charleston after they're on board. You'll still arrive on time. Explain everything to Corrie. He'll understand."

Andrew went to the construction site, which fortunately had only negro workmen present. He asked Gabriel, a carpenter, to build two boxes, five-and-a-half feet long by four feet wide by three feet deep, with holes drilled in the sides and on top, and to put lumber, saws, hammers, and a shovel in one of them.

"Dat mos' de stuff ah got, brudduh Andrew. Ah cyan' wu'k widout 'em."

"I realize that, Gabriel. Please do me this favor. I'll replace them later today. I'll return here in an hour. When you see me, tell the other workmen to go for a walk."

Andrew went home and found Dante still shaking in the privy. "I'll be right back, Dante. I'm getting you out of here." Andrew ran into his house and rolled up one of Patience's dresses and cotton bonnets. He went into a closet, lifted a loose floor board and removed some gold coins. He returned to the privy. "Listen Dante, my dray is out front. I'm taking you to the construction site. We can't take any chances of you being seen. Put this dress and bonnet on."

Dante recoiled at the sight of the clothes. "Ah yent dressin' luk no wommin!"

Andrew slammed the dress into Dante's chest. "Oh, yes, you are. Your only other choice is to hang. I'll bring your clothes along and put them in the box with you. After you change, we're walking to the dray. Keep your head down, hold my arm, and walk like a lady."

"Wut box?"

"I'll explain on the way."

As they rode to the site, Andrew revealed the plan to Dante. He said, "I put sixty dollars in gold pieces in your trouser pockets. You'll need them in Africa. When you land, catch a ship to Liberia. That's where Jumbo is. When we get to the site, jump off and stay on the sidewalk next to the wagon so no one can see you. Gabriel will bring a crate over. You get in it."

"An' den?"

His eyes fixed on the road, Andrew answered, "And then you pray to God. You pray for your very soul. This is the last chance I'll have to talk to you. Take care of yourself, Dante."

Dante's buried his face in his hands. "Ah 'poluhgize, Andrew."

Andrew said, "There's no reason to. I know you didn't kill Down."

Before Dante could confess that he had put a conjure on him, Andrew parked the wagon by the two boxes. They climbed down and Gabriel approached them. Andrew said, "Gabriel, go away. I don't want you to see this."

Andrew looked around and said, "Get in the box right now!" Dante did as he was told and lay flat on his back, sobbing. Andrew placed Dante's clothes next to him, picked up the cover, and nailed it shut. He heard a moan from inside. Andrew kneeled and said into the air holes, "Don't give up, Dante. You'll be safe soon. God bless you."

Andrew then called to Gabriel, "Help me get these boxes on the wagon."

"Here are the supplies you wanted, Master Charles," Andrew called out as he pulled up to the Eastern Wharves.

"It's about time," Charlie said loudly. "You lazy negroes can't do anything on time. Boys, get those boxes on that ship, and hurry. We're an hour behind!"

Four workmen ran to the back of the dray and removed the two boxes. Andrew caught Charlie's eye and nodded at the box holding Dante. Charlie directed the two men carrying that crate to go first. They started lugging it up the pier to the tug. Andrew breathed a sigh of relief.

"Hold on one minute," yelled a man with a clipboard in his hand as he ran down the pier after the workmen.

Lamar hurried after the customs inspector and called, "George, they're just some boxes of building supplies I'm sending up to Charleston. They have no value. Not even Howell Cobb would put a duty on them."

George waited for Charlie to catch up. "Are they on the manifest, Charlie?"

"No, George. I just got a telegram from Lafitte in Charleston. He needed some saws and hammers, so I got this together. That's all."

George walked around the boxes to inspect them. "Why do they have holes?"

"I've used these boxes for everything, even transporting my dogs to the country."

George studied the boxes for a moment. "They look new to me. Open 'em up, boys."

Charlie nodded to the men closest to the collector. They opened the box, revealing carpenter's equipment. "See? I'm telling you the truth, George. It sort of hurts that you don't believe me." Charlie slapped George on the back and shook his hand. George put his right hand in his pocket and then withdrew it.

"Charlie, every merchant in Savannah wants me to ignore their last-minute shipments. That's when things get smuggled out. Open that other box and you can be on your way."

Charlie nodded at the workmen standing by Dante's box, as he prepared himself to act shocked at the sight of a negro. The men started to remove the nails.

"Sorry for being so late Charlie, George," yelled Dr. Turner, the city health officer, as he ran up the pier. "I'm way behind today. Please gather the crew so I can inspect them." Because fevers brought havoc to so many cities, the crews of ships had to be inspected by a health officer for contagious diseases before departing a port. The health officer issued a bill of health, which had to be presented at the next port of call to gain entry to the harbor.

Charlie seized the opportunity. "Captain Farnum, get the crew together. Dr. Turner is in a hurry. He doesn't have all day!" All the men ran to board the steam tug and lined up outside the pilot house, leaving the boxes on the pier unattended.

George followed the men to the tug, watched the inspection, and signed the doctor's bill of health and the manifest. He then collected the fee for the support of the pest house, and bade good day to Charlie. As George and the doctor left the wharf, the workmen carried the boxes to the ship, and the steam tug *Lamar* was on its way. Andrew and Charlie exhaled together.

Andrew went home and told Patience that Dante had run away yet again after she had left the house that morning. He said he didn't think Dante would return. Patience was relieved but asked Andrew how he could be so sure. Andrew said he just had a feeling. When left alone, Andrew closed his eyes and prayed that Dante's escape would be successful. He had lied to too many people, people he loved.

When the tug cleared the mouth of the river, one of the crewmen opened the box. Dante popped out as if propelled by giant springs. The men gathered around him and laughed at the negro in the frilly dress. One man said, "I think I'll enjoy my night with this wench."

Another man pinched Dante's arse. Dante was so happy to be out of his coffin he laughed as well. Then Dante stepped back and tore off the dress to the whistles and hoots of the crew. He threw the dress and the bonnet overboard, and, standing in his drawers, watched as the wind carried them into the choppy whitecaps.

He then reached into the crate and pulled out his trousers and shirt and hurriedly put them on. He heard the coins clinking. "Ah yent dressin' luk no wommin."

"All right, let's get to work. Have you never seen a negro before?" Farnum said as he walked over to the gathering.

"Si, Capitan Farnum," one of the crewmen said, and they all dispersed.

Farnum said to Dante, "You, see that bucket over there? I want you to take it and start scrubbing this deck."

"Massa, ah yent know how tuh scrub no . . . ."

Dante never saw Farnum's fist bury into his stomach. He simply doubled up like a triggered animal trap and fell to the deck, bent tightly with his head to his knees. He tried to cry but nothing came out of his mouth except saliva. He couldn't breath. He felt himself being lifted into the air and the next thing he knew, he was slammed against the pilot house, his head bouncing against it. He saw stars. Farnum's face was inches from his.

"Now you listen to me, boy. When I give you an order, you do it. You don't think about it. Do you understand?"

Dante still couldn't talk, but he nodded his head. That wasn't enough for Farnum. He pulled Dante slightly forward and slammed him back against the wall of the pilothouse. "Speak, nigger! Do you?"

Dante gasped, "Yassuh, massa! Yassuh!"

"Good. Now let me tell you something else. I don't give a damn about Lamar's promises. If you do anything to annoy me, I'll cut your arms and legs off and throw you to the sharks. Do you doubt me?"

"No, suh!"

Farnum released his hold on Dante, who remained on his feet but crouched over, clutching his abdomen. He staggered to the bucket, dropped to his knees, and swabbed the deck. Lord, how he missed home.

It was eight o'clock at night when the tug approached Charleston Harbor. Dante, who had been scrubbing for ten hours, heard Farnum's voice. "Get in the crate!" Dante dropped the brush and jumped in. "I see you're capable of learning a lesson. What's your name?"

Dante looked up from the box. "Dante, massa."

"All right, Dante. You lie still in this box, and don't make a sound. When we dock, we're going to move you to another ship. If you don't do as I say, I'll kill you." A crewman put the top of the box back on and hammered it shut.

Three hours later, after the crate had been carried, set down, and carried again, the top of the box was removed. Dante saw four men looking down at him. One was Master Farnum. Dante didn't dare move.

"Get out of there," Farnum ordered.

Dante scrambled out of the box and stood erect. One of the other men, dressed in a dark blue jacket with a red, white, and blue patch on the pocket, and white pants inspected Dante and said, "Is Lamar out of his mind?"

Farnum explained, "Charlie said he owed someone a big favor." Farnum pointed to Dante. "This is the favor. Charlie said this boy murdered a white man."

Corrie, his eyes still on Dante, said, "Remarkable. Tell me, Farnum, how did Lamar escape the lunatic asylum all these years?"

"That's s good question, Captain Corrie."

Corrie finally spoke to Dante, politely. "What's your name, boy?"

"Dante, massa." Dante found himself feeling slightly comfortable with this man.

Corrie sunk his hands into his jacket pockets. "Dante, we're sailing to Africa tomorrow morning. It's a long trip, six or seven weeks. The last thing I want to deal with at ports of call is a smuggled negro murderer. I'll have to assign one of my men to watch you because I don't trust you. But if I throw you overboard, no one will know. I'll tell Mr. Lamar everything went as planned. Dante is back in Africa swinging from trees with his ancestors." Corrie then said to the two other men, "Tie him up."

Two of the men grabbed Dante, tied his hands, and pushed him onto a chair. Corrie said, "Thank you, Captain Brown, Mr. Brooks."

Dante dropped his head and started to cry.

Corrie asked, "Did I say something to upset you, Dante?"

Dante looked up. "Massa, ah nebuh kill dat man. Ah gwine cook een uh restran' een Sabannah wid Miss Amy."

Corrie let Dante wail for a bit. "I understand you're a good cook. Is that so?"

Dante nodded furiously. "Yassuh, massa. Fuh sutt'n."

Corrie explained, "Dante, I don't want to kill you. I'm merely suggesting you could be a rather large obstacle on this trip. You see my point of view, don't you?"

"Yassuh, massa, ah sholy do." He lowered his head again.

Corrie grabbed a clump of Dante's hair and pulled his head up. "Of course, we could always use another cook. Has Captain Farnum here explained the rules of the voyage?" Corrie released Dante's head.

Dante kept his head raised. "Yassuh, massa, he sholy do, mussy boocoo."

Corrie, Farnum, Brown, and Brooks laughed at the illiterate negro's use of French. "Good. If I can, I intend to honor my partner's request and take you to Africa. You're an inconvenience, but I'll work around that. My advice to you is not to make one second of this trip troublesome for me, my guests, or my crew."

"Massa, oonuh gladdee ah yuh, ah prumis'!"

"Good. We still need to depart Charleston tomorrow morning. So you're going to have to get back in that crate when the pilot boards. Remember, not a peep."

"Ah hate dat box, massa."

Farnum took a step towards Dante but Corrie blocked him with his arm. "I don't care. After we get out of here, you'll sleep in a storeroom, cuffed to a post. And you can show us what a good cook you are."

The next day, Friday, July 3, 1858, just before departing, Corrie sent a telegraph to Charlie saying the journey was going as planned. At 1:30 in the afternoon a pilot came on board to guide the ship out of the harbor. By three o'clock they were bound for their first port-of-call, Trinidad, Port of Spain. Dante was let out of the box. He was on his way to Africa.

With the Fourth of July celebrations over, and with the *Wanderer* safely on its way, Charlie decided it was time to tell Howell Cobb how he felt about him. Charlie would make the letter public by also sending it to the newspapers of Savannah and Charleston. First, he wanted Trow to see it.

"Chollie, you can't send this letter to the Secretary of the Treasury of the United States!" Trow said, shaking his head, as he laid the thirteen-page document on Charlie's desk. "I know you're angry with him, but it won't do us any good to have him angrier. We planned for his refusal. Everything's falling into place."

"He insulted me as no gentleman should. He'll pay for that. He's lucky I'm not seeking satisfaction."

"He's family, Chollie. You don't speak to family like that. Not in public."

"He spoke to me that way in public, Trow," Charlie said calmly.

Trow sighed, knowing he could not change Lamar's mind. Charlie's statement described his three applications for clearance of the *Cobden*, and Cobb's reasons for rejecting each one. Then Charlie refuted Cobb's reasoning, insisting there was no law against importing emigrants into America, whether from Europe or Africa. Charlie said it was an abuse of executive power to withhold any rights of citizens by assuming illegal motives. Charlie accused Cobb of making laws to suit his views.

If Charlie had stopped there, the matter might have been forgotten. But that would not have been Charlie. He went on to admit that he had planned all along to drop the Africans at the levee at New Orleans and to let the law decide if he had acted legally. But Cobb's way of handling the matter—dodging the main issue and appeasing the North by opposing slavery—was the work of a little man. Charlie told Cobb that the slave-trade laws were forced upon the South by the North, and he intended to violate them. He ended by challenging Cobb to "Let your cruisers catch me if they can."

Charlie read the letter again and chortled. The *Wanderer* was on its way, in the hands of a professional, and would return in five months with the answer to all his problems. Then he would write another letter to Cobb, asking, "Where were your cruisers, Mr. Cobb, where were your mighty ships?"

Charlie excused himself from Trow and went to the post office to mail the letter. He was in such a good mood he decided to visit Andrew to tell him Dante was safely on his way home. Charlie was the only man in Georgia who could have accomplished that.

"Hello, Andrew. The fireworks were better than ever this year," Charlie said as he approached Andrew at the Abraham House building site.

Andrew stood to greet Charlie. Lamar stepped close to him and said, "Everything went as planned. Now it's our little secret."

Andrew wiped his brow. "Thank you so much, sir. It will remain a secret, believe me."

As Charlie was about to tell Andrew how well everything had gone, he was interrupted. "Hello, Charlie. What brings you here today?" Mr. McBain asked.

Charlie shook McBain's hand. "Sir, how are you this fine day?"

"Very well. And you?"

"I'm thinking of building a new stable. Would you know of a good bricklayer to help me?" Charlie laughed at his cleverness.

McBain laughed too, but his smile quickly dissolved. He turned to Andrew and said, "There's good news. I just came from the marshal's office. It seems that Mrs. Down's niece saw Mr. Down's murder. She went into shock and could do nothing but cry for days. She finally told the marshal that it was Hank that killed Down and Dante had tried to stop Hank. The marshal says Dante is in the clear. If you see him, tell him everything is all right. He can come home now. We need to get him back home."

"Ye . . . yes, sir. I'll do that. If I see him, I'll do that."

"Thanks, Andrew. Good seeing you again, Charlie."

"Er . . . good seeing you, Mr. McBain."

CHAPTER 23

Dante Goes Home

July-September 1858

"He'll be back, one way or another," Patience said to Andrew as they dressed to visit the McBains the day after learning Dante was not wanted for murder. Patience turned to Andrew for a response, but saw him fumbling to button his shirt. She felt his tension from across the room.

Andrew had said little since the previous day. He hadn't told Patience that he helped Dante, especially in concert with Charlie Lamar, knowing how much it would anger her. "I'm worried about him. As long as he thinks he's wanted, he'll take desperate actions."

"Don't be worried. He runs to you as soon as he gets in trouble, and you put your life at risk to help him. If he'd listened to you in the first place and had gone to Master McBain, he'd be fine today instead of on the run. I feel a tremendous burden off our backs. That was the worst day of my life." She stepped over, kissed his cheek, and said, "Now, let's get to the McBains. We don't want to be late."

Twenty minutes later they were standing in the McBain family parlor. Mr. McBain asked, "Andrew, I gather there's been no word from Dante?"

"No, sir," Andrew replied, feeling his stomach tighten as he lied.

"Where in the world could he have gone?" Amy pondered. "He has no idea of the world beyond Savannah."

"He could be hiding at one of our maroon sites at Tybee," Joseph offered. "He liked to fish and climb the trees there."

McBain said, "I've put advertisements in several South Carolina and Georgia papers offering a reward for his return. I can't imagine Dante being so resourceful he'd avoid capture."

They speculated a while longer. Though it was not her place, Patience wanted to steer the conversation away from Dante. "Miss Amy, what are you going to do about the restaurant?"

Amy studied Patience for a moment before replying, "I'm still going to open it. If Dante doesn't return, I'll have to find another cook."

*   *   *

At Captain Corrie's request, Gisseppe the cook took Dante on a tour of the ship. At the very rear or aft part, occupying its entire width, was Corrie's cabin. The door was open and they peeked in. There were mirrors on the walls, satin-wood furniture, lace curtains, gold-leafed picture frames, packed bookshelves, and gleaming brass navigational instruments. Dante thought it was as fancy as the big house.

They proceeded up the passageway between two smaller staterooms, where Corrie's guests, Mr. Brent and Mr. Beman, slept. Dante had to stop for a moment and place a hand against the bulkhead to steady himself as a wave rolled the ship. They walked around the aft companionway into a wood-paneled room with a dark, polished, rectangular table surrounded by eight high-backed chairs. Gisseppe called the room the salon, the dining room for the captain and his guests. Dante asked why rooms on a ship had different names than those in a house. Gisseppe laughed, and told Dante to use ship words on board.

They next walked between a library on the port side, with shelves of books and a table with charts spread upon it, and a small stateroom on the starboard side, where Captain Farnum and Captain Brown slept in bunk beds. Forward of these was the galley, or kitchen. Dante stopped and inspected the room and thought how small it was compared to the kitchens at the Heritage or the house on Pulaski Square. He noted the cooking ware, knives, cutting boards, and how they were all secured with straps or wooden fasteners.

They then entered the crew's salon, much smaller than the captain's. Forward of that, on either side, were the crew's staterooms with six bunk beds each. They stopped at the fore companionway and Gisseppe pointed beyond it to a privy, a storeroom which would be Dante's bedroom, and, at the very front of the ship, the forepeak, where masts, riggings, and other sailing gear were stored. Gisseppe told Dante there were many casks of food and supplies stored under the floor boards.

Dante bounced up the companionway to the deck, excited at learning so many new things and the way Gisseppe talked to him as if he were one of the crew.

Once on deck, Gisseppe said, "We get to work now, Dantino. Very much work."

"Yassuh, Massa Joe Soupy."

"Dantino, you no call me 'massa,' prego. Call me Joe.

"Yassuh, Joe."

Dante couldn't help but cross paths with the other men in the confines of the ship. During his first days at sea, he counted sixteen men in addition to Joe and himself. He soon learned there were three captains. Captain Corrie appeared to Dante to be the massa. Joe told him that Captain Farnum was the super cargo, the man in charge of the finances. Captain Brown ran the sailing of the ship and set its course. There was also a sailing master named Brooks, who worked for Captain Brown.

There were two British guests, Brent and Beman, who spent most of their time with Corrie and Farnum fishing, shooting rifles from the deck, playing card games, reading, drinking, and eating, though Corrie did spend time with Brown and Brooks charting their course.

The remaining ten men were crew, and spoke in many accents. Joe said they came from Portugal, Spain, and Greece, places Dante had never heard of. Of course, their real identities and nationalities didn't match the crew list Corrie submitted to the port collector in Charleston.

As Dante cleared dishes from the table in the captain's salon after their first supper at sea, Corrie said, "Dante, this meal was delicious. Did you help Gisseppe cook the shrimps and rice?"

Dante almost came to attention. "Yassuh, Massa Capin, see boo play."

Corrie swirled the wine in his glass. "Where did you learn to cook?"

"Mos' f'um Miss Jinny at de Huhtage." Dante saw Corrie look blankly at him. "Een Sabannah. Massa McBain. Dey mek bricks."

Corrie asked incredulously, "He was going to let you open a restaurant?"

Dante shifted the dirty dishes in his hands. "He daa'tuh, Miss Amy, she buy it. Miss Amy say ah de massa chef. Ah fin'lly at las' de massa." The men laughed.

Corrie sipped his wine. "You cook very well, Dante."

"Mussy boocoo." Dante returned to the galley, dishes piled on his arms, beaming from the compliment. Dante was determined to please Captain Corrie.

After Dante left, Corrie said to Farnum, "That negro makes me laugh."

Farnum replied, "As long as he stays out of trouble."

Corrie excused himself, returned to the quiet of his cabin, and enjoyed his after-supper glass of brandy. He was on his way to making a handsome profit, one that would guarantee him a comfortable life for many years. The expedition would also satisfy his need to face and conquer danger. There were laws declaring slave traders pirates, punishable by death. And there were naval squadrons on the coast of Africa, but that only increased his excitement. Corrie knew he could out-smart any naval commander. And he had the fastest ship on the seas to do it with.

Dante kept a busy schedule. At 5:30 in the morning, Joe woke him and uncuffed him from a post in the storeroom where he slept, brought him onto the top deck, and made certain he washed. Dante told Joe that the missus made him and all the house servants wash every day. Dante spent the next fourteen hours preparing food, cooking, serving, cleaning, sweeping, and scouring the galley. This was far more than he ever worked at the Heritage or in Savannah. He fell asleep the instant he hit the storeroom floor, and didn't wake up until Joe opened the door.

Joe taught Dante how to cook at sea, including building a brick stove on the top deck. Fires were not permitted below. He also showed Dante how to cook with garlic, an herb that the crew loved in their food. Dante's stomach growled whenever he used garlic, and he would take a little for his food. Somehow, Joe always knew when he had eaten it.

After a few days, Joe gave Dante an old pair of white trousers, a white shirt, and a tall, white chef's hat to wear when he worked in the kitchen.

Gisseppe appreciated Dante's assistance, and enjoyed his humor. Like the time he told Dante he was born in Geneva, and Dante asked him if the *Wanderer* would stop there. Gisseppe lived most of his life in Europe, but had recently settled in New Orleans, where the higher-paying work on slavers was plentiful. He spent most of his adult life at sea, and treasured his short time at home with his wife and four children, of whom he talked often with Dante.

The other crewmen were not as nice. They appeared as if they were going to or coming from a fight. This was especially true of Juan and Miguel, two Spaniards. They looked like brothers to Dante, both several inches shorter than he, and wiry, with curly brown hair. Juan had a slight limp and Miguel had a pockmarked face.

Dante tried to avoid them, but on a ship, that wasn't easy. On the sixth day, the seas became rough, and Dante vomited over the side of the ship to the laughter of the crew. As he sat on the deck recovering, Juan, in poor English, asked Dante if he liked to swim. Dante said he did. Juan and Miguel then grabbed Dante by the ankles, lifted him as if he were a feather, and held him over the side of the ship. Dante screamed for his life, and Joe tried to get them to stop. Fortunately, Captain Farnum was near and ordered the men to pull him up. It took Dante's heart about ten minutes to slow down. He noticed that Juan and Miguel were grinning at him, enjoying his fear. He didn't doubt they would have dropped him into the ocean if not for Farnum.

Dante soon got used to the ship's movement. He began to value the time he spent on deck. When no one was looking, Dante gazed out over the endless ocean, wondering how far it stretched, and what country existed at the end of it. He watched other ships glide across the ocean's sparkling surface, and wondered if their passengers might be looking back at him. He loved the oily smell of the ship and the sounds of creaking masts and snapping sails. He became convinced he wanted to spend the rest of his life at sea.

Three weeks after her departure from Charleston, the *Wanderer* sailed into Port of Spain, Trinidad. The crew gathered on deck to see the harbor and the small town overlooking it. Dante, standing in back of the others, asked excitedly, "Dishyuh Affricky?"

The men laughed. By then, Dante was used to asking serious questions and being laughed at. Joe said, "No, Dantino. Thees-a Trinidad."

"Oh," was all Dante could say, never having heard of Trinidad. He didn't want to ask where that was and get laughed at again.

That night, while Dante was removing dishes from the captain's table, Corrie asked in his usual, kindly manner, "Tell me, Dante, are you enjoying your trip at sea?"

"Si, Massa Capin." Dante said loudly, using a word he heard Juan use.

Corrie smiled. "Bueno. You'll soon face another test. We'll be in Trinidad for a few days and I'll be entertaining on board. In the presence of my guests, you are not to say a word. If you do, you'll go back in the box."

Dante grimaced. "Pray go, Massa Capin, don' pit me een dat box, see boo play."

Farnum pointed his knife at Dante. "Then keep your mouth shut."

The *Wanderer* stayed in the Port of Spain for five days and took on water and provisions. Corrie entertained locals every night. Dante didn't utter a word when he was in the salon. Early on the sixth morning, while Dante was helping prepare breakfast, the *Wanderer* suddenly set sail and left Trinidad. Dante asked Joe why they were leaving. Joe said he didn't know.

Dante really didn't care. He was getting closer to Africa, and freedom.

*   *   *

"Don't you ever take a break?" the blue-eyed man with dark brown hair, shiny-white teeth, and a dimpled chin said to Amy as she placed the plates on the table.

"Not when there's work to do," Amy said politely, concentrating on the settings.

It was mid-September and Dante's Place had been opened almost two months. Just when Amy thought the restaurant wasn't going to make it, word about the delicious food had spread around town. Even though many of the wealthy residents were still at their summer residences, the establishment started to fill its tables.

Amy had waited a week after Dante disappeared before she decided to act. With all the work she had put into the project, she wasn't about to give up. With Andrew's permission, she asked Patience to be the cook. Patience was anxious to help the woman who had done so much to help manumit Andrew and to give him his first chance as an architect. Patience also wanted to start working again, though evenings were not her preference. But when Emily offered to have Chloe take care of Truvy until Andrew finished work, she accepted Amy's offer.

Things did not go so smoothly at first. The waiters were slow in tending to customers, most of whom were the McBains and their friends. Patience and her assistant cook had trouble coordinating the serving of the dishes for each table. Amy had difficulty creating a menu. Amy couldn't seem to buy the right quantities of ingredients. But Amy, Patience, and the head waiter met every night after the last diner left, and every evening before they opened. In time, they resolved the major problems. Amy visited every hotel in town, telling them of her new restaurant, and put up signs at the two railroad depots. By September, she was confident of success.

"Now, that's dedication. I hope the owner appreciates it," said the same man, one of four at the table.

Amy replied, "I am the owner."

Four sets of eyebrows arched at Amy's statement. The man continued. "I guess that explains it. It's encouraging to see a successful businesswoman."

Amy said, "Thank you," and darted to another table in the crowded room. The man looked after her, as his three companions smiled at one another.

"Forget it, Bob," one of them said. "Any southern woman that beautiful is married with ten screaming children at home. Even if she isn't, she won't have the time of day for a Yankee."

Bob said, "Nothing ventured, nothing gained, Dr. Salter," and started on his venison.

Amy returned in five minutes to pour wine in the men's empty glasses. Bob got to the heart of the matter. "Who's the Dante in 'Dante's Place,' your husband?"

Amy, who was having a hectic evening, threw her head back and laughed out loud. "No, just some boy who saved my cat."

Bob held his knife and fork like flagstaffs. "You named your restaurant after a boy who saved your cat?"

Amy concentrated on pouring. "It's a long story."

Bob said, "I have time." Amy glanced at Bob, and then finished pouring the wine.

Dr. Salter tried to do his part for Bob. He said to Amy, "Bob here is a painter, the best I've ever seen."

Amy held up the empty bottle and asked Salter, "Would you like another, sir?"

Salter replied, "That's an excellent idea."

Before Bob could talk about his painting, she was gone. One of the men, Hunter, said, "I don't fancy your chances, Bob. But you made her laugh, even though you didn't mean to."

After supper Amy asked the men how they enjoyed their food. Bob said, "This is the best meal we've had in the South. You should be proud of this establishment. You'd be a sensation in New York."

Amy finally managed a smile for the handsome man trying to engage her in conversation. "Thank you. May I get you anything else? A piece of pie?"

Before anyone could respond, Patience appeared from the kitchen and said, "Miss Amy, we're out of peach pie."

The men's eyes followed the beautiful negro lady as she hurried away. Amy said, "May I get you some pie, other than peach?"

The fourth man, Ted, slurred, "Is she your slave?"

Amy winced at the comment. "I asked if you wanted a piece of pie."

"Well, is she?" Ted persisted. Bob kicked him under the table, while Hunter told him to shut his mouth. Ted, too deep into the wine, did not care.

Amy folded her arms. "If you think that's your business, no, she's not."

"Who owns her then?" Ted demanded.

"Her husband!"

Ted pondered his wine glass and uttered, "She's married to a white man?"

Amy started to leave. Dr. Salter said, "Please excuse Ted. He doesn't mean to be rude, but some of us find slavery cruel, and we can't help but comment on it."

Amy looked at the nearby tables, and said to the men, "I'd advise you to lower your voices. The last thing we need is a group of arrogant Yankees who've just visited the South for a few days to offer their opinion. Now may I get you anything else?"

Hunter looked at the others and said, "No. We have to get to the prize fight."

Amy's nose wrinkled in a sneer. "So you find slavery cruel and you're going to a prize fight?" She shook her head and left.

After paying the bill, the men stood to leave. Bob wanted to bid goodbye to Amy, but she was tending to another table, and not about to return. He said, "Thanks, Ted."

*   *   *

On the next part of the voyage, Dante faced the harsh reality of life at sea. Day after day passed without any mention of landfall. One night, well after the ship had left Trinidad, as Dante was serving dinner in the captain's salon, Corrie asked, "Tell me, Dante, when we reach Africa, what do you intend to do?"

"Dunno, massa. Ah kin ketch de ship fuh Libeery. Ah kin cook een uh restran'."

The men at the table laughed. Corrie said, "These African towns along the Congo River aren't like Savannah, Dante. They're poor little crap holes with one run-down hotel at best. Most Africans are very poor and eat dog meat on a good day. There are a few rich traders who live in big houses outside of town, and they have slave cooks."

Dante asked, "Dey slabes een Affricky?" Again, the men laughed at him.

A few weeks later, while Dante was preparing supper for the crew in the galley, he heard loud voices. Joe called him topside. Dante saw the men facing east. Far in the distance was the hazy outline of land. Joe turned to Dante and said, "Dantino, thees-a is Affricky."

Later that day, Dante asked Joe the date. It was one he wanted to remember forever; the first day he set eyes on Africa. Joe told him, "September 15, 1858."

The next day, the *Wanderer* sailed into the Congo River. It was far wider than the Savannah, and was lined on both sides with walls of green trees. There was no sign of a town. Once, Dante saw a plume of smoke rising above the trees, but that was about it. After a few hours, the river began to narrow. Villages appeared every few miles, with black people squatting by the shoreline, almost naked, fishing or washing clothes.

At one point, a large inlet appeared on the south side of the river. Joe shook Dante's shoulder and pointed. "Mangroves!"

Dante was about to ask Joe what mangroves were when someone called, "Ship to port!" A ship about the size of the *Wanderer* was floating adrift with no colors, smoldering from a fire somewhere in its bowels, and no sign of life. The name was painted over. The crew watched in silence as they passed her by. Dante saw Captain Corrie on deck, frowning.

The Webster-Ashburton Treaty, which established a British-American squadron for the coast of Africa, was far from perfect. There were too few ships for so large an area, and, worse, the two countries didn't trust each other. American businessmen were convinced the British would use the treaty as a guise to harass their merchant ships. The Americans' concern might have been well-founded, but there could be little doubt that the British did take fighting the slave trade seriously.

Still, the American government had made its position clear. It considered any boarding of an American ship by a foreign vessel a violation of maritime law and would not allow it. The British felt that that was a boon to the slave traders. After all, flags were cheap. A slave ship captain from another country could fly the American colors and proceed unmolested.

To counter this problem, the British boarded suspected slavers flying the American flag, demanding the captain to show papers authenticating the ship's ownership, country of registry, and its manifest. If the papers were fraudulent or "lost," the British searched the ship, and, if they deemed her a slaver, seized it.

If the papers authenticated American registry, yet the British sensed signs of the slave trade, such as the stench of hundreds of humans stowed below, they would detain the ship and send for the American Squadron to handle the crisis.

There were some British captains who didn't give a damn about flags and papers. If they suspected a ship to be a slaver, American or not, they searched her and worried about the consequences later. This was on the minds of the crewmen of the *Wanderer* as they stared at the hulk of the ghost ship in the middle of the Congo River.

By evening, the *Wanderer* reached its first destination, Pont du Lain, a village on the south bank of the Congo River. Dante saw many funnels of smoke rising in the air, as well as a narrow pier made of uneven logs sticking twenty yards into the river. The crew dropped anchor.

After supper Corrie told Dante they would be in the river for about a week and he, Corrie, would be entertaining each night. After that, Dante was free to go.

As Dante lay in his storeroom that night, he heard the cries of animals on land. Some sounded almost human. For the first time, Dante tried to picture what Africa looked like beyond that thick wall of trees. In his daydreams, he pictured the world looking like Georgia. But now he saw Africa was different. It even smelled different, a strange mixture of smoke, something rotten, and the sweet scent of blooming flowers. A loud yet distant scream interrupted his thoughts. He wondered where he would stay his first night on land. Where and what would he eat? Who would he talk to? Dante hardly slept.

The next morning, four crewmen rowed Corrie, Brent, Beman, and Farnum to shore. When they reached the pier, they were surrounded by twenty African boys, in all shapes and sizes, wearing tattered loincloths, trying to grab the men's rifle cases, and making more noise than a tent full of children at the circus. The white men held their rifle cases high over their heads. The children still reached for them, like hunting dogs jumping at feeding time. One shout and the boys fell silent. A bald African man, wearing beige trousers and a white-flowered, purple shirt, strode up the pier. The boys moved aside to allow him through.

The African, taller, heavier, and more muscular than any of the whites, approached Corrie, who, despite the suffocating morning heat was wearing white trousers and his blue New York Yacht Club jacket. The black man asked, "You need help, boss?"

Corrie said, "We were told King Rumba would take us hunting."

"Yes. Me sabe, boss. Welcome to Pont du Lain. Me, Benny. Please, come." He pointed to the largest boys and said, "They carry for you." The men handed over their rifles. Benny smiled and walked down the pier, the Africans boys following, all struggling to get a grip on one of the cases. The white men brought up the rear, with Corrie caressing a small, soft-covered valise.

The pier led to a dirt street that ran parallel to the river and was lined with one-story, ramshackle, wooden huts. Skeletal dogs, with swarms of flies hovering around them, lay in the shade, their tails swiping ineffectually at the insects. A few older, toothless negroes in loincloths meandered aimlessly. As Benny marched west along the street, the visitors took in their dismal surroundings. They looked ahead and saw, standing out like a mare in a herd of jackasses, a two-story, colonial-looking, white house with a front porch and a second-story piazza overlooking the street and the river beyond. Mr. Beman said, "It's not Brighton, but it will do in a pinch."

Benny walked towards the house. As they passed an alley between two crumbling buildings, a stench of garbage and human waste almost buckled the visitors' knees.

They reached the house and climbed the three steps to the front porch. Benny pointed to four white rocking chairs. The men squinted into the windows, but it was too dark inside to see. Corrie, Brent, and Beman sat down while Farnum stepped back into the street and inspected the outside of the out-of-place building.

"Kensington Palace Hotel," Farnum read to the others.

Benny said, "Yes, world class hotel, boss, believe me. You like some drink?"

The men declined, content to watch the life of the near-lifeless town. A group of fifteen shirtless young black men in light brown shorts, with rusty muskets over their shoulders, passed by. The group acknowledged Benny and disappeared down an alley.

Moments later, two African women of undetermined age, dressed in colorful but soiled wraps, one as fat as a water buffalo, the other as thin as a heron's leg, appeared out of nowhere, and giggled towards the visitors. Benny yelled something and they walked away, the thin one making a rude facial gesture at Benny.

Benny smiled at the men, pointed at the women, and asked, "You like, boss?"

The men laughed. Brent said, "Not on my worst day, Benny, and I've had some dreadfully bad days."

They were distracted by the arrival of a wooden coach drawn by two horses. Benny opened the door and waved the men in. Corrie still clutched his valise. The helpers secured the rifle cases on top of the coach and they were off. The boys ran after them for a bit, waving and shrieking, before giving up.

After a bumpy twenty-minute ride through a dense jungle of thick trees, bushes, and vines, the coach pulled into a clearing and stopped. The men stepped out and saw another coach ten yards away. The door opened and a negro boy dressed in a white robe appeared. He opened a parasol, and a short, rotund black man, also in a white robe, emerged. He walked to the visitors, the negro attendant trotting by his side, keeping every ray of sunlight off him. "I am King Rumba. Welcome. How may I be of service?"

Corrie stepped forward. "Hello, King Rumba, I'm Captain Corrie. This is Dr. Brent, Mr. Beman, and Captain Farnum."

"Yes, Captain. It is a pleasure to meet you. Please excuse my English." Rumba, who had attended a university in England, fished for a compliment.

Corrie gave it. "Your English is excellent, King Rumba. Here is a gift for you, for the fine hospitality you have shown us." Corrie handed Rumba the small soft valise.

Rumba unbuckled it. His face beamed at the yards of fine Italian silk. "Thank you, Captain Corrie. This is very kind of you. I will treasure this fine gift. Shall we get out of this dreadful sunlight and conduct our business?"

Rumba and his parasol-toting servant headed to his carriage. Corrie, Beman, and Benny followed. They all climbed in, the white men sitting on one bench, and Rumba and Benny the other. Corrie negotiated the purchase of five hundred Africans, at least three-quarters male, between the ages of fourteen and thirty-five. They agreed on a price, which averaged forty-five dollars, to be adjusted based on the number, health, ages, and sex of those finally delivered and accepted. Fortunately, Rumba spoke English and Mr. Beman's translating skills were not needed.

Corrie gave Rumba a leather bag of gold coins as down payment. Rumba handed the bag to Benny, who counted the contents. Benny nodded to Rumba, who thanked Corrie, then, eyeing Corrie up and down, said, "I do admire that uniform, Captain."

Corrie noted that he had something the king wanted. "Oh, it's the outfit of the New York Yacht Club, one of the finest in America. It's probably the first time one has seen the light of day in Africa."

Rumba laughed. "I think you are right, Captain." Rumba's eyes inspected the jacket for a few seconds. He then said, "You may expect delivery in four weeks. It's much more difficult now, with so many French ships."

France had made slavery and the slave trade illegal, though French planters had a tremendous demand for labor at their plantations in the West Indies. To get around its own laws, France had recently adopted the African apprentice system to supply that labor. The French government assured the world that the imported Africans would be free men, treated humanely, indentured for only ten years, and could opt to return to Africa after their indenture. However, the apprentices were still captured in tribal wars, sold at the factories on the coast, and stuffed into holds of ships, like all other slaves.

Rumba continued, "I have about 150 at my factory now. I am expecting a Foulah caravan here in two weeks with about two hundred more. In two days my army and I are going on a hunt. We will capture enough to fill your request. As you may know there are no tribes worth hunting in this area. They have been wiped out by the trade. We must travel far inland, at least a week's journey, to find villages of any size. It will take at least two weeks to return because we must march our captives back, always a slower process. If the chiefs don't willingly give us men and women in tribute, we will need to conquer them. But we are fortunate. The tribes we shall visit are at war with one another, and will not come to each other's assistance when we attack. That always makes the mission easier."

Corrie asked, "How big is your army, King Rumba?"

The king took the pouch from Benny. "About three hundred men. Fifty are on horses. Plus, we have slaves who carry equipment, perform necessary tasks, and cook for the soldiers. They are assembling now and we'll be ready in a few days. I first need to find some non-fighting men, a blacksmith and a cook. But we will get these hands soon. I have some influence in this area." Rumba winked.

Corrie smiled. "I may be able to help you out with a cook, King Rumba."

Rumba pulled his head back in surprise. "How might you do that, Captain?"

Corrie explained. Rumba welcomed the offer and asked Corrie to deliver the cook to Benny at the pier in three days. Rumba then left the white men to prepare for the hunt.

Capturing slave ships was just one way the British tried to stop the trade. Another was by strangling the supply, which at that time was provided by other Africans. Stronger tribes conquered weaker ones, keeping a few of the vanquished for themselves, and bringing the majority to African or white-owned factories near the coast.

Soon after England banned slavery in its possessions in the West Indies in the 1830s, it embarked upon an effort to convince the kings and tribal leaders of West Africa to stop capturing and selling their fellow Africans. However, the demand for slaves was still huge. Though every country had banned the slave trade, three still permitted slavery within its borders: the United States, Cuba, and Brazil.

England began its efforts to stop the trade where it had the most influence, on the Upper Guinea coast, which included British West Africa, where a majority of the slaves in the first half of the nineteenth century had been captured. Using various methods of persuasion on the tribal chiefs, such as pleas to humanity, pay-offs, trade deals, and destruction of the factories, the British had signed slave-trade suppression treaties with most of the tribes in the area. Only the sadistic King of Dahomey refused.

Naturally, the slave traders looked for other sources. They only had to go south to the Lower Guinea coast.

England did not have the same influence in this area as it did to the north. In fact, claim to much of that territory was disputed between the British and the Portuguese, who had first explored the Congo River basin in the late-fifteenth century. Many European countries, including Portugal and England, had friendly trading relations with the local tribes, who supplied products like palm oil, nuts, copal, gums, dry goods, fish oil, and lumber. Neither Britain nor Portugal wanted to risk a conflict that would disrupt those mercantile interests, and left control of the area in the hands of the tribal kings, many of whom were happy to supply the slave trade.

The most powerful tribe in the Central African region was the Foulah. They were not negroes, but bronze-colored with fine hair, and they were Mohammedans. Wherever they settled and conquered, they spread the word of Islam. They were skilled merchants, and prodigious slave hunters. It was commonly believed that if the Foulahs could be convinced to end their role in the trade, it could be virtually eliminated in Africa. However, no European country had such powers of persuasion.

So the squadrons began to spend more time in the Congo River area looking for suspected slavers, supplied by the likes of Rumba.

After Rumba had departed, the men tried their hand at hunting with two guides and Benny. Though they had hoped to find big animals, they only shot some game birds. By early evening, in the sweltering heat, they headed back to town and the ship. As they passed the Kensington Palace Hotel, they saw a line of coaches parked in front, with the African drivers standing about, dressed in western-style shirts and trousers, and smoking cigarettes. Their coach stopped and Benny opened the door. "Boss, you want to have a drink, meet some Europeans?"

Corrie looked at the other men, who nodded their sweaty heads. Benny led them into the noisy bar, which fell silent upon their entry. When their eyes adjusted to the darkness of the room, they saw about twenty-five white men staring at them. Suddenly, the bar patrons burst into cheers, walked over to Corrie and his men, threw their arms around the newcomers, and insisted on buying drinks.

These men were the core of the white community of Pont du Lain. They were the traders and agents for the legitimate and illegitimate products shipped from the port to the Americas, West Indies, and Europe. They worked hard in this desolate spot of the world, surviving the heat, fever, disease, bugs, animal life, and tribal wars to make their fortunes. They lived each day as if it were their last, partying, drinking heavily, gambling, and performing dangerous stunts on a dare. Life in Africa had that effect. Nothing, save the arrival of new, young prostitutes or a supply ship from Europe, caused more excitement than the sight of some white men with news of the outside world. Soon they all were drinking and laughing like long-lost friends.

The merchants were from many countries. They were mostly English and German, but also a few Dutch and Portuguese, as well as a Scotsman, a Frenchman, an Israelite, and a Spaniard. They all complained about the palm oil crop for the year, but had high hopes for the next year. They also bemoaned the high price of everything, the weather, and the natives. But none said they wanted to leave, except the Frenchman, the champion complainer. These men were addicted to this outpost of civilization; its remoteness, beauty, danger, and potential riches.

After an hour of joviality and naughty jokes, Corrie shouted to the men at the bar, "Gentlemen, you are all invited tomorrow evening on my yacht, the *Wanderer*! I shall expect you at seven. Please bring a wife, a mistress, or both!"

Another cheer erupted. These men liked a party.

Corrie and his men said goodbye and headed for the door. Just then, three men in white naval uniforms walked through, the first bumping into Corrie. The man said, "I'm ever so sorry, old chap. I didn't see you."

Corrie responded, "No need to apologize. I should watch where I'm going."

The man offered his hand. "I don't believe we've met. I'm Commodore Wise of the *HMS Medusa*. Of the British Squadron. My guess is that you're from the schooner in the river."

Corrie shook the man's hand. "Yes, I'm Captain Corrie. I own the *Wanderer*."

The men exchanged greetings. Then Corrie said to Commodore Wise, "I'd like to stay and chat, but we must be getting back to the ship. I'm having a party tomorrow night on the *Wanderer* with our new friends here. Can you and your officers join us?"

Wise said, "Unfortunately, we'll be on patrol all day tomorrow."

Corrie saw Wise as an opponent, one who had to be challenged and defeated. "Then come the night after for supper, Commodore."

Wise said, "Very well, then. We'll be there."

"Excellent. Let's say eight." Corrie and his men departed.

Commodore Wise and his men acknowledged the other patrons in the bar with slight nods and sat at a table, where they drank by themselves.

*   *   *

"Good evening," Amy said to the customer as he entered the restaurant. It took a second for her to recognize him. "Oh. Did you enjoy the prize fight?"

"Good evening. Not really." Bob smiled, hoping for a friendly start with Amy.

Amy was not about to give it to him. "That's a shame. My brother told me there was plenty of blood and smashed teeth. It sounded like a perfectly delightful evening for the enlightened northern sportsman."

Bob realized the enormity of the challenge ahead. "A table for one, please."

"Certainly. Follow me." Amy led Bob to a small table in the corner. She pulled out the chair for him. He thanked her and sat. Then he held out two red roses. She didn't take them. "What are they for?"

Bob still offered the flowers. "For you. One's from me. I want to apologize for the other night. My friends were very rude. You shouldn't have had to put up with that. I've felt guilty the past few days. The other is from Dr. Salter. He apologizes as well. He left town with the others and asked me to give it to you. I'm staying a few extra days to paint a landscape."

Amy looked at the flowers as if they might have thorns.

Bob had hoped the roses might generate a smile. "I hope I'm not making you uncomfortable. My name is Carson, Bob Carson."

Amy finally took the flowers. "Thank you, Mr. Carson. I'm Miss Amy McBain. You're not the one who needs to apologize. I'll get your waiter."

Well, at least she was polite, thought Bob. That was a start.

*   *   *

The next night, the white community of Pont du Lain was lavishly entertained on the *Wanderer*. Dante and Gisseppe served food and drinks on the top deck. The guests talked about business, hunting forays, and life in Africa.

But the most popular topic of conversation was the *Kate Ellen*, the ship that the *Wanderer* crew had seen adrift in the river. The men of Pont du Lain had seen slavers come and go, but the circumstances around the *Kate Ellen* were unusual. Several rumors had reached the community. One was that the ship had been captured by the British Squadron ship, the *Viper,* the previous day, but the British found her deserted, though a slave deck had been laid. There were no papers or colors, and her name had been painted over. No one knew what happened to the crew.

Another rumor had the *Viper* seizing the *Kate Ellen* and its hull full of slaves, stranding the crew on shore, and leaving the ship floating in the river to send a signal to other slavers.

If that story were true, the rescue certainly would have exhilarated the captured tribe people. But it would have raised a problem for the British: what to do with the liberated Africans. They couldn't be taken back to land to find their way home because they had no idea where their homes were. They'd been captured many miles inland. Besides, they'd be seized again by a local king within yards of where they'd be let off. The Africans were village-less and homeless.

The British would have two choices: take them to the British West Indies where they could be "hired" by plantation owners, or take them to Sierra Leone, a country founded by England along the Upper Guinea Coast in 1787 to settle displaced American negroes after the Revolutionary War.

The men of Pont du Lain were convinced of one thing: Commodore Wise was not to be fooled with. He was a man with a purpose, and he did not like to lose.

As the night progressed, the *Kate Ellen* was forgotten when two drunken guests jumped overboard into the crocodile-infested waters on a bet. They were quickly rescued by the Africans sitting by in the rowboats used to ferry the men to the ship. An argument ensued as to who won the wager, and the evening on the *Wanderer* soon ended when the men of Pont du Lain took their dispute to the bar of the Kensington Palace Hotel.

The next day, Corrie told Dante he had found work for him as a cook for an African king. Dante's face lit up as he thanked Corrie. Cooking for a king was worthy of his talents. He figured the king would entertain other kings, and Dante's reputation would spread throughout Africa.

Corrie explained to Dante, "I'm entertaining some officers from a British naval ship tonight. I want that to go well. Tomorrow morning, we'll take you ashore. My deal with Mr. Lamar will have been fulfilled."

Dante again thanked the captain and started to leave. Corrie called, "One last thing." Dante stopped and turned. "I believe you, Dante. I don't think you'd kill a man."

"Grassus, massa."

At supper that night, Corrie, Farnum, Brent, Beman, and their British guests sat in the salon. The fine wines relaxed everyone. Corrie talked about their around-the-world hunting and sight-seeing adventure, and their visits to Trinidad and St. Helena. Of course, the *Wanderer* had never called at St. Helena, site of Napoleon's grave, but Corrie had told authorities in Trinidad that was his next port-of-call before departing without clearance, and stayed with that story.

The British officers talked about life on the coast of Africa, with the same complaints as the white traders. It was the worst duty in Her Majesty's navy.

After supper, Corrie asked Commodore Wise about the local hunting.

Wise said, "That depends, Captain. What are you looking for?"

Corrie unfastened the top button of his shirt. "Big game. Cats and antelope."

Wise nodded. "You'll find them, if you have time and a good guide."

Corrie then asked, "How about elephants?"

Wise smiled without humor. His eyes did not leave Corrie's face. "Are you interested in ivory, Captain?"

Corrie answered without letting the commodore know he understood the word "ivory" was used interchangeably with slaves. "We're just eager for an exciting hunt."

Wise responded, "You will find that, Captain." He then stood and his two lieutenants followed. "We enjoyed your hospitality very much. You must allow me to return the courtesy. If we can assist you in any way while you're here, please let me know. Now, if you'll excuse us."

Corrie escorted the officers to the top deck and watched them board their rowboat. He then went to his cabin for a brandy, knowing he had delivered a masterful performance in out-smarting the commodore.

When the British officers returned to the *Medusa*, Commodore Wise said to one of his lieutenants, "That British merchant ship in the river, the *Sea View*, is leaving tomorrow for Loanda. See the captain first thing and ask him to tell that baboon's backside, Officer Conover, a schooner's in the river, and she's a slaver."

The lieutenant responded, "Sir, she's too small to be a slaver."

"Lieutenant, I can smell a slave ship captain from across an ocean, and Corrie is one. The *Wanderer* is either a slaver or an auxiliary carrying supplies for a slave ship. You tell the *Sea View* captain to deliver that message to the American! If Conover doesn't get one of his ships up here to search the *Wanderer*, I will."

Corrie watched as Dante cleared the breakfast dishes from the table. "Well, Dante, this is your last day with us."

"Yassuh, massa," Dante said with a trace of sorrow.

"Finish up and get your belongings. You'll be taken ashore. When you get to the pier, a man named Benny will take you to your new place of employment." Corrie reached into his pocket and pulled out a coin. "And Dante, here's something for you. You may need it."

Dante took the gold coin from Corrie's hand. "Ten dolluh?"

Corrie laughed at the simple negro. "Yes. From us. Use it wisely."

Dante turned the coin over in his hand. "Yassuh, Massa Capin. Mussy boocoo."

Dante gathered his small bundle of belongings, including his chef's hat. He said goodbye to Joe Soupy who, after Andrew and Hercules, was his best friend. Gisseppe wished him luck. "When I come to Liberia, I find you, Dantino. Yes?"

Dante said he hoped so. They shook hands and Dante departed for the lifeboat. He passed some of the crew, who nodded to him. Even Juan and Miguel offered small hand salutes. Dante had made them laugh.

As he was rowed to shore, Dante turned to look back at the *Wanderer*. He felt sad that he would never see her again.

When they reached the pier, Dante thanked the oarsmen and climbed the ladder. He was a free man.

CHAPTER 24

Neeka

October-November 1858

The *Wanderer* remained in the Congo River for a week after Dante departed. Captain Corrie and his guests hunted and saw the sights during the day and entertained the local whites and the *Medusa* officers on the yacht at night. Then Corrie decided to explore the coast while awaiting delivery of the cargo. As the ship left the river, Corrie sat in his cabin and reveled in all he had accomplished so far. He was not aware that the *Sea View* had arrived at St. Paul de Loanda, the major city along the lower Guinea coast, about two hundred miles south of the Congo River, and that her captain had delivered Wise's message about the *Wanderer* to Flag Officer Conover of the American Squadron.

$*$ $*$ $*$

Dante stood on the pier, his small bundle of clothes under his arm. Somehow, the morning sky seemed bluer and the trees greener. He could hear the river flowing and the birds singing. Everything appeared more real to him. He started whistling with the birds. No one would control his life anymore. And he wouldn't hang.

Dante saw a black man in white trousers and a green-flowered shirt walking towards him. Dante had the urge to hug the stranger, the first Dante encountered as a free man. The negro marched up to him and asked, "You Dante?" Dante nodded. The man said, "Me Benny. Follow me, sabe?" Benny turned and walked down the pier. Dante had to trot to keep up.

Benny headed east from the pier, away from the Kensington Palace Hotel. They entered a narrow jungle path cut through green, leafy bushes so tall that Dante could hardly see their tops. He smelled flowers with fruity fragrances stronger than Miss Amy's perfume. Africa seemed a magnificent place. He wished he could tell Andrew and Hercules about it.

In fifteen minutes they entered a clearing. Dante saw a building that looked like the City Market. It was a four-sided, one-story house made of light reddish-brown clay around an open center. Its roof was thatched. Benny pushed through a door in one wall and marched through the central courtyard. He moved through a door in the opposite wall to an area of circular mud huts. He walked over to one and said, "You sleep here tonight, sabe?"

Dante stepped in the doorway of his new quarters, no bigger than his room at the McBain house in Savannah. A straw mat covered part of the dirt floor. Dante saw a brown bug as big as his palm scuttle across the mat and disappear into a small hole at the base of the wall. He put his bundle of clothes on the floor and sat on the mat. Benny yelled, "No sit! Time to work! Come with me." He walked away and Dante scrambled after him.

Benny re-entered the courtyard, approached a wooden door in another wall and knocked. A voice beckoned from within. Benny opened the door and waved Dante into a long room with beams in the ceiling, animal skins hanging on white-washed walls, and many cushions on an unevenly tiled floor. Benny grabbed Dante by the shoulder and pushed him towards a hammock in the middle of the room. Rumba was lounging in it, wearing a small red vest laced with gold patterns, which was unable to conceal several rolls of belly fat. He also sported short, white, puffy Turkish pants that reached his calves. A black woman sat on the floor beside him. Rumba tapped her shoulder. She stood and left.

Benny swatted the back of Dante's head. "Kneel to the King!"

Dante kneeled on the spot. "Pray go, Massa King!"

Rumba studied Dante and ordered, "Get up, boy! Captain Corrie tells me you're a good cook and need work. Is that so?"

Dante stood at attention. "Yassuh, massa."

The king pulled on a rope hanging from a beam in the ceiling, enabling him to swing back and forth. "Is there anything else you can do? Fire a musket? Wield a knife?"

Dante scratched his head and thought. "Ah kin clime trees lukkuh cat."

The king spat, "What good is that? Tonight, you help Sammy cook. Tomorrow, we're going on a trip with the general. I'll decide what to do with you when we return."

"Massa, ah gwine tuh Libeery aftuh dis, see boo play." Dante was about to open negotiations on his wages when the king held up a hand.

Rumba said, "You're going where I say you go. Now get to work."

Benny grabbed Dante's shirt, turned him around, and guided him out the door. Dante tensed up in anger. This wasn't the treatment he expected. He thought he would be cooking royal meals for a king, his wives, and his princes.

Dante helped prepare supper by peeling yams and cooking rice in a yard in back of the house with chickens pecking about. There was a large stone stove. Rumba's cook, Sammy, a tall, thin black man with gray hair, spoke English. He took an interest in the American slave returning to Africa, and asked Dante many questions about life in Georgia. This made Dante feel better. He thought Sammy would be his friend, just like Gisseppe.

The king did not call upon Dante after the meal to receive compliments. In fact, after Dante cleaned up, he was ordered to his hut for the night. He did not sleep well. He heard loud screeches from the jungle and rustling outside his hut. Things crawled over him. He missed the storeroom on the *Wanderer*.

He was awakened at sunrise by Benny kicking his leg. He stood, went outside, and looked around. He had to blink his eyes. Beyond the huts, in an open field, hundreds of men were assembling, wearing shorts or loin clothes with machetes hanging at their waists and old muskets over their shoulders. There were about fifty men on horses, similarly dressed. One short, thin black man on horseback, wearing a light brown uniform with medals covering the entire front of his shirt, was inspecting the other men. Dante figured him to be the general. Rumba, in a similar uniform but without medals, and wearing a wide-brimmed straw hat, sat on a horse beside the general. A parasol-carrying negro, in a white robe, was on a horse by Rumba's side. Two white men in white hunting outfits on horseback waited on the other side of the general.

There were about fifty unarmed black workers standing by ten donkey-drawn wagons full of equipment and sacks.

Benny told him to join the group by the wagons. Dante dressed in the shirt and pants given him by Joe and bundled his others. He had to decide what to do with his seven gold coins, leave them wrapped tightly in a kerchief in his pocket, as he usually did, or stick them up his anus for safety. His personal "safe" involved unique problems and he opted for his pocket. But he was ready to do anything to protect his only assets.

The army moved out, the general, Rumba, and the whites leading, the horsemen following, then the foot soldiers, then the wagons. Dante marched alongside one of the supply wagons, wondering where he was heading. After the first hour, he took off his shoes. By midday he removed his shirt. In the afternoon, he rolled up his trouser legs.

Hours later, when they finally stopped, Dante and the workers tended to the soldiers. Dante helped build fires and then cooked rice with three other cooks in giant boiler pots carried in the wagons. No one spoke to Dante, other than one worker who yelled orders at him, though Dante couldn't understand a word. After the meal, the workers hauled the equipment back onto the wagons and the army moved on.

When they camped in the evening, the workers repeated the process. Many of the soldiers disappeared in the brush and caught monkeys and small furry animals that looked like rats, which they cooked over their own fires. Sammy cooked for Rumba, the two white men, and the general, who slept in tents. Fortunately, they always camped near a river, and Dante was able to swim and bathe. He slept on the ground next to a wagon.

After a week, Dante considered sneaking over to Sammy and asking where they were going. However, in the middle of the eighth day, the general ordered the army to stop in the middle of an open plain, and pointed straight ahead. Far in the distance was an immense forest. The general gave a signal and the army moved ahead.

In three hours they reached it. Dante had never seen such a natural miracle, a flat plain of high grass on one side of a line and dense, towering trees on the other side. The jungle was so thick Dante thought there was no room for a person, no less a horse, to squeeze through.

The general ordered the foot soldiers into the forest. The men moved in slowly, and disappeared from view as if they had passed through a curtain to another room. The horsemen followed. Rumba, the general, and the white men waited a few moments before entering. Sammy joined them. The workers, including Dante, dropped their loads and sat.

After thirty minutes, Dante heard a scream, followed by loud shouts and musket blasts, arousing his curiosity. Ten minutes later, Sammy ran out, took Dante by the arm, told him to hush, and led him into the forest.

Once past the initial wall of trees the area opened into a different world. It was cool, moist, and dark. Dante could smell the moldy earth. A few needles of light pierced through the thick tree cover. There was an endless number of soaring trees, their shafts thick, brown, and glossy, broken at regular intervals of perhaps ten feet by a group of thick branches, with the first level of branches starting at fifteen feet.

Dante and Sammy walked towards Rumba and the general, who were looking up at the treetops, when a scream shattered the stillness. They stopped in their tracks, fifteen yards from Rumba. Beyond the king, one of the soldiers was turning in a circle with a small arrow sticking between his shoulders, trying to pull it out. Dante didn't think it had penetrated very deep, but he was certain it was painful. The soldier fell to the ground. Another soldier tried to yank it out, causing the wounded man to yell even louder.

Dante heard a chorus of chants from the heavens. He looked up and saw hundreds of black men and women, standing on the upper limbs of trees about ninety feet above them, chanting and taunting Rumba's army with spears and bows in their hands.

The general told his men to move back, out of range of the forest people's arrows and spears. Then fifty of his foot soldiers stepped forward and pointed their muskets to the sky. The people in the trees jumped into large baskets nestled between the branches or hid behind the shafts. The soldiers fired. The ear-splitting noise echoed through the jungle. A cloud of burnt powder hovered over the soldiers. The tree people re-emerged unscathed and resumed their taunts. Dante examined the trees. He saw no baskets on the first two levels of branches, then a few on the next five levels, and then many on the higher levels where most of the people stood.

Dante whispered to Sammy, "Who dey?"

Sammy whispered back, "The Bimeré tribe."

"Dey lib een de trees?"

"Not always. They live near, in a village. But they know the hunters come. So they hide in trees where the hunters can't reach them." Sammy pointed up. "See those big baskets on the branches? They are thick and strong. The Bimeré live in them. They keep their food, water, goats, and dogs there. Arrows can't penetrate the baskets, and our soldiers are not good with muskets, which are very old."

Dante recalled the stories he heard from Heritage slaves of runaways who lived in the trees of the Georgia swamps to hide from their massas and blood hounds. Dante asked, "Sammy, wut dey huntin'?"

Sammy looked twice at Dante. "What do you think? We hunt for slaves."

Dante stared at the army. He felt his insides loosen and thought he might soil his pants. He was on a slave hunt, led by a black man, no less.

Sammy said, "I don't know how the king can capture them. King Rumba won't chop down the trees. The wood is very hard and there are too many. Bimeré shoot all the choppers with arrows and spears. But king and general come a long way. They don't give up easy."

The general shouted and one of the soldiers ran to a tree with a rope ladder over his shoulder. The soldier started to shimmy up the tree, slowly, Dante thought, and almost got to the first level of branches when a veil of arrows rained down on him. He fell from the tree and writhed on the ground in agony from the seven small, crude arrows that pierced his body. Two soldiers rushed to him and carried him away. The Bimeré resumed mocking Rumba's army.

One of the white men with Rumba stepped forward and aimed his musket skyward. He took a while before pulling the trigger. The explosion reverberated through the forest. A branch beneath the Bimeré on the eighth level shattered. The tribe chanted and shook their spears.

The white man turned to the general and, pointing to the musket, spoke angrily in a foreign language. Sammy whispered to Dante, "The man does not like the weapon. He says he needs to get closer."

Dante turned to Sammy and whispered, "Wuffuh dey wan' dis tree so bad? Dey udda, smalluh trees tuh clime."

"Bimeré king is in that tree. If they capture him, others give up."

They watched as another soldier ran to the tree with a rope ladder. He climbed safely to the first level. But as he tried to tie the ladder around the branch, he lost his grip and it fell to the ground. Dante heard the king and the general groan. The soldier then shimmied unmolested to the second level of branches. Sammy told Dante the general was trying to determine the locations of the Bimeré. The soldier next climbed towards the third level. As he neared it, a Bimeré man suddenly appeared and speared the encroaching soldier in the shoulder. The soldier cried out, but lunged, grabbed the Bimeré's ankle, and pulled. Both men fell thirty-five feet to the soft earth, landing with a thud. Rumba's soldiers charged the Bimeré and hacked at him with machetes. His screams were quickly silenced. Dante saw the man's head roll on the ground. Rumba's men each picked up a piece of the body and danced in place, waving the bloody parts high over their heads. Dante turned away and vomited. The stunned Bimeré in the trees fired more arrows, scattering Rumba's men.

The general ordered another soldier to the tree. The Bimeré didn't respond. The soldier, his musket over his shoulder, climbed to the second level. Fifty soldiers on the ground fired their muskets at the baskets on the lower levels to give the soldier protection. He immediately climbed towards the third level and was about to mount the thick branch when a Bimeré warrior with a small sack ran to the soldier. He emptied its contents onto the soldier, who screamed, swiped at his neck, screamed again, then fell to the ground. A few of Rumba's soldiers ran to help, but took one look at him and ran away, hollering in fear. The fallen soldier's eyes bulged, his face contorted, his body convulsed, and his mouth exuded saliva.

The general rode over, ignoring a hail of arrows, got off his horse, and with his sword, hacked at the ground. He picked up something and taunted his soldiers, who scattered like frightened rats. The Bimeré danced in the trees.

Sammy said, "Eeeeeyah! A tape snake. It bite, you die." He stepped backwards in fear even though the snake was dead and thirty yards away.

The general returned to the king and the two white men. They huddled, deep in conversation. One of the white men pointed at the lower level of branches.

Dante felt weak in the knees and wished the Bimeré would defeat King Rumba and his savages. He decided it was time to leave the forest world. He didn't know why Sammy got him in the first place. He took about five steps when he heard, "Dante!" He turned around. Rumba pointed a finger at him. "Come here!"

Dante pointed to his own chest. "Me, massa?" The king nodded. Dante ran to him.

The king leaned forward. "You say you can climb trees?"

"Uh, no suh, massa. Ah jes' foolin'. No suh! Nebuh clime uh tree befo'. Ah 'fraid uh dem." The general leveled his rifle at Dante's chest. "Which tree, massa?"

Rumba said, "You wait here. Don't say another word."

The general barked orders and twenty of his men ran out of the forest. They returned in an hour with five stiff wooden mats, about six feet square, made of sticks and small branches and bound together by strands of hide. Dante thought they looked like small roofs. A soldier tied a length of rope to one of the mats.

The king then said to Dante, "This is what I want you to do." Dante listened intently to the instructions. He looked around to see if there was any way to escape. But he was trapped. Either he did what Rumba ordered, or he was a dead man.

Dante carried one of the wooden mats over his head and a rope ladder over his shoulder, and ran to the Bimeré king's tree. He dropped the mat at the base of the tree, put the free end of the rope in his teeth, and shimmied up to the first level of branches at a speed that amazed everyone. The Bimeré watched, giving only a few war hoots. Dante pulled up the mat, rested one end on the branches and laid it at an angle against the tree, forming a shield, under which he took shelter. The Bimeré, sensing trouble, unleashed a torrent of spears and arrows at Dante, who shivered with fear, but they bounced off or stuck in the wood. Under the protection, Dante tied the rope ladder to the main branch by the tree shaft. Then he untied the rope from the mat.

When the storm of arrows stopped, two soldiers ran to the base of the tree with another rope ladder and held a wooden mat above their heads. Dante lowered one end of the rope which the men tied to the mat. Dante slowly pulled it up, protecting the soldiers as they climbed the ladder one by one to the shield on the first level.

About fifty soldiers moved forward, and pointed their muskets up in different directions. Dante wrapped the second rope ladder around his upper body, grabbed hold of the second mat in his left hand, and said a prayer. He heard the general shout and heard an explosion of musket fire. Using his legs and one free arm, he shimmied up to the second level. The instant he reached it, he leaned the mat against the tree as he had done on the first level. As Dante breathed in relief, he felt a slicing pain in his leg and cried out. He saw an arrow sticking in his calf, his blood oozing out. He fought to avoid puking in front of three hundred soldiers and the Bimeré tribe.

Dante gritted his teeth and yanked. The pain shot through his body and he almost fell off the tree. He sat under the shelter for a minute and finally summoned the courage to look at his wound. Despite the blood, the cut wasn't deep, and his dizziness subsided. Dante unwrapped the rope ladder from his body and tied it to the main branch.

Another soldier, holding a third wooden mat over his head, ran to the tree and climbed the rope ladder to the first level as the Bimeré arrows bounced off. After a brief rest, he climbed the ladder with the mat to the second level, twenty-five feet above the ground.

Another soldier, holding the fourth mat over his head, ran to the tree and ascended the ladder to the first level.

Then, two soldiers held the fifth mat over one of the white men's head and escorted him to the tree as arrows poured from the sky. When they got to the base, the soldiers on the first level lowered their free mat till it hovered over the white man, and slowly raised it as he climbed the ladder. The white man then climbed similarly to the shelter of the second level, as soldiers on the ground fired their muskets at the trees.

The process was repeated for the second white man until both of them were huddled under the shield on the second level with Dante and a soldier. To make room, the soldier descended one level.

One of the whites removed his musket from his shoulder, peeked from behind the shield, carefully aimed towards the upper level of branches, and fired, the boom of the blast scaring the hoe cake out of Dante. One of the Bimeré sank to his knees. The white man yelled, "Yavoul!" The wounded man fell forward, off his branch, and to the earth. He tried to move, but was instantly set upon by machete-wielding soldiers, who hacked the man to pieces. The soldiers grabbed the man's body parts and performed their macabre dance. Dante was beyond puking.

The second white man switched positions with the first and fired his musket, the ball tearing into one of the giant straw baskets. A scream engulfed the forest. Three Bimeré rushed to the basket. An old man emerged and helped pull out a younger woman. She was holding her shoulder and crying. One of the Bimeré was about to pick her up when a blast from the first white man's musket frightened everyone. The woman shrieked and dropped from the tree, only to wedge between two branches on the third level. She dangled upside down, lifelessly, as Dante and the white men listened to her blood splatter on the shield above them.

Yet another blast fired by the second white man dropped another Bimeré.

The old Bimeré man called out from high above in a native language. Sammy translated for Rumba and the general. The general shouted to the white men to stop firing. In moments, hundreds of men and women appeared from baskets and from behind branches and started descending rope ladders. The two white men shook hands. The king of the Bimeré had surrendered. His queen and two sons were dead.

As the defeated tribe reached the ground, the general's soldiers tied their hands and marched them out of the forest and into the plain. They were separated into two groups, one for healthy boys and men and another for women, children, and older men. The boys and men in the first group stood in a line, and Rumba inspected each one, nodding at those he approved. The few he rejected were sent to the other group.

Rumba, through Sammy, spoke to the Bimeré king, a frail, round-shouldered man with short white hair and collapsed cheeks. He tried to stand straight and maintain his dignity, though tears ran down his face. He nodded as Sammy talked to him. Then, he approached the group of women and small children and spoke. Several of the women, some with children, formed yet another group. They had chosen to join their husbands on a cruel journey to a strange land, and a lifetime of bondage. In all, the hunt led to the capture of 120 Bimeré.

The soldiers put wooden yokes around the male captives' necks, and connected the yokes with rope of vines and tree roots, forming a coffle or slave train. As Dante trembled in horror, Rumba rode over and commended him for his contribution. "Very good, Dante. When I visit this tribe again in fifteen years, I will be certain to bring you."

Then Rumba, his army, and his bounty marched to the next target, leaving the defeated king and his shattered remaining subjects to watch their departure.

Over the next two days, Rumba visited two more tribes. The kings of both decided to pay tribute rather than fight Rumba's superior army. With 212 slaves in tow, Rumba began the return to his factory on the coast.

The march back was a nightmare for Dante. He couldn't look into the faces of those he helped capture as he dished out rice for them. On the first night, he lay on the ground, and thought about home. He wondered about Andrew, and if Miss Amy had opened the restaurant.

*   *   *

Joseph dreaded approaching the table, but Amy said he had to. The restaurant was so busy she couldn't switch things around. She promised she would help him. He took a deep breath. "Good evening, gentlemen. May I get you something to drink?"

"Joseph!" Charlie Lamar yelled, "Since when did you become a waiter?"

Joseph hoped the burning sensation in his face didn't reveal itself to the people at the table. "Since another waiter got sick an hour ago and Amy needed help."

Charlie said, "I guess helping out the wife around the house came in handy."

John Tucker, bank director and new owner of Drakies Plantation on the Savannah River, said, "Well, you make a fine looking one, if I must say." The other men at the table, Richard Akin, John Montmollin, George Wylly, Nelson Trowbridge, Henry Dubignon, and Daniel Stewart, laughed in chorus.

Joseph said, "Very funny, John. Now, who'd like a drink?"

Charlie said, "Why not bring us a few bottles of red wine. Some French stuff."

Joseph said, "Three bottles of red French stuff it is," and walked away.

Charlie called out, "Thank you, garçon!" The others chortled.

Charlie was in good spirits. Joseph knew it couldn't be due to his financial situation. That was as bleak as ever. More likely, it was due to his recent notoriety.

The first seizure of the *Rawlins* as a suspected slaver made newspapers in the South. But Charlie's application to bring in African apprentices and his subsequent public rebuke of Howell Cobb brought Charlie's name to folks around the country.

A second mission by the *Rawlins* the previous May didn't fare any better. During a stop in St. Thomas, the supercargo absconded with the ship without clearance, leaving the abandoned captain cursing on the pier. The ship eventually appeared in Savannah in late July without papers and was seized. Newspapers throughout the country reported that Lamar's ship had deposited a cargo of Africans in Cuba. Joseph doubted this.

On top of that, Charlie had become involved in the *Echo* controversy. The *Echo* was a slave ship that picked up 473 slaves in Africa in early July 1858, and was caught off the coast of Cuba in late August with only 318 souls still alive. The ship and the survivors, many of whom were malnourished and sick with dysentery, were taken to Charleston and kept in quarantine.

While the crew of eighteen awaited trial, officials had to decide what to do with the surviving Africans. There was no place in America for them to go. By law, they couldn't remain in South Carolina. The only option was to send them back to Africa.

The American Colonization Society asked the government for fifty thousand dollars to settle the survivors in Liberia and train them in industrial pursuits.

Charlie wrote a letter to several newspapers saying he would *pay* the government fifty thousand dollars for the Africans for a term of years and teach them industrial pursuits. Charlie's offer was widely read but never considered.

Charlie was still broke, but he had gained a national reputation.

The evening wasn't as bad as Joseph had expected. Once he served Charlie's table, the men ate, talked in low voices, and ignored Joseph. When Joseph brought the bill at the end of the meal, Charlie laid down some money and asked, "Joseph, are you going to help us on the fair this year? It's already October."

Joseph, annoyed that Charlie paid for the dinner but was unable to repay him, said, "I don't know, Charlie. I'm pretty busy, but I'll try."

Charlie said, "Try to join us. We can use you."

As the men left the restaurant, Charlie saw Amy, smiled, and said, "Miss McBain, the food was excellent and the service even better. And I do like the name."

Amy's eyes followed Charlie as he left the restaurant. She wondered what he meant by that. And she wondered if Dante were still alive.

*   *   *

One evening during the return march, Dante sat by himself, his head hanging between his knees, still depressed by the hunt. He was startled by a light tap on his head. He looked up to see a young girl he guessed to be five years old. She was naked with wide white eyes, short black curly hair, and a finger lodged in her nostril. She coyly twisted her body back and forth.

Dante asked her name. She looked blankly at him, still twisting. Dante pointed to himself and said, "Dante." Then he pointed to her. Twist, twist. Dante pointed at himself again. "Me, Dante." She said something that sounded like "Neeka," and Dante decided to call her that. He then tried to make the little girl laugh. He made faces, rolled on the ground, tried to make a figurine out of a twig, but Neeka just stared at him.

For the rest of the trip, whenever they camped, Neeka stood by Dante's side. Sometimes, he picked her up and let her help stir the pot. He gave her his chef's hat to wear. It was so big it rested on her shoulders, so he cut two holes in it for her eyes. After that, Neeka never took her hat off, except to sleep. She sat with it, marched with it, stirred rice with it, bathed in the river with it, even tried to eat with it on, though she had to tilt it up to reveal her mouth.

When it was time to sleep, Neeka returned to her mother. She walked by her mother's side during the march. Occasionally, she tried to visit her captive father, but she was chased away by Rumba's guards.

Finally, after ten dusty, dry, sweaty days, they reached Rumba's compound. Rumba, Sammy, the white men, and Dante stayed while the general and the rest of the army marched the captured Africans to the prison-like barracoon, where they would be held with others until Corrie picked them up.

It saddened Dante to wave goodbye to Neeka, and he let her keep his hat. But his heart had been torn apart many times in the past weeks, and there was nothing left to tear.

That night, lying in his hut, Dante decided to tell Rumba he was leaving for Liberia. He became angry thinking about the role Rumba played in capturing Africans. He never wanted to see another slave. He wanted to live among free men.

The next morning, October 15, Dante, still perturbed at Rumba, went to the king's house and told the African he was leaving. Rumba said he had many uses for Dante, the great cook and tree climber. Dante said he was still leaving. Rumba told Dante to go to his hut. Dante, his anger raging, called Rumba, "Uh fat, nigguh slabe catchuh."

Rumba screamed, "Benny! Benny! Come here now! Bring your rifle!"

In seconds, Benny charged into the room. Rumba said, "Shoot this little pig."

Benny grabbed Dante by the hair and pulled him to the door. Dante hollered as he tried to wrestle from Benny's grip.

Rumba shouted, "Wait, Benny. I have a better idea." Benny threw Dante to the floor. Rumba whispered in Benny's ear. Benny laughed so loud, he had to sit.

*   *   *

The *Wanderer* sailed down the African coast, stopping at some ports along the way, before anchoring off Benguela, about two hundred miles south of St. Paul de Loando. Captain Brown sent his men ashore to walk on land, get drunk, and let off masculine steam with African prostitutes. The voyage back to America would be long and trying, and the men needed some excitement to see them through it.

It was during their stop in Benguela when Gisseppe started to feel feverish. At first the men laughed at Joe, saying the African princess of his dreams with whom he had spent a passion-filled ten minutes had left him something to remember her by. Demetry the Greek asked Joe if he would kindly avoid stirring the evening stew with his dick. Joe laughed along with the men, but sensed his fever had nothing to do with his love-making.

Dr. Brent, who had been hired to provide medical treatment to the crew and slaves, gave Joe medicine and told him to rest. But a few days later, when the *Wanderer* raised anchor to sail back to the Congo River, Joe was unable to stand to cook the evening meal. He lay in his bunk, alternately shivering and burning up. It took all his strength and concentration to pray for his family. A few days later, as the ship neared the mouth of the Congo, Joe died. He was given a proper burial at sea, wrapped in a sheet.

There was a pall among the crew. The loss of a good mate and cook had a sobering effect. Basseli the Greek, who helped Gisseppe in the galley after Dante had left, took over the cooking duties. Despite his claims, Basseli was no cook, and the crew soon began to dread the voyage to America. Corrie was also concerned.

He didn't want to eat slop for six weeks either. But he had bigger problems to deal with.

The *Wanderer* returned to the mouth of the Congo River early on the morning of October 11. They passed the *Rufus Soule*, an American merchant vessel, and they exchanged salutes. By the afternoon, they were near Pont du Lain. They dropped anchor and the crew started on another critical part of the mission. They had to lay the slave decks in four days without being boarded by a squadron ship.

Slave decks were the architectural wonder of the illegal slave trade. They allowed the seemingly impossible: the stowing of an unimaginable number of people in an extremely limited space. In a macabre sense, the decks required symmetry and proportion. But instead of monumentality, they commanded inhumanity.

When the foreign slave trade was legal in America, ships were built with the purpose of transporting large numbers of Africans. When the trade became illegal, ships, usually mercantile vessels, had to be converted to slavers. Several issues governed these conversions. First, the ship could not look like a slave ship, lest they draw the attention of the squadron in Africa or the revenue cutters in America. Second, they had to be fast enough to outrun a government ship. Third, the hull had to be convertible to carry slaves, since, until the ship was ready to board human cargo, it had to look like a commercial vessel to snooping officials. The *Wanderer* introduced another challenge; it had been designed as a luxury schooner, not a cargo carrier.

Corrie had all the bulkheads in the hull taken down. The crew built a sturdy, new bulkhead creating an aft section twenty feet long and fore section about seventy feet long, excluding the forepeak.

Corrie and his sixteen men would live in the aft section. As they would work in shifts, all the men would not be present at one time. Still, the voyage back would be cramped.

The five hundred Africans would stay in the fore section. The crew built ten-foot-wide shelves along the port and starboard bulkheads. Each shelf allowed two rows of seventy Africans, lying on their sides, spoon style, toe to head, for a total of 280 people. The remaining 220 would sleep on the hull deck.

This slave deck design differed from the traditional one, which placed a deck around the entire interior perimeter of the ship about four feet beneath the underside of the top deck. However, Captain Corrie did not want sick Africans living above him.

By the afternoon of October 15, the decks were completed. As the ship received its final delivery of water and wood, Corrie, Brent, Beman, and Farnum went ashore to see their friends in Pont du Lain one last time. They were greeted warmly and toasted in the Kensington Palace.

The locals talked about the sinking of the American merchant ship, the *Rufus Soule*, three days before. The British Squadron ship, the *Viper*, had boarded it on the evening of October 11, slightly north of the mouth of the Congo. The British opened the hatches, took the American flag down, and removed the crew to the *Viper*. The British then set the *Rufus Soule* aflame. The next morning they fired cannon into her side and watched her sink. The *Viper* then sailed to Kabenda, about 30 miles north of the Congo River, and on the morning of October 14, landed the crew of the *Rufus Soule*, which included two Americans, on a beach.

This discussion convinced Corrie to leave immediately. He and his men bade farewell and headed for the rowboat. As they crossed the street, they saw Benny walking towards them, prodding a bound and blindfolded black man with the barrel of a musket. As they got closer, Corrie could see that the man was Dante.

Corrie stepped in front of them. "Benny! Is that Dante?"

Benny looked up and spotted Corrie. He grabbed Dante by the shirt to stop him. "Yes, boss. I'm taking him to Foulah musselman. A gift from Rumba."

Dante moved his head side-to-side towards the voice. "Massa Capin?"

Benny poked Dante hard with the rifle. "Keep mouth shut, sabe!"

Corrie asked, "What's wrong, Benny? Wasn't Dante a good cook?"

"Massa Capin . . . Ooouch!"

"I say, quiet!" Benny yelled after another hard jab. He said to Corrie, "When he return from trip, he insult the king. Make Rumba very, very mad, I tell you, boss. First, Rumba want me to kill him. Then he say, give Dante to Foulah king. Rumba say maybe sore arsehole rest of life help cure big mouth."

Farnum, Brent, and Beman had to turn away to hide their laughter.

Corrie wanted to laugh, too, but he had another thing on his mind. "Listen, Benny. I'm responsible for sending Dante to Rumba. I'll take him back."

"I don't know, boss. He want Dante to be a slave to Foulah musselman."

Corrie reached into his pants pocket and pulled out a coin. "Benny, I want you to do me a favor. Take this gold coin." Benny stared at Corrie's hand, but took the coin. Then Corrie removed his jacket. "Benny, Rumba liked this New York Yacht Club jacket. Take it to him as a gift from me. Tell him I apologize for Dante, and I will punish him worse than any Foulah king could ever do. You have my word."

Benny took the jacket. "Rumba like jacket very much. But you must promise to punish Dante very bad."

Corrie placed his hand on his chest. "You have my word, Benny."

"Okay, boss. Me sabe." Benny pushed Dante towards Corrie and said, "I see you in a few days." He returned to Rumba's palace, yacht club jacket in hand.

Farnum removed the blindfold from Dante and untied his hands. Dante got on his knees and started to cry. "Massa Capin, Lawd hab mussy."

Corrie said, "Get on your feet, Dante. We're in a hurry."

As they rowed back to the *Wanderer*, Dante said, "Massa Capin, ah gladee ah yuh. Massa Rumba nuttin' but uh slabe huntuh. Wus' t'ing ah eber see." Dante explained his experience, though the white men showed little interest.

Corrie then told Dante about Gisseppe. Dante had difficulty swallowing when he heard the news.

The crew stood bug-eyed as they watched Dante climb up the ladder to the ship. When Dante reached the deck, he waved to the stunned men.

Corrie said to Captain Brown, "Pull the anchor and set the sails. Let's get out of this river." Brown yelled orders, and Brooks repeated them. The crew scurried to their stations. Then Corrie said to Dante, "Come with me, Dante. I need to have a word with you. Join us, Captain Farnum."

They took the aft companionway to the newly designed sleeping quarters, with all the beds and bunks crammed in. Before Dante could say a word, Corrie asked him to be the cook on the return voyage.

Dante didn't hesitate. "Massa Capin, ah cyan' gwi' tuh Jawjuh. Dey hang me."

Corrie didn't want to see Dante hang, but he needed a cook for the return trip, and the negro was his only choice. He said, "We're not going to Georgia, Dante. We're going to Cuba, where you'll be free with other negroes. Cuba's a beautiful place!"

"Den ah cook fuh oonuh, Massa Capin. Oonuh sabe me f'um de Foulah man."

Corrie slapped Dante on the back. "Excellent, Dante. I knew I could count on you. Now let me apprise you of some things. There have been some changes. You will notice that we redesigned the ship. After you cook tonight and tomorrow, I want you to return here to your bunk. I won't be locking you in a storeroom, but I don't want you coming on deck till I tell you. During the trip, you'll do a lot of cooking. Plan on serving the crew and me at seven in the morning and four in the evening. We'll pick up some guests in a day or two. They take their meals at nine in the morning and at five in the afternoon. Because we have many new guests, we need to feed them in shifts. Some of the crew will help you."

Dante exhaled and relaxed. Anything would be better than the slave hunt.

The *Wanderer* reached the ocean by the morning of October 16, and sailed ten miles south of the Congo's mouth. Captain Brown kept one eye on the coast for the signal, and the other eye on the ocean, for the squadron. At about four o'clock in the afternoon, he saw three fires on the shore, each about one hundred yards apart.

"That's it, they're ready!" Brown called, looking through his scope. "Brooks, take her in. I'm getting Captain Corrie."

Brooks maneuvered the *Wanderer* to about forty yards from shore, as close as her nine-and-a-half foot draft allowed, and dropped anchor. Corrie, Farnum, Beman, Brent, and four of the crew took a lifeboat to shore. Benny was there to greet them. He escorted them beyond the tree line to an open area, which was packed with naked African men, women, and a few children. Their heads and bodies had been shaved to prevent the spread of lice and disease. Because there was only one purchaser, they did not have to be branded.

Rumba was there, wearing his New York Yacht Club jacket, ready to conclude the business. The *Wanderer* men were not smiling. This was the most crucial part of the trip. They had to inspect the Africans, settle with Rumba, and board five hundred people and additional equipment without being detected by the squadron.

Dr. Brent examined each captive, pulling at lips to inspect teeth and gums, and feeling heads and bodies for lumps. Farnum and Benny kept a count of the sex and estimated age of each African approved by the doctor. The accepted slaves, hands bound, were taken to one of Rumba's rowboats. Two of Rumba's soldiers stood guard at each end of the large boats. As soon as twenty-eight people were boarded, Rumba's men rowed out to the *Wanderer*.

The Africans climbed the rope ladder onto the deck, where they were greeted by three shotgun barrels. They were led to the fore hatch and directed down into the darkness of the companionway, where they saw three more barrels.

Juan had them step from the companionway onto the port slave deck and walk along it as far as possible. There, Miguel had them lie down on their right sides, one by one, knees bent, tucked up against each another. Once the space along the port bulkhead had been packed, they started another row on the same shelf, head to toe. Dante, lying in his bunk, heard footsteps and banging, and wondered if the crew was boarding livestock.

More slaves were placed similarly on the port hold deck, underneath the slave deck. Next, the starboard slave deck was filled with males. Lastly, the women and children were placed on the remaining space of the starboard hold deck. When the operation was completed, 490 souls had been crammed into the stifling tomb.

With Juan, Miguel, and Demetry standing guard, three other crewmen brought down three tubs, each about four feet long, three feet wide and three feet deep, and placed them in the center aisle. Miguel clapped his hands and the Africans craned their heads to see him. Miguel then squatted over the side of one of the tubs, gave a little grunt and pointed into the tub, and nodded his head affirmatively. He wasn't sure he made his point, so he lowered his trousers and urinated in the tub. The Africans understood.

By late morning of October 17, 1858, all the slaves had been boarded and stowed. Corrie had done it. He had out-smarted them all, the port collectors, the squadron, the British. He considered having an early glass of brandy when he heard Brown shout, "Captain Corrie, a ship to starboard. It's under steam and it's making right at us!"

*   *   *

Flag Officer Conover had one of the more thankless jobs in the United States Navy. He had but four ships to patrol thousands of miles of coast, rivers, and inlets. Assigning his ships was difficult, often requiring guess-work. The weather was stifling hot, fevers rampant, supplies scarce, and there were no places nearby for his men to rest and recover. On top of this, Conover had to deal with the British boarding American vessels.

The captain of the *Sea View* had passed Commodore Wise's message about the *Wanderer* to Conover on September 25 at St. Paul de Loando. But it was not until October 7 that Conover gave written orders to Commodore Totten of the *SS Vincennes*, and it was not until October 9 that the ship left St. Paul de Loando. By October 14 the *Vincennes* was sailing in the waters off Kabenda when Totten spotted the *HMS Viper*, which had just deposited the crew of the *Rufus Soule* on a desolate, nearby beach. Totten boarded the British ship. The British Commodore gave a full account of the *Kate Ellen* without mentioning the *Rufus Soule* incident. Satisfied with the report, Totten continued to search for slavers along the coast of Kabenda.

Early on the morning of October 17, Totten decided to sail to the south of the Congo River, just as the *Wanderer* was loading its human cargo. Before he could give orders, a small boat rowed up to the *Vincennes* and delivered a message stating that two Americans had been taken from the *Rufus Soule* by the British ship *Viper* and had been stranded on a nearby beach. Totten sent men to retrieve the Americans. By late morning, the *Vincennes* finally headed south, looking for the *Viper* and an explanation about the *Rufus Soule*. Then they spotted a ship, a beautiful yacht, lying off the coast. Totten knew it had to be the *Wanderer*. He ordered his men to seize it.

Corrie called, "Let's get out of here, Captain Brown!"

Brown yelled commands to the crew, and they jumped to action. "Hurry mates, they're getting closer."

Corrie looked on as the *Vincennes* got within range of their guns. But the *Wanderer's* sails finally billowed. Once she was under way, the *Vincennes* didn't have a prayer of catching her, even with a swollen belly. Let your cruisers catch me if they can!

Once Corrie was certain the ship was safe, he visited Dante below and explained that the *Wanderer* was carrying 490 Africans to Cuba, to a better life, away from slave hunters like Rumba. Corrie said the Africans were depending on Dante to cook for them. After Corrie left, Dante sat in a daze. He had been so happy to be back on the *Wanderer* and headed for Cuba. Instead, he was cooking for slaves again. Captain Corrie had lied to him. Dante went topside.

The deck looked as it always had: sails unfurled and snapping in the breeze and the crew at their stations, though Miguel and Juan were standing at the fore hatch holding shotguns. He started to build a fire in the brick stove. He heard shouting from below. Then he heard an explosion. In a minute, Demetry emerged backwards from the hatch with a shotgun pointed down. Then a black male appeared, also ascending the companionway backwards, and bent from the waist. He was carrying something, as it turned out, a pair of black arms. Soon, the top half of an African man's body, its head swaying lifelessly, was in clear view. Then another African appeared, holding the legs. As the men gained the deck, Demetry motioned them to the side of the ship. They tossed the body into the ocean. The Africans returned to the hold.

The crew had to set an example right away. This would be a long journey across an ocean while guarding many people. Absolute, immediate subservience to every command was critical. The first African man who hesitated at an order was shot.

Dante hunched over, started cooking, and prayed to God.

In less than an hour, the first batch of food was ready. Brown shouted to Miguel, who yelled into the hold. About one hundred naked or near-naked women and children climbed out of the hatch. They walked single-file towards the middle of the deck, where Dr. Brent examined them. Those whose health was questioned were given medicine. They were then released to eat. Mr. Beman, in addition to acting as Corrie's interpreter and counsel in dealings with African kings, kept count of the slaves at each meal.

The prisoners went to a pile, took a wooden spoon and dish, and walked by Dante, who, with head down, scooped out rice and beans for each. The women sat in groups on the deck. When they finished, they returned their spoons and dishes to the pile. They walked to a wooden tub and were each given a pint of water to drink. After they finished, the women and children were allowed to remain on deck.

Then a group of fifty males in leg chains climbed on deck, and, under guard, followed the same process as the women. However, the men were ordered back into the hold after their water ration, and the next group emerged. The process continued for three hours without incident until everyone was checked, fed, and given water. Dante realized the crew was experienced in controlling a ship full of captives.

As Dante watched the women on deck, his mouth dropped open. He thought he recognized some of them as the Bimeré he had fed for ten days. He waited to make sure, since their shaved heads changed their appearance. But he had no doubt. He looked at the children. Staring at him was a hairless Neeka. He called out her name.

She held up her little hand and slowly opened and closed it in a wave. Neeka said something to her mother, who nodded, and the girl walked to Dante. He picked her up and hugged her.

The next few weeks were orderly. Each day was the same as far as Dante was concerned: wake up at 5:30, wash, cook for the crew, cook for the slaves, clean up, cook for the crew, cook for the slaves, clean up, and go to bed at ten o'clock.

Dante tried to be friendly to the captives, but many of the Bimeré tribe recognized him as being a part of Rumba's army and ignored him. Some of the crew occasionally nodded to him, but Corrie was the only one to engage him in conversation, however slight.

There were aspects of the voyage that especially disturbed Dante. In the morning and the evening, African men carried the three tubs from the hold and emptied them off the back of the ship. The stench of so much human waste was overpowering. Of course, that's how the hold always smelled. In time it seeped into the rest of the ship.

Even worse was when an African became ill, most commonly from dysentery. As soon as anyone was too weak to leave the hold, or complained of bloody diarrhea, Dr. Brent issued medicine. If it wasn't effective, the slave would get so weak he couldn't make it to the tubs. Soon, he would be covered in his own waste, making the hold even more objectionable. Other Africans would have to carry the sick person onto the deck for one last examination. If Brent determined that recovery was unlikely, the slave was thrown overboard.

One time, after becoming immune to the procedure, Dante watched the body as it hit the water. In seconds, a shiver of sharks was at the surface, tearing away at it. The water turned red, and stayed that way, even after the body was gone. Dante wondered if the horrors of the trip would ever end.

Four weeks into the journey, Neeka's father became ill with dysentery. Dr. Brent's medicine didn't take hold, and the African got worse. He was carried on deck, given a final examination, and unceremoniously tossed overboard. His wife was on deck and screamed. She had to be restrained by other black women. Neeka quietly watched her hysterical mother.

Neeka's mother never recovered. She sat on the deck during the day and moaned, taking notice of only Neeka, who she kept by her side. After refusing food and water for several days, Neeka's mother grew too weak to walk by herself, and had to be carried by the other females. Neeka walked by their side, holding her mother's toe in her hand. Dr. Brent gave a last examination to the dying woman. He peered into her open but cloudy eyes and felt her wrist. He pinched her neck and she jerked, but immediately returned to her sleepy state. Brent nodded to Juan and Miguel, who picked up the woman and threw her into the ocean. Neeka ran to Dante and wrapped her arms around his leg. Dante felt her tremble and patted her back.

After that, Neeka spent all her time on deck near Dante, but she soon stopped eating. Three mornings later, the black woman who had been caring for her brought the frail girl to Dr. Brent. Brent examined her, felt her pulse and heart, and then said some words to Beman. Brent then turned to Juan and nodded. Juan moved to pick up the child.

Dante, observing this, ran over and stepped in front of Juan before he could take the girl. Dante turned to the doctor and pleaded, "Please, massa, don' hu't dat gal chile. Ah tek huh."

Dr. Brent said, "Get the hell out of here, Dante."

Juan clutched Dante by the arm and tried to pull him away, but Dante pushed Juan to the deck. Juan got up and charged Dante, and the two started to wrestle, almost falling on Neeka. The crew shouted, drawing Captain Farnum to the scene. He separated them.

Dante held Farnum's arm, "Please, massa. Leabe dat chile."

Dr. Brent spoke up. "The girl's near death, Captain. It's just a matter of time."

Farnum pulled his arm away from Dante's grip and grabbed a clump of his hair. "You heard the doctor, Dante. Get back to work. Don't make me tell you again, or you'll join her."

Corrie, hearing the commotion, walked over. "Do we have a problem?"

Farnum released Dante and explained, "Both this child's parents have died and the girl's stopped eating. Dr. Brent says she's about to die. It's time for a bath."

Dante lifted the dying girl from the deck and rocked her in his arms. "Ah kin git she tuh eat, Massa Capin. Ah hab money. Ah buy she an' tek she wid me tuh Cooba. She muh chile."

Corrie shook his head. "Dante, the girl wants to die, or she'd eat. The doctor says she's suffering."

"Ah kin git she tuh nyam, massa." Dante handed the girl to Dr. Brent, ran to the pots, scooped out some rice in his hand, and returned. He took Neeka from the doctor, cradled her in one arm and squatted on the deck. He put some rice on her lips and whispered, "Please, Neeka. Eat dese rice fuh me. Please." Neeka, her eyelids half shut, didn't respond. Dante gently pressed more rice on her lips. "Please, Neeka." Everyone on the deck, Africans included, stopped to watch as the white kernels, one by one, fell from Neeka's lips and stuck onto her bony black chest. Dante tried to press rice into her mouth, but the child made no attempt to chew. Dante kissed her cheek and sobbed.

The men stood by and let Dante cry for a minute. Corrie kneeled next to him and said, "I'm sorry, Dante. There's no hope." He stood and nodded to Juan, who took Neeka from Dante without a fight. Juan carried the girl to the side of the ship and threw her away.

Corrie said, "Dante, you need to get to work." Dante wiped his eyes on his shirt, stood, and returned to the potboilers.

Farnum followed Corrie below and asked, "He still thinks he's going to Cuba?"

Corrie said, "No one's told him otherwise."

"What happens when we get to Georgia? We're only a few days away."

"We'll deal with it when we get there."

Farnum said, "There's nothing to deal with. I'll do it before we land."

Two days later, on the afternoon of November 28, after forty-three days at sea, Brooks spotted land. Dante stood away from the crew and admired the long-awaited sight. He was almost there. He studied the tide.

By six p.m. the *Wanderer* dropped anchor near the Cumberland Island lighthouse on the Georgia coast. Corrie lowered his spyglass and said to Farnum, "Let's wait here for ten more minutes. The pilot is supposed to be waiting for our arrival to take us in. If he doesn't show, we'll have to take a lifeboat in and find one."

Farnum took the spyglass from Corrie, scanned the water, and lowered it. "I agree. I better take care of Dante."

Corrie asked, "You're sure there's nothing we can do?"

Farnum gave the spyglass back to Corrie. "He knows too much."

Corrie turned away and squinted into the spyglass. "Be quick about it."

Thirty minutes later, Farnum returned. Corrie, still scoping the water, said, "No sign of a pilot. I've got to go ashore and find one. Did you take care of Dante?"

"No. I searched all over. Not a trace of him. No one else has seen him."

Corrie turned to Farnum. "No trace? Where in the world could he be?"

Farnum shrugged. "If he's on the ship, we'll find him as we unload the Africans, or when we clean it up. If he's in the water, he'll never survive long enough to reach shore."

Corrie said, "No, I imagine he couldn't."

Dante lay on the bulkhead plank as it bobbed in the ocean. He didn't trust Corrie. He couldn't risk that the captain would let him stay in Cuba, and Dante couldn't go back to Georgia. So he stuffed his gold coins up his anus, took a large board from the hold, jumped overboard in the darkness as the tide went in, and floated to a new life in Cuba.

CHAPTER 25

Cashing In

November 1858-January 1859

"Chollie, they're here!"

Lamar looked up and saw Trow standing in his office doorway, smiling like a boy on Christmas morning. Behind him, looking like the wild man from the circus with months of hair growth and a deep sunburn, was Captain Nicholas Brown. Charlie murmured, "Thank God."

Despite national fame from his efforts to import Africans, Charlie never strayed far from financial ruin. His last hope was the *Wanderer*. Over the past week, he doubted he would ever see her again. But instantly invigorated at the sight of Brown, Charlie bounced into action. "Let's get to work. We don't have a moment to spare. Trow, find Captain Stevenson at the wharf and tell him to have the steam tug ready by nine o'clock. I'll get Tucker, and I'll send word to Montmollin that we'll have the Africans to him in a few days. Meet back here at ten to nine."

Charlie watched Trow run from the office. He waved Brown in and closed the door. "How did it go, Captain?"

Brown said, "Almost as planned. Captain Farnum said 409 were landed. A few are sick and may not make it."

Charlie grinned. That meant a gross of about two hundred fifty thousand dollars. "Well done. Stay here and make yourself comfortable. You can tell me all about it on the way to Jekyl."

It took several hours for the tug owner to find a captain, but by one o'clock in the morning of December 1, Charlie, Trow, Brown, and Tucker were finally on their way. As Captain Christie piloted the *Lamar* out of the river and along the coast, Brown described the voyage. "It was difficult at the end. We were almost out of food and water. We got to the coast just in time. One more breath of air from that hold and I was going overboard."

Charlie wrinkled his nose at the thought. "Exactly when did you reach Jekyl?"

Brown said, "November 28, two days ago, at six o'clock, almost dark."

"Was a pilot at the lighthouse to take you in?"

Brown shook his bushy head. "No. Apparently, there was a problem."

Charlie stoked his freshly trimmed beard. "What problem?"

Jekyl Island is about seventy miles south of Savannah and had been owned by the Dubignon family since the 1790s. The plantation's main crop was sea island cotton. By 1858 John Dubignon, Henry's older brother, was the only family member residing there, living in a house on the northwestern side of the island, overlooking Jekyl Creek. He and an overseer ran the plantation, the net proceeds from which were divided amongst John, Henry, and their sister Catherine Dubignon Hazelhurst.

The island measures about eight miles long and one-and-a-half miles wide. The sandy eastern shore faces the Atlantic Ocean. The western side is separated from the Georgia mainland by Jekyl Creek and several miles of tidal marshlands. Two miles south of Jekyl, across the St. Andrews Sound, is Little Cumberland Island. John Dubignon was connected to civilization by a five-mile boat ride north to Brunswick harbor.

Other than John Dubignon, the overseer, and family members, no one had reason to set foot on Jekyl, though on rare occasions duck hunters tried to use it.

Lamar knew he needed a desolate place to land the Africans. There were few more so than Jekyl, and Charlie enlisted the services of his friends John and Henry Dubignon.

They planned to bring the *Wanderer* to the coast, have a pilot navigate her through St. Andrews Sound, past the southern tip of Jekyl, to the mouth of the Little Satilla River, which is hidden from the coastal shipping lanes, and land their cargo. To ensure that there would be no surprise visitors when the *Wanderer* was due, John Dubignon placed a notice in the *Savannah Morning News* on November 23, warning against any trespassers or hunters coming on the island.

Once the *Wanderer* had been piloted to the mouth of the Little Satilla, she could only be spotted by local fishermen. The sooner the ship was on the western side of the island, the better. A ready pilot was critical.

Brown explained, "Captain Corrie and Brooks took a lifeboat to the lighthouse but only a keeper named Harris was there. Corrie said he needed a pilot to take a yacht across the sound. Corrie looked so ragged that Harris got suspicious and said he couldn't do it, but said he knew a pilot, James Clubb, on Jekyl who could. The three rowed across St. Andrews Sound in the dark and found the pilot at the Jekyl lighthouse. Corrie told him he was the captain of the *Wanderer*, which was in distress and out of provisions and water. Clubb was also suspicious and refused. Corrie suggested they go to John Dubignon, who would vouch for him. Clubb agreed. The Dubignon brothers and Trow were at the house. Clubb consented to bring the vessel in. Then Corrie admitted the ship carried a cargo of Africans, figuring it was best not to surprise him. Clubb demanded five hundred dollars for the job."

Trow confirmed this. "That's right, Chollie. I said no, it's a twenty dollar job, but Henry and John said they'd pay it to land the Africans before anyone saw them."

Charlie nodded. Brown continued, "Clubb said he'd have to wait for daybreak and Corrie and Brooks returned to the ship. Clubb came as promised and in a few hours he brought the *Wanderer* to the Little Satilla, about two hundred yards from the Jekyl shore."

"I wonder why Dubignon didn't have a pilot?" Charlie mused out loud. He then asked Brown, "Who else knows about the *Wanderer*?"

"Just Harris and Clubb, the lighthouse keeper and the pilot, as far as I know."

Charlie exhaled loudly. "And then?"

"We used the two *Wanderer* lifeboats and Dubignon's yawl to bring the Africans ashore. That took much of the day. We built a camp off the beach where no one could spot the Africans from the water. They're there now, with half of the crew."

Charlie asked, "Where's the ship?"

Brown replied, "Clubb brought it a few miles up the Little Satilla, completely hidden from the coast. The other half of the crew is there, cleaning her and putting her back to her original condition. It's going to take some doing to get the stink out, tear out the slave decks and replace all the bulkheads."

"How are the Africans?"

"Most are healthy. A few need attention. Dr. Brent and Mr. Beman took off for Brunswick the moment we hit land and Captain Farnum paid them. So Henry Dubignon fetched his brother-in-law, Dr. Hazelhurst, to look at them."

Charlie slowly rubbed his hands together, pleased with Brown's report. He turned to Trowbridge. "Trow, when is the other boat arriving?"

"In a day or two. They're anxious to pick up their share."

Charlie yawned and extended his legs. "Anything else, Captain?"

Brown yawned as well. "That's all I know. After the Africans were set up in the camp, Trow and I caught the *St. Johns* just past midnight to get you."

Charlie said, "Good. Let's get some rest and we'll talk more at Jekyl." He pulled the front of his hat over his eyes. All he had to do was distribute the slaves to his customers and get the *Wanderer* back to Charleston. Things were finally turning his way.

After a brief stop at Brunswick, the *Lamar* entered Jekyl Creek and arrived at Dubignon's Landing on the afternoon of Wednesday, December 1. John and Henry Dubignon, Corrie, and Farnum were there to greet Charlie. They went to Dubignon's one-story, tabby house while the tug took Brown south to the camp.

The men sat around a table in the dining room. Charlie congratulated Corrie, who looked as wild as Brown. "Captain Brown informed me of your trip. Well done. It's time to cash in, and not a moment too soon. How many Africans are in the camp?"

Corrie held a piece of paper with numbers on it and replied, "At last count, 404. Eighty died in passage. Five have died here. When are you going to take yours away?"

Charlie said, "I told Montmollin that we'd arrive late on December 3." Charlie took the paper from Corrie's hand and studied it for a moment before handing it back. He then asked, "When are you taking the ship back to Charleston? We've got to get her out of Georgia without raising any suspicions. Aside from the Africans, she's the biggest piece of evidence"

Corrie slapped Charlie's shoulder. "All taken care of. The men are working on the ship right now, getting her back to her original state. She had some damage to the main mast the day before we arrived. We should have no problem getting her to Brunswick. We'll probably need to tow her to Charleston. Repairs might take too long."

Charlie's brow creased at the mention of repairs, but he had no choice. "As soon as I get back to Savannah, I'll arrange to have her towed. Do you anticipate problems getting clearance?"

Corrie grinned. "I just sailed half way around the world and back without a problem. I'll get her cleared through Brunswick as well."

Charlie always liked Corrie's attitude. "I guess I needn't have asked." Lamar turned to Trow. "When are you taking your Africans, Trow?"

"I'm arranging that with Akin. Should be in a few days."

Charlie commented, "Good. That will get all the Africans out of here. Captain Farnum, do you have money left to pay the men and yourself?"

Farnum dangled a pouch and laid it on the table. "Yes, and a little left over."

Corrie said, "Put a hundred dollars aside for a pilot to bring the *Wanderer* to Brunswick."

"When does the crew depart?" Charlie continued.

Corrie explained, "The men still here on Jekyl will load the Africans and accompany you to Montmollin's plantation. After that, they'll leave. Since we'll tow the ship to Charleston, the men cleaning the *Wanderer* will disappear after the ship docks at Brunswick."

Satisfied with the plan, Charlie stood, stretched his arms and said, "I need some sleep. Then, I just might find some time to write my next letter to Howell Cobb." The men laughed. "Tomorrow, I'll have a look at our Africans."

The next morning, the men took John Dubignon's yawl to the camp. When Charlie entered it, he froze in his tracks, and then let out a triumphant holler. The sight of four hundred Africans chattering in languages he could not understand, and dancing around a big fire was the most beautiful he had ever seen. His financial woes were over.

Farnum said, "They seem happy to be here, and they're well behaved. Towards the end of the voyage, we removed their cuffs and let them roam the deck. They didn't cause any trouble."

Corrie waved one of the Africans over. He was about fourteen years old, black as coal with a round face that had some markings under each eye. The boy smiled at the white men. Lamar, as proud as a new father, asked, "What's your name, young man?"

The boy said, "What's your name, young man?"

Lamar looked at Corrie and the other men, who were giggling like children. He turned back to the boy and said, "Did you have a pleasant journey?"

The boy replied, "Did you have a pleasant journey?"

Corrie explained to a wide-eyed Lamar, "It's amazing. The negroes from one of the tribes can repeat everything said to them, even though they have no idea what they're saying."

Lamar said to the African, "It was nice talking to you."

"It was nice talking to you."

Charlie was thinking of another clever thing to say to the boy when he noticed an unfamiliar white man talking to John Dubignon. Charlie patted the young African on the head, approached Dubignon, and said, "I don't believe I've met your friend, John."

"Charlie, meet James Clubb. He piloted the *Wanderer* in."

Charlie offered his hand. "I've heard about you, Mr. Clubb. It's my pleasure."

Clubb took Charlie's hand. "Nice to meet you, Mr. Lamar."

Lamar gripped Clubb's hand and said, "I understand you charge quite handsomely for your services, sir?"

Clubb tried to free his hand but Charlie wouldn't loosen his hold. "I do charge a little more for money-making ventures, Mr. Lamar."

Charlie pulled Clubb closer, till their noses were inches apart, and spoke through clenched teeth, "What you call *a little extra*, sir, I call extortion. But you made a deal with my partners, and I must honor it. Consider that little extra the cost of your absolute silence. If you ever say a word about your activities here with us, I will personally take that little extra out of your greedy, thieving hide. Do I make myself clear, Mr. Clubb?"

Clubb's cheek started to twitch. "Ya . . . ya . . . yes sir, Mr. Lamar." Charlie released his hand and Clubb slunk away.

Over supper at Dubignon's, Charlie kept after the details: moving the Africans, paying expenses, collecting debts, towing the *Wanderer*, and coordinating explanations of events to nosey authorities. Corrie lifted his glass of wine and said, "Charlie, have a drink and relax. Everything is working out. This is a success!"

Charlie sighed. "You're right. But we can't afford to make any mistakes. That reminds me, what happened to that slave you took to Africa?"

Corrie and Farnum eyed each other, but didn't answer. Charlie went on. "As it turned out, he didn't murder that man after all. I never had to sneak him out of the country."

Corrie and Farnum shouted in unison, "What!?"

Charlie laughed so hard at their reaction he nearly fell backwards off his chair. When he regained his composure, he said, "Don't fret. It was good practice for when we return Howell Cobb's negroes to Africa." Charlie used his hand to dry his eyes. "So, what happened? How long after you cleared Charleston harbor until you threw him overboard?"

Corrie and Farnum sat stone-faced. After a long swallow of wine, Corrie told Charlie the story. "Captain Farnum went to take care of him. We never found him."

Charlie's mouth opened like a trap door. "He came back? He saw everything and he came back? And you don't know where he is? Are you joking?"

Corrie said, "Don't worry, Charlie. He never could have gotten to shore. He jumped overboard two miles out. He's in a shark's belly right now."

Charlie folded his arms across his chest and scowled at the men. He wanted everything to be perfect. Now this.

*   *   *

Dante floated on the plank for two hours. The water was still warm from a summer that had lasted through October. He was scared, but he wouldn't give up. Though it was dark, he had seen land from the *Wanderer* and was certain he would reach it by riding the tide. He would make it to Cuba and start a new life. He owed it to Neeka and the other Bimeré.

Soon, he washed up on a shore. The late November night air was made colder by the wind against his wet body. He crawled onto the beach and walked till he was surrounded by trees and sheltered from the breeze. He took off his soaked clothes and sat with his arms around himself, shivering. He covered himself with palmetto fronds. Despite the discomfort, Dante thanked God. He had made it safely to his new country.

He slept until first light, when beach crabs started to pinch his body. He jumped up and swatted furiously at the hungry invaders. He realized that he, too, was hungry. He walked along the beach but found nothing. He picked some leaves off plants and chewed them, but spit them out. He had seventy dollars in gold coins buried safely away, yet he couldn't buy a kernel of rice.

As the sun cleared the horizon, he saw a rowboat about a hundred yards from shore. He ran to the water's edge and jumped up and down, naked, waving his arms over his head. The two men rowed towards him. Dante gathered his clothes and ran into the water to meet them. He smiled when he saw they were black! One pulled Dante in.

Dante said, "Grassus. Dishyuh Cooba, po' fabaw?"

The two men looked at each other and laughed as they rowed away from the beach. Dante looked around. He saw a large ship just like the *Wanderer* disappear behind the southern part of the island.

Dante said, "Cooba sholy look same lukkuh Jawjuh."

The men started laughing again. One said, "Oonuh een Jawjuh, nigguh!"

Dante shouted, "Yuh? Jawjuh?" Both men nodded.

Dante was confused. He was certain he was in Cuba, but these two men looked and talked like Georgia negroes. He decided not to say anything until he knew where he was.

Dante put on his clothes, which were still damp and uncomfortable. He examined the boat. There were several large burlap sacks lying on the deck and undulating. After ten minutes, the men stopped rowing, and one of them pulled from the water a wire cage with five crabs. The other man held open one of the sacks and the contents of the trap were emptied into it. They dropped the trap back into the water and started rowing again.

After handling a few more traps, one of the men asked Dante, "Oonuh run'way?"

He replied, "No. Ah fall f'um de ship."

The men laughed. They rowed for a while, pulling up traps along the way, until they reached a harbor and pulled to a wharf. Dante thanked the men again, climbed up the ladder, and walked along the pier.

He passed four negroes sitting around a fire, frying fish in a skillet, and stopped. One man saw Dante smacking his lips. He took a fish out of the pan, put it on an old, stained metal dish, and handed it to Dante. "Fuh oonuh."

Dante thanked him and ate hungrily with his fingers, burning his mouth in the process. Dante finished the food and handed back the dish. He sucked the grease from his fingers, wiped his hands on his pants. He wanted to pay the man, but he would have to pull coins out of his arse, a gesture he was certain would not be welcomed. He told the man he had no money. The man said payment was not necessary. Dante then asked if he was in Cuba.

The men laughed, as Dante had expected. The kindly negro said, "Oonuh een Brunswick, Jawjuh." He pointed to the harbor. "Cooba way fudduh yonduh."

Dante squinted at the harbor as if he were trying to spot Cuba in the distance while he tried to comprehend the nightmare to which he had just returned. Dante thought that wherever he was, it must have an Oglethorpe Ward like Savannah, where the coloreds live. If he could find it, he could hide until he found a way to get to Cuba. He asked, "Weh de town?"

The negro pointed to the end of the pier.

Dante gave a parting wave and left. He didn't get far. As soon as he exited the pier, a white man on a horse came by and appraised the disheveled, long-haired, bearded negro. He asked Dante who owned him. Dante didn't respond. He couldn't tell the truth or he'd be sent to Savannah, and the gallows. His hesitation was all the marshal needed.

As they entered the jail, the marshal announced, "Got us a runaway, boys. Says his name is Joe Soupy. He can't remember who owns him. Throw him in the cell. I'll put a notice in the paper. If no one claims him in a year, we'll auction him off."

*   *   *

On Friday morning, December 3, the six *Wanderer* crewmen who had remained on Jekyl Island packed 175 of the Africans onto the deck of the *Lamar,* to the astonishment of Captain Christie, who was fighting his nervousness by pulling hairs from his ear. Lamar said to him, "You were not to be involved in this, Captain, but now you are. We will proceed up the coast today, but we are not to enter the Savannah River until it's completely dark. We'll pass Savannah town and you will let me off at Coleraine Plantation six miles above the city on the Georgia side. Then you will continue eight more miles to the South Carolina side. Mr. Tucker will instruct you. After the passengers are unloaded, return to Savannah and forget this ever happened. Is that clear?" Charlie placed a gold coin in Christie's jacket pocket.

"Yes, Mr. Lamar. It's absolutely clear," Christie's voice wavered.

Lamar, Tucker, Brown, Farnum, and the *Wanderer* crew boarded the boat. The trip went as planned. They entered the Savannah River at night and no customs officer thought to stop the familiar tug. In the early morning of December 4, Christie went home, happy to forget.

After the *Lamar* departed Jekyl Island, another steam tug anchored off Jekyl beach and boarded another 185 Africans. The ship immediately chugged up the Satilla River to its headwaters. The Africans were then transported overland, at night, in covered wagons to various plantations in Georgia, Alabama, and Mississippi, swallowed whole and rendered invisible by the peculiar institution.

Thirty-six Africans remained on Jekyl. They were taken to a camp on the grounds of the Dubignon house and awaited their move to a sugar plantation in Louisiana by Trow and Akin.

The other *Wanderer* crewmen scrubbed and re-scrubbed the ship and restored the *Wanderer* to her original state by the evening of December 4. John Dubignon hired a pilot to take her to Brunswick the next morning. When they arrived, Corrie paid the crew and they disappeared like frightened bugs. He only had to wait for a tug to tow the ship to Savannah.

Corrie visited Brunswick Port Collector Woodford Mabry in the wooden Custom House that overlooked the harbor, and asked for clearance to Charleston. Mabry put on his jacket and followed Corrie. Mabry walked quickly through the ship and sniffed loudly a few times, but said nothing. Then he examined the *Wanderer's* previous port clearances, one from Charleston to Port of Spain, another from Port of Spain to St. Helena, and the final one from St. Helena to Charleston. The latter had no consular seal. Corrie explained that the consular official was on leave when the *Wanderer* anchored in St. Helena. Mabry nodded and gave clearance.

Later that day, as Mabry prepared to go home, his assistant ran into the office and told him of a rumor that a ship had recently dropped off a cargo of Africans in the area. Mabry put on his jacket, walked to the *Wanderer,* and asked Corrie if he could inspect the ship again. Corrie said yes, but as it was late, they made an appointment for the morning.

That night, Captain Corrie worried about the port collector's request. He second-guessed his decision not to sail to Charleston, despite the damage to the ship.

The next day, Monday, December 6, Mabry more thoroughly inspected the *Wanderer* and still found no evidence of slaving activity. He told Corrie the clearance papers were still good and went back to his office. As he prepared his second pot of coffee of the day, his assistant charged into the building and told him there was a new rumor that a steamer had taken a load of Africans from Jekyl Island to Savannah. Mabry put on his jacket, walked back to the *Wanderer,* and asked Corrie again for the old clearance papers. Upon closer inspection, he noticed the papers clearing the ship from Trinidad to St. Helena did not have a consular seal either. That meant two of the three clearance papers were improper. He revoked the clearance to Charleston and told Corrie to sit tight while he made some inquiries. Corrie said he was happy to cooperate while the administrative problem was resolved.

After Mabry left, Corrie paced the stateroom, searching his mind for a way to outsmart the authorities. No idea surfaced. Either the tug appeared very soon, or it was time to pack and find passage to Charleston.

When Mabry reached his office, he wrote a letter to United States District Attorney Joseph Ganahl in Savannah requesting guidance. Ganahl was born in Savannah in 1828 to a prominent family. His father had been the largest German cotton buyer in the town. His brother Charles was a respected doctor who had served as a city alderman with Charlie Lamar. Joseph, who had chosen to practice law over medicine, was guided by one principle: that America was a nation of laws. He intended to see that people lived by them.

*   *   *

After the Africans and their escorts were dropped off on the South Carolina side of the Savannah River, they all marched to John Montmollin's plantation. It took two days to settle the Africans and get a doctor to inspect them.

Those members of the *Wanderer*'s crew who went to Montmollin's had completed their jobs. They collected their final pay and departed for various coastal towns for a few weeks of heavy drinking before finding their next employment. Farnum traveled by coach and train to Charleston, where he boarded a ship to New York. Brown, Juan, and Miguel caught a ride on one of Montmollin's flat boats to Savannah on December 7, planning to sail to New York the next day. They checked into the City Hotel. Their sunburned, lined faces, long hair, and filthy clothes did not surprise the desk clerk. This was the normal appearance of seamen who had just returned from a long voyage.

By late afternoon the three were in Price's Clothing Store, purchasing fancy suits. Brown paid with gold coins and had them delivered to the hotel. They had supper, and then returned to the hotel to sleep and await their ship at noon the next day.

On December 8 District Attorney Ganahl received Woodford Mabry's letter. Minutes after he read it, he heard from Mr. Price that three seamen had bought costly clothing at his store and were living high at the City Hotel. Ganahl decided to investigate. He and U. S. Marshal Daniel Stewart went to the hotel just before noon, spotted the seamen in the lobby, and questioned them about their recent activities. Brown answered Ganahl as vaguely as possible. Ganahl, a veteran of many cross examinations, knew a liar when he heard one. He arrested the men and took them to the U. S. Commissioner's office in the Custom House a half block away.

As Ganahl watched the clerk prepare the affidavits and warrants, John Owens, the most noted criminal defense lawyer in Savannah, entered the office. "Excuse me, Mr. Ganahl, but I represent these men. Exactly why are they being charged?"

Ganahl pulled a watch from his pocket. "That didn't take long, sir. Just fifteen minutes."

Owens turned up his nose. "I will ignore that comment, Mr. Ganahl, other than to remind you that I defend falsely accused individuals and protect them from over-zealous prosecutors."

Ganahl let out a laugh that scared the clerk, making him draw an unintended line across one of the warrants. "For clarification, let me say that I am not surprised to see the attorney for Charlie Lamar appear in the commissioner's office minutes after I've arrested three men for violation of the Slave Trade Act of 1820 for the illegal importation of Africans into the country."

Owens's voice rose. "That's preposterous! Where's your proof?"

Ganahl pointed to the affidavits on the clerk's desk. "I don't need to reveal that to you now. But as a professional courtesy, I'll tell you what I know. There are rumors that Africans were landed on Jekyl Island about ten days ago. There's even talk that some of them were subsequently shipped and landed up the Savannah River. Then these three check in at the City Hotel, looking like they've been to sea for months, and within a few hours are buying gentlemen's clothing with gold coins."

Owens scoffed. "You call that evidence? You've got to do better than that."

"I will, Mr. Owens, believe me. There'll be a hearing in front of the commissioner in ten days to determine if the case should be given to a grand jury. Of course, you know all that. In the meantime, they'll be the guests of Mr. Van Horn." Charles Van Horn, the builder and blind and sash maker, had since become the city jailer.

Owens shouted. "I demand bail for my clients."

Ganahl pointed to an office door. "Speak to the commissioner. I'm not a gambling man, but for a charge of piracy I'd wager you won't get it." Owens walked past Ganahl to the office. As he was about to knock, Ganahl called out, "Mr. Owens?"

Owens faced the district attorney. "Sir?"

"Please send my regards to Mr. Lamar. Tell him I hope to see him soon."

Owens growled and entered the commissioner's door without waiting for an invitation.

Ganahl was correct. Bail was denied. Owens was allowed to speak privately to the men, although only Brown understood English. Owens assured them that every effort would be made to defend them and gain their freedom.

After all the legal papers had been processed, Marshal Stewart escorted the prisoners to the Hall Street county jail. Van Horn put them in a damp cell. That night, the men dined on steak, fried oysters, and peach pie, ordered from the most popular restaurant in town, Dante's Place. Brown paid. They finished the meal with claret and segars and talked about renovating the cell to eliminate the dampness.

The news of the *Wanderer* spread through town like a call to a fire. Joseph told Andrew about it as they watched their boys play in Monterey Square one evening. Joseph said it was Charlie Lamar's schooner, but no one knew if he was involved in the plot. Andrew felt nauseous. He had put Dante on a slave ship. He told Joseph he wasn't feeling well and took Truvy home.

Andrew did not say much over supper. He went to bed, lying on his side, facing away from Patience. He prayed that the ship dropped off Dante in Africa before they took on the slaves. Patience broke his concentration.

"Andrew, it's Sunday, my night off."

Andrew said he was tired. He felt his wife's warm hand slide down the front of his drawers and stroke him. Then he felt his wife kissing his back. He became aroused, lay on his back, and forgot about Dante, at least for the night.

*   *   *

Charlie Lamar watched in horror as his *Wanderer* scheme started to crumble. Brown and the two Spaniards were in jail, awaiting a hearing. The tug he sent to Brunswick to tow the *Wanderer* had arrived just hours after the yacht had been seized.

But as far as he knew, Corrie and all the other crew had escaped from Georgia, and the *Wanderer* had been restored to its original state. No Africans had been captured. He had just received word that the slaves at Montmollin's were shipped further up the river near Augusta to his cousin's plantation in South Carolina. They would soon be sold to buyers. Charlie was still hopeful that no case could be made against him.

But Charlie had to do more than just stay out of jail. The venture had to succeed financially or he was finished. This much was certain: he could not allow anyone to talk, or Africans to be captured. He had to prevent that at any cost.

The rumors continued to fly, and they grew wilder by the day. The *Wanderer* had brought in eighty Africans, or three hundred, or five hundred, or none at all, or acted as a decoy for the real slave ship. Some Africans died on the voyage, or none had died. African sightings were reported in Macon and Augusta. However, Joseph Ganahl could not deal with rumors. He had three men in jail and just days to build his case before the hearing. After he had ordered Port Collector Mabry to seize the *Wanderer*, he sent a deputy marshal to Brunswick to subpoena anyone who might be connected with the importation or had witnessed it.

Ganahl also told the deputy marshal to spend a day on Jekyl Island to search for Africans. Ganahl needed, more than anything, living proof that Africans had been imported into the country. Having the *Wanderer*, a few of its crew, and some eyewitnesses was far from conclusive. But a jury would have difficulty refuting living, breathing evidence, no matter what their feelings about slavery or the trade.

News of the landing spread far beyond Savannah. Newspapers in all major cities carried the reports, and editorials demanded justice for those responsible. Word even reached President James Buchanan, who publicly decreed that all proper and necessary means must be used to enforce the law. He had Attorney General Jeremiah Black assign Savannah lawyer Henry Rootes Jackson, who had recently served as the United States ambassador to Austria, as a special prosecutor to assist Joseph Ganahl.

By the time the hearings began, Ganahl still had not captured any Africans, but he had found some witnesses. And he did not yet have to prove the defendants' guilt; he only had to convince the U. S. commissioner that the case should be sent to a grand jury.

On Saturday, December 19, with Commissioner Charles Seton Henry presiding, the hearing began. For four days, Ganahl called witnesses. Men like Woodford Mabry were forthcoming, but others, like Dr. Hazelhurst, Henry Dubignon's brother-in-law, who had examined the Africans after they had landed, were less so. Lighthouse keeper Horatio Harris refused to testify for fear of criminating himself. Ganahl and Jackson realized they needed more time to prepare and gather evidence, and asked the commissioner for a postponement.

The commissioner obliged and delayed the hearings until December 28. The prosecution and defense lawyers left the Custom House but ignored each other. As they descended the steps, they noticed a crowd standing on the bluff across the Bay, looking towards the harbor. The attorneys stopped as they saw a revenue cutter with a large, graceful schooner in tow.

John Owens said to no one, "She sure is a beauty."

Joseph Ganahl shook his head. "That's a matter of opinion, counselor."

*   *   *

Christmas day at the plantation was still special for Joseph and Amy. In their adult years, they spent less and less time there. But whenever they rode down the avenue of oaks, they felt nostalgic for their youth.

After the gift-giving to the servants, Andrew, still despondent over learning he had consigned Dante to a slave ship, Patience, and Truvy went outside to have the traditional roast pig with Hercules and the other servants while the McBains settled down to their Christmas supper in the big house.

James McBain spoke of how tiring running the plantation had become. That was the last thing Emily wanted to hear. She knew that once her father-in-law could no longer manage the plantation, Joseph would have to. As beautiful as the Heritage was, she didn't want to live with two hundred slaves. She might even be called upon to manage the house servants in place of Sarah. Emily didn't want to think about it. She asked Amy, "Are you still receiving mail from your painter friend in New York?"

Amy conceded, "Yes, but I'm so busy I can't respond to them all." She waited for her mother to say something.

"I hope he understands that," Sarah said, looking at Amy. Sarah didn't care if Bob was a New Yorker. She could tell Amy was interested in him. He could be from the moon, as long as he and Amy, soon to be forty, married, lived in Savannah, and gave Sarah grandchildren.

In fact, Amy liked Bob quite a bit based on the few times she met him at the restaurant. He was handsome, charming, and enthusiastic. His letters were interesting and friendly without being cloying. And he wasn't obnoxious like his friends. She was glad she had consented to his request to let him write to her.

"Is he going to do anything besides write letters?" Joseph said as he raised and lowered his eyebrows several times.

Amy fluttered her eyes in return. "He said he's thinking of moving south to paint landscapes on commission. He'll do portraits to put bread on the table."

James McBain inwardly groaned. While he was fond of Emily, one New Yorker in the family was enough. "I don't think artists make much money."

Amy took her father's hand. "There are other things in life than money, Father. Besides, painters don't starve. Look at Mr. Cerveau. He lives comfortably. And please, I hardly know Mr. Carson. Don't marry me off just yet. You all know that isn't easy to do." Sarah pursed her lips.

After dinner, Hercules drove Joseph and Andrew and their families back to Savannah. As they traveled through town on Broughton Street, they saw a crowd of people standing on the sidewalk along Drayton Street.

Amy asked, "What in the world is going on?"

Joseph called to Hercules to park the coach. Amy, Andrew, and Joseph got out. People were lined up for blocks trying to get into George Wylly's office. Joseph asked a stranger what was happening.

The man responded, waving his hands as he spoke, "A wild African! They caught one on Jekyl Island. The sheriff brought him up yesterday. Marshal Stewart put him in the jail, but moved him here today for his health. Mr. Wylly is letting the public see the boy." George Wylly, who had just been elected a city alderman with John Tucker, was also a property broker who dealt in slaves. Clients often brought their negroes to his office, where he had a holding cell.

Joe Ganahl was so excited by the capture of the African he had sent a telegram to Attorney General Black, informing him of the critical piece of evidence.

Joseph asked Andrew and Amy, "Are you interested in seeing a wild African?"

"Not really," answered Amy. "The poor thing."

Andrew said, "Actually, I'm curious."

"So am I," Joseph admitted.

Amy returned to the coach, and Hercules took the women and children home. Andrew and Joseph got on line, and moved with it in silence, exhausted by the day's activities. Then Joseph accidentally bumped into the woman in front of him.

The woman turned and said loud enough for everyone in Savannah to hear, "Why don't you look where you're going!"

Joseph said, "I'm awfully sorry, madam. That was clumsy of me."

"Clumsy and rude! I hope the African isn't as wild as you!" She turned back to her husband and said, "Herbert, they aren't raised with manners any more. On Christmas day no less. I know Jesus must be weeping."

Andrew shook Joseph's arm. Then it dawned on Joseph. It was Gruesome Woman, grayer and heftier, and difficult to recognize under her bonnet and topcoat.

Soon they were in a room with the African boy, who was sitting on a stool, smiling at the people passing by. He had scar markings high on his cheeks. Andrew's stomach began to churn as he thought about the boy being captured and crammed into a ship. He didn't think it was right for him, a negro, to gawk at the boy like an animal at the circus. He wanted to leave.

Mr. and Mrs. Young stopped to stare at the boy. She was driven to comment, "What an ugly, savage-looking beast."

To which the boy replied, with a toothy smile, "What an ugly, savage-looking beast."

Mrs. Young shrieked, "Did you hear what he called me, Herbert? I won't tolerate that. I'll have him whipped!"

The boy said, "Did you hear what he called me, Herbert? I won't tolerate that."

The woman shrieked again and her husband pulled her away while Andrew, Joseph, and the other people in the room roared with laughter.

Joseph said to the boy, "Very good show, young man."

"Very good show, young man." The African beamed at the crowd.

Andrew was glad he stayed to see the African boy make a fool of Mrs. Young.

The next morning, as Joseph walked to work, a friend stopped him on the street. "Joseph, have you heard the news? The wild African boy! He's been stolen!"

"How? By whom?"

"The word is George Wylly closed his office at eleven o'clock last night, put the boy in a cell, and left his night watchman in charge. About midnight, there was a knock on the door. When the watchman opened it, he saw a pistol pointed at his face. Two white men wearing kerchiefs over their faces took the African. There's hell to pay. Ganahl's lost his evidence. He wants to hang Marshal Stewart by the balls. It was the marshal who took the boy from the jail to Wylly's place for the boy's health, but he was better protected in the jail."

Joseph nodded and thought, "Well, Charlie's friendship with Stewart and Wylly is still coming in handy."

The stolen African sent the *Wanderer* prosecution team scrambling. An embarrassed Ganahl wired Attorney General Black in Washington, explaining the theft and blaming Stewart. He assured Black their case was still strong.

Special prosecutor Henry Jackson wired Treasury Secretary Cobb, requesting help in the investigation and a new federal marshal. Cobb assigned James Spullock as special agent and also appointed him the new federal marshal for the district of Georgia, to become effective upon Senate confirmation and Spullock's posting bond. Until then, Stewart, who refused to resign, would remain as marshal.

On December 29 the *Wanderer* hearings resumed. Ganahl and Jackson had spent the past week preparing. Not only did they want the case sent to a grand jury, they also wanted to send a message to anyone in the South who might be thinking of participating in the slave trade.

The commissioner called the hearing to order and swore in the pilot. Ganahl asked the witness, "Mr. Clubb, would you mind telling the court your occupation?"

Clubb answered from memory. "I cannot do so, sir, without criminating myself."

Ganahl smiled at the witness. "Yes, you can, Mr. Clubb. There is no way you can criminate yourself by answering this question. Please tell us your occupation."

"I cannot do so without criminating myself."

Ganahl turned to the commissioner. "Your honor, would you please inform the witness that by answering my question, he would not be criminating himself."

Before Commissioner Henry could respond, attorney John Owens stood, cleared his throat, and announced, "It's all right, Mr. Clubb. You may answer that question."

Everyone in the courtroom stared at Owens. Ganahl, red in the face, gasped, "Who in the world do you think you are, counselor, to interfere with my examination of the witness?"

"I'm trying to move things along here, sir. I'm helping you out."

Ganahl took a step towards Owens. "Helping me? You little piece of . . . ." Ganahl caught himself. He pointed at Owens. "You have no right to interfere with my questioning of a witness here, either by objecting to my questions or telling the witness which questions he is free to answer. If you don't know that, you don't belong in this room, other than to sweep it!"

Owens had wanted to hit a sore spot, and he found the mark, though at the expense of legal decorum. "I am within my rights as counsel for the defense to ask the court to allow or prevent a witness to answer a question that might criminate him. It's a universal practice!"

Ganahl replied, "Oh, really? In which legal swamp is it universally practiced?"

"Order! Order! That's enough!" Commissioner Henry broke in, banging his gavel. The lawyers stopped, but the gallery was making more noise than a locomotive. "Quiet in the courtroom!" added Henry.

The attorneys could hear the commissioner breathing. He glared at Owens. "Counselor, it is the duty of the court to inform the witness as to what is required of him. You have no right to interfere with prosecution's questioning. Please take your seat and let the prosecution continue."

Owens obeyed. Ganahl still stared at the defense. Owens smirked.

Ganahl turned back to the witness chair. Clubb, who looked as if he had never before worn a necktie in his life, tugged at the collar of his shirt. "Mr. Clubb, would you please tell the court your occupation?"

"I cannot do so, sir, without criminating myself."

Commissioner Henry groaned. "Sir, this court requires you to answer the question, or you will be found in contempt of this court and committed to jail."

Clubb looked around the room like a lost boy. "I cannot, sir, without criminating myself."

As the commissioner was about to speak, Henry Jackson stood and said, "I would like to say something, your honor!"

The commissioner, exhausted by the previous incident, told Jackson to go ahead.

Up to this point, Ganahl had asked all the questions in the hearing, and Jackson, known throughout Georgia as a great orator, had not yet spoken. The spectators froze in anticipation.

Jackson began, "Your honor, as you may know, I have long served the system of justice in this community, and in this country. I did so and do so proudly, for the civility and progress of this country is based upon the proper administration of the law. In all my years of serving the courts, I have never seen any behavior more abhorrent to the system of justice than that just displayed by the counsel for the defense." Jackson didn't look at Owens, who rolled his eyes, and rested his clasped hands on his stomach.

Jackson continued. "Making a mockery of our law is detestable, but not illegal. What is almost as disturbing as the antics of the defense is that the court too often overrules the objections of the prosecution."

If dead silence could become quieter, Mr. Jackson had just made it so. Henry leaned forward in his chair, and moved his spectacles lower on his nose, all the while staring at Jackson.

Jackson continued, slowly raising his voice until he ended his declaration with a shout. "Just now, the court has ruled that a witness has been in contempt of court. Let me say this, Commissioner, if I were still sitting on the bench of the Superior Court of Chatham County, I would rule the counsel for the defense in contempt of court!"

The spectators erupted. Henry resorted to the gavel. "Order, order!"

Owens stood without being recognized. "Your honor, I have not made any improper interference. I am defending the prisoners, and I have certain rights in this hearing. The *assistant* for the prosecution objects to the system of justice if he doesn't get his way."

Jackson looked at Owens and felt the urge to pummel him.

The commissioner yelled, "Enough! I have heard enough! Marshal, take this witness to jail." Marshal Stewart and two bailiffs moved to Clubb.

Ganahl stood and said, "Your honor, please do not remove the witness just yet. I would like to bring some additional charges against him!"

Owens jumped to his feet. "Objection! Objection! The prosecution has no right to suspend this examination in order to allow another prosecution to be commenced! I have never seen such outrageous behavior in a court in my life." Owens stuck the dagger in as deep as he could before twisting it.

Before Ganahl or Jackson could speak, the commissioner said, "Objection sustained!"

The government attorneys gawked at Henry. Finally, Jackson said, "Sir, if you continue to overrule us, we will be forced to *nolle prosequi* the case. Yes, we will request permission not to prosecute. And the responsibility will not be upon us. When the president, the attorney general, the Senate, and the House of Representatives hear that the case against the blatant, illegal importation of Africans against all the laws of this country, humanity, and God has been terminated, this court will be the shame of the country!"

The commissioner pointed his gavel at Jackson. "Do not threaten me, counselor, or I will find *you* in contempt of court! Now, marshal, take this prisoner to jail. We will commence with these proceedings."

Ganahl and Jackson sat. Their heads were spinning. It was going to take more than good law, witnesses, and evidence to win.

The next witness, Captain Hillary Frazier, was more forthright and his non-contentious testimony restored calm to the courtroom. He told how on December 12 or 13 he picked up about 170 negroes fifteen miles above Savannah on the South Carolina side and took them to a point three miles below Augusta on the South Carolina side, a distance of about two hundred miles. The negroes did not speak English.

Captain Luke Christie next took the stand and Ganahl, back in control of his emotions, began his questioning. "Mr. Christie, what is your occupation?"

"I'm a pilot for the steam tug *Lamar*, sir."

"Have you recently piloted the tug outside of the Savannah area?"

"Yes, sir. I took her to Brunswick area recently, at the beginning of this month."

Ganahl looked at his notes on the table. "Can you tell us something about it?"

"Sir, I cannot answer any further in fear of criminating myself."

A gasp shot through the courtroom. Ganahl waited for quiet. "And just why do you think you might be criminating yourself, Captain?"

"Because I may have transported illegally imported Africans within this state."

"I think you are misconstruing the law, Captain. In no way were your acts criminal. Now, can you tell me more about your trip to Brunswick?"

"I cannot, sir."

Ganahl turned to Commissioner Henry. "Sir, please explain to the witness that he is not criminating himself."

"Counselor, I am not convinced he is not. I need time to research the issue further. Therefore, I am adjourning the hearings for the day. I will advise the witnesses tomorrow. Case adjourned." The spectators charged for the exits to spread the word about the hearing.

"One moment, Mr. Commissioner," Ganahl said. "May I have permission to speak?"

Mr. Henry sighed and said, "If you must." The spectators rushed back to their seats.

Ganahl said, "Thank you, sir. I just want to take a minute to give notice to the people." Ganahl then turned to face the courtroom, his hands on his hips. "I want everyone to know, both inside this room and without, that if you had anything at all to do with this violation of the law, I have my eye on you. I don't care how big or small you are, or how powerful or powerless you are, I am coming after you with all the force and energy the good Lord and the government have given me. Witnesses may refuse to testify, juries may be afraid to decide, and even the courts may fail to meet their mark. But that will not deter me. If anyone should doubt me, he will be in for a very rude surprise. The government that stands behind me has the time, means, and resolve to see this case prosecuted to the very end of the law."

Ganahl turned back to Henry. "That's all I have to say, sir."

Ganahl walked out of the courtroom with a pain in his stomach, when his assistant came bounding up the steps of the Custom House with news. A deputy marshal in Macon had seized two Africans the day before. Marshal Stewart had sent ten officers to meet the Macon authorities at Seventy-nine Mile Station to bring the Africans back to Savannah. They would arrive that night. Ganahl vowed these two would not escape. His pain began to fade.

That night, Stewart awakened Van Horn at the city jail to deposit the two Africans. He also handed the jailer a letter from Ganahl stating that the Africans were to remain in jail at any cost and under any circumstances, until he said otherwise.

The hearings of December 30 were scheduled to commence at eleven o'clock. By eight, hundreds of people crowded onto the steps of the Custom House. Word of the previous day's proceedings had spread through town like a hot summer wind.

The commissioner entered the hearing room, had Captain Christie sworn in as a witness, and then made a proclamation. "I have examined the applicability of the

Act of 1820 to transporting illegally imported slaves within the State of Georgia as it pertained to yesterday's testimony of the witness. While most of the act does not pertain to the witnesses' testimony, there are a few clauses that are so worded that I cannot comfortably tell the witness that his testimony would not criminate himself." The commissioner talked about these clauses.

Ganahl stood. "Your honor, I must tell the court that I too have examined the Act of 1820 and can find no way in which Captain Christie had done anything in violation of the law. He must be told by this court that he can answer the prosecution's questions without fear of criminating himself. If not, I am afraid that the rulings of this court will prove to defeat the ends of justice"

Commissioner Henry's voice cut through the courtroom. "That is enough, Mr. Ganahl! I have made my interpretation of the law. It is not open to debate."

Ganahl practically pleaded, "Would the court at least tell the witness that the mere internal transportation of negroes is not a crime in the eye of the law?"

"Yes, I will charge the witness with that information." Commissioner Henry turned to Captain Christie and said, "Do you understand that point, Captain?"

Christie looked at Henry, wiped his forehead, and finally squeaked, "Yes, sir."

With that, Christie testified in great detail. He explained everything he had observed from the time he picked up Lamar, Trowbridge, Tucker, and Brown in Savannah to the time he dropped the men and Africans off on the South Carolina side of the river.

Ganahl and Jackson were elated. Not only had the crime been established, but Lamar was identified as part of it.

Though additional witnesses testified that day and on the next hearing date, after Christie's testimony there could be no doubt about the commissioner's decision. On January 3, 1859, he pronounced that his court would commit the prisoners to the grand jury of the next term of the U. S. District Court.

After the hearing was adjourned, Joseph Ganahl shook Henry Jackson's hand and whispered, "I wonder if Charlie Lamar just felt a little tightness around his neck?"

CHAPTER 26

The Auctions

February-November 1859

"Hello, Mr. Carson. I didn't see you come in." Amy tried to conceal her smile as she stood near the entrance to her restaurant. Bob had written to tell her he was coming to Savannah in early February for several months to paint. He was as handsome as she'd remembered.

Bob stepped closer and offered Amy a camellia. "You were busy with customers. I didn't want to interrupt you."

Amy accepted the flower. "Thank you. It's beautiful. When did you arrive?"

"Yesterday. I checked into the Screven House and looked for a studio today. I found a nice situation by Johnson Square. It's small and on the second floor but meets my needs. It's good to see you again."

"It's nice to see you. Come. I'll seat you." Bob followed Amy to a table. She held a chair, making him feel uncomfortable. He wanted to be holding a chair for her. She looked around to see if she was needed elsewhere, then sat with him. "I wish you luck with your painting."

"Thank you. I'm anxious to get started." Bob surveyed the room and asked, "How is the restaurant business, Miss McBain?"

"We're very busy. We have many regular customers. We started offering meals for people to take home to eat. And the *Wanderer* case is bringing people like lawyers, witnesses, spectators, and newspaper reporters to town. Have you heard about it?"

"The *Wanderer*? I certainly have. The newspapers in New York print the reports from the southern papers. It's an incredible story. It's captivated the nation."

That was not an understatement. The incident had especially captivated the government. Much had happened since the commissioner's hearing. In early January the U. S. Senate passed a resolution demanding that President James Buchanan release all information available on the *Wanderer*. The House of Representatives passed a similar resolution a few weeks later. Buchanan responded that he was not yet prepared to comply.

Under intense criticism from local newspapers for clearing so many ships involved in the slave trade from the port of New York, U.S. Marshal Isaiah Rynders had to explain to President Buchanan why he had released the *Wanderer* the prior June.

With all the coverage, pressure from Washington for convictions grew. Joseph Ganahl had spent every waking minute gathering evidence and witnesses for the upcoming grand jury hearings in February. He thought he had enough to convict the three crewmen and William Corrie. However, Corrie was not in his custody. The captain had caught a ship to South Carolina as the *Wanderer* was seized in Brunswick. Ganahl sent an affidavit to the district court judge in Charleston for Corrie's arrest and extradition. The judge had Corrie arrested, but ruled that South Carolina had jurisdiction and would try him. Ganahl was furious. Convicting Corrie was critical to the overall success of his prosecution. He had to bring Corrie to Savannah.

Above all, Ganahl wanted to get Charlie Lamar. He hated Lamar's arrogance and disregard for the law. Ganahl still smarted from the theft of the African boy the previous Christmas, which he thought Lamar had planned.

The prosecutor's major challenge was to link Lamar to the ownership of the *Wanderer*. Ganahl had filed a libel of information with the Admiralty Court, over which John Nicoll, Charlie's father-in-law, presided. It required all persons having any right of title or interest in the *Wanderer* to come forth and interpose their claims. Corrie, the sole owner according to the permanent ship registry, wired from South Carolina that he claimed just one-eighth interest. Ganahl needed other ways to connect Lamar to the ship.

Bob said, "We read a lot about a Charles Lamar. Supposedly he's a wealthy businessman behind the expedition. I gather he's a Fire-eater, a secessionist, and wants to re-open the slave trade."

Amy scanned the restaurant before whispering, "Charlie and his friends eat here a lot. So do the lawyers who are trying to put him away. I always have to be on guard. Charlie puts on a good appearance, but as a legitimate businessman, he's a failure. The word is he's broke and has to pay thousands in legal fees to defend the crewmen of the ship as well as himself. I can't say how much of his involvement in the slave trade is based on his Fire-eater principles and how much is based on his need for money. But his financial embarrassment must be playing a big part."

Actually, Charlie was in worse shape than anyone knew. In addition to legal costs, one of his business partners, James Gardner, was threatening to take Charlie to court. He was in another legal battle over patent violations regarding his cotton press. One of Charlie's ships was sitting at the wharf with only a partial cargo, incurring demurrage costs of $150 per day. Of course, his notes were still floating all over town. And little money was coming in. The South Carolina purchasers of the Africans were slow in paying, and one buyer refused to remit anything.

Bob was surprised to hear about Lamar's financial difficulties. He asked, "He's not considered a hero here?"

Amy shook her head, her long hair swaying back and forth. "Of course not. He's just a blowhard, and has been most of his adult life. A few people like him for spitting in the face of the North, but most think he's a bully and they hate the attention he's brought upon us. We're not a town of slave-traders."

Bob asked, "Would you consider him dangerous?"

Amy nodded, "To his enemies." She then saw the crowd building in the restaurant and excused herself to assist them.

While Bob ate supper, he watched Amy handle her customers with grace. He knew she was a special woman. As he left, he told Amy he would return the next night.

Bob went directly to his hotel room, sat at the table, and started writing notes about Savannah and the *Wanderer* for his real employer, the *New York Democrat* newspaper, based on Amy's account. Bob felt terrible about deceiving Amy. Seeing her again convinced him that he had done the right thing taking the Savannah assignment. But he couldn't reveal himself, at least not yet. It was just too dangerous in a town with the likes of Charlie Lamar.

Bob finished his report the next day, after the grand jury, in front of Judge John C. Nicoll, returned true bills for piracy against Corrie and crewmen Nicholas Brown, Miguel Arguirvi, and Juan Rajesta. The trial was scheduled for the May term. Bob signed the story using the pen name "Oglethorpe" and mailed it, as the telegraph could expose him. It would appear in the newspaper one week later. He doubted anyone in Savannah would ever see it, as northern papers rarely circulated in town.

Over the ensuing weeks, Amy remained on Bob's mind, whether he was painting or writing. He had supper most nights at the restaurant, but she was always too busy to chat for long. Finally, he asked her if they might be able to dine together one night. Amy consented, but wanted to have it at her restaurant, as she wouldn't be comfortable away from it, and she wanted to invite her brother and sister-in-law. Bob couldn't refuse.

When the night came, they sat at a corner table, with Amy purposely facing away from the room so she wouldn't be distracted. She had given instructions to the workers not to disturb her except for an emergency. She had asked Joseph and Emily to come a half hour after Bob so she could have some time alone with him.

Bob said, "It's hard to believe I'm actually sitting at a table with you, instead of looking up at you, ordering."

Amy twirled the camellia Bob had brought her. "This is a good test, to see if I can relax while I'm here. I've not been able to do that. You have to be a certain kind of person to run a restaurant. I'm not sure I'm it. Fortunately, I have an excellent cook."

"You seem to be doing very well. The restaurant is always full when I've been here, and the food is delicious." Always the reporter, Bob was anxious to learn more about Amy. "Miss McBain, does your family live in Savannah?"

"Yes. My father owns a plantation a few miles outside of town. He makes bricks and has a saw mill and iron foundry."

That sounded prosperous to Bob. "Do you have to work so hard?"

"No, but I always have. I've been lucky in finding work that I've enjoyed. My first position was in the state lunatic asylum."

Bob's eyes lit up. "Really? I worked in an asylum in New York when I was younger!" For the next thirty minutes the two traded stories. Amy was thrilled to meet someone who shared her experiences. Most men thought her work in the asylum was odd or amusing. But not Bob. He seemed more compassionate than any man she'd ever met, and as eager to listen as to talk.

Bob then asked Amy something that had been on his mind since they first met. "Are you going to tell me how the restaurant got its name?"

Amy told the story to a wide-eyed Bob. She concluded, "By the time the marshal cleared him, he was gone. We have no idea where he is."

Bob said, "What a sad story," and wondered if he could possibly write an article about it without revealing himself. He decided he couldn't.

Amy changed the subject. "So tell me, Mr. Carson, how are you able to pick up and move to Savannah so easily?"

"Miss McBain, it would please me if you called me Bob, and I called you Amy."

Amy smiled. "It would please me, too."

Bob continued. "My wife died two years ago during childbirth. Since I'm on my own, I can move around more easily." This part of Bob's story was true, as was his skill at painting.

Amy put her hand to her mouth. "Oh, I'm so sorry. May I ask about the child?"

Bob cleared his throat. "I lost my son, too." He took a drink of water and said, "I look forward to living and working in a new setting. It's what I need. Savannah is a beautiful town."

Emily and Joseph appeared at the table. Amy embraced them both and introduced Bob. After everyone sat, Joseph asked, "How are you enjoying life in Savannah, Mr. Carson?"

Bob said, "I've spent most of my time setting up my studio. But I've seen many of the squares. Savannah is a town like no other. I'm looking forward to painting it. Everyone I've met has been friendly, though I see wariness in some people's eyes when they first hear me speak."

Joseph laughed. "There are many Northerners here, visiting or living, including my wife. You'll have no problem. I'll be happy to introduce you around. Do you like sports? Boating, horses, quoits, hunting?"

Bob replied, "Yes, all of those."

Joseph smiled. "That will make things easier. This is a sportsman's town."

For the next two hours, they dined and talked. Emily asked Bob about New York, especially the new Central Park. Bob said it was opening that winter with carriage-ways, winding pedestrian walkways, and equestrian paths, all set amidst a treed and flowered landscape. The roadways traversing the park for cross-city traffic were sunk below the surface to be less noticeable to park dwellers.

After the dishes had been cleared, two men approached the table. One of them said, "Good evening, Miss McBain, Mrs. McBain, Joseph."

Joseph stood and greeted the men. He then introduced Henry Rootes Jackson and Joseph Ganahl to Bob. Bob was impressed that Joseph knew them both. Joseph told Ganahl that Bob liked to play quoits and would have to join them at the club. Ganahl agreed. They chatted for a few minutes and the lawyers returned to their table.

Bob asked softly, "Joseph, is that Henry Jackson, the former minister to Austria?"

Joseph said, "Yes. I served with him in the militia. He's a genius. He's assisting in the prosecution of a slave ship case. Have you heard of the *Wanderer*?"

Bob replied, "As I told Amy, one can hardly avoid it."

Emily leaned forward and whispered, "They've already charged four of the men and they're going to charge more at the next hearing in April, including the leader, Charlie Lamar." Joseph patted his wife on the back to calm her down. She looked at Joseph and sat back.

Bob replied, "I've read of him in the New York papers. But I wonder if the government will be able to prosecute such an influential man."

Joseph nodded in the direction of the lawyers' table on the other side of the room. "Ganahl detests Lamar. He'll do anything to put a noose around his neck."

Bob knew that a report of a face-to-face discussion with Charlie Lamar would make a great story for his paper. He asked, "Joseph, do you know this Lamar?"

Joseph glanced at Emily before answering. "I've known Charlie since we were boys. I've been involved with him on several committees. You could say we're friends, though I've had less contact with him since he got involved in the slave trade."

Bob sensed he was entering on sensitive grounds, but forged ahead. He said, "I've heard Lamar's father-in-law is the federal district judge here."

"That's true, but Judge Nicoll is an honorable man. I can't believe he'd compromise his reputation for Charlie. Just yesterday there was an Admiralty Court hearing on the ship, which had been seized. Everyone suspects it's Lamar's, though his name isn't on any ownership papers. Judge Nicoll presided and ruled the *Wanderer* was involved in importing Africans illegally and ordered it forfeited. It's being auctioned next month."

Emily perked up. "Speaking of auctions, Mr. Carson, there's going to be a big slave auction in a few days. The Butler auction. Have you heard of it?"

Pierce and Fanny Butler, the bickering couple with whom James and Sarah McBain shared a boned turkey so many years ago at the Coupers, finally divorced in 1849, with Pierce getting custody of their two daughters. Fanny resumed her acting career in America to be near her girls. Pierce moved back to Philadelphia, but kept his Brunswick plantations. After the financial panic of 1857 he was forced to sell them, including 436 slaves. Through a Savannah broker, he had arranged to auction the slaves at the Ten Broeck race track. Hundreds of people from all over the South were expected to attend.

"A slave auction?" Bob's editors had asked him, if possible, to write an article on one. It seemed as if he'd be getting his chance. "No, I haven't." Bob asked Joseph, "Are you attending?"

"I haven't decided. I need to consult with my father."

Emily narrowed her eyes and whispered, "Joseph! You're not really going, are you? It's the most despicable thing I've ever heard of."

Joseph held his wife's hand. It was obvious to him that in the presence of another New Yorker, she was feeling freer to express her sentiments about slavery. "Please relax, dear." She frowned. He then asked Bob, "Why do you ask?"

Bob said, "I'd be interested in seeing it, but I wouldn't want to go alone."

"Of course. I'll let you know if I go."

After supper, on their way home, Joseph and Emily agreed that Bob and Amy made a handsome couple. Amy went home thinking how charming Bob was, and wondered what it would be like to have him in her bed. Bob wondered if Amy liked him as much as he liked her. Then he started to write notes on Charlie Lamar and the upcoming slave auction.

James McBain asked Joseph to go to the auction on behalf of the Heritage. Though most of the negroes were cotton and rice field hands, there were a few mechanics in the gang. Joseph invited Bob. As Joseph drove the gig to the track, Bob explained that he had learned to paint from his mother. He then earned money by painting portraits of the children of wealthy New York clients of his mother. Since then, he never doubted how he wanted to earn his livelihood.

The track wasn't as crowded as race or fair day, but it was still busy. Certainly, the crowd was different. Instead of gaily-dressed men and women, it was full of hard-looking, cursing, segar-smoking slave brokers.

Joseph perused the program. All 436 slaves had spent their entire lives on Butler's plantations. They were to be sold in families, as was the custom. While this seemed a humanistic gesture, the family was defined as a husband, wife, and their children. If a slave had parents, brothers, or sisters in the lot, he or she would likely be separated from them forever.

Joseph and Bob watched as the families were paraded one by one onto a stand, sold, and marched away to a new owner. Bob felt queasy and glanced at the floor to avoid looking at the strained, pleading faces of the slaves. After a while, he left the auction area and walked to the sheds where the negroes were kept and inspected by prospective buyers before taking the stand.

Joseph also found the auction disturbing. He wasn't sure why. He'd been to auctions before. But watching family after family stand before the crowd with no control over their futures had left him sad. Maybe it was because Bob was with him and Joseph knew what he must be thinking. In addition, there was a rumor circulating that Butler had given each servant a dollar in gratitude for a lifetime of servitude. Joseph thought it was a pathetic gesture.

Joseph didn't make a purchase. He looked for Bob and found him talking to two men who, Joseph learned from the introductions, were planters from Mississippi. Bob and Joseph then returned to town. They spoke little during the ride back. Joseph didn't feel like defending the peculiar institution. Bob was thinking that the auction and his interview with the planters would make an excellent report.

They entered town at five o'clock. Joseph said, "I usually stop by a bar after work for a drink. It's a good way to learn what's going on. Do you want to join me?" Bob accepted.

They went to Southcott's and Joseph saw James Hamilton Couper, in town for the auction, and his son, Hamilton. Hamilton was practicing law in Savannah and frequently played quoits with Joseph. Joseph introduced Bob.

They discussed the auction. Hamilton Couper than asked Joseph, "Have you heard the news about the Africans who were captured in Telfair County?"

Joseph replied that he hadn't. Bob edged closer. Hamilton explained that a deputy marshal had just arrested Charlie Lamar's friend Richard Akin, three of Lamar's slaves, and thirty-six Africans as they were crossing Georgia in wagons. The deputy marshal telegraphed Marshal Stewart to determine what to do with the Africans. Stewart in turn telegraphed officials in Washington City for advice though, legally, the Africans were the property of Georgia.

The men shook their heads in wonderment about Charlie's stability. The talk soon turned to sports. Joseph was eager to take Bob to the quoits club, and Hamilton said he'd gladly join them. They agreed to play the next evening and departed the bar.

At the quoits ground the following day, they saw a beaming Joseph Ganahl, and Hamilton Couper asked the district attorney to join them. Hamilton asked Ganahl why he looked so happy. In a moment of candor, Ganahl revealed that he wrote to the governor of Georgia advising him that the federal government was temporarily claiming the Africans captured in Telfair County. Ganahl boasted that he had the two Africans in the county jail and the thirty-six in Telfair County. With Lamar's three negroes and his friend Akin in custody, Ganahl was confident he could link the Africans and the *Wanderer* to Lamar.

After the game, Bob went to his studio as giddy as Ganahl. The story was becoming more incredible with each passing day. He wrote a report on the auction and the seized Africans.

*   *   *

"Thank you, Jinny," Joseph said as she laid the plates on the table. He turned to Emily. "What was that you were saying, dear?"

"I said I think Amy is sweet on Bob. I saw her today and she actually talked about Bob without me asking. She's never done that with a man before."

Joseph laughed. "Where did you see Amy?"

Danny, in his nightshirt, ran into the room to his mother. She lifted the three-and-a-half-year-old onto her lap. "Today at the restaurant when I went shopping by Market Square. I met the nicest man, a shoe store owner. He moved here from Massachusetts ten years ago. I told him I had worked as a school teacher in New York and at Mrs. Church's. He said he instructs illiterate adults to read at night at his store. He asked me if we had any old books to spare."

Joseph offered, "I'm sure we have a few for him."

Emily stood and handed Danny to Joseph, who placed the boy on his lap and kissed the top of his head. "Getting back to Amy, she's going to invite Bob to have supper with your parents and us in a few weeks. That must mean something." Joseph didn't respond. Emily asked, "Joseph, do you like Bob?"

Joseph nodded. "Yes, very much. He's easy to talk to and he's a good sportsman."

"But?"

"But nothing." Joseph chewed his pork chop, and saw Emily staring at him. "Well, I do think something about him is odd. He asks more questions than any man I've ever met. But I don't worry about it." Changing topics, he asked, "Did you hear the latest about Charlie Lamar?"

"Lord, no! What now?"

Joseph explained that earlier that day, Charlie Lamar and John Tucker had visited the county magistrate's office. Lamar demanded possession of the two Africans in the county jail, claiming they were his property. The magistrate prepared a writ of possession, which provided that, unless Lamar's claim of ownership was contested, the negroes were his. Daniel Stewart, still the U.S. marshal as his replacement had not yet posted bond, the jailer, Charles Van Horn, and the Africans were summoned to the magistrate's office. The magistrate told Van Horn they were having a hearing to determine ownership of the blacks. Van Horn explained that he had written orders from the district attorney not to let the Africans out of the jail and said he would find Mr. Ganahl. But the magistrate refused to let him leave, stating that the Africans were under his charge and he could not abandon them. Van Horn asked Stewart to fetch the district attorney. Stewart left and returned in twenty minutes, saying Ganahl was busy. The magistrate called the hearing to order. Tucker testified that the negroes were the property of Lamar, and the magistrate awarded them to Charlie. Minutes later, Lamar and Tucker drove off with the Africans.

When Ganahl learned of the hearing later that day, he ran to the magistrate's office to protest. The district attorney claimed Stewart never tried to find him and held Stewart and Van Horn responsible for the release of the Africans. The magistrate ignored Ganahl's complaints.

Lamar had outsmarted Ganahl publicly once again. The district attorney was not looking forward to writing his next letter to Washington.

Van Horn, never an admirer of Lamar, despised Charlie even more for using him to get the Africans and damaging his reputation. He wanted revenge as badly as Ganahl.

Emily said, "Lamar should be put away forever."

Joseph said, "Let justice take its course, Emily. Justice will prevail."

Emily put her hands on her hips. "Well, it certainly didn't prevail in the magistrate's office. Thank God they took his ship away. When is the auction?"

"Next week. I'm taking Bob. And Andrew expressed an interest in going."

*   *   *

Joseph and Andrew were working together in Joseph's office when Bob entered a half hour before the auction of the *Wanderer*. Joseph introduced the two and told Bob they'd be with him shortly. Bob took a seat as the negro explained an architectural design to Joseph. Bob could not help but notice how articulate and well versed on architecture Andrew was.

Andrew was showing his plans for the First African Baptist Church to Joseph. The church elders had recently decided to begin construction, and Andrew was selected as the architect and builder.

Andrew considered the church the most important project of his life. He would be instrumental in bringing spiritual salvation to generations of Savannah's negroes. His objective was to create a functional building for worship, not an architectural trophy. He would not have crews of artisans, but church members devoting their spare time. Andrew would not be paid for his efforts.

Andrew had designed a rectangular, front-gabled brick building with a main auditorium over a ground floor. There were three evenly spaced entrances across the front elevation. Each door was set back, and capped by a simple entablature, which sat beneath a shuttered window, all set within a recessed arch. The front doors were reached by a side stairs which led to a front walkway. The pediment held a semi-circular window. The sides of the church had six tall shuttered windows set within recessed arches. It was powerful and monumental in its simplicity.

The interior drawings had twenty-five rows of pews with galleries at the sides and end, supported by thin columns with Corinthian capitals, all designed to seat seven hundred worshippers. The basement would be used as a lecture room and Sunday school.

Joseph stood and said, "The plans are excellent, Andrew. Father will want to see them. It will be as handsome as any church in Savannah." Joseph put his arm around Andrew's shoulders and squeezed. "I'm proud of you, friend. Real proud. Now let's go to the auction."

Bob could sense the affection between the two men. As they left Joseph's office, Bob asked Andrew where he had learned so much about architecture. Andrew replied that it was a long story. Bob smiled. He was determined to learn it. As they walked, Bob told Andrew how impressed he was with the buildings of Savannah. Andrew explained that Savannah was like an architectural museum, where one could see fine examples of Colonial, Georgian, Adam, Federal, Greek Revival, Gothic Revival, and Italianate, all within a few blocks.

Bob told Andrew how he thought the paired, Greek Revival townhouses with intricate ironwork on the west side of Monterey Square looked remarkably similar to townhouses on the west side of New York's Gramercy Park. Andrew said John Norris, the architect for whom he was working, had designed the buildings on Monterey Square, and lived in New York. Bob said the next time he visited New York he would sketch the Gramercy Park buildings for Andrew.

Joseph led Bob and Andrew through the crowd of several thousand to the front of the Exchange, and stood next to Charles Van Horn, who merely nodded at Joseph.

U. S. Marshal Stewart, still waiting for his successor to post bond, stepped onto a stand, faced the crowd, which packed the intersection of Bay and Bull streets, and held up his hands. When the people hushed, he still had to shout to be heard. "All right, gentlemen! Upon the order of Judge Nicoll of the Admiralty Court, the yacht *Wanderer*, confiscated by the government of the United States of America, is to be auctioned. The payment must be made in cash, ten percent today, and the rest upon delivery. If you wish to bid, stick your hand high in the air so's I can recognize you. If you don't intend to bid, don't raise your hand. Now let's get started."

"Wait a minute, Daniel!" a voice cried out. Charlie Lamar hopped onto the stand and Stewart stepped aside. He removed his hat and addressed the gathering. "Good morning, my fellow Savannahians." The crowd groaned. When it quieted, Charlie announced, "Confiscated by the government, my sweet arse! Stolen is more like it!"

That got the folks cheering. Joseph looked at Andrew and shook his head. Bob gawked at Lamar's performance.

"I needn't remind you that this is my ship. You should all know that I will be bidding to get back what is rightfully mine. No true gentleman would bid against me." Charlie folded his arms across his chest and surveyed the throng. He added, "Do I make myself understood?"

Someone shouted back, "We hear ya, Charlie," prompting more cheers.

Charlie jumped from the podium to his place at the front of the anxious crowd.

Stewart said, "Thank you, Mr. Lamar. Now let's start the bidding for this fine craft. I'm beginning with five hundred dollars. Do I hear five hundred?"

Charlie raised his hand.

"We have five hundred dollars from Mr. Lamar. Do I hear one thousand dollars for this one-of-a-kind ship? One thousand? Going once; going twice . . ." Stewart raised his gavel.

"One thousand dollars," a voice shot into the cool March morning air, piercing it like a hot tipped arrow. Two thousand heads turned to see Van Horn's raised hand.

Stewart looked at Charlie and shrugged. "Mr. Van Horn bids one thousand dollars. Do I have fifteen hundred?" Charlie's hand shot up. "I have fifteen hundred from Mr. Lamar. Do I have twenty-five hundred dollars? Twenty-five hundred? Going once, going twice . . ."

"Twenty-five hundred!" Van Horn hollered, ignoring the stares of the crowd.

Joseph whispered to Andrew, "Is Van Horn out of his mind?" Andrew shrugged.

Stewart cleared his throat. "Mr. Van Horn bids twenty-five hundred dollars. Do I have twenty-six hundred?" Charlie raised his hand. "I have twenty-six hundred from Mr. Lamar. Do I have four thousand dollars? Four thousand? Four thousand going once, going twice . . ."

"Four thousand!"

Lamar stood on his toes and glared over the heads and hats of the crowd to find his adversary. Van Horn fixed his eyes on Stewart. Lamar turned back to the podium. Stewart looked at Charlie, who nodded. "I have four thousand dollars from Mr. Van Horn! Do I have four thousand and one dollars?" Charlie raised his hand.

"I have four thousand and one dollars. GoingoncegoingtwicesoldtoCharlie Lamar!"

The crowd fell silent. Van Horn called out, "Hey, what's going on?" He turned to those around him, including Andrew and Joseph and said, "Did you see that? He didn't give me a chance to bid. This was fixed. Joseph McBain, you're my witness. I was about to bid. I never had a chance." He called to Stewart, "I protest this auction!"

As Van Horn ranted, the people parted to let Lamar make his way to Van Horn. When Charlie reached him, the jailer said, "You fixed this. I was going to bid."

"You want to bid? Here, bid on this." Lamar threw a right hand that landed flush on the jaw of Van Horn, dropping him to the ground like a felled pine. He struggled to get up but as he regained his feet, he fell flat on his back again.

Someone called out, "Charlie hit him once, and knocked him down twice!"

Charlie stood over Van Horn for a moment, looked up, and said, "Hello, Joseph, Andrew. Enjoying the auction?" He then pushed his way to the front of the Exchange.

Joseph turned to a frozen Bob Carson and said, "Well, now you've met Charlie Lamar."

Charlie bounded onto the stand and called out, "I believe Mr. Van Horn has learned to act like a gentleman." The folks hooted and hollered.

Joseph was about to leave when he saw Charlie smiling and waving wildly in the direction of the Custom House. Joseph looked towards the building. Standing on the top step, scowling down at Charlie, were Joseph Ganahl and Henry Jackson.

Bob said he had to return to work. Joseph told Bob he would see him on Sunday at his parent's house for supper. He knew the auction would make for a lively conversation.

As they watched Bob leave, Joseph asked Andrew, "What did you think of the auction?"

Andrew replied, "I hope Master Charles uses the ship to sail away. Far away."

Sunday supper at the McBains was pleasant considering it was an interview. Amy would do what she pleased regarding Bob, but she still desired her parent's approval. A handsome, well-mannered, intelligent, employed man Amy's age should not have raised any concerns. But Bob's northern roots changed things.

Pre-dinner conversation in the parlor was light, as James McBain tried to determine if Bob were a Republican by asking subtle questions such as, "So what do you make of this Lincoln fellow?" and "Don't you believe the Constitution is a fairly explicit document?" Bob handled the inquiries deftly, talking for minutes without revealing his true position. Amy caught Joseph's eye during the discussion and smiled at their father's tactics. McBain did ask Bob about the painting business, to which Bob talked at length, especially in explaining why he preferred oil-based paints over watercolors. Bob offered to paint McBain's portrait, and McBain accepted.

The conversation soon turned to the *Wanderer*. The day after Ganahl watched Lamar buy the ship, he received a telegraph. The Africans being held in Telfair County had been freed. Marshal Stewart claimed he never received a reply to the request he sent to Washington seeking guidance, so, without informing Ganahl, he telegraphed Deputy McRae in Telfair County to set the Africans free. McRae released them to Akin, relieving Ganahl of his last living evidence.

"What do you think of this *Wanderer* business, Mr. Carson?" McBain asked.

Bob again answered politically, but honestly. "I think many things, sir. But most of all, I think it's beyond belief. If I'd written a book about what's happened so far, it would be passed off as fiction. And every day, it gets more unbelievable. I have trouble keeping up with all the captured Africans, all the witnesses, all the law-breaking, and all the legal maneuvering. I've no doubt something will happen in the next few days that will test the imagination further."

At the evening's end, Joseph and Emily drove Bob home. The two men talked about Mr. Heenan's recent boxing exhibition at Oglethorpe Hall. Sarah told her daughter that Bob was very charming. James kissed his wife and Amy goodnight and had his port on the piazza. He needed to prepare himself for another northerner-in-law.

Bob was correct about another unbelievable event. It took ten days.

Joseph Ganahl was so angered over Lamar's theft of his evidence and other antics that he lost sleep. Ganahl revealed his anger to Jackson as they prepared for the upcoming grand jury hearings in their office on the second floor of the Custom House one late March morning.

As they talked, Ganahl stood at the office window overlooking the corner of the Bay and Bull Street. He said, "I'm glad we've had this talk, Henry. You've given me the proper perspective on this . . ." Ganahl paused, gasped, and cried out, "Holy mother of God!"

Jackson jumped from his chair and joined Ganahl at the window. Several hundred people encircled a buggy in front of the Exchange. The driver was Charlie Lamar. The passenger was a black boy in his younger teen years, wearing a smart suit of clothes and a top hat, which he kept tipping to the people in the crowd.

"Why that no good son of . . . . I'm going down there!" Ganahl whipped his jacket from the coat tree and hurried out of the office, with Jackson following.

They pushed their way through the crowd to the buggy. Lamar was taunting the stammering port collector, John Boston. Charlie spotted the lawyers. "Well, if it isn't the protectors of our southern way of life."

"Just what do you think you're doing, Lamar?" Ganahl shouted.

Charlie grinned. "We're just taking a little ride around town, enjoying this lovely day. And yourself, Mr. Ganahl?"

"Just who is this fellow?" Ganahl demanded, looking at the young black boy with bright white teeth and markings under each eye.

"Just who is this fellow?" replied the boy, before Lamar could answer.

"Oh, just a boy I've taken a liking to. His name is Corrie. Corrie, please say hello to Mr. Ganahl and Mr. Jackson."

"Yas, Mass' Charl." The boy tipped his hat. "Mass Gonna, Mass Jackson."

Lamar said, "It's been fun chatting, gentlemen. I hate to take you away from your work. Good day." Lamar yelled to the crowd, "Move aside!" and snapped the reins. Corrie tipped his hat to Ganahl and Jackson as the buggy pulled away. The lawyers stared after them.

"Mr. Ganahl?" Boston interrupted.

"What!?" Ganahl barked.

"If that boy is an African, shouldn't we seize him as evidence?"

Ganahl slapped his forehead. "Yes. Of course. Get Marshal Stewart. No, not him. Get Agent Gordon. Have him seize that boy." Ganahl kicked at the dirt of the street and stomped back to the office.

When they returned, Jackson said to Ganahl, "Calm down. Remember what we just talked about. Please have a seat. I was about to tell you before Lamar rolled by, I'm going to Washington tomorrow to see Attorney General Black. John Egbert Farnum is rumored to be in New York City, and about to publish his memoirs on the *Wanderer* incident. I want Black's permission to arrest him and bring him here for trial."

Ganahl's eyes lit up. "Farnum? That would be excellent. Yes. I'd love to see Lamar's face when Farnum walks into the courtroom. Indeed! Have a successful trip, Henry." The men shook hands and Jackson left.

Six hours later, Agent Edwin Gordon found Ganahl alone in his office. "Sir, I finally located Lamar. He said the boy wasn't his and that he gave him back to his owner, who had already left for Columbus."

Ganahl threw his pen down on the table, and it bounced up and landed on his shirt, staining it with ink. He put his head in his hands and groaned. Gordon tip-toed from the office.

Ganahl bemoaned the prospect of another sleepless night. He couldn't let Lamar defeat him. He sat up and prepared grand jury subpoenas for five of the Telfair County men who had captured the Africans. Their testimony would bring a true bill against Lamar. Ganahl felt better, so he prepared the paperwork to charge Lamar with holding an African boy named Corrie. At nine o'clock he closed the office and headed home. He slept after all.

Bob's next article started with, "New York readers aren't going to believe the latest development in the *Wanderer* case, but . . . ."

A week later, Joseph was having an after-work drink with some friends at the Our House barroom. Hamilton Couper mentioned that articles about Savannah, particularly the *Wanderer*, were appearing in a New York newspaper. They were written by a reporter calling himself Oglethorpe. Couper passed the latest article to the others to read. It was about Butler's slave auction. Joseph's friends believed it was written by a reporter living in the North based on rumors and other reports, as was so often the case.

Joseph thought the article had too many details to be written anywhere but in Savannah. And the report appeared to be accurate. Joseph handed the paper back to Couper.

*   *   *

The grand jury hearings were scheduled to begin on Monday, April 11. However, due to late-arriving witnesses, the hearings were delayed four days. Five of the tardy witnesses were the men from Telfair County.

Charlie Lamar had been aware of those men's subpoenas to testify and filed affidavits for their arrests, claiming they had unlawfully taken his property. Justice Phillip Russell issued the warrants. When the Telfair County men finally stepped off the train, two constables greeted them, placed them under arrest, and escorted them to Justice Russell.

The outraged men demanded to see the district attorney. Ganahl was informed and rushed to Russell's office. Twitching with anger, he told the men to be calm while he tried to figure a way to free them.

The hour being three o'clock, Justice Russell allowed the men to go to dinner under the care of a constable. When they returned, Russell held a hearing. Lamar testified that the men had stolen his property worth over thirty thousand dollars. The constable then testified that the men had admitted over dinner that they had stolen Lamar's negroes. The men hollered in protest, but to no avail. Russell committed them. Stewart, in a show of sympathy for the lawmen's plight, became their security in lieu of one thousand dollars each, and the defendants were released.

The night before the opening of the grand jury, Joseph Ganahl got little sleep. His spirits didn't improve when Henry Jackson returned from Washington with no government commitment to arrest Farnum.

The grand jury finally convened in mid-April. Over the next few weeks, Ganahl accomplished much of what he had intended. Since he could not prove that Lamar owned the *Wanderer*, and because Lamar didn't make the trip to Africa, Ganahl couldn't charge him with piracy. But he did convince the jurors to find three true bills against Lamar, one for holding an African boy named Corrie, one for holding the two Africans captured in Macon, and one for holding thirty-six Africans captured in Telfair County. Lamar wouldn't hang, but he'd go to jail for many years.

The grand jury also found true bills against Richard Akin, John Tucker, Nelson Trowbridge, John Dubignon, and Henry Dubignon for the holding of African negroes, and one more against Nicholas Brown for importing African negroes. Ganahl and Jackson were satisfied. Some prominent men who thought they were above the law would be judged by it.

A trial date for Corrie, Brown, Arguirvi, and Rajesta for the charge of piracy was set for May 5. Conviction was punishable by death.

Ganahl left the courthouse with a bounce in his step, looking forward to a good night's sleep. During the hearings he had seen the exhaustion and strain in Lamar's eyes. Ganahl had finally started exacting his revenge. The true bills were just the start. The trials and the convictions would be the real pearls.

As Ganahl reached the sidewalk, he saw attorney John Owens and Lamar. He wanted to tell Charlie to have fun in hell, but that would be unethical, so he passed them by. He heard someone call, "Mr. Ganahl, I have something for you to read."

Ganahl stopped in his tracks, unprepared for the gall of Lamar to talk to him. He snarled, "I don't think it appropriate for us to communicate, Mr. Lamar."

Owens, also surprised at Lamar's conduct, said, "He's right, Charlie."

Charlie pouted. "I'm not trying to communicate with him, John. I just want to give him something to read." Charlie thrust the *Daily Morning News* at the district attorney. Ganahl reflexively took the paper but didn't know what to do with it. Lamar continued, "There's an interesting article on King Gezo of Dahomey. He'd captured thousands of fellow-Africans for the slave trade in his time, before his unfortunate, recent death. He was so fond of human sacrifices that his loving son slaughtered eight hundred Africans in tribute to his dear father. Now, were those Africans better off in Africa or in America on a Christian plantation, Mr. Ganahl?"

Ganahl threw the paper back at Charlie. "Have fun in hell, Lamar!" he yelled and walked away. Sleep eluded the district attorney that night.

On May 3, in front of a gallery full of spectators, the trial of Corrie, Brown, Arguirvi, and Rajesta for the charge of piracy was called, with Associate Supreme Court Justice James Moore Wayne and District Judge John C. Nicoll presiding. There was only one problem. William Corrie remained in South Carolina. The district court judge still refused to give him up for trial in Georgia. Ganahl was forced to ask Wayne for a continuance of the trial until the next term of the court in November. Wayne granted the request, agreeing that the four men should be tried together, but declared he would not delay the trial past November. Wayne refused the defense request to grant the three prisoners bail. They would spend the next six months, which included the sickly summer and autumn seasons, in a cell.

Ganahl and Jackson were disappointed in the delay. They wanted to strike while they thought they had public opinion on their side. They would have to try to rekindle local passions against the law-breakers in six months.

An early summer brought the kind of heat Savannahians could almost chew, and a respite from the *Wanderer* affair. The grand jury hearings and Charlie's antics had exhausted the town. Residents, including the McBains, had until November to proceed with their normal lives.

Most significantly, the old, wooden First African Baptist Church on Franklin Square was torn down. On July 5, with Andrew and Patience, the McBain family, Patience's parents, and Bob Carson in attendance, the cornerstone to the new church was laid. Reverend S. G. Daniel of the white First Baptist Church presided over the ceremonies.

After the dedication, while having lemonade, Bob again asked Andrew about growing up on the plantation and how he learned so much about architecture. The two sat on a bench in Franklin Square and Andrew modestly described his life. Bob thought this was yet another great story that had to be told—a negro who surreptitiously gained an education and was a gifted architect, but had to conceal it. His editor would have to put it on the front page.

Bob's painting business did well enough to provide a cover for his other activities. He advertised in the *Daily Morning News* and the *Savannah Republican* and made acquaintances through Joseph and Mr. McBain. Bob painted a portrait of James McBain and a landscape of the house at the Heritage. Amy hung the landscape on the wall of the restaurant, which resulted in several commissions.

Bob spent most of his summer in New York conferring with his editor and visiting his aunts and cousins. He even took a day to sketch the paired houses by Gramercy Park for Andrew. The absence from Savannah made Bob realize how much he missed Amy. He thought about proposing, however that would require a confession about his true employment. He feared that might cause Amy to terminate their friendship. Bob decided to wait until he was confident she would not leave him when she learned the truth.

The restaurant trade slowed for the summer, for which Amy was grateful. She was proud to have created one of the most popular eateries in town, though the hours and night work drained her. Still, her spirits were high, as she had fallen in love with Bob. She enjoyed his company more than that of any man she had known. He was so different. Bob, through his paintings, talked about flowers that harmonized, trees that mourned, and birds that meditated, while most other men talked about the price of middling cotton.

Amy expected Bob to propose, and she would happily accept, though there were potential problems. What if Bob wanted to go north? She would go wherever he wanted, but she couldn't imagine leaving her home.

Sarah spent the summer at Tallulah Falls and prayed that Amy and Bob would marry and start a family, if Amy could at age forty. She also tried to convince her husband to hire an overseer and join her at the falls. McBain promised his wife he would join her the following year.

In August Patience told Andrew she thought she was pregnant. The couple was overjoyed at their blessing. The next day they visited Joseph and Emily to deliver the news.

Just three weeks later, when Bob returned from New York, James, Joseph, Emily, Amy, and Bob visited Andrew and Patience. Bob presented Andrew with the sketch of the Gramercy Park building. Then Emily revealed her news—she was pregnant, too.

Of course, there was nothing normal in Charlie Lamar's life. He lost his court case and twenty-three thousand dollars over his violation of a cotton press patent. The trial had to be held in Charleston because of Lamar's relationship to Judge Nicoll.

Charlie did find time to take several friends to Havana on the *Wanderer* in the hope of selling it. He invited Joseph, who declined.

Charlie also arranged for Leonidas Spratt to speak in Savannah about re-opening the African slave trade. The South Carolinian, considered one of the best orators of his day, held his large audience spellbound.

Joseph did have contact with Charlie again when he decided to re-involve himself in the agricultural fair and the jockey club, much to the displeasure of Emily. But Joseph had always enjoyed the work, the contacts, and the friendships that that work offered. He assured Emily that he would not be involved with Charlie beyond the committee meetings.

Emily continued volunteering at the Savannah Female Asylum, and collected reading material for Mr. Fisk. One evening in mid-October, she brought him a box of books.

"Why, thank you, young lady. You can't imagine how much this helps." Fisk paused a moment to study the pretty woman before him. He then asked, "Have you heard the news about this Harpers Ferry incident?"

Emily did not expect to be asked that. She responded warily, "Only a little. It just happened."

Word had been filtering by telegraph into Savannah that the night before, Sunday, October 16, a group of abolitionists had taken control of the Harpers Ferry, Virginia, federal armory with the intent of arming the local slaves and creating an uprising. Southerners were aghast at the boldness of the act.

Fisk nodded, "It's a shame these things have to happen." He looked around his own shop and said in a hushed voice, "But we're fortunate there are men as brave as those patriots."

Emily exhorted, "Oh yes, we are!"

That's what Fisk wanted to hear. "Mrs. McBain, would you like to do more than donate books? As a school teacher, you could help me instruct."

Emily's smile broadened. "Mr. Fisk, I'd love to help people read."

Fisk held her hand in his. "Mrs. McBain, I could tell the first time you walked in here that you were a special person."

Emily blushed at the compliment. "That's very kind of you to say, Mr. Fisk."

"I read to them after the work day, two nights a week. Could you come by tomorrow at nine? Just for an hour? Would that be satisfactory with Mr. McBain?"

"I'll ask him, but I'm certain it will be, Mr. Fisk." With that, Emily left the shoe shop, bubbling with excitement.

Joseph hadn't seen his wife so animated in a long time as she told him of Fisk's offer. He realized teaching illiterate adults would be the perfect opportunity for her talents. And if she was happy, he was happy.

That night Joseph lay in bed waiting for sleep to take him. He felt his wife remove his nightshirt. Then he felt her naked body on top of his. She stretched his arms out to the sides and whispered in his ear to close his eyes, not move a muscle, and pretend he was floating on a cloud. She sat on him, leaned forward and kissed his forehead. She moved down slowly, letting her breasts slide over him as she kissed his lips, ears, neck, nipples, and belly. His last coherent thought was that perhaps Emily might consider teaching five times a week.

The next night, Jefferson drove Emily to Market Square. "Ah waitin' yuh, Missus," Jefferson said as he helped her step from the carriage onto the deserted dark street.

"I'll only be an hour." Emily walked to the store door and was greeted by Sewall Fisk.

As he led her through the darkened store, he said, "I've heard some more about Harpers Ferry. A hero of the Kansas operation named John Brown is leading the insurrection. They're trapped inside the armory. But they have God on their side." Fisk then opened a storeroom door. "In here, Mrs. McBain."

Emily walked into the dimly lit room, removed her shawl, and froze. She stared at the three male and three female adults sitting on the floor and turned to the New Englander. "Mr . . . Mr. Fisk. I had no idea. Did I not understand you correctly?"

Fisk took Emily's trembling hand. "You're a special person, Mrs. McBain. Our challenge is enormous. We have so much work to do."

He spoke to the six students. "Scholars, please meet our new teacher, Mrs. McBain."

They replied, "Ebnin', missus."

Emily stammered, "Good evening." She turned back to Fisk. "Sir, as much as I want to help, this is against the law."

Fisk squeezed her hand. "Not against the laws of humanity, Mrs. McBain. Not against the laws of God. There are higher authorities than the State of Georgia."

Emily withdrew her hand and wrapped her shawl around her shoulders. "I'm so sorry, Mr. Fisk. I really can't. I have my family to think of."

"I understand, Mrs. McBain. But please, as long as you're here, just help tonight. That's all. They've been counting on you."

Emily stared at the negroes looking up at her. She didn't want them to think she was unsympathetic. She removed her shawl again. "I guess since I'm here."

Fisk pulled over a small wooden chair for Emily. While he sat in the corner and read *Uncle Tom's Cabin* to two of the blacks, Emily sat between two men and two women. Their body odor was unbearable, and Emily had to breathe through her mouth. Her heart pounded like a drum. She thought of getting up and leaving, but she couldn't. She started with the alphabet. They all had trouble pronouncing the letters, but after awhile, they improved. One of the women was able to recite the first six letters by memory, and used a Gullah word containing each one. Emily was so excited at the woman's progress that she leaned over and hugged her. Before she knew it, Fisk interrupted her. It was ten o'clock.

Emily stood and the negroes thanked her. Emily's heart ached for the poor souls.

As Fisk led her to the front door, he said, "You can always change your mind, Mrs. McBain. And God bless you."

Though Emily was elated at helping the negroes, she felt guilty about breaking the law. She had to tell Joseph the truth, but was too nervous to do it that night. When she arrived at the house, Joseph asked how the teaching went. She told him, "Nicely," then hurried to see Danny in his bedroom. She joined the growing number of Savannahians who were not sleeping well.

The next morning Joseph and Emily were in the carriage; he on his way to work, she to shop. Joseph told Jefferson to drop him at the corner of Bull and Bay. As Jefferson pulled the carriage to the curb, she said, "Joseph, I need to talk to you about last night. About Mr. Fisk."

Joseph sat back. But just as Emily started to explain, Joseph glanced out the window and saw Charlie Lamar run out of the Exchange, across the Bay and up the stairs of the Custom House. Joseph stuck his head out the window and called to him. Lamar spotted Joseph and yelled, "Joseph! Please help me out! Some damned rascal just stole the *Wanderer*!"

Joseph turned to Emily. "Did you hear that? Let me find out what's happening. Can we speak tonight?" Before she could reply, Joseph shot out of the carriage and up the Custom House stairs. Emily was relieved she didn't have to tell the story, but was angry that Joseph would dash off, and for Charlie Lamar no less.

That night, Joseph explained to Emily that a man named David Martin had come to town a few weeks ago looking to buy a ship. He had heard the *Wanderer* was for sale and negotiated with Charlie to buy a share in it. Though Martin hadn't paid Charlie any money, he raised a crew for a fruit run to the Caribbean. The night before, Martin called the entire crew to the ship, where a few of his mates forced the rest of the men to set sail towards the ocean. Charlie learned of the heist the next morning and heard that the ship was aground ten miles down river. Charlie was on his way to the Custom House to ask the port collector for use of a revenue cutter to give chase when he hailed Joseph. As it turned out, they were too late. Martin and the *Wanderer* had escaped.

Emily asked Joseph why he would lift a finger for a criminal like Lamar. Joseph said that he detested Charlie's slave trade activities, but Charlie had put him on the spot and he couldn't refuse. Emily decided not to confess about her visit with Sewall Fisk. If Joseph could help a law-breaker, however innocently, so could she. She decided to assist Fisk again.

Two weeks later, in early November, two groups were discussing Lamar and the upcoming trial over supper at Dante's Place.

Joseph Ganahl and Henry Jackson sat at a corner table. Ganahl was upset. The Harpers Ferry incident had fired up many in the South. With John Brown trapped inside the armory, the marines, led by Lt. Colonel Robert E. Lee, had stormed the building and took Brown prisoner while killing a handful of his followers. A week later, Brown, whose men killed both innocent blacks and whites during their attempt, stood trial in Virginia. On November 2, 1860 he was found guilty on all charges and was sentenced to hang one month later. Ganahl worried there would not be many southern jurors willing to convict anyone of piracy after a Northerner showed such total disregard for the law.

Also, Ganahl still had been unable to extradite William Corrie. Ganahl accepted that the trial, due to start in two weeks, would have to proceed without the most important defendant.

At another table, the McBains talked of Emily's pregnancy, and how well she looked. They also talked about the recent theft of the *Wanderer*. Amy said she'd heard that Martin had bragged a few days before he left that he was going to Africa for a cargo of slaves, and the theft was a charade, with Lamar in on it. Joseph said, "He didn't act like he was in on it when I saw him trying to recover the ship, though Charlie might be a better actor than I know."

Bob, who had just written to his paper of the Martin incident, said to the others, "I know I've said this before, but I feel we're in a theatre watching a play. What in the world could possibly happen next?"

*   *   *

The marshal called out to the crowd in front of the Glynn County courthouse in Brunswick. "Alrighty! Next we have this fine negro runaway. No one's answered the notices we ran in the papers over the past year, so the lucky purchaser will have title free and clear. He goes by the name of Joe Soupy. He claims to be a thirty-six year-old cook. A mighty fine cook, I might add. This is no broken-down, lazy field nigger. Now I want a good offer on Joe, who has many good fryin' and stewin' years ahead of him. Who will start the bidding at five hundred dollars?"

"Why does he look familiar?" James Hamilton Couper said to his son, Hamilton, as they attended the public auction near the Couper plantation.

"Five hundred dollars! I have five hundred. Do I hear six fifty?"

"A cook? Do I know anyone missing a cook?" the elder Couper mulled.

"I have six fifty. Do I hear seven hundred? I have seven hundred. Do I hear seven fifty?"

Couper froze. "I know! It's James McBain's negro. I've met him several times. I saw him just a few years ago in Savannah. I'm certain of it. His name is Dante."

"Seven hundred dollars going once, going twice . . ."

Couper raised his hand and shouted, "Wait a minute! Hold it! I know that boy!"

The marshal stared into the crowd. Dante wondered who would know him in Brunswick.

Couper pushed to the courthouse steps. The marshal asked, "Mr. Couper, are you bidding on Joe?"

"No, I'm not. You can't sell this negro. James McBain of Savannah owns him. His name is Dante, not Joe."

The marshal looked at Dante. "Is that true, Joe?"

Dante looked at Master Couper. He was caught. It was all over. He was going to die. He hung his head, took a deep breath, and charged down the stairs, but was caught by the crowd. The marshal yelled at his deputy to take Dante to the jail. He then announced to the crowd, "The sale of Joe Soupy, or Dante, is off until we can determine who he is, and who owns him!"

The next day, James Hamilton Couper greeted James McBain at Brunswick harbor and drove him to the jail. The marshal led them to a cell. "Right in here, Mr. McBain. He's been very quiet. Don't talk and hardly eats."

The marshal, McBain, and Couper walked into the small cell. McBain saw a negro sitting on the floor with his head in his hands. The marshal said, "I'll leave you gentlemen alone with him. I'll be just around the corner."

McBain stood for a few seconds waiting for the black man to look up. "Dante?"

Dante lifted his head and saw McBain. He rose slowly with his hands on his chest. "Ah nebuh killum, massa, ah swaytuh Gawd." Dante's body shook.

"I know you didn't, Dante. I know. We all know."

Dante cocked his head and said, "Wut? Oonuh know, massa?"

"Yes. Mr. Down's niece saw the whole thing. She was so frightened she couldn't speak for days. She said she saw Hank stab him and you tried to stop it. She cleared you."

Dante's mouth opened. He held McBain's arm. "W'en, massa? W'en she say dat?"

"Just a few days after it happened. We looked all over, but couldn't find you. Where have you been? Dante? Marshal! Marshal! Dante just fainted!"

CHAPTER 27

The Trial

November 1859-May 1860

The first glass of water in the face opened Dante's eyes. The second made him lift his head off the brick floor. He saw the marshal standing over him and Masters McBain and Couper sitting on wooden chairs, watching him. The marshal pulled Dante onto a chair. His shoulders slumped. Water dripped from his chin onto his lap.

McBain said, "Just relax, Dante. You're all right." Dante nodded without raising his head. After a few minutes, he said he was feeling better. Couper and McBain helped the negro stand up and Couper drove the two to Brunswick harbor.

On the voyage to Savannah, while most passengers stood by the railing and studied the ocean, Dante sat on a bench next to McBain and gazed into space. He'd hardly said a word since he'd been revived. He was happy he was not wanted for murder, but was stunned that he had gone through the past seventeen months of hell for nothing.

McBain left him alone at first. Dante, always slim, was nearly gaunt and the corners of his eyes and forehead had grown lines of age and worry. His curly hair grew in tube-like bundles, and stuck out like the fronds of a palmetto tree.

Eventually, McBain asked, "Where did you go, Dante? Where did you hide?"

Dante knew he would be asked that question. He looked straight ahead. "Een de swump. Een de trees, massa. Dey udda run'ways. Dey laa'n me tuh trap an' fish."

McBain put his hand on Dante's shoulder and squeezed it, causing the negro to wince. "I know you were scared, Dante. But if you ever have a problem again, you come to me. You don't run away. Do you understand me?" McBain loosened his grip.

Dante again hung his head. "Yassuh, massa."

"When we get back to Savannah, you rest a while. Then you can cook again. That will make you feel better."

Dante followed McBain down the gangway on a warm November afternoon. Amy, Joseph, Andrew, and Hercules were there to greet him. Amy stepped forward and took his hand. She said, "Welcome home, stranger." Joseph, Andrew, and Hercules echoed the sentiment. They climbed into the coach, and Dante sank into the upholstered seat. He hadn't been on anything so soft for a long time. As the coach started moving, Amy explained how much everyone had missed him. No one had ever told him that before. He was glad to be home.

When they got to the house, the other servants welcomed Dante. Andrew asked Mr. McBain if Dante could have supper at his house that night. McBain agreed, knowing that if Dante opened up to anyone, it would be Andrew. Andrew, of course, had been thrilled at the news of the discovery of Dante. The guilt he had held for the past year was gone.

Three hours later, after a haircut from Celia and a bath, Hercules drove Dante to Andrew's house. Hercules asked him if he were feeling better. Dante said he was, but offered nothing more. Hercules sensed the cook brought back a dray load of trouble with him. He wondered what it might be.

Dante and Andrew sat in the parlor. "Dante, I don't know what to say. I'm relieved you're back and safe. No one knows how you escaped. Not even Patience. I told Hercules I helped you, but not how. What did happen? Did you get on the ship? Did you go to Africa?"

Dante didn't answer. He wasn't ready to tell the story. "Weh Miss Pay'shun?"

"At Miss Amy's restaurant. She's the cook. She prepared dinner for us before she left."

Dante looked at Truvy playing on the floor. "Dey whales maw small den dat chile."

Andrew said, "We're having another. Patience is pregnant again."

Dante smiled. Then he dug into his pocket and handed Andrew six shiny gold coins. Andrew blinked at them in confusion. Dante said, "T'ank oonuh, but ah yent need 'um."

Andrew pocketed the coins and they sat for dinner. Dante ate noisily, involved in his meal. Andrew watched him and said, "Whenever you feel like talking, go right ahead. I won't force you."

Dante was about to take another bite of ham when he stopped, placed his fork on the plate, and said, "Ah ready, Andrew."

Over the next two hours, Dante talked. He told the story stoically, except when he described the voyage home, and the tossing of the Africans and Neeka overboard. Then he choked up. He finished by describing his escape from the ship, thinking he was swimming to Cuba. He shook his head. "Ah uh dum' nigguh, Andrew."

Andrew, stunned to speechlessness by the tale, pushed the blueberry pie towards Dante, who tried to remove a slice, but it crumbled in the pie dish. Dante said, "T'ank de Lawd it obuh."

Andrew cut an intact piece and placed it on Dante's plate. "You're alive, that's the important thing. But it's not over, Dante."

Dante lifted a piece of pie on his fork. "Wut oonuh say, not obuh?"

"The ship you were on, the *Wanderer*. It landed the Africans on Jekyl Island. Some of the men were caught, and they're being tried in Savannah. The case is all anyone talks about."

The pie fell off Dante's fork and splattered on his plate. "Wut men?"

"Brown, an American, and two Spaniards named Rajesta and Arguirvi."

"Ah know Capin Brown. Oonuh know de fus' names ub de Spany?"

"I think Juan and Miguel. Do you remember them?"

Dante gasped. "Miguel trow Neeka een de oshun. Dey try tuh kill me." Dante reached for a glass of water. His hand shook as he lifted it, spilling water on his hand and the table. "Oonuh yeddy Capin Cowie aw Fahnum?"

Andrew tried to calm Dante. "I haven't heard anything about a Farnum. Corrie is in jail in Charleston. The district attorney is trying to bring him here to stand trial."

Dante drained his glass of water in one swallow. "Ah nebuh wan' tuh see Capin Fahnum agin. He wussuh den de Spany. Andrew, ef dey laa'n ah yuh, dey gwi' kill me, fuh sutt'n."

"They won't know you're here. They're in jail. Besides, black men aren't allowed to testify. You're no threat to them." Dante's fear was obvious. Andrew steered the conversation away from his journey. "Do you want to see the restaurant?"

Dante nodded. They put the dishes in a bucket of water. Andrew grabbed one of Joseph's pre-signed passes and they left. Dante carried Truvy. When they arrived at the restaurant, Andrew pointed to the sign hanging over the door. "What do you think?"

Dante looked at the sign and said, "'Bout wuh?"

Andrew stepped over to the sign. "It says 'Dante's Place. A Restaurant of Distinction.'"

Dante stared at the sign, trying to make sense of it. "Duh stink shun? Andrew, ah need uh fabuh. Ah need tuh laa'n tuh read."

Andrew smiled. "As long as you never mention to anyone that I'm helping you."

The men embraced. Dante walked home, worrying about the *Wanderer* men.

*   *   *

When Associate Supreme Court Justice James Moore Wayne arrived in town, the first of the *Wanderer* cases was set to be called. William Corrie still had not been extradited and would not be tried with the three other defendants.

The delay of six months did not diminish the interest in the trial by Savannahians. Large crowds occupied every foot of the Custom House steps, trying to gain entry to the limited spectator seats available. Reporters and workers had to fight their way through. There was a slight hint of tragic-comedy behind the proceedings. After all, there was no *Wanderer*. No one knew where it was. And on the first scheduled date of the trial, with people awaiting entry to the courthouse, a local man dressed as a woman strolled back and forth on the sidewalk in his best feminine gait, drawing howls and whistles from the crowd.

There was no humor in the proceedings to Joseph Ganahl and Henry Jackson, both of whom had labored so hard in preparation. Despite not having an African, they were confident they had gathered enough evidence to prove their case. They just had to prevent disruptive behavior by defense lawyers John Owens and Thomas Lloyd.

Finally, at four o'clock in the afternoon of November 16, a jury of twelve men had been sworn, and with Judges Wayne and Nicoll presiding, the trial began.

Spectators Joseph McBain and Bob Carson listened intently to the first witness, Horatio Harris, the lighthouse keeper on Little Cumberland Island. Harris recalled events with great detail, much as he had at the pre-trial and grand jury hearings. Before the defense lawyers could cross-examine the witness, Judge Wayne adjourned the court for the day, letting Harris's words sink into the minds of the jurors.

The next day, Harris continued describing how he had seen the Africans, Charlie Lamar, John Tucker, Nelson Trowbridge, and John and Henry Dubignon on Jekyl Island beach. However, Harris suddenly had trouble positively identifying Brown, Arguirvi, or Rajesta because they looked so different in the courtroom than they had on Jekyl Beach the prior year, having not bathed, shaved, or had a haircut for so long.

Ganahl and Jackson thought Harris was playing dumb. Jackson asked, "Mr. Harris, throughout your previous testimony you referred to the prisoners as being on the beach. Why do you no longer say the men on trial are the same men you saw on the beach at Jekyl Island?"

"Objection, your honor!" shouted John Owens as he leapt from his chair. "The prosecution is trying to get the witness to imply identity. Can the counsel confine his questioning to what the witness knows, not what he infers."

Jackson, who had warned Ganahl not to let Owens's behavior distract him, ground his teeth. He turned to Judge Wayne and said, "Your honor, I wasn't aware that the counsel for the defense was the one to tell me how I should conduct my questioning. The witness spent enough time around these defendants on Jekyl Island to be well acquainted with them and honestly believes the defendants are the same men. There must be some explanation why the witness says these are the men but will not swear to their identity. It's apparent undue influence had been brought to bear on the witness."

Owens jumped to his feet again and called out, "Objection, your honor, objection! What is the prosecution implying or accusing? What evidence does he have that any pressure has been put on any witness? I demand to hear that evidence, or I demand an apology! Is that how the counsel plans to conduct this trial? If he hears testimony he doesn't like, to charge tampering with the witness? This is outrageous."

Jackson pointed a finger at Owens. "I did not charge anyone with tampering."

Owens took a step towards Jackson and pointed back. "That was your language!"

"Order! The both of you come to order!" the flush-faced Judge Wayne hollered. Judge Nicoll groaned. The lawyers quieted and faced the judge. "Mr. Jackson, if you insist on making such charges in this court, you better have evidence to back them up. If not, don't make them. Now let's proceed."

Owens, satisfied with the chaos he had sown, grabbed the lapels of his jacket and sat. Bob turned to Joseph and whispered, "Mr. Owens is good. Very good."

Joseph whispered back, "So are Mr. Jackson and Mr. Ganahl. You'll see."

Bob said, "I have five dollars that says Owens is better."

Joseph said, "I'm not sure the best man wins this fight. I won't bet."

The testimony of Horatio Harris, while clearly establishing that there was an illegal landing of slaves in the state of Georgia, had less clearly implicated the prisoners.

The prosecution called other witnesses, who delivered vague testimony tying the defendants to the voyage of the *Wanderer*. A ship captain *thought* he had picked up Brown at Jekyl Island on the night the Africans had been landed on the beach. Captain Luke Christie told how he took Trowbridge, Lamar, Tucker, and Brown to Jekyl Island on a steam-tug. Christie saw the Africans on the beach and saw them loaded onto the steam-tug for the return trip. He *thought* he saw the defendants on the beach with the negroes, and *thought* they helped load them on his ship. He *thought* they made the return trip with the Africans and were let off with the others fourteen miles above Savannah on the South Carolina side of the river. He was not positive about anybody's identity but Brown's.

James Clubb, who piloted the *Wanderer* across St. Andrew's Sound, told of seeing Brown on Jekyl Island, but could not identify any other of the crew.

Over the next four days, almost thirty witnesses were called. The lawyers gave their closing arguments in one day. On Tuesday, November 22, at 4:30 p.m., after Judge Wayne had charged the jury and had all the testimony re-read, the jury retired to the jury room, not to eat or sleep until they reached a verdict.

Bob had attended each day of the trial, and when on his own, took thorough notes. Joseph only had time for two days of testimony, the lawyers' summation, and the judge's charge to the jury. As they left the Custom House after the jury started deliberations, both agreed the defendants were guilty, but Bob said Owens had succeeded in planting enough doubt in the jurors' minds. Joseph said that was true only if the jurors were looking for doubt. They agreed to meet when the jury reached a decision.

Joseph was sitting in his office at 11:30 on Wednesday morning when Bob charged into his office. "They've reached a verdict, Joseph! Judge Wayne's called the court in session at noon. We'd best get over right now!" They ran from the office, with Joseph wondering how Bob had learned so quickly of the jury reaching a decision.

They claimed the last two seats of the spectator section in the packed courtroom. Ten minutes later, Charlie walked into the courtroom with Tucker, Henry Dubignon, and Trowbridge and sat in the seats behind the defense attorneys.

As Ganahl and Jackson entered the room from a side door, all chatter stopped. Everyone rose as Judges Wayne and Nicoll appeared.

Wayne said, "Please be seated," and nodded to a bailiff, who brought the jurors into the courtroom. The judge asked the foreman, "Mr. Belden, has the jury reached verdicts in the case of the United States against the defendants?"

"Yes, your honor, we have."

"In the case of the United States against Nicholas Brown for the true bill of piracy, what is your verdict?"

"Not guilty, your honor."

"In the case of the United States against Juan Rajesta for the true bill of piracy, what is your verdict?"

"Not guilty, your honor."

"In the case of the United States against Miguel Arguirvi for the true bill of piracy, what is your verdict?"

"Not guilty, your honor."

The courtroom erupted in a mix of cheers and gasps. "Order in the court," Wayne called as he rapped his gavel. "The prisoners are still to be tried on other bills and are to be remanded to jail to await those trials. This court is now dismissed."

Lamar and his friends converged on the defense lawyers, slapping their backs and shaking their hands. Judges Wayne and Nicoll viewed the celebration and walked away shaking their heads. As they entered the judges' chambers, Wayne said, "If a local jury won't convict strangers with all that evidence, they're not going to convict Georgians."

Ganahl and Jackson collected their papers and quickly retired to their office across the hall. Ganahl sat at his desk and stared out the window at the Exchange. Jackson perched on the edge of the desk and said, "You performed admirably, sir. The jurors made up their minds before the trial began. Forget this case. We have others coming up."

Ganahl nodded without looking at Jackson. Jackson patted Ganahl on the shoulder and left the district attorney deep in thought. He bade good day to Joseph and Bob as he passed them on the Custom House steps.

As Jackson walked away, Bob whispered to Joseph, "Even though I knew Owens would triumph, Ganahl and Jackson impressed me. They did everything to win the case."

Joseph replied, "I guess that wasn't enough."

*   *   *

"It's disgusting, Joseph. They stole 490 lives, killed ninety of them, and were acquitted," Emily said as she pushed her supper dish aside. It was the evening of the verdict.

Joseph chewed his food slowly. "It's not that clear-cut, Emily. The witnesses couldn't identify them. Their appearances had changed from the beach to the courtroom."

"That's nonsense, and you know it." Emily looked away from her husband.

Joseph said. "Just remember what Bob said. He's never heard of a conviction handed down by a New York court in a slave trade case either. And there have been plenty."

Emily retorted, "That doesn't make these verdicts right. A horrible crime's been committed and the people involved get off just like that."

"Poppa, what's wrong?" four-year-old Danny asked, standing in the doorway in his nightshirt. Joseph and Emily turned to their son. Chloe came by and picked up the boy.

Joseph said, "Nothing, son. Mother and I are just talking."

Emily said, "It's bedtime, darling. I'll be right up to read a story to you." Chloe carried the boy away.

Joseph waited to hear footsteps on the stairs. He lowered his voice. "Emily, I agree the verdicts were bad. But this is how the justice system works in the North *and* the South. There was a trial with witnesses and evidence presented to a jury. They didn't convict. How else would you have it?"

"A southern court had no trouble convicting John Brown, a man doing good."

Joseph swallowed his food without chewing. His voice rose again. "Doing good!? Are you serious? A man who murdered innocent people? He shouldn't have been convicted?"

Emily turned her chair sideways and said, "It's becoming unbearable here."

Joseph winced. "What do you mean by that?"

"Nothing. Are you still planning on going to the agricultural fair tomorrow?"

"Yes. I'm going with General Harrison. Then Andrew wants to show me the church. I haven't seen him in a while. After that I have a jockey club meeting. Emily, what did you mean by it becoming unbearable here?"

"Nothing. I shouldn't have said it. If you're going to be out tomorrow night, then I'm going to help Mr. Fisk."

*   *   *

"It looks great Andrew," Joseph said as the two walked around the building site.

"Thank you. I'm glad you could come by." The congregation had raised and spent five thousand dollars, a little less than half of what they would need to complete the church. But despite limited funds and irregular hours, by December 1859 Andrew and the negro workers had completed much of the framing. They planned to have the structure enclosed in a few months, and Sunday services could be held in the basement. Andrew was proud of the progress and had been anxious to show it to Joseph.

Joseph stood by his gig on Montgomery Street and examined the front of the partially completed building. "I've been attending the *Wanderer* trials. Have you followed them?"

Getting hold of a newspaper was not easy for negroes, but Andrew managed to find one occasionally. And the trial was the topic of conversation in town, even for the blacks, so he had a good idea of the proceedings. "As best I could. I know that the men were found not guilty."

"Yes, despite a shipload of evidence against them."

Andrew stared at the front façade as well. He had more knowledge of the *Wanderer* voyage than Joseph could imagine. He decided to offer his opinion. "I agree, Joseph. Everyone knows Africans were brought into Georgia on the *Wanderer*. I understand there was testimony placing the three defendants on the ship. Yet no one was convicted. What can I do? Get angry? That's just the way things are."

Joseph thought about Andrew's comment. Of course, that was how any negro would react. If he, Joseph, was angry at the verdict, he couldn't fathom how a negro must have felt. But what could anyone do? Joseph said, "The church will be the finest in all Savannah, Andrew. And everyone knows Andrew McBain designed it. I've got to go to the race track. I'll see you soon."

A few days later, in front of just a handful of spectators, one being Bob Carson, Captain Brown was tried on a second charge of importing African negroes. The jury foreman took ill during deliberations and Judge Wayne declared a mistrial. He ordered a retrial for the May term. Brown was released on bond and left Savannah.

Also, District Attorney Ganahl failed to convince a grand jury to find another true bill against Rajesta and Arguirvi. Judge Wayne discharged them from custody. They immediately disappeared from town. The remaining *Wanderer* cases were continued to the Spring 1860 term.

No one was more relieved at the news than Dante. Soon after he returned to Savannah, he began working in the restaurant. It was good timing. Patience was pregnant and didn't want to work at night. She taught Dante the routine of cooking in a restaurant before she left. His dream of being an important cook had finally come true. But he still feared the men of the *Wanderer*. When he learned from Andrew that Brown, Juan, and Miguel had left Savannah, he thanked God.

*   *   *

At eleven a.m. on December 2, 1859, as Judge Wayne was releasing Nicholas Brown on bail, a hangman in Charles Town, Virginia, was releasing the trap door beneath John Brown's feet in front of two thousand enthusiastic spectators. Word spread quickly over the telegraph. It was a joyous day in the South. There was one less abolitionist. A message had been delivered.

That night, Emily watched men outside taverns celebrate the event as Jefferson drove her to Mr. Fisk's store. The sight, on top of the *Wanderer* verdicts, had made her more determined than ever to help. She spent the next hour teaching the slaves, whose number had grown to eight. She was pleased with their progress, and left the store proud of her efforts.

As she was about to step into the coach, a man with a hat pulled down over his kerchief-covered face, grabbed her arm, startling her and causing her to yelp. The man told her not to say a word. Her heart raced. Then she heard someone else say, "You stay right there, boy." She saw another similarly dressed man with a pistol pointed up at Jefferson, who was coming to Emily's aid.

The man holding her arm said calmly, "Mrs. McBain, don't you ever come back here again. Now, please go home."

Emily was so frightened she could hardly climb the three steps to the cab. As soon as the masked man closed the carriage door behind her, Jefferson drove away. She looked out the window and saw three men walk towards Fisk's shoe store.

The men entered the store and told the negroes to go home. They gagged and bound Fisk, carried him outside, and threw him into a wagon which carried three other men. They drove for an hour to a deserted field on the east side of town, ignoring Fisk's muffled screams.

In the chilly night air, the masked men cut off all of Fisk's clothes with a knife and set them on fire. Five men held Fisk while the sixth cut his hair with scissors. Fisk's eyes almost bulged out of his head when he saw the cauldron of hot tar. He wriggled like an unearthed worm to break his bonds, but it did no good. Two of the men, using sticks, slapped the black substance over Fisk's naked body. The abolitionist moaned as he tried to suppress any acknowledgement of pain, but cried out when the steaming black mass was spread over his genitals. A bag of loose cotton was opened and the men took turns pressing handfuls onto Fisk's sticky coating.

When they finished, the men stood aside and watched the New Englander writhe on the ground. They cut the cloth over his mouth and the rope around his ankles, leaving only his wrists tied together, and left. Fisk yelled, "Sinners. You'll burn in hell! All of you!" He could hear their laughter over the clanking of the wagon wheels.

Fisk lay on the ground for a while, praying. He then staggered to his feet and felt the weight of the tar, like a suit of armor, pressing his body down. He started the freezing, five-mile trek back to town, one ponderous step after another. Many times he sank to his knees from exhaustion and pain. But he knew Jesus couldn't rest on his last walk, and neither would he.

"Joseph, something happened to me last night. I need to tell you about it," Emily said to her husband over breakfast the next morning. She had wanted to tell him when she returned home the night before, but he hadn't gotten back from a jockey club meeting until after she had fallen asleep. Not that she slept well. She knew she was breaking the law yet continued to help Fisk. And she was caught doing it. She was afraid for her family and had to tell Joseph.

"Certainly," Joseph said, trying to cut a piece of bacon.

"When I left Mr. Fisk last night, a man in a hat and a mask stopped me and said I shouldn't go there anymore." Emily covered her face with her napkin and started to cry. "I'm scared, Joseph."

Joseph went to his wife and held her. "Don't worry, darling. Nobody's going to hurt us. Do you know why he did that? Why would he have a problem with you teaching people to read?"

Emily looked up at Joseph, tears pooling in her eyes. "Because they're colored."

Joseph went back to his chair and collapsed in it, like a defeated prize fighter. "You've been teaching negroes at Fisk's and you never told me?"

Emily nodded. Joseph walked to the doorway to make sure the servants weren't listening. He returned to his chair and asked, "Emily, how could you do such a thing? Did you think of Danny or my family?"

Emily rubbed her cheekbones with trembling hands. "I thought I was going to teach whites. When I went the first time, he took me to a back room and there were negroes. I told him I couldn't, but he convinced me to do it just one time. That's all I did. I didn't go back. But then I got so angry at the *Wanderer* verdicts." She covered her face in her hands.

Joseph saw his wife in pain, hunched over in her chair, and reached for her hand. "Who else knows of this?"

"No one. Jefferson took me to Fisk's but he doesn't know what I was doing. Last night, when the man stopped me, Jefferson came to my aid, but another masked man pointed a gun at him. I told Jefferson not to mention a word to anyone."

Joseph gasped, "Holy Mother of God!"

They sat quietly for a while, he looking at her, she at her lap. Finally, Emily sobbed, "You taught Andrew, didn't you?"

"Yes, but that was one boy on a plantation, far away from any authorities, not in a secret room in town with many negroes. And I was a boy, too. Don't you see the difference?" Emily nodded, then shook her head in confusion.

They were interrupted by Chloe. "Excuse me, Master Joseph. Jefferson says he needs to see you outside right away, if you don't mind."

Fisk reached the outskirts of town at Liberty Street and East Broad at six a.m., while it was still dark. His cotton-covered body was a dirty white except for his posterior, hands, elbows, and knees, which were dark brown from repeatedly falling to the ground. He paused for a minute to gather the strength to get to the city hospital on Drayton and Huntingdon.

He struggled to Drayton and Liberty as the sun was just rising and the residents of the area were starting their days. By the time he had reached Drayton and Taylor, one block away from Joseph's house, there was a group of squealing children following him.

Jefferson was preparing the coach when he heard the commotion and went to observe it. He didn't know it was Fisk, but he knew, based on the man's condition, what he had been accused of. That's when Jefferson asked Chloe to fetch Joseph.

Emily followed Joseph outside. Jefferson told them a man who'd been tarred and cottoned was walking on Drayton towards the hospital. The three started running. When they reached Fisk, he was clomping along, his head swaying side to side, and mumbling prayers. Joseph almost puked when he saw that the only uncovered areas on the victim's entire body were his eyes, nostrils, and mouth. Joseph said, "Sir, we're here to help you!"

Though she doubted it would provide any comfort, Emily removed her shawl and wrapped it around the pitiful man. He whimpered, "May God bless you."

Joseph said, "Sir, the hospital's right here. We'll help you to it. Can we notify anyone? What's your name?"

"Fisk, sir. Sewall Fisk."

Emily turned her back and howled like a wounded animal.

*   *   *

"Did you hear about the shoe store owner, Henry?" Joseph Ganahl asked Henry Jackson in their office as they filed their paperwork the day after the conclusion of the fall session.

Jackson sorted a stack of papers into two piles on his desk. "Yes. It's a sad day for us all when lawlessness reigns," Henry replied. "Savannah is full of good, honest, God-fearing people."

Ganahl replied, "My guess is Charlie Lamar and his mob had a hand in it."

Jackson explained, "Marshal Stewart insists he investigated. Charlie was at a jockey club meeting. Claims he has witnesses."

Ganahl laughed at the thought of Stewart investigating Lamar. "Then it was Charlie's charming friends. I heard Joseph McBain and his wife got Fisk to the hospital. She became ill at the sight of him. The doctors are still trying to get all the tar off. He's losing skin."

Jackson placed one pile of papers in a desk drawer. "Apparently, the incident is having its intended impact. Did you read William Price's letter in the *Daily Morning News*?" Price was the clothing store owner who had sent word to Ganahl about the three, free-spending ragged men, which helped lead to their arrest. He also gave testimony against Brown during the trial. After the news of Fisk had spread, rumors started to circulate that Price had abolitionist sympathies. The clothier was so frightened that he wrote a letter to the editor of the newspaper claiming he was as ardent a supporter of slavery as had ever lived.

Ganahl replied, "I did," as he examined the back of his hand. It looked like it belonged to an old man. The trial still weighed on his mind. He knew prosecutors lost some cases. But he had won convictions with less evidence than he had against the *Wanderer* defendants.

Jackson said, "Joseph, I need to inform you that I'm going to Washington in a few days to ask Attorney General Black to remove me from the case. It's not because we lost these first trials. The heart of the trade is in the North. This charade is giving the Northerners just what they want, the eyes of the nation on the South, away from them. This case is a waste of my time if the government won't support us in getting the real criminals like Farnum."

"I agree. But Lamar is from the South. So is Corrie. Just because they're minor players, they can't be allowed to break the law. What kind of message does that send?"

Jackson picked up the remaining papers on his desk and placed them in a case. "I'm not suggesting we let them beat the law. You can handle these cases. You don't need me stepping on your toes. I have to get my message through to Washington, and I have no idea how to do it other than by resigning." Jackson dusted his empty desk.

Ganahl stood and offered his hand. "I wish you luck, Colonel. It's been an honor working with you."

Jackson went to Washington and delivered his resignation letter to Attorney General Jeremiah Black. He stated that he could not work on the case as long as the government had no interest in bringing J. Egbert Farnum to justice. Jackson's ploy worked. President James Buchanan, after learning of Jackson's resignation, authorized him to go to New York with special investigator Lucien Peyton to arrest Farnum. A week later Captain John Egbert Farnum was sitting in the Chatham County jail.

*   *   *

Emily asked, "Do you think a jury will convict Farnum?" as she gently ran her hands over her pregnant belly. They were sitting in Amy's restaurant just two days before Christmas. Joseph had just explained the latest event in the *Wanderer* saga.

The prospect of the baby helped bring Joseph and Emily closer together after the experience with Mr. Fisk. Joseph gave up his after-work drinks to spend more time with Emily and Danny. Emily did her best to withhold her comments on slavery.

However, Joseph hadn't forgotten the Fisk incident. Though he was angry that Emily had lied to him, he was far more incensed that anyone would admonish his wife or tar and cotton another human for any reason. But he couldn't complain to the police or the marshal about Emily being accosted because he would have to admit that his wife was educating negroes, a crime for whites as well as blacks. He would somehow have to find the culprits himself. In the meantime, Emily never went out at night alone.

Emily couldn't forget, either. She wondered about Mr. Fisk's recovery, but didn't dare return to the store to find out. And the police hadn't found the criminals who attacked him. She wondered if she could raise her children in such a society.

Joseph said, "We'll have to wait and see. But that's not all the *Wanderer* news. I heard the ship's been found."

Emily said, "Oh, no. Where?"

Joseph explained, "As I understand it, after David Martin high-jacked the *Wanderer* he headed for the coast of Africa for a cargo of slaves. As the ship neared Africa, Martin hailed a passing ship for supplies. As he and four crewmen rowed to it, the first mate on the *Wanderer* gave the order to sail back to America, leaving Martin behind. A few days ago the *Wanderer* entered Boston Harbor."

Emily asked, "Who told you that story?"

Joseph said, "Charlie. I saw him at a jockey club meeting this afternoon. He's happy, but says he has to go to court to get his ship back. More legal fees." Emily closed her eyes upon hearing that Joseph still had contact with Lamar, but refrained from commenting.

Amy whispered, "Speak of the devil."

They looked up and saw Lamar walk in with ten other men. He was still taking great pleasure from the court victory the prior month. And he had finally started collecting for the sale of Africans, which removed some financial pressure.

Charlie spotted the McBains and walked over with City Marshal Daniel Stewart. Joseph and Bob stood to greet them. When Joseph sat down, Emily kicked his leg under the table. Joseph asked Charlie what they were celebrating.

Charlie replied, "Nothing. We just had a meeting at Masonic Hall. We're organizing a Southern Rights Vigilance Association right here in Savannah." Joseph had recently read about the group in the paper. It was dedicated to the preservation of southern rights and institutions by those concerned about northern attacks on slavery, Northerners' refusal to return runaways, and abolitionist propaganda. "You should join us, Joseph."

Joseph turned pale. "Thanks, Charlie, but the fair and jockey club take all my time."

Charlie said, "Well, you can always change your mind. Enjoy your evening." He and Stewart bowed to the ladies and returned to their table.

Amy said under her breath, "That's just wonderful. Of all the people to be taking it upon himself to defend the southern way of life."

Joseph thought the group might have already started with Mr. Fisk. He decided to have a chat with Charlie about the men who accosted Emily. It was an ominous sign for the New Year.

But 1860 held great promise for many. Dante was reveling in his role as a chef.

Joseph Ganahl was sleeping soundly again. He had had enough. In January he resigned as district attorney and returned to private practice. Hamilton Couper was appointed to replace him.

Andrew McBain and his workers finally enclosed the church and Reverend William Campbell was able to lead his worshippers in the basement. A call went out to the white Christian community to help raise the remaining six thousand dollars to complete the building.

In late March and early April, three weeks apart, two McBain babies entered the world. Patience first gave birth to a boy, Gully Palladio, and then Emily gave birth to Charlotte Sarah. The celebrations in the McBain households were long and joyous.

Savannah itself was faring well. The economy had returned to vibrancy. There was so much cotton being harvested in Georgia that the Central of Georgia Railroad had to borrow one hundred freight cars and seven locomotives from other lines to carry the product to the port.

The upcoming *Wanderer* trials didn't even get much attention in barroom chatter. The year's cotton crop, the Kansas situation, and the upcoming presidential election were the main topics of concern.

Not everyone was content. Farnum had not adjusted well to life in jail. He was not shy about letting the jailer, his lawyer, or Charlie know of his displeasure. Charlie had assured him that a release on bond would be forthcoming, but Charlie was no lawyer, and it never came.

Farnum was finally able to breathe fresh air for a day in April. After four months in jail, he attended his grand jury hearing. The jurors quickly found a true bill against him for piracy. Bail, always doubtful, was no longer possible.

*   *   *

Danny and Truvy sat on their fathers' shoulders on the Bay. Both boys waved the Georgia flag as the militia units in their bright uniforms marched by. Joseph wished that Emily was with him to see the May Day parade, but she was home with baby Charlotte. Patience was at home with Gully.

Bob was impressed with the large number of smartly dressed, well-armed men marching with precision. He knew many in the North assumed that the southern states' militias were groups of ill-trained, shoeless farmers armed with shovels.

After all the groups had passed by, Andrew started to leave. At Joseph's request, Andrew consented to bring Danny to Emily so Joseph and Bob could have a drink.

Joseph and Bob went to the Pulaski bar and saw District Attorney Hamilton Couper. They chatted with him and Bob made plans to get together soon with him for a game of quoits. Then Couper left for his office to prepare for the upcoming *Wanderer* trials. He seemed to have the same confidence Joseph Ganahl once had.

Joseph and Bob were about to leave when Charlie Lamar and an ever-present crowd of followers flowed in like a high tide. Joseph cursed his luck of running into Charlie yet again, but chance meetings were not unusual in Savannah where gentlemen frequented the same barrooms.

Charlie invited them to join him. Before Joseph could decline, Bob accepted, which puzzled Joseph. They followed Charlie to a table. Charlie introduced his friends to Joseph and Bob. Joseph knew most of them, including John Tucker, Richard Akin, William Hone, and James Middleton. Charlie then asked, "Joseph, do you know Carey Styles?"

Joseph replied, "No, I don't believe we've ever met."

"Carey, meet my good friend Joseph McBain. And this is his painter friend, Bob Carson. Joseph and I serve on several committees together. Joseph has the first dollar he ever made, and a million others." The remark drew laughter. "Joseph, Carey is from South Carolina, but he's been living in Brunswick for the past few years. Just what Georgia needs, another lawyer."

As Joseph shook Styles's hand, the name dawned on him. Styles had shot and killed a man two years before at a political meeting in Brunswick and was charged with murder. The case gained greater attention when Styles was elected mayor of Brunswick a few months later. After a courtroom battle involving some of the state's most prominent lawyers, the jury returned a verdict of not guilty. Joseph thought Styles made an ideal friend for Lamar—clever and dangerous.

The men drank and joked. Bob seemed to pay close attention to their every word. Joseph was about to bid goodbye when Lamar announced, "You know, Captain Farnum would enjoy being here now. I bet he has some stories to tell."

Styles raised his glass. "I concur. Let's bring him here."

Lamar looked at Styles. "It stinks in that jail. The man is locked up, and for what? Violating laws that that damned Congress had no right passing? Well, piss on Congress! Piss on the jail! I'm bringing Egbert back here for a party." Charlie stood. "Who's coming with me?"

Three of the men stood. Charlie said to the others, "Rent a room. And get some women. We'll be back in a flick!" With that Charlie, Styles, Middleton, and Hone left.

Bob and Joseph watched the other men go to the hotel lobby to rent a room. Joseph turned to Bob and said, "I can't believe that even Charlie would be this reckless. Freeing a prisoner from jail and bringing him to a party in town? And then what?"

Joseph and Bob went to the bar, where Joseph recognized Mr. Cevor, a recent resident and an aeronaut. They started chatting about Cevor's latest balloon ascension and were so enthralled by the adventure, they forgot about Lamar. Forty minutes later, just as Mr. Cevor left, Charlie and his group, which had increased by one man, barged into the lobby.

Bob and Joseph watched the men walk upstairs. Joseph rubbed his chin in thought. He wished he had gone home earlier. "Bob, if that extra man was Farnum, and I'm certain it was, a crime—a jail break—has just been committed. I'm getting Hamilton Couper at his office. This might get ugly. You're still an outsider here. It will be safer if you leave." Joseph left the bar.

Bob was in a quandary. He knew Joseph was correct, but this was turning into an enormous story. He decided to stay in the bar and wait for Joseph and Couper to return.

Couper put on his jacket as soon as Joseph explained the situation. Couper, who as a young man had idolized Lamar as a fun-loving sportsman, was repulsed by his conduct in the *Wanderer* affair, and was doing all in his power to lock him up. Ganahl had warned Couper that Lamar was a tough criminal and would test Couper as soon as he got the chance. That warning was coming true.

Joseph and Couper entered the hotel just as the jailer, Charles Stone, and two deputies did. Stone said, "Mr. Couper, Charlie Lamar and some of his friends forcibly removed Captain Farnum from the jail. They held down the deputy and snatched his keys. I heard they're here."

Couper said, "I've just been informed of that as well. Let's find Mr. Farnum."

Couper got the room number from the desk clerk and the lawmen ascended the stairs. Joseph knew he should go home, but he just couldn't leave without learning the outcome of the confrontation. Against his better judgment, he followed Couper up the stairs. Bob trailed behind.

Couper knocked on the door and waited. He knocked again. The door opened and the noise and smoke hit them like a bucket of waste in the face.

Holding the door handle, William Hone said loudly, "Well, look who's here. Please come in, Mr. District Attorney."

The room quieted as Couper, Stone, and the two deputies entered. Joseph stayed in the doorway. Couper spotted Farnum sitting on a chair with a woman on his lap. Couper said, "Let's go, Farnum. The party's over."

Styles said, "The captain isn't going anywhere, sir."

Couper looked at the grinning Styles and said, "Someone told me you were a lawyer, an upholder of the law. I guess he had lost his mind."

The smile drained from Styles' face. "Couper, don't you have other things to do to amuse yourself?"

"I'm taking Captain Farnum back to the jail. That will be amusement enough."

Someone else said, "No, you're not, Hamilton. So why not leave now, unless you want to join us for a drink."

Couper knew that voice belonged to Charlie Lamar and ignored it. He said to the escapee, "Let's go, Farnum. Don't make me ask you again."

Couper heard the unmistakable clicks of pistols being cocked. He turned and saw Lamar, Hone, Styles, and Middleton pointing their guns at his head. Charlie spoke again. "It's you that's leaving, Hamilton. You and your friends."

"Lamar, do you think you can break a man from jail and keep him? Are you that crazed?"

Charlie pointed his gun inches from Couper's ear. "I didn't say I want to keep him. I want to throw him a party. That's what I'm doing." Lamar lowered his pistol. The others followed. "Let the captain stay here tonight, Couper. We'll return him to you tomorrow. He'll apply for bail, and he can have some freedom before his trial. Isn't that fair?"

Couper didn't feel like explaining to Charlie that a man being held on a charge of piracy could not post bond. He looked around the room. "Who else here is defying the officers of justice? Please step forward and identify yourselves." No one moved. "Let's go, Farnum."

The four revolvers once again leveled at Couper's head. Lamar said, "Sir, I thought you were a smart man. I've just made a fair proposition." Charlie looked around the room and spotted Joseph in the doorway. "Joseph, can you reason with Hamilton? You two go back a long way."

Joseph, transfixed by the contest of wills occurring before him, said, "Charlie, you're breaking the law. I've got to draw the line there."

Lamar replied, "Oh? Do you draw the same line with your wife?"

No one but Joseph knew what Lamar was talking about, but the question still stunned everyone in the room. They all looked at Joseph, who said, "What damned business of that is yours, Charlie?"

Couper shouted, "Stay out of this, Joseph!" Couper then said to Farnum, "I'll see you tomorrow morning, Captain." Once again the revolvers lowered and Couper, publicly humiliated by Lamar, walked out of the room, followed by Joseph and the lawmen. Joseph saw Bob in the hallway and asked if he heard the confrontation. Bob nodded.

Joseph did not sleep well that night. He would have to have a talk with Charlie.

Hamilton Couper did not sleep much, either. Men had openly defied the law and he had been powerless to stop it.

Couper got to his office at seven o'clock the next morning and waited for Farnum. When he didn't show by noon, Couper walked across the Bay to the Exchange, told the mayor about the previous night, and asked him to place men at his disposal if he had to retake Farnum by force. The mayor promised twenty officers.

Couper then sent a messenger to the Pulaski House to inform Farnum that he was waiting. At two o'clock, Farnum entered Couper's office and requested bail. Couper told Farnum that his lawyer had to request it through the courts, but he would likely not get it. He then escorted the escapee to jail. Couper breathed a sigh of relief as he saw Farnum locked in his cell.

Though a grand jury of the United States Circuit Court found true bills against Lamar, Middleton, Hone, and Styles for rescuing Farnum, the story of the party at the Pulaski House spread throughout Savannah and America. Charlie Lamar had faced down Hamilton Couper.

*   *   *

Captain Farnum conferred with his lawyer the evening before the May term of the district court was scheduled to begin. The lawyer assured Farnum he had nothing to worry about. Farnum said he couldn't wait to get out of the hell-hole.

The jailer stuck his head in the door and informed Farnum and the lawyer that their supper had arrived. The lawyer removed his papers from the table.

The jailer entered the room followed by Amy. He said, "Right here, Miss McBain."

Amy stepped to the door and said, "In here."

Farnum looked up as the negro with his arms full of dishes stepped into the room.

Dante stepped to the table, smiled at the diners, and dropped the dishes piled with food to the floor. "Dante!" Amy shrieked.

"Massa Fahnum?"

"Oh, shit!" replied Farnum.

CHAPTER 28

The Witness

May 1860-Jan 1861

"Dante, do you feel like talking yet?" Amy asked as the wagon creaked past the Free School on Whitaker Street on their way back to the restaurant. Dante sat next to her, hunched over as if he had a stomachache. Amy snapped the reins. "How in the world do you know Captain Farnum? I can't help you unless I know."

Dante had prayed he'd seen the last of the *Wanderer* men. Then Farnum appears, and would surely try to kill him. Dante knew that he could not run away again. Only the McBains could protect him. "Ah bin dey, on de ship."

Amy brushed her hair from her ear. "What!? You were on the *Wanderer*?"

"Yessum, Miss Amy."

Amy whispered, "My Lord," as they pulled up to the restaurant. She held Dante's arm before he could jump from the wagon. "Dante, we don't have time to talk now. I have to get food back to the jail and a crowd is forming here. But we have to talk later."

Amy sent a messenger to tell Joseph to meet her at the house on Pulaski Square at eleven o'clock that night, and to notify their father, who was in town, to be available as well.

Dante slumped in the chair as he told the McBains about his experience on the *Wanderer*. To protect Andrew he lied about how he got onto the ship. He explained that he had gone to Andrew for help, and Andrew told him to go to Master McBain. Too scared to do that, Dante went to the river and hid in Lamar's cotton warehouse. He overheard men talking about boxes being loaded on the next ship. When they left, he saw a box with holes, removed and hid its contents, crawled in, and pulled the top over him. Soon he felt the box being carried and set down again, heard a ship's whistle, and felt the rolling motion of being on water. After many hours, he pushed away the lid, and scared the wits out of four men standing nearby. They were going to throw him overboard until he told them he could cook. They made him work day and night for the rest of the voyage.

The McBains peered at each other. The story was unbelievable, yet Dante knew too many details of the voyage and its participants. James McBain went to the cabinet and fumbled for a bottle of whiskey. He looked at Amy and Joseph, who both nodded. He poured and handed out the glasses. They sipped as Dante stared at the floor.

McBain said, "You've been through a terrible experience, Dante. But you'll have to speak to the government lawyers. They'll be interested in your story, even though you can't testify. That's the price you pay for not trusting me."

"Massa, please. Dey kill me."

"No one will harm you, Dante. You have my word. If necessary, you can stay at the Heritage. That will be all."

After Dante left the room, McBain said to Amy and Joseph, "Who knew? Dante is much stronger than any of us thought."

*   *   *

Hamilton Couper was at his desk preparing for the next round of *Wanderer* trials when Henry Jackson rushed into the office. "You see this, Hamilton?" Jackson said, out of breath, as he dropped the *New York Times* on the desk. Staring at Couper was an article entitled, "The Fine Young Southern Gentleman."

Hamilton read silently. The cynical article described Farnum's escape from jail and the lenient treatment he received from the federal authorities in Savannah. The writer, who based his article on reports in southern papers, implied that Charlie Lamar ran the justice system in the town. Couper's face turned red. He pushed the paper away as if it were a plate of rotten food.

"Now read this," Jackson said, pointing to a different article.

Couper read, "The New York Slave Trade." It described how corrupt New York officials were bribed to clear a slave ship from New York for the coast of Africa. The article ended with the following: "One thing, however, is certain—that if we cannot find officers of the law in New York honest and energetic enough to prevent slavers leaving our ports, we must cease denouncing Lamar, and other slave-trading gentlemen of the South. This port is, beyond question, the headquarters of the traffic, and on the authorities here devolves the duty of rooting out the nest of malefactors who furnish the ships and money to sustain it."

Jackson slapped his hand on the newspaper. "This is what I've been saying all along. Even the *New York Times* acknowledges it. New York is the center of the slave trade. Yet when a pest like Charlie Lamar lands Africans here, the North has a fit."

Couper shrugged. He felt the same as Joseph Ganahl had. "Henry, it's our job to prosecute violators of the law here, regardless of what's happening in New York."

Jackson rolled up the paper and held it like a club. "Hamilton, Southerners are seriously talking about secession. Only a small number own servants and very few own ten or more. Yet Southerners are willing to leave the Union. It's because of the arrogance of the North in matters like this. They have to live by the same laws we do."

Couper let Jackson's words dissipate in the stuffy office air. "Henry, there's nothing we can do about that. We need to prepare our cases."

Jackson sat. "That reminds me. I received a message from James McBain. He says he needs to speak to us about the *Wanderer*."

Couper shook his head. "We don't have time. The trials start tomorrow. Whatever it might be, we won't be able to use it now. Tell him we'll contact him after the term is over. Besides, I have to reply to the *Times*." Couper held out his hand. Jackson gave him the paper.

The district court session began on May 14. The first case was the United States against Nelson Trowbridge for holding African negroes. A successful prosecution was critical to set the tone for the succeeding trials. Couper and Jackson had as much evidence against Trowbridge as against Lamar and Farnum.

With Judges Wayne and Nicoll presiding, a jury was selected. The prosecution presented its case, calling on twelve witnesses during the course of the day. The next day, the defense and prosecution summed up their cases and Wayne charged the jury, who then retired to deliberate. The following evening, after twenty-eight straight hours in the jury room, the foreman advised Wayne that the jurors were unable to agree on a decision, and never would. Also, several of the jurors had become sick and were unable to stand more confinement in the stifling jury room. With the consent of the counsels, Wayne declared a mistrial. This was not the start for which Couper or Jackson had been hoping.

The second case was the United States vs. John Dubignon, the resident planter of Jekyl Island, for holding, and abetting in the holding of, African negroes. Once again, a jury was selected, witnesses testified and were cross-examined, summations were made, and the jury was charged. These jurors needed only twenty-eight minutes. The verdict: not guilty.

After one week, the government had failed to win two cases for which it believed it had ample evidence to convict. But Couper and Jackson could not be discouraged. The case against J. Egbert Farnum for piracy was next.

Jury selection took all of the first day. Witness testimony began on the second day with many of the men who had testified at the earlier trials. While there was evidence that Farnum had embarked on the *Wanderer* at Charleston, no one had seen him on Jekyl Island during or after the landing of the Africans. He was not placed in the area until he boarded a ship leaving Charleston for New York two weeks later. The prosecution needed more than the same witnesses who had testified at the earlier trials. It had one: Edwin W. Moore, a former commodore in the Texas Navy and currently a businessman in Galveston.

Hamilton Couper's heart started to race when he called Moore to the stand. Couper let Moore sit for a minute for everyone in the courtroom to see before he asked his first question. "Sir, how do you know the defendant?"

Moore: "I met Captain Farnum during the Mexican War."

Couper: "Have you ever had discussions with the defendant regarding his involvement in the voyage of the *Wanderer*?"

Moore: "Yes, sir." The courtroom buzzed. Until this point, none of the testimony appeared damaging to Farnum.

Couper: "Could you describe the discussion?"

Moore: "Yes. It took place in Washington nine months ago. I was there on business and I ran into Farnum at the Metropolitan Hotel. We had a drink and he told me how he had led a voyage to Africa for negroes aboard the *Wanderer*. He described how they fooled the British and American Squadrons, sailed back to Georgia and landed over four hundred Africans. He said he was planning to write a book about it."

Couper: "Did he mention the names of anyone else on the voyage?"

Moore: "Just a Captain Corrie."

Couper: "Did he mention how the Africans were sold, or to whom?"

Moore: "No, he said nothing more than I have already told."

Moore was dismissed. The prosecution had testimony that put Farnum on the *Wanderer* and at its landing. Couper had to suppress his smile.

Wayne adjourned the court for the day and Moore left the courtroom without meeting Farnum's eye. As he entered the lobby, he heard someone say, "I thought men from Texas knew when to speak and when not."

Moore eyed the speaker. "And just who might you be, sir, to judge what I say?"

"The name is Charles Augustus Lafayette Lamar. I believe you knew my deceased uncle, Mirabeau." The former president of Texas had died six months earlier.

A crowd, including Joseph, Bob, and Couper, gathered around the two men. "Yes. I knew General Lamar well. You must be the family lunatic I've heard so much about. Sir, I am in a hurry. I'd like an apology now so I can get on with my business."

Charlie said, "You'll get no apology from me, sir. I said you talk too much, and I meant to add you're a damnable liar."

"Really? And who will your second be?"

Charlie looked around and saw his lawyer cringing. "Mr. Owens. And yours?"

Commodore Moore knew few men in town. "District Attorney Couper."

Lamar grinned at Couper, then pointed to Joseph and said, "Mr. McBain can officiate." Charlie walked away.

Joseph was stunned that he had just been impressed into Charlie's duel. Bob saw Joseph's pale face and slapped him on the back. "I think you need a drink."

It took a few seconds, but Joseph finally turned to Bob. "I think you're right."

Owens and Couper went to Couper's office and negotiated the terms of the duel. Couper also regretted his involvement. He had a trial to run. But he didn't decline when Moore selected him, and he was honor-bound to fulfill the role. They scheduled it for the morning after next, Thursday, at seven a.m. at Screven's Ferry. They would duel with pistols, one shot apiece. A doctor would be present.

The court reconvened on Wednesday with more witnesses for the prosecution. After a recess, the lawyers began their summations. But all the talk outside the courtroom was about the duel the next morning.

The men appeared at Lamar's Cotton Press on the river at 6:30 a.m., just as the sun was peeking above the horizon. Lamar and Owens stood at the front of one boat and were rowed by two of Charlie's negroes. Moore and Couper, sitting, followed in another. Joseph and Dr. Arnold trailed in a third boat, listening to the creaking of the oars. No one spoke as they glided over the mist covered river to the dueling grounds.

Emily had called Joseph crazier than Charlie when he informed her that he was officiating a duel between Lamar and a witness at the trial. Joseph explained that unless he had a strong excuse, as a gentleman he was obliged to honor the request. She reasoned, "Well, maybe Charlie will be killed. That would be a glorious outcome."

The three boats reached the South Carolina bank and the men walked to an open area nearby. Owens and Couper presented the weapons in their mahogany, cloth-lined cases for inspection. They then discussed the direction in which the principals would step off their paces.

Joseph chose a starting point and waved Charlie and Moore over. "Do either of you have anything to say before we commence?" Joseph asked in a final attempt to settle the dispute.

"I only wish to state that since Mr. Lamar is a relative of my departed friend General Lamar, I will only shoot him in his right shoulder," Moore claimed.

Charlie announced, "I have nothing to say."

Joseph said, "You will have one shot each, at five paces each. I will count with the following cadence: one . . . two . . . three . . . four . . . five. At the count of five, I will say, 'Wheel and fire!' Are you ready?"

The men stared at each other and nodded. They looked as if they were posing for portraits, chins up, and stern. Joseph said, "Stand back to back." The men did, each holding their pistol with a bent right arm, so their weapons were at chest level and pointing to the heavens.

Joseph then stood next to the seconds and Dr. Arnold, his medical satchel at his feet. Joseph thought Moore appeared relaxed, while he could see every muscle and vein in Charlie's neck and jaw. Joseph called out, "Gentlemen, prepare yourselves." Joseph took a deep breath and started the count. "One . . . two . . . three . . . four . . . five. Wheel and fire!"

Moore spun like a dervish. A puff of smoke escaped from his pistol. The ball blazed so close to Lamar's right ear that he flinched. But Charlie was still standing. Moore had missed! The Texan's eyes widened. He slowly lowered his weapon to his side. He had no honorable choice but to stand like a man and be killed.

Charlie sneered and aimed, closing his left eye. He waited a few seconds before pulling the trigger so Moore could squirm during his last moments on earth. The report echoed in the still morning air. Charlie, his arm extended, waited for his opponent to sag to the ground. But the former captain of the Georgia Hussars came closer to hitting a passing gull than his adversary. Charlie eyed his pistol.

Owens, Arnold, and Joseph breathed deeply. Couper silently cursed his luck. Joseph stepped forward. "Gentlemen, by the articles agreed upon, this duel is over."

Lamar, still looking at his pistol, scratched his head. Owens announced to Couper, loud enough for all to hear, "I now have a duty to perform. I am authorized by Mr. Lamar to say to Commodore Moore that the language complained of was used by him under excitement and misapprehension and that he now withdraws and regrets it."

Couper said, "I'm glad to hear it."

Commodore Moore approached Lamar and the men shook hands. As they walked back to the boats, the combatants talked casually, like old friends. Joseph could hear Moore telling Charlie a story about his Uncle Mirabeau at the battle of San Jacinto.

Couper returned to the Farnum trial. The lawyers gave their closing arguments and Judge Wayne charged the jury. He spoke of the horrors of the slave trade and the misery it brought to the captured Africans. He also told the jury that the Act of 1820, which made participation in the slave trade an act of piracy, was constitutional and had withstood all legal arguments contesting it. At 8:30 p.m., the jury retired to deliberate.

Wayne then announced that the other cases on the docket would be called the next morning beginning with the United States vs. Lamar, Hone, Styles, and Middleton for removing Farnum from the Chatham County jail.

Friday morning, Lamar and his co-defendants were escorted into the courtroom. The case was called and Wayne asked the defendants how they pled. John Owens spoke for his clients. "Guilty, your honor."

Couper looked at Jackson. They had a victory, a conviction against Lamar. It had nothing to do with the voyage of the *Wanderer*, but it still felt uplifting. Judge Wayne pronounced that sentencing would take place at the close of the term.

Wayne then called the next case: The United States vs. Charles A. L. Lamar for holding an African named Corrie. When Lamar pleaded not guilty, indicating that there would be a trial, Judge Nicoll, Charlie's father-in-law, stood and marched from the silent courtroom, withdrawing from the case. Charlie watched him disappear through the door to the judges' chambers. Charlie felt a trace of guilt for putting Nicoll in that situation. But just a trace.

Jury selection started, but before it could be completed, as it was late, Wayne adjourned the court for the weekend.

No sooner had Judge Wayne sat for supper at his home that evening than a messenger came to his door with a letter from the jury foreman in the Farnum case. Wayne read it and told the messenger to notify the lawyers and the defendant that the court would reconvene at nine o'clock that night.

After Wayne called the court to order, he asked the jury foreman to confirm what had been stated in the letter: that the jury was unable to reach a verdict and there was no probability they ever would. The foreman complained that the jurors had not had any food in thirty hours and had been in the same room together for almost twenty-six. Wayne declared a mistrial. Farnum would have to be tried again.

On Monday, May 28, the trial of Charlie Lamar for holding an African named Corrie resumed with Judge Wayne still presiding alone. The jury included painter Firmin Cerveau. All the familiar witnesses were called. By this time, these men could give testimony in their sleep.

Before the afternoon recess, Wayne told Couper and Jackson that to prove their case they had to establish that the *Wanderer* left from the United States, picked up African slaves, returned to Georgia, and that Lamar had some ownership.

The last point was the problem. They had no proof that Lamar had any interest in the ship at the time of the crime. During the recess, Couper and Jackson made the inevitable decision. When the court reconvened, Couper requested permission not to prosecute. *Nolle prosequi* was granted by Wayne. Then, Couper requested *nolle prosequi* for the remaining cases against Lamar, Akin, Tucker, Randolph Mott, and Henry Dubignon. The court approved.

Two years after the *Wanderer* left on its illegal, deadly voyage to Africa, Charlie Lamar was exonerated for his role in it. He celebrated with the other *Wanderer* defendants that night at the Pulaski Hotel bar. He had personally struck a blow to the nose of the hypocritical North.

On May 31, the end of the spring term of the court, Judge Wayne sentenced Lamar, Styles, Middleton, and Hone to thirty days imprisonment and $250 each plus court costs, for rescuing Farnum from jail. They could serve their time in an apartment over Lamar's office.

There were more *Wanderer* cases to be tried in the November term against Corrie, Farnum, Brown, Trowbridge, and Martin. Farnum was allowed to post bail of five thousand dollars and Brown one thousand dollars. But the powder was out of the cannon. The government, despite its resources, witnesses, and evidence, had won only a minor conviction.

The morning after the term ended, Couper and Jackson sat in their office and reflected on the results. "Well, Henry, we're fortunate Lamar and his cronies pleaded guilty to one of the charges. I don't think we'd have won a conviction if it had gone to a jury."

Jackson pondered. "I agree. I wonder why he did it?"

Couper said, "Who knows how Lamar thinks? That reminds me. Remember James McBain had something to tell us? He's coming by this morning."

One hour later, James and Joseph McBain were seated in the office, exchanging pleasantries. "What is it we can do for you, sir?" Jackson asked McBain.

"It's a long story. But to get to the point, one of my servants, Dante, tells me he was on the *Wanderer*, going and coming. He saw almost everything."

The lawyers stared at McBain, who nodded as if to say, "You heard me right."

Couper said, "The negro who my father and I saw at the auction in Brunswick?"

McBain said, "The very same," and then recounted the circumstances of the murder of Mr. Down and the highlights of Dante's story.

Couper said to McBain, "Sir, I don't know where to begin. It's incredible, if true."

"I agree. But he couldn't have made up that story. He knows the men and so many facts. He also fears for his life."

Jackson said, "We do want to speak to him. Negroes aren't allowed to testify against whites, but that's a state law. I'm not certain if there's any precedent for a federal trial. I'll have to research it. The Dred Scott decision ruled that negroes were not citizens and couldn't bring suit in court, but I don't know about being a witness."

Joseph asked, "And if there is a precedent and he's allowed to testify?"

Couper interjected, "We'd still have a problem. A white jury would never believe a slave's testimony against the likes of Lamar's friends."

Jackson added, "Yes, but it may be all we have. We have until November to ponder it."

*   *   *

While the government's case against Charlie Lamar and the *Wanderer* defendants was falling apart, so was the Democratic Party. They held their presidential convention in Charleston in April. Many in the party assumed that Senator Stephen Douglas of Illinois would easily secure the nomination. But the delegates from the cotton states insisted that the platform include a federal slave code which would give citizens the right to bring slaves into the American territories. Douglas felt this was a losing issue, and favored a policy of popular sovereignty, as had been used in the Kansas and Nebraska territories. But with Kansans about to vote to become a free state, the cotton states could not accept that. After a contentious debate and political maneuvering, the Douglas platform was selected, prompting fifty southern delegates to walk out. Afterwards, despite fifty-seven ballots, no nominee could muster the required two-thirds majority. The convention ended in shambles. The factions agreed to meet again in mid-June in Baltimore.

Passions did not cool in the intervening six weeks. At the Baltimore convention, over one hundred southern Democrats stomped out over the right to bring slaves into the territories. The remaining Democrats nominated Douglas.

The southern Democrats held their own convention in Richmond later that month and nominated John Breckinridge of Kentucky.

The Democrats were hopelessly split, making the upcoming election a free-for-all. Adding to this confusion, former Whigs in the upper South who had nothing in common with the other parties and wanted to maintain the Union, formed the Constitutional Union Party. They nominated John C. Bell of Tennessee.

The fledgling Republican Party met in mid-May in Chicago, gleeful of the Democrats' problems. Instead of electing front-runner William H. Seward of New York, they chose, on the third ballot, the well-spoken, humble Abraham Lincoln of Illinois.

Despite the Democrats' disarray, most in the party were not concerned about the Republicans. Many Democrats echoed the sentiments of one Virginia newspaper after Lincoln's nomination: "When four years ago the Republican Party sacrificed to expediency by nominating Colonel Fremont, they were supposed to have done a very foolish thing . . . . Nobody, therefore, would have expected the party to repeat the experiment in a more extravagant form. Yet they have done this in choosing Abraham Lincoln . . . . Colonel Fremont had, perhaps, some claims of qualification for the office . . . . Lincoln possesses [none] . . . . A year ago he was an unknown out of his own State . . . and all his recent reputation rests upon his popularity as a stump orator in canvassing Illinois as the Republican opponent to Mr. Douglas' return to the Senate . . . . His record as a public man is brief and obscure. His private record is that of a third rate politician . . . ."

*   *   *

Joseph and Emily avoided discussions about the upcoming election. She favored Abraham Lincoln, though he had proclaimed that he would not interfere with the institution of slavery in the states where it currently existed. But he stood fast on prohibiting its spread to the territories. Emily thought it was a good first step.

Joseph had accepted that slavery would have to end one day. He even wanted it to. But he wanted the South to come up with the solution, and no politician offered one. He was also confused about the deep South's stand on the federal slave code. As it was, the South was short of slaves. There was no excess to take to the territories, certainly no amount worth seceding over. Above all else, Joseph felt the Union had to be maintained, whatever the issues.

However, the election was months away and Emily had other things on her mind. She and the children were going to Tallulah Falls with Sarah in a week and she was busy packing. One June evening, as they were preparing to go to the Pulaski Square house for supper, Emily asked, "Joseph, do you promise to visit?"

Joseph replied, "Yes, in August and September, with Father. He's hired an overseer for two months. He certainly needs the rest, though I don't know how he'll be able to stay away for so long."

Emily said, "He was as excited as Danny today, taking him to see the aeronaut." Mr. Cevor was making an ascension in his new balloon, the *Forest City*, from the yard at the military barracks on Bull and Liberty streets. Danny had seen the ascension of Mr. Cevor in the *Montpelier* a few months before and had begged his grandfather to take him.

A knock at the front door interrupted them. Moments later Chloe appeared in the parlor. "Master Joseph. It's Hercules. He's here to take you to the hospital. It's Master McBain!"

Three weeks later, Joseph sat in his study, drinking whiskey and staring at the globe. He gave it a spin and waited to see on which country it would stop. His father had finally been released from the hospital and was recovering in the house on Pulaski Square. James McBain had stood in the hot June sun for three hours waiting for the balloon ascension. When he and Danny returned to the house on Pulaski Square, he collapsed. Sarah put wet towels on his face and Hercules rushed him to the hospital. He regained consciousness after a few hours but was weak, unable to stand or talk. His left side was numb. Dr. Arnold told Sarah that James was to remain hospitalized until he recovered.

Joseph, who had spent every day since his father's collapse at the Heritage and every night at the hospital, slept little despite those long, grueling days. The sight of his father, always so strong and in command, lying helplessly in a hospital bed shocked him.

Emily entered the study and watched her husband. She was concerned about her father-in-law, but knew she and Joseph had reached a critical point in their lives. "What are we going to do, Joseph?"

Joseph concentrated on the globe. "Pray for a full recovery."

Emily sat next to him. "Of course, dear. But the Heritage? Who will run it?"

Joseph sighed. "I will. Isaac and the drivers are good, but they can't run the place long without supervision. And they can't keep the records."

Emily ran her hand over Joseph's back. "You know how difficult that will be for me. It's hard enough with the few servants we have here. I'll try, but you know I won't be happy."

Joseph spun the globe. "I'll hire a permanent overseer. Then we can move back to town, and I can visit there as necessary." Joseph was weary. He didn't want to argue with his wife. He finally faced Emily. "Until then, I have no choice. My father is sixty-six years old and ill, and we have a family business to manage. If you wish, stay here with the children, and I'll come in as often as I can."

Emily took his hand. "I just wrote my parents to say we'd visit them at Christmas so they could see the baby. You haven't seen them since our marriage seven years ago."

"It's unlikely I'll be able to with my father's health. You go on your own. I'll visit next summer, I promise."

Emily didn't want to upset Joseph. She hugged him and left him spinning.

Sarah and Emily abandoned their plans for the mountains of Georgia. Joseph spent the rest of the summer at the Heritage. Sometimes, he brought Danny out. The boy loved the plantation life and playing with the other children. Joseph managed to come to town a few nights a week to see his family and father, who slowly regained feeling in his side and face.

Before her father fell ill, Amy had considered closing the restaurant for the summer and accompanying her mother and Emily. Business was slow, and Bob was spending much of his time in Charleston. Now, Amy felt alone. She wanted Bob with her, holding her. She wondered if Bob would ever propose, and what his plans for them were.

Bob made many trips to Charleston under the guise of painting landscapes. South Carolinians were making the most noise about seceding from the union if Lincoln should win, and with the *Wanderer* trials over until November, the bigger stories were to the north.

Bob's mind was always on Amy. He wanted to propose. However, he had painted himself into a corner and couldn't get out. If he asked for her hand in marriage, he felt honor bound to confess his real purpose in Savannah. But he was still afraid that she might hate him for deceiving her and refuse to see him anymore. On the other hand, if he didn't propose, he was certain Amy would leave him. One thing was clear—he had to make a decision soon.

James McBain recovered slowly, and by the end of September he regained all the feeling in his body and wanted to return to work. Dr. Arnold told him to wait until the weather cooled. McBain was confident in Joseph's ability to run things, but was acutely aware that Emily rarely went with Joseph to the plantation.

Sarah realized her husband's life had to change, and sensed the strain Joseph and Emily were under. In her mind there were two solutions—hire a white overseer to run the Heritage, or sell it. She intended to speak to James about it as soon as he was up to it.

Andrew continued to work on the church, which took more time than normal because of the slow flow of funds and the availability of the volunteer workers. But it was taking shape, and he still felt he was creating something special. He also worked closely with John Norris's new associate, Dewitt Bruyn, on General Hugh Mercer's house, as Norris made frequent trips to visit his family in New York.

Andrew was saddened by Mr. McBain's illness and visited his former owner every evening. McBain's eyes glowed each time Andrew walked into his room. The experience made Andrew realize how much he loved the family that gave him so many opportunities. It pained him to see any McBain suffer. He would do anything in his limited power to prevent it.

"Andrew, you scared me half to death!" Bob said, looking up from the desk in his studio. "Please, come in. Have a seat."

Andrew sat stiffly and said, "I'm sorry about that, Mr. Carson. But I need to have a word with you." Andrew looked at the writing paper in front of Carson.

Bob noticed Andrew's eyes, straightened the papers, and put them aside. He asked, "Is there something I can do for you?"

Andrew said, "I'll get right to it, sir. I have reason to believe you're writing for a New York newspaper."

Bob felt the blood rush to his face. He leaned back in his chair, trying to hide his embarrassment. "Andrew, whatever gave you that idea?"

Andrew pulled from his jacket pocket the newspaper that Norris had given him after his last trip north and placed it on the desk. One headline read, "A Negro Makes Good in the South." The first line read, "Could a negro slave in the South become a master builder and architect?"

Bob picked up the paper and squinted at the article, pretending he was reading it for the first time. "This is about a slave in Charleston."

"Mr. Carson, that story is about me and it is based on our conversations. We both know it." Bob and Andrew stared at each other for an uncomfortable moment. Andrew asked, "Does Miss Amy know?" Bob shifted in his chair. "Mr. Carson, I don't care if you write secret reports about Savannah for a northern newspaper. I'm glad you are. But don't you dare hurt Miss Amy or her family. That's my only concern."

Bob placed the newspaper back on the desk. "My intentions towards Miss McBain are sincere, Andrew, I can assure you. But there's no other way to find out what's really happening in the South than to see it first hand. To do that, some reporters have to live secret lives. Surely, you must understand that."

Andrew stood and put the newspaper back in his pocket. "Sir, you can keep it secret from anyone you want, but not from Miss Amy. She deserves to know the truth. Now, you fess up to her. That's what a man would do. Have a good evening."

Bob watched Andrew leave. He had waited long enough. He silently thanked Andrew.

Amy took hold of Bob's hand as they sat on a bench on the Strand overlooking the river. She smiled and said, "So, Mr. Carson, what is so important that you need to sit in such a romantic place while the restaurant is open?"

Bob gently squeezed her hand. "I just wanted to tell you how special you are. And that I can't live without you."

"Really?" Amy swiveled closer to Bob so their sides were touching. "When did you realize that?"

Bob leaned over and kissed Amy on the cheek. "Oh, about two years ago, when I first saw you." Amy looked around the area before returning the kiss. Bob removed a ring from his pocket. "Amy, I want to put this ring on your finger. I want you to be my wife."

Amy stared at the ring for a moment. Then she wrapped her arms around Bob. "Of course I'll marry you."

Bob waited for Amy to sit back. Beaming, he placed the ring on her finger. "I'll need to talk to your father."

Amy held up her hand and inspected her ring. She shifted her hand to see the stone sparkle. "Oh, I believe he'll say yes."

Bob lifted Amy's hand to his lips. "We'll be married wherever and whenever you say. I just want it to be as soon as possible."

Amy said, "Me, too. My parents will want a big wedding. They missed out with Joseph. But it doesn't matter to me. If I rush, maybe I could organize everything in a month or so."

Bob covered Amy's hand in both of his. "That seems like forever, Mrs. Carson. I'll try to be patient. I'll have to write to my aunts and cousins in New York and invite them, though I'm not certain they'll make the trip."

Amy smiled at the sound of her soon-to-be name. "If they can't make it on such short notice, we can visit them after we're married." Amy looked to the harbor in thought. "We can live at Harris Street. One of my tenants is moving out next month. And after we marry, I'll hire a manager for the restaurant so we can be together more."

Bob kissed Amy's hand again. "I have another idea. Let me be your manager."

Amy straightened. "What do you mean?"

"Just what I said. I'll take fewer commissions, and only ones in Savannah. I'll help you out in the restaurant. We'll be together."

Amy relaxed and laid her head on Bob's shoulder. "That would make life easier."

They sat in silence for a few minutes. Then Amy asked, "Bob, what happens if Lincoln wins and Georgia secedes? What do we do?"

Bob had considered that. He wasn't going to lose Amy over anything. "My life is with you, Amy. If you're here, I'll be by your side."

Amy knew that Emily had expressed the same sentiment to Joseph so many years before and their differences were now causing problems. But she didn't mention that to Bob. After all these years, she had met a man she loved and wanted to marry. If he insisted on moving back north, she would do it. But she didn't want him to know that. She didn't want to leave Savannah and her family unless it became absolutely necessary.

They kissed and walked back to the restaurant, arm-in-arm. Bob still had to reveal his writing career to her, but now it would be much easier.

Later that night, Bob asked McBain for permission to marry Amy. McBain's brush with mortality had changed his perspective. He wanted his daughter to have a husband, even a New Yorker, and a family. He stood, shook hands with Bob, and said, "Welcome to the McBain family, Bob. Let's have a drink." After a toast, they had a long chat. Sarah and James were thrilled to hear that Bob was going to help Amy manage the restaurant, which committed the couple to remaining in Savannah. They talked of Amy, and all she had accomplished, and of her confidence and resolve. Bob told James he had never met a woman like her. Sarah told Bob that his creativity was a perfect complement to Amy's energy.

Over the next month, Amy, Emily, and Sarah planned the wedding, making all the necessary arrangements for Amy's dress, the church service, and the reception. It was a hectic time for all the McBains, but it was a happy diversion from health issues, the plantation, and politics. In mid-October 1860 Bob and Amy were married at the Independent Presbyterian Church. They held a reception at the Pulaski Square house for two hundred guests, including Andrew and Patience.

During the reception, Bob took Andrew aside and thanked him for their earlier conversation. Bob assured Andrew that he was quitting his job. The two shook hands and smiled at each other.

*   *   *

One could not forget about politics for long. The feeling in the South that Lincoln was unelectable fizzled. The Republican candidate was drawing huge, enthusiastic crowds wherever he campaigned in the North. In state elections in early October, Pennsylvania and Ohio, two critical states in the upcoming presidential contest, went Republican. It had become clear. Short of a miracle, Abraham Lincoln would be the next president of the United States.

Some Southerners were quick to react. As early as September, Governor William Gist of South Carolina recommended that his state secede if the Republican were elected. Shortly after that, Charlie Lamar wrote a letter to Gist offering to raise one hundred men, armed, equipped, and ready for service if South Carolina seceded.

Even Northerners were concerned. In New York, the non-Republican parties formed a fusion movement to try to prevent Lincoln from carrying the state.

It was all in vain. On November 6, 1860, Abraham Lincoln was elected president. He didn't garner even 40 percent of the popular vote, but he did receive 59 percent of the electoral vote, a resounding majority. Two nights later the largest demonstration in Savannah's history—in support of secession—was held in Monument Square. The Southern Rights flag was unfurled, speakers called for secession, patriotic songs were sung, and bonfires were lighted.

Both Joseph and Emily had seen the gathering as they returned home from Amy's restaurant. "What's going to happen, Joseph?" Emily asked as they sat in the parlor. She was thrilled about the election, but tried to conceal it from her husband. It would mean changes to their lives, but she couldn't guess what they might be.

"I really don't know, Emily. Everyone needs to calm down and not act rashly."

Emily pointed to the day's paper on the table. "South Carolina's governor has already called for a special session of the legislature. They're going to secede."

"That's the mood now, but secession is insane. The Democrats may keep control of the Senate. As long as we all remain in the Union, Lincoln will be limited in what he can do. When everyone thinks about it, they'll come to the same conclusion."

Emily shook her head. "Joseph, you can be so naïve. Do you think Southerners are all going to sit down and have a nice little chat over tea? At this very moment, thousands of people are crammed into Johnson Square screaming for secession. Do you believe they'll change their minds tomorrow, just like that?"

Joseph stood and poured himself a drink. He didn't know what anyone would do. His confusion was understandable. Lincoln's victory had a contradictory effect on white Savannah. Most dreaded his election, but celebrated it because it forced them to consider secession.

Black Savannah celebrated as well, though much more discreetly. Politics and elections were things that never impacted black folk, except when they tightened control over their lives. But the news of the election of a man who didn't believe slavery should spread any more than already existed was a good thing.

The Sunday after Lincoln's election, Andrew was mobbed by the other church-goers as he walked through the doors. They knew that he was educated, could read, and had close ties to many whites. They were anxious to learn what the consequences of the election might be.

He told them what he knew, which wasn't much, and said it was too early to make much sense of it. But Andrew saw the excitement, the hope, in their eyes, and he became excited, too. Maybe he and his brothers and sisters wouldn't have to wait for heaven to become truly free.

$$*\quad*\quad*$$

The day before the election, Hamilton Couper and Henry Jackson talked with Dante about his experience on the *Wanderer*. His story was so convincing that they decided to ask the court to approve him as a witness. They knew their chances were slim, and that a jury wouldn't believe him even if he did testify, but it was their only option. Their previous evidence and witnesses had failed them. Maybe Dante's account would captivate the jury, too.

As it turned out, Dante never had to testify. A week after the election, on the first day of the November session of the district court, Couper decided to ask permission not to prosecute the remaining *Wanderer* defendants. He knew that no local jury would convict them after Lincoln's victory, regardless of anyone's testimony. Permission for *nolle prosequi* was granted by Judge Wayne. William Corrie, who had never been brought to Georgia, John Egbert Farnum, Nelson Trowbridge, and Nicholas Brown were free to go on with their lives. The trials of the *Wanderer*, excepting David Martin, were over. No one would pay for the crime.

The *Wanderer* news no longer caused even a ripple of interest. All the cotton states had called for special sessions of their legislatures to deal with the crisis of a Republican president. South Carolina was the first to take action, calling for an election of delegates on December 6 to a secession convention beginning on December 17.

Georgia was not far behind. The governor called a special session of the legislature for November 12 to debate the issue. After ten contentious days, a state-wide election was scheduled for January 2, 1861, to elect delegates to a secession convention two weeks after that. There would be two tickets, one for supporters of immediate secession, called "Secessionists," and one for supporters of negotiation with the government before seceding, called "Cooperationists."

The debates took to the streets and taverns of Georgia in anticipation of the election. Governor Joseph Brown and Georgia's representatives in the Congress, as well as Howell Cobb, campaigned for secession. It seemed certain that Georgians would vote to leave the Union.

*   *   *

Ever since the confrontation between Lamar and Couper the night Couper tried to capture Farnum, Joseph had avoided Charlie. He ended his association with the agricultural fair and the jockey club, to the great relief of Emily. He stayed away from bars and ate less in Dante's Place. If Joseph saw Charlie on the street, he acknowledged him and moved on. Though Joseph still fumed over Lamar's remark about Emily, and Charlie's possible role in the assault on Fisk, Joseph never confronted Charlie. He hoped that avoiding Lamar would be message enough.

So Joseph's stomach bunched up into a knot when Charlie dropped by his office one day in early December. Joseph relaxed when Charlie said, "Joseph, I wanted to tell you to present the note at my bank. It will be honored."

Joseph was ecstatic to be getting the twenty-five hundred dollars. He thanked Charlie and was about to usher him out of the office when Charlie said, "These are great times, Joseph. We're finally removing the yoke of the North from our necks."

Joseph sat back. "I guess, Charlie. But breaking up the Union is a mistake. Maybe the Democrats can take back the Senate in the next election." Joseph's argument for caution had convinced no one.

"That's in two years. It's better to be masters of our destiny now!" Charlie paused and pointed to a portrait of Danny on the wall behind Joseph's chair. "That's new."

Joseph turned and looked. "Yes. Bob did it."

Charlie stood and walked around the desk to inspect it up close. "I like it. He certainly is talented. Maybe I'll talk to him about portraits of my daughters." Lamar returned to his chair. "Say, Joseph, are you planning on joining a militia unit with all the excitement?" Joseph had resigned from the Jasper Greens after Danny was born.

Joseph replied, "Yes, I've been speaking to Hamilton Couper about the Oglethorpe Light Infantry. Why do you ask?"

Charlie sneered at the mention of Couper. "I wanted to tell you that I've received permission from Governor Brown to form a mounted rifle company of one hundred men. If you don't go with the Oglethorpes, you could join me. I'll make you an officer. We could inflict considerable harm on those Yankees."

"I'll consider that, Charlie," Joseph lied.

Charlie moved his chair closer to the desk. "Joseph, there's another thing we need to talk about." Charlie cleared his throat. "Joseph, I hear some of the boys are worried about you."

Joseph moved his chair forward as well and placed his arms on the desk till their faces were just a few feet apart. "Really? How so, Charlie?"

"Joseph, first listen to what I have to say before you go off half-cocked. Your father's cook talked to the government about a boat ride he took. And someone who calls himself Oglethorpe has been writing uncomplimentary stories about Savannah and me for a New York newspaper. The boys think it's Bob Carson."

"Bob? Do you have any proof that he's writing them?"

Charlie spoke in a hushed tone. "Joseph, you're a good friend. I'm doing all I can to protect you. Please don't make any more foolish mistakes. Like your wife helping that Fisk fellow spread abolitionist propaganda to negroes."

Joseph pointed his finger, almost touching Lamar's nose. "You know, Charlie, if anything happens to my wife or family, I'll find the persons responsible and kill them. And I mean anyone. You know that, don't you?"

"Joseph, don't look at me like that. We've known each other our entire lives. I would never touch a McBain. Our enemy is up north. We need to fight them, not ourselves."

Joseph said, "You just mind what I say, Charlie." He stood, went to the door, and opened it. "Deliver that message to the boys. Now I must get back to work." Joseph ushered Charlie from his office. He tried to work but couldn't concentrate. He walked home, dizzy with anger.

*   *   *

Many people became dizzy trying to follow the events of November and early December 1860 and pondering the future of the Union. To no one's surprise, a tide of pro-secession candidates triumphed in the election to the South Carolina convention. The result of the convention in mid-December promised to be a formality.

Two days before the convention, Joseph and Emily stood on the deck of the ship Emily and baby Charlotte were taking to New York for Christmas. Emily told Joseph she was scared. Five-year-old Danny was rubbing his eyes with his knuckles. He didn't want to see his mother leave. Danny had pleaded with her to be allowed to spend Christmas with his father and grandfather on the plantation. She finally relented. Now neither she nor Danny was so sure.

Joseph tried to ease her fears. "Don't worry. Even if South Carolina secedes, there won't be civil war. She'll come back to the Union with her tail between her legs. Enjoy your time with your parents. We'll know more when you return in January."

The ship whistle blew. Emily handed Charlotte to Joseph, bent down, kissed Danny, and said, "You be a good boy and take care of your father."

"Yes, mommy," Danny whimpered.

Emily hugged and kissed Danny again, and took Charlotte from her husband. Joseph asked, "Do you promise to write every day?"

Emily said through her tears, "Of course, darling. And there had better be a letter waiting for me when I arrive in New York." They both smiled.

They kissed again and Joseph and Danny left the ship. Father and son stood on the wharf and waved as the ship sailed away. Joseph felt empty in his gut, but he lifted his son to his shoulder and asked, "How about some ice cream?"

On December 20 the delegates to the South Carolina secession convention voted 169 to zero to secede. Not a single man thought it wise to negotiate with the North before leaving the Union. Over thirty years of frustration exploded in the legislative halls. South Carolina was free to govern herself. Celebrations erupted throughout the state.

But breaking from the Union wasn't that easy. Details had to be resolved. There were federally owned facilities such as forts, arsenals, courts, post offices, and custom houses on South Carolina territory. Ownership had to be negotiated. Also, there were federal troops and employees at these installations, and their status had to be resolved.

South Carolina officials maintained that their state had sent many thousands of dollars over the years to the federal coffers in tariff payments. They contributed to the financing of federal installations, and the ones in South Carolina were rightfully theirs.

The federal government disagreed. Nor did it think any state had the constitutional right to secede. South Carolina didn't care what the government thought. It wanted all the federal property, especially the forts, which sat at strategic sites in Charleston harbor. It could not let a foreign power have a presence on its own doorstep.

Governor Francis Pickens sent three commissioners to Washington to demand ownership of the federal forts in Charleston harbor—Moultrie, Sumter, and Castle Pinckney—and to request the government to evacuate Moultrie, the only garrisoned installation. Government representatives said they needed time to consider the demands, and both sides agreed not to make any aggressive moves against the other until the negotiations had been completed.

As President Buchanan and his cabinet discussed the crisis, Major Robert Anderson, the commanding officer at Fort Moultrie, evaluated his situation. He felt too exposed at Fort Moultrie. If South Carolina troops ever decided to attack, he wouldn't be able to defend his position, which was so close to the batteries on the mainland. He had a duty to protect his seventy men and their families. The almost-completed Fort Sumter, outfitted with cannon, and being further from the land batteries of the city, would be much safer. Anderson knew he wouldn't receive permission to transfer, and it would be impossible to sneak to it undetected.

Instead, he received permission from South Carolina to move the wives and children to Fort Johnson on James Island. On Wednesday evening, December 26, three barks and a couple of barges docked at the Fort Moultrie wharf and boarded the men, women, and children, loaded all the stores, supplies, munitions, and armaments they could carry, and headed for Fort Sumter. They made several trips. In hours, the troops and families were within the walls of the safer fort.

South Carolinians were outraged when they learned of Anderson's deception. Not only did he break the agreement in deserting Fort Moultrie, he spiked the cannons he could not take with him, and burned their carriages. Governor Pickens wrote an angry letter to the President.

While President Buchanan, who was counting the minutes until he could leave town for good, said he had not approved the move, he soon claimed that he supported Major Anderson's actions since the officer had reason to fear South Carolina's intention to take control of Fort Sumter. South Carolina, incensed at the bad faith of the government, seized Forts Moultrie and Castle Pinckney and the federal arsenal at Charleston. This news spread like poison ivy throughout the South. The government couldn't be trusted.

On January 2 Georgians cast their ballots to send electors to the state convention. Fifty-seven percent voted for candidates representing immediate secession. This was closer than predicted, but the secessionists still had the upper hand going into the convention two weeks later.

On the same day of the special election, Governor Brown ordered the First Regiment of Georgia Volunteers, consisting of the Savannah Volunteer Guards and the Oglethorpe Light Infantry, to take control of Fort Pulaski at the mouth of the Savannah River. Secession fever was contagious.

*   *   *

"Good afternoon, Mr. Molyneaux. Please come in," Sarah McBain said and led the dapper man into the formal parlor. Edmund Molyneaux was the British consul in Savannah. He had lived there for thirty years and was well respected in the town. He had sent a note to the McBains two days before that he had an important matter to discuss.

Sarah apologized that her husband had to travel to the Heritage and was unable to meet with him. As they shared cups of tea, Sarah asked Molyneaux about his and his wife's recent trip to London. Molyneaux inquired about the health of Mr. McBain.

Mr. Molyneaux then revealed the reason for the visit. "I have quite interesting news, Mrs. McBain." He pulled two envelopes from his jacket pocket. "I just received these letters from England, from her Majesty, Queen Victoria. Apparently, your Andrew wrote a letter to the Queen about two or three years ago. A remarkable letter, really, passionately requesting the Queen to knight James Oglethorpe posthumously. Andrew also mentioned his interest in architecture. The Queen's lady in waiting passed the letter on to her. Her Majesty, a lover of architecture, was fascinated by a negro slave who had earned his freedom in the South, and was an admirer of classical architecture, no less Oglethorpe." Molyneaux paused to sip his tea.

"About a year ago, the Queen wrote to me in confidence about the character of Andrew. Of course, I know that Andrew did the beautiful brickwork on my house for Mr. Norris. I investigated him further and felt completely confident in the man. I responded to the Queen in the most positive way. Yesterday, I received these letters from her. One is for me and one is for Andrew McBain in care of James McBain. While the letter to Andrew is to be delivered sealed, I am aware of its contents." He paused, heightening the drama.

"It is an invitation for Andrew and his family to be the guest of the Queen in London. I believe she is seriously considering knighting Oglethorpe."

Sarah McBain dropped her tea cup on the carpeted floor. Fortunately, it was empty. She gasped and picked it up. "Please excuse my clumsiness, sir. But this is astonishing news. Our Andrew? Invited by the Queen? Are you serious?"

"Yes. Andrew would work with the surveyor general for a period of two years for a generous stipend. At the end of that term, Andrew may choose to remain in England or return to America. Or one of Her Majesty's colonies, if he would prefer. The only issue I can foresee is if he decides to return to Georgia. Would he be allowed back? But I think I can resolve that, if that would be his choice."

Sarah was so excited she started fanning herself. "I don't know what to say, Mr. Molyneaux. Andrew is like a son to us, but he is also a free man and can do as he chooses. We would never stand in the way of such an opportunity. We would only encourage it. I'll inform my husband this evening."

Molyneaux stood and picked up his hat. "Very good. I've never heard of Her Majesty doing anything like this before. You and Mr. McBain should feel very proud. I'll leave the letter to Andrew with you. Once he decides, please have him come to my office and I'll work out the travel arrangements. Have a good day, Mrs. McBain. And my regards to Mr. McBain."

Andrew sat in the parlor and read the letter for the third time to Patience, who bounced baby Gully on her knee. Truvy, seeing his parents so excited, ran around the room in circles.

"I don't believe it, Patience. An invitation from the Queen of England to practice architecture. After all these years, she finally replies. I had given up hope. Now I get a reply, and she invites us to go to England. If only Grampah were here to see it."

Truvy leaped onto his father's lap, laughing. Patience hugged her husband. "I'm so proud of you, Andrew. God is rewarding you for being such a good man. I'll have to do some sewing if I'm going to meet the Queen. And I have to buy her a gift. What should I get?"

"I don't know. Maybe a turban?"

"Really? Do you think she'd wear a turban if I tied it for her?"

Andrew started to laugh, and Patience hit him playfully. "Andrew McBain, you're making fun of me. But I'll bring her one anyway, and when we get there I'll cook a peach pie for her, just in case. When are we going?"

Andrew tickled Truvy's sides, sending him into a giggling fit. "I'll want to see the church finished. That will take about four months. Tomorrow we'll ask the McBains what we have to do. They'll help us. I can't wait to tell Joseph."

As Andrew and Patience celebrated in their bedroom, Joseph arrived home from the office, sat in the parlor, and opened his daily letter from Emily.

January 10, 1861

My Dearest Joseph,

I cannot postpone this letter any longer, though it grieves me so to write it. We have read the news about the election to the convention. Georgia is almost certain to leave the Union. The country is falling apart.

South Carolina wants war, Joseph. You must know about the firing on the *Star of the West* when it tried to deliver provisions to the poor women and children in Fort Sumter. And the rebel army in Florida is poised to attack the federal troops at Fort Pickens.

President Buchanan will not lift a finger to do anything about the seceding states, but Lincoln will as soon as he assumes office in March.

Joseph, I cannot expose our children to the dangers of war. That would be contrary to all natural laws of motherhood. I am not returning to Georgia. I guess I should have known seven years ago that our marriage could not work there. But I loved you so much I thought I could change you. I now know I could never do that.

I'm begging you to send Danny to me, where he will be safe. I also pray that you will come with him. You are so smart, darling, you would be a success in any business endeavor you try here. I don't want to live another minute without you, but we can never be, not in the South.

My heart is breaking as I write this, for I fear I know your decision, and I will never see you again. You must believe me when I tell you I love you with all my heart and will wait for you always. Please give my love to your parents, Amy, Bob, Andrew, Patience, and the others.

Your loving wife forever,

Emily.

"Daddy, what's wrong?" Danny asked as he walked into the study and saw his father with his head in his hands.

"Oh, hello, Danny. I'm sad because I miss your mother." Joseph dried his eyes with two swipes of his handkerchief and pulled together for his boy. Joseph guessed Emily's parents had persuaded her to stay in New York, otherwise she would never have left Danny behind.

"When is she coming home? I miss mommy, too."

Joseph had to lie to his son. "Soon. She says she misses you very much."

"Can you read the letter to me? I want to hear mommy talking."

Joseph picked up his son, placed him on his knee and kissed his forehead. "Not now, son. We have to go to Grampah's and Gramah's for dinner. I'll read it to you later."

CHAPTER 29

Abraham Lincoln

January-April 1861

"Have you stopped smiling since you got that letter?" Hercules asked as he drove Andrew to the McBain house a few days after the Queen's invitation arrived. Mr. McBain was having a party at his house and had asked Andrew to help William welcome the guests.

Andrew's white teeth glowed in the darkness of the January evening. "I guess not. But at least I can sleep. Patience is so excited, she can't." He adjusted his necktie and smoothed out his suit. "How do I look?"

Hercules saw Andrew fussing with his clothes and said, "Fit for a queen, nigger."

They pulled to the front of the house and saw ten carriages parked along the square. Andrew gasped, "Good Lord, Hercules, we're late! I thought you said seven o'clock?"

Hercules said, "I can't understand it. Those carriages weren't here thirty minutes ago when I left to pick you up. You better git while I pull into the carriage house."

Andrew jumped off and bounded up the front stairs. Joseph opened the door before Andrew could knock. Joseph's face was tight with anger. "Dang, Andrew! You're late. Father is peeved. Come on."

Andrew's heart sank as he followed Joseph. "Joseph, I'm so sorry. Hercules picked me up just fifteen minutes ago."

Joseph grabbed the knob to the door of the formal guest parlor. "I don't want to hear it, Andrew. Now, go in and apologize."

Joseph pulled open the door and a sweating Andrew stepped in.

"*Surprise!*" shouted the room full of white men.

A grinning Mr. McBain stepped up to Andrew, who stood with his arms stiff at his sides, and said, "Welcome, Andrew. You've made Savannah proud. Some folks wanted to congratulate you personally on your achievement."

Joseph stepped up first and, unable to control his devilish smile, said, "I never want you to be late again," and hugged his friend. The other men cheered.

"Joseph, you nearly had me in tears."

McBain said, "There will be no tears tonight, Andrew. Now let these other men greet you." One by one, the men commended Andrew and wished him well: John Norris, his assistant DeWitt Bruyn, Andrew Low, James Hamilton Couper, Hamilton Couper, Edmund Molyneaux, Solomon Ziegler, manager of Engine Number 4, Firmin Cerveau, Bob Carson, Dr. Richard Arnold, Shamus Riley, looking quite uncomfortable in a suit, and several local builders. Joseph also invited the editors of the *Savannah Morning News* and *Savannah Republican*, two men who had no love for each other.

Only at Reverend Andrew Marshall's funeral had so many white men in Savannah gathered to honor a black man. After each man had words with Andrew, James McBain toasted him. He talked of Andrew's life at the Heritage, his heroism, his accomplishments, his wife and children, his life-long devotion to the McBains, and his faith in God. He then handed Andrew a gift of a pocket watch. The men applauded.

When Andrew spoke, he stood as tall as he ever had. He thanked Master McBain for the watch. He told them he was proud to represent Georgia, and that he would not disappoint them. He thanked them for this show of support, and he thanked his parents, Grandfather McBain, and Reverend Marshall, who were not with them anymore. And he thanked God. The men raised their glasses and called, "Hear, hear."

The guests stayed another hour lauding Andrew before they left. Andrew, Joseph, and James sat on the piazza smoking segars and talking about Andrew's trip. James told Andrew that Amy would rent his house, collect the rents, pay his taxes, and that he could leave his wagon and horse at the Heritage.

Joseph said, "Andrew, you'll actually be able to visit Oglethorpe's home. How grand."

Andrew nodded. "Yes. But I'd enjoy it even more if you and Mrs. Emily visited us. We could show our children Oglethorpe's birthplace, gravesite, and old estate together. What an experience that would be for them! And us!"

Joseph gulped. "That would be something, wouldn't it?"

The next night, Joseph explained to his parents, Amy, and Bob that Emily wasn't returning because of the prospect of war. Joseph didn't tell them that she wouldn't live in a slave society any longer.

Sarah asked, "When will I see my granddaughter again?" and began to cry.

Bob said, "I'm sorry to hear that, Joseph. Let's hope her fears soon prove to be unfounded and she returns." Bob, like Joseph, believed there would not be war, but the chances had increased considerably since he and Amy had married. He had begun evaluating their choices if fighting erupted, but hadn't discussed them with Amy.

Amy reached over and held Joseph's hand. She knew how heartbreaking and humiliating this was for him.

James McBain asked, "What are you planning to do, Joseph?" McBain had recovered from his illness and was working again but was looking to hire a full-time overseer to lessen his and Joseph's work load. He was not surprised that Emily had left.

Joseph shook his head. "My only choice is to go there and convince her to return. If she refuses, I at least want my daughter back. I'll litigate if I have to, but I'm not certain how easy that will be, if New York and Georgia are in different countries."

The American landscape had changed since Emily decided to remain in New York. Under increasing pressure from Northerners to re-supply Fort Sumter, President Buchanan approved sending the *Star of the West* to South Carolina in early January. As the ship entered Charleston harbor, batteries from Fort Moultrie and on Morris Island opened fire. At the sight of the first splash by the bow, the captain of the ship reversed course and headed back north.

Both sides were outraged. The federal government considered the attack on the vessel an act of war. South Carolina Governor Andrew Pickens claimed the attempt to reinforce Sumter was a hostile act and sent a representative to Washington to demand surrender of the fort.

Then Mississippi, Florida, and Alabama passed ordinances of secession between January 9 and 11, raising the number of rogue states to four.

The attention of the nation turned to Georgia. She was the key to a strong confederacy. If Georgia didn't secede, the other four would be islands of discontent. However, if Georgia left the United States, the confederate states would be a more formidable union, a solid block geographically, economically, and militarily, and more attractive to the undecided slave states.

The Secessionists had a majority of the delegates at the Milledgeville convention, but not an insurmountable one. At the start, the leaders of the Cooperationists tried to pass a resolution delaying a vote on secession to gain time to change minds. They failed. Two days later a resolution in favor of secession passed by a count of 166 to 130, far from the unanimity of South Carolina, but enough to defeat the Cooperationists.

An ordinance of secession was then crafted and adopted the next day by a vote of 208 to eighty-nine. Within days, all of Georgia's members of Congress resigned and left Washington. The only notable Georgian official to defy his state and remain with the Union in Washington was Supreme Court Justice James Moore Wayne.

Savannah celebrated her new beginning with gun salutes, fireworks, and bands. They had taken a stand for independence, just as their forefathers had eighty-five years before.

Joseph said, "I also reminded Emily that New York City might secede from the Union." Many Southerners had been amused to learn that the mayor of New York City in early January had recommended to the city council that the municipality secede and become independent with commercial ties to both the North and South. The mayor stressed it was not worth going to war over, but felt it was in the economic interest of the city not to be tied politically to either side.

McBain laughed. "That was interesting, but Mayor Wood won't have his way. In any case, you must convince Emily to return. Wives should never leave their families. Never. Besides, she'll be as safe in Georgia as anywhere on earth."

Joseph stared at his supper plate, his sadness obvious to all. "She writes to me every day, as if she's on holiday. I want my family back, but I'm angry she'd do such a thing."

Sarah's eyes were edged with thin red lines. "Dear, what about Danny?"

Joseph tapped the table with his knuckles. "I'm not giving him up, that's for sure. He's my son. He was born a Georgian and he'll remain a Georgian." Joseph sighed and added, "He still doesn't know his mother's not coming home. I'm going to have to tell him sometime, but I keep holding out that Emily's next letter will say she's returning." Joseph didn't want to talk about his shattered family anymore. "She did say she visited Gazaway Lamar recently. She's always had a soft spot for him since he attended our wedding. She's worried for his safety."

The last few years had not been easy ones for Gazaway, as he watched from afar the tribulations of his son. In fact, Gazaway had been sucked into the *Wanderer* quagmire after the ship was returned to Boston in December 1859. The vessel, having been involved in the slave trade, was seized yet again. After it was appraised at six thousand dollars, Gazaway posted sureties and became the legal claimant. Gazaway then transferred ownership back to Charlie. In December 1860 Nelson Trowbridge took the ship to Cuba where he sold a half-interest on behalf of Charlie. Gazaway cursed the *Wanderer* as the albatross that wouldn't fly away.

Charlie also learned he'd have to stand trial for Martin's voyage. Though he claimed he had no part in it, as owner of the craft he was legally responsible for it.

But the *Wanderer* issues were not as troubling to Gazaway as the dissolution of the Union. As he witnessed the states secede from one thousand miles away, he knew he would soon have to return to Georgia. However, his wife was too sick to move, so, in the relatively calm aftermath of the nation's split, Gazaway continued to live in New York.

As a wealthy merchant, director of the Lamar Fire Insurance Company, and president of the Bank of the Republic, he was ideally situated to assist southern associates in financial matters and had done so for years. He was called upon to help again in the fall of 1860, though in a different way. In October he helped South Carolina Governor William Gist purchase ten thousand muskets from the federal government. Under ordinary circumstances, this would not have been unusual, since each state received an armaments allotment. However, the prospect of secession clouded the propriety of the transaction. Then, after Lincoln's election but before South Carolina's secession, Lamar similarly helped order muskets for

Georgia Governor Joseph Brown. Northerners were infuriated when they learned of the sales.

McBain said, "Emily's right. Gazaway had better be careful. New Yorkers won't take kindly to a Georgian in their midst brokering armaments for the South."

Joseph replied, "Yes, but Gazaway is a tough old cock. He can handle himself."

Sarah cleared her throat to get everyone's attention. She wasn't ready to abandon the topic of her grandchildren. "Joseph, when are you going to New York to see Emily?"

"I don't know. First, I have to go to Charleston to see the Floating Battery."

"The floating what?" Sarah asked.

"Floating Battery. It's supposed to be the most amazing thing." Joseph explained that after Major Anderson moved his troops to Fort Sumter the previous Christmas, South Carolina immediately planned to retake it. As the fort was over three miles from the mainland, the generals worried they'd have trouble bombarding it with land batteries. They started building an indestructible floating fort which could be towed and moored within easy range of Sumter. Iron plates were needed and the Heritage had contracted to produce some of them.

Amy folded her arms. "This is becoming frightening. South Carolina is seriously considering going to war on her own against the United States?"

James McBain shrugged. "It appears so."

Bob said to Joseph, "You must look up my friend Dr. Salter while you're in Charleston. He just moved there. I'll write a letter of introduction for you. He's well-connected and as sharp as a tack. You'll enjoy his company."

Joseph replied, "Thanks, Bob. It's always nice to know someone when visiting another city." Bob excused himself and retired to the study to prepare the letter.

As Bob wrote it, Joseph bade goodnight to Amy and his parents, and asked his mother if she could keep Danny while he was in Charleston. Sarah finally smiled. She loved nothing better than taking care of her grandson.

*   *   *

A few evenings later, Joseph stood at the Pritchard Street boat yard in Charleston, tongue-tied. The Floating Battery was massive, as big as two houses side-by-side. He guessed it to be about one hundred feet long about fifty feet wide. The framing was near completion, with the hold and deck made of solid southern pine. The front or gun wall slanted back at a slight angle and was made of fibrous palmetto wood. The builder, Mr. Marsh, explained to Joseph that the plan was to cover the wall with six layers of iron plates, making it four feet thick.

An iron-plated roof would extend from the gun wall to provide complete cover from retaliatory fire. Four gun holes were cut to allow for the cannon. Three magazines in the rear, well-protected by the side walls and the roof, stored the powder and the thirty-four- and forty-two-pound cannon balls. There were six entrances to the hold, in which two hundred men could fit. It would be moored between Morris and James islands, four hundred yards from the most exposed side of Sumter.

Joseph inquired if Major Anderson would allow South Carolina forces to tow the fort so close without firing at it. The smile left the builder's face. "I guess we'll see."

Joseph and Marsh then resolved a few details regarding the dimensions of the plates. Joseph assured Marsh that production was on schedule and the Heritage would have its share of the plates ready in a few weeks.

Joseph returned to the Planter's Hotel. He had a messenger deliver Bob's letter to Dr. Salter with a note suggesting they dine one night. The messenger returned with a note from Salter saying he would meet Joseph at the hotel's dining room at eight that night.

Dr. George H. C. Salter was in his early thirties, a few inches shorter than Joseph, with a barrel chest and a head and full beard of black, shiny hair. His loud voice was loaded with the certainty of a cannon ball in flight. "Of course I remember Miss McBain; an elegant woman, even while attending to crass patrons, including yours truly."

Joseph laughed. "She and Bob are happily married. He now helps Amy attend to those patrons. He still paints a little."

Salter took a deep puff on his segar. "Yes, so I read in Bob's letter." He held up his glass of whiskey. "To their happiness." As they drank, Salter wondered how smitten Bob must have become to leave the newspaper and remain in the South, especially in the current environment. Salter, recently married, knew that love was a powerful motivator. He also knew there were many North-South marriages that had to come to terms with the times.

Salter asked, "And what brings you to Charleston, Mr. McBain?"

Joseph spoke about supplying materials for the Floating Battery. Salter was a good listener and Joseph got the idea the doctor soaked up every word he said.

"That beast will bring considerable mayhem to the equation, as they say. Tell me, Mr. McBain, are you pleased with the disunion movement in Georgia?"

Joseph admitted he had been a Cooperationist, but would abide by the voice of the majority, as would any true Georgian.

Dr. Salter rolled his segar in his mouth for a moment, and blew out a thin stream of smoke. "You're willing to risk all for the institution of slavery?"

Joseph waited for the waiter to serve the food before replying. "Disunion is about much more than slavery, sir, though I'm sure you've been told the same here in Charleston. Our ways of life are different. Those who favor disunion don't believe our interests—be they tariffs, trade, international relations, territorial expansion, or, yes, slavery—can ever be reconciled with the North. However, I personally think that, as one union we're stronger economically and militarily and must negotiate our differences. We owe that to the founders of our country."

Salter cut his steak into pieces all at one time. "There aren't many who think like that in the Palmetto State."

"I guess not. Sir, you sound like a northern man. What brings you here?"

Salter devoured a piece of beef. "My family is from Portsmouth, New Hampshire, though I was born in New York City, and have lived there for years. Now, I'm a correspondent for the *New York Times*."

Joseph almost choked on his food. He took a large swallow of water. He leaned forward and spoke softly, "The authorities here allow a reporter from the North?"

Salter was not the type of man to whisper for any reason. He boomed, "Certainly, and why not? I seek and report the truth. I damn when it's due and praise when it's earned. Early indications are the people here respect that. I do have a prejudice for the stars and stripes, but I am eminently fair. Still, I use a pen-name. I am the Jasper."

Joseph raised his eyebrows. "A famous South Carolina name! You're a doctor?"

"Yes. I recently spent several years as a surgeon on a ship that ran between New York and France." Salter then pointed his fork, which held a chunk of steak, at Joseph and said, "But my interest now is reporting, especially in these historic times. And I don't quit until I get the information I need." Salter mouthed the meat off the fork.

Joseph didn't doubt him. He enjoyed Salter's honesty, even if it bordered on the arrogance so common in Northerners. He asked, "What's your impression of Charleston, sir?"

Salter finished his meal, sopping up the last trace of gravy with a chunk of bread. He pushed his chair back and crossed one leg over the other, causing his napkin to slide to the floor. "Actually, I'm impressed with the spirit of the gamecocks, especially the rich, elderly planters who have left their plantations to join in the preparations for war. They work right alongside their negroes, I might add. If my friends in the North think they can sail down here, knock these folks around, and force them back into the Union within a few days, they're in for a surprise."

Joseph wondered if the straightforward answer was just simple boasting. "Do you plan on writing about that in your paper, sir?"

Salter replied, "I certainly do. Ask Bob Carson about my reporting."

Just then, two men entered the dining room, catching Salter's eye. The doctor excused himself and walked over to them, leaving Joseph alone. Joseph thought about Bob. He was friends with a correspondent of the *New York Times*. Was Charlie Lamar right? Could Bob be a reporter, too? He always asked many questions, especially about the *Wanderer* and Lamar and life in Savannah. He went to every *Wanderer* trial and hearing and befriended Couper and Ganahl. Joseph was convinced the article he read about Savannah by Oglethorpe was written by someone residing in the town.

"You must forgive me, Mr. McBain," Salter said, jolting Joseph from his thoughts. "But if I see someone who might have information, I must approach him. As I'm new here, I must make acquaintances right away. There's no time to be shy."

At the end of the evening, Salter told Joseph that he was leaving in a few days on a turtle-hunting trip to Florida and would return in two weeks. He hoped to see Joseph again.

Joseph boarded a train two days later. A rail link between Charleston and Savannah had recently been completed, allowing travel between the two cities in seven short hours. During the ride Joseph considered the mood of Charleston. The people were preparing for war and seemed excited about it. He heard no talk of negotiation and compromise. The unimaginable had become a possibility. Americans, family members, friends, and business associates might soon be killing one other.

Joseph also thought about Bob. He composed a note to him suggesting they have a drink one evening. There was only one sure way to find out if Bob was a reporter. Ask him.

*   *   *

Bob read Joseph's note as he waited in the post office to mail his final report to his newspaper. When Bob resigned, his editor had asked him to write just a few more articles, concluding with the secession convention and the reaction in Savannah. After that, the paper would no longer keep a correspondent in that town. Bob was anxious. He couldn't live the lie any longer. He planned to confess to Amy at the next opportunity.

Bob owed much to the paper, yet he didn't feel guilty about quitting. It was either the paper or Amy, whom he assumed would never leave the South. There were good jobs up North, but there were few women whom he could love, and who would love him in return. Being with her was more important.

Bob thought meeting Amy was fate. He hadn't seen a woman socially in New York for over a year after his wife died. He took a vacation to the South with some friends and met an unmarried, beautiful, intelligent woman. Then his employer assigned him to Savannah.

Marriage made him feel young again. He and Amy wanted to have children, and they eagerly worked at it almost every day. Because they were at the restaurant most nights, they made love in the daytime, which Bob thought so much more erotic than in the dark.

Work at the restaurant was harder than Bob had imagined. There was something to do every moment. However, Amy had the process so well organized that he simply followed her direction. He sometimes shopped at the city market with Amy and Dante. Dante selected the fish, meat, and fowl while Amy bought vegetables, rice, and other cooking ingredients. Often, he would see them standing by a food stall, conferring on the preparation of a dish, pointing fingers at tomatoes or beans or carrots.

As it turned out, he enjoyed greeting, seating, and hosting diners. Savannahians were friendly, gracious people and they often complimented his paintings that hung on the wall.

Bob's presence allowed Amy to leave the restaurant early whenever she got tired or wanted to see her family. When Bob arrived home, he gave her an accounting of the night's receipts, which Amy could guess within ten dollars based on the number of diners.

Bob finally posted the letter to his editor, and concluded to meet Joseph in two days. He didn't notice the two men watching him as he left the post office.

The next night, Bob closed the restaurant by himself, and strolled through Chippewa Square towards their house on Harris Street. He saw a flash of light. It seemed to come from behind him. He tried to touch the back of his head, but couldn't because he was lying on the ground. He heard someone say, "Write about this, Mr. Oglethorpe." He felt a pain shoot through the side of his head, and his ear started to ring so loudly he couldn't hear another sound. He vaguely felt his body being lifted and carried. Then he felt himself being dropped to the ground.

He opened his eyes and saw a white ceiling. He turned his head to the side and saw Amy sitting on a chair, a book in her hand. He croaked her name. She heard him, came to his bedside, and held his hand. He could hardly hear her say, "You'll be all right, dear. You'll get better," over the noise in his ears.

Bob closed his eyes and thought about where he was and how he got there. His head throbbed. He realized he had been jumped from behind. Bob propped himself on his elbows and groaned, "Damned cowards! I'll find them and kill them!"

He struggled to throw his feet over the side of the bed, but Amy held him down. She pleaded with him, "No, Bob. Please rest. Please!" Bob fell back onto the bed, felt a stabbing pain in his ear, and mumbled to himself. He vowed to find his attackers.

Fortunately, after he was smacked on the back of the head with a brick and kicked, two policemen came by, spoiling the ambush, and preventing a tar and cottoning.

*   *   *

"I don't know what to do, Joseph. Someone's trying to harm him," Amy said as the two talked in the restaurant before opening. It was two days after Bob had been assaulted. He had just left the hospital and was convalescing at home. He kept a pistol in the night-table drawer. Bob had suffered a cut and deep bruises, and still had ringing in his ear, but Dr. Arnold expected him to recover.

"It could have been random, Amy. Some thieves trying to rob him."

Amy pulled a piece of paper from her purse and waved it like a fan. "I got this letter today. Unsigned, of course. It says northern newspaper reporters belong in the North. If he doesn't leave town on his own, someone will help him."

Joseph took the note and read it. "That sounds like the Vigilance Committee. It's time to have to talk with Charlie."

Amy said, "As bad as Charlie is, do you think he'd attack a member of our family? We've known him for years. You and Andrew saved his life. He considers you a close friend."

"I'm not saying it was Charlie. But he might know who it is." Joseph paused, and then asked, "Amy, could he be, you know, a reporter?"

Amy glared at Joseph. "How could you say such a thing? Bob runs the restaurant with me. He's a painter!"

"I mean before that. He did spend a lot of time at those *Wanderer* trials."

"Well, so did you! So did many other men in Savannah. I don't know, Joseph, and I don't care. He's my husband. Even if he were a reporter, he doesn't deserve to get his head knocked off." Amy sniffled.

Joseph held Amy's hand to calm her. He had pushed too far. He also knew he could not confront Bob so soon after being attacked. "I'm sorry, Amy."

"Maybe we should move."

Joseph jerked his head back. "Amy, you can't! Savannah is a good town. It has a few criminals, just like any other place. If you leave, you admit defeat and cede the city to them. We must find whoever is responsible and have them locked up. Father's trying to do that."

James McBain, who was not aware of the anonymous note, had reported the attack to the city marshal and the chief of police, and had advertised a reward of two hundred dollars for information on the persons responsible. No one had yet come forward. James also offered to let Hercules stay at Amy's house for a while, but she declined.

Amy replied, "What do I do until they're caught, if ever? Let them beat up Bob and feel good because we didn't leave?" Amy rested her face in her hands. Bob was a proud man. When she suggested they leave Savannah, he said he'd never run from cowards. Amy said he couldn't fight who he didn't know. Bob said he'd find them.

Joseph pressed, "If you move, where would you go?"

"I don't know. I'd consider New York City, Bob's home. We're going there in a few weeks so I can meet his aunts and cousins."

"Amy, do you think you'll get better treatment up there than he got here?"

Amy sighed. "I don't know. But we can't be looking over our shoulders for the rest of our lives here." The two sat quietly for a moment. Then Amy said, "Please don't tell Mother and Father about that note. I don't want them to be suspicious of Bob as well."

Joseph moved his chair next to Amy's and put an arm around her shoulder. "You know the difference between you and Emily? You stand by your husband. I can't lose you, Amy. First Grandfather, then Emily and Charlotte, and soon Andrew and Patience."

Amy used a napkin to dab at her eyes. "I feel the same way. But Bob's my husband. I love him." Amy laid her head on Joseph's shoulder. "I'm frightened, Joseph."

Joseph hugged his sister. "Don't worry. I'll protect you, Amy. Things will work out."

Joseph left the restaurant and went straight to Charlie's office. An assistant told Joseph that Charlie was out of town for a few days. Joseph told the assistant he'd be back.

A few nights later, after visiting Bob, a weary James McBain took his newspaper and port to the piazza and read about the Montgomery Convention.

Representatives of the six seceded states—Georgia, South Carolina, Mississippi, Florida, Alabama, and Louisiana—were gathering to form a new union. Texas would join them soon. Howell Cobb was appointed the convention president. Within a week the men had drafted a constitution. It was similar to the Constitution of the United States, and an ordinance was passed continuing all laws of the United States in force as of November 1, 1860, until repealed or altered by the Southern Confederacy. While the constitution recognized the right to hold slaves, it prohibited the importation of African negroes from any foreign country other than the slaveholding states of the United States.

The convention unanimously elected Jefferson Davis of Mississippi president, and Alexander Stephens of Georgia vice-president.

Committees were established for finance, foreign affairs, military and naval affairs, commerce, and patents. They set to work on pressing issues such as a tariff to raise revenues to support the new government and establishing a military. More than a few eyebrows were raised in the North at the speed and determination under which the new confederacy was formed.

McBain closed his eyes and wondered what his grandfather and father would think of the prospect of Americans warring against each other. He fell asleep in the chair with an ache in his chest for his family and country.

*   *   *

Amy hugged her parents and Joseph on the wharf. She assured her mother there was nothing to look after. She had closed the restaurant temporarily and paid the employees for the three weeks she and Bob would be in New York.

Bob kissed Sarah on the cheek and shook Joseph's and James's hands. He promised his in-laws that he would take good care of Amy.

The whistle blew and Amy and Bob started down the pier to the ship. Bob heard a voice say, "Have a good voyage."

Bob stopped and turned. He saw a man slightly shorter than he, nor as muscular, with a full beard, wearing a baggy suit and a hat pulled down over his forehead, barely revealing his eyes and a grinning mouth. Though Bob had never seen the stranger before, there was something about the man. Bob asked, "Excuse me? What did you say?"

The man replied, "You heard me." Two other bearded men, dressed like the first, with hats pulled down, stepped to his side.

Joseph moved next to Bob and said to the leader, "You speak with an unfortunate tone, sir, and I don't appreciate it. Identify yourself so I may find you later."

The leader smirked. "You don't need to bother finding me, sir. I'll find you."

One of the other men pointed at Bob's swollen ear and asked, "What happened?"

Some sixth sense told Bob he was facing the cowards who had ambushed him. Unable to control his anger, he stepped forward and fired his right fist at the inquisitive man's cheek, staggering him backwards and spinning his hat sideways.

Amy and Sarah screamed as James rushed to restrain Bob. The leader charged Bob but Joseph landed a punch flush on the man's temple, dropping him onto the wharf.

Joseph was held back by two workmen who were trying to stop the confrontation.

The three men gathered themselves. The leader straightened his hat and pointed at Bob. "You get on that ship and don't come back." He then looked at Joseph and said, "You and me have a score to settle." They hurried to a wagon and drove away.

Amy yelled after them, "Animals! This isn't your town to tell people what to do! Go to hell, all of you!" She started to cry and Bob held her.

The workmen released Joseph. He grabbed Bob's arm, and yelled, "Let's go after them. I'll get Hercules. He's just up the street."

Joseph started to run down River Street. Bob released Amy and followed him. Amy screamed after him, "Bob! Come back! We have a ship to catch!"

Joseph and Bob stopped and watched the back of the cowards' wagon kick up dirt as it gained speed. They returned to Amy, Sarah, and James.

Amy said, "Bob, are you crazy? We can't miss the ship." Bob didn't want to argue with Amy, but he would have gladly missed it to catch those men.

Joseph asked the workmen and other observers, "Does anyone here know those men? I'll pay for their names." The people looked at each other and shook their heads.

James said, "Bob, they talked like they knew you. Why would he order you to get on the ship and not come back?" Joseph heard the question and waited for Bob's answer.

Bob shrugged. "I don't know, sir. I think they were the ones who jumped me."

The *Adjustor*'s whistle blew again. Amy hugged her parents and Joseph once more. She said to her brother, "I love you, Joseph. Please be careful."

Joseph held his sister tight. "Don't worry, Amy. I can take care of myself."

James said, "I got a good look at one of them. We'll find them."

Amy and Bob walked to the ship and soon disappeared inside it. The lines were released and the ship was towed away by a steam tug. Sarah, James, and Joseph waved until the *Adjustor* reached the middle of the river, and then moped away. As they were crossing River Street, someone nearby shouted, "Look!"

The McBains turned and saw the revenue cutter *Dobbin* pull alongside the *Adjustor*. Uniformed men in the *Dobbin* called up to the captain. Soon the *Adjustor* was tugged back to the pier. Amy and Bob weren't leaving Savannah quite yet.

After Georgia purchased muskets through Gazaway Lamar the previous December, her leaders realized they needed even more guns. After secession, the only way to accomplish this was through private arms dealers in the North. This was not difficult. Trade between the North and the South continued much as it had before the break-up of the Union. The ship and train schedules between the two regions didn't change. Many northern businessmen stationed in the South remained, as did southern businessmen living in the North, though they had to keep their opinions to themselves. And while the seceded states had to establish their own currency, as well as banking, postal, and customs organizations, the lack of them hardly inhibited commerce between the regions.

So it certainly wasn't odd to see ships in New York harbor being loaded with goods bound for southern ports. However, on a late January day, a New York policeman noticed musket cases being loaded onto the *Monticello*, bound for Savannah. He notified his superior officer and within hours, thirty-eight boxes were opened and the muskets were seized.

When Governor Brown learned that the legally purchased goods had been confiscated, he sent a message to New York Governor Edwin Morgan demanding their release within three days. Brown never received a reply, and ordered Colonel Henry Rootes Jackson to seize all the ships in Savannah harbor belonging to residents of New York. On February 8 Jackson took control of five vessels. Brown apprised Morgan of his actions and declared the ships would be freed when the arms were delivered to Georgia's agent, Gazaway Lamar.

Two days later, Lamar was told by New York authorities that the arms had been released. He telegraphed the port collector in Savannah, who released the five ships. Everyone breathed a sigh of relief. A serious confrontation had been avoided.

The sighs were brief. After the vessels had departed, Lamar was informed that the police supervisor had never released the arms, and would only do so through the legal process. Lamar telegraphed Governor Brown with the news.

On February 21 Governor Brown once again ordered Colonel Jackson to seize all New York ships in Savannah Harbor. Amy and Bob were on one of the three.

The McBains returned to Pulaski Square and sat in the parlor as Amy and Bob considered their options. Amy was too frightened to return to their house on Harris Street. Bob wanted to get in the wagon and find the three men. Joseph agreed, but James prevailed. He had Hercules take Amy and Bob to the Heritage to wait the two days until the next ship for New York departed. Then he and Joseph went to the police chief, who promised to renew his efforts.

*　　*　　*

"Joseph! Come on in! I heard you stopped by recently." Charlie Lamar stood and shook Joseph's hand. Charlie sat back down, but Joseph kept his feet. "I want to thank Emily for keeping in touch with my father. He appreciates that. I understand she's staying in New York for a while."

Joseph didn't want to discuss his private life with Charlie. "Yes."

"I also heard Andrew is going to England to work at the invitation of the Queen. You must congratulate him for me."

"I'll do that. I didn't come here to chat, Charlie. You know some criminals jumped Bob Carson from behind and almost beat his head in a few weeks ago?"

Charlie stroked his beard. "Yes, I heard."

"I told you if anyone attacked my family I'd kill him."

"Joseph, why come to me? I said I'd never harm a McBain. I'd fight to defend you!"

Joseph tried to keep calm. He couldn't tell if Charlie was toying with him. "A few days ago Amy and Bob were about to sail to New York. Three men I didn't recognize were there to wish them well. Do you know anything about that?"

Charlie placed his hands flat on the desk. "Joseph, I don't know everything that happens in this town. I spend all my time with the Mounted Rifles, preparing for war."

Joseph moved around the desk and stood over Charlie. "Who is responsible? Was it 'the boys' you said were so worried about me? The ones that suspected Bob was a reporter?"

Charlie leaned back. "Joseph, I told you I don't know. Where is Bob now?"

Joseph bent forward, not giving Charlie any space. "He and Amy caught another ship yesterday. Charlie, you either tell me who did it, or you help me search for them now. I got a fair look at one of them at the pier."

Lamar pushed his chair back so he could stand without bumping into Joseph. "Joseph, I know how you feel. A few days ago my father was accosted on the streets of New York by a so-called citizens committee. They told him he must leave the city. Father had recently resigned from the bank and had every intention of moving. He told them his wife was too sick to travel. The mob threatened him. They were probably Lincoln's damned Wide-Awakes." Charlie was referring to a political club of Lincoln supporters who were distinguished by a uniform with a glazed cape and cap.

"It's too bad your father had to experience that. But thugs in New York aren't my problem. The ones here are. Now tell me who they are or get into my gig."

Charlie grabbed his hat and walked to the door. Joseph drove Charlie around the east side of town where poor whites lived: by the wharves all the way to Lamar's Creek, around the Trustees' Garden, up and down East Broad, East Boundary, Reynolds, Arnold, Randolph, and Anderson streets, around the Savannah Albany and Gulf Railroad Depot. Joseph eyed every man he saw. They went into three barrooms. On two occasions Charlie had Joseph stop the gig so he could question acquaintants on the street if they knew of the mystery men. They came up empty. After two hours, Joseph drove Charlie back to his office, thanked him for his time, and promised to return in a few days to continue their search in the southern part of town.

Joseph left Charlie and went to the post office to pick up the mail, and Emily's daily letter. They were much the same; how she missed him, the cute things Charlotte did, and a plea to send Danny to her. The letters made Joseph anguish for the loss of his family. He had been planning to go to New York in a few weeks to bring his wife and daughter back to Savannah. However, Joseph had a strong sense that this missive might be the one saying she was coming home. He opened it the moment he sat in his study.

February 21, 1861

My Dearest Joseph,

Life without you is torture. Charlotte has your eyes, and I am reminded of you every time I look at her, which is one thousand times a day. I continue to pray every night that you and Danny will come to us.

I have the most fabulous news. You're not going to believe what I'm about to tell you. President Lincoln arrived in New York two days ago on his train journey from Springfield to Washington. A procession of thirty-five carriages escorted him from the Hudson River Railroad Station to the Astor House. That's where we spent our first, very romantic night of marriage together! Do you remember? I think of it all the time.

Yesterday, Lincoln was welcomed at City Hall by Mayor Wood, the idiot who proposed that the city secede from the Union. I had taken Charlotte downtown in the wild hope of meeting the president, and we waited on line in the blustery weather for two hours! (Don't worry, Charlotte was bundled up.) There must have been two thousand people, and though I was well situated, I wasn't sure I'd have the chance to see him. But we finally got into the building and the reception room. As we inched closer to the President, I felt my knees shaking.

Finally, I was next. The man in front of me was very tall, and when he greeted the president, Mr. Lincoln asked him to turn around. Lincoln also turned and the two stood back to back. The president looked at me and said, "Ma'am, who is taller?" I could hardly talk. I told the president he was. Mr. Lincoln winked at me and said, "I saw him stretching himself to make the question, so I thought I would try it."

Everyone nearby laughed. He extended his hand to me and said, "It's a pleasure to meet you. You are an excellent judge of height." He then took Charlotte from my arms, held her and gave her a kiss on the cheek! He said, "What a beautiful child. May I ask where her father is?"

I told him you were home in Georgia and that I was afraid to go there because there might be war. I started to cry and he put his arm around my shoulders. He assured me there will not be war. He asked for my name and yours, and where you live in Georgia. I told him and a man sitting at a nearby table wrote it down.

I was so excited at meeting him, I guess I was confused. I thanked him and started to walk away. He said, "Mrs. McBain, here," and handed Charlotte to me. Everyone, even Mayor Wood, laughed. I turned red as a tomato.

Joseph, President Lincoln is the smartest, kindest man alive. If anyone can heal this nation, he can. But the South must trust him. I pray that this can happen. Please write as soon as you receive this. I miss you so much.

Your loving wife for eternity,
Emily

Joseph didn't bother to smell the perfumed paper. He barely held onto the letter in his dangling hands. Was she crazy, being away from him yet writing all those letters? He wondered if he could live with her again if she ever returned. Joseph decided not to respond to Emily, and reconsidered his trip to New York.

Two weeks later, the day the South had dreaded came to pass. Abraham Lincoln was inaugurated as the sixteenth president of the United States. Despite fears of violence, the day passed without incident.

James Buchanan was probably the happiest man in America. His presidency was full of stormy political issues, from the reaction to the Dred Scott decision and its impact on slavery in the territories, to the Kansas situation, to the Financial Panic of 1857, to the rise of the Republican Party, to the strife within his own Democratic Party, and, finally, to secession.

He had been criticized endlessly in the North for not sending supplies or reinforcements to the federal troops at Fort Sumter after the failure of the *Star of the West* mission.

In the South he had been blasted for not evacuating the fort and handing the keys to South Carolina or the Confederacy, as he could easily have done. He even proclaimed that Major Anderson was justified in evacuating Fort Moultrie and occupying Fort Sumter. And when members of his cabinet—Cobb, Floyd, and Thompson, all sympathetic to the South—resigned, he didn't replace them with like-minded men.

But Buchanan had found his backbone too late, and there was no way he, in his final months as president, would do anything to throw the country into civil war.

Now, it was Lincoln's turn to deal with the situation. But the new president didn't move precipitously. Like Buchanan, he wanted to avoid a bloody war. Nor did Lincoln want to do anything that would cause the eight slave states still in the Union to join the Confederacy. Lincoln's dilemma was a sensitive one.

The country waited.

CHAPTER 30

No Turning Back

March-April 1861

Joseph and Andrew strode into Mr. Camp's clothing store on Congress Street. Andrew, dressed in his best suit, drew little attention from the other patrons. Mr. Camp smiled at both men and addressed Joseph. "Good day, Mr. McBain. How may I help you today?"

Joseph put a hand on Andrew's shoulder. "My friend Andrew is moving to England. He'd like two tailored suits made of your finest materials, cashmere or fine wool. And please put this on my account."

Mr. Camp said, "Of course, sir. We've read about Andrew. We're very proud of him." He took a step back to examine Andrew. He then fitted Andrew for two suits and five shirts.

The two then went to Wood's Shoe Shop on Broughton where Andrew insisted on paying for new pairs of shoes and boots. They next walked around the City Market, bought apples from a vendor, and ate them as they made their way to the Strand. They stood at the edge of the bluff as they had so many times as boys.

Joseph said, "You're going on one of those adventures we always dreamed of."

"I can't believe this is happening, Joseph. And I can't believe it won't be with you. You must visit us in England!"

Joseph bent down and picked up a clover. He pulled a leaf from it and flicked it over the side of the bluff. "Whenever we've been separated in the past, I've always been the one to leave. I knew I'd be back. Now, it's you who's leaving and I'm not so sure I'll see you again."

"What do you mean?"

Joseph flicked another leaf. "If you like England, you can stay. I don't know what it's like there, but maybe you can be an architect without hiding it. Maybe you can vote, too. Maybe your children can go to school, and you can walk the streets at night without a pass. If you can have all that, it would be difficult to return here."

Andrew pondered that. Next to his family, he loved Joseph more than anyone. They had shared their lives, albeit unequally, like brothers. He couldn't imagine life without him. "I've thought about that, Joseph. What you say may be true, but don't forget I'm a Georgian, too."

Joseph smiled. "We're both children of Oglethorpe, aren't we?"

Andrew laughed. Then he frowned. "What's going to happen to the country, Joseph?"

Joseph looked at the river. The harbor looked so peaceful as the ships glided around. "I don't know. Most of the seceded states have ratified the new constitution. I don't see us ever becoming part of the United States again, unless we're defeated in war and are forced back in. Then the bitterness would be unbearable. Hopefully, a settlement can be negotiated so we can live peacefully as neighbors. But I'm not so sure anymore."

"Do you really think there'll be war?"

Joseph took a deep breath. "South Carolina troops are pouring into Charleston. I was there last week and a doctor friend of Bob's arranged a tour for us of the batteries around the harbor. There are about fifteen of them, all packed with artillery. It will take a large fleet of ships to break past them. And you should see this Floating Battery. It's an ironclad fort on water. It even has its own hospital. The generals must be itching to use their power. The longer they go without reaching an agreement on Sumter, the more likely fighting will start."

Andrew leaned his forearms on the fence. "I know Mr. Norris was worried about the situation. That's why he moved." Norris had recently left Savannah for New York. He thought that war was unavoidable, and placed the house for General Mercer in the hands of his associate, DeWitt Bruyn. Before Norris departed, he told Andrew that if he desired, he could come to New York and work for him after he returned from England. "It just seems so extreme to resort to war. You've always said so."

"Yes, but the peace committees in the Senate and the House haven't solved anything. The South is drunk on our new-found independence. It won't take much to light the fuse."

"What are you going to do, Joseph?"

"You know how I feel about Georgia, Andrew. I'll fight for her if called upon. I've joined the Oglethorpe Light Infantry." Joseph slapped Andrew on the back. "You're leaving here at the right time, my friend. The next year or two could be very dangerous."

"What about Danny?"

Joseph exhaled through his mouth, and his lips fluttered. "Danny might be safer in New York, and his safety is my biggest concern. The Confederacy will fight to defend her rights and territory. We have no designs on conquering other states. The North, however, will try to crush us and everything we have. But I'm worried that if I send Danny to New York, I may never see him again. War will change everything. Many families won't survive. Friendships will be destroyed."

The men stood quietly for a minute. Andrew asked, "Joseph, do you still wear your necklace, the one that Toonahowi gave your great-grandfather?"

Joseph threw the clover stem away, undid a shirt button, and revealed the sacred family possession of stones and animal teeth, now considerably yellowed. Andrew said. "Our friendship is like that necklace. It will endure."

Joseph put his arm around Andrew's shoulder. "You're right. Friends forever."

*   *   *

"It took a while, but we're finally getting together," Bob said to Joseph at the bar in the Marshall House on Broughton Street. Bob and Amy had returned to Savannah from New York the day before and he contacted Joseph right away.

Joseph pulled a barstool next to his, and Bob sat. Joseph asked, "How was your trip?"

Bob picked up the beer that Joseph had ordered for him and took a long swallow. "Very pleasant. My aunts love Amy. Why wouldn't they? She'll tell you about it tonight at supper."

Joseph sipped his beer. "I'm certain she will. I hope you got some rest. It looks like your wounds have healed."

Bob nodded. "Yes, but I haven't forgotten."

Joseph said, "I didn't think you would. I'd protect myself if I were you."

Bob pulled his jacket aside, revealing a revolver.

Joseph arched his eyebrows and said, "It looks like you're prepared." He then asked, "Have you made any decisions about your future?"

Bob got off the barstool and leaned his back against the bar. "Not yet. I don't want to leave until I find those men. But Amy's scared. It won't take much for her to leave. We'll travel to and from the restaurant at night together. Your father has offered Hercules to escort us."

Joseph held his beer but didn't feel like drinking. He had a headache since he received Bob's note suggesting they finally meet. Joseph had lost his desire to question Bob about working for a newspaper. He was more concerned about his sister's safety. But he needed to know if he was defending a man who had been deceiving him and his family. "Bob, why were those men at the wharf so intent on getting you out of town? If they were the men who accosted you in Chippewa Square, they didn't try to rob you."

"I don't know, Joseph. I guess they're not fond of Northerners."

"Bob, I have to know one thing, and I want the truth. Are you a reporter for a northern newspaper?"

Bob turned to order another round of drinks. He watched the bartender refill the glasses and place them on the counter. He then looked Joseph in the eye. "I was. I'm not any longer."

Joseph grimaced. What he suspected had been confirmed. He glared at Bob. "How could you do that? Befriend us, dine with us, and come into our homes?"

Bob glanced around, but no one was in earshot. "Yes, I deceived you. My employer sent me here and didn't think I could safely reveal my identity."

"Dr. Salter works openly as a reporter in Charleston."

"Yes, but he's one of the few in the South who does. And not everyone there knows he's the writer for the *New York Times*. He uses a pen-name. I think he's crazy." Bob clutched Joseph's arm and said, "By God, Joseph, don't the incidents of the last month bear me out?"

Joseph didn't reply. When Bob released his arm, Joseph took a sip of beer.

Bob continued to defend himself. "I fell in love with Amy and I made a choice. I married your sister, I left my post at the paper, and we're living in Savannah. What more can I do to prove my intentions?"

"Does Amy know that you were a reporter?"

"Yes, I told her in New York. The truth, Joseph, just as I've told it to you."

"How did she react?"

"She was very angry at first. But she understands what I gave up for her. She's glad I chose her over my position and my home. She's forgiven me. That's what I'm asking of you." Joseph didn't reply. Bob added, "I even showed her some of my reports. Have you read any of them?"

Joseph looked at his glass. "I read an article by Oglethorpe. Was that you?"

Bob whispered, "Yes. They were straight reporting on the *Wanderer* trials and life in Savannah. There were no lies or fabrications. I praised Ganahl, Jackson, and Couper for their dedication to justice. I wrote about the bravery of many of the witnesses. I commended James Moore Wayne and John Nicoll on the way they ran the trials. I condemned Lamar, Farnum, and some of the other defendants. Was I wrong to do so?"

Joseph suddenly felt exhausted. He rubbed his eyes. Bob had lied, but he did give up everything for Amy. And his life was in danger in Savannah, yet he was staying with her. Joseph wanted to drop the matter, now that he knew the truth.

Bob broke the silence. "Emily sends her love."

Joseph perked up. "Emily?"

"We dined with her in New York. She and the baby are well. She says she misses you and can't wait to see you in New York."

Joseph felt even sadder. He told Bob he was tired and would see him later at his parent's house. They shook hands and Joseph went home, no less confused about his life.

At supper, Amy talked about meeting Bob's relatives and about New York, its theatres, restaurants, and the Central Park for most of the evening, much to the chagrin of her parents. But she said nothing about leaving home, and seemed excited about reopening the restaurant in a few days. Amy did ask Joseph about the Heritage businesses, and he told her about the Floating Battery. He said he planned to visit Charleston soon to see the finished product. He also told Bob he was looking forward to seeing Dr. Salter again.

* * *

A few weeks later, on Tuesday, April 9, Joseph checked into the Mills House in Charleston and sent a note to Dr. Salter inviting him to supper. Joseph then walked to the wharf behind the Custom House on East Bay Street where the Floating Battery was docked. Mr. Marsh escorted him to it. Joseph was no less awed than the first time he had seen it. The front looked like a stable made of iron, but instead of heads of horses peaking out the windows, there were four thick, black, shiny cannon barrels. Soldiers sweated freely as they loaded barrels of gunpowder and cloth bags with charges into the magazines.

Before Joseph could utter a word, a captain hurried over and said, "I'm sorry, sir, but you'll have to leave the area. This is for military personnel only."

Marsh said, "This is Mr. McBain, Captain. His company supplied some of the material for the battery."

"Pleased to meet you, Mr. McBain. Thank you for your assistance," the captain said as he pointed to the gate. "But I'm afraid you'll still have to leave."

Joseph apologized and left. As he returned to the hotel, he felt a great sense of excitement in the town. The stores were empty of customers. Everyone was in the streets, talking about the Sumter situation. He passed the office of the *Charleston Mercury*, where at least one hundred people were bunched on the sidewalk, reading the bulletin board with the latest wires from Washington and Montgomery.

Joseph decided to visit the Battery, the southern tip of the peninsula on which Charleston was located. It provided a sweeping view of the harbor, including Fort Sumter, three and one-quarter miles out. Large cannons manned by cadets from the Citadel, called the West Point of the South by South Carolinians, lined the sea wall. Hundreds of men and women stood, casually chatting as if they were at the Ten Broeck track between races. Joseph squinted at the structure on the horizon that was the center of the nation's attention.

A man standing next to him said, "I hear seven federal vessels are off the bar and five thousand men are headed here from the interior. It won't be long now." Joseph nodded but didn't pursue the conversation. After an hour, he returned to his hotel. The clerk handed him a note. Dr. Salter would meet him for supper at eight.

"It's good to see you, Dr. Salter," Joseph said as he stood at the table to greet the reporter.

"Likewise, Mr. McBain. Please excuse my tardiness," Salter replied as the men shook hands. "How are Mr. and Mrs. Carson? I haven't heard from Bob in a while."

Joseph told the doctor about the assault on Bob, and explained that Bob had fully recovered and, after a visit to New York, was back in Savannah.

Salter shook his head. "Tell Bob I wish him well. Maybe it's time for him to consider moving. It's not a healthy place for a Northerner."

Joseph asked, "Sir, are you having a similar problem here?"

Salter sipped his whiskey. "Remember that tour we took of the Confederate batteries around the harbor last month? Well, I wrote about it for the *Times*. Since then, the *Mercury* has attacked my paper and me as abolitionists. Others have called the *Times* a 'vile, Black Republican sheet.' Still others demanded that the local Vigilance Committee watch my every step, and that I should be asked to leave the city."

"Then why don't you leave? Before you get hurt? These Vigilance Committees can get quite nasty. Surely, your work here isn't worth physical harm."

"Charlestonians! Those threats come out of one side of their mouths. Out of the other side comes exclusive information, often during suppers in their homes or at soirees, when they act like I'm a beloved member of their family." Salter held up his empty glass to the waiter.

"The men here behave like little children. They seceded not to keep their niggers, but because they wanted absolute free trade, including a few who want the slave trade. They hated the federal tariff, yet install one just like it after they leave the Union. They denounce Major Anderson for his deceit in taking Fort Sumter, yet they allowed him until recently to buy fresh produce every day at the market. That is not rational behavior, my good man."

Joseph peered around the dining room to see if anyone could hear Salter. "What's your opinion of the situation here, in terms of war, doctor?"

The waiter brought Salter's refill, which he instantly consumed. As he talked to Joseph, his eyes darted to people entering the dining room. "I'm afraid to say bloodshed is inevitable. Once it starts, no one knows when it will end. I hear General Beauregard will accept only surrender from Major Anderson. Anderson won't do anything without orders. The word is the federal government has decided to send ships to re-supply Fort Sumter, by force if necessary. Draw your own conclusions." Salter drained the last drops from his whiskey glass, even snaking his tongue inside the vessel to help the effort. "Tell me, sir, how long will you be in town?"

Joseph replied, "I'm supposed to leave in a few days, on Friday. My business is finished. I really came up here to see the situation first hand."

Salter patted his mouth with his napkin. A man in a suit came up to them, whispered in Salter's ear, and walked away. Salter said to Joseph, "If you stay, please let me know. I'd enjoy chatting some more, but you must excuse me right now. I need to be someplace." With that, the Jasper placed the napkin on his plate, leaving his half-finished meal and Joseph.

The next two days Joseph walked around the city, fascinated by the constant movement of troops through the streets, the rumors of impending attacks, the mass of people at the Battery and newspaper offices, and, with the exceptions of taverns and restaurants, the halt in business activity. Strangers stopped him on the street to announce the latest news, or to ask him if he had any to offer. He spent the nights at the Battery, surrounded by thousands of others, waiting for war to begin.

On Thursday night, his last in Charleston, as he watched the twinkling firelights from the batteries surrounding Sumter, he wondered what the scene would look like the next time he visited. As he walked back to his hotel, he felt his stomach churning.

As Joseph slept, three representatives of General Beauregard rowed to Fort Sumter to ascertain if Major Anderson had changed his mind about an immediate evacuation. Anderson wrote a note stating that he would evacuate in three days if he was not re-supplied or given different instructions from his government. The Confederate men conferred and finally wrote back to Anderson at 3:30 a.m., saying that their forces would commence firing in one hour. They boarded their boat and left.

Joseph awoke to the sound of cannon fire. He dressed and darted into the hall just as ten other men did. They ran down the stairs together without speaking, cramming the stairwell with other men from the lower floors. They charged down Meeting Street towards the Battery, joining hundreds of others leaving their abodes.

When Joseph reached the Battery, he saw streaks of fire across the black sky, rising from six or seven Confederate batteries. He saw no return fire from Fort Sumter. When a shell burst into the walls of Sumter, a cheer erupted from the crowd that jammed the area.

After about an hour, Joseph noticed cannon fire from the water near the fort blasting into the side of Sumter. He knew the Floating Battery—made of his own iron—was unleashing its destructive force.

Two and one-half hours later, at daybreak, the federal forces, under Captain Abner Doubleday, opened the guns of Fort Sumter. The skies were alive with red-white meteors and explosions, like a distant summer thunderstorm.

The daylight brought gray, rainy skies, but the people didn't leave the Battery. Joseph tried to find a less crowded spot and walked up East Bay Street to Adger's Wharf, which also afforded a good view of the harbor. He stood for hours as both sides blasted away without let-up.

At 10:30 a.m., Joseph spotted Dr. Salter on the wharf. "There's no turning back now, Mr. McBain," shouted the reporter. "I'm afraid we are about to experience a painfully bloody chapter in our history." Salter held his field glasses to his eyes and said, "Still no sign of the federal ships. They're leaving Major Anderson to squirm."

Joseph was in a daze. His mind was no longer on the battle. It was on his family. He realized he might never see Emily or Charlotte again. And he would have to decide once and for all about Danny's safety. All he could think to say to Salter was, "I had better get back to Savannah, to my unit."

Salter said, "We all have different priorities now, Mr. McBain. Hopefully, we will meet again, sooner rather than later, and as friends and fellow countrymen. But my gut tells me it will be later. Much later."

Joseph looked out to the battle raging in the harbor and turned back to Salter. "What are you going to do, doctor?"

"I'm a reporter, Mr. McBain. I'll go where my employer tells me, where events happen that Americans should know about. After I file my story I'm going to my room for a little rest. I've been up all night. Please take care of yourself. We're in for a rough ride." The men shook hands and went their separate ways.

Joseph returned to his hotel. He slept for a few hours, packed, checked out, and took the hotel omnibus to the train station. As the carriage moved along deserted Meeting Street, Joseph could hear the booms of the bombardment, still at peak fury. The carriage traveled two blocks when Joseph saw eight soldiers escorting Dr. Salter along the street. Joseph could hear the correspondent yelling at the soldiers.

Joseph called to the driver to stop. He ran to Salter but the soldiers prevented him from getting next to their prisoner. He walked alongside the circle of men. "Dr. Salter, what's the problem?" The soldiers kept marching, prodding Salter along.

Salter laughed derisively, "I've just been arrested as a federal spy!"

Joseph looked at the sergeant for an explanation, but was ignored. "Is there anything I can do for you, doctor?"

Salter waved an arm at the soldiers. "If you have no authority over these rebels, I'm afraid not."

Joseph stopped and watched the doctor force-marched towards the guard house. Then he proceeded to the train station.

War had begun. There was no turning back.

CHAPTER 31

A Free Man of Color

April-May 1861

Joseph sat in the family parlor with his parents the day after his return and described his days in Charleston. His father stared into space. Major Anderson had surrendered and Sumter was in Confederate hands. James feared the consequences of war, even with a southern victory. The sacrifices in terms of family, friends, and wealth were too much for him to comprehend. Sarah was red-eyed and subdued. Her only son would most certainly be marching off to war.

James informed Joseph of the latest news of that day. As South Carolina and the six other Confederate states celebrated the great victory, Abraham Lincoln had issued a proclamation calling for the militia of the remaining Union states to supply seventy-five thousand men to help suppress the rebellion. He also called on both houses of Congress to convene the following July 4 to consider the measures to be taken. And there was talk of a Union blockade of southern ports.

The slave states that had not declared for secession finally had to make a choice: furnish men for the Union or fight with the Confederacy.

Joseph said, "I have to report for drills tomorrow afternoon, and every day after that except Sundays. We'll probably be called in May. How is the overseer?"

McBain closed his eyes for several seconds, as if in prayer. "After Sumter fell, he joined the Republican Blues. He won't be here long. Any man who can lift a gun will be called to duty. I'll have to manage on my own."

Sarah asked, "Joseph, what are you going to do about Danny?"

"Leave him with you. He'll be safe here."

Danny, not yet six years of age, ran into the room and hopped onto the couch next to his father. Joseph put his arm around his son. The boy had his father's light brown hair, which flopped up and down as he ran, and the freckled face and dark brown eyes of his mother. Danny asked, "Can I play with Truvy?"

Joseph mussed his son's hair. "In a little while, son. You have a piece of cake, and then we'll see Truvy." Joseph watched his son run from the room.

Joseph saw the day's paper on the table next to his father and asked, "What's the latest from Montgomery?"

James picked up the paper and held it in his lap. "Everyone expects Virginia, North Carolina, Tennessee, and Arkansas to secede. Kentucky and Missouri could go either way. There are plenty of secessionists and unionists in both. Maryland and Delaware will probably stay in the Union. Speculation is that Davis will move his headquarters to Virginia, where most of the fighting will take place."

Joseph stepped to the cabinet, poured himself a drink, raised the glass to his lips, held it there for a few seconds without drinking, and placed it back on the table. He walked to the window overlooking Pulaski Square. "How are Amy and Bob?"

Joseph heard his mother sniffle. He sat on the arm of the settee next to her and placed his hand on her shoulder. "What's wrong, Mother? Is she all right?"

Sarah looked up at her son. "She's having a baby."

Joseph's eyes widened. "That's fabulous, Mother! That's no reason to cry."

Tears trickled down her face. "She and Bob are moving to New York. They've decided Bob can't stay here during a war. Amy's afraid for him and the baby."

Joseph returned to the window. He wasn't surprised, but he was still saddened at the news. "When is she leaving?"

McBain answered, "As soon as she sells the restaurant."

No one spoke. Sarah kept her kerchief pressed against her eyes. Joseph gazed out the window. James examined the paper in his lap, as if looking for something hopeful in the news. The McBain family was breaking apart and it seemed nothing could save it.

Joseph finally said, "This mess will resolve itself faster than anyone thinks. A few battles, some casualties, and everyone will realize how senseless fighting is."

Sarah straightened. "Is that so, Joseph? If those casualties are your friends and fellow soldiers, will you leave it at that? Or will you want revenge?"

Joseph took a deep breath as he considered his mother's question. Danny ran back into the room with yellow cake crumbs bordering his lips. Joseph said, "All right, son. Let's see Truvy." He reached down and took his son's hand. As they reached the door, Joseph said to his parents, "Thank God Andrew and Patience are getting away." Joseph took Danny to see Truvy, and then went to congratulate Amy and Bob.

*   *   *

The May Day celebration of 1861 for the eleven volunteer militia corps of Savannah was the largest anyone could remember. After the morning parade, the Oglethorpe Light Infantry marched to Lover's Lane, where they took target practice for the rest of the day. In the afternoon, they held a competition, and Joseph and Private T. W. Bennett tied for the first prize. Each was awarded a pair of Colt's Repeaters. Danny, upon viewing his father's performance, strutted in front of the other children. Joseph let his son run his hand over one of the pistols. The boy looked at his father as if the guns were magical.

At the end of the day, First Lieutenant J. J. West addressed the men. He told them that the group would continue to drill daily at 4:00 p.m. in Forsyth Park. He explained that although a few politicians had tried to find a solution after the taking of Fort Sumter, a battle in Baltimore had dashed any hopes for reconciliation.

West was referring to the incident a week after the shelling of Sumter when a regiment from Massachusetts was on its way to Washington City. The soldiers had arrived in Baltimore and had to transfer to another station across town. In doing so, the rear of the regiment was attacked by thousands of pro-Confederate men, resulting in several deaths. The first gun battle of the war, though small, had elevated passions on both sides.

Lieutenant West concluded by saying that in all likelihood the unit would be ordered to Virginia within weeks, and all members should prepare to leave at a moment's notice. Joseph knew this would be the case, but felt tightness in his gut anyway. He knew the time left with his son was dwindling. He went home and spent the rest of the day teaching Danny how to play town ball in Monterey Square.

That night, Amy told Joseph that George Wylly had found a buyer for the restaurant. The man wanted to retain all of the employees. Dante would still be the head chef. If everything went well, she and Bob could move in a few weeks.

*   *   *

Sunday, May 5, 1861, was a great day for the First African Baptist Church and for all of Savannah's negroes. As people flowed in for the dedication services, they stopped in front to admire the building, true to Andrew's original design. It was amazing to all that the local slaves, with limited funds and manpower, could construct something so impressive. And all but fifteen hundred of the eleven thousand dollar cost had been paid. It was the first brick negro church in Georgia. Black residents of the town felt a tremendous sense of pride, and congregated in front of the church, shaking each others' hands. They knew that now they were on equal footing with whites in their faith and house of worship.

The services were held at noon so non-members of the congregation, particularly whites, could first attend their regular services. All of the McBains sat together in the fifth row of pews, alongside the Lows. Deacon and Polly Low, with Andrew and Patience, and their two children sat in the first row.

The people fanned themselves on the warm May day as they looked around the freshly painted interior of the church, with its side and end galleries, oak pews, oil-clothed aisles, and white pulpit. The mahogany organ in the balcony played and the choir began to sing. The negroes stood and clapped their hands, while the whites sang sitting down. Reverend S. G. Daniel of the First Baptist Church led a prayer.

He was followed by a reading of scriptures, hymns, and a sermon by Reverend S. Landrum. Finally, there was the dedicatory prayer, doxology, and benediction.

At the end of the service, Reverend Campbell took the pulpit and thanked Andrew McBain for his efforts on behalf of the church and announced what most in attendance already knew, that Andrew was going to England in three days to work for the Queen of England, and to represent all Savannah. Following Joseph's and Amy's lead, everyone rose and applauded. Andrew stood, faced the people, smiled, bowed at the waist, and lifted Gully in his arms.

Afterwards, people crowded around Andrew to congratulate him and wish him well. Deacon James Low clasped his hands behind his back and nodded approvingly. His daughter had married well.

The people moved down the aisle to the celebration in Franklin Square. At the door, Mr. Molyneaux appeared and said, "That was a most beautiful ceremony, Andrew. Congratulations on this fine building." Molyneaux was standing with a man in a blue ship captain's uniform. Molyneaux said, "Andrew, I'd like you to meet Captain Vaughn of the *Kalos*, the ship you'll be taking to England."

Andrew and the captain shook hands, and Andrew introduced his family.

The captain said, "This is an extraordinary circumstance, quite extraordinary. But as I look at this church, I understand why. Your talents are obvious and to be admired."

Andrew put one arm around Patience's waist and another on Truvy's shoulders and replied, "Thank you, sir."

Captain Vaughn said, "Andrew, you must tell me all about your story. I've only heard bits and pieces. Would you and your wife be free to join my wife and me for supper tonight on the ship? And you too, Mr. Molyneaux?"

Molyneaux declined because of a prior commitment, but Andrew gladly accepted.

Vaughn made arrangements with Andrew to pick him up at the pier at seven o'clock.

Andrew and his family walked into Franklin Square, where many of the congregation had gathered. Andrew found Joseph and asked, "I'm having supper with the captain of the ship that's taking us to England. I'll need a pass for the night. I'm out of the pre-signed ones."

Joseph patted Truvy on the back. "No problem. How are you getting to the harbor? Your horse and wagon are at the Heritage." Andrew shook his head. Joseph said, "Then I'll drive you and pick you up. What about the children?"

"Could you first drop them off at Patience's parents? Mrs. Low allows that."

Joseph said, "Certainly. And don't forget we're all having supper together tomorrow, your last night here." Patience said she would never forget that.

*   *   *

That night, as Andrew helped Patience from the gig, Joseph said, "I'll be back at ten."

Andrew and Patience thanked him and left. Joseph watched as they walked to the end of the pier to the rowboat in which Captain Vaughn was standing and waving. He also noticed two white stevedores eyeing the well-dressed negroes as they ambled along the wharf. When Andrew and Patience reached the boat, Joseph left for his parents' house, wondering how life in England would be for Andrew and his family, and if he would ever see his friend again.

Supper at the McBain house was subdued. Amy announced that she and Bob would move to New York in a week. Joseph said the Oglethorpe Light Infantry expected orders for Virginia any day. Sarah simply nodded as the others talked. She had already cried too much. However, everyone's spirits rose as they reflected on Andrew's life and the incredible turn it had taken, and toasted him. Amy suggested that they all travel to England in a year and visit him. It would be a grand reunion. They all agreed.

Joseph looked at his watch. "My Lord! It's already ten o'clock. I've got to pick up Andrew and Patience." He excused himself, kissed his mother and Amy, and left.

Joseph arrived at the wharf at 10:15. In the gaslight, he saw several men at the end of the pier standing close to Andrew and Patience. Joseph jumped off the gig and ran to them. As he approached he realized that three white men were blocking Andrew from leaving the pier.

"What's going on here?" Joseph called. The three men turned around.

The leader said, "Well, look who's here. I shoulda known these'd be your niggers."

Joseph stopped in front of the men, his fists clenched and his heart pounding. "So, you shaved your beards. I'm not surprised. That's what cowards do, hide their identities." Without waiting for a response, Joseph said to Andrew and Patience, who were behind the three men, "Andrew and Patience, walk over here. Now!"

Andrew put his arm around his wife and pushed passed the startled men, who had turned away from them to face Joseph. In a second, Andrew and Patience were standing behind Joseph.

When the men realized what had happened, the leader pointed at Andrew and said, "Those darkies aren't going anywhere."

Joseph said to the man, "That's not for you to decide." Keeping an eye on the men, Joseph turned his head sideways and asked, "Andrew, what's going on?"

Andrew said, "The captain brought us back in the lifeboat. A gang of men was here. One told the captain to get out and ordered the two oarsmen to return to the ship and stay there or he'd kill them. He told these three to guard us and make sure the oarsmen didn't come back. Then he and the others took the captain away."

Joseph faced his antagonist. "If you're a man and not the coward I think you are, you'll be here in ten minutes so we can settle our differences once and for all."

The man said, "Why not now, sir?"

"Because I'm taking my friends home. Then I'll return for you. You have my word."

"You're not going anywhere." The man called to the other men, "Harold, grab hold of the captain's honored guests." When Harold was abreast of Joseph, Joseph lunged and drove his shoulder into the man's chest, sending him, with hands and legs flailing, into the water.

Joseph turned to Andrew and said, "Let's go."

Joseph heard a click. He stopped and turned back. He saw a pistol pointing at his head. The leader sneered, "As I said, sir, you're not going anywhere."

The third man squatted, grabbed Harold's forearms, and pulled him back onto the pier. Harold, lying flat on his stomach, shouted, "Shoot the bastard, Willie."

Willie said, "Not yet, and lower your dern voice. I have a score to settle with this one. I want to have some fun doing it."

Joseph looked at the gun. He could hear Patience's muffled sobs behind him. He said, "Let my friend and his wife go. Then it'll just be us."

Willie pointed the gun at Joseph's chest. He craned his head to see Andrew and Patience. He then raised the gun to Joseph's head, and lowered slowly to Joseph's stomach. He smiled and started to whistle. He finally said, "I just can't make up my mind where to fire this shot. Could you help me, sir? Do you want it ripping through your heart, your stomach, or your balls? I'll be happy to grant your last wish."

Joseph couldn't charge the man without getting shot. But it looked as if only Willie was armed. He hoped that if they stood long enough, someone would come by or something would distract Willie, and Joseph could make his move. Until that happened, he had to get Patience and Andrew away. He called, "Andrew!"

"Yes, Joseph?"

"You and Patience walk down the pier to my gig and get out of here. If you hear a shot, don't stop. Ride on. I'll see you later."

Andrew had his arm tightly around Patience's shoulders and could feel her trembling. She clutched her arms against her chest.

Willie said, "Don't you move, Andrew, or I'll kill Joseph where he stands. I'm interested in him, not you. I just don't want you running for help."

While keeping his eyes on Willie, Joseph said, "Go, Andrew! When I say 'one,' take a step back"

Beads of sweat grew on Willie's forehead. With the gun still pointed at Joseph's chest, he said, "Don't you move, Andrew, or I'll shoot."

"One." Patience and Andrew took one step back together.

Willie's eyes darted from Andrew and Patience back to Joseph. He raised his pistol to Joseph's face. Joseph saw Willie's hand shaking. He felt sweat running down his neck.

"Two." The negroes stepped back again.

Willie blinked several times. He clutched the gun with both hands, but they still shook. He shouted at Joseph, "No more, sir, or you're a dead man. Don't try me!"

Joseph said, "Andrew, you both walk backwards to my gig. I'm staying here."

Andrew called, "Joseph!"

Joseph's mouth was as dry as a cotton ball. "Do as I say, Andrew. We have no time to discuss this. Now go!"

Andrew stepped in front of Patience. Then they stepped backwards, single file.

Willie stepped to the side to see past Joseph, but Joseph also stepped, blocking Willie's path and line of sight. Willie, his pistol still pointed at Joseph, said, "Stop them, Harold! You too, Sam."

Harold and Sam took a step forward and Joseph yelled, "Stop!"

The men froze in their tracks. Willie said, "Don't listen to him! Now, get them niggers!"

As Harold and Sam walked by Joseph, he charged them, hoping to send them and himself in the water, but this time the men were ready and grabbed hold of him. They wrestled as Willie stepped to them. Willie shouted, "Hold him still!"

As Joseph struggled, he hollered, "Andrew, run!"

Harold and Sam were each able to grab an arm and pull so that Joseph was spread armed, crucified. Willie pointed the gun at Joseph's chest. Joseph tried to pull his arms loose, but couldn't. He kicked at Willie, who sidestepped Joseph's foot. Sam hollered, "Shoot him, dammit!"

Harold, panting and wheezing, gasped, "Blast him now!"

Willie put the barrel inches from Joseph's chest just as Andrew slammed into him, sprawling both of them on the deck and sending the gun flying down the pier. They scrambled to their feet and ran towards the weapon about ten yards away. Joseph broke free from the grasp of his distracted captors and ran after the gun with Harold and Sam in pursuit. As the five men charged for the weapon, Willie stumbled and fell, and the other four tripped over him and tumbled onto the deck. Willie crawled on his hands and knees and got to the gun just before Joseph, who couldn't regain his footing and stumbled again. Joseph rolled over onto his back, and in the dim gaslight saw Willie on his knees, his teeth bared and his jaw trembling, pointing the gun at him. Then something blacked out Willie from Joseph's view. The explosion thundered in the night air. Joseph heard someone shout, "Let's get out of here," and heard footsteps race down the pier.

Joseph tried to get up to give chase, but something heavy was holding him down. He pushed up and the weight rolled off him. He heard something knock on the pier next to him. He saw Andrew's white eyes looking skyward. Then he heard Patience running towards them, screaming.

Joseph, lying on his stomach, reached over and touched Andrew's head. It rolled lifelessly, facing Joseph. Joseph hollered, "Andrew! Noooooo!"

The sound of the gunshot drew two policemen. Joseph asked one to get the chief and James McBain of Pulaski Square. He asked the other to fetch Dr.

Arnold. Joseph then kneeled next to Patience and tried to console her as she hugged Andrew's body.

Chief L. L. Goodwin and James McBain arrived simultaneously, almost ten minutes later. Dr. Arnold was not at home, but it didn't matter.

McBain looked down at Andrew's body and gasped, "Oh, no! Mother of God! No!" Joseph embraced his father, who cried unabashedly on his son's shoulder. Hercules, who had driven McBain, kneeled next to Patience, placed one hand on Andrew's bloody chest, and the other on Patience's back.

Patience cradled Andrew's head and prayed, "Come back to me, Andrew. Please come back to me. Don't leave us. We need you here. I need you. Your children need you. Please, please, please!"

Chief Goodwin sent his deputy to fetch Mr. Bogardus, the undertaker, and asked Joseph what had happened. As a dazed Joseph finished his account, Bogardus arrived with some helpers and carried Andrew's body away.

Joseph, James, and Hercules helped Patience to the carriage. McBain took Patience to Mr. Low's house to be with her parents and children. Joseph drove his gig to his sister's house.

McBain walked Patience to the front door and knocked. Tom Milledge opened the door and saw Patience, huddled over, leaning against McBain, and sobbing. He led them into the parlor and ran to get her parents. As Patience curled up on the settee, Andrew Low came into the room. McBain whispered the story to him. Low stared at the floor and shook his head. Then James and Polly Low entered the room, Bibles in hand. Everyone knelt and the deacon led them in prayer. Then McBain got up and left.

When James and Hercules returned to Pulaski Square, James went upstairs to tell Sarah, who buried her face in the sheets and cried for hours. Hercules went downstairs to tell the servants. They all held each other except Dante, who fell to the floor in a fetal position and howled like a dying dog.

Joseph arrived at Amy's house as she and Bob were getting ready for bed. Amy took one look at Joseph at the door and asked what was wrong. He guided them into the parlor and asked them to sit. In a broken voice, he told them. Amy held her chest and gasped for breath. Bob grabbed her as she fainted and fell sideways. She regained consciousness in a minute and Bob carried her into the bedroom.

When Joseph returned from Amy's, he, James, and Hercules sat in the family parlor. Joseph tried to explain the events of the night. He gasped, "It was my fight, my business, not Andrew's. And then he gave his life for me. Why?"

James told his son to go to bed. He would need all his strength for the days to come.

Joseph couldn't sleep until after he had drunk a half bottle of whiskey. When he dozed, he dreamed of Andrew, alive, laughing, working with bricks, lying on his back and studying the clouds. He woke up and wondered if Andrew was really alive and he was waking from a nightmare. Then reality dawned. Andrew was gone. Forever. Joseph went to the basin and vomited.

The next morning, Joseph had Hercules drive around the streets of Old Fort looking for the men. After four hours, they gave up. Then Hercules drove Mr. McBain and Joseph to the Heritage where McBain addressed the plantation. McBain gave the servants the rest of the day off to pray for Andrew's soul.

For the next two days, Joseph spent his time at the plantation with Isaac, his bushy beard and hair now completely white, designing and constructing a tombstone for Andrew. He also wrote letters to Emily and John Norris.

The citizens of Savannah were outraged at the tar and cottoning of a British sea captain and the murder of a prominent negro. The sitting grand jurors for the Superior Court of Chatham County called on the city and state authorities to put an end to the lawlessness and disgraceful disregard of the laws of the land and punish severely all those detected in the commission of those acts. The mayor and the city council offered a reward of five hundred dollars for information leading to the arrest of the individuals involved.

James McBain offered two thousand dollars more.

British Consul Molyneaux added a reward of one thousand dollars. He also wrote to the Queen explaining why Andrew McBain would not be visiting England.

Two days after Andrew's murder, Joseph returned to Savannah and visited Patience at her house, where she had been staying with the children and her mother. He embraced her and then picked up Truvy. When he put the lad down, the boy ran into another room.

He and Patience sat in the parlor room. "Patience, I hate to do this now, but I have to." She nodded, her kerchief at her nose and mouth. "Andrew left a will, as you know. He left all his possessions to me."

Patience gently cleared her throat. "I know, Master Joseph. Andrew discussed his will with me and why he wrote it as he did." She knew she was property and would be inherited.

"I want you to know that you may continue to live in the house. Legally, it's mine, but practically it's yours. That's how Andrew wanted it. All of Andrew's savings and other property as well. It's all yours."

Polly Low came in the room, holding a whining Gully. When she handed the baby to Patience, the baby stopped crying. Patience looked up. "Thank you, Master Joseph."

Truvy returned to the room and sat pouting on the couch next to his mother. He looked as if someone had taken all his toys. His mother had told him his father had gone to heaven and wouldn't be home for a long time. Truvy, not yet six years of age, was sad he would not be seeing his father for a while, but was unable to comprehend the sorrow of the adults around him. He had learned that heaven was a good place, a beautiful place.

Joseph continued. "Andrew saved enough money that you won't have to work for many years. If you wish, I'll give you a set amount each month. If you need more, just let me know. If you choose to work, you may keep all your earnings."

"Thank you, sir."

"You also know that Andrew wished to be buried next to his parents at the Heritage?" Patience nodded. "We're keeping space next to him. And I've designed a tombstone for him."

Patience handed Gully back to her mother, put her face in her hands, and started to sob. Truvy wrapped his arms around her. It took all of Joseph's self-control not to break down as well. Joseph knew that Andrew had given his life for him, and wondered if Patience resented him for it. That thought made Joseph feel even worse.

She soon stopped, dried her eyes, and said, "Thank you for taking care of that, sir."

"I guess that's it. If I have to leave Georgia, my parents will take care of you. We're still doing everything we can to catch those men. The marshal thinks they may have left the state."

Joseph and Patience stood and embraced. He felt her body quake and held her until she calmed down. Then Joseph left, picked up Ulysses the barber, and returned to the Heritage to finish the tombstone for Andrew.

On the morning of the funeral, Hercules went to fetch Dante to go to the church. As Hercules entered the room, he saw Dante on his knees, pushing something under the bed. Dante heard Hercules and stood up stiffly. Hercules looked at Dante's feet and saw the handle of a pistol sticking out from the bedcover. Dante tried to kick the gun further under the bed with his foot. Hercules nodded towards the article and said, "What's that?"

"Wut?"

"Don't fool with me, Dante. That thing at you feet." Dante didn't move or speak. Hercules stepped over and picked up the gun, a six-shot revolver. He balanced the weapon in the palm of his hand. "Where did you get this?"

"Dat muh 'fair."

"What's it for?"

Dante stepped past Hercules and closed the door. He then faced the coachman. "De buckra dat kill Andrew."

"What are you talking about?"

"Jes' wen ah leabe de restran' dat night, ah yeddy uh bang, lukkuh gunshot. Wen ah walk fuh yuh, 'long Whitakuh Street, uh dray dribe by. Almos' run me obuh. Dey t'ree men een it."

Hercules shouted, "You saw the men that shot Andrew?!"

"No. It berry daa'k. But ah see de wagon. It hab uh big maa'k 'long de side, lukkuh hawss. Ef ah see de wagon, ah fine de men." Dante lifted the gun from

Hercules hand. "An' den ah kill 'um." Dante kneeled and slid the gun under the bed. He stood to face Hercules.

Hercules looked at the floor and then at Dante. "Are you crazy? You just get caught with that gun, you go to jail. Maybe for good."

Dante grabbed the bigger, stronger Hercules by the lapels of his suit jacket. "Ah ain' lettin' dis pass, Huhclee. Eben ef ah hab tuh die, dem buckra gwine pay. Ah owe dat tuh Andrew. Now, oonuh gwine jine me?" Dante released Hercules.

Hercules smoothed his lapels and said, "We have to bury Andrew. We can talk later."

Every Savannah negro, free and slave, seemed to attend the funeral, as well as many whites. Reverend Daniel and Reverend Campbell delivered sermons and led prayers. Joseph McBain eulogized his friend from written notes. Every time his voice started to break, he breathed in as deeply as possible and exhaled slowly. He talked about how he and Andrew had grown up and shared their lives together. He spoke of Andrew's accomplishments in his life, his love of Oglethorpe, his faith, and his family. Then Joseph could talk no more.

Reverend Campbell stepped from the pulpit. The casket was carried up the aisle by James McBain, Joseph, Hercules, Dante, Deacon Low, Isaac, Jefferson, and Ulysses. Patience, who carried Gully and held Truvy by the hand, her mother, Sarah, Amy, and Bob followed. The other mourners fell in behind them. Outside the church, the pall bearers placed the coffin on a hearse. The procession moved along Montgomery Street to the Bay, then east a few blocks to the bluff across the street from the City Hotel.

At Joseph's request, the procession stopped so Andrew could have one last look over the bluff and to the harbor, and the mysterious world beyond. Reverend Campbell asked the people for a moment of silent prayer. During his prayer, Joseph raised his head and saw someone walking from the sidewalk to the hearse. Charlie Lamar placed a red rose on Andrew's coffin, patted Patience on the arm, and offered her his condolences. He then stepped next to Joseph and said, "I'm sorry, Joseph." Joseph noticed the dark circles under his eyes. Charlie then disappeared into the crowd of onlookers. Joseph knew he would have to kill Charlie.

They proceeded down the Barnard Street ramp to the public pier and placed the casket in McBain's flat-bottom boat. The McBains, Patience and her children, her parents, and some of the Heritage negroes stepped on the boat. Reverend Campbell led the throng of mourners in a last prayer and a hymn.

With the men standing and the women sitting, the boat pushed off and the oarsmen guided it up the river towards the Heritage. Joseph stood next to the coffin, placed his hand on it, closed his eyes, and lowered his head, trying to feel his friend inside. As they passed the rice fields of Hutchinson Island, Joseph heard singing.

Lawd tek muh han' an' ease muh burden
Oh ay mah ay mah ay
Tek muh han' an' show me heben
Oh ay mah ay mah ay
Mah ay mah ay oh ay mah ay
Mah ay mah ay oh ay mah ay

Joseph looked up, but the fields were empty.

The boat docked at the steam mill wharf, where the Heritage servants waited. The casket was lifted from the boat and the pall bearers carried it to the foot of the freshly dug gravesite in the negro cemetery.

The tombstone was a replica of the front of an ancient Greek temple, made of Savannah Greys and covered in stucco. It was five feet wide and almost five feet high. It had six columns in the Doric order. Sculpted in relief in the tympanum of the pediment was:

Andrew McBain
Loving Husband, Father and Friend
March 20, 1820 to May 6, 1861
He Builds with the Ancients

Isaac led the people in prayer, and Joseph delivered another eulogy.

The casket was lowered into the ground. Joseph and Hercules covered it with dirt.

Patience walked forward and kneeled at the foot of the grave, bent forward and placed both her hands on the loose soil and cried. Truvy placed his hand on her shoulder. As she tried to rise, Joseph and Deacon Low helped her up.

Patience stood between Joseph and her father and held each of their arms. With Polly holding the deacon's other arm, they started walking towards the river, with the other McBains following. The servants parted as they walked through.

Patience said to Joseph, "Thank you so much for everything you did for Andrew, Master Joseph. You know how much he loved you." Joseph was unable to speak. Patience asked him, "What's going to happen to you now, with the war?"

"I'm leaving for Virginia in a few days. My parents will be here for you in my absence."

Patience squeezed his arm. "Please take care of yourself, Master Joseph. Promise me you will."

Before Joseph could respond, Truvy interrupted, "Ma, can Danny and I play now?"

Patience wiped away her tears and said, "Yes, dear, but don't go far. We'll be leaving soon."

Both boys went running towards the river. Joseph and Patience could hear their calls.

Truvy yelled, "Let's play explorer. I'll be Oglethorpe! You're Tomochichi."
Danny called back, "No, I'll be Oglethorpe!"
Truvy answered, "All right. I'll be Oglethorpe tomorrow."

#####

APPENDIX

Listing of non-fictional characters

The following appendix presents the non-fictional characters in the book, listed by last name, first name, and a brief description.

Please note the following abbreviations used in the description column:
CAL—Charlie Lamar
GBL—Gazaway Lamar
JEO—James Oglethorpe

Akin	Richard	Friend of CAL; sportsman, city sheriff, clerk of city council
Anderson	John W	Savannah businessman and state legislator
Arguirvi	Miguel	Mate on the *Wanderer*
Arnold	Dr. Richard	Savannah mayor, doctor, newspaper owner
Ash	Dr.	Passenger on the *Pulaski*
Bacon	Marshall	New York Tombs lawyer; friend of J. E. Farnum
Ball	Colonel	Passenger on the *Pulaski*
Baty	Thomas	Free negro and fireman with Engine No. 4
Belden	William	Foreman of first *Wanderer* trial jury
Beman	Mr.	Passenger on the *Wanderer*
Black	Joseph	U. S. attorney general
Black Cloud		Charlie Lamar's horse
Bogardus	Mr.	Savannah undertaker
Boston	John	Savannah port collector
Bourke	Thomas	Glynn County sportsman
Brailsford	William	Glynn County sportsman
Brent	Mr.	Passenger on the *Wanderer*
Brooks	William	Sailing master of the *Wanderer*
Brown	Henry "Box"	Virginia slave who escaped bondage in a box via U.S. Mail
Brown	John	State legislator from Baldwin County
Brown	Mr.	Passenger on the *Pulaski*
Brown	Captain Nicholas	Sailing captain of the *Wanderer*
Bruyn	DeWitt	Savannah architect; associate of John Norris
Bryan	Andrew	Founder of the First African Baptist Church
Bull	Colonel William	Surveyor general of So. Carolina. Helped JEO layout Sav.
Butler	Fanny Kemble	British actress; married to Pierce
Butler	Pierce	Owner of Butler Island and Hamilton Point plantations
Camp	Mr.	Clothing store owner
Campbell	Reverend William	Rev. of First African Baptist Church after Rev. Marshall
Cant	John	Shipyard owner

Caroline		Servant of Dr. Stewart; passenger on the *Pulaski*
Castell	Robert	English architect; friend of JEO; wrote *Villas of the Ancients*
Cerveau	Firmin	Painter and artist
Cevor	Professor Charles	Aeronaut and employee of Central of Georgia Railroad
Christie	Luke	Steam tug captain
Church	Mrs.	Owner of Savannah private school
Clubb	James	Pilot on Jekyl Island
Cluskey	Charles Blaney	Greek Revival architect
Cobb	Howell	Georgia lawyer, judge, congressman, secretary of treasury
Cobb	Mary Lamar	Wife of Howell; cousin of GBL
Conover	Flag officer	Commander of American Squadron in Africa
Cooper	Dr. David	Superintendent of Georgia State Lunatic Asylum
Corrie	William C	Washington lobbyist and sportsman; partner of CAL
Corrie		African boy brought to America on the *Wanderer*
Couper	Carolyn Wylly	Wife of James Hamilton Couper
Couper	Hamilton	Son of James Hamilton; U.S. district attorney
Couper	James Hamilton	Rich planter and amateur architect from Glynn County
Cunningham	Henry	Negro minister of Second African Baptist Church
Daniel	Rev. S. G.	Minister of First Baptist Church in Savannah
Dubignon	Charles	State legislator from Glynn County
Dubignon	Henry	Friend of CAL; member of family owning Jekyl Island
Dubignon	John	Part owner and manager of family plantation on Jekyl Is.
Dubois	Captain	Captain of *SS Pulaski*
Dure	Mr.	Owner of Savannah's oldest house
Eastman	Moses	Savannah jeweler and owner of Cluskey designed house

Jackson	Henry Rootes	Savannah lawyer, judge, military officer, special prosecutor
Jay	William	English architect; practiced in Savannah 1817-1822
Johnson	Colonel	Louisiana planter; original owner of the *Wanderer*
Johnston	Mr.	Louisiana planter who bought slaves from CAL, Trowbridge
Jones	Dr. George	Savannah doctor: devoted member of anti-dueling society
Lafitte	John B.	CAL's shipping agent in Charleston, SC
Lamar	Caro Nicoll	Wife of Charlie; daughter of John C.
Lamar	Caroline	Daughter of Gazaway; younger sister of Charlie
Lamar	Charles A. L.	Son of Gazaway; Savannah businessman and sportsman
Lamar	Eliza	Niece of Gazaway; passenger on *Pulaski*
Lamar	Gazaway Bugg	Prominent Savannah businessman. Father of Charlie
Lamar	Geo. Washington	Brother of Gazaway. Lived in Augusta
Lamar	Harriet Casenove	Second wife of Gazaway
Lamar	Jane Cresswell	First wife of Gazaway
Lamar	Lucius Q. C., Jr.	Lushe; cousin of Charlie
Lamar	Lucius Q. C., Sr.	Circuit court judge; cousin of Gazaway; father of Lushe
Lamar	Martha	Younger sister of Charlie; passenger on the *Pulaski*
Lamar	Mirabeau	Cousin of GBL; second president of Republic of Texas
Lamar	Rebecca	Younger sister of Charlie; passenger on the *Pulaski*
Lamar	Rebecca	Sister of Gazaway; Aunt of Charlie
Lamar	Thomas	Younger brother of Charlie; passenger on the *Pulaski*
Lamar	William	Younger brother of Charlie; passenger on the *Pulaski*
Lamar	Zachariah	Plantation owner from Milledgeville; father of Mary

Lemmon	Jonathan	Virginian who lost slaves in court case in New York
Liele	George	Negro minister; held services on Brampton Plantation
Linville	Henry	Second manager of Engine No. 4
Lloyd	Thomas	Defense attorney; partner of John Owens
Long	Dr. Crawford W.	Georgia doctor; discovered anesthesia
Low	Andrew	Wealthy English merchant living in Savannah
Low	Hattie, Amy	Andrew Low's daughters
Low	Sarah Hunter	Andrew Low's first wife
Luftburrow	Matthew	Savannah builder
Lyons	James	President of 1856 Southern Commercial Convention
Mabry	Woodford	Port collector in Brunswick, Georgia
Manigault	Charles	Owner of Argyle Is. (Gowrie Plantation) in Savannah River
Marsh	Mr.	Builder of Floating Battery
Marshall	Andrew	Minister of First African Baptist; free person of color
Martin	David	Tried to buy an interest in the *Wanderer*
Massie	Peter	Scottish planter; left bequest for a Savannah public school
McDonald	George	Governor of Georgia
McRae	Mr.	Passenger on the *Pulaski*
Mercer	General Hugh	Purchaser of Italianate mansion on Monterey Square
Mesmerization	Professor of	Performing hypnotist
Middleton	James Mott	Friend of CAL
Milledge	Tom	Andrew Low's butler
Miller	A. N.	Chief of Savannah Fire Company
Minis	Dr. Philip	Doctor; grandson of first male Hebrew born in Sav.
Mirault	Aspasia	Free person of color; owner of confectionary store
Moko		Mentally challenged, homeless African American woman
Molyneaux	Edmund	British consul in Savannah

Montmollin	John	Plantation owner, bank director, auctioneer, friend of CAL
Moore	Edwin Ward	Commodore in Texas Navy; Galveston businessman
Nicoll	John C	Sav. mayor and district court judge; CAL's father-in-law
Noah		Based on a Negro passenger on the *Pulaski*
Norris	John	New York architect practicing in Savannah
Oglethorpe	James Edward	The founder of the colony of Georgia
O'Neill	Father Jeremiah	Catholic priest
Owens	George Welshman	Owner of a William Jay designed house
Owens	John	Defense attorney
Parkman	Samuel	Savannah businessman; passenger on the *Pulaski*
Pearson	Captain	Sailing master of *SS Pulaski*
Peter	Jesse	Black minister; ordained Andrew Bryan
Peyton	Lucien	Special investigator for Treasury Department
Price	William	Clothing store owner
Purse	Thomas	Savannah bookseller and state legislator
Rajesta	Juan	Mate on the *Wanderer*
Russell	Phillip	Magistrate and manager of white engine company
Ryerson	Mr.	Drugstore owner
Rynders	Isaiah	U.S. marshal, southern New York district
Salter	Dr. George H. C.	New York Times correspondent in Charleston
Sans Foix		Chef of John Couper, father of James Hamilton
Scarbrough	William	Partner in *SS Savannah*; later worked for GBL
Scudder	Amos	Sav. builder and alderman; investor in Savannah canal co.
Sheftall	Sheftall	Revolutionary war hero; dressed in his army outfit
Sims	William	Early business partner of Charlie Lamar
Smith	Mr.	Passenger on the *Pulaski*
Smith	Mrs.	Passenger on the *Pulaski*
Spaulding	Randolph	Wealthy Glynn County planter and sportsman
Spratt	Leonidas	Charleston lawyer; advocated reopening slave trade
Spullock	James	U. S. Marshal

Stark	James Jones	Legislator and businessman from Glynn County
Stevenson	Captain	Owner of steam tugs in Savannah
Stewart	Daniel	Friend of CAL, U.S. and city marshal, fireman
Stewart	Dr.	Passenger on the *Pulaski*
Stone	Charles	Deputy marshal, city jailer
Styles	Carey	Friend of CAL; Brunswick lawyer and mayor
Telfair	County	Telfair County witnesses (5)
Tomochichi		Chief of Yamacraw tribe; let JEO settle in Savannah
Toonahowi		Tomochichi's nephew
Totten	Benjamin	Commander of *SS Vincennes*
Trowbridge	Nelson	Friend and business partner of CAL
Tucker	John	Friend of CAL; merchant, plantation owner, bank director
Turner	Dr.	Health officer
Ulysses		Barber and carver; based on 20th-century Ulysses Davis
Van Horn	Charles	Builder, sash and blind maker; city jailer
Vaughn	Captain	Captain of British ship *Kalos*
Vitruvius	Marcus Pollio	Roman architect and engineer; wrote book on architecture
Waring	Dr.	Savannah doctor and mayor
Wayne	Henry	Son of James M Wayne; wanted to bring camels to Texas
Wayne	James Moore	Savannah lawyer, politician, and judge
Williams	William Thorne	Bookstore owner; five-time mayor of Savannah
Wilson	Edward	City clerk
Wise	Commodore	Commodore of British Squadron in Africa
Woart	Mrs.	Passenger on the *Pulaski*
Woart	Reverend	Passenger on the *Pulaski*
Wofford	William B	State legislator; president of the senate
Woolhopter	Philip	Charlie Lamar's assistant
Wylly	George	Property broker, auctioneer, partner of John Montmollin
Ziegler	Solomon	White manager of Engine No. 4

BIBLIOGRAPHY

It is not possible in the space permitted to list all the newspaper articles, letters, diaries, pamphlets, historical journals, personal interviews, special collections, and books used in researching this book over the past five years. However, for the reader who may want to explore further the historical events and non-fiction characters in this story, the following sampling of references is given. Further inquiries should be directed to the author at *jjordan0408@charter.net*.

The fictional Heritage plantation is based upon the real-life Hermitage plantation (now destroyed), owned by Henry McAlpin. Descriptions of the Hermitage can be obtained in "The Hermitage Plantation" by the Georgia Writers' Project, *Georgia Historical Quarterly* 28 (March 1943), 55-87; and an essay entitled the "Souvenir of the Hermitage," at the Georgia Historical Society, Vertical File "Savannah-Historic Houses-Hermitage."

For positive white views of plantation life in antebellum Georgia, read "The Testimony of Margaret Ketchum Ward on Civil War Times in Georgia," edited by Aaron M. Boom, *Georgia Historical Quarterly* 39 (September 1955), 268-93, and (December 1955), 375-401; the "Old Canoochee-Ogeechee Chronicles" by Julia Harn, *Georgia Historical Quarterly* 15 (December 1931), 346-60, 16 (March 1932), 47-55, (June 1932), 146-151, (September 1932), 232-9, and (December 1932), 298-312; and "The Antebellum and War Memories of Mrs. Telfair Hodgson," edited by Sarah Hodgson Torian, *Georgia Historical Quarterly* 27 (December 1943), 350-6.

For a different view of plantation life, read *Journal of a Residence on a Georgian Plantation in 1838-1839* by Frances Anne Kemble, and edited by John A. Scott (Athens: The University of Georgia Press, 1984). The trip to Georgia in 1840 during which the Butlers had supper with the Coupers and McBains as described in chapter 11 is fictional, but Fanny's four-month trip the prior year (1838-1839) was the basis for her journal.

For insights of slaves into plantation life, access the Slave Narratives online at the Library of Congress Web site at http://memory.loc.gov/ammem/snhtml/snhome.html

Reminiscences by residents of life in Savannah are particularly good. The memoirs of Charles Olmstead are reported in several issues of the *Georgia Historical Quarterly*. See 1 (September 1917), 243-252, 42 (December 1958), 389-408, 43 (March 1959), 60-74, (June 1959), 170-86, (September 1959), 261-80, (December 1959), 378-96. Olmstead wrote of Moko and the Professor of Mesmerization. Also excellent is "Reminiscences and Recollections of Old Savannah" by Charles Seton

Henry Hardee, *Georgia Historical Quarterly* 12 (June 1928), 158-76, (September 1928), 255-88, (December 1928), 353-89. Among many things, he describes maroons and Mrs. Mirault's ice cream. Both Olmstead and Hardee wrote of townball, obviously an early form of baseball, being played in the 1830s and 1840s. Other interesting depictions are presented in "Glimpses of Savannah" by Mrs. Paschal N. Strong, Sr., *Georgia Historical Quarterly* 33 (March 1949), 26-35; and *Recollections of a Long and Satisfactory Life* by William Harden, (Savannah, Georgia: Press of Review Printing Co., Inc., 1934).

Another fine source is *Cerveau's Savannah* by Joseph Frederick Waring (Savannah: Georgia Historical Society, 1973). Waring describes the town and some of its residents in 1837, the year Cerveau completed his beautiful painting which now hangs in the main hall of the Georgia Historical Society and graces the cover of this book. Cerveau did indeed paint the same scene from the bell tower of the City Exchange in 1853 and had it lithographed. However, a copy has never been located, despite efforts by the author and Dr. John Duncan.

For descriptions of Savannah by Northerners, read *Pleasure and the Pain; Reminiscences of Georgia in the 1840s* by Emily Burke (Savannah, Ga.: Beehive Press, 1978); and "The 1849 Memoirs of Second Lieutenant John C. Tidball," edited by Eugene C. Tidball, *Georgia Historical Quarterly* 84 (March 2001), 116-38.

There are several good accounts of life in Savannah for African Americans, free and enslaved, before the Civil War. *Black Savannah 1788-1864* by Wittington B. Johnson (Fayetteville: The University of Arkansas Press, 1996) is excellent, as are the books of local authors Charles Lwanga Hoskins and Dr. Charles J. Elmore, professor and department chair at Savannah State University.

Several accounts of the *SS Pulaski* disaster exist. Rebecca Lamar (Mrs. Hugh McLeod when scribed) wrote a lengthy memoir years after the incident in the "The Loss of the Steamer Pulaski," *Georgia Historical Quarterly* 1 (1917): 63-95; Gazaway Lamar wrote of his experience in a letter dated July 6, 1838, to Sarah Mackay, whose brother lost his wife and two children. See the C. L. Woodbridge Papers, folder 3, item 3, Georgia Historical Society, Savannah. James Hamilton Couper's account, "Loss of the Steamer Pulaski," can be found in *The Historical Collections of Georgia* at the Georgia Historical Society, 353-64. For the account of the people on the raft who were first rescued by the *Henry Camerdon*, see the pamphlet *Narrative of the Loss of the Steam Packet Pulaski*, H. H. Brown 1838 at the New Hanover County (Wilmington, North Carolina) Public Library.

A description of the Georgia State Lunatic Asylum and its first patients was found in *But for the Grace of God* by Dr. Peter G Cranford (Augusta, Ga.: Great Pyramid Press, 1981).

Sources for the illegal African slave trade include *The Suppression of the African Slave Trade to the United States of America 1638-1870* by W. E. B. Du Bois (Baton Rouge: Louisiana State University Press, 1896); *American Slavers and the Federal Law 1831-1862* by Warren S. Howard (Berkeley: University of California Press, 1963);

and "The Revival of the African Slave Trade in the United States, 1856-1860" by Harvey Wish, *The Mississippi Valley Historical Review* 27 (March 1941), 569-88.

The slave hunting scene in chapter 24 is based on an article titled "Slave-Hunts in Central Africa," which is based on accounts by German traveler Dr. Nachtigal, from *Harper's New Monthly Magazine* 48, issue 287 (April 1874), 710-17. It is available online at the Web site of the Cornell University Library.

For those interested in the history of the American Colonization Society, I recommend *The American Colonization Society, 1817-1840* by Early Lee Fox (New York: AMS Press, 1971). To learn more about free Negroes in America, read *Slaves Without Masters* by Ira Berlin (New York: The New Press, 1974).

For a basic understanding of American architectural styles and their elements, see *A Field Guide to American Houses* by Virginia and Lee McAlester (New York: Alfred A. Knopf, 2000). For an excellent history of classicism in early American architecture, read the first three chapters of *Greek Revival Architecture in America* by Talbot Hamlin (New York: Dover Publications Inc., 1944). Another good source on architectural history is *Western Architecture* by Ian Sutton (London: Thames and Hudson, 1999). For Savannah architecture, see *Savannah Revisited History & Architecture* by Mills Lane (Savannah: Beehive Press, 2001), and *The National Trust Guide to Savannah* by Roulhac Toledano (New York: John Wiley & Sons, 1997).

Different dialects were used by Africans and their descendants along the coast and Sea Islands of Georgia and South Carolina as well as in the interior. I relied on *Gullah Fuh Oonuh* by Virginia Mixson Geraty (Orangeburg, S.C.: Sandlapper Publishing Co., 1997).

Several papers have been written about Gazaway Lamar, who continued to be an important influence in southern business and politics during and after the Civil War. "Gazaway Bugg Lamar, Confederate Banker and Business Man" by Thomas Robson Hay, *Georgia Historical Quarterly* 37 (June 1953), 89-128, presents a good profile of the man. Robert Neil Mathis wrote "Gazaway Bugg Lamar: A Southern Entrepreneur" for his doctoral dissertation for the University of Georgia, Athens, in 1968.

Two book accounts of the *Wanderer* have been written: Tom Henderson Wells's *The Slave Ship Wanderer* (Athens: University of Georgia Press, 1967), and, more recently, *The Wanderer: The Last American Slave Ship and the Conspiracy that Set Her Sails in Motion* by Eric Calonius (New York: St. Martin's Press, 2006).

The first *Wanderer* trial was covered extensively in the *Savannah Daily Morning News* and the *Charleston Mercury*.

Relatively little has been published about Gazaway's son, Charlie. Mr. Wells writes about Charlie in *The Slave Ship Wanderer* and in "Charles Augustus Lafayette Lamar, Gentlemen Slave Trader," *Georgia Historical Quarterly* 47 (June 1963), 158-68. Mr. Calonius also writes about Lamar. Both have basic information on Charlie, but both omit major aspects of his life which are critical to understanding Lamar's possible motivations for his crimes. A complete biography of Charles Augustus Lafayette Lamar is still needed.

The most frequently quoted letters of Charlie Lamar are contained in "A Slave-Trader's Letter-Book," originally published in the *North American Review* 143, issue 360 (November 1886). It is a compilation of selected letters Lamar wrote between 1855 and 1860. The story of the discovery of this source is incredible. In 1886, twenty-one years after Lamar was killed in one of the last battles of the Civil War, a northern man somehow rescued a letter-press copy-book from the "maw of a New England paper-mill." What the man was doing at the paper-mill and how he happened to pick out Charlie's letter-book from a pile are not explained. The discoverer supposed that the letter-book got from Georgia to New England in the hands of a Union soldier after the Civil War. One historian, Warren Howard, in *American Slavers and the Federal Law* (see above), claims the letter-book is a fraud, that the journal printed it to embarrass Charlie's cousin, L. Q. C. Lamar, Jr. (Lushe), who was the United States secretary of the interior in the Grover Cleveland administration. Mr. Howard says the letters offer nothing new about Charlie. Mr. Wells, in *The Slave Ship Wanderer*, says he is positive the letters are legitimate.

I tried to resolve the issue by locating the actual-letter book, or a copy of it. However, the *North American Review*, now published by the University of Northern Iowa, has no records from that period. Nor does the Houghton Library at Harvard University, the only other known holder of the *Review's* old records.

I believe there never was a letter-book. There's no original or copy, and the circumstances around its discovery are just too unbelievable. Also, if Lamar went through the trouble of having his letters printed in a letter-book, why did he never have it published or distributed, as he did with his rebuke of Howell Cobb? The Charlie I believe I know would have been proud of his thoughts and would want as many people as possible to read them. Also, none of the original Lamar letters I reviewed during my research are in the letter-book.

However, many the letters read just like documented Lamar letters in attitude and style. If they are fraudulent, someone very familiar with Lamar expended a lot of time and effort to produce them. It is possible that the publisher or some other person got hold of some of Lamar's letters and published them under the guise of a letter-book. An analysis of these letters, often edited and sometimes undated, would be a worthy scholarly endeavor.

For actual Charlie Lamar letters, access the Charles A. L. Lamar papers at Special Collections & Archives in the Robert W. Woodruff Library at Emory University, Atlanta. Fascinating letters between Lamar, Nelson Trowbridge, and James Gardner are found in the James Gardner Papers at the Georgia State Archives. Chroniclers of Lamar usually state that he was a wealthy businessman who entered the trade solely as a matter of principle. These letters show his many failures as a businessman and his financial woes as he entered the slave trade. They also reveal his and Trowbridge's involvement in the Louisiana legislature's failed attempt to import African apprentices into the country.

There is no better way to get a feel for a period than to browse the newspapers of the day. This is how I learned of the aerial balloon pioneer, Dr. Cevor, the tar and cottoning of Sewall Fisk and Captain Vaughn (which actually occurred in February 1861), Firmin Cerveau's second view of Savannah, the Floating Battery, and Dr. George H. C. Salter.

Museums also supplied valuable information. It was at the Beach Institute in Savannah that I saw the fabulous works of local barber Ulysses Davis (1913-1990), who carved the busts of all of the presidents of the United States from George Washington to George H. W. Bush.

ABOUT THE AUTHOR

Jim Jordan received his BBA and MBA from Pace University in New York City and is a certified public accountant. He spent most of his professional career in New York and England working as a financial analyst and financial systems consultant.

He has lived in the lowcountry of South Carolina with his wife Kathleen since 1994. In 2001 he began a second career conducting history and architecture tours in nearby Savannah, Georgia. *Savannah Grey* is his first novel.

Do you have questions or comments about the book? Contact Jim Jordan at *jjordan0408@charter.net*